A GUIDE TO THE
GENERAL CAHIERS OF 1789

WITH THE TEXTS
OF UNEDITED CAHIERS

A GUIDE TO THE
GENERAL CAHIERS OF 1789

WITH THE TEXTS
OF UNEDITED CAHIERS

BY

BEATRICE FRY HYSLOP

(New Printing, with Additions and Corrections)

1968
OCTAGON BOOKS, INC.
New York

Reprinted 1967

by special arrangement with Columbia University Press

OCTAGON BOOKS, INC.
175 FIFTH AVENUE
NEW YORK, N. Y. 10010

LIBRARY OF CONGRESS CATALOG CARD NUMBER: 67-18769

Printed in U.S.A. by
NOBLE OFFSET PRINTERS, INC.
NEW YORK 3, N. Y.

TO MY FATHER

PREFACE TO THE OCTAGON EDITION

Since this volume was originally published in 1936, the author published a *Supplément au répertoire critique des cahiers de doléances pour les Etats Généraux de 1789* in the official series of "Documents inédits sur l'histoire économique de la Révolution française," Paris, 1952, and in 1955 an article in the *Annales historiques de la Révolution française,* pp. 115-23. Nine additional general cahiers had come to light between 1936 and 1955, but none since then. Parish cahiers have been found, but losses incurred in archives during World War II have not been filled by such discoveries.

Corrections and additions to data given in the first edition are being provided in this edition (preceding the index), but unfortunately, provision for publishing the nine texts not hitherto known or available could not be made, since the texts would have added unduly to the length of the revision. The author hopes to publish them elsewhere, especially those that remain in manuscript. Also in the interest of brevity, minor typographical errors in the original edition will not be cited. The revisions that are important are statistics involving numbers of cahiers, where they can be found— in other words, the scholarly apparatus for consultation of the *cahiers de doléances* of 1789.

The author has found no material or published discussions that require revision of the original analysis of the convocation of 1789, of the cahiers as documents, and of their value. There is a renewed interest in these documents of 1789, not only for parish cahiers, which are now considered less reliable for peasant opinion, being more influenced by lawyers, local administrators, and rich proprieters, but also for the general cahiers as a reflection of bourgeois opinion. Search for cahiers of the urban lower classes excluded from the gilds has not been fruitful. The convocation did not provide for assemblies and cahiers of journeymen or apprentices, but if these workers met the general qualifications of age and tax payment, they could attend town assemblies of the unorganized townsmen. They were as apt to be influenced by local officials and prominent citizens as the peasantry were in the parishes. Attention might be called to the lists of cahiers of the curés and of gilds provided in the *Supplément,* pp. 198 and 194-95.

The cahiers will continue to be an important gauge of public opinion on the eve of the Great Revolution in France.

August, 1967   BEATRICE F. HYSLOP
Hunter College of the City University of New York

PREFACE

A la simple lecture des divers mandats des députes de toutes les provinces, on pourra presqu'infailliblement en augurer le sort des Etats-
généraux et la destinée de la Nation.—Servan, *Idée sur le mandat des
députés aux Etats-Généraux,* s. l. 1789, p. 4.

Qu'ils resteront comme le textament de l'ancienne société française,
l'expression suprême de ses désirs, la manifestation authentique de ses
volontés.—De Tocqueville, *L'Ancien régime,* Paris, 1866, *avant-propos,*
pp. iii-iv.

Let us imagine, for the moment, that in the fall of 1932, during
the critical presidential campaign that brought Franklin D. Roosevelt
to the White House, all the voters of each electoral district met together and drew up a statement of the reforms that they wished the
future president to carry out. In place of party platforms made in
national party conventions, there would be thousands of documents
representing the consensus of opinion in each of the electoral assemblies. We should consider such documents a unique source for
appraising public opinion at that period of national crisis. Fortunately, other sources for determining popular opinion exist today, but in
the France of 1789, before mass opinion had become vocal through
the development of a press or of regularly established representative
bodies, a process similar to that imagined for our last national election actually took place.

Political, social, and economic conditions had reached a crisis.
When other methods to bring about recovery failed, the national
representative body—the States-General, which had not met for one
hundred and seventy-five years—was summoned to pull France out
of its depression. The years immediately preceding had witnessed
many difficulties analogous to those of present-day America. There
had been a poor harvest and consequent famine, aggravated by the
maldistribution of such food supplies as existed. The peasants bore
the brunt of taxation and of hard labor. Tolls, duties, and a multitude of restrictions obstructed the marketing of their produce and
put the profits in other pockets. Small farm owners were scarcely
better off than agricultural tenants, upon whom seigniorial dues were
still levied. Serfdom, nominally abolished, still existed in some parts
of France. The peasants were awakening, however, to a consciousness
of their disproportionate burdens. The old industrial organization of

gilds was breaking down, partly as a result of the spread of economic liberalism, but even more as a result of practical economic development. Industry and commerce had expanded beyond possible control by a system that had flourished when government was weak and commerce largely regional. The gildsmen were caught between a growing capitalism and rebellious labor. The old horizontal organization of industry would soon have to choose between economic liberalism and a vertical form of organization. Industrial conditions were further prejudiced by unsuccessful competition with English manufactures and commerce. Overproduction, followed by curtailment and unemployment was the consequence of the commercial treaty of 1786. While the economic status of the productive groups within France had declined, the government itself could not balance its budget. Income from taxation decreased, while expenses mounted by leaps and bounds. The only remedy that the ministers of Louis XVI suggested was the raising of new loans, which meant an increased debt. New taxes upon property, which had escaped under the existing régime, were successfully opposed by an appeal to traditional privileges. Economically, France was at cross purposes with herself.

In the government, traditional procedure had culminated in a deadlock. The Parlements obstructed reforms proposed by the king's councils, if the privileges of any of their members or of the corporate whole were endangered. Edicts were issued and then withdrawn, leaving conditions more confused than before. The king's ministers could effect no constructive reforms without involving some privileged group, whose opposition usually caused the immediate downfall of the ministers, as the brief ministry of Turgot well illustrates. Even Necker, who had won the confidence of the active business public, was no prestidigitator and could not conjure away accumulated debt and abuse. Confidence in the central government had weakened, and provincial units were striving to solve their local problems without reference to neighboring areas or to national complications. Increased regionalism became a defense against the arbitrary despotism of the central government, and yet each province was hindered in its efforts to put its own house in order by a cumbersome, outworn, bureaucratic control on the part of the central government. Constitutional reform was desperately needed.

Amid political and economic depression and confusion, social conditions reflected a similar instability. Eighteenth century enlightenment had fostered a loosening of religious ties. Local associations, clubs, and the *salons* became centers of active discussion of the political and social principles which the philosophers advanced. While the old aristocracy fluttered between Le Petit Trianon and the Grand Château of Versailles, active affairs were dealt with by an increasing *intelligentsia,* independent of hereditary title. Egalitarian ideas from eighteenth century philosophy were stimulating revolt against traditional castes and rules.

Along every line, France had been passing through a great depression, and, with the summons of the States-General, came the opportunity for a comprehensive national reorganization. What was the popular program of national regeneration? It is just such a question that the *cahiers de doléances* of 1789 can help us to answer.

Elections to the States-General in 1789 were carried out in successive stages; each assembly drew up instructions for its delegates to the next larger unit. These programs were called *cahiers de doléances.* Such a practice had grown up during the fifteenth and sixteenth centuries, when the States-General had been frequently summoned. Since 1614, when the States-General had last assembled, many changes had taken place. During that interval, there had been the long reign of the Grand Monarch, the growth of a colonial empire and trade, innumerable European wars, and the spread of philosophical enlightenment. Nevertheless, when the States-General was summoned to meet in 1789, much of the traditional procedure was revived, and the practice of giving written instructions to deputies was followed. These documents present us with an invaluable cross section of public opinion on the eve of the Revolution.

There are many drawbacks to using the *cahiers de doléances* as sources. Historians have differed widely upon their utility. While some have relied too much upon the cahiers, uncritically used, others have denied them any value as expressions of collective opinion, and still others have rejected any objective information contained in them. Documentary criticism of the *cahiers de doléances* began in the late nineteenth century under the aegis of Aulard and Brette, and has progressed steadily since then. Nevertheless, information about these documents and the documents themselves are widely scattered, and a great many of the cahiers have been lost. There is an obvious need of classification and verification. It seemed desirable to the author, therefore, to set forth in sequence the material pertinent to an accurate use of the cahiers.

The number of cahiers drafted in the elections of 1789 totals more than twenty-five thousand, and can probably never be exactly determined. This group of documents falls naturally into two classes—the cahiers drawn up in the preliminary electoral assemblies, and those written as instructions for the deputies to the States-General. The more one works with the cahiers the more differences may be noted between these two large groups—that is, between the *preliminary* and the *general* cahiers. Most discussions or analyses of the cahiers have ignored these differences, and, in the twentieth century, have tended to disregard the *general* cahiers altogether. Generalizations about the value of the *preliminary* cahiers do not necessarily hold for the *general* cahiers, either as to their documentary value or their content. Certain aspects of the *general* cahiers are more significant than of the *preliminary,* and it is obviously desirable to assemble in one volume the information that may be necessary for any careful utilization of the *general* cahiers.

The task of validating the *general* cahiers as a gauge of public opinion in France in 1789 is five-fold. It is first necessary to define the cahiers as a set of documents and second, to determine the number of general cahiers; third, documentary verification is necessary to discover and to make available for accurate use the texts of all known general cahiers; fourth, an analysis of the value of each cahier is requisite; and lastly, the limits and the advantages of general cahiers as sources must be ascertained. Thus, the present study is a manual to aid in using the general cahiers, and to enable the student of conditions existing on the eve of the French Revolution to test the pulse of the French electorate.

Attention is here called to seven publications which are indispensable for a study of the cahiers. The present volume is interpretative of them, and is also supplementary. The seven publications are as follows:

Champion, Edme, *La France d'après les cahiers de 1789* (Paris, 1897).
Brette, Armand, *Recueil de documents rélatifs à la convocation des Etats-Généraux de 1789* (Paris, 1894-1915, 4 vols.), and *Les Limites et les divisions territoriales en France en 1789* (Paris, 1907).
Documents inédits sur l'histoire économique de la Révolution française, the volumes of the official series in which cahiers are edited, and especially the following volume of this series: Hyslop, Beatrice, *Repertoire critique des cahiers de doléances pour les Etats-Généraux de 1789* (Paris, 1933).
Hyslop, Beatrice, *French Nationalism in 1789 according to the General Cahiers* (New York, 1934).

Mavidal, J., and Laurent, E., *Archives parlementaires de 1787 à 1861* (Paris, 1867-75, 7 vols.).

With these volumes at hand, the student can readily consult the general cahiers of 1789.

The author wishes to acknowledge the generous coöperation of librarians and archivists in France, and especially of M. Camille Bloch, professor at the Sorbonne, former supervisor of the departmental archives and former curator of the Musée de la Guerre mondiale. Professor Carlton J. H. Hayes, of Columbia University, during the supervision of the author's doctoral dissertation, offered helpful suggestions, and Professor Charles Downer Hazen has read and criticised the present manuscript. Thanks are also due to Virginia Thompson (Ph.D., Columbia University), and to Mary Bradshaw (Ph.D., University of Wisconsin) for discussion and criticism. Stephanie Locke (M.A., Teachers College) gave technical help on the Appendix, and R. T. Miller drafted the maps. Acknowledgment is also made to those who have copied manuscripts, typed unedited texts, and contributed many other services toward the preparation of this volume. A generous grant of the Columbia University Council for Research in the Social Sciences has made possible the publication of this volume.

BEATRICE FRY HYSLOP

KINGSWOOD SCHOOL CRANBROOK,
  BLOOMFIELD HILLS, MICHIGAN
  JANUARY 2, 1936

CONTENTS

CONTENTS

CONTENTS

ILLUSTRATIONS

MAPS

CHARTS

ABBREVIATIONS

Arch. Nat. Archives Nationales at Paris.

Arch. Dept. Archives Départmentales. Sometimes, *Arch.* has been followed simply by the name of the department whose archives have been consulted.

AP *Archives Parlementaires,* edited by Mavidal and Laurent (Paris, 1867-75), 7 vols.

Bib. Mun. Bibliothèque Municipale.

Bib. Nat. Bibliothèque Nationale at Paris.

C¹ lower clergy.

CN clergy and nobles (combined).

CT clergy and third estate (combined).

D.I. A volume in the official series of *Documents inédits sur l'histoire économique de la Révolution française.*

Gen. généralité.

MS manuscript.

N nobles.

NT nobles and third estate (combined).

PR printed.

p.v. *procès-verbal,* or *procès-verbaux.*

T third estate.

U the three orders (combined).

V *ville,* or town.

3 O the three orders.

References to specific electoral districts and quotations from cahiers have been given according to the class and the name of the district, without designation as to whether its official status in 1789 was a *bailliage, sénéchaussée, comté, gouvernance, intendance, siège royal,* etc. The official status may be checked with Brette, A., (*Recueil des documents relatifs à la convocation des Etats-généraux de 1789,* Paris, 1894-1915, Vol. I), or Hyslop, B., (*Repertoire critique des cahiers de doléances de 1789,* Paris, 1933). The omission has been made in order to save space and to eliminate unnecessary detail.

When reference has been made to the electoral districts, the word which applied to the majority of districts, the *bailliage,* has been used.

Attention may be called to the fact that French accents are not generally used with capital letters. Consequently, such names as Etampes, Etain, etc., appear without an accent over the "e."

I
THE ELECTORAL PROCESS OF 1789

WHEREVER representative or advisory bodies have existed, recommendations and information for the members have been offered or demanded. Before the development of the press or of modern political machines, such advice was generally given voluntarily and by individuals, or else was specifically solicited. In France, however, the custom of giving instructions to governmental bodies developed during the early modern period. Written recommendations or memoranda bore the title of "cahiers," whether they were designed for the Provincial-Estates[1] or for the States-General, but it was especially in connection with the latter, the national body, that their composition assumed a legal character. Laws for the convocation of the States-General prescribed and defined the making of *cahiers de doléances*. The king and his councilors, who issued the call, were not concerned with what posterity might do with these documents; they only sought to learn the needs and desires of their subjects. Many of these documents have, however, been preserved and their existence affords historians an invaluable type of source.

When the States-General was summoned in 1789, some contemporaries looked upon this move as revolutionary. To our eyes, the Revolution lay not in its summons but in the unprecedented events which occurred after its meetings began. The convocation of the States-General on the eve of the Revolution was, in fact, even to the making of *cahiers de doléances*, a revival of the traditional institution which had flourished prior to 1614. For an understanding of the *cahiers de doléances* as sources, it is first necessary to recall the early States-Generals in France with which written instructions were inseparably associated.

THE EARLY STATES-GENERALS

In response to a demand from an official commission on historical works, Georges Picot made a very scholarly study of the early States-Generals in France.[2] It would be superfluous to repeat here what he

---

[1] Provincial-Estates will be used to translate *états-provinciaux*, in order to avoid confusion with the *assemblées provinciales*.

[2] Picot, Georges, *Histoire des Etats-Généraux* (Paris, 1888, 5 vols.).

3

has written, or to summarize his five volumes. A comparison of his work with available sources[3] brings out, however, certain developments pertinent to the convocation of the States-General in 1789, and to the practice of making *cahiers de doléances*.

From the point of view of the existence and functioning of a national representative body with partial legislative powers, French history falls into five periods: (1) prior to 1484, a period of the beginnings of the States-General and of the formulation of traditions; (2) 1484-1615, a period of productive activity; (3) 1615-1789, an era when the French kings governed without the national representative body;[4] (4) 1789 until the third French Republic, a period of alternative régimes, now government with a national representative body, now government with a body or bodies whose membership and powers were entirely controlled by a dictatorial committee, emperor, or king; (5) the third French Republic, with its parliamentary régime. With the exception of the States-General of 1789, the last two periods are irrelevant to our present study.

The records for the first period are scanty, and the debatable problems relating to the States-General do not concern us here.[5] By 1484, the beginning of the second period, the following practices had been evolved: royal summons by classes within geographic areas, the granting of specific powers to the deputies; the composition of *cahiers de doléances* as guides for the deputies; the presentation to the king of summaries of the reforms solicited by each class; bargaining by the king with the States-General for money in return for a promise of reform, and the issuance, after the adjournment of the States-General, of a reform ordinance based upon the cahiers.

During the second period of French constitutional history, 1484-1615, there were six important meetings of the States-General. These were held in 1484, 1560, 1576, 1588, 1593-96, and 1614. With the convocation of 1484, election by *bailliage*[6] was definitely substituted for the personal, royal summons. The early promise of this States-General did not materialize, because of the intervention of the Princes and an unwise grant of money by the States-General before any reforms had been promised.[7] The two succeeding French kings, Louis XII and Francis I, carried out the reforms which had been

---

[3] *Cf.* Bibliography under "Early States-Generals."

[4] There were two abortive attempts to hold States-Generals in 1649 and 1651.

[5] For example, the origin of the States-General (Carolingian council, feudal assemblies, military assemblies), etc.

[6] *Bailliage* will be used, rather than its nearest English equivalent, "bailiwick."

[7] *Cf.* Picot, G., *op. cit.*, Vol. I, pp. 345 *et seq.*, and Vol. II, *passim.*

solicited in 1484, and evaded the nebulous claims of the States-General to an exclusive right to authorize new taxes. Louis XII summoned it only once, in 1506, not for general reform, but to face the problem of breaking the Hapsburg marriage alliance.[8] The States-General showed such unanimity of opinion among the orders and with the king, that it voted to call Louis XII the "father of his people."[9] Francis I avoided summoning the States-General altogether. Louis XII and Francis I, like their Tudor contemporaries in England, sensed the spirit of the times, and received popular support for their rule, without recourse to the national representative body.

The meetings of the States-General in France of 1560, 1576, 1588, and 1593-96 formed a part of the intricate history of the French civil wars, in which religious, constitutional, social, economic, and national issues were mingled. Due to the wise policy of L'Hôpital in carrying out the principles laid down by the States-General of 1560, the meeting of that year resulted in the Ordinance of Orléans, a strengthening of the Salic law, and the demand for an oath of regency. At this time also, the practice of limiting the powers of deputies to the States-General received additional sanction.

Although the Protestants abstained from participation in the States-General of 1576, that national body reflected popular feeling at the time. The interest of France as a whole was made paramount over religious or sectional claims, while the third estate held the balance of power between the other two orders. Further sanction was given to the holding of separate sessions for each order, in place of the joint session held in 1484, and at the same time, the third estate was granted double the number of representatives of the privileged orders.

The States-Generals of 1588 and 1593-96 further demonstrated the weakness of that body. The result of quarrels over procedure and over the extent of the deputies' powers was a deadlock. With the failure of the latter meeting, Henry IV inaugurated a period of personal rule. By relying on the Assembly of Notables, in place of the three orders as represented in the States-General, and by carrying out the reforms demanded by the States-Generals of 1560, 1576, and 1588, he ruled without summoning a new meeting of the national body.

In 1614, when the treasury was depleted during the regency of

---

[8] The States-General advocated breaking the alliance, and substituting the betrothal of Claude of Lorraine with Francis, who later became Francis I.

[9] Cf. Picot, op. cit., Vol. II, pp. 141 et seq.

Marie de Medici, another States-General was called. It failed to accomplish anything by reason of quarrels between the orders, the uncompromising attitude of the third estate, the time wasted in settling minor matters of procedure, and the successful evasion of definite measures by the regency. The deputies and the institution of the States-General, as well, were discredited, and thereafter the king could rely directly on popular support. For the succeeding one hundred and seventy-five years, except for abortive attempts in 1649 and 1651, during the *Fronde*, the French kings ruled without the States-General.

Despite the intermittent history and inglorious failures of the States-Generals, the traditions developed before 1484 were strengthened and elaborated during the active period 1484-1615. Convocation by *bailliage* was the accepted method, and *cahiers de doléances* were drawn up in all electoral districts. While summaries of the *bailliage* cahiers for each order were prepared and sent to the king, the common method of deliberation in the States-General had come to be by the orders meeting separately. Hereditary monarchy, the Salic law, and Catholicism were among the accepted principles of French law, but the powers of the States-General continued to remain vague. Failure to establish by law the relative status of the three orders and to achieve constitutional definition of the powers of the States-General *vis-à-vis* the monarch, resulted in the triumph of the latter. After 1614, came absolute monarchy. Certain checks existed, but their operation depended largely on the personal force and character of the monarch himself. Under Louis XIV, these restraints were negligible. Under Louis XVI, their operation created a deadlock and such governmental ineffectiveness, that a reversion to the traditional States-General seemed to be the only way out of the *impasse*.

PRELIMINARIES OF THE CONVOCATION OF 1789

Historians have disagreed concerning the date of the first official promise to convoke the States-General for 1789. Brette took as the point of departure for his study of the convocation, the order in council (*arrêt du conseil*) of July 5, 1788[10] and this seems to be the logical approach. A royal commission, which had studied the early States-Generals, concluded that the method of convocation used

[10] It will be more convenient to refer to the reprint of documents in Brette than to originals at the National Archives in Paris. For the text of the order in council, *cf.* Brette, Armand, *Recueil des documents relatifs à la convocation des Etats-Généraux de 1789* (Paris, 1894-1915), Vol. I, p. 19.

in 1614 could not be applied in its entirety in 1789. The royal council wanted information to supplement that already studied, and also desired some expression of opinion from French subjects. Consequently, an order in council was issued directing the royal officials throughout France to search in local archives and libraries for information regarding the past States-Generals.[11] Provincial-Estates, universities, learned societies, and other groups were also invited to send any pertinent information they might have to the Keeper of the Seals. These materials, conscientiously gathered and sometimes accompanied by summaries and recommendations, furnished the royal councils with comprehensive materials on the traditions and practices of the States-Generals.

The order in council had a further result not altogether foreseen. It contained no prohibition against publication of the materials so gathered: there was an implicit grant of freedom to the press. Hitherto, delays attendant upon obtaining permission to print, refusal of permits by royal censors, and arbitrary action by means of *lettres de cachet* against authors held suspect, caused many inconveniences and acted as a check on the quantity as well as the content of publications. The great philosophers of the eighteenth century had evaded this censorship by using printers in Amsterdam, Antwerp, Basle, and Geneva. After the order in council of July 5, 1788, however, France was inundated with pamphlets dealing with the history of the States-Generals and with discussions of contemporary problems. One authority has estimated that no less than five hundred pamphlets appeared between July 5 and December 27, alone.[12] A bibliography of those published after December 27 and before May 6, 1789, when the States-General actually opened, has not yet been made, but there are many evidences that the flood of pamphlets became even greater after the method of convocation had been determined. After that date, they dealt less with the States-General than with the problems it would have to face.

The order in council of July 5 appealed to French history and tradition, but also to contemporary opinion. Between its issuance and the promulgation of the rule for convocation, bearing the date of January 24, 1789,[13] four developments took place, which are significant for their influence upon public opinion during that period.

[11] *Idem*, pp. 19 *et seq.*
[12] Garrett, Mitchell E., *A Critical Bibliography of the Pamphlet Literature. . . .* (Birmingham, Alabama, 1925), p. 2.
[13] *Cf. infra*, p. 12 *et seq.*

On August 8, 1788, an order in council promised the opening of the States-General for May, 1789, and suspended the operation of the May edicts for judicial reform during the electoral period.[14] These edicts had been designed to carry out much needed reforms toward a simplification of judicial procedure, amelioration of criminal justice, and a diminution of the obstructive power of the *Parlements*.[15] The Parlements had formerly been the chief bulwark against monarchial absolutism, in the absence of the States-General. There had existed thirteen Parlements, of which the Parlement of Paris had the largest jurisdiction and a dominant influence. When the king issued an order, it had to be registered by each Parlement before it could be applied within its jurisdiction. Although the king could virtually overcome opposition by holding a *lit de justice*,[16] nevertheless, the Parlements had held up measures prejudicial to a given area and had prevented hasty action. In recent years, however, the Parlements had been recalcitrant and had actively opposed royal measures. Consequently, according to the May edicts of 1788, the power of the Parlements to register laws was to be given to a plenary court whose members would be appointed by the king. With the exception of this item, the reforms of the May edicts were in line with the demands of the eighteenth century jurists, but the Parlements were still too strong to be supplanted without resistance, and were looked upon as a needed check against arbitrary action by the monarch.

The *Journée des Tuiles*, June 7, 1788, had witnessed an alliance of the masses with the magistrates of the Parlement of Grenoble against the May edicts.[17] Opposition to the royal measures increased in each center where a provincial Parlement met. The suspension, therefore, of the plenary court in the order in council of August 8, was a concession to the opposition, and an evidence of the weakness of the royal government. At this moment of triumph, the Parlements might have assumed leadership of the popular movement and

[14] *Cf.* Brette, *op. cit.*, Vol. I, pp. 23-25.

[15] On the May edicts, *cf.* Seligman, Edmond, *La Justice pendant la Révolution* (Paris, 1901), Vol. I, pp. 111 *et seq.*

[16] When the Parlement refused to register an edict, the king might add to the number of magistrates and, by choosing those who would support his edict, could overcome the opposition. Such a procedure was called a *lit de justice*. The very threat of this was sometimes sufficient to win over the Parlement.

[17] For events in the Dauphiné, *cf.* Champollion-Figéac, A., *Chroniques dauphinoises* (Vienne, 1884), Vol. I, *passim*.

have directed it, but they did not. Whereas the Parlements had been spokesmen for reform, these bodies soon became reactionary. Instead of seeking the welfare of France, they sought the maintenance of their own privileges and prestige. The leaders of the Revolution were not parlementarians. The Parlements soon lost their early popularity, and were, in fact, dissolved early in the Revolution.[18] The other judicial reforms promised in the May edicts remained unenforced, but many of the detailed measures reappeared in the legal reforms enacted by the National Assembly. Thus, an attempt at constructive reform by Louis XVI was defeated by the Parlements, and these problems were added to the many which the future States-General would have to face.

A second important development of this interval, already forecast, was the defection of the Parlements from the ranks of the progressive movement. The Parlements began censuring pamphlets which they considered too revolutionary. The Parlement of Paris denounced the pamphlet by Linguet, *Annales politiques, civiles, et litteraires,* on September 27, 1788,[19] and other Parlements followed suit. Condemnations became more frequent after December, 1788.[20] This action aroused opposition among the revolutionary forces, led to distrust of the Parlements and contributed to their subsequent destruction. Such a reëstablishment of arbitrary censorship contributed to the ferment of public opinion.

A third important event in the six-month interval between July 5 and the royal convocation was the second meeting, on October 5, 1788, of the Assembly of Notables, summoned by royal order to discuss the convocation.[21] The subdivisions of the Assembly considered many questions, but on December 27, Necker made a report to Louis XVI summarizing only three of their recommendations.[22] The minutes of the assembly were not published at the time, so that the public received Necker's report as the opinion of the Notables. He made three recommendations: (1) that representation in the States-General be according to *bailliage,* as in 1614, but proportionate to the population; (2) that the third estate have a number of representatives equal to that of the clergy and nobles taken together,

---

[18] The National Assembly dissolved the Parlements on November 3, 1789.

[19] *Cf.* Brette, *op. cit.,* Vol. I, p. 31.

[20] *Ibid.,* pp. 31 *et seq.*

[21] *Ibid.,* Vol. I, p. 32. The assembly had met in 1787.

[22] For the text of what was later made public, *cf. Archives parlementaires,* (Paris, 1867-75), Vol. I, pp. 390-484. Necker's report is given, pp. 489. *et seq.*

known as "the doubling of the third;" and (3) that each order choose its deputies exclusively from among its members. Since only one of the six bureaus of the Assembly of Notables favored doubling of the third estate, Necker gave the public a more liberal impression of the recommendations of that body than was warranted by the facts.[23]

The result of Necker's recommendations was an order in council of December 27, 1788, adopting the first two principles, but ignoring the third.[24] The last was of minor importance, but Necker and, after him, the king's council, made a fatal error in the omission of any ruling about the method of voting in the States-General. The Assembly of Notables was overwhelmingly for maintenance of the traditional method of voting (that is to say, vote by order),[25] while the Parlement of Paris had avoided the issue in their declaration of December 5.[26] The King and Necker may have realized the danger of openly sanctioning the old method. It was perhaps safest at the moment to avoid the thorny question of the method of voting, but the evasion left a problem of prime importance for the States-General itself to settle. In the interval, before the first sessions, the revolutionary forces had increased.

The immediate result of the king's pronouncement on December 27, 1788, was universal enthusiasm, especially among the third estate. It was only when far-sighted leaders pointed out the illusory advantage of representation according to population and the doubling of the third estate, without vote by head, that popular discussion turned from consideration of numerical representation to the method of voting. The conservatism of the Assembly of Notables and the evasion by Necker and Louis XVI, stimulated revolutionary agitation. Vote by head became the cry of radicals.

The fourth general development of the period was an increased ferment throughout France. The classes who were to play a dominant rôle in the States-General were busy reading, writing, and discussing. A great interchange of ideas, impossible under a strict censorship, was going on. In addition, the popular reaction to the grain shortage, presaged in the notices of disorders in the market places, seizure of supplies, and sabotage in the rural districts,[27] gave some forewarning

[23] Garrett, Mitchell, "The Call for Information Concerning the States-General in 1788," in *American Historical Review*, April, 1932, pp. 510-11.

[24] *Cf.* Brette, *op. cit.*, Vol. I, pp. 37-38.

[25] Garrett, Mitchell, *op. cit.*, note 23.

[26] *Archives parlementaires*, Vol. I, p. 550.

[27] The despatches of the British ambassador made frequent mention of the disturb-

of the future significance of the economic element in shaping the thought of the French masses. While the royal councils were studying the traditions of past States-Generals and were attempting to steer a middle course, radical mutterings were growing in volume. The six months following the first official announcement relative to the States-General showed a revival of French traditions, a popularization of eighteenth century philosophy, a leavening of the masses, and the appearance of new popular leaders.

THE CONVOCATION OF 1789

National popular elections are such a common occurrence today, that it is hard for us to imagine ourselves in the France of 1789. There, an institution in abeyance for one hundred and seventy-five years was revived amid changed circumstances. The program of convocation actually adopted, after all information had been assembled and discussed, was a compromise between the traditional method, which bolstered class and regional privileges, and the principles of uniformity and equality.[28] Convocation by *bailliage,* or the equivalent judicial unit, was applied to all districts that had been represented in the States-General of 1614, but some reclassification of the districts was undertaken. The same rule was applied to some of the districts added since 1614, but a slightly different procedure was applied to most of them, as well as to numerous *pays d'états.* An attempt was made to assign representation proportionate to the population of the various districts, which were very different in geographic area,[29] and although a type rule was issued for four-fifths of the territory of France, modifications and local variations neutralized this attempt at uniformity. The result was a most intricate system, whose irregularities were further increased by variations in local application. The analysis of the convocation which follows is intended to clarify the nature of the *cahiers de doléances,* and focuses, therefore, principally on the number of indirect steps applied in the elections of the different electoral units.

The convocation, as actually carried out, applied seven types of

---

ances outside of Paris (Browning, Oscar, *Despatches from Paris* (London, 1909-10), Vol. II, *passim.* The correspondence of the intendants and local officials indicated increasing ferment as the date for the opening of the States-General approached (*cf.* correspondence in the folders of each *bailliage, Arch. Nat.* Ba 9- Ba 87).

[28] *Cf.* in addition to the articles of the convocation regulations, the preamble of the January edict, *op. cit.,* Vol. I, pp. 66 *et seq.*

[29] *Cf.* map. p. 30.

procedure.[30] By means of this classification, the distinction between preliminary and general cahiers will be clear. The seven groups hereafter described are as follows: (1) all *bailliages*[31] which proceeded according to the type regulation of January 24, 1789; (2) districts which united in a common center for elections, but whose separate cahiers were given to the deputies; (3) districts where the Provincial-Estates carried on the elections; (4) privileged towns; (5) several small districts that had been included within *bailliages* already convoked, but which, after protest, received the right of direct representation in the States-General; (6) districts which had rulings peculiar to themselves; and (7) districts, chiefly the French colonies, for which there was no royal convocation, but which held elections subsequently recognized by the National Assembly. The accompanying map shows that the greatest geographic area, with a correspondingly larger proportion of the population, came under the first type. Privileged cities were scattered, but the remaining types of convocation were applied chiefly to frontier areas.

THE FIRST TYPE OF CONVOCATION—THE GENERAL REGULATION

The first group, which comprised the greater part of France, proceeded according to the regulation of January 24, 1789,[32] or applied the same method under rulings issued at later dates.[33] Innumerable, small modifications were issued for individual districts, but the same general procedure was used.

Louis XVI intended that a very wide suffrage be applied, but different qualifications and privileges for each of the three classes was an inevitable result of the class distinctions of the time. For

[30] Brette's four-fold classification (the *pays d'élection* that obeyed the January regulation, *pays d'état* that followed the same method, *pays d'état* that had special convocation, and districts that received no royal convocation), does not clarify the problem of the cahiers and does not bring out common likenesses and differences in the procedure used. (*cf.* Brette, *op. cit.*, Vol. I, *passim.*).

[31] The term *bailliage* will be employed as the type term for the electoral unit, although some districts were called *sénéchaussée, comté, gouvernance,* etc.

[32] For the entire text of the January 24, 1789 edict, see Brette, *op. cit.*, Vol. I, pp. 64-87. Brette gives useful tables showing what districts followed the same procedure as in 1614 and also the modifications of the type rule. (*loc. cit.*, Vol. I, *passim*).

[33] The following districts have been included in the type classification because they followed the same procedure, although the convocation orders were issued later: Paris *hors-les-murs* (March 28, 1789, *loc. cit.*, p. 110); Colmar and Schlestadt, Haguenau, and Belfort and Huningue, all of Alsace (Feb. 17, 1789, *loc. cit.*, p. 217); Aix, Arles (*sénéchaussée*), and Marseille, all of Provence (March 2, 1789, *loc. cit.*, p. 239).

GENERAL ELECTORAL DISTRICTS
OF 1789

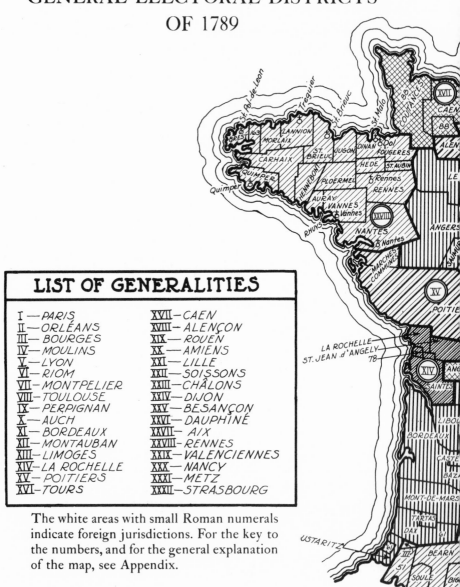

LIST OF GENERALITIES

I — PARIS	XVII — CAEN
II — ORLÉANS	XVIII — ALENÇON
III — BOURGES	XIX — ROUEN
IV — MOULINS	XX — AMIENS
V — LYON	XXI — LILLE
VI — RIOM	XXII — SOISSONS
VII — MONTPELIER	XXIII — CHÂLONS
VIII — TOULOUSE	XXIV — DIJON
IX — PERPIGNAN	XXV — BESANÇON
X — AUCH	XXVI — DAUPHINÉ
XI — BORDEAUX	XXVII — AIX
XII — MONTAUBAN	XXVIII — RENNES
XIII — LIMOGES	XXIX — VALENCIENNES
XIV — LA ROCHELLE	XXX — NANCY
XV — POITIERS	XXXI — METZ
XVI — TOURS	XXXII — STRASBOURG

The white areas with small Roman numerals
indicate foreign jurisdictions. For the key to
the numbers, and for the general explanation
of the map, see Appendix.

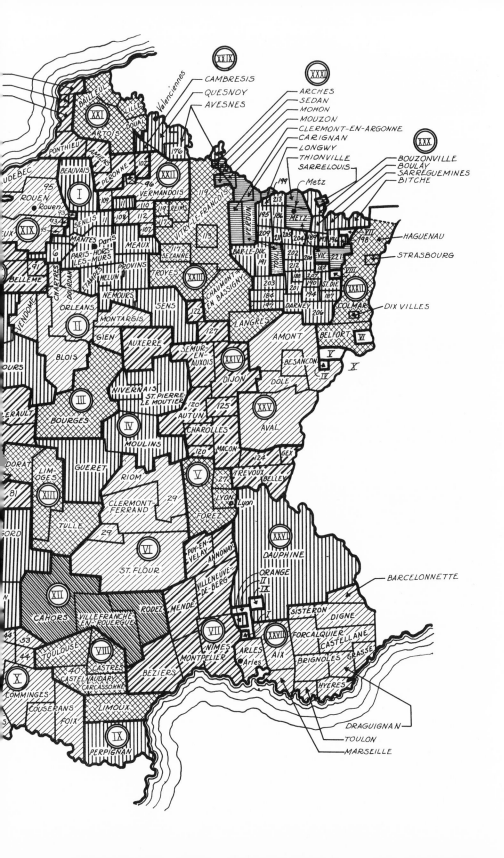

the clergy, all Catholic ecclesiastics were eligible for the assemblies of the clergy (arts. 9-12, 14-19).[34] All nobles possessing fiefs, or those without fiefs, but born French or naturalized, resident in the district, twenty-five years of age and possessing acquired or transmissible nobility,[35] were eligible for assemblies of the nobles (arts. 12, 16-17, 20-21).[36] In the assemblies of the third estate, were all nobles not possessing transmissible nobility, and all members of the third estate who were eligible. The qualifications for the latter were (1) French birth or naturalization, (2) twenty-five years of age, and (3) residence and registration on the tax rolls (arts. 25-30). The regulation of January 24 provided for very nearly universal manhood suffrage.

The wide suffrage was, however, modified and restricted by two other features of the convocation, plural voting and indirect election. Clergy and nobles possessing fiefs had the right to be represented wherever they held property, by appearing in person in one assembly and by a representative in the others (arts. 17, 21). This privilege was particularly significant in such cases as that of the Duke of Orléans, whose active campaigning for election was thereby facilitated, and his influence increased by representation in several *bailliages*.[37]

The inclusiveness of the primary suffrage qualifications was further neutralized and controlled by the system of indirect elections. As Necker had recommended, the jurisdiction of the *bailliage* was the electoral unit according to the regulation of January 24, but the districts were classified into principal and secondary *bailliages*. A principal *bailliage* formed one electoral unit, and either comprised a single judicial area, or might have several subordinate jurisdictions dependent upon it. Any *bailliage* subordinate to another electoral unit was called a secondary *bailliage*. After the method of election for the principal *bailliage* without secondary areas has been made clear, the slight difference between these and principal *bailliages* with secondary *bailliages* will be noted. Since judicial units were used,

---

[34] The articles of the January 24 regulation will be cited, without the page reference. *Cf.* note 32 for general page references.

[35] On titles of nobility, see article *Noblesse* in Marion, M., *Dictionnaire des institutions de la France au dix-septième et dix-huitième siècle* (Paris, 1923).

[36] Attention may be called to the fact that French citizenship was not required of nobles holding fiefs. Accordingly, German princes holding land in Alsace, and Swiss holders of fiefs in Franche-Comté might take part in the elections.

[37] *Cf. infra*, p. 57 on the Duke of Orléans.

transmission of the royal convocation orders and administration of the electoral assemblies was the duty of the royal judicial officers, the *baillis, the lieutenants-généraux,* and their *subdelegates.*

In the elections of a principal *bailliage,* there were two steps for the clergy; one step for the nobles; and two, three or four steps for the third estate. The regular clergy, the chapters, and ecclesiastics not holding an office, held preliminary assemblies and chose delegates to the general assembly of the clergy of the *bailliage* (arts. 9-11, 15). In the latter, curates,[38] bishops, and all the higher clergy appeared in person or by personal substitutes. For the nobles, all those who were eligible, appeared in person or were personally represented (arts. 12, 16-17, 20-21). Women owners of fiefs and orders of nuns were represented in the general assembly of the nobles, or of the clergy, by procurators (art. 20). A contrast between the elections of the privileged orders and those of the third estate will be evident at once in the greater complexity of the latter, and in the machinery which separated the deputies to the States-General from the ordinary voter. First, the parishes of a *bailliage* elected delegates to the assembly of the *bailliage* (art. 25). When towns of a *bailliage* possessed gilds, each gild assembled and chose a number of delegates to a general assembly of the town, while non-members of gilds met in an assembly and also chose delegates (arts. 26-28). A general assembly of the town composed of the delegates from these two types of assemblies chose delegates to the *bailliage* assembly. The general assembly of the third estate of a *bailliage* comprised, therefore, representatives of the parishes and towns. If this assembly numbered more than two hundred members, it was required to reduce itself to two hundred.

All delegates or members of the general assemblies of a *bailliage* convened first in a joint assembly of the three orders, which was opened by the chief judicial officer of the *bailliage* (art. 40).[39] The roll of members was taken, and then each order separated and held its own assembly. The convocation permitted the three orders or two of them to unite in the composition of the cahier, but the elections

---

[38] Any curate whose parish was at a great distance from the town where the general assembly met was required to send a delegate, while he remained in his parish to perform his religious duties (art. 14).

[39] The majority of *bailliages* kept a separate *procès-verbal* of the opening and closing session of the three orders, but occasionally the minutes of the assembly of the third estate were inserted between the two meetings.

14

BAILLIAGE OF THE FIRST TYPE

GENERAL ASSEMBLY OF THE THREE ORDERS FOR OPENING

First Degree | Second Degree | Third Degree | Fourth Degree

CLERGY

First Degree
1. Assemblies of ecclesiastical chapters^[a]
2. Assemblies of each of the regular orders^[b]
3. Assemblies of ecclesiastics without office^[c]

Fourth Degree
General Assembly of Clergy of *bailliage* composed of:
1. Deputies from 1, 2, 3
2. Curates^[d]
3. Higher Clergy^[e]

NOBLES

Fourth Degree
General Assembly of Nobles of Bailliage composed of:
1. Nobles^[f]
2. Procurators of C and N possessing fiefs^[g]
3. Procurators of women owners^[h]

THIRD ESTATE

PRINCIPAL BAILLIAGE

Second Degree
1. Parish assemblies^[i]
2. Towns without gilds^[j]
3. Towns with gilds^[k]: assemblies by gild and assembly of unorganized citizens

Third Degree
4. Assembly of town composed of gild deputies and unorganized deputies^[l]

SECONDARY BAILLIAGE

Second Degree
1. Parish assemblies
2. Towns without gilds
3. Towns with gilds: assemblies by gilds and assembly of unorganized citizens

Third Degree
4. Assembly of town composed of gild deputies and unorganized deputies

Third Degree
5. Preliminary assembly of principal *bailliage* for reduction to one quarter composed of deputies from 1, 2, and 4
6. General assembly of secondary *bailliage* composed of deputies from 1, 2, and 4

Fourth Degree
General Assembly of Third Estate of Principal with Secondary *bailliage* composed of deputies from 5 and 6

---

a One deputy for every 10 canons, 1 for every 20 assistants (art. 10).
b One deputy for each order (art. 11).
c One deputy for each 20 members (art. 15).
d Cf. art. 14.

e Cf. art. 12.
f Cf. art. 12 and 16.
g Cf. art. 17.
h Cf. art. 20.

i Two deputies for every 200 "*feux*." Cf. art. 31.
j Two deputies for every 100 members. Cf. art. 25.
k One deputy for every 100 gild members, 2 deputies for every 100 unorganized citizens. Cf. arts. 26, 27.
l Deputation according to population. Cf. art. 28.

were to be held separately by orders. In the majority of cases, each order drew up its cahier and elected the number of deputies allowed by the royal convocation. A joint assembly of the three orders, in which the deputies took an oath and received their election papers and cahiers, terminated the electoral process in all general *bailliages*.

For principal *bailliages* with secondary *bailliages*, the difference of method affected the third estate only. The clergy and nobles of the secondary *bailliages* appeared at the assembly of the principal *bailliage*, just as did members of these orders of the principal *bailliage*. An additional indirect step was, however, added for the third estate. The primary elections within the secondary *bailliages* proceeded in the same manner as in the principal *bailliages* without secondary districts (art. 38). In the principal *bailliages* a preliminary assembly of the delegates from the parishes and towns was held, in which the number of delegates was reduced to one quarter (arts. 33-34).[40] The general assembly of all the principal and secondary districts was composed of the reduced number of delegates from the preliminary assembly of the principal *bailliage*, and the delegates from the general assemblies of the secondary *bailliages* (four steps). It was this assembly which elected deputies to the States-General for the third estate of the entire area, principal and secondary *bailliages*.

The accompanying chart may help to visualize the complicated system of indirect elections. Many principal *bailliages* had two or more subordinate ones, but as the system was the same for each of the latter, the diagram is made with only one as a type. The method just described, and pictured in the chart, was typical of all districts to which the regulation of January 24 applied, or to other districts included in the first group.

Each of the assemblies legally constituted as electorates had the right to draw up *cahiers de doléances*.[41] In addition, curates and ecclesiastics appearing in person in the assemblies of the clergy might present cahiers. Thus, for the first type of convocation, there were for the clergy: cahiers of the curates, of chapters, of monastic orders, of seminaries, of priests without office, of the higher clergy, and a cahier of the united clergy of the *bailliage*. For the nobles, without indirect election, there was only the cahier of the assembly of the nobles. For the third estate, there were: parish cahiers, gild cahiers, cahiers of unorganized townsmen, town or city cahiers, cahiers of

---

[40] In actual fact, the reduction was not always carried out.
[41] *Cf.* on the cahiers, text for Jan. 24, arts. 21, 24, 28, 33-34, 38, 40, 43-45, 49.

secondary *bailliages,* cahiers of preliminary assemblies of principal *bailliages,* and cahiers of the principal *bailliage* united with its secondary *bailliages.* A vast number of cahiers resulted from the number of assemblies prescribed by the royal convocation.

THE SECOND TYPE OF CONVOCATION—REUNION OF BAILLIAGES

The second type of convocation, which for convenience will be called *reunion of bailliages,* applied the same unit of election, the *bailliage,* the same qualifications for voting, and the same privilege of plural vote, as the first type.[42] The difference between the two came in the addition of an indirect step in the elections for all three classes. In this type, the convocation rule was not based on the regulation of January 24, but separate summons were sent to each of the districts. The districts included in the second type, though widely scattered geographically, applied the same method.

For the second type of convocation, there were no principal and secondary *bailliages.*[43] All *bailliages* were, in a sense, principal *bailliages,* within which the elections proceeded just as in the first type of convocation. The difference came in the final step taken after these elections. All *bailliages* of the second type were classified into groups around a center of reunion.[44] The representatives of each of the three

[42] For the regulations which determined the centers of reunion, and details of the convocation of the second type, *cf.* Brette, *op. cit.,* Vol. I, pp. 231 *et. seq.,* pp. 238 *et seq.,* pp. 220 *et seq.*

[43] There were three exceptions to this statement. Verdun, Carignan and Sedan had each a small secondary district dependent upon them, but this did not affect the part of the election which differed from the first type of convocation.

[44] The following groupings indicate the procedure for the second type of convocation.

Generality of Aix

Draguignan : Castellane, Draguignan, Grasse.
Forcalquier : Barcelonnette, Digne, Forcalquier, Sisteron.
Toulon : Brignoles, Hyères, Toulon.

Generality of Metz

Metz : Longwy, Metz, Sarrebourg and Phalsbourg, Sarrelouis, Thionville.
Sedan : Carignan, Mohon, Mouzon, Sedan.
Toul : Toul, Vic.
Verdun : Clermont à Varennes, Verdun.

Generality of Nancy

Bar-le-Duc : Bar-le-Duc, Bourmont, Briey, Commercy, Etain, La Marche, Longuyon, Pont-à-Mousson, St. Mihiel, Thiaucourt, Villers-la-Montagne.
Mirecourt : Bruyères, Charmes, Châtel-sur-Moselle, Darney, Epinal, Neufchâteau, Mirecourt, Remiremont, St. Dié.
Nancy : Blamont, Lunéville, Nancy, Nomény, Rozières, Vézelise.
Sarreguemines : Bitche, Boulay, Bouzonville, Château-Salins, Dieuze, Fénestrange, Lixheim, Sarreguemines.

orders of the various *bailliages* assembled at a center of reunion, where they chose deputies to the States-General. This made an additional step for the clergy and nobles as well as for the third estate. The significant fact for a study of the *cahiers de doléances* is that the assemblies at the centers of reunion did not draw up *cahiers de doléances*.[45] These assemblies elected deputies directly to the States-General, but instead of making joint cahiers of all the *bailliages* united (as happened in districts of the first type where there were secondary *bailliages*), the cahiers of each of the subsidiary *bailliages* were given to the deputies.

Again for clarity, a diagram is given. It will be remembered that the first steps within the *bailliages* were the same as in the first type of convocation; they have not been repeated in this diagram.

BAILLIAGES OF THE SECOND TYPE

BAILLIAGES		CENTER OF REUNION (No cahiers made)

The result of this type of convocation was a larger number of general cahiers in relation to the area of the districts and to their population than was produced by the first type of convocation. A glance at the map, especially at the sections of the *generalities* of Nancy and of Metz proves this statement.[46] Whereas there were thirty-five

[45] *Cf.* the respective royal regulations, Brette, *op. cit.*, Vol. I, p. 220, art. 4; p. 231, art. 4; p. 239, art 6. Brette has given only the summary of these royal regulations, which are more explicit in the full texts. *Cf.* for example, the complete text of the convocation for Provence, *Arch. Nat.* Ba 69.

[46] *Cf.* Map p. 12. There were 57 *bailliages* in the second type of convocation as against 139 in the first, but the area and population of the latter was much greater.

general cahiers for the *generality* of Paris and only seven for the *generality* of Poitiers, there were ninety-three for the *generality* of Nancy, which was no larger in area than either of these.[47] This fact should not be overlooked when the opinions expressed in the cahiers are weighed.

THE THIRD TYPE OF CONVOCATION—PROVINCIAL-ESTATES

The convocation according to the third, fourth, fifth, and sixth types was a concession to the privileges of the areas concerned. The third type provided for elections by the Provincial-Estates, and was applied in three districts—the Dauphiné, Béarn, and Navarre. Despite this common feature, however, each of these districts displayed local peculiarities of procedure.

The Dauphiné has sometimes been called the cradle of the Revolution. There had been open resistance to the establishment of a Provincial-Assembly under the edict of 1787, and also to the May edicts. The dominant group in the Dauphiné desired the continuance of the traditional Provincial-Estates, but asked for reform in its composition. A reorganization of this body was authorized by an order in council of October 22, 1788.[48] The new Provincial-Estates began meetings in December, 1788,[49] and was composed of deputies of all three orders, with the third estate represented by double the number of either of the first two orders. The suffrage was more liberal for the clergy and more restricted for the nobles and third estate than elsewhere in France. In the case of the clergy, clerical office was the necessary qualification, but both the higher and lower clergy held preliminary assemblies and chose deputies to the Provincial-Estates. A stricter interpretation of titles of nobility and a higher tax qualification were imposed for the nobles, who met by district and chose representatives to the Provincial-Estates. A higher tax qualification was also applied for the third estate, which held preliminary assemblies within the six *élections* (districts similar to the *bailliage*) into which the Dauphiné was divided.

The Provincial-Estates so composed, and meeting as one chamber, held elections and drew up a joint cahier for the States-General. The elections took place early in January, 1789, without previous royal

---

[47] *Cf.* the table on p. 12.

[48] *Cf.* Brette, *op. cit.*, Vol. I, pp. 286 *et seq.*

[49] *Cf.* p. v. of Provincial-Estates, *Arch. Nat.* Ba 74 MS, and printed. Part of the minutes are reprinted, AP (*Archives parlementaires*), Vol. III, pp. 80-83.

authorization, but were eventually legalized.[50] Thus, the procedure in the Dauphiné antedated that of the general convocation and took place as a part of the reorganization of the Provincial-Estates. Although the elections were by indirect steps, there were no preliminary cahiers for the Dauphiné, but a body of documents of a similar nature does exist. After the adjournment of the Provincial-Estates, an Intermediate Commission, appointed to carry out the measures adopted by the Provincial-Estates, sent questionnaires to all the communes (parishes) of the Dauphiné.[51] The answers, often composed by the municipal or communal council, gave details of local conditions comparable to parish cahiers in other districts of France. Many of these documents have been preserved.[52] There was, however, only one *general* cahier for the Dauphiné.

Béarn was a second example of election by the Provincial-Estates. An effort to apply election by *bailliage* failed,[53] and a second convocation order was issued for elections by the Provincial-Estates. The regular body was augmented,[54] sat in two chambers—the clergy and nobles in one body, called the *Grand Corps,* and the third estate apart in a second chamber. Each of the two chambers made a cahier, but the elections for the States-General of each order were separate. In addition, the lower clergy were authorized to hold special elections, at which they made a joint cahier.[55]

The third district where election by Provincial-Estates was applied was Navarre. Like Béarn, the original convocation by *sénéchaussée* was withdrawn and a convocation by the Provincial-Estates authorized.[56] The third estate of the existing Provincial-Estates refused to approve the plan of the clergy and nobles for additional representation.[57] This raised the constitutional question as to whether the consent of all three orders was necessary. The problem was referred to the king, and resulted in a reproof administered to the third estate.[58] An augmented Provincial-Estates met in July, 1789,[59] which

---

[50] *Lettre du Roi,* of April 7, 1789, *Arch. Nat.* B III 163, pp. 539 *et seq.*

[51] Cf. p. v. of the Intermediate Commission, *Arch. Isère,* III C 4.

[52] *Cf.* Hyslop, B., *Repertoire critique des cahiers de doléances de 1789* (Paris, 1933), pp. 223 *et seq.*

[53] *Cf.* Brette, *op. cit.,* Vol. I, pp. 291 *et seq.,* and Vol. IV, pp. 209 *et seq.*

[54] *Idem,* Vol. IV, pp. 213 *et seq.* The qualifications for suffrage were determined by the law of Béarn. There were preliminary cahiers for Béarn.

[55] *Cf.* Brette, *op. cit.,* Vol. I, p. 297.

[56] *Cf.* Brette, *op. cit.,* Vol. I, pp. 213 *et seq.*

[57] *Cf.* p. v., of the Provincial-Estates, reprinted by Brette, *op. cit.,* Vol. IV, p. 184.

[58] *Cf.* letters of the king's representative, summarized by Brette, *op. cit.,* Vol. IV, pp. 195-96.

elected a deputation to present the cahier of Navarre, drawn up by the three orders jointly, to Louis XVI.[60] Sentiment was so provincial that there was no election of deputies to the National Assembly, and Navarre remained unrepresented throughout that body's existence. The deputies chosen to present the cahier to the king did consider applying for admission, but realized that their powers were insufficient. In the interest of tranquility in Navarre, no new summons of the Provincial-Estates was made.[61]

In all three cases where the Provincial-Estates held the elections for the States-General (in the case of Navarre, for deputation to the king), this involved indirect representation and the balance of power in the hands of a conservative *bloc*.

THE FOURTH TYPE OF CONVOCATION—PRIVILEGED CITIES

In the fourth type of convocation were the privileged cities. According to the regulation of January 24, 1789, Paris alone was to elect deputies direct to the States-General,[62] and all other cities were to be included in some *bailliage*. This statement was later ignored, and special direct elections were subsequently granted to seven cities: Arles, Lyon, Rouen, Valenciennes, Metz, Strasbourg, and the Ten Imperial Cities of Alsace (one district).

The royal convocation for Paris *intra-muros* was tardy, and did not appear until April 13, 1789.[63] The completion of its elections actually overlapped the opening of the States-General. According to the convocation, the preliminary assemblies of the clergy of Paris followed the same rule as the clergy under the January regulation (art. 1).[64] The nobles held preliminary assemblies in twenty departments of the city (arts. 7-11). The third estate, for whom additional suffrage qualifications were required,[65] held preliminary assemblies by districts of which there were sixty (art. 12). The deputies of the preliminary assemblies of each order met in general assemblies for Paris, similar to the general assemblies of the *bailliages* of the first

[59] *Ibid.*, Vol. IV, pp. 197 *et seq*. The suffrage depended upon the law of Navarre. There were no preliminary cahiers, however.

[60] *Cf.* Brette, *op. cit.*, Vol. II, p. 524, footnote.

[61] *Ibid.*, Vol. IV, pp. 201-2.

[62] *Ibid.*, Vol. I, p. 78, art. 29.

[63] *Cf.* Brette, *op. cit.*, Vol. I, pp. 113 *et seq*. Paris *hors-les-murs* followed the first type of convocation.

[64] *Cf.* complete description of the elections of Paris *intra-muros* in Brette, *op. cit.*, Vol. III, pp. 289 *et seq*.

[65] *Ibid.*, Vol. III, p. 290, footnote 1.

type of convocation, and each order made a cahier and held elections for the States-General. In addition, the municipal council of Paris, presiding over forty deputies representing all three orders, was authorized to draw up a cahier for the city of Paris (arts. 10-12). Unlike the gilds in other towns of France, the gilds of Paris had no official rôle in the elections. They were permitted to draw up petitions, but they did not elect deputies to the general assembly of the third estate.[66] Thus, for Paris *intra-muros*, there were preliminary cahiers for all three orders, three general cahiers, and one cahier of the municipality of Paris.

Whereas the *sénéchaussée* of Arles came under the first type of convocation, the city of Arles was granted a special convocation by royal regulation of April 4, 1789.[67] By its terms, the clergy of the town elected a deputy and made a cahier. The nobles and the third estate held separate preliminary assemblies, in which electors were chosen for a joint assembly of the two orders. This assembly elected a deputy from each class and made a joint cahier to be taken to the States-General. Thus, the town of Arles sent two general cahiers to the States-General, one for the clergy, and one for the nobles and third estate united.

The city of Lyon was authorized to insert its own cahier at the end of the cahier of the *sénéchaussée* of Lyon, although the elections were to be made in common with the assembly of the third estate.[68] The city of Rouen received similar authorization.[69]

The third estate of the town of Valenciennes was authorized to send direct representatives to the States-General, according to the last two articles of the regulation for the province of Hainaut.[70] This allowed the making of a general cahier.

The city of Strasbourg was given a special convocation in the royal regulation for Alsace.[71] The clergy and nobles took part in the assemblies of their orders held at Haguenau (art. 7), while the third

[66] The royal regulation allowed anyone or any group to present petitions and opinions to the officers of the municipality, which were, in fact, turned over to the electoral assemblies. These pamphlets and petitions do not have the official character of gild cahiers, such as gilds in other towns made.

[67] Brette, *op. cit.*, Vol. I, pp. 242-44.

[68] Brette, *op. cit.*, Vol. I, pp. 129-30.

[69] *Ibid.*, Vol. I, p. 157-58. There is no positive evidence in the general cahier nor in the *procès-verbal* of the assembly that the cahier of the town was sent with the general cahier.

[70] Brette, *op. cit.*, Vol. I, p. 216, arts. 6, 7.

[71] *Ibid.*, Vol. I, pp. 217-18.

estate held separate elections and made a cahier to send directly to the States-General (art. 6).

The city of Metz solicited direct representation like that of Strasbourg. Although the town had already taken part in the general elections of the *bailliage* of Metz, a second assembly was authorized to elect deputies to the States-General and to make a general cahier.[72] The special convocation and the assembly took place in April, 1789.[73]

The last of the privileged cities was the group of Ten Imperial Towns of Alsace. As in the case of Strasbourg, the special regulation formed a part of the rule for Alsace.[74] The third estate in each town of the ten[75] elected deputies to a joint assembly at Schlestadt, where two deputies for the States-General were elected, and a general cahier made.

THE FIFTH TYPE OF CONVOCATION—SUPPLEMENTARY AUTHORIZATION FOR DIRECT REPRESENTATION FOR SMALL DISTRICTS

The fifth group of the convocation comprises three small areas in the southwest of France (Couserans, Quatre-Vallées, and Rustaing) and one secondary *bailliage*, Rochefort-sur-Mer. In all four cases, the district had been included in the regular convocation of January 24 but was dissatisfied with a subordinate status. After protest, direct representation was authorized.

The country (*pays*) of Couserans, which was convoked as part of the district of Comminges,[76] protested against the center chosen for its general assembly. The King subsequently made Couserans a separate electoral district, authorized special elections, with one deputy for each order,[77] and the right for each to make a cahier.[78] It would appear from the *procès-verbaux* of the assemblies that the nobles and third estate agreed to make one cahier together,[79] but the

---

[72] *Ibid.*, Vol. I, pp. 227-28.

[73] *Cf.* p. v. and cahier, *Arch. Nat.* B III 86. Also, Abbé Lesprand, in the *Annuaire de la Société d'histoire et d'archéologie lorraine*, 1903, p. 192.

[74] Brette, *op. cit.*, Vol. I, p. 218, arts. 8, 9.

[75] The Ten Imperial Cities were: Colmar, Haguenau, Landau, Munster, Kayserberg, Oberehnheim, Rosheim, Schlestadt, Turckheim, and Wissembourg.

[76] Brette, *op. cit.*, Vol. I, p. 144.

[77] *Ibid.*, Vol. I, pp. 145-46.

[78] This is a notable exception to the doubling of the third estate.

[79] Unfortunately, the cahiers of Couserans were either lost in a fire in the archives of Ariège, or they were never properly placed in the local archives. We cannot, therefore, verify the *procès-verbaux* with the documents, and the former are slightly vague. Nevertheless, both the minutes of the assembly of the nobles and of the third estate speak of

clergy insisted upon working alone. The assemblies were held in May.

The third estate of the district of Quatre-Vallées found itself excluded from the assembly at Auch, to which it was convoked. Protest to the king resulted in the grant of a new assembly,[80] which met at the end of May,[81] elected a deputy to the States-General, and drew up a cahier.

The country (*pays*) of Rustaing felt itself excluded from the elections of Bigorre, of which it formed a part. After petition, royal consent was given for an assembly,[82] which met in July, 1789, drew up a cahier, and designated one of the deputies of Bigorre as its special representative.[83] This assembly represented all three orders, although the guiding hand was that of the third estate.[84]

Rochefort-sur-mer, *siège royal*, secondary to the principal *sénéchaussée* of La Rochelle, received special permission, by a modification of the January rule, to send its cahier to the States-General, although its elections were to be in common with the principal *sénéchaussée*.[85] This measure was carried out at the same time as the regulation of January 24.

coöperation to make a joint cahier. The *procès-verbal* of the nobles makes no further mention of the cahier, but the *procès-verbal* of the third estate (for May 27) mentions the reading and adoption of "le Cahier de réunion de leur Doléance." This is an unusual wording to adopt unless the two orders were united. "Réunion" was only used in this connection when secondary *bailliages* united with the principal *bailliage* for the general cahier, or when two or three orders united. As there were no secondary *bailliages* associated with Couserans, the phrase would seem to indicate that the nobles and third estate not only began, but also completed, a joint cahier. The evidence for such a conclusion is slight, but it is all that is available in view of the loss of documents and the vagueness of those that have been preserved. The point is only important in its bearing on the number of general cahiers actually made in 1789, since the cahiers themselves had been lost.

Cf. p. v. of each order, *Arch. Nat.* Ba 43, or summaries in Brette, *op. cit.*, Vol. IV, pp. 115 *et seq.* Brette accepts the supposition that each order made one cahier, and it is necessary to consult the original minutes to find the phrase quoted above rather than the summaries given by Brette.

[80] Brette, *op. cit.* Vol. I, pp. 146-47.

[81] *Ibid.*, Vol. IV, pp. 91 *et seq.*

[82] Brette, *op. cit.*, Vol. I, p. 207.

[83] *Ibid.*, Vol. IV, p. 144. Barère de Vieuzac was the deputy of the third estate of Bigorre designated by the country of Rustaing to be its special representative.

[84] The third estate invited property holders of the district belonging to the clergy and nobles to join the assembly. *Cf.* p. v. in Brette, *op. cit.*, Vol. IV, p. 144.

[85] Brette, *op. cit.*, Vol. I, pp. 132-34. This regulation resembled the privileges granted to the town of Lyon, but involved a whole secondary *bailliage* rather than a town.

THE SIXTH TYPE OF CONVOCATION—BRITTANY, CORSICA

The two areas of Brittany (*Generality* of Rennes) and Corsica had regulations peculiar to themselves. Both methods were partially borrowed from the first and second types of convocation.

Brittany, like Béarn, had entirely separate elections for the higher and lower clergy.[86] The higher clergy and the nobles of the entire provinces were convoked to an assembly at St. Brieuc.[87] As events transpired, they assembled, protested against the method of convocation, refused to elect deputies, and made no cahier.[88] The lower clergy were convoked to assemblies by the nine dioceses of Brittany;[89] as in the rest of France, the curates appeared in person or by proxy, while the chapters, seminaries, and regular clergy held preliminary assemblies and sent delegates to the assembly of the diocese.

The convocation of the third estate of Brittany was very complex and involved more indirect steps than was the case for the other classes.[90] The royal regulation was not explicit regarding the composition of the cahier, with the result that the different districts of Brittany followed one of three procedures. There were six districts that made direct elections to the States-General,[91] like the *bailliages* without secondary *bailliages* of the first type of the convocation. Three districts proceeded in the same manner as the principal *bailliages* with secondary ones, of the first type of convocation.[92] These held elections and made a joint cahier at the center of the principal *sénéchaussée*.[93] Four districts proceeded after the manner of the second type of the convocation—the reunion of *bailliages*.[94] In these last,

---

[86] *Cf. supra*, p. 20.

[87] *Cf.* the ensemble of regulations for Brittany, Brette, *op. cit.*, Vol. I, pp. 246 *et seq.* *Cf.* on the final convocation, pp. 259-65. The articles on the higher clergy and the nobles are nos. 10 and 11.

[88] *Cf.* p. v. and declarations of each order, *Arch. Nat.* Ba 25.

[89] *Cf.* text of regulation, *loc. cit.*, arts. 12-13. The nine dioceses were: Dol, Nantes, Quimper, Rennes, St. Brieuc, St. Malo, St. Pol-de-Léon, Tréguier, and Vannes.

[90] Brette, *op. cit.*, Vol. I, p. 260, and tables, pp. 263-64.

[91] Brest, Dinan, Hennebont, Lesneven, Ploërmel, and Rennes.

[92] The difference in procedure between this group and the one that follows is ascertained not by the royal regulation but from the *procès-verbaux*. Carhaix (with secondary: Châteaulin, Châteauneuf-du-Faou, Gourin, Quimperlé), Nantes (with secondary, Guérande, and Quimper (with secondary, Concarneau), were the principal *bailliages*.

[93] Fougères was the center of reunion for Hédé and St. Aubin-du-Cormier; Morlaix, for Morlaix and Lannion; St. Brieuc, for St. Brieuc and Jugon; and Vannes, for Auray, Rhuys, and Vannes.

[94] There was no mention of a joint cahier in the p. v. of Fougères (*Arch. Nat.* C 19/77). Should such a cahier be discovered, Fougères would then be classified with the

no joint cahier was made; the elections took place at the principal center and the cahiers of each of the *sénéchaussée* represented were given to the deputies.[95] Otherwise, in the matter of parish assemblies, gilds, and so forth, the method was the same as for the rest of France.

Corsica was the only district outside of the mainland of France for which a royal order of convocation was issued. The island was divided into eleven jurisdictions, within which the procedure followed the same steps as *bailliages* without secondary districts.[96] The deputies elected by each of the three orders of the eleven districts met in a joint assembly for the island of Corsica, at Bastia. This method meant two or three steps in the elections of the clergy, two for the nobles, and three for the third estate. Choice of joint or separate action at Bastia was allowed by the royal regulation, but actually, as it worked out, each of the three orders held their elections separately and made separate cahiers.[97]

THE SEVENTH TYPE OF CONVOCATION—DISTRICTS WITHOUT ROYAL CONVOCATION

The seventh group of the convocation is misnamed, as it includes the districts for which no royal convocation was issued, but which held elections subsequently recognized by the National Assembly. In this group were two districts in France (the principality of Arches and Charleville, and Bassigny-Barrois) and five of the French colonial possessions (St. Domingue, Martinique, Guadeloupe, Pondichéry, and the Islands of France and Bourbon).

The ignorance of the royal councils of the actual administrative units of France was often displayed in the convocation regulations, and was still further demonstrated by the total omission of Arches and Charleville. This ignored district near the Flemish frontier waited, but finally held elections and made a cahier in December, 1789.[98] Bassigny-Barrois was not made a unit in the general

---

sénéchaussées of Carhaix, Nantes, and Quimper, and the cahiers of Héde and St. Aubin-du-Cormier would have to be subtracted from the number of general cahiers. Both of these and the cahier of Fougères are missing.

[95] *Cf.* the royal convocation, Brette, *op. cit.*, Vol. I, pp. 266 *et seq.*

[96] The eleven districts were: Ajaccio, Aléria, Bastia, Bonifacio, Calvi and Balagna, Cap Corse, Corte, La Porta d'Ampugnani, Nebbio, Sartène, and Vico. *Cf.* table, Brette, *op. cit.*, Vol. I, p. 279.

[97] Cf. p. v. of each order, *Arch. Nat.* C 18/60[1].

[98] *Cf.* Brette, *op. cit.*, Vol. I, p. 300, and p. v., MS, *Arch. Nat.* C 33/280.

convocation of the Barrois.[99] It held an assembly, however, and designated the noble who had been elected by the *bailliage* of Bourmont to represent its interests and to present its cahier.[100] In both these cases, the election was held by the three orders united.

The French colonies received no convocation. As soon as the promise of the States-General had been made, representatives of colonial interests in St. Domingue, residing in Paris, began to agitate for convocation.[101] Their efforts were, however, unsuccessful. In default of royal summons, the French colonials in five colonies organized elections. St. Domingue took the lead, and its action served as a model for the other colonies of the western hemisphere. One class alone took part—the white property owners of French extraction. Any attempts of the native population to hold elections were actively suppressed.[102]

Committees for the colonists were organized in Paris, made up of commercial agents or colonial property owners. These groups worked as steering committees. In the case of St. Domingue, the Paris committee, under the conspicuous leadership of Gouy d'Arsy, exceeded the wishes of the colonists.[103] Deputies to the National Assembly were elected both by the committee in Paris, and in the three sections of St. Domingue, the north, west, and south. A part of each deputation was eventually admitted to the National Assembly.[104] Martinique authorized the committee in Paris to act for it, and the elections and cahier for that colony were made by it.[105] The Paris elections of the Guadeloupe committee were denounced in the colony, and elections were held there.[106] As in the case of St. Domingue, part of each deputation was admitted to the National Assembly.[107]

[99] *Cf.* on the Barrois, *ibid.*, Vol. I, pp. 231 *et seq.* Bassigny-Barrois comprised the general area of Bourmont and La Marche. *Cf.* Map, p. 12, and annotation, p. 154.

[100] *Ibid.*, Vol. I, pp. 300-301.

[101] On the elections of St. Domingue, see the volume in the official series, Maurel, Blanche, *Cahiers de doléances de la colonie de Saint Domingue* (Paris, 1933). The text of the work of the Paris committee may be found MS and printed in *Arch. Nat.* B III 135 and Ba 38.

[102] *Cf.* the papers of all three colonies. For St. Domingue, *loc. cit.*, note 101; for Martinique, MS, *Arch. Nat.* C 32/270, printed, *Bib. Nat.* 8° Le 23.183; for Guadeloupe, *Arch. Nat.* C 30/247.

[103] The analysis of the elections of St. Domingue by Paul Boissonnade (*St. Domingue à la veille de la Révolution*, Paris, 1906), is helpful, but has now been superseded by the official volume by Blanche Maurel. See note 101.

[104] Brette, *op. cit.*, Vol. II, pp. 301 *et seq.*

[105] P. v. of Paris committee, *Arch. Nat.* C 32/270. Two of the five deputies elected were admitted. *Cf.* Brette, *op. cit.*, Vol. I, pp 307 *et seq.*

[106] *Cf.* p. v. of the colonial assemblies, *Arch. Nat.* C 30/247.

[107] Brette, *op. cit.*, Vol. I, p. 306.

In both St. Domingue and Guadeloupe, the colonial assemblies met according to the administrative divisions of the islands, without holding an assembly for the whole.[108] In St. Domingue, the north took the lead, while in Guadeloupe, the *Grande-Terre* assumed leadership, but coöperation, not rivalry, existed among the various sections. Martinique acted as a unit.

In the eastern hemisphere, white French colonials of Pondichéry and of the Islands of France and Bourbon each held elections, and some of the deputies elected were subsequently admitted to the National Assembly.[109] The first deputies chosen by the Islands of France and Bourbon were lost at sea, so that its representatives were not admitted to the National Assembly until February, 1791.[110]

Cahiers were drawn up by the electoral groups in the colonies and by the Paris committees, but several of these documents have been lost. The committee for St. Domingue at Paris made no cahier, but the petition for admission to the National Assembly is a valid substitute.[111] In the colony, the cahier drawn up by the assembly of the north of the island, supplemented by remarks drawn up by the west, is the general cahier for the colonials.[112] The cahier of the Paris committee for Martinque has been preserved, and the colonials did not make any.[113] Although the cahier drawn up at Petit-Bourg in Guadaloupe has been preserved, the cahiers of the other two parts are now unknown.[113] The cahier made at Pondichéry has been preserved.[113] The documents for the electoral assembly and the cahier of the Islands of France and Bourbon were lost when the vessel carrying the first deputies was shipwrecked.[114]

Because of the lack of royal convocation, delays which resulted from distance and the difficulties of transportation to France, elections in the colonies took place at various dates between 1789 and 1791. In its attitude toward the colonies, the National Assembly compromised between recognition of the active colonial agents in Paris and desire that the colonists be consulted directly.

[108] Brette, *op. cit.*, Vol. II, pp. 540-41. In St. Domingue, the West adhered to the action of the North, while the South tacitly approved of it. See the Introduction of Maurel, B., *Cahiers de doléances de la colonie de Saint Domingue* (Paris, 1933).
[109] Brette, *op. cit.*, Vol. I, pp. 308, 309, and Vol. II, p. 542.
[110] *Idem.*
[111] The text has been reprinted in the Appendix, p. 418.
[112] Maurel, B., *op. cit.*, Introduction and texts.
[113] *Cf.* annotation *infra*, under the name of the colony, pp. 130 and 363.
[114] *Cf.* Brette, *op. cit.*, Vol. I, pp. 309-10.

Significant Characteristics of the Electoral Process

From the foregoing discussion of the convocation and elections for the States-General of 1789, five points should be noted. In the first place, four-fifths of France followed the ruling of January 24, and therefore carried out a relatively uniform method. The districts applying the second method differed little from the first in respect to numerical representation, but they sent a larger number of cahiers to the States-General. The remaining districts of France, convoked according to the third, fourth, fifth, and sixth types of convocation, evidenced the dominance of privilege and tradition over uniformity.

So great was the complexity of reviving an old institution that throughout the electoral period, local royal officials corresponded regularly with the royal council in regard to the difficulties involved in applying the general convocation to each specific district. The greatest diversity in minor details prevailed and helped to make the labyrinthine electoral regulations even more complex in their execution.

The time element in the elections is a second item worthy of attention. The districts where the more uniform procedure applied—the first type—held their elections at the end of February and early in March.[115] The greater the divergence from the principle of uniformity, the later the elections were held,[116] with the notable exception of the Dauphiné whose early elections have already been noted.[117] The assemblies of the districts of the second type of convocation were held in April. The significance of the time element lay in the influence that one district might have on another, and also in the effect of the seasonal obstacles of spring sowing, late snows, and weather hindrances to travel and communication upon a rapid and a careful electoral procedure.

A third element to be noted is the electoral suffrage. The method of indirect elections and plural representation modified the original measure of almost universal suffrage, and resulted in a more direct voice and wider influence for the higher clergy and the nobles. Although the curates nearly always outnumbered other ecclesiastics

[115] This fact is quickly ascertained by examination of the p. v. of the electoral assemblies.

[116] The earliest regulation for the second type of convocation was issued on February 17 (for the Barrois, Lorraine, Trois-Evêchés, etc.), but the distance of these districts from Paris caused additional delays in the publication by the local authorities.

[117] *Cf. supra*, p. 19.

in the general assemblies of the *bailliage,* they seldom formed a *bloc* hostile to the other members. Although the majority of deputies chosen by the clergy were curates,[118] their numerical predominance in assemblies of the *bailliages* is seldom evidenced in the cahiers. Only in matters of the ecclesiastical hierarchy and jurisdiction and an occasional *rapproachement* with the third estate, do the cahiers of the clergy indicate the predominance of the curates in individual assemblies.

An eventual result of the convocation of the third estate was the election of urban deputies to the States-General. This insured a more direct representation for the towns than for the rural classes. Lawyers and merchants made up the overwhelming majority of deputies for the third estate.[119] Thus, although any man's vote was good in an electoral assembly, the peasants, as a result of the system of indirect elections for the third estate, delegated the representation of their interests to the upper *bourgeoisie.*

The wish of the King, expressed in the introduction to his letter of convocation, which accompanied the regulation of January 24, 1789, was actually fulfilled. He had uttered the hope "that all the most noteworthy persons of each province, *bailliage* or *sénéchaussée* come to the States-General."[120] By and large, the prominent members of each order in the various electoral districts were chosen as deputies to the States-General. Although the elections of 1789 presented some advancement toward democratic representation over the method employed in 1614,[121] they were still aristocratic as carried out.

A fourth important factor in the elections of 1789 was the modification of Necker's original promise that representation should be based on population. The method of indirect elections and concessions to privileged areas, combined with ignorance or inadequate information as to the distribution of population, counteracted his efforts for representation on a numerical basis. Although the third estate often exceeded the numbers of the privileged orders, it received only double representation.[122] In respect, therefore, to numerical representation, the elections were also aristocratic.

[118] *Cf.* the pedigrees of deputies to the National Assembly, Brette, *op. cit.,* Vol. II, *passim.*

[119] *Idem.*

[120] Brette, *op. cit.,* Vol. I. p. 65.

[121] This is true not only with respect to the classification of principal versus secondary *bailliages,* but also as to the qualifications for suffrage. *Cf.* Picot, *Histoire des Etats-Généraux,* Vol. V, pp. 264 *et seq.*

[122] This can be checked by the lists of members of the *bailliage* assemblies.

THE METHOD OF CONVOCATION OF 1789

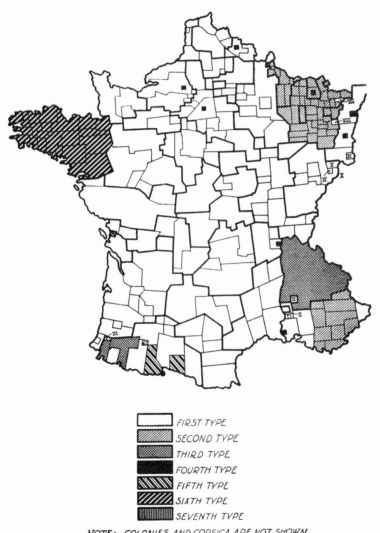

FIRST TYPE
SECOND TYPE
THIRD TYPE
FOURTH TYPE
FIFTH TYPE
SIXTH TYPE
SEVENTH TYPE

NOTE:— COLONIES AND CORSICA ARE NOT SHOWN

A fifth significant fact, resulting from the nature of the convocation was the great number of *cahiers de doléances*. Every electoral assembly had the right to make a cahier.[123] It is these documents that are our chief concern.

[123] Only about 20,000 cahiers are now in existence. *See* Hyslop, Beatrice, *Repertoire critique des cahiers de doléances de 1789* (Paris, 1933).

II

THE TEXT OF A CAHIER DE DOLEANCES

THE WORD "cahier" is, of course, an ordinary French word, meaning notebook. Historically, the term has been applied to petitions to various governmental bodies,[1] and has been used in the title of pamphlets, collections of essays, and even of magazines.[2] In view of the development of the French States-General, however, the word "cahier" has acquired a special historical connotation.

More than a century elapsed after the composition of the last official cahiers before adequate criteria provided a basis for distinguishing these electoral documents from the huge mass of pamphlets which appeared during 1788 and 1789,[3] as well as from all other documents or literature bearing the title of cahier. M. Brette defined a *cahier de doléances* in 1897,[4] in the first volume of his monumental work on the convocation of 1789; but in 1905, the commission of the French Ministry of Public Instruction, under whose official supervision the various volumes of the *Documents inédits sur l'histoire économique de la Révolution française* have appeared, gave a simpler and yet more complete definition. According to this official definition, a cahier is—

l'ensemble des écrits contenant voeux, plaintes, doléances rédigés en 1789 dans les assemblées électorales qui avaient un caractère de légalité reconnu, soit parcequ'elles avaient été convoquées en exécution d'ordres royaux, soit parceque les députés élus en conséquence de ces assemblées furent admis à l'assemblée nationale.[5]

[1] For example, petitions or memoranda prepared for or by a Provincial-Estates were often called "cahiers."

[2] Many of the pamphlets issued as electoral propaganda in 1788 and 1789 used "cahier" in their titles. Barrès wrote a series of essays published under the title of *Mes cahiers*, while serial publications have appeared under the titles *Cahiers belges, Cahiers de la Quinzaine*, etc.

[3] *Cf. supra*, p. 7 and *infra*, p. 64.

[4] *Cf.* M. Brette's definition in *Recueil de documents relatifs à la convocation des Etats Généraux de 1789* (Paris, 1897-1915), Vol. I, p. lxx. Minor differences in the two definitions will be referred to as the analysis proceeds. The major difference is the omission, by M. Brette, of recognition by the National Assembly as a criterion of the legality of an electoral assembly.

[5] *Cf.* circular sent out by the commission, reprinted in the *Révolution française, revue*, 1908, Vol. LV, p. 74.

The essential feature of both definitions is that a cahier must emanate from a legal electoral assembly. Unless an assembly was authorized by royal convocation, or was subsequently recognized by the National Assembly,[6] it was not legal, and therefore any documents issued by it were not official cahiers. The importance of the entire electoral process now emerges. A cahier was, therefore, a collective composition produced as an integral part of the elections to the States-General. As such, the cahiers were included in the official archives of France. From this primary distinction follow differences in the nature, preservation, value, and use of the cahiers which eliminate confusion with other materials.

A *cahier de doléances* always included two documents and sometimes three. The commission's definition mentions an "ensemble des écrits." Besides the minutes or *procès-verbaux* of the electoral assembly and the cahier proper, the assemblies composed a grant of power or mandate, which might appear in one of the foregoing documents, or alone.

THE PROCÈS-VERBAL

The royal convocation of 1789 required that minutes be kept for every electoral assembly[7] and sent out forms of procedure for the various assemblies prescribed in the indirect method of election.[8] A *procès-verbal* should exist, therefore, for every assembly held.

An almost uniform procedure was followed. The parish assemblies and those of the lower clergy conformed more closely to the prescribed formula, and the former often used the printed forms and merely filled in the spaces for names, dates, and so forth.[9] The general assemblies of the *bailliages* were not only larger, but longer in duration, so that the minutes of their sessions often covered many pages of manuscript.[10] In the first place, there were minutes for the opening and closing assembly of an electoral district, at which all three orders were present. The *procès-verbal* began with the date

[6] *Cf. supra,* note 4, which calls attention to Brette's failure to include recognition by the National Assembly in his test of legality. This is of special significance for the seventh type of the convocation.

[7] *Cf.* regulation of January 24, 1789, in Brette, *op. cit.,* Vol. I, p. 86, art. 49.

[8] *Cf.* reprints of forms in *Archives parlementaires* (Paris, 1867-75), Vol. I, pp. 626 *et seq.*

[9] See, for example, the *procès-verbal for T. Gourin* (secondary to Carhaix), *Arch. Nat.* Ba 25.

[10] Official paper was prescribed, but due to shortage or to other reasons, it was not always used. (*Cf.* Brette, *op. cit.,* Vol. I, p. 76, art. 23 and footnote.)

and place, enumeration of the royal officers of the *bailliage,* and a list of all the delegates of the three orders present at the formal opening. For the closing meeting, the names of the deputies elected by each order were given and the administration of an oath and investiture of the deputies with their powers was recorded. Some times a religious element was added in one of these sessions by a prayer or a chant. The *procès-verbal* of the three orders was signed by the officers, usually by the deputies, and sometimes by all members of the assembly.

When the three orders separated, each kept the minutes of its own assembly.[11] The usual procedure was to confirm the powers of the presiding officers provided in the convocation rule, or to elect new ones.[12] The orders then chose a committee to verify the elections of the members or verified them in an assembly of the whole. The same committee or, more often, a second one was chosen to prepare a draft of the cahier. When this committee had finished its work, the order reassembled. The draft of the cahier was read aloud, discussed, and finally adopted. The members affixed their signatures to the text of the cahier. After the completion of the cahier, every assembly proceeded to the election of deputies. Whereas the business of the assemblies had been carried on orally up to this point, the election of deputies was by written ballot.[13] When the prescribed number of deputies had been chosen, a grant of powers was made and the assembly of that order was ready for the closing assembly of the three orders.

Such was the skeleton procedure provided for all general assemblies, but many variations with interesting details were recorded. In the first place, as regards the authenticity of the *procès-verbaux,* some of the registrars were careful and others lax in fulfilling the prescriptions of the royal regulation. The list of members was not always clear, nor did they always sign the *procès-verbal.* The presiding officers should have recorded their verification of the *procès-verbal,* but this record does not always appear. Only in rare cases is

[11] According to the regulations, the registrar (*greffier*) of a *bailliage* was *ipso facto* secretary of the general assembly of all three orders and also of the assembly of the third estate. Probably for this reason, one often finds the minutes of the latter assembly inserted between the opening and closing sessions of the three orders. *Cf.* for example, T. Beziers, *Arch. Nat.* C 16/30.

[12] On the presiding officers, *cf. infra,* p. 53.

[13] See procedure for election of deputies, regulation of January 24, 1789, in Brette, *op. cit.,* Vol. I, pp. 85-86, arts. 46-48.

the judicial seal still appended.[14] Nevertheless, it is a simple matter to ascertain whether a given document is the *procès-verbal* of an authentic electoral assembly and what step in the convocation the given assembly represented. The dates, officers, and elections may be checked with the procedure prescribed for that district by the royal convocation. The dates are especially significant for the third estate, since the method of indirect elections provided for several assemblies to be held in the same town.

Some hint of the kind of information which a *procès-verbal* may convey is implied in the foregoing description. By means of the list of members, one may add a name to the genealogy of a French family,[15] while facts about the profession, office, or social standing of members were sometimes appended. Individual variations in the general procedure, as well as the detailed execution of the usual formula, often throw light upon personalities and circumstances influencing the electoral period in a given area.

The election of officers caused occasional difficulty.[16] The papers of some delegates were not in order, which caused delay in their admission or their exclusion.[17] Some assemblies were careful to exclude any persons not authorized as members of the assembly, others were indifferent about this.[18] Some discussed the cahier at length, modifying and amending it, while others rushed it through. The election of deputies sometimes required a series of balloting, or conversely, it went through with despatch. Petitions were sometimes submitted and discussed, or passed on to the committee for the cahier. Communications were often exchanged by the three orders of a *bailliage,* either as an effort to make one joint cahier, a desire of the upper classes to apprise the third estate of a renunciation of tax privileges, or as a general means of maintaining friendly relations and letting the other orders know what had taken place in the

[14] For example, see p. v. from all three orders of Calais, *Arch. Nat.* C 17/39 MS.

[15] It was actually in connection with a point of genealogy that the author discovered a reprint of the text of the cahier of the nobles of St. Jean d'Angely, about which neither archivists nor any of the books on the cahiers had given information.

[16] *Cf.* for example, C. Meaux (*Arch. Nat.* Ba 51), C Moulins (*Arch. Nat.* C 21/109), etc.

[17] *Cf. for example,* C. Douai (*Arch. Nat.* B III 62, p. 85 *et seq.*) and C. Toul (*Arch. Nat.* C 24/157).

[18] The curates of Bouzonville (*Gen.* of Nancy) complained, with respect to the assembly of the third estate of that district, that "strangers to the assembly entered indecently with pipe in mouth, and elbowed, made speeches, and influenced the elections." *Arch. Nat.* Ba 77.

assembly.[19] When doubt arose over a point of procedure, business stopped until the proper royal officer could give an authoritative decision.[20] It was even necessary, occasionally, to write to the keeper of the seals for an interpretation of the royal convocation.[21]

One might continue to cite *ad infinitum* many details which appear in the *procès-verbaux* and which make them valuable sources, instead of mere formulae. Our chief interest in them is, however, their usefulness for verification of the cahier proper and for any light which they throw upon the opinion of the assembly.

THE CAHIER PROPER

The second and chief document of the "ensemble des écrits" was the cahier proper, or list of grievances, instructions, or recommendations given to the deputy to serve as a guide for his actions. These documents had certain common characteristics, both because cahiers from the early States-Generals had been discovered and circulated, and also because a common legal framework was required.[22]

Various titles, such as "cahier de doléances . . . ," "cahier d'instructions," "pouvoirs et instructions," or other variations, were given. The title was followed by a short paragraph indicating the order and the district that had made the cahier. In addition, the names of the deputies to whom the cahier was entrusted might be given, and also a statement added that the cahier was to be taken to the next successive assembly, or to the States-General itself.[23]

The form in which the main part of the cahier was to be cast was not prescribed.[24] Although it usually started with a short preamble

[19] *Cf.* for example, C, N, T, Montargis; C, N, T, Aval; C, N, T, St. Jean d'Angely, etc.
[20] See, for example, question of substitute chairman, C. Douai, *Arch. Nat.* B III 62, pp. 88-89.
[21] See the correspondence between the local officials and the keeper of the seals in almost any *dossier, Arch. Nat.* Ba 9-Ba 86.
[22] On the procedure for making the cahier, see regulation for January 24, 1789, in Brette, *op. cit.,* Vol. I, pp. 84-86, arts. 44, 45, 49.
[23] Brette called attention in his definition of a cahier to the misleading character of many of the titles to cahiers. The assembly was occasionally misinformed as to where the cahier was to be taken, and also the title did not always make clear what assembly adopted the cahier. The title must be checked with the ending of the cahier and with the *procès-verbaux.*
[24] The king wished to leave perfect freedom to the electorate to express its wishes. This was clear in the *Lettre du Roi* accompanying the convocation regulations, and in his instructions to the officials who supervised the elections in the *bailliages. Cf.* Brette, *op. cit.,* Vol. I, pp. 64 *et seq.,* 66 *et seq.,* 317 *et seq.*

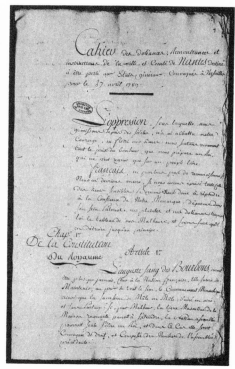

THE COVER AND FIRST PAGE OF
THE GENERAL CAHIER OF
THE THIRD ESTATE OF
NANTES

addressed to Louis XVI or to the States-General, or both, these statements were never identically worded. After the preamble, most of the committees chosen to draft the cahier voiced the will of the assembly in a series of numbered articles, concisely worded and without detail or explanation. Some, however, adopted paragraph form and interspersed the demands with illustrative detail or supporting argument.

The cahier ended with certain prescribed information. The adoption of the cahier by the assembly was recorded with the date. If any changes or additions were made, these were mentioned. Alterations of the text might be made on the manuscript by erasures, insertions, or marginal comments signed by the secretary of the assembly, or by the members of the committee for the cahier.[25] The adoption of the cahier was followed by the signatures of the committee, the officers of the assembly, and the members of the assembly. Finally, a paragraph of authentication by the chief royal officer of the district was added. As with the *procès-verbaux*, a few cahiers have been preserved to which the original judicial seal with wax and ribbon still adheres.[26]

Despite these many gauges of authenticity for a genuine cahier of 1789, confusion has arisen because electoral pamphlets sometimes adopted titles and forms similar to the official documents, and also because individual texts seldom include all the marks of identification. The original texts of the cahiers were manuscripts in the handwriting of the members of the commission, the secretary of the order, or of an official scribe. A text was given to each deputy, while a copy was kept in the local archives. The copyists must have been hurried at times, for frequently we find their texts incomplete or embodying errors.[27] Many assemblies, especially those of the general *bailliages*, voted to print the cahier, the *procès-verbal*, or both. In some cases, the original manuscripts have been lost and we know the documents only through their printed editions. The various authentic marks both for manuscripts and for printed texts should be corroborated by corresponding information in the *procès-verbaux*. The crucial test is the adoption of the cahier, accompanied by the date, and by the names

[25] For example, see manuscripts of T. Nemours (*Arch. Nat.* C 21/112²).

[26] *Cf.* for example, the cahier of T. Nantes, reproduced on preceding page.

[27] *Cf.* for example, the various texts in the *dossier* for C, N, Angers in *Arch. Nat.* Ba 13, C 14/8; or compare texts of T. Besançon in *Arch. Nat.* Ba 21 and *Arch. Doubs* B. 9501.

of the presiding officers of the assembly, but all doubt is eliminated when these various indications are accompanied by the signatures of the members of the assembly.[28] There can then be no question that the given text is not merely a draft of the committee, but is the one actually approved by the assembly. Because of the omission of some of these means of identification, doubt must be cast upon the validity of certain of the texts which have come down to us.[29]

The pertinence of the foregoing discussion as to the nature and value of the cahiers may best be illustrated by comparing several of the texts of cahiers reprinted in the Appendix. For example, note the cahier of the lower clergy of the diocese of Nantes, reprinted from an edition inserted in the printed *procès-verbal* of the district.[30] This text meets all the requirements of authenticity, when compared with the *procès-verbal*, and illustrates an orderly and concise series of articles. Contrast the verbose text of the third estate of Longwy which is likewise authentic and which is reprinted in the *Appendix* from the manuscript text.[31] On the other hand, the cahier of the third estate of Sarreguemines did not bear the signatures of the assembly, and yet it has sufficient other marks of authenticity.[32] The various types of documentary identification of a cahier may be seen by comparing several of the unedited texts in the Appendix.

The cahier proper and the *procès-verbal* are complementary documents, and both are necessary for the interpretation of opinions in the body of the cahier.

THE MANDATE

There was a third portion to the "ensemble des écrits"—the mandate. The cahier contained specific recommendations, but in addition an assembly usually made a grant of powers. This might be written as the concluding paragraph of a cahier,[33] or made into a separate document.[34] In most cases, however, the mandate was transcribed in the *procès-verbal* of the assembly.

The *Lettre du Roi* preceding the regulation of January 24, and all other regulations applying to other districts of France, contained the following statement:

[28] See the facsimile of signatures at the end of the cahier of the third estate of Calais, facing p. 86.

[29] *Cf. infra*, p. 86. [30] *Cf.* Appendix, p. 374.

[31] *Cf.* Appendix, p. 331. [32] *Cf.* Appendix, p. 391.

[33] For example, N. Artois (AP, Vol. II, p. 85, art. 7), or at beginning, T. Amiens (AP, Vol. I, p. 744).

[34] For example, N. Aix, *Arch. Nat.* Ba 9.

et seront les dits députés munis d'instructions et pouvoirs généraux et suffisants pour proposer, remontrer, aviser et consentir tout ce qui peut concerner les besoins de l'Etat, la reforme des abus, l'établissement d'un order fixe et durable dans toutes les parties de l'administration de chacun de nos sujets.[35]

The king wanted the instructions for the deputies to be general and their specific interpretation left to the deputies. Similar statements had appeared in the rules for convocation of the early States-Generals,[36] and yet the failures of these very assemblies led the electorate of 1789 to write mandates to supplement the cahier proper.

There were actually three types of mandates given to the deputies. The first, which may be called a general mandate, repeated the formula quoted from the *Lettre du Roi*. In such cases, the paragraph often appeared in the preamble of the cahier, in its conclusion, or in the minutes of the assembly at the point where it was recorded that the deputies were invested with power. A second type may be called the special mandate. This repeated or emphasized certain articles of the cahier or added other items. The terminology of special mandates was more forceful than the general mandates. The third kind of mandate—the imperative—was the significant type. It differed from special mandates only in the peremptory command of obedience.[37] The deputies were threatened with repudiation if they exceeded or failed to carry out either the full instructions of the cahier or particular items. The importance of the mandate is at once obvious in an interpretation of the cahier proper.

When consulting the *cahiers de doléances*, therefore, one should study the *procès-verbaux* of the assemblies, the cahiers proper, and the mandates. Occasionally, an assembly voted to append memoranda to the cahier,[38] while some general assemblies voted to give all *preliminary* cahiers, as well as the *general* cahier, to the deputies to the States-General.[39] Only by using all of these documents in conjunction with the general cahiers can one make a fair estimate of public opinion, and of conditions in 1789 as presented in the cahiers.

[35] *Cf.* reprinted text, Brette, *op. cit.*, Vol. I, p. 65.

[36] *Cf.* regulations in Lalourcé et Duval, *Forme générale et particulière de la convocation et de la tenue des Assemblées Nationales ou Etats-Généraux de France* (Paris, 1789), Vol. II, pp. 30, 33, 49, 91.

[37] *Cf infra* on imperative mandates, pp. 99 *et seq.*

[38] For example, the *Mémoire* on provincial government, sent with the cahier of the third estate of Senlis, *Archives parlementaires*, Vol. V, pp. 736-47.

[39] *Cf.* table of sources in Appendix, p. 113, under Agen, Aix, Alençon, etc.

III

THE NUMBER OF GENERAL CAHIERS

THE INTRICATE method of the convocation, the procedure followed in making the cahiers, and the use to which these documents may be put, suggest two large classifications of the cahiers of 1789: *preliminary* cahiers and *general* cahiers. The latter were the final series of cahiers made for the deputies to take directly to the States-General. All cahiers other than these were preliminary to them—that is to say, all the cahiers composed in the successive assemblies before the *general* assembly. To this group belong cahiers of church chapters, curates, monastic orders, parishes, gildsmen, towns, secondary *bailliages* and preliminary assemblies of principal *bailliages*.

GENERAL VERSUS PRELIMINARY CAHIERS

Failure to distinguish between these two groups of the cahiers of 1789 has led to many inaccuracies. Differences in the length, scope, composition, influence, number, printing, preservation, and use of them should be recognized. Preliminary cahiers were almost invariably shorter and more restricted in scope. Although some parish cahiers advocated general reforms for the national government, they devoted more space to local and rural problems. A gild cahier might deal exclusively with industry and commerce. Cahiers of the lower clergy dealt almost entirely with minor matters of ecclesiastical hierarchy and jurisdiction. On the other hand, general cahiers dealt with all phases of national reorganization and devoted less space to local or class matters.

The method of convocation in 1789 provided for indirect elections for the clergy and for the third estate, and for direct election for the nobles. Hence, there were no preliminary cahiers of the nobles. Furthermore, the general cahiers of the clergy and third estate were intended to be syntheses of the preliminary cahiers of their locality. The committee which drafted the cahier was given the preliminary cahiers upon which to base their draft.

Besides differences of length, scope, and procedure, the two classes of cahiers displayed differences in the education of the members who made them. Whereas there was evidence of illiteracy in parish assemblies,[1] this was rarely the case in general assemblies.[2] Perhaps because of this, wholesale adoption of electoral models, or of prepared texts was greater in the preliminary assemblies than among the general ones.[3] The same pamphlet literature was in circulation for the preliminary as for the general assemblies, but plagiarism may be more often detected in the documents issuing from the less educated assemblies.[4]

A corollary to the varying degree of education was the difference of language used in the two groups of cahiers. Preliminary cahiers displayed an imperfect knowledge of French, the presence of a local dialect or bilingualism more often than did the general cahiers. French had to be interpreted for Breton peasants,[5] while some of the parish cahiers of the northern communes were written in Flemish.[6] Even where French was used, grammatical imperfections and lack of clarity indicate a poor command of French by the secretary of the assembly, who was naturally better educated than some members of the assembly. The bilingual areas were the northeast (French and German), the north (French and Flemish), Brittany (French and Breton), the south (French and Basque), and Corsica (French and Italian). The members of general assemblies were usually better versed in the official idiom,[7] even where two languages were in use.

A fourth difference between preliminary and general cahiers is their numerical diversity. Whereas the convocation provided for two hundred and thirty-four general electoral districts (including Corsica, but not the French colonies),[8] the number of preliminary

---

[1] The official formula for parish assemblies contained the phrase "qui a été signé par ceux des dits habitants qui savent signer." If there were few signatures at the end, the natural conclusion is that the other members of the assembly could not write.

[2] Only six out of approximately six hundred general assemblies used the same phrase as the parish *procès-verbal* (see note 1) and thereby suggested the presence of illiterates. These six were T.—Agen, Annonay, Cambrésis, Hyères, Sisteron, and Toulouse.

[3] *Cf.* introductions to official editions of cahiers.

[4] Contrasts and similarities in style and content are outstanding in parish cahiers.

[5] For example, T. p. v., Châteaulin, *Arch. Nat.* Ba 25.

[6] *Cf.* comments in Sagnac and St. Leger, *Histoire de la Flandre maritime* (Paris, 1906), Vol. II, p. ix.

[7] The originals of only three *general* cahiers were in languages other than French; the third estates of Strasbourg and of the Ten Imperial Cities wrote the original texts in German but had French translations made, while the nobles of Corsica wrote theirs in Italian. The third estate of Corsica made theirs in both French and Italian, but there was no indication of which was written first. The cahier of the clergy of Corsica has been lost, and the *procès-verbal* is not clear on the language used.

[8] *Cf.* list of districts in Appendix p. 144.

assemblies was in the thousands. There were many secondary *bailliages*, and the number of assemblies of parishes, religious orders, chapters, gilds, and so forth baffles the statistician.

The number of general cahiers actually made in 1789, as well as the number that are still available, is an ascertainable quantity,[9] but the number of preliminary cahiers will probably remain unknown. Approximately 20,000 parish cahiers have been preserved, but the diversity in the number of parishes within the various electoral districts was so great that no accurate estimate can be computed from the collections still existing.[10] Several hundred preliminary cahiers of the clergy and of gilds have also been preserved, but as yet no effort has been made to determine how many were actually made in 1789.[11]

Although individual cahiers may be useful for the study of a specific district, their real significance as sources lies in their revelation of collective opinion. The utility of the general cahiers is best found in a comparison of all available general cahiers, and for this reason the number should be as complete as possible. As will be seen later, about eighty-five per cent of the general cahiers have been preserved,[12] while approximately only one-third of the electoral districts of 1789 have today relatively complete collections of parish cahiers.[13] Thousands of the preliminary cahiers have been lost. Too many loopholes make it impossible to discover opinion for the whole of France from preliminary cahiers. The fragmentary character of such

[9] *Cf. infra*, p. 144.

[10] *Cf.* Hyslop, B., *Repertoire critique de cahiers de doléances de 1789* (Paris, 1933). The index of parishes, which contains only those for which the cahier is known, includes about 20,000 names. Whenever the parish cahiers of a *bailliage* have been officially edited, the editors have determined the number of parishes for the given district. Also, M. Brette did this for the various districts treated in his four volumes. Nevertheless, it would be a laborious process to try to compute the number for the whole of France, both because of discrepancies between local records and the *procès-verbaux*, double representation, and disparity between districts.

[11] The inventory cited in note 10 does not contain an index of preliminary cahiers of the clergy or of the gilds. References to them may be found under the names of the districts where such cahiers have been preserved.

[12] *Cf. infra*, p. 150.

[13] By turning over the pages of the official inventory, cited p. 000 note 10, some idea of the number of districts where large numbers of parish cahiers have been preserved may be obtained. The smaller districts comprised few parishes, and one would have to be generally informed on the matter to arrive at any accurate estimate. There exist today fairly complete collections of parish cahiers for about 150 of more than 400 *bailliages*. A comparison might be made between the parish cahiers of the one hundred and fifty *bailliages*, but this would leave many gaps for a synthesis for the whole of France.

an attempt would be even more marked for the preliminary cahiers of the clergy, or for the gild cahiers. The contrast in the number of cahiers in the two big groups, as well as the loss of documents, affects the utility of both classes of cahiers.

Printing is a factor of primary importance in the preservation of texts. Whereas nearly half of the total number of general cahiers were printed in 1789,[14] comparatively few of the preliminary cahiers were published during the electoral period.[15] Copies of the general cahiers were kept in the local archives, while the originals were taken by the deputies to the States-General with the result that, in many cases, copies now exist in both the departmental and the national archives. In some cases in which the original manuscripts have been lost, printed editions have survived.[16] Less care was shown in the conservation of preliminary cahiers. If the text was transcribed on the municipal register it may still be seen in the communal archives, but, in most cases, the texts used by the committees for drawing up the general cahiers were turned over to the local archives and are now in the departmental archives. The loss of preliminary cahiers through fires, failure to keep together the electoral documents of local districts, ignorance of the importance of the manuscripts, carelessness in preservation,[17] and many other causes cannot be offset by printed texts if the originals have disappeared. Only in rare cases does a printed edition exist for which the original has been lost.

The printing of the cahiers of 1789 was important not only in the preservation of these documents, but also for extending their contemporary influence. Preliminary cahiers could exert little influence except in oral discussion among the members of an assembly which composed it. Unless texts were printed, there was little chance that they would become known outside of the *bailliage*. By contrast, the general cahiers received wide circulation because they were printed, and also because they exerted an influence upon the procedure of the States-General and National Assembly.

Just as proportionately more of the preliminary than of the general cahiers have disappeared, and also as relatively fewer of them were

---

[14] *Cf. infra*, p. 151.

[15] Note examples of printed preliminary cahiers in the official inventory. They are quite rare.

[16] For example, text of T. Ten Imperial Cities, T. St. Dié, etc.

[17] For example, the parish cahiers of the *bailliage* of Chinon, subdivision of the *bailliage* of Tours, were probably destroyed among papers that were allowed to rot away in the cellar of the archive building.

printed in 1789, the modern editing of preliminary cahiers has been slower than the publication of the general ones. Valuable collections of parish cahiers for different *bailliages* have now been made available through the efforts of the official commission of the Ministry of Public Instruction. Many previous reprints were isolated and based upon inadequate documentary criticism. There remain important collections to be edited.[18] Nearly all the general cahiers have now been reprinted, even though their publication in the *Archives parlementaires* has serious drawbacks, while the few unedited texts which remain are given in the appendix of this volume.[19] For those, therefore, who cannot travel to the numerous departmental archives where original manuscripts are to be found, the general cahiers are more accessible for research than the much larger group of preliminary cahiers.

In every careful appraisal of the cahiers, there appears some discussion of their objective and subjective value. Objective value means the utility of a cahier as a source of facts and conditions, while subjective value means the use of the cahiers as a gauge of the state of mind of the electorate. The objective value of the preliminary cahiers is relatively greater than of the general cahiers. Inasmuch as parish cahiers gave more attention to local details and to descriptions of local conditions, they serve as sources for rural conditions and institutions.[20] Even if conditions were not as bad as indicated, the peasants believed them to be so. We may, therefore, discover from preliminary cahiers not only the psychological background of the Revolution among the rural population, lower clergy, and townsmen, but we may also learn a great deal about actual conditions in different areas.

With respect to the general cahiers, their subjective value outweighs their objective value. As they were more concerned with general principles and represented the consensus of opinion from a large

[18] *Cf.* the official inventory, Hyslop, B., *Repertoire critique des cahiers de doléances* . . . (Paris, 1933).

[19] On the publication of the general cahiers, see *infra,* p. 158, and the unedited texts in the appendix, pp. 202 *et seq.*

[20] A controversy has raged over the value of the cahiers. No distinction has been made in such discussions between the two types of cahiers. Three general attitudes were taken: rejection of any great value in the cahiers as source materials (e.g., Wahl, Loutchizky, etc.); belief in their greater objective value (e.g., Sagnac); and belief in their prime subjective value (e.g., Sée, Onou, and nearly all editors of official collections).

area, they devoted little space to description of existing local institutions. They were concerned chiefly with national reform and a new régime. Their prime importance is subjective.

In view of all the differences between the two groups of cahiers of 1789—their length, scope, composition, influences, textual language, number, printing, preservation, and value—each group has its own value as source material. Since previous discussions of the cahiers have failed to appraise the groups separately, and since the general cahiers offer certain advantages over the preliminary, attention in this volume will be centered upon the first group alone—the general cahiers. The first problem which arises is to determine the number of general cahiers.

THE NUMBER OF GENERAL CAHIERS

Public opinion, as represented in the cahiers carried by the deputies to the States-General, was expressed in a definite number of documents, and all of these were *general* cahiers. In order that no district be represented by more than the officially recognized number of documents, it is important to know how many general cahiers were made in 1789 and also how many of them have been preserved. Two circumstances affect the number made: the royal convocation and variations in its local application. The foregoing analysis of the convocation was designed to clarify the number of general cahiers authorized. There were also other determining circumstances. Two or three classes in a *bailliage* might unite to make a joint cahier, or an occasional assembly might decide not to make a cahier. Other minor irregularities occurred.

After careful consideration of all attendant circumstances, it appears that six hundred and fifteen *general* cahiers were made in 1789, not including colonial cahiers.[21] To date, the only scholarly attempt to compute the number was made by Aulard in a brief article for the *Révolution française*,[22] of which he was then editor. According to his calculations there were six hundred and forty-three *general* cahiers, but he included colonial cahiers, failed to take into

[21] It has seemed desirable to treat the colonial documents separately, since each colony represented certain special conditions. *Cf. infra*, p. 144.

[22] *Loc. cit.*, 1895, Vol. XXIX, pp. 150 *et seq.*, under the title of "Quels sont les cahiers qui nous manquent?" The computation of Vialay in 1911 (455 general cahiers) was quite inaccurate (see Bibliography, p. 460).

consideration districts where two or three classes made joint cahiers,[23] and some sections of Brittany where joint cahiers were made by several districts of the third estate.[24] Some typographical errors in his list also affected his total estimate.[25]

Five hundred and twenty-three out of six hundred and fifteen general cahiers are still available in some form, either in the original manuscript or printed edition of 1789 or in reprint.[26] A few of the originals have disappeared since their reprinting.[27] The accompanying map illustrates the varying number of cahiers sent by the various *generalities* to the States-General, and shows the larger proportion from the north, the northeast, the extreme south, and Brittany. It also reveals the proportionately greater loss of general cahiers from the *generalities* of Auch, Aix, Rennes, Valenciennes, Nancy, Metz, and Strasbourg. A proportionately larger number of cahiers of the clergy have disappeared.[28] Although general texts may yet be discovered as the work of classification of departmental archives proceeds,[29] or may be revealed among private archives,[30] nevertheless,

[23] Aulard did not observe that the clergy and nobles of Sarrelouis made a joint cahier; the three orders of Clermont-en-Argonne (à Varennes), one cahier; and the nobles and third estate of Couserans a joint one.

[24] Aulard overlooked the existence of a joint cahier for Carhaix with Châteaulin, Châteauneuf-du-Faou, Gourin and Quimperlé, and the joint cahier of Quimper and Concarneau. He also did not know that the lower clergy of St. Pol-de-Léon made no cahier.

[25] Some cahiers appear in the list of those which Aulard had newly discovered, and they were repeated among those that were still missing; for example, U. Mouzon, T. No26 Note y, etc.

[26] Note the correction of the number of general cahiers available, given as 522 in Hyslop, B., *French Nationalism in 1789 according to the General Cahiers* (New York, 1934), pp. 9 and 244. The change is due to the discovery of the general cahier of the third estate of Rouen.

[27] For example, T. Belley, N. St. Jean d'Angely, etc.

[28] Whereas 18 per cent of the cahiers of the clergy have been lost, 15 per cent of the nobles and barely 10 per cent of the third estate are missing.

[29] The consolidation of departmental archives is still going on, with a corresponding continuance of classification. For example, only recently, legal archives of the district of Château-Thierry among which electoral documents of 1789 would appear, were turned over to the departmental archives of the Aisne. A first superficial inventory failed to reveal any cahiers. On the other hand, the general cahier of the third estate of Rouen has only just come to light at the archives of the *Seine-Inférieure*. Note that the number of general cahiers available has been corrected in this volume to include this cahier hitherto missing.

[30] In rare cases, a deputy to the States-General kept one set of the electoral documents which have been handed down by his descendants. See, for example, Aval, in Appendix, p. 207. Eventually, such collections should find their way to state archives, but isolated cahiers or electoral documents may be hidden away in private collections whose owners have not realized their value.

DISTRICTS FOR WHICH
CAHIERS ARE MISSING

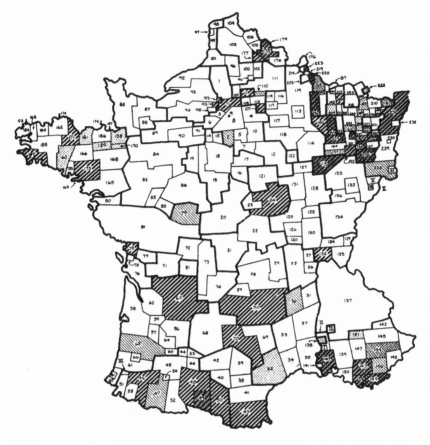

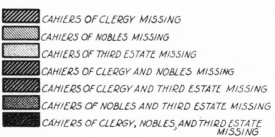

CAHIERS OF CLERGY MISSING

CAHIERS OF NOBLES MISSING

CAHIERS OF THIRD ESTATE MISSING

CAHIERS OF CLERGY AND NOBLES MISSING

CAHIERS OF CLERGY AND THIRD ESTATE MISSING

CAHIERS OF NOBLES AND THIRD ESTATE MISSING

CAHIERS OF CLERGY, NOBLES, AND THIRD ESTATE
                                    MISSING

every effort has been made to find missing cahiers, and few are likely to appear after the present exhaustive research.[31]

With respect to colonial cahiers the number is less certain than for the electoral districts of France itself. Since there was no royal convocation, we can estimate the number only by means of the electoral documents themselves or related documentary material. Many of these documents have disappeared, so that details of these elections are only partially available. It appears from such information as is available, that there were seven general cahiers for the colonies, of which five have survived.[32]

In spite of the various gaps left by the loss of *general cahiers*, the number of available texts is large and provides some expression of opinion from nearly every corner of France.[33]

[31] Information supplied to the author, during the preparation of the official inventory, and the efforts of archivists at that time, should have uncovered any hitherto unknown documents.

[32] *Cf.* table, in Appendix, p. 150. Note the need of correction of the figure given in Hyslop, B., *French Nationalism in 1789 according to the General Cahiers* (New York, 1934), pp. 243-44.

[33] Even where the cahier proper is missing, the *procès-verbal* has nearly always survived. The latter have been entirely lost for only twenty-six assemblies (*cf.* table, in Appendix, pp. 113 *et seq.*).

IV

THE VALUE OF THE GENERAL CAHIERS AS
SOURCE MATERIALS

EVER SINCE the cahiers were drawn up, a controversy has raged over their utility as sources. During the Revolution and for more than half a century thereafter, a reverent attitude prevailed. The cahiers were looked upon as oracles of French opinion and conditions. A number of cahiers, chosen at random, were read, and the resulting impression was deemed to represent the whole of France. After this undiscriminating period, documentary criticism began, which was followed by revaluation of the meaning and utility of the cahiers. None of the analyses of the cahiers have however, distinguished between the two large groups of cahiers. In the preceding chapter, the discussion of the distinctions between *preliminary* and *general* cahiers indicates clearly that differences exist in their respective value and use. Here we are concerned only with the *general* cahiers, and we will proceed, therefore, to analyze the value of the *general* cahiers alone, without repeating or summarizing previous discussions.[1]

The problem of the value and utility of the general cahiers involves three questions—their originality, their sincerity, and an evaluation on the basis of these factors.

THE PROBLEM OF ORIGINALITY

A fundamental ambiguity in the appraisal of the cahiers has arisen from confusion over the meaning of the word "originality." The general cahiers were a collective product and intended to represent the consensus of opinion of the assembly which made them. They were not the exposition of unique schemes or original ideas of single members. Furthermore, the members of assemblies of the clergy and of the third estate were delegates of smaller units, and their instructions were used in preparing the general cahier. Thus, the general cahiers for these classes were influenced by the preliminary cahiers and were, therefore, inevitably unoriginal. Even in as-

[1] Although most of the points that will be made hereafter were touched in a general way in previous analyses of the cahiers, they assume greater definiteness when applied to the general cahiers alone, and an actual appraisal has been attempted here.

semblies of the nobles, for whom there was only one stage in the elections and for whom there were no preliminary cahiers, the members represented class interests quite as much as personal interests. None of the general cahiers was original in the sense of being individual creative writing.

In addition to this fact, a complex set of influences affected the content of the general cahiers. Various circumstances influenced the members of the assemblies and conditioned their expression of opinion; consequently, no ideas were expressed that had not been voiced already in the literature of the eighteenth-century or in its popularization by electoral pamphlets. In a second sense the general cahiers were not original, for they evinced no new theories or demands.

Influences affecting the content of the cahiers fall into four groups: time, attendant circumstances, personal and literary influences.

THE TIME ELEMENT

The time element in the making of the cahiers affected the body of the text both in the care in composition and in the influence of one district upon another. The royal instructions for the convocation intended that the cahiers be composed very carefully, but delays in the issuance of the regulations exerted pressure upon the composition of the cahiers.[2] In the first place, the regulations for the parts of France farthest from Versailles were issued later than those for the first type of the convocation,[3] and the distance of the former made it necessary to expedite matters in order that the deputies might reach Versailles for the official opening. Without railroads and aeroplanes, travel was difficult except along the chief highways, as Arthur Young attested. Furthermore, the time when the general assemblies were held involved weather conditions. While late snows hindered communication and delayed the arrival of deputies for the general assembly of St. Flour,[4] in some cases, the rural delegates were anxious to get home

[2] Even the regulation of January 24 was delayed in publication. The first notice of its issuance cited by the British ambassador was on February 5, (Browning, O., *Despatches from Paris* (London, 1909-10), Vol. II, p. 155, Letter of Dorset to Carmarthen), while the *Gazette de France* reprinted the convocation orders several days after their issuance. Added time was taken to send the royal regulations to the various parts of France.

[3] Whereas the type regulation was dated January 24, the interpretative orders were most of them dated early in February. The first rule of Alsace and Trois-Evêchés, was dated February 7, while other *pays d'état* received their regulations later still.

[4] See comments of Mège, F., in *La Dernière Année de la province d'Auvergne* (Paris, 1904), p. 159.

for spring planting.[5] The regulation for Paris was issued so late that the elections were still going on when the States-General convened.[6] Although time and distance might have exerted a marked influence upon the cahiers, by causing undue hurry, the general cahiers present rare evidences of this. There were only a few cases in which the assembly altered the official procedure by delegating the power to make the cahier without a final vote by the whole assembly, or by holding the elections before the cahier had been completed.[7] Some reservation, therefore, should be made upon the representative value of the particular cahiers involved.

The amount of time spent upon the making of the cahier, both by the committee and by the assembly itself, had a bearing upon the care given to the composition. A great variation in the time required by the committees was evidenced by the *procés-verbaux*.[8] In the case of the clergy of Crépy-en-Valois and of the third estate of Amiens, the committee was ready with a draft after a few hours of consultation, whereas a ten-day interval elapsed between the election of the committee and the submission of a draft to the assembly of the third estate of Chatellerault and of the nobles of Bordeaux.[9]

The length of time taken by the committee is not directly related to the length of a general cahier, but it is helpful in determining other influences. If a very complete cahier was turned out in a phenomenally short time, we should suspect that a model had been adopted or that some influential person had dictated the contents. The cahier of the third estate of Nemours, although exceptional, is a case in point. The assembly chose sixteen members for the committee, whose minutes have been preserved, and who spent six days in making the cahier.[10] The cahier is, however, exceptionally long.[11] It would appear virtually impossible to compose in a period of six days so long and so careful a compilation of the parish cahiers as is evidenced by the text, and at

[5] *Cf.* for example, T. Riom, p. v., *Arch. Nat.* C 23/136; T. Bar-le-duc, p. v., *Arch. Nat.* B III 21, pp. 238 *et seq.;* T. Perpignan, p. v., *Arch. Nat.* C 22/124; etc.

[6] See Brette, *op. cit.,* Vol. I, pp. 113-14.

[7] These exceptions were C. Toulon, C. Poitiers, C. (lower) Nantes, N. Hyères, T. Perpignan.

[8] The length of time taken may be calculated from the interval between the choice of the committee and the submission of the draft.

[9] See the respective *procès-verbaux.* For their call number, consult the table of sources in the Appendix, pp. 113 *et seq.*

[10] P. v., *Arch. Nat.* C 21/112¹.

[11] *Cf.* reprint of the text covering 113 pages, *Archives parlementaires,* Vol. IV, pp. 112-215. Note the effort to show the opinion of preliminary cahiers in the footnotes.

the same time to include long philosophical discussions. The fact that Dupont de Nemours, the Physiocratic propagandist, was a member of the committee, explains the embellishment of the demands of the parishes with lengthy philosophical phrases. The assembly approved the cahier, but it is quite probable that Dupont added to the text after its adoption. The demands were authentic, but the phraseology was that of an individual. The action of the committee is a partial index of other influences upon the content of the cahier. For the most part, the committees were very conscientious.[12]

Time was also consumed in the discussion of the cahier by the assembly. Here again, we discover a variety of procedures. Some assemblies took pains to read the draft of the cahier several times before approving it, with or without alterations.[13] Some assemblies approved the draft unanimously.[14] It is impossible to tell whether attention to the reading of the draft was perfunctory in the assemblies where the cahier was adopted without changes or additions, but information in the *procés-verbaux* indicates that most assemblies were conscientious and took pains to have the cahier conform to the collective will.[15]

The time element in the convocation also made possible the influence of the elections of one district upon another district. The elections were spread out over the months of February, March and April; later elections were exceptional. Among the three orders of a single *bailliage,* the texts were often exchanged, compared, and modified in accordance with comments.[16] Between *bailliages,* however, a general spirit and action might be influential, but direct influence of cahiers upon other *general* cahiers is not evident. In the first place, there could be no wide circulation of cahiers without printing, and that took time. There is evidence that some districts communicated with others before the electoral assemblies[17] and that certain districts knew what

[12] For examples of careful committees, see C. Verdun, C. Beziers, N. Colmar, N. Limoux, T. Dijon, etc.

[13] For example, three readings—N. Angers, C. Pont-à-Mousson; two readings—C. Nîmes, N. Villefranche-en-Rouergue, N. Cahors, T. Douai, etc.

[14] For example, T. Sens, T. Dorat, C. Tulle, etc.

[15] For example, N. Alençon, N. Gien, T. Nîmes, C. Condom, N. Saumur, C. Angers, etc.

[16] *Cf.* for example, C, N, T, Saintes, N, T,· Villefranche-de-Beaujolais, etc.

[17] There exists in the *Bibl. Rouen,* carton 217, a manuscript entitled: *Etat de toutes les municipalités du royaume où il a été envoyé des mémoires relatifs à la tenue des Etats-Généraux.* The document lists the provinces of France with the number of *mémoires* sent to each; for example, Normandy 47, Burgundy 30, Artois 10, etc. These pamphlets were sent out in October, 1788.

was in other cahiers,[18] but it is more likely that similarities in the phraseology or unusual demands were due to a common model rather than to direct plagiarism.[19] There are no examples among the *general* cahiers of an admitted borrowing from other *general* cahiers.

ATTENDANT CIRCUMSTANCES

Among the circumstances which influenced the contents of the cahiers was the method of choosing a committee for their preparation. Either the most prominent members of the assembly were chosen by virtue of their reputation or one of two principles prevailed, *i.e.*, geographic or functional representation.[20] In assemblies of the clergy, the committee was often recruited according to ecclesiastical rank,[21] while the nobles chose their prominent members.[22] The third estate selected the committee more often by geographic area, according to the subdivisions of the *bailliage,* and less often by function—(gild, nonmember of gild, or rural delegates).[23] The personnel of the committee and the method of its composition influenced the preparation of the cahier, inasmuch as these modified the influence which a single individual could exert. In many assemblies of the third estate, the cahier of the principal *bailliage* or of the chief town was read aloud in the assembly and taken as a point of departure by the committee.[24]

PERSONAL INFLUENCES

By far the most tangible influence upon the content of the general cahiers was exerted by individuals. The rôle played by persons of

[18] The N. Charmes knew the terms of the cahier of N. Bordeaux (*cf.* p. v., *Arch. Nat.* Ba 53). T. Vermandois knew what T. Villers-Cotterets was doing (*cf.* p. v., *Arch. Nat.* B III 154). Most of the districts knew about the elections and activity of the Dauphiné (*cf.* for example, T. Charolles, in its cahier, *Archives parlementaires,* Vol. II, p. 619), etc.

[19] *Cf.* for example, the phrases that a man or a citizen was "franc et libre" in N. *Etain*, AP, Vol. II, p. 214, and CT, Bruyères, AP, Vol. IV, p. 10.

[20] Only a minority of the *procès-verbaux* indicate the method of selecting the committee.

[21] *Cf.* for examples of choice by rank: C. Aix, Belley, Bordeaux, Cambrésis, etc. Five assemblies chose the committee by geographic area: C. Alençon, Caen, Moulins, Ponthieu, and Toulouse.

[22] Six assemblies of the nobles chose the committee by geographic area: Caen, Coutances, Limoges, Périgord, Rouen, and Villeneuve-de-Berg.

[23] At least thirty-six assemblies of the third estate chose the members of the committee according to geographic area (*cf.,* for example, T. Aix, Angers, Artois, etc.). The third estate of Loudun chose by function.

[24] *Cf.,* for example, p. v., T. Dijon, in p. v. of the three orders, *Arch. Nat.* C 18/66.

dominant character was often facilitated by the holding of office in the electoral district, by selection to serve on the committee, or by the direction of an organized group whose opinion carried weight by virtue of its organization. For convenience, the influence of individuals will be treated under the following headings: royal officials, prominent individuals, and organized groups.

Royal officials

The complex provisions of the convocation brought all the local judicial hierarchy of royal officials into action.[25] The central government appreciated the power and the responsibility of the local officials, as was indicated in a letter from the Keeper of the Seals to the lieutenant generals: "It is in a measure in your hands that the fate of the convocation lies, since it is on the execution of the regulation that depends the exact representation which His Majesty has wished to procure to all his subjects."[26]

The rôle played by the royal officers varied with the different *bailliages* and with the particular officers. Such was the confusion of jurisdictions, that many controversies arose over the exact duties of each officer and considerable friction ensued.[27] In fact, official rivalry appeared to engage more time and energy than did direct efforts to dominate the electoral assemblies.

The *bailli*, by virtue of the convocation, presided over the general assembly of the three orders and was chairman of the assembly of the nobles.[28] The former rôle gave him an excellent opportunity to set the tone of the local elections. With the royal instructions in view, many of the *baillis* opened the general assembly with a speech appealing to law and order and patriotism, and urging harmony among the orders.[29] While exhorting the assembly to carry out the royal instructions, the *baillis* might also give interpretations of them. In rare cases the *bailli* went so far as to suggest the major problems

---

[25] *Cf.* Brette, *op. cit.,* Vol. I, pp. 68 *et seq.*

[26] *Cf.* MS, *Arch. Nat.* Ba 1 (project) or reprint in Brette, *op. cit.,* Vol. I, p. 324.

[27] Correspondence between the central government and the local officers shows that the former was often ignorant of vacancies, of the extent of jurisdictions and of the powers actually exercised. There were quarrels between the *baillis* and the lieutenant-generals, between the latter and the *procurors du roi,* while officials not named in the convocation were anxious to play a part. The regulation of January 24 expressly prohibited other officials from taking any part in the electoral procedure (*loc. cit.,* arts. 8, 30, 51).

[28] *Loc. cit.,* arts. 40, 41.

[29] For example, 3 O. p. v., Melun, *Bib. Nat.* Le 23.78.

which the cahiers should discuss.[30] Such advice was no more influential, however, as far as the results show, than the mass of electoral pamphlets in circulation or the personal influence of prominent members of the assemblies. Gouy d'Arsy, grand *bailli* of the *bailliage* of Melun and Moret, was perhaps the most voluble of these officers and radiated more personal influence through his office than most.

The lieutenant general had a similar chance of influencing the tone of elections, both because he frequently substituted for an absent *bailli*[31] or filled a vacant office,[32] and because he presided over the assembly of the third estate.[33] In actual practice, the lieutenant generals were more active than the *baillis,* for most of the correspondence between the Keeper of the Seals or central bureau and the *bailliages* was carried on by the lieutenant generals. They also appeared more in the *procès-verbaux,* and they more often verified and sealed the electoral documents. The lieutenant general sometimes opened the assembly of the third estate with a patriotic speech and occasionally gave specific advice, but there is not a single instance in which such advice was adopted under official pressure.[34]

It is certain that few of the royal officers took themselves as seriously as Caignart du Rotoy, the lieutenant general for Vermandois, who gave dinners for fifty of the delegates to the general assembly each evening, so apportioning the invitations that the number of members of the third estate was always double that of the privileged orders.[35] If his gastronomic generosity bespoke an ambition to be chosen deputy, the expense was wasted, for he was not elected.[36] The Marquis d'Espagne, *bailli* of Couserans, also gave dinners to delegates, but he steadfastly refused to accept election. He appears to have been disinterested and to have had a conscientious desire to promote harmony.[37] Similarly, the lieutenant general of Beziers refused to give advice when it was solicited and claimed that the king

---

[30] For example, p. v. for Commercy, *Arch. Nat.* Ba 19.

[31] For example, St. Jean d'Angely, Brette, *op. cit.,* Vol. IV, p. 414.

[32] For examples, elections in Comté de Foix (Brette, *op. cit.,* Vol. IV, pp. 162 *et seq.*); Dax (*ibid.,* Vol. IV, pp. 355 *et seq.*), etc.

[33] See regulation of January 24, art. 41, in Brette, *op. cit.,* Vol. I, p. 83.

[34] The lieutenant-general of Châtel-sur-Moselle recommended seven articles for the constitution and urged that local matters be omitted from the cahier, but his advice was not adopted exclusively. *Cf.* 3 O. p. v., and the cahiers. There were no other cases of such definite advice.

[35] *Cf.* letter of Caignart du Rotoy to the Keeper of the Seals and the latter's reproof, *Arch. Nat.* B III 154.

[36] *Cf.* Brette, *op. cit.,* Vol. II, *passim,* for list of deputies.

[37] *Cf.* correspondence, *Arch. Nat.* B III 55, pp. 220 *et seq.*

intended freedom of action for the assemblies.[38] The records show both types of officials: those who used their office to further their personal ambitions and to dominate the elections, and those who acted as impartial arbiters of the royal regulations and who promoted peace and harmony.

The local registrar was official secretary of the assembly of the three orders of a *bailliage* and also of the assembly of the third estate.[39] His chief influence upon the elections lay in his method of recording the *procès-verbaux*. His carelessness or his accuracy both affected the official record, and facilitated or hindered the future utilization of these documents. Occasionally the registrar put something of his own enthusiasm[40] or ambition[41] into the interpretation of the minutes, and his preference for one faction or another may have colored his report, but there is no evidence that the local registrars influenced the content of the general cahiers.

An examination of the pertinent sources corroborates the statement that the royal officers exerted no tangible influence upon the articles of the general cahiers which can be attributed to their official status. This was certainly true of the officers of the central government who interpreted the regulations to local officials, and it was also true of the *baillis,* lieutenant generals, and other local officials. There is no denying that the action of the royal officers was a factor in the electoral assemblies, but their influence was rather upon the general tone, upon matters of procedure, and upon the actual elections, than upon the articles and demands of the cahiers.[42]

Influential individuals

Many writers have spoken of the composition of the cahiers as if one person in the electoral assembly had written the cahier, and then

---

[38] 3 O. p. v., *Arch. Nat.* C 16/30.

[39] See regulation of January 24, Brette, *op. cit.,* p. 84, end of art. 41.

[40] For example, p. v., T. Château-Thierry, *Arch. Nat.* C 17/52.

[41] For example, p. v., T. Riom, *Arch. Nat.* C 23/136, and comments of Mège in *La Dernière Année de la province d'Auvergne,* pp. 89 *et seq.*

[42] One might challenge the denunciation of the intendants in many cahiers, the absence of similar disapproval of the *bailli,* lieutenant generals, and other officials of the convocation, and the request for more presidial courts as due to influence of these local officers, but it would be impossible to prove. According to Onou, in "Les Elections de 1789 et les cahiers du tiers-état" (in *La Révolution française,* 1909, Vol. LVI, p. 509), the officers of the central authority were neutral and impartial, but the local officials often used arbitrary power in support of the nobles and upper *bourgeoisie.* Onou was not distinguishing between the two classes of cahiers. There is insufficient evidence with respect to the general cahiers to warrant his statement.

the assemblies had passively accepted the text submitted to them. Even editors of the series of *Documents inédits* . . . have sought to fasten authorship upon some particular individual.[43] This approach puts a false emphasis upon the prominence of individuals in the electoral period of 1789. To be sure, each *bailliage* produced local leaders. Practically all the men who became prominent in the National Assembly later, displayed leadership in the assemblies of their respective classes, and were often members of the committees which drafted the cahier.[44] Although it is important to identify the dominant personalities in each district, it is far more significant to determine how carefully the assembly discussed the draft of the cahier. Thus, whether one man composed the draft or the whole committee worked harmoniously is of less importance than what modifications of the text the assembly saw fit to make.

The foregoing statement is well illustrated by the cahier of the third estate of the *sénéchaussée* of Nîmes. The editors of the cahiers of that district assign authorship of the general cahier of the third estate to Rabaut St. Etienne, a prominent Protestant, who had already written several pamphlets.[45] The cahier in question is philosophical in tone and conformed in its general outlines to the program of reform advanced by Rabaut St. Etienne, but the *procès-verbal* of the assembly informs us that the text of the cahier was read aloud twice and discussed before final adoption.[46] If, therefore, the general cahier of the third estate of Nîmes expressed the ideas of Rabaut St. Etienne, it did so with the full knowledge and approval of the assembly, and we may, therefore, conclude that the cahier represents faithfully the collective opinion. The predominant influence of one person is no reason, in this case, for rejecting the cahier as unrepresentative of the collective will.

The cahier of the third estate of Longuyon[47] is a less well-known

[43] For example, Le Moy, *Cahiers de doléances* . . . *d'Angers* (Angers, 1915), Vol. I, pp. clxvi *et seq.*, and especially, clxviii-clxix.

[44] The Lameths, Malouet, Mounier, Talleyrand, Rabaut St. Etienne, Siéyès, Dupont de Nemours, etc., are examples in point.

[45] Bligny-Bondurand, *Cahiers de doléances* . . . *de Nîmes* (Nîmes, 1908), Vol. I, pp. xxx-xxxi. Note especially the sentence "Tous ces cahiers des villes et des campagnes . . . Rabaut St. Etienne, député de Nîmes, les prit et les fondit en un monument remarquable, qui devint le cahier du Tiers-Etat de la sénéchaussée." This is entirely misleading. The editor lists the publications of Rabaut St. Etienne which he claims to have been the direct inspiration of the parish cahiers.

[46] P. v., *Arch. Nat.* C 21/114.

[47] The text is reprinted on p. 331.

illustration of the same circumstances. The *procès-verbal* of the assembly mentions that a Monsieur Guillaume wrote the cahier, but then indicates that the text was adopted by the assembly only after careful discussion and some modifications.[48]

In a few cases, the cahiers give internal evidence of the influence of prominent individuals such as, for example, the cahiers of the third estate of Rennes, of Riom, and of Nemours.[49] Some individuals were recognized leaders, whose spontaneous leadership was approved by the assembly. Some were working for their own advancement, but in such cases their efforts were directed toward influencing the elections rather than the cahiers. Most of these individuals had become known by their writings, whose influence will be discussed hereafter. The whole procedure prescribed for the composition of the cahier was designed to check the individual and to insure the expression of the collective will. All evidence available leads to the conclusion that personal influences were no more prominent than are inevitable and natural in all elective systems. The cases of undue influence in which the will of the assembly was overridden were exceptional; the cahiers affected thereby are listed among those that are regarded as unrepresentative.[50]

The Duke of Orléans enjoyed an exceptional position, and something must be said of his influence. The cousin of Louis XVI was active both in electioneering and in propaganda for the cahiers.[51] He profited by the right of plural voting, was himself elected deputy by three districts,[52] and worked to have his agents chosen in other districts.[53] The important fact for the cahiers lies, however, in the

[48] *Arch. Nat.* Ba 19, under "Longuyon."

[49] In their introduction to the official edition of cahiers of the *sénéchaussée* of Rennes (*op. cit.*, Vol. I, Introduction, p. civ), Sée and Lessort recognize that the demands of the cahier of the third estate of Rennes coincided with the wishes of the parishes, but they believe that the phrasing was the work of Lanjuinais.

The need of supplementing the *procès-verbal* with other electoral material is particularly marked in the case of T. Riom, since Malouet the secretary, recorded the minutes so as to emphasize his own predominant rôle. The adoption of the cahier was not unanimous as he reported. See Mège, *op. cit.*, p. 93. See p. 88 on T. Nemours.

[50] *Cf. infra*, p. 87.

[51] Louis Philippe Joseph, duc d'Orléans, later known as Philippe Egalité.

[52] The Duke was elected by the nobles of Paris *intra-muros*, Crépy-en-Valois, and Villers-Cotterets, but he chose to represent Crépy. The nobles of Villefranche-de-Beaujolais would have elected him had they not heard of his election by the other districts. *Cf.* Brette, *op. cit.*, Vol. II, p. 260.

[53] See the references by the British ambassador, Letter from Dorset to Carmarthen, February 26, 1789 (Browning, O., *op. cit.*, Vol. II, p. 164).

instructions which he sponsored. The Duke of Orléans distributed a pamphlet, *Instruction donnée par S. A. S. Mgr. le duc d'Orléans à ses représentants aux bailliages, suivie de délibérations à prendre dans les assemblées,* the first part of which has been ascribed to Choderlos de Laclos, and the second to Siéyès. These instructions must have received wide circulation, inasmuch as they went through several editions.[54]

The Duke's pamphlet did not contain unique advice. The first section urged the representatives of the Duke to have inserted in the cahiers articles for the organization and guarantee of a constitutional monarchy,[55] while the second section (the part ascribed to Siéyès), after criticising the royal convocation, developed various ideas under three headings—national needs, needs of the *bailliage,* and needs of the classes. Aside from many reforms asked for in a great deal of the electoral propaganda, the following items were distinctive[56] of the Instructions sent out by the Duke: (1) emphasis upon a complete reorganization of the method of elections with the new system based on a symmetrical, uniform series of successive steps;[57] (2) desire for individual liberty to travel, emigrate, or migrate; (3) recommendation that the third estate elect as representatives only members of its own order; (4) challenge to the third estate to act alone if the upper classes did not coöperate; (5) approval of divorce; (6) denunciation of imperative mandates.[58] What internal evidence do the general cahiers give of influence from the Instructions?

In the first place, acknowledgment of the Instructions of the Duke of Orléans appeared in only three general cahiers (and in a few *procès-verbaux*). The nobles of Chartres agreed with the attitude of the Duke on *capitaineries,* but otherwise the various articles of the cahier cannot be traced exclusively to his Instructions.[59] The third

[54] There were at least four editions. Martin, in *La Franc-maçonnerie de la Révolution* (Paris, 1926), believed that 100,000 copies were in circulation (Part iii, p. 156).

[55] M. Bloch has given an excellent summary of the Instructions in the introduction to the official edition of the cahiers of the *bailliage* of Orléans (*op. cit.,* Vol. I, pp. xi et seq.).

[56] Inviolability of property, liberty of the press, taxation by the States-General only, reform of the civil and criminal code, etc., were advocated by so many different writers that direct influence on any common demand could only be identified by peculiar phrasing. *Cf.* also chart, p. 66.

[57] Although other pamphlets advocated successive steps, the introduction of the canton as a unit was not common.

[58] Other items might be given, but they would be less distinctive.

[59] *Cf.* the Instructions and text of cahier, AP, Vol. II, pp. 626-29.

estate of Villefranche-de-Beaujolais took a similar attitude on *capitaineries* but did not include the same articles that might be traced to the Duke's influence[60] as did the nobles of Chartres. The third estate of Marseille thanked the Duke for his instructions, approved of them, but specifically rejected the demand for divorce.[61] Following this introduction, the first portion of the cahier, dealing with liberty, was clearly inspired by the Duke's Instructions, but thereafter none of the characteristic features were repeated. Some of the ideas that appeared in the Duke's Instructions, such as convocation of the States-General in case of a regency, approval of a writ of *habeas corpus,* denunciation of intendants, were given, but these recommendations were also made in other electoral pamphlets. The general cahier of the third estate of Marseille was in no sense a slavish adoption of the Duke's Instructions.

What of the characteristic demands of his propaganda? It is impossible to know exactly what districts received the Duke's Instructions. We do know, at least, that they were sent to all districts where the Duke held property or exercised rights of suzerainty. A statement of the property held by the Duke in 1790 gives us some idea of what electoral districts this included.[62] On this basis, it is reasonable to suppose that at least twenty-five of the general districts received the Instructions of the Duke of Orléans.[63]

The *bailliages* of Villers-Cotterets and Crépy-en-Valois were home territory of the Duke, and inasmuch as he was elected by the nobles of both districts we should expect to find a marked influence of his ideas upon the cahiers. In the case of Villers-Cotterets, although the cahiers of all three orders resembled each other closely, and by identical demands[64] strongly imply some common influence, none of the cahiers revealed traces of the Duke's Instructions. Furthermore, the third estate of Villers-Cotterets was the only assembly of that

[60] *Cf. ibid.,* AP, Vol. II, pp. 282-86.

[61] *Cf. ibid.,* Fournier, D. I., *op. cit.,* pp. 358 *et seq.*

[62] See the *Compte-Rendu* for October 18, 1790, *Bilan ou état des biens et revenues de tout nature dont jouit M. d'Orléans* (s. l. n. d., in 8° and in 4°), examples in *Arch. Nat.* AD X 11.

[63] Avesnes, Amiens, Alençon, Blois, Coutances, Crépy-en-Valois, Chaumont-en-Bassigny, Chartres, Château-Thierry, Châlons-sur-Marne, Dourdan, Etampes, Lille, Marseille, Montargis, Nemours, Orléans, Paris *hors-les-murs,* Paris *intra-muros,* Péronne, Riom, Soissons, Vermandois, Villers-Cotterets, and Villefranche-de-Beaujolais.

[64] The attitude toward the existence of classes, and the articles and order of the demands of the first parts of the cahiers are the chief similarities. See texts, AP, Vol. VI, pp. 187-93.

order that approved of vote by order, a demand quite contrary to the Duke's advice for the third estate. Similarly, all three cahiers of Crépy-en-Valois bore some signs of a common inspiration,[65] but a demand about *capitaineries* was the only one by the clergy that might be traced to the Duke; three demands (relative to *capitaineries,* convocation of the States-General in case of a regency, and alienation of the royal domain) in the cahier of the nobles were the only impress of his influence; and the cahier of the third estate bore no resemblance at all to the Duke's Instructions.

Let us consider the most characteristic demands of the Duke's Instructions: first, approval of divorce. The third estate of Marseille is the only cahier to mention it at all, and then only to oppose it.[66] Another distinctive demand of the Duke was that the third estate elect only members of its own order as deputies to the States-General. Thirty-four cahiers of the third estate approved this principle.[67] Only six of these were from *bailliages* where the Instructions were unquestionably sent.[68] A third demand of the Duke's Instructions was for individual freedom to come and go, and to move about in France. Twenty-four general cahiers asked that the principle of liberty of personal movement be established.[69] Four of these cahiers came from districts where the Duke held property.[70]

One might continue through the entire list of articles distinctive of the Duke's Instructions, but the outcome would always be the same. The conclusion follows that either his Instructions were sent to all *bailliages* where any of these demands occur, which would include nearly every election district in France,[71] or the appearance of these demands is not directly due to his Instructions. As a matter of fact, the evidence of method of procedure, of the texts themselves,

---

[65] Compare Instructions and texts of cahiers, AP, Vol. III, pp. 73-79. Similar statements were made relative to venal offices, venality and the nobility, reaffirmation of legislation since 1614, etc.

[66] *Cf. supra,* note 61.

[67] The list is given in Hyslop, B., *French Nationalism in 1789* . . . (New York, 1934), p. 192, note 261.

[68] Chartres, Châlons-sur-Marne, Coutances, Paris *hors-les-murs,* Paris *intra-muros,* Villefranche-de-Beaujolais.

[69] The list is given in Hyslop, B., *French Nationalism in 1789* . . . (New York, 1934), p. 93, note 174.

[70] Alençon, Dourdan, Nemours, Marseille.

[71] Inasmuch as each of the distinctive articles of the Duke's Instructions appeared in a slightly different set of general cahiers, the total number of general cahiers that expressed one or more of the items is very large.

and a comparison of texts, supports the latter alternative. Although the Duke's Instructions were widely circulated, they were only one of the many electoral pamphlets. The Duke undoubtedly contributed to general enlightenment, but the very fact that the earmarks of his Instructions were scattered throughout a cahier proves that such ideas were expressed without conscious reference to the Duke.

An anonymous pamphlet was circulated in 1789[72] ascribing a very wide influence to the Duke and arguing that he was responsible for such attitudes as insubordination by the curates, a spirit of revenge among the orders, denial that France possessed a constitution accompanied by praise for the English Constitution and the principle of the separation of powers, aspersions on royal authority, demand for freedom of the press, free movement and emigration, inviolability of the post, abolition of *lettres de cachet,* divorce, and the irresponsibility of the States-General. Many of these tenets may be found elsewhere than in the Duke's Instructions. No one general cahier displayed consistently all of these attitudes, and frequently, though adopting one or two, showed opposite tendencies in the other items. This is especially true with respect to imperative mandates, which the Duke denounced. No evidences that have been available thus far corroborate the claims of the anonymous writer, at least as regards the *general* cahiers.[73] Although isolated articles in specific cahiers may have been inspired by the Duke of Orléans's Instructions, the assemblies displayed independence and voluntary choice in the contents of their cahiers.

Although influential individuals, including the Duke of Orléans, exerted an influence upon the contents of the cahiers, nevertheless, the *procès-verbaux* and the cahiers themselves afford convincing proof that the assemblies discriminated among the recommendations urged upon them, and never submitted passively to dictation.

Groups

Among the organized groups which exerted an influence on the cahiers was the Masonic order, of which the Duke of Orléans was

[72] *Aux français sur les instructions de M. le duc d'Orléans* (s. l. n. d., in 8-vo.), example in *Arch. Nat.* AD I 9.

[73] Direct borrowings from the Duke's Instructions can be detected more easily in parish and curate cahiers than in the general ones, and the argument of the anonymous writer may be justified with respect to the preliminary cahiers. For example, see official editions of parish cahiers for Coutances, Marseille, etc.

then official head.[74] Gaston Martin, who has given the best analysis of Masonry in France, refutes the theory of preceding writers that there was a Masonic plot.[75] He contended that the Masonic groups formed centers for the spread of eighteenth-century philosophy, served as laboratories of political training, and during the elections discussed the demands to be put into the cahiers. They received electoral propaganda and later helped to circulate the cahiers themselves. As far as the *general* cahiers are concerned, the argument of Martin is justified.[76] Most of the leaders of the Revolution were Masons, but Masonry served as only one of the many centers of propaganda and discussion.

Other groups, such as local academies and agricultural societies, were similar agencies for the dissemination of propaganda. There is no evidence in the minutes of the assemblies or in the cahiers themselves of any direct influence. Although there were patriotic groups in formation, and although there was a *"parti bouregois"* here,[77] a coterie of lawyers there,[78] the work of all these groups was the preparation of the general state of mind, rather than pressure brought to bear during the electoral assemblies upon the content of the general cahiers.

Two organized groups did carry on propaganda which bore definite fruit in the cahiers. The committee for St. Domingue at Paris issued a steady stream of correspondence, appeals, letters, and addresses, to stir up interest in the colonies and especially to refute the propaganda against slavery issued by a second influential group, the *Société des Amis des Noirs*. This latter organization, under the leadership of Condorcet and Brissot, promoted a humanitarian program. It is highly probable that the demands about colonial problems and denunciation of slavery were directly due to the activity of one or both of these societies.[79]

---

[74] The Duke was made Grand Master of the Grand Orient when it was formed in 1773. Although Masonry became active thereafter, the Duke appears to have had little to do with it (*cf.* Britsch, *La Jeunesse de Philippe-Egalité*, Paris, 1926, ch. VII, part iii).

[75] Martin, Gaston, *La Franc-maçonnerie et la Révolution* (Paris, 1926). He refutes the Abbé Barruel, *Mémoires pour servir à l'histoire du Jacobinisme*, and also L., Amiable, *La Franc-maçonnerie et la magistrature en France à la veille de la Révolution.*

[76] Among other evidences, an address of the masons of Draguignan to the National Assembly, undated (MS, *Arch. Nat.* C 123/398) supports Martin's view.

[77] See introduction, Le Moy, *Cahiers de doléances . . . Angers.*

[78] See on Dijon, Cochin, A., and Charpentier, C., *La Campagne électorle en 1789 en Bourgogne* (Paris, 1904).

[79] N. and T. Paris *hors-les-murs* acknowledged the propaganda of the committee from St. Domingue; T. Vermandois acknowledged the propaganda of the *Société des Amis*

Prominent personalities, whether holding royal offices, enjoying prestige by virtue of wealth, literary or political activity, or as members of organized groups, assumed leadership in the electoral assemblies of 1789. This was inevitable, especially in view of the fact that the French people had at that time had little training in political activity. Although many individuals offered advice or advocated the adoption of certain principles, the cahiers were selective, and on the whole, expressed the collective will of the assembly which adopted them.

LITERARY INFLUENCES

Time, circumstances, and personal influences all played a part in swaying opinion in the assemblies when the cahiers were made. A far more significant factor is the literature which formed the intellectual background of the members of the electoral assemblies. It was not likely amid the turmoil and hurry of the actual election period that the deputies to the *bailliage* assemblies would find time to peruse the writings of the eighteenth-century, or even the many contemporary publications. Political writings had already been leavening and educating the masses, while popular education was intensified during the electoral period.

Models

First among the writings that contributed to the formation of public opinion should be mentioned several semiofficial models which received nation-wide circulation. Although the central government studiously avoided giving out models of cahiers (formulae for the *procés-verbaux* were, however, distributed to all electoral districts[80]), pronouncements by governmental bodies did carry a certain official weight. Thus, Necker's summary of the second Assembly of Notables, presented to the King on December 27, 1788, made not only three recommendations regarding the convocation of the States-General, but discussed some of the reforms that should be made.[81] This report was printed and must have been widely circulated, in view of the number of cahiers which specifically acknowledged Necker's state-

---

des Noirs, while the first gave colonial demands and the last denounced slavery. These are a few of the examples that might be cited. Demands relative to the colonies took the form of request for colonial representation in the States-General, or demand for reform of colonial trade.

[80] *Cf. supra*, p. 33, note 8.

[81] The report is reprinted in the *Archives parlementaires*, Vol. I, pp. 489 *et seq.*

ments.[82] Another semiofficial program, giving fuller reforms than those of Necker, was embodied in the act of the Parlement of Paris of December 5, 1788.[83] The General Agents of the Gallican Church also sent out an official program of church reforms.[84]

Pamphlets

Throughout the latter half of 1788 and during the first half of 1789, an extensive pamphlet literature was interpreting eighteenth-century philosophy for the layman and applying its principles to the concrete reforms which the States-General should carry out. The wealth of such material and the confusing fact that much of it was issued anonymously and without date, make it impossible as yet to determine the total quantity of electoral propaganda, its authorship, and to what extent circulation of particular pamphlets was local, regional, or national.[85] We may only indicate which were the best known and which appear to have been the most influential.

Nearly every discussion of the cahiers has summarized more or less fully the general purport of the best-known pamphlets. Our present interest is not, therefore, to repeat what has been adequately done by Sée, Champion, Denys-Buirette, Lavisse,[86] and others, but to call attention to certain facts about the influence of the electoral propaganda, whose significance has hitherto been overlooked.

In the first place, it was altogether normal that there should have been a leavening of the popular mind prior to the meeting of the States-General. Propaganda, in its sinister twentieth-century connotation, was not then known. It was, however, a natural concomitant of the electoral period that political thinkers and writers should put

[83] Districts from different parts of France acknowledged Necker's report; e.g., N. Agen, T. Ustaritz, T. Nîmes, T. Loudun, T. Vannes, T. Boulay, C. Vic, etc.

[83] Reprinted in the *Archives parlementaires*, Vol. I, pp. 550 *et seq.*

[84] It has been impossible to determine just what instructions the Gallican Church sent out. It is possible that the papers merely included reports of the programs and protests sent to the king by the General Assemblies of the clergy. *Cf. Remontrances du clergé de France, assemblé en 1787, au Roi, sur l'edit du mois de novembre 1788, concernant les non-catholiques* (Paris, 1788, 8°, 37 pp.), copy in Princeton library; and reprint of other remonstrances in *Archives parlementaires*, Vol. I, pp. 373 *et seq.*

[85] Mitchell B. Garrett, who prepared the bibliography of pamphlets issued between July 5 and December 27, is preparing a bibliography on the later period.

[86] Sée, H., "Les Idées philosophiques du dix-huitième siécle et la litérature prérévolutionnaire," in *Revue de synthèse historique*, Vol. VII (1903), pp. 178-90; 278-90; Carré, Sagnac, and Lavisse, *Histoire de France depuis les origines jusqu'à la Révolution* (Paris, 1926), Vol. IX, pp. 366 *et seq.* For Champion and Denys-Buirette, see bibliography, pp. 460, 461.

their views into writing. The motive was more often that of patriotic service than of self-advancement.[87] The same creative spirit stimulated the publicists on the eve of the Revolution, as had motivated Voltaire, Montesquieu, and Rousseau. Voltaire hoped to arouse opposition to abuses by his satire and subtle praise of better conditions. Montesquieu demonstrated some of the good features of the English system of government in the hope that France would profit by the example. Rousseau hoped to revise social conventions and bring about a return to a natural and simple state of society. Just so the pamphleteers believed in certain principles or special reforms and set about educating the masses. Arthur Young bears witness to the popularity of bookstalls, printers' shops, and cafés where electoral material could be procured.[88] Neither the royal censors nor the Parlements could control and stem the pamphlet output, nor could the printers satisfy the demand. Although most of the electoral pamphlets could be read in half an hour, their recommendations would furnish discussion throughout eternity. Such discussions were the prelude to the electoral assemblies.

A second significant fact about the pamphlet literature is the repetition of many of the same ideas and reforms. The more electoral pamphlets one reads, the harder it is to discover original features in single publications. In order to demonstrate the repetition of ideas, a table has been prepared, utilizing some of the more prominent propaganda and revealing the appearance of twenty-five principles or demands in each pamphlet, or in several works of one author. Care has been taken to consider only such pamphlets as would have exerted an influence during the electoral period.[89] It is at once obvious from the tabulation that a number of ideas were so often advocated by different electoral pamphlets that it is small wonder that the general cahiers repeated, and hence agreed on many of these topics. It is proof not only that "common abuses engender common remedies," but also that the perusal of many pamphlets in 1789 created common currents of thought. One cannot, therefore, point out one particular pamphlet as the source of recurring ideas. The chief problems perti-

---

[87] This is borne out not only in introductory phrases, but also in the fact that many pamphlets were issued anonymously. The latter could hardly contribute to self-publicity, or to election to the States-General, unless the authorship were uncovered.

[88] Young, A., *Voyages* (Paris, 1931), Vol. I, pp. 272-73, June 9.

[89] Internal evidence is not always conclusive for undated, anonymous pamphlets. Care has been taken to consider only the pamphlets that appeared before the cahiers were completed.

CHART OF OPINIONS IN COMMON PAMPHLETS OF 1789

	Parlement	Decl. of Dec. 27	Rennes	D. of O. Instructions	Antraigues	Bergasse	Condorcet	La Révellière	Mirabeau	Pétion	Rabaut St. Etienne	Servan	Siéyès	Target	Thouret
1. E. G. periodic	√	√		√		S	√	√	√	√		√	√		√
2. Tax by E. G.	√	√		√	√		√	√	√	√		√	√		√
3. Const 1st				√	√	√				√			√		√
4. Separation of powers				√		√		√	√	√		√			
5. Anti-monarchical		×		√	√		√	×		√	×	×			×
6. Resp. min.	√	√		√	√		√	√				√	√		
7. Verify nat'l debt				√	√		√				√	√	√		√
8. Prov.-estates					√	√	√	√		√	√	√	√		√
9. Vote by head			√	S	×	S	√	√		√	√	√	√	√	√
10. Elective principle					√	√	√	√		√		√	√		
11. C+N=T	√	√		√				√			√	√	√	√	√
12. Deputies own order	√	√	S							√	√	√	√		
13. T=nation	√	√		√	√						√	√	√		
14. Three classes					√		×				S			√	√
15. Equal tax liability	√		√	√	√	√	√	√	√	√	√	√	√		√
16. Renun. of privilege				√	√	√	√			√	√				
17. Decl. of Rights				√			√					√	√		√
18. Individ. lib.		√		√	√		√		√			√	√		√
19. Lettres de cachet			√	√	√		√			√		√	√		
20. Inviol. of prop.				√	√		√		√		√	√			
21. Lib. of press	√	√		√	√	√	√	√	√	√	√	√			√
22. Religious toleration		√			√	√						√			
23. Anti-clerical					√		√				√				
24. Imperative mandate			√	×	√	S	√			√			×	×	×

A check means approval of the item. A cross means disapproval of the item. An "S" means that there is some remarkable feature about that item in the works of the given author. Bergasse asked for permanent States-Generals, not periodic; he opposed vote either by head or by order, favored a legislative body in two chambers elected by all three orders jointly. Rabaut de St. Etienne states in one of his pamphlets that France was divided into three classes according to the constitution, but he denied it in another. The Duke's Instructions did not want the third estate to elect clergy or noblemen unless they had renounced their privileges.

PAMPHLETS USED FOR CHART

Arreté du Parlement, du 5 décembre 1788, sur la situation actuelle de la nation (See AP, Vol. I, pp. 550–51).

Rapport fait au roi par M. de Necker . . ., December 27, 1788 (See AP, Vol. I, pp. 489–98).

Délibérations du Tiers de Rennes des 22–27 décembre, 1788. Reprinted in Sée and Lessort, *D.I.*, *op. cit.*, Vol. I, pp. lxxi *et seq.*

Duc d'Orléans, Instructions envoyées par le duc d'Orléans, suivie de Délibèrations à prendre dans les assemblées de bailliage . . . (s. l. 1789).

Antraigues, Comte de, Mémoire sur les Etats-Généraux, Second Mémoire sur les Etats-Généraux.

Bergasse, Nicolas, Mémoire sur les Etats-Généraux, Lettre sur les Etats-Généraux.

Condorcet, M. J. de, Déclaration des droits . . . ; Examen sur cette question: est-il utile de diviser une assemblée nationale en plusieurs chambres?; Lettre d'un gentilhomme à Messieurs du tiers-état; Lettres d'un citoyen des Etats-Unis à un français; Réflexions sur les pouvoirs et instructions à donner par les provinces à leurs députés aux Etats-Généraux; Sentiments d'un républicain sur les assemblées provinciales et les Etats-Généraux.

La Révellière-Lépeaux, Louis M. de, Doléances, voeux et pétitions pour les réprésentants des paroisses . . . ; Plaintes et désirs des communes tant de ville que de campagne.

Mirabeau, Comte de, A la nation provençale; Dénonciation de l'agiotage; Sur la liberté de la presse.

Pétion de Villeneuve, J., Avis aux français sur le salut de la patrie.

Rabaut St. Etienne, J. P., Considérations très-importantes sur les intérêts du tiers-état . . .; Question de droit public: doit-on recueiller les voix dans les Etats-Généraux par ordres ou par têtes de délibérans?

Servan, J. M. A., Avis au public, et principalement au tiers-état; Avis salutaire, au tiers-états . . . ; Idée sur le mandat des députés aux Etats-Généraux; Exhortation pressante aux trois ordres de la province de Languedoc.

Siéyès, Abbé, Qu'est-ce que le tiers-état? Délibérations à prendre . . .

Target, G. J. B., Les Etats-Généraux convoqués par Louis XVI.

Thouret, J. G., Avis des bons normands . . . ; Suite de l'avis.

KEY TO THE ITEMS CHARTED

1. The States-General should have periodic meetings.
2. All taxes must be voted by the States-General.
3. A constitution should be made before other business is undertaken.
4. Approval of the principle of the separation of powers.
5. Anti-monarchical sentiment.
6. Responsibility of the ministers.
7. Verification of the national debt.
8. Establishment of Provincial-Estates in all provinces.
9. Approval of vote by head in the States-General.
10. Approval of the elective principle.
11. The number of deputies allowed the third estate should be equal to the number allotted to the clergy and nobles combined.
12. Each order should elect deputies only from its own class.
13. The third estate is the French nation.
14. The French nation was, and should be, divided into three classes.
15. Equal tax liability irrespective of class.
16. Renunciation of privileges.
17. Declaration of Rights.
18. Individual liberty.
19. *Lettres de cachet*.
20. Inviolability of property.
21. Liberty of the press.
22. Religious toleration.
23. Anti-clerical demands or spirit.
24. Imperative mandate.

67

nent to the originality of the cahiers is, therefore, whether pamphlets were actually in the hands of the committee and whether or not principles or wording borrowed from the pamphlets were imposed counter to the will of the assembly.

In the first place, there is no instance of the verbatim adoption of an entire pamphlet as a *general* cahier. There are examples of direct appropriation of specific articles or demands, but even in the most patent of these the variations and deviations of the rest of the cahier prove that the pamphlet was used merely as a guide. The wording of the pamphlet was adopted in such cases, it is reasonable to suppose, because it expressed the will of the committee, and it was then approved by the assembly.

Let us examine some concrete illustrations. Monsieur Bloch in his edition of the cahiers of the *bailliage* of Orléans, calls attention to identical paragraphs in the cahier of the town of Orléans, the *bailliage* of Orléans, and of the grand *bailliage* of Orléans.[90] The first of these took over large excerpts from the cahier of the unorganized inhabitants (*habitants libres*) of the town, who seem to have adopted a pamphlet which the editor did not identify.[91] A close examination of the various texts reveals minute variations. Similarities and differences were both voluntary and deliberate. When so much was borrowed, it would have been less arduous to have adopted the whole without alteration. Instead of following the easiest policy, the committees not only omitted or added to particular articles, but also included new items. The general cahier of Orléans (i.e., of the grand *bailliage*) is, therefore, one illustration both of direct borrowing and of the independence of the assembly.

Le Moy has done a similar piece of editing for the general cahier of the third estate of Angers. He shows passages in the general cahier adopted from the town cahier and from the more influential pamphlets known to have been in circulation in the district of Angers.[92] The striking feature of these adoptions is that the earlier parts of the cahier borrow more frequently from the pamphlets, while the later parts resemble the town cahier more closely. Likenesses and differences both prove that the general cahier was not a prearranged pro-

[90] Bloch, C., *D.I., Cahiers de doléances . . . d'Orléans* (Orléans, 1907), Vol. II, pp. 287 *et seq.*, and see also, pp. 251 *et seq.*

[91] *Cf.* models cited in introduction to Vol. I, and the text, pp. 251 *et seq.*

[92] Le Moy, *D. I., Cahiers de doléances . . . d'Angers* (Angers, 1915), Vol. I, pp. ccv *et seq.*

gram put across by the *parti bourgeois,* but the selective will of the assembly acting under enlightened guidance.

The two illustrations cited have been chosen because the editors of those particular volumes of the *Documents inédits* . . . have been at considerable pains to demonstrate the point we wish to make. Only three or four other volumes of the official series permit similar comparisons.[93] Such a study should be made for each *bailliage.* The *procès-verbaux* sometimes state that such and such an individual presented memoranda or a pamphlet to the assembly, and that this material was turned over to the committee,[94] or they acknowledge indebtedness for certain propaganda,[95] but a great deal of the local material must be examined to get the full intellectual background of any particular assembly. Obviously, it is impractical in the present study to establish the background for each of the two hundred and thirty-four electoral districts. Fortunately, in the widespread literature on the electoral period in specific areas, some information is given, even if seldom utilized, for a minute comparison of texts. Available details only corroborate the conclusion reached in the two official volumes cited (Bloch and Le Moy). The general cahiers did borrow from pamphlets not only ideas but also phraseology, but in every instance the borrowing was selective.

Aside from the analysis of the influence of the Duke of Orléans's propaganda, and the cahiers of the third estate of Orléans and of Angers, some other illustrations may be given as proof of the foregoing statement. The Comte d'Antraigues, whose pamphlet on the States-General was published early in the electoral period and received a very wide circulation,[96] was secretary of the committee which drew up the cahier of the nobles of Villeneuve-de-Berg.[97] That cahier, however, shows none of the distinctive features of his pamphlets[98] and

[93] For example, consult Jouanne for Alençon, Mourlot for Caen, and less carefully, Cauchie and Lesueur for Blois, Bridrey for Coutances, Le Parquier for Le Havre, Martin for Mirecourt, Etienne for Vézelise, Savina and Bernard for Quimper, Laurent for Sézanne, and Vernier for Troyes.

[94] For example, N. Alençon, see the p. v., *Arch. Nat.* Ba 11.

[95] For example, T. Vermandois acknowledged the reception of a memorandum from the *Société des Amis des Noirs* (*cf.* p. v., *Arch. Nat.* C 25/170); T. Caudebec-en-Caux acknowledged the reception of a pamphlet sent to them from Rouen which they desired to have suppressed as libelous (*cf.* p. v., *Arch. Nat.* C 17/46), etc.

[96] *Mémoire sur les Etats-Généraux* (s. l. 1789).

[97] P. v., PR, *Arch. Nat.* Ba 85.

[98] The following ideas or expressions were characteristic of his pamphlet: monarchy is appropriate for large states, popular sovereignty, the third estate is *le peuple,* man is

furthermore displays a class spirit and regionalism entirely contrary to his teaching.[99] On the other hand, the nobles of Mantes spoke of monarchy and large states in much the same terms as did the Comte d'Antraigues, but there is no evidence that his pamphlet was used by either the committee or the assembly.[100]

Internal evidence from the cahier of the nobles of Ponthieu furnishes a patent example of borrowing from a pamphlet, but of retaining at the same time independence of thought. Although there is no proof that Thouret's *Avis de bons normands à leurs frères tous les français* was actually used, the only logical conclusion is that it inspired the following words of the cahier. Compare the following expressions:

Thouret

Si vous êtes étonnés du peu d'utilité des précédents Etats généraux, lisez les anciens cahiers des bailliages; vous reconnaîtrez presque toujours une des grandes causes de la défectuosité des Etats dans l'imperfection et les vices des cahiers.

On y voit d'une époque à une autre des contradictions sur l'ordre constitutionel dont on connaissait peu les principles. On n'y aperçoit jamais le dessein d'établir fiximent cet ordre sans lequel toute administration devient nécessairement versatile, arbitraire et incohérent; toujours, l'idée superficielle de recrépir les parties en détail a éloigné du soin plus essentiel d'ordonner l'ensemble et de rectifier les bases. Il semble que chaque assemblée de bailliage

Cahier

On s'étonne quelquesfois du peu d'utilité des précédents Etats généraux. Qu'on lise les anciens cahiers des bailliages: on y reconnaîtra les causes du peu de fruit de ces assemblées nationales. Les véritables principes n'étaient pas alors connus; les cahiers ne présentent, d'une époque à l'autre, que les contrariétés sur l'ordre constitutionnel; et d'ailleurs, chaque bailliage s'isolant dans l'étendu de son ressort, et ne s'occupant que de ses intérêts particuliers, n'égligeait d'embrasser du même coup d'oeil la France entière.[101]

---

in slavery (this was probably borrowed from Rousseau), need of a defensive army, liberty, patriotism.

[99] See the text, AP, Vol. VI, pp. 177-82.

[100] *Cf.* cahier, AP, Vol. III, p. 661, col. 1, and p. v., *Bib. Nat.* Le 23.231, and notes of Brette, *op. cit.*, Vol. III, pp. 344 *et seq.* This idea had been expressed, of course, by Montesquieu.

[101] [Thouret] *Avis de bons normands à leurs frères tous les français* (Rouen, 1789), pp. 290-291. Pétion rejected an appeal to French history, but no similarity of idea or phrasing can be drawn (*Avis aux français sur le salut de la patrie*, ch. ii).

bornée à la vue de son district était
incapable d'embrasser du même
coup d'oeil la France entière.
Chaque cahier, réduit étroitement à
l'intéret de son bailliage, ne s'élève
jamais à la perspective de l'universel
de la nation et les vues fécondes qui
auraient produit la restauration en
grand sont partout remplacées par
un amas indigeste de doléances locales, futiles et intéressées.[102]

The identity of idea in the two documents and the numerous identical
phrases are the more conspicuous in view of the fact that this idea
occurs in no other general cahier and in no other pamphlet. What of
other advice in the *Avis*? Although some of the recommendations of
the cahier of the nobles of Ponthieu may be found in the pamphlet,
these were not unique in Thouret's proposals, while the nobles gave
their deputies an imperative mandate, which was directly contrary
to the advice of Thouret, and they omitted any development of the
idea of national representation which was a cardinal note of the pamphlet. Despite the one borrowed idea, the cahier was not a slavish
copy of a model.

Let us compare the model for a cahier written by Servan with the
cahier of the third estate of Aix, where he was chosen deputy.[103] One
might expect his pamphlet to exert a marked influence. There is a
mild similarity. Beyond the first article, however, the third estate
of Aix made different demands relative to the army and gave a detailed program of reform for commerce and agriculture, neither of
which did Servan discuss. Furthermore, the cahier is distinctly anti-
clerical, while Servan did not mention religion in this model. More-
over, the cahier failed to include at least one of the distinctive features
of Servan's advice, namely, that the deputies of each province band
together in the States-General as a means of preventing corruption
of the deputies by the court.[104] In other words, the writings of Servan

---

[102] AP, Vol. V, p. 431, col. 1.
[103] Servan, *Idées sur le mandat des députés aux Etats-Généraux* (s. l. 1789), and the
cahier, AP, Vol. I, pp. 695-97. Servan's *Project de déclaration proposé aux députés des
communes aux Etats-Généraux de France* (s. l. 1789), develops only a few points, and
its outstanding feature, measures for publicity for the constitution, does not appear in
the cahier. Some pamphlets ascribed to Servan were anti-clerical.
[104] *Loc. cit.*, pp. 5-6.

were not the sole source of inspiration among the third estate of Aix.

Chassin implied that the anonymous pamphlet published by Pétion de Villeneuve, *Avis aux français sur le salut de la patrie,* was influential in the *bailliage* of Chartres.[105] This pamphlet of two hundred and fifty-four pages could not be read as quickly as most of the electoral propaganda. It began with a patriotic appeal to put aside all *esprit de corps* for "la passion du bien public est la seule qui soit permise dans cette grande circonstance."[106] The first and second chapters deny the value of looking back into French history to discover the path of reform, and describe the government of France as it then functioned. It took Pétion about a hundred pages to reach his more definite suggestions of reform, and throughout his pamphlet his style is literary and philosophical. The cahier of the third estate of Chartres is notably concise and direct, while the style of the cahiers of the two privileged orders bear no mark of Pétion's style.[107] None of the general cahiers of that district was anticlerical, whereas the pamphlet of Pétion was characterized by a bitter attack upon the clergy. Aside from several articles that were not unique in the advice of Pétion, the cahier of the third estate and the pamphlet both contained similar statements against the registry of laws by the courts[108] and against the issuance of *lettres de grâce.*[109] On the other hand, the cahier of the third estate of Chartres contained a long section on the establishment of an intermediate commission, which Pétion does not even mention. There is even less direct influence between the cahiers of the privileged orders of Chartres and the *Avis.* If the pamphlet of Pétion was used by any of the three classes, other models were also used.

Let us look at the question of influences from another point of view. The cahiers seldom mentioned paper money. An opinion favoring the issuance of "papier national" was expressed by Brissot[110] but did not appear in other pamphlets that were widely circulated during the electoral period. Among the cahiers including any statement on paper money are districts as widely scattered as T. Toulouse, T. Troyes, N. Mâcon, T. Dôle, T. Alençon, C. Agen, and T. Lesneven. It is

[105] Chassin, C., *Le Génie de la Révolution* (Paris, 1864), Vol. I, p. 409.
[106] *Loc. cit.,* opening sentence. Princeton University has a copy of this pamphlet.
[107] C. Chartres, AP, Vol. II, pp. 623-26; N, *ibid.,* pp. 626-29; T, *ibid.,* pp. 629-35.
[108] Pétion, *op. cit.,* pp. 179 *et seq.;* T. Chartres, AP, Vol. II, p. 629, art. 8.
[109] Pétion, *op. cit.,* pp. 135 *et seq.;* T. Chartres, AP, Vol. II, p. 630, art. 23.
[110] Brissot de Warville, *Précise adressé à l'Assemblée des electeurs de Paris* . . . (s. l. n. d.), p. 15.

problematical whether Brissot's pamphlet was used by the committees for these particular cahiers. The dispersion of the topic seems to reënforce the argument that the pamphlet literature of the electoral period leavened public spirit and developed the political thought of the members of the assemblies but was seldom actually utilized directly in the composition of the cahiers.

Consider, for a moment, the request for the introduction of juries into French judicial procedure. Twenty-eight general cahiers of 1789 asked for their institution,[111] but these twenty-eight documents came from all parts of France—from Sarrebourg in Trois-Evechés, Rustaing on the Spanish border, Artois on the Flemish frontier, and Draguignan on the southeast. Who inspired the demand for juries? The Instructions of the Duke of Orléans, Condorcet, La Révellière-lépeaux, and Servan all advised their adoption in France. The only conclusions from the geographic distribution of distinctive demands and their repetition by several writers, are that there was widespread circulation of the electoral propaganda and also ultimate independence of the electorate.

Le Moy, in the volume on Angers already cited,[112] has indicated that La Révellière-lépeaux and two friends of his were very influential during the electoral period in Anjou. Despite the indebtedness of the general cahiers of Angers to these sources, there is a noticeable omission of La Révellière-lépeaux's demand for juries and for justices of the peace; there is no praise of Louis XVI as "liberator and regenerator," and no evidence of an anticlerical tone. No general cahier repeated La Révellière-lépeaux's suggestion that the Catholic clergy be allowed to marry.[113] On the other hand, the interest of the third estate of Angers in nationalization of the army and their demand for the publication of the minutes of the States-General may have been drawn from his pamphlets.

There is still another point of view. Groups of cahiers occasionally displayed textual resemblances which lead us to suspect a common inspiration even though we cannot discover it. The cahiers of the clergy and third estates of Soissons, of all three orders of Crépy-en-Valois, and of the third estate of Villers-Cotterets all asked that

---

[111] See Hyslop, B., *French Nationalism in 1789 according to the General Cahiers* (New York, 1934), p. 81, note 102.

[112] *Cf. supra*, p. 68.

[113] Cf. reprint of La Révellière-lépeaux's pamphlets in Le Moy, *op. cit.*, especially Vol. I, pp. clxxv-clxxxix.

73

peasant holdings be limited to four *charrues*.[114] In several cahiers of the *generality* of Auch, appeared articles utilizing the phrase, *"nul seigneur sans titre."*[115] The third estates of both Blois and Gien asked that muzzles be not required for dogs.[116] The nobles of Laon and the third estates of Crépy-en-Valois and Villers-Cotterets made identical demands for revision of all laws issued since 1614.[117] The third estates of Angers, Nantes, and Rennes stipulated that no deputy be elected to two successive States-Generals.[118] The third estates of Digne and Draguignan used similar phraseology with respect to the registration and publication of laws.[119] In all of these cases and many others that might be cited, the originality of the demand and the identical phraseology point to a common source, but in other respects each cahier differs from the others.

Aside from specific resemblances of particular articles, one may discover general similarities in tone, method, or program among several cahiers of a *generality*. Thus, there are resemblances between the cahiers of clergy, nobles, third estate of Châtillon-sur-Seine and of nobles and third estate of Dijon; of nobles and third estates of Armagnac and of Auch; of the nobles and third estates of Comminges and of Bigorre, etc.[120] Occasionally, the cahiers of the different orders of the same *bailliage* also displayed a similar tone, as for example, the cahiers of the three estates of Rodez, of Moulins, of Forez, or of nobles and third estate of Mâcon.[121]

The cahiers themselves seldom acknowledged the source of their inspiration. In view of the purpose of the cahiers and a resulting advantage in brevity, for the deputies could not be expected to consult prolix instructions, this is not surprising. Specific references to Necker's report of December 27, to the instructions circulated by the General Agents of the Gallican Church, to action taken (and known

[114] See respectively, AP, Vol. V, p. 770; Vol. VI, p. 698, art. 68; Vol. III, p. 74, cols. 1 and 2; Vol. III, p. 79, art. 65; Vol. VI, p. 193, art. 29.

[115] For examples, T. Auch, T. Bigorre, T. Quatre-Vallées, etc.

[116] T. Blois, Cauchie and Lesueur, *D. I., op. cit.*, Vol. II, p. 454, and T. Gien, AP, Vol. III, p. 408, art. 25.

[117] See respectively, AP, Vol. VI, p. 141, art. 13; Vol. III, p. 76, art. 4; Vol. VI, p. 192, art. 24. The district of Laon is also known as Vermandois.

[118] See respectively, AP, Vol. II, p. 39, art. 15; Vol. IV, p. 94, art. 6; and Sée and Lessort, *D. I., op. cit.*, Vol. IV, p. 243, art. 18.

[119] See respectively, AP, Vol. III, p. 348, art. 8 and p. 255, art. 4.

[120] See composite table pp. 113 *et seq.* under each name, for page references to each cahier.

[121] *Idem.*

through publication) by the third estate of Rennes in December, 1788, and to events in the Dauphiné were the only citations appearing in several cahiers.[122] All other contemporary influences must be deduced from internal evidence or from hints in the *procès-verbaux* and supplementary sources.

The great philosophers of the eighteenth century were specifically cited in some cahiers,[123] but their ideas appeared elsewhere without acknowledgment. The doctrine of natural rights was frequently expressed, while Rousseau's "contract" served as the basis for numerous demands. Montesquieu's emphasis on nationality, approval of the English monarchy, the separation of powers, and his appeal to the French sense of honor recurred constantly. Skepticism and anticlericalism may bespeak the influence of Voltaire. One could try to trace the parentage of all ideas of law reform to the works of the Baron d'Holbach, or of Beccaria; the educational reforms to the *Emile*, La Chalotais, or Rolland; the written constitution and the contents of a declaration of rights to the American Revolution; emphasis upon agriculture, simplification of taxes, and property qualifications for suffrage to the Physiocrats. The ideas of eighteenth-century philosophers were common currency to the makers of most of the general cahiers, but the expression of such principles was attributable to some members of the assembly already steeped in eighteenth-century writings, or to a pamphlet popularization, rather than to any consultation of the weighty volumes at the moment of the composition of the cahier. There is no way to discover, for example, unless a cahier mentions the source (and this it seldom does), whether references to a social contract came from reading Rousseau's famous volume or from concise statements of the theory by Servan.[124] Servan, Condorcet, and the Comte d'Antraigues must have drawn

---

[122] *Cf. supra*, p. 19. C. Castellane (p. v., *Arch. Nat.* Ba 39, in folder for Draguignan), acknowledged the instructions of the Gallican Church. The action taken by the third estate of Rennes is summarized in Sée and Lessort, *D. I., Cahiers de doléances . . . de Rennes* (Rennes, 1909-12), Vol. I, pp. LXXI *et seq.* This action was widely known in Brittany, as the cahiers of T. Lannion, Lesneven, Morlaix, Ploërmel, Quimper, Rennes, and St. Brieuc, attest. In cases where propaganda or action is acknowledged, the assemblies usually did not repeat the details of the program approved. The deputies were expected to know the significance of the citation.

[123] Only a small number of general cahiers referred to any of the philosophers by name. For examples of references to Montesquieu, see T. Boulogne-sur-Mer (AP, Vol. II, p. 432); C. Péronne (AP, Vol. V, p. 347); to Quesnay, T. Nemours (AP, Vol. IV, p. 144, etc. Rousseau was not mentioned by name.

[124] *See* especially, Servan, *Projet de déclaration. . . .*

their inspiration from Montesquieu when describing monarchy as the most appropriate for large empires and for the geographic character of France, and the appearance of this idea in scattered cahiers was more probably due to the pamphlet popularization than to the *Esprit des lois*.

Historians have continually traced a link between eighteenth-century philosophy and the French Revolution. Influence there undoubtedly was, but it passed into the French consciousness through the channels of the electoral propaganda with a corresponding modification. One of the pamphleteers himself testifies to the change in the French public in the months prior to the opening of the States-General. Rabaut St. Etienne remarked:

I am undertaking a serious discussion; but I do not speak to those Frenchmen whom a long enduring despotism had condemned to turn to pleasant or frivolous reading, the rare wisdom that they had received from nature. Three months have changed the nation.[125]

Later in the same work, he said:

They [conservatives] had not observed that enlightenment had already made sufficient progress for a mass of citizens to be capable of studying the science of taxation, its abuses, and their causes, and to delve into such questions to the point of causing their patriotism to burst forth at this moment.

They have not paid attention to the fact that the French of today are no longer those of preceding centuries; enlightenment, in improving the mind, has made known to man his dignity; that the third estate, filled with enlightened men . . . can no longer be led like a flock of slaves. . . .[126]

In view of the nature and extent of the pamphlet material, no one should be surprised to detect ideas from eighteenth-century philosophy in the cahiers, and these documents were themselves a prophecy of the Revolution.

Some historians have ascribed a strong influence upon the French Revolution to American thought and experience. Here again, influence was probably conveyed through the pamphlet literature. To be sure, spectacular figures like Lafayette must have radiated a certain personal influence; and Franklin, Washington, Jefferson, and other

[125] Rabaut St. Etienne, *Question de droit public* . . . (Languedoc, 1789), p. 3.
[126] *Ibid.*, p. 42.

prominent Americans were known to the *intelligentsia,* but the influence of American ideas upon the cahiers was more than likely traceable to reference and expositions of American practice in the works of Condorcet, Brissot, and others.[127] It is significant that America was nowhere specifically mentioned in the general cahiers. Rare demands for a special constitutional assembly,[128] or demand for a two-thirds or three-quarters majority for the passage of laws may have been of American origin,[129] but whether from America or from Rousseau, it is probable that the electoral pamphlets served to draw attention to these particular ideas.

All the foregoing data illustrate the diverse influences which created an atmosphere or acted directly in the electoral assemblies to affect the contents of the cahiers. Time, procedure, education, presiding officers, influential members, electoral propaganda, electoral incidents, all fused (or failed to fuse) to create a particular collective spirit in each electoral assembly. This *état d'esprit* is reflected in the general cahiers. The various influences were natural and legitimate to the extent that they did not prevent a representative expression of opinion. The crucial question for the value of the cahiers is not, therefore, the originality of the cahier, but rather its representative quality. The conclusion from a study of the internal and external evidence is that the overwhelming majority of the general cahiers were selective and did express fairly accurately the *état d'esprit* of the respective elective assemblies.

THE PROBLEM OF SINCERITY

Although the general cahiers expressed no original ideas, were they the sincere expression of the electoral assemblies?

Voltaire has said that people like to air their grievances and take pleasure in exaggerating them. Some general cahiers did describe the heavy tax burden, the poverty of the soil, the unbearable local conditions, in order to give weight to their plea for *egalitarian* reform, but such pessimistic descriptions were much less frequent in the gen-

---

[127] Condorcet, *Lettres d'un citoyen des Etats-Unis à un français* . . .; Brissot, *De la France et des Etats-Unis.* . . .

[128] It is well to recall that the American Constitution had been ratified but that Washington had not yet taken office when most of the electoral assemblies were meeting in France. See for example of possible American influence, T. Paris *hors-les-murs,* AP, Vol. V, p. 240, art. 38.

[129] For example, N. Mantes, AP, Vol. III, p. 661, col. 2.

eral than in the preliminary cahiers.[130] Bewailing local conditions did not add force to reforms demanded for the whole of France. One is struck, rather, with the optimistic tone of the *general* cahiers. Although some officers and institutions were denounced,[131] the same cahier that denounced them usually suggested positive reforms to remedy existing abuses. Within the limits of their brevity and generalizations, the general cahiers concentrated upon a constructive program; expressions of confidence in the king as leader in reform and national regeneration were well-nigh universal.[132] Where pessimism was strongest, the local sentiment was also strongest, but the majority of general cahiers were national in focus and at the same time optimistic.

The general cahiers have been reproached with another kind of exaggeration, that of using stock phrases and current overstatements. Certain formulae for addressing the king were prevalent, and in the ferment of the electoral period many patriotic phrases and reform slogans were voiced. The trinity of liberty, equality, and fraternity had not yet been verbally associated; however, at this time each term was a rallying cry. Such demands as that for a regular convocation of the States-General, equal liability for taxation, guarantees of individual liberty, were popular slogans as widely accepted and probably as imperfectly understood as was the phrase "making the world safe for democracy" in war-time America. In 1789, all classes desired the establishment of a constitutional monarchy and displayed a surprising unanimity as to the general methods necessary to achieve this. At the time that the cahiers were made, expressions of class fraternity, of patriotism, of equality and liberty, were consonant with the agreement of the classes upon major reforms, and they are, therefore, no

[130] Less than fifty general cahiers displayed a notably pessimistic attitude. The three strongest illustrations are C. Sisteron, T. Castelmoron d'Albret, and T. Longwy, but even these devoted some attention to general reforms. By contrast, let us take for example the parish cahiers of the principal *bailliage* of Coutances. Forty-nine out of one hundred and sixteen parish cahiers of the *bailliage* displayed pessimism, while fifty-four (not all identical with the forty-nine cited) devoted their entire attention to local conditions and reform. These figures were arrived at by a careful reading of the parish cahiers in the official volume, Bridrey, E., *D. I., Cahiers de doléances . . . de Cotentin*, Vol. I; only the figures for the principal *bailliage* are given.

[131] For example, denunciation of the office of intendant was usually accompanied somewhere in the cahier by the assignment (tacitly or expressly) of his functions to the Provincial-Estates to be instituted. E. g. C. Beauvais, N. Angers, and T. Poitiers.

[132] *Cf.* the discussion of the king as reformer in Hyslop, B., *French Nationalism according to the General Cahiers of 1789* (New York, 1934), pp. 157, *et seq.*

evidences of insincerity or duplicity. The brevity of the cahiers, inevitable in view of their purpose, the method of composition, and the pressure of time lend force to the accusation of the use of stock phrases; but a comparison of the cahiers with the pamphlet literature, the budding journalism, and subsequent speeches in the National Assembly leads one to believe that such expressions were an honest reflection of current opinion.

Inconsistency or contradiction in the articles of a single cahier has sometimes been considered an evidence of insincerity. How could the same cahier ask for an equal status of all districts of France, and at the same time request maintenance of all its local privileges, or combine class spirit with fraternity?[133] Few cahiers were the unanimous opinion of all members of an assembly. Men often agree on general policies but differ on details, and it is only logical that the synthetic product of so many minds should diverge in some particulars from the principles of any one member of the assembly. Contradictory articles may have been included because the opinion of the assembly was actually divided upon the subject,[134] while in other cases, the brevity may be misleading, or the articles may have been adopted without a full realization of their significance.[135] Self-deception or a house divided against itself, rather than insincerity, is the explanation for such cases.

The cahiers have also been accused of misrepresentation and, consequently, of insincerity. Ignorance of actual conditions may have led to misrepresentation in a few cases. The presence of royal officers, prominent business men, and the better educational qualifications of the members of general assemblies exclude ignorance of conditions as an explanation for most general cahiers.[136] The fact that the cahiers were a collective product also formed a check on misrepresentation. It is not logical to suppose that the assembly, knowing the amount of

[133] Compare the discussion of regionalism and class spirit, in Hyslop, B., *op. cit.*, pp. 183-93.

[134] For example, T. Poitiers with protest, T. Agen accepted by small majority, C. Amiens, etc.

[135] Note, for example, contradictions of patriotism, regionalism, fraternity, and class spirit in N. Annonay, AP, Vol. II, pp. 47-49; brevity in C, T, Tours (*infra*, pp. 87-88); N. Mirecourt, Martin, *D. I., op. cit., pp.* 261 *et seq.*

[136] The general cahiers gave less descriptive material than the parish cahiers. Even in the case of the parish cahiers, however, numerous editors have found that their information on taxes and local administration coincided with other contemporary sources. Note statistics given in general cahiers of N. Limoges and T. Longwy.

existing taxes, voted to state double that sum in the cahier.[137] It is also unreasonable to assume that an assembly asked for reforms that it did not want. Ignorance of corresponding conditions in other *bailliages* may have led to overemphasis upon the harmful conditions in the one *bailliage* and also to self-pity, but there is no evidence of deliberate misrepresentation.

The cahiers cannot be accused of satire or cynicism. Their makers were in deadly earnest and largely devoid of humor. Ardent reformers are seldom, if ever, humorous, and the cahiers present no exception.

Were the general cahiers of the clergy and the third estate (supposedly a compilation of preliminary cahiers), actually a faithful reproduction of the preliminary cahiers? To determine whether they were or not requires a comparison of these documents for each *bailliage,* but it is impossible to make such a study for every *bailliage* in France, because of the loss of preliminary cahiers. For a study of various districts where they have been preserved, several characteristics are apparent which it is reasonable to suppose apply to other districts as well. As a result of the comparison, one generalization holds for the cahiers of both clergy and third estate—that proportionately greater space was given to national problems or reforms in the *general* cahiers than in the preliminary cahiers. Can this be true and the *general* cahiers still be considered representative of opinion for either class within a *bailliage?*

Let us take first the cahiers of the clergy. Parish problems were the natural interest of the curates. For example, a majority of the cahiers of the curates of the *bailliage* of Auxerre either devoted entire attention to ecclesiastical affairs, or offset such affairs only with an interest in the secular administration of the parish.[138] Demand for increase in revenues or salaries for curates, pensions, reform in the collection of the *dîme,* reapportionment of the costs of parochial improvements, and a more important position for curates in the ecclesiastical hierarchy, were the chief interests of curates of this district. When the local lay administration attracted attention, demands were

---

[137] Attention may be called to the errors in reproducing the statistics of the cahier of the nobles of Limoges, committed by the *Archives parlementaires;* see *infra,* p. 178. The cahiers of a general region were a check upon each other as regards misrepresentation.

[138] By a careful reading of the cahiers of the curates reprinted by Porée, C., *D. I., Cahiers des curés du bailliage d'Auxerre* (Auxerre, 1927), it was discovered that out of forty-eight cahiers, sixteen devoted entire attention to church affairs, nineteen to parish problems, lay or ecclesiastic, while only four gave major attention to national organization.

made for reform in seigniorial administration and justice, denunciation of, or reduction in, various local taxes, and other measures to improve the life of the rural peasant. A similar proportion of preliminary cahiers from cathedral chapters, *chanoines,* and groups of regular clergy concentrated attention on local or ecclesiastical reform.[189] The *general* cahier of the clergy of Auxerre does not show a similar emphasis. Inasmuch as this cahier is very much longer than any of the preliminary cahiers, and gave a detailed program of national reform, the relative importance of ecclesiastical reform, and especially of rural reform, was greatly reduced. Porée claimed that the *general* cahier of the clergy is a fair representation of the preliminary cahiers.[140] That is certainly true as regards the general tone, when all the preliminary cahiers are taken together, but the needs of the lower clergy and their demands for the parishes fall into the background as compared with the national program. We must remember, however, that the curates or their personal representatives appeared in the general assembly and at Auxerre actually formed a majority.[141] Consequently, the political demands of the general cahier were approved by them when the cahier was adopted by the assembly, even though these demands had received little or no attention in their original cahiers. Thus, the *general* cahier of the clergy of Auxerre, although not reproducing the preliminary cahiers in their entirety, was, on the whole, representative.

As Porée noted, very few collections of the preliminary cahiers of the clergy have been preserved,[142] but by a similar comparison for a few other districts, the foregoing generalization holds true. Whereas the needs of the lower clergy were detailed in their preliminary cahiers and often formed the entire subject matter, they were condensed into a few articles in the general cahier. While the *general* cahiers repeated the wishes of the preliminary cahiers, they assigned a different rela-

---

[189] The cahier of the cathedral chapter of Auxerre, and that of the *chanoine* Clément de Bizon were primarily national and secular, but the other eleven preliminary cahiers, not from curates, were predominantly ecclesiastical or local. Cahiers of the regular clergy were notably so.

[140] Porée, C., *op. cit.,* pp. cxxix-cxxxi. For the text, see *ibid.,* pp. 359 *et seq.*

[141] Porée also claimed that although the curates were in a majority, many of them were subservient to Mgr. Cicé, the bishop of Auxerre. On the representation of curates in the electoral assemblies, *cf. supra,* p. 30.

[142] The volume of Porée is the only official editing of preliminary cahiers of the clergy. His statement is to be found, *op. cit.,* p. i. Other collections of manuscripts or reprints may be ascertained by examination of the *Repertoire critique des cahiers de doléances de 1789* (by Hyslop, B., Paris, 1933).

tive importance to these items. With this reservation, therefore, the general cahiers of the clergy fairly represented the opinion of the general assemblies which adopted them[143] and to a large degree of all ecclesiastics in the *bailliage*.

The relationship between preliminary cahiers of the third estate and the *general* cahier of the *bailliage* necessitates some additional considerations. Whereas curates appeared in person at assemblies of the clergy, the parishes were represented by elected delegates. An analysis of several cases shows that the rural or peasant element and the gild element of towns were progressively eliminated by the indirect steps of the elections.[144] The general assemblies of the *bailliages* were composed largely of petty officials, lawyers, and the upper *bourgeoisie*. To be sure, the parishes and gilds were free to choose their own delegates, and if they chose to be representd by men who were locally prominent rather than by peasants or gildsmen, it was their own fault. Undoubtedly, delegates were cognizant of the wishes and conditions of their electorate, and they would tend to have a wider vision and a more national focus than peasant or gildsman. Thus, for the general cahier of the third estate, three questions arise: were the general cahiers true reproductions of the parish cahiers, were they representative of opinion in the general assembly, and were these two identical?

Let us take the question of the parish cahiers and the general cahiers first. Parish cahiers devoted most of their attention to rural and local problems. Questions of the *gabelle, dîme, corvée,* method of tax collection, feudal dues, feudal justice, roads and communication, fuel, and forests and hunting rights consumed most of the space.[145] If any items of reform in the national government were given, the treatment was very brief. In the general cahiers, on the other hand, national reform took an inverse proportion of the space. Rural needs were either consolidated into a few articles, or overbalanced by a long program of national reform. Where a conscientious effort was made to compile the parish cahiers, two methods

---

[143] The general cahiers were less opposed to seigniorial justice than the cahiers of the curates.

[144] For example, see the analysis for Caen by Mourlot, F., *Le Cahier d'observations et doléances du tiers-etat de la ville de Caen en 1789* (Dreux, 1912).

[145] *Cf.* p. 78, note 130. If the same district is used for an illustration, i.e., the principal *bailliage* of Coutances, only twenty-seven out of the hundred and sixteen preliminary cahiers gave major attention to national problems, and many of these were traced to the same or similar influences. The others gave chief attention to such items as have been mentioned.

were open to the committees. They might include only the articles upon which there was general agreement, or else might list all demands in any preliminary cahier.[146] In the first case, many demands for rural reform would be omitted, and national reform would thereby assume a proportionately more prominent rôle. In the second case, there would be equal emphasis on all articles irrespective of their prominence in the parish cahiers. Thus, even where compilation was undertaken, emphasis and omission tended to alter opinion in the general cahier, so that it rarely presented a complete picture of the parish cahiers.

The same thing happened with respect to gild and town cahiers as represented in the general cahier. Although the cahier of the chief town of a *bailliage* was often used as a starting point for the general cahier,[147] the gilds chose few of their own members as delegates to the town assembly, and both the town and the general cahier contained few demands relative to the gilds or industrial organization. The city proletariat was no more vocal in the general cahiers than were the peasants.

Did the *general* cahiers represent opinion of the general assembly, if not of the *preliminary* cahiers? The answer depends on the adoption of the cahier by the assembly, which is the crucial test of any cahier. In so far as the members of the third estate adopted the text of a cahier submitted to them by the committee, the cahier may be said to reproduce the ideas of the members or their interpretation of the wishes of the electorate. In some cases, the general cahier was a faithful mirror of the preliminary cahiers,[148] but far more frequently

---

[146] Many assemblies voted to give the preliminary cahiers to the deputy to supplement the general cahiers; this was a tacit admission that the general cahiers were not identical with the parish cahiers, and that the latter contained demands not repeated in the general cahiers.

The general cahier of the third estate of Blois illustrates the policy of including all topics treated by the preliminary cahiers, without apparent consideration of how important the article was. The general cahier contains an article asking that there be no obligation to put muzzles on dogs, unless in sections where the grapevines would be harmed. (Cauchie and Lesueur, *D. I., op. cit.,* Vol. II, p. 454, last item of art. 16). Of the more than two hundred parishes of the *bailliage* of Blois, only two parishes (Thiville, p. 329, art. 26; Flacey, p. 376, art. 13) protested against the action of feudal lords in putting muzzles on peasants' dogs. The parish cahiers of this *bailliage* had a good deal to say about hunting rights and the destruction to agriculture by wild game, but only two brought up this particular item, and it reappears, therefore, with disproportionate importance in the general cahier.

[147] For example, T. Orléans, T. Dijon, etc.

[148] Several authors of official editions of parish cahiers have affirmed that the general cahier represented faithfully the preliminary cahiers; e.g., Bridrey, Sée, etc.

it reproduced with even greater accuracy the opinion of the general assembly. In other words, the majority of general cahiers of the third estate were sincere representations of dominant opinion in the *bailliages* rather than of the entire third estate. They portrayed the program of those influential persons, the *intelligentsia* and upper *bourgeoisie,* who were to engineer the Revolution. The determining factor in evaluation of the cahiers of all three orders, with respect both to originality and to sincerity, was the adoption of the text by the assembly. The minutes of the assemblies provide information about discussions of the text, alterations and additions, and even in some cases of the insertion of dissenting opinion.[149] In many cases, the draft of the cahier was read several times before its final adoption.[150] Evidences of the alteration of the committee's proposals, appearing as marginal insertions or in the deletion of articles on the original manuscript, have sometimes disappeared in the printed or reprinted texts.[151] In the majority of cases, the assemblies took very seriously the business of making the cahier, and only set their approval upon the final text after careful consideration.[152] This is true of the nobles, as well as of the clergy and third estate.

In view of the foregoing remarks, the claim may be made that the *general* cahiers of all three classes[153] were sincere representations of opinion in the general assemblies and hence of the dominant groups in each class of the electoral districts. In some cases, further claim may be made that this opinion coincides with the opinion of the entire class, while in other cases, the general cahier reproduces rather the opinion of a minority in the general assembly. These latter cases constitute cahiers which must be used with reservation.[154] With due consideration of the various influences that played a part in the electoral assemblies, a careful study of available material justifies the conclusion that by and large the general cahiers faithfully reproduced dominant opinion in the *bailliages.*

[149] For examples, C. Avesnes, p. v., *Arch. Nat.* C 15/18; T. Barcelonnette, p. v., *Arch. Nat.* B III 66², etc.

[150] For instance, C. Villefranche-de-Beaujolais (p. v., *Arch. Nat.* Ba 85); C. Avesnes (p. v., *Arch. Nat.* C 15/18), etc.

[151] For example, see annotation and the form of the cahier, U. Bourg-en-Bresse (*Arch. Nat.* Ba 23 MS, and reprint, AP, Vol. II, pp. 452 *et seq.*); T. Nemours (*Arch. Nat.* C 21/112², MS (overlooked by Brette) and AP, Vol. IV, pp. 112 *et seq.*), etc.

[152] Examples of very careful adoption are T. Melun, N. Paris *hors-les-murs,* T. Sens, C, N, Gien, etc.

[153] The cahier of the nobles was not based upon preliminary cahiers. It represented dominant opinion of the general assembly.

[154] *Cf. infra,* p. 87.

THE VALUE OF THE GENERAL CAHIERS

ESTIMATION OF THE REPRESENTATIVE CHARACTER OF EACH GENERAL CAHIER

The foregoing analysis has taken all of the general cahiers as one group. Anyone who wishes to consult the cahiers as sources would want to know which of the texts are reliable. We are here concerned with the reliability of the cahiers as gauges of public opinion, not as sources for specific information about existing institutions and conditions. Other contemporary records, such as tax rolls, court records, administrative reports, gave fuller details of the existing régime than the general cahiers which were chiefly interested in the reforms to be made. The cahiers were designed as instructions for the deputies, not as encyclopedias of facts or almanacs of conditions. Such information as the general cahiers convey is interesting, but it needs checking with pertinent sources. It is obviously an impossible task to attempt to verify every objective fact of every general cahier, and therefore it is impossible to classify them upon such a basis. The significant fact about the cahiers is their expression of collective opinion, and hence our concern is to determine how accurately each of the general texts reproduced opinion of a particular assembly.

Classification according to reliability as expressions of opinion involves a division of the *general* cahiers into three groups: those that are generally reliable, those for which some reservation is necessary, and those for which such serious reservations must be made that they can hardly be deemed reliable sources of opinion.

The overwhelming majority of general cahiers belong to the first group—those which may be considered reliable gauges of dominant opinion in the various classes for their respective areas.[155] All cahiers were subject to various influences and possess common limitations on their utility,[156] but such reservations may be said to neutralize each other. If a cahier bears witness to the influence of some individual member of the assembly, but was adopted by the assembly, it may be considered reliable.[157] If the committee took only a very short time in the preparation of a text, which, however, was carefully discussed by the assembly before adoption, the cahier has been

[155] Consult the composite table, pp. 113 *et seq.*, column 14, for indication of cahiers belonging to the second and third groups. Any not included in those classifications naturally belonged to the first, or reliable group. Four hundred and twenty-one of the available general cahiers were reliable.

[156] Cf. *infra*, p. 89.

[157] For examples, C, T, Mantes, C, Nancy, N, Draguignan, T, Longuyon, T, Rennes, etc.

considered a valid source.[158] If the official marks of authenticity at the end of a cahier are incomplete, but when checked with the *procés-verbal*, give reasonable evidence that the text extant is the original, the cahier has been adjudged trustworthy.[159] For nearly all cahiers some such doubt could be raised, but enough other factors may also be found to justify their classification as reliable sources.

A word may be said about seventeen cahiers of this group[160] which, though reliable, should be considered apart because they were composed subsequent to the regular electoral period or after the opening of the States-General. Whereas most of the general cahiers represent opinion current during the months of March and April, these seventeen cahiers probably represent beliefs of a later date. In some cases the assembly which made them was cognizant of events in Paris, and sometimes it was not.[161] In either case, a special interest attaches to these cahiers for their reflection of the development of opinion throughout 1789.

The second class of the general cahiers—those for which some reservation is necessary—comprises seventy-seven cahiers, not including those that have been lost.[162] Although the colonial cahiers have been considered separately in estimating the total number of general cahiers,[163] they would fall into this group in regard to their reliability.

Two main drawbacks lead to the placing of a cahier in this second group: doubt that the cahier expressed a majority opinion of the assembly which sponsored it and suspicion regarding the authenticity of the text now extant, because of incomplete or irregular authentication. In cases in which the royal officers exerted undue pressure,[164] in which propaganda was especially potent,[165] in which protests were made against the cahier as slighting some particular interest,[166] in

---

[158] For examples, T. Bar-le-duc, C. Saintes, etc.

[159] For examples, C. Aix, NT. Arles, T. Avesnes, T. Bar-le-duc, etc.

[160] The list is as follows: U. Arches et Charleville (December, 1789); CN, C¹, T, Béarn (May); U. Navarre (July); C, N, T, Paris *hors-les-murs* (May); C, N, T, M, Paris *intra-muros* (May); T. Quatre-Vallées (May); U. Rustaing (July); C, N, T, Soule (June). To this should be added C, NT, Couserans (May) which are missing.

[161] C, N, T, Soule did not know; U. Rustaing did.

[162] See table *infra*, pp. 116 *et seq.*, column 14.

[163] *Cf. supra*, p. 144.

[164] For example, T. Dax, T. Limoux, etc.

[165] For example, T. Angers, T. Dijon, N. Limoux, etc.

[166] For example, T. Bellême, where a complaint was lodged that the towns and agricultural interests were inadequately represented.

86

FACSIMILE OF THE SIGNATURES AT THE END
OF THE CAHIER OF THE THIRD ESTATE OF CALAIS

which the cahier or certain articles were adopted with a slight majority,[167] the cahier probably reflects minority rather than majority opinion of the assembly and is, therefore, less representative than the cahiers of the first group. Secondly, when the text of the cahier now surviving does not agree with the *procés-verbal* as to its date of adoption, lacks signatures, or raises further doubt that the existing text was not the one adopted by the assembly in 1789 and yet for other reasons has been accepted, such cahiers should also be used with caution.[168]

Several of the colonial cahiers should be included in this group, both because of the exceptional circumstances accompanying colonial elections and because of their tardy composition.[169] The documents for Pondichéry are the most reliable, but they represent opinion in March, 1790. The colonial cahiers that have been lost would be subject to similar reservations.[170]

The third group of the general cahiers is the most significant, for the twenty-seven cahiers (including two cahiers that have been lost) so classified should be used only with great caution.[171] The reasons for rejection of these cahiers as reliable testimony of opinion in the respective electoral assemblies are both stronger and more numerous than those applying to the second group of cahiers. In cases in which disorder in the assembly and protest are unaccompanied by adequate authentication of the cahier,[172] the text belongs in this third group. If the procedure for the composition and adoption of the cahier was irregular, with insufficient evidence that the assembly approved of the text, doubts as to its reliability must be raised.[173] In a few cases there is reason to believe that the text of the cahier was tampered with or that another text was substituted.[174] In a few other cases the original has been lost, and only summaries with incomplete authen-

---

[167] For example, T. Mâcon (cahier adopted by plurality); C. Thionville, N. Dijon, N. Comminges (certain articles approved with difficulty or protest).

[168] For examples: C. Bitche, T. Bordeaux, T. Carcassonne, T. Forcalquier, etc.

[169] *Cf. supra,* p. 27 and *infra* under each colony pp. 116 *et seq.*

[170] Guadeloupe (Paris committee), Iles de France et de Bourbon.

[171] For the complete list of cahiers of the third group, see table *infra,* pp. 116 *et seq.,* with comments.

[172] For example, C. Amiens, T. Chaumont-en-Bassigny, C. Dijon, etc.

[173] For example, N. Hyères (text missing), C. Nantes, C. Toulon (text missing). In the cases of C. Paris *intra-muros* and N. Rouen, the procedure was irregular, but the assembly finally approved the text, so that these two cahiers have not been included in the third group.

[174] For example, C. Beziers, N. St. Pierre-le-Moutier.

tication are now extant.[175] The exceptional circumstances of the electoral period, combined with the contents of the particular cahiers, lead one to distrust the text. Although the various texts in this group have generally been accepted among the cahiers, they should be used with some reserve.

Two cahiers of this group were exceptional with regard to the period of their composition: U. Bassigny-Barrois, and U. Dauphiné, the former after the change of the States-General into the National Assembly,[176] and the latter prior to the normal electoral period.[177] In addition, it is desirable to recall here the cahier of the third estate of Nemours. Attention has already been called to its exceptional length, careful compilation of parish cahiers, and also to the undoubted influence of Dupont de Nemours upon its contents and phraseology.[178] Although there is an authentic manuscript of the cahier, and the ordinary tests of reliability obtain, this text is exceptional and hardly comparable with other general cahiers.[179]

Although only four-fifths of the extant general cahiers may be used without reservation,[180] these documents still constitute a unique source of the opinion prevalent on the eve of the Revolution.

An Evaluation of the General Cahiers as Source Materials

The lack of original ideas, the varying weight of extraneous influences, and the degree of sincerity evident in each electoral assembly affected every general cahier and gave it more or less value as an expression of dominant opinion in 1789. In addition to these considerations, there are certain other limitations which the cahiers possess as a class of source materials. Some of these qualifications are inherent in the cahiers themselves, and some may be removed by proper verification.

[175] C, T, Tours, U. Dauphiné.

[176] Deputies elected by Bassigny-Barrois were admitted to the National Assembly in August, 1789 (Brette, *op. cit.*, Vol. IV, pp. 300-301), but the cahier bears no date, and there is no *procès-verbal* of the assembly.

[177] *Cf. supra*, p. 19.

[178] *Cf. supra*, p. 57.

[179] The p. v. states that the committee was given power to polish up the text (p. v., *Arch. Nat.* C 21/112^1). It is quite unlikely that so long a cahier was actually read aloud in the assembly before approval was given.

[180] There were 615 general cahiers, not including colonial cahiers, of which 523 survive. Four hundred and twenty-one belong to the reliable group.

THE VALUE OF THE GENERAL CAHIERS

LIMITATIONS

Four limitations must be noted. In the first place, the cahiers form a definite class of documents,[181] and therefore cannot be expected to reveal all sides of French life on the eve of the Revolution. Other contemporary sources, such as records and correspondence of the king's councils, intendants, and local royal officials, texts of laws, court proceedings, legal papers, letters, and diaries, possessed similar limitations, and no one class should ever be used alone, if a full picture of conditions just before the end of the old régime is desired. The cahiers, in particular, dealt chiefly with political affairs and need to be supplemented with further material regarding the cultural and social development. In view of their purpose, the cahiers were surprisingly wide in scope, but they were, nevertheless, limited in their contents.

Closely allied to the first limitation is the brevity and directness of the general cahiers. Since they were composed as platforms of reform, the more concise they were, the wider the range of topics that could be treated, and the more expeditiously could the deputies consult the instructions of their electorate. A result, therefore, of the purpose of the cahiers and also of the method used in their composition was the enumeration of specific demands with little descriptive material and little argument. The majority of general cahiers comprise a series of articles which total perhaps three thousand words[182] and can be read in fifteen minutes to half an hour. It is surprising, in view of their brevity, purpose, and form, that so many philosophical phrases, descriptive glimpses, and justificatory explanations are included. One must know from other sources the institutions which the cahiers asked to have reformed, for the general cahiers seldom explained existing conditions,[183] with which the representatives were more or less familiar. Even the reforms or new institutions advocated were often outlined in a very summary fashion. As similar motives sometimes led to opposing demands, and different reasoning to the same request, one may judge of the ideas behind the demands

[181] They cover three or four pages in the *Archives parlementaires*.

[182] In French departmental archives, the cahiers have been classified among judicial papers, but in the National Archives, with the legislative papers.

[183] It was taken for granted, for example, that the deputies knew what the *banalité*, the *capitainerie*, etc., were, as well as the jurisdiction of *gros-décimateurs*, *huissiers*, intendants, etc.

only if some explanatory phrase has been added.[184] Ideas in the cahiers are fragmentary and often detached, so that the philosophical background of each assembly is only partially revealed in the cahiers.[185]

A third limitation of the general cahiers also arises from their nature. No two cahiers were identical. Indeed, if they were, there would be good reason to doubt their reliability.[186] In a measure, each cahier differs from every other. The remarks addressed to Louis XVI which open most of the cahiers, were expressed in the greatest variety of words and actually reveal several shades of meaning. After this, came a series of articles, sometimes more than a hundred of them.[187] Various items were treated. Even most obvious demands were sometimes omitted.[188] The most widely expressed single idea was equal liability for taxation (or the contrary), but not all cahiers included such a statement.[189] Even such demands as that for the establishment of a periodic States-General, of Provincial-Estates in all provinces, of ministerial responsibility, or guarantees of personal liberty, did not appear in all cahiers.[190] When such demands were omitted, does it mean that the electoral assembly did not desire those reforms? We cannot say with finality, but because of the method of compilation

---

[184] For example, compare the motives for vote by order (C. Etampes) with motives for vote by head (any T. cahier); motives for abolition of slavery (C. Mont-de-Marsan, N. Châteauneuf-en-Thimerais, NT, Péronne).

[185] This is best illustrated by a perusal of two or three of the unedited texts given in the Appendix.

[186] There is one exception to this. The cahiers of the nobles and third estates of Châteauneuf-en-Thimerais were nearly identical, but the *procès-verbaux* explain that the two orders started to make a joint cahier, but could not agree on hunting rights or on the keeping of dovecotes, so that they handed in separate cahiers which differ only in those respects (*cf.* p. v., N, *Arch. Nat.* Ba 32; T, *ibid.*, C 17/51).

[187] Not all cahiers numbered the articles or set off different topics by separate paragraphs. The N. St. Pierre-le-Moutier, for whose cahier there is grave suspicion about authenticity, has left a text of only two articles, whereas N. Château-Thierry gave a very full program in seventy-four articles. For page references, consult the table *infra*, pp. 123 and 138, under the name of the district.

[188] It would be reasonable to suppose that every cahier would express an opinion on the method of voting to be applied by the States-General, vote by head or by order. Nevertheless, ninety-two assemblies failed to record their preference (See Hyslop, B., *French Nationalism* . . . p. 68). On this particular question, it is, of course, possible that these groups wished to avoid the thorny question, just as the King and Necker had avoided it.

[189] Approximately 480 of the general cahiers made this demand. See Hyslop, B., *op. cit.*, p. 257.

[190] Consult the same work, Hyslop, B., *op. cit.*, for information on the cahiers and these various topics.

and the fact that the general cahiers were collective products, they included whatever ideas were uppermost in the minds of the assemblies. Omission signified that the articles itemized were considered more important than those omitted. Had the central government sent out a questionnaire to be answered in a systematic fashion, all the general cahiers would have contained a like number of articles, bearing upon identical subjects.[191] Actually, the central government studiously avoided models for the cahiers, and consequently, the variety and the combination of demands in the five hundred and twenty-three general cahiers make a synthesis of their contents extremely difficult.

A first reading of a dozen or so of these documents impresses the reader with their great similarity. This is the inevitable result of their similarity of form, their brevity, and the identity of the major problems with which almost all of them dealt. Yet a closer examination shows a great variety of measures, full and brief items, complete and short programs, with a corresponding omission of many and of only a few items. The cahiers that may be classed together for their like opinions on one topic (for example, on the powers of the States-General) may be quite disparate on another topic (such as, for example, judicial reorganization).

The fourth limitation also concerns difficulty in consulting the cahiers, but it is hoped that this has been decreased by the present analysis. Although much has been written on the subject, both the secondary works and the texts of the cahiers, original or reprinted, have been scattered. It has been virtually impossible in the past to consult the complete number of texts and to give due consideration to the relative value of the various texts. The present analysis makes clear the number of general cahiers and those which are now extant and where the authentic cahiers may be found.[192] Information that has hitherto been scattered or has not been treated has been brought together into a few tables in the appendix.

A composite table has been designed to include essential documentary information.[193] This table lists the electoral districts

---

[191] Events in the Dauphiné illustrate the meaning here. We may recall that the elections and the cahier were made by the Provincial-Estates, augmented in numbers, but without primary elections similar to the rest of France. The Intermediate Commission of the Provincial-Estates sent out questionnaires to the communities of the Dauphiné, and the replies to these are substitutes for the preliminary cahiers of the rest of France. As answers to questionnaires, however, they give information on identical problems. See bibliography, p. 446, under Guillaume.

[192] *Cf.* Appendix, pp. 113 *et seq.*   [193] *Idem.*

alphabetically with the *generality* to which each belonged and the type of convocation. A third column indicates whether Brette[194] or volumes of the official series have dealt with the particular district. Succeeding columns indicate where a text of the *procès-verbal* may be found, where the mandate may be located, the type of mandate, manuscript and printed editions of the cahier proper, and the best reprint of the cahier. The *Archives parlementaires* contain nearly all the general cahiers, but are notoriously defective.[195] Each reprinted text has been verified with the original, and if omissions or errors affect the meaning, a separate list of such corrections has been made.[196] The composite table includes an indication whenever this list should be consulted. The final column of the table gives comments on the elections and cahiers of the district. By means of this table, the student may now consult the general cahiers with ease and accuracy.[197]

The way in which the cahiers are read has a direct bearing upon their utility. The general cahiers should be read by *generality*,[198] and the cahiers of all three orders of a single *bailliage* should be reviewed consecutively. By this means, similarities between the cahiers of a given locality and also between those of the different orders can be detected. Such a method is the only one by which impressions of regional opinion may be drawn together so as to reveal national opinion. Furthermore, this method provides a necessary check upon the differing conditions of the various *generalities*. If, for example, one were examining the general cahiers for their attitude toward the abolition of internal barriers, one would naturally expect differences in the reforms solicited, depending upon whether the given district was included in the *cinq grosses fermes,* the *pays réputé étranger,* or the *pays étranger effectif*.[199] Silence in such a case may mean one thing for one district and quite another thing for a different district.

---

[194] It is very unfortunate that Brette was unable to complete his masterly study before his death. Volumes III and IV of his work summarize the elections and documentary details of the cahiers for sixteen *generalities,* but seventeen (including Corsica) remain to be done. These loopholes have been partly filled by volumes of the official series on specific *bailliages,* but many districts remain without adequate treatment.

[195] Consult the introductory remarks to the list of corrections, p. 158.

[196] See *infra,* p. 159.

[197] Explanatory notes at the beginning of the table should be consulted.

[198] The royal convocation was issued to the grand *bailli* of each *generality,* who distributed the regulations to the *bailliages* of their jurisdiction.

[199] See the discussion of this very topic, Hyslop, B., *French Nationalism in 1789 . . .* pp. 56-57.

It is possible to ascertain special conditions governing the various areas and thereby to throw light upon the brief demands of the cahiers from a given *generality*. A table showing the election districts by *generalities* may be found in the Appendix.[200]

The arrangement of the *generalities* should depend upon the object of the research. The logical procedure for any general topic is to start with the *generality* of Paris, proceed clockwise through all the *generalities* that were *pays d 'élection* and then through the *pays d'état*.[201] If on the other hand, for example, opinion of the north of France were to be contrasted with that of the south, it is obvious that all northern *generalities* should first be taken together and then all the southern ones together. The table in the Appendix gives the essential classification of districts, and the order of the *generalities* may be shifted according to the aim of the reader.[202]

Material included in the present study should eliminate the major difficulties that have prevented use of the general cahiers with historical accuracy. These documents possess certain advantages which counterbalance their limitations and often outweigh them, such that the general cahiers remain valuable and, indeed, necessary sources of information about France on the eve of the Revolution.

ADVANTAGES

The outstanding advantage of the general cahiers is that they provide a gauge of public opinion. Some objective value may attach to individual cahiers, but the significant fact is that the makers of the cahiers thought the conditions to be as they presented them, while the changes that they desired to institute are a further index of public opinion. Electoral pamphlets outlined the ideas of individual writers, but the general cahiers were expressions of the group mind of the electorate of 1789. We may be interested to know the range of ideas in the cahiers, but the greater value of these documents lies in the repetition of ideas by different districts, or different classes. The general cahiers are sources, *par excellence*, of popular opinion, not of individual opinion. We have seen that it would be inaccurate to claim that the general cahiers offer a complete mirror of the entire

---

[200] *Cf. infra,* p. 145.

[201] This is the order used in the table in the Appendix, and in the analysis of the general cahiers for nationalism, Hyslop, *op. cit.*

[202] *Cf. infra,* p. 145, and map, p. 12.

population of France, but they do represent the state of mind, relative to the forthcoming States-General, of dominant groups from all parts of France.

The importance of this fact is increased by the absence of any better contemporary source of collective opinion. Today, in order to appraise popular opinion, we study the newspapers and assume that their readers agree with the principles expressed therein. Before the Revolution there existed in France only two national newspapers —the *Gazette de France* and the *Mercure*. The former was the social column of monarchial France. Most of its pages reflected the movements of the royal court, with particular attention to persons, costumes, and court etiquette, although some notice of royal edicts and measures was inserted. Similar notes about other European states were included. The *Gazette* was the official organ of the king and included no light upon popular conditions or opinion.[203] The *Mercure* gave some internal and national political items, but most of the space was devoted to literary comments and essays.[204] Neither of these was a gauge of popular opinion.

The present-day practice of sending letters to the president and to other public officials,[205] as well as to radio stations, has developed to such an extent in recent times that it forms an additional fund of popular opinion which is accessible, however, only to the recipients. Under the old régime in France, the king constantly received petitions, which were sometimes individual, sometimes collective,[206] but these were more likely to be congratulatory or laudatory than remonstrative. Such petitions would have little in common with regard to the ideas treated, individuals or groups presenting them, the geographic area represented, or the time of presentation. These

---

[203] The *Gazette* changed little even after the Revolution had begun, for one would search in vain among its issues for adequate reporting of the proceedings of the States-General and National Assembly, or indeed, of such an outstanding event as the capture of the Bastille. *Cf.* copies of the *Gazette* for the first seven months of 1789, *Arch. Nat.* Y II 1.

[204] For a collection of the issues of the *Mercure*, see *Bib. Nat.* 8° LC². 39. Arthur Young commended the *Mercure* but expressed a very poor opinion of the *Gazette* (*Voyages*, Vol. I, p. 353, July 27, and p. 420, Sept. 5).

[205] The newspapers of the United States have called attention to the astounding increase in the number of letters sent to the president since Franklin D. Roosevelt took office.

[206] For example, on April 20, 1789, Raup de Baptestin gave the king a memorandum on the establishment of honorary awards. The *Six Corps* of Paris often presented petitions to the king. The presentation of petitions and letters of commendation from different parts of France seriously handicapped the procedure of the National Assembly, and is one of many reasons why that body progressed so slowly with its business.

documents would in no way take the place of or improve upon the general cahiers as sources of popular opinion.

Reports of intendants might contain local reactions to particular measures, but such information would not be furnished by all intendants for every *generality* of France at a similar time, while the report would naturally be colored by the personality of the intendant himself. Discussions and activities of the provincial-assemblies, established in 1787, were partial gauges of opinion where such assemblies existed,[207] but their minutes were seldom printed,[208] and since these bodies were often impotent and since they wasted time on technicalities of procedure, any of their papers would leave a great many gaps. Court records would give even less information about popular opinion than other contemporary records cited. In view of the absence of a better gauge, the general cahiers assume greater importance as sources.

Furthermore, a fairly complete number of cahiers has been preserved. The general cahiers offer official documents for all parts of France, drawn up according to as fully a representative basis as was possible in the eighteenth century. The fact that they were written exclusively in March and April of 1789 and that they had a common purpose in view, led to the inclusion of opinions (even though divergent) on all the major problems confronting France at that time. There are enough fundamental characteristics in common to furnish a basis of comparison. Consequently, despite the various limitations which we have noted, the general cahiers stand ahead of any other contemporary records as sources of dominant opinion.

A fourth advantage lies in the opportunity of comparing the general cahiers of 1789 with cahiers of early States-Generals and hence of discovering the onward march of ideas over several centuries. Attention has already been called to the fact that by 1483, election by *bailliage* and the making of cahiers were integral parts of the convocation of the States-General.[209] For the century and a half after that year, cahiers were drawn up at each summons. Unfortunately, few of the *bailliage* cahiers are now extant, but there is a complete

---

[207] These provincial-assemblies (*assemblées-provinciales*) were not truly representative. On their composition, work, and ultimate failure, consult Renouvin, P., *Les Assemblées provinciales de 1787* (Paris, 1921).

[208] Mirabeau complained that the minutes were withheld by arbitrary censorship. See Mirabeau, *De la liberté de la presse*, in *Œuvres* (Paris, 1834), Vol. III, p. 282.

[209] *Cf. supra*, p. 4.

collection of the national cahiers—that is, of the summaries of the *bailliage* cahiers drawn up by each of the three classes in the States-General for presentation to the king.[210] Those early States-Generals were not deliberative bodies in the modern sense. In return for grants of money, the classes drew up the lists of reforms which they expected the king to act upon. Consequently, whether the king did actually carry out reform or not, these documents were as reliable sources of information on the reform programs of the leading groups of early States-Generals as the general cahiers were for 1789.

There is evidence that some of the electorate of 1789 expected the traditional procedure to be followed.[211] They believed that each order would draw up a national program based on the general cahiers of its own class. Had the traditional procedure been followed, there would, of course, have been no Oath of the Tennis Court, no transformation of the States-General into the National Assembly, and revolutionary measures would certainly have been postponed. The summary of the general cahiers, presented by Clermont Tonnerre in behalf of the committee on the Constitution,[212] is evidence of the force of the traditional procedure even in the National Assembly and of the idea that cahiers should actually form the basis of action by the national representative body. The summary itself is not, however, comparable to the national cahiers of the early States-General.

With some allowance for the fact that the national cahiers were syntheses of *bailliage* cahiers, and therefore one step farther from the electorate than the general cahiers of 1789, a comparison is illuminating and a helpful check upon the latter as sources. Similarities and differences throw light upon the history of French institutions and upon the development of philosophy and principles during the centuries involved. Since the reforms asked by the cahiers were never granted in full, even when a reform ordinance was issued after the adjournment of the States-General, many problems were recurrent, and led to the repetition of the same or nearly the same demand or of the same principle, by successive States-Generals.[213] Indeed, in a

[210] A complete bibliography of early *bailliage* cahiers has not been attempted. Only a few have been reprinted, while isolated examples of manuscript texts are scattered among different liasses at the *Archives Nationales.*

[211] For example, see C. Belfort and Huningue (p. v., *Arch. Nat.* B III 27, p. 191); see also cahiers of C. Aval, St. Quentin; N. Alençon, Nancy; T. Lyon.

[212] *Cf. infra,* p. 104.

[213] For example, the demand for uniformity of weights and measures, abolition of *annates,* the removal of interior customs barriers, etc.

comparison of the early cahiers with those of 1789, one is struck first with the similarities: the similar form, identical problems, expressions of confidence in the king and of hope that reform would be effected, insistence upon the right of the States-General to vote the taxes, and a desire for a systematic judicial system. Some conflicting aims between the nobles and third estate on the subject of feudal justice were apparent in the early cahiers, as they were in 1789 on the seigniorial régime.[214] On the other hand, the whole development of eighteenth century political philosophy made itself felt in the tone, the phrases, and in the demands of the cahiers of 1789. The possibility of a detailed comparison for different historic periods adds value, therefore, to the general cahiers of 1789.

The fifth special value of the general cahiers includes several factors, all of which arise from the use to which those documents were put in 1789. The first important fact was the publication of the cahiers. Two hundred and sixty-three general cahiers and one colonial document, that is to say, nearly half the entire number, were printed at the command of the electoral assembly.[215] Patriotism and the desire of the electorate to make their aims known to their contemporaries motivated publication.[216] The size of these editions varied greatly. The average edition was four or five hundred, but more than fifty assemblies ordered more than one edition,[217] while a few rare districts voted to issue several thousand copies.[218]

The class and geographic distribution of printed editions is interesting. Two facts emerge with regard to the former: the much larger number of cahiers of the nobles than of the other two orders, and the large percentage of joint cahiers that were printed. This predominance may have been due to the cost of printing, which must have deterred many assemblies of the third estate from ordering publication.[219]

[214] See Hyslop, B., *French Nationalism* . . . pp. 114 *et seq.*

[215] See the composite table, *infra*, pp. 116, *et seq.*, column 10. A concise alphabetical list of the printed general cahiers was given in Hyslop, Beatrice, *French Nationalism in 1789* . . . pp. 244-45. A list of printed cahiers by *generality* is given *infra*, p. 151.

[216] See vote to print in p. v. of T. Château-Thierry, N. Perche, T. Bailleul, etc.

[217] The *procès-verbaux* furnish information about the number of copies voted. See table *infra*, pp. 116 *et seq.*, column 10 for cases of two and three editions.

[218] The united orders of Bourg-en-Bresse appear to have voted for 3,000 copies, possibly in three editions of 1,000 each (p. v., *Arch. Nat.* C 16/35). T. Bailleul voted an edition of 5,000 copies (p. v., *Arch. Nat.* Ba 18), but as this would have been very unusual, perhaps the figure was a typographical error on the part of the secretary and only 500 copies were desired.

[219] See comment of Arthur Young, *Voyages*, Vol. I, pp. 272-73.

The distribution of printed editions among the *generalities* is also significant.[220] The frontier sections, except for those directly north, printed their cahiers less frequently in proportion to the number of cahiers from each *generality;* while the southern *generalities* were particularly backward. By contrast with the *generality* of Aix, where only a third of the general cahiers were printed, two *generalities* (Lille and Rouen) printed all but one cahier, and nine *generalities* (Paris, Orléans, Moulins, Lyon, Montpellier, Limoges, Tours, Valenciennes, and Strasbourg) printed more than half their cahiers.

The distribution of printed texts among the classes of each *generality* is also significant. All three orders adopted publication in about equal proportions in six *generalities*.[221] In three *generalities* there were printed more cahiers of the third estate than of the nobles.[222] By contrast, only one of the twelve cahiers printed in the *generality* of Orléans came from the third estate.[223] Such information is pertinent to the type of ideas in circulation in a given area, for some cahiers were conservative, some progressive, others radical.[224] When the cahiers were first printed, they probably circulated locally before being sent to other sections of France.

The printing of so many general cahiers made it possible for these texts to be widely read and to exert an influence outside the assemblies which made them. Contemporary diaries bear witness to the fact that there was a great desire to see, read, and discuss these expressions of collective opinion.[225] Although many were printed locally, the Parisian printers were the busiest, and many visitors asked at the bookstalls for all available texts. Newspaper discussions of cahiers and, later, published summaries added to the general knowledge of the cahiers.[226]

A measure adopted by more than a sixth of the electoral assemblies in 1789 made possible a wider influence of the cahiers—the appointment of committees of correspondence.[227] Various motives led

[220] For a table of printed cahiers by *generality*, see *infra*, p. 151.

[221] Paris, Limoges, Rouen, Amiens, Lille, and Dijon.

[222] Auch, Valenciennes, and Strasbourg.

[223] T. Dourdan.

[224] For an analysis of national sentiment in the general cahiers, consult Hyslop, B., *French Nationalism in 1789. . . .*

[225] For example, Arthur Young mentioned the crowds at the printer's Desenne, gatherings in cafés, etc. (*Voyages*, Vol. I, pp. 272-73).

[226] For example, the *Mercure de France* discussed the cahiers in an article, May 2, 1789.

[227] *Cf. infra*, in composite table, column 8, pp. 116 *et seq.*

to the selection of committees: a desire to keep tab on the deputies,[228] to furnish the deputy with supplementary information about the *bailliage*,[229] to perpetuate the electoral assembly,[230] and to secure a method of receiving information from the deputies which could be relayed to the constituents.[231] The fullest exposition of motives, and hence of functions, for a committee of correspondence was given by the united orders of Montfort l'Amaury:

> These bureaus have no other functions than to carry on correspondence and to serve as intermediaries in communications between the deputies and the parishes which compose each of the two *bailliages*,[232] with power to put in order the material sent on the part of the parishes to the deputies, or on the part of the deputies to the parishes; and if the States-General or the deputies are disturbed in the exercise of their functions, the said bureaus of correspondence will be authorized to ask the *bailli*, or the lieutenant-general for him, to demand the convocation of the assembly of the *bailliages*, and at the same time, they will be empowered to write circular letters to all the clergy, nobles, and deputies of the parishes.[233]

Information upon the actual activities of these committees of correspondence is so scanty,[234] that it is impossible to say at present how far these committees succeeded in the work for which they were chosen.[235] They may have served as centers of the later federative movement. It is altogether probable that they served as intermediaries for the circulation of cahiers in the provinces.

The general cahiers were intended as instructions for the deputies to the States-General, and their actual use was significant. Aside from being read throughout France, they were read and obeyed by the deputies, and hence they influenced the early course of the Revolution.

The history of the nullification of imperative mandates was, in a measure, the story of the triumph of the third estate. The knowledge

[228] For example, T. Bellême, p. v., *Arch. Nat.* C 22/121.

[229] For example, T. Douai, p. v., *Arch. Nat.* C 18/70.

[230] For example, 3 O, Charolles, N. p. v., *Arch. Nat.* Ba 31.

[231] For example, T. Sedan, T. Marseille, etc.

[232] Montfort l'Amaury had a secondary *bailliage*, Dreux.

[233] P. v., *Arch. Nat.* Ba 54.

[234] Minutes for the first few meetings, of a routine nature, exist for the committee of Charolles (*Arch. Nat.* Ba 31). It is possible that departmental archives possess pertinent material, not yet explored.

[235] It is significant that so many assemblies of the third estate of Brittany appointed such committees, and that the *Club breton* at Versailles was so active in May and June.

of the difficulties and failures of previous States-Generals led many assemblies to adopt restricted mandates.[236] Three motives led to the grant of imperative mandates. In the first place, they were adopted in order to prevent corruption of the deputies. The assemblies feared that court influence, the grant of pensions, offices, or other rewards, would make the deputies disregard the wishes of their constituents. A second desire was to reënforce the deputies collectively in the States-General and thereby assure effective reform before the dissolution of that body. Such mandates made the promulgation of a constitution before other business imperative, or insisted on a verification of the finances before taking up legislation with regard to taxation. A third motive for restricted mandates arose from class spirit or regionalism. A fear that the rights and powers of one of the privileged orders might be sacrificed, and the desire of the third estate to insure itself a voice commensurate with its importance led each of the classes to make imperative the demands favorable to itself. In some cases, also, provincial or local spirit led to a demand for the protection of regional privileges.

The difference between general, special, and imperative mandates lay in the degree of pressure put upon the deputy.[237] Four methods were suggested to coerce deputies into obedience to imperative mandates: the grant of power for a limited time only, after which the deputy could be supported by a new grant of power or a substitute could be chosen;[238] a requirement that deputies return to their districts at the adjournment of the States-General to answer for their work to the constituency;[239] insistence that the deputy keep in correspondence with a committee constituted in the *bailliage*, and to which he would be held responsible for his action;[240] and a threat that the deputy would be disowned if he acted contrary to the mandate.[241] The last method was the most severe, as it meant recall of the deputy, non-payment of his salary and expenses, and the sending of a new, more

---

[236] *Cf. supra*, p. 38.

[237] Talleyrand, in defending a motion on mandates in the National Assembly July 7, 1789, distinguished two types of mandates, limited and imperative; but his two types overlapped and left some loopholes. (The official *procès-verbal* of the National Assembly was very brief on this point, but the *Point du jour* gave a fair résumé. *Loc. cit.*, Vol. II, no. 6, p. 100). The full report was printed separately (*Bib. Nat. Le 29. 46A*).

[238] For example, T. Gien, Mandate, MS, *Arch. Nat.* Ba 43.

[239] For example, N. Nivernais, p. v., *Arch. Nat.* Ba 58.

[240] For example, T. Bellême, p. v., *Arch. Nat.* C 22/121.

[241] For example, N. Carcassonne, p. v., *Arch. Nat.* C 17/41.

obedient representative. An oath, administered to each deputy, made the mandate binding, however severe.[242]

A great many of the clergy and nobles had received imperative mandates prescribing vote by order, with the result that they refused to compromise with the third estate in the month of May and early days of June. The Oath of the Tennis Court automatically repudiated imperative mandates for those who took the oath, while in order to safeguard deputies against violence or perversion, which had been one of the motives for issuing imperative mandates, the newly formed assembly declared the persons of the deputies inviolable.[243]

Three lines of conduct were open to those whose mandates forbade vote by head, and therefore, union with the third estate: withdrawal from the States-General, in which case the *bailliage* would be unrepresented for that class; secondly, disregard of the mandate, for which the deputy risked repudiation; and thirdly, staunch support of the losing party which advocated separate chambers. A way out of the *impasse* was offered in the report of the king in the royal séance of the States-General, June 23:

The king permits those deputies who believe themselves hindered by their mandates to ask their constituents for new powers; but his Majesty enjoins them to remain in the States-General, while waiting, in order to assist in all the deliberations on pressing matters of state, and to give their consultative voice.[244]

The next step after this declaration was an order in council of June 27, declaring that imperative mandates were null and void and that new mandates must be sought.[245] New assemblies of the clergy and nobles were convoked where imperative mandates had been given. Thus, the machinery for the grant of new mandates was set in motion, and at least ten assemblies of the clergy and eighty-two assemblies of the nobles were held.[246] The fact that some of these

---

[242] See, for example, the oath administered in the assembly of the three orders of Clermont-en-Beauvoisis, p. v., *Arch. Nat.* C 17/57.

[243] *Procès-verbal de l'Assemblée Nationale Constituante* (Paris, 1789 on), Vol. I, no. 5, p. 3. June 23, 1789.

[244] In the minutes of the royal séance, art. 5, *Arch. Nat.* AD I 11.

[245] Reprint of text, Brette, *op. cit.*, Vol. I, pp. 56 *et seq.*

[246] The minutes of these assemblies exist in cartons of documents by *bailliage, Arch. Nat.* Ba 9- Ba 87. The following districts held new assemblies:

Clergy: Autun, Bazas, Boulogne-sur-mer, Clermont-en-Beauvoisis, Lille, Limoux, Nivernais, Nîmes, Toulouse, Villers-Cotterets.

assemblies did not meet until September, October, and November is indicative of the strong hold of imperative mandates.[247] Adherence to them was evidence of the reliance upon tradition and conservatism as over against the Revolution.

Was the royal regulation final, or was it necessary for the National Assembly to declare imperative mandates null and void? This question was raised several times and then came up for lengthy discussion on July 7 and 8. The discussion was opened by a proposal from Talleyrand[248] that the National Assembly declare its sovereignty and deny the right of the *bailliage* to obstruct or nullify by means of imperative mandates.[249] A discussion and many other proposals followed. Gaultier de Biauzat[250] presented a text even more sweeping than that of Talleyrand. Lally-Tolendal, the deputy of the nobles of Paris *intra-muros,* who had had difficulties with regard to his own mandate, proposed a delay for the reception of new mandates. Barère[251] approved of the Talleyrand text and called attention to the fact that once the National Assembly declared imperative mandates null and void there would be no need for new assemblies to grant general powers. He believed that such assemblies would be dangerous to the prestige of the National Assembly. Siéyès,[252] always the theoretician, stated that there was no need to deliberate on the question; that, by virtue of the sovereignty of the National Assembly, im-

---

Nobles: Agen, Alençon, Amont, Annonay, Armagnac, Artois, Auch, Autun, Auxerre, Bar-sur-Seine, Bazas, Belfort, Bellême, Besançon, Bourg-en-Bresse, Bourmont, Caen, Cambrésis, Carcassonne, Cahors, Castelmoron d'Albret, Castelnaudary, Castres, Châlon-sur-Saône, Charmes, Chartres, Chaumont-en-Bassigny, Clermont-en-Beauvoisis, Colmar, Comminges, Condom, Coutances, Crépy-en-Valois, Darney, Dax, Dijon, Dorat, Douai, Dourdan, Epinal, Fénestrange, Foix, Gien, La Marche, Langres, La Rochelle, Libourne, Limoges, Limoux, Loudun, Le Mans, Mâcon, Mende, Mirecourt, Montargis, Mont-de-Marsan, Moulins, Nérac, Neufchâteau, Nivernais, Périgord, Poitiers, Remiremont, Riom, Rivière-Verdun, Rodez, St. Dié, Saintes, St. Flour, Sarreguemines, Semur-en-Auxois, Sézanne, Soule, Toul, Toulouse, Trévoux, Tulle, Vendôme, Villefranche-de-Beaujolais, Villefranche-en-Rouergue, Villers-Cotterets, Vitry-le-françois.

[247] The majority of assemblies took place between July 15-30. The clergy of Lille did not meet until Oct. 15; C. Boulogne-sur-mer, Nov. 9; N. Auch, Sept. I; N. Soule, Sept. 16. See the cartons for each *bailliage*.   [248] Deputy of the clergy of Autun.

[249] All the proposals exist in MS, Arch. Nat. C 28/217. Talleyrand's was also printed (*Bib. Nat.* Le 29.46 A). The official version of the minutes of the National Assembly, edited by Baudouin, *Procès-verbal de l'Assemblée Nationale,* no. 17, gives the most complete account of the discussion. The *Point du Jour* is fuller for earlier discussions. Consult nos. 9 and 12 for séances before July 7, and no. 15 for July 7, 8.

[250] Deputy of T. Clermont Ferrand.   [251] Deputy of T. Bigorre.

[252] Deputy of T. Paris *intra-muros.*

perative mandates were *ipso facto* null and void, and that consequently no resolution was necessary. The session of July 7 ended
without a decision.

On July 8, Siéyès reaffirmed his contention. The Archbishop of
Bordeaux[253] proposed a draft declaring that mandates could not sus-
pend the action of the National Assembly, and that admission to it
would be conditional upon submission in advance to the decrees of
the Assembly. Pros and cons were voiced,[254] and finally, when a vote
was taken, Siéyès' opinion carried.[255] This was a negative acceptance
of the sovereignty of the National Assembly and a repudiation of imperative mandates. It signified the recognition of the deputies, once
admitted, as deputies of the nation at large, not as the representative
of a particular class or *bailliage*. Despite the action by the National
Assembly, supplementary assemblies of the clergy and nobles continued to meet to extend the powers of their deputies, and the con-
servatives continued to cite their mandates against the sovereignty of
the National Assembly.

The legal rejection of the practice of written instructions and the
establishment of a law providing for national representatives with
deliberative powers, as contrasted with regional delegates with
limited powers, was foreshadowed in the declaration of the abolition
of provincial privileges on the night of August 4.[256] Several times
during the discussion of the Constitution, statements were made de-
nouncing imperative mandates,[257] and the principle was finally embodied in the Constitution of 1791, in the following words: "The
representatives nominated in the departments will not be representatives of a particular department, but of the entire nation; no mandate may be given."[258] What had been a traditional practice under
the old régime was repudiated in the new, and with the nullification
of mandates came also an end to the making of *cahiers de doléances*.

[253] Champion de Cicé.

[254] Several proposals, not given in the printed minutes, exist in MS, *Arch. Nat.*
C 28/217.

[255] According to Bailly's *Mémoires*, the motion was carried 731 votes against 81
(*loc. cit.*, Vol. II, p. 37).

[256] *Bulletin des lois*, August 4-11, 1789, Vol. I, p. 3, art. 10.

[257] For example, on December 3, 1789 (*Procès-verbal de l'Assemblée Nationale Constituante*, Vol. VIII, no. 141, p. 5, art. 2); April 19, 1790 (*ibid.*, Vol. XVIII, no. 264,
p. 6).

[258] The best reference text of the Constitution is in Duvergier, *Collection des constitutions, chartres et lois fondamentaux* (Paris, 1830), Vol. I, p. 105, chap. i, title 3, sec.
3, art. 7.

The fact that imperative mandates were repudiated did not mean, however, that the cahiers ceased to exert an influence upon the procedure of the National Assembly. The deputies had them constantly in mind, but their influence was informational and psychological rather than obligatory. The committee on the Constitution studied them, and on July 27, 1789, in behalf of that committee, Clermont-Tonnerre[259] presented a summary to the National Assembly.[260] It was assumed that the consensus of the cahiers would be used as a guide in the order of business. The summary which Clermont-Tonnerre made was both astute and concise. He began with the statement that all the cahiers agreed on the need of regeneration for France, but that they differed on the means to achieve that end. Some cahiers demanded reform of the existing Constitution, while others asked for a new Constitution incorporating a declaration of rights. After this introduction, the report continues under two divisions: the articles on which the cahiers agree, and those on which there was no general consent.[261] Since the summary was to serve as guide in the discussion of a Constitution, only the fundamental problems were dealt with, and all the exhaustive detail of the cahiers was passed over. Clermont-Tonnerre could not have consulted a complete number of the general cahiers, but his generalizations hold true with regard to the entire number now available.

The articles on which the cahiers agreed, according to Clermont-Tonnerre's report, were the fundamental principles of the monarchy, the power and composition of the States-General, and the rights of citizens. In respect to the first, France was a monarchy, hereditary through the male line. The person of the king was inviolable and his agents were responsible for their actions. The king held the executive power, and his approval was necessary for the validity of law. The cahiers likewise agreed that the legislative power lay in the States-General, with the royal sanction. The consent of the States-General was considered necessary for loans and taxes, and the term of the latter should be only from one session to the next. The persons of the deputies should be inviolable.[262] Provincial-Estates should be

[259] Deputy of N. Paris *intra-muros.*
[260] *Procès-verbal de l'Assemblée Nationale Constituante,* Vol. II, for complete text. The *Point du jour* barely mentioned the report (*loc. cit.,* Vol. I, pp. 315 *et seq.*), and the *Journal des Etats-Généraux* made no mention of it (*op. cit.,* Vol. II, pp. 196-210).
[261] For text, *loc. cit.,* from note 260.
[262] This demand actually appeared in less than seventy-five cahiers.

established in all the provinces of France. Furthermore, Clermont-Tonnerre pointed out that the cahiers agreed almost unanimously upon the rights of citizens—personal liberty, inviolability of property, security of the mails, and personal security from arrest.

In addition to these topics, Clermont-Tonnerre summarized briefly the articles relative to the States-General upon which there was disagreement: questions about representation by orders, procedure in the States-General, permanence versus periodicity, and the right of the king to dissolve the States-General.

The fact that it was considered desirable to take the time of the National Assembly for a summary of the cahiers indicates that they were then considered representative of public opinion, and that deference to the wishes of the nation at large was the policy of the National Assembly. Clermont-Tonnerre's report assumed a minor importance in the minutes of the National Assembly,[263] but the knowledge that the National Assembly was consulting the cahiers could not fail to win approval from the provinces.

From time to time, after July 27, reference was made to the cahiers in speeches on the constitution,[264] but less frequently as the Revolution progressed. Three facts attest the continued importance placed upon the general cahiers: the publication of summaries,[265] a complete manuscript summary (unfinished) made at the command of the Keeper of the Seals,[266] and references to the cahiers in contemporary *mémoires* and histories.[267] The limitations upon the objective and subjective value of the cahiers, which historians now recognize, were not taken into consideration in 1789, or for many years thereafter. This fact adds to their subjective value because of the influence of the general cahiers upon the minds of the deputies and, therefore, upon their action. The general cahiers were undoubtedly factors contributing to the sentiment of national unity and regeneration which marked the beginnings of the Revolution.

[263] Mounier's draft of a constitution took much more space (*Procès-verbal de l'Assemblée Nationale Constituante*, Vol. II).

[264] For example, note references in the quotations selected on the question of the veto, in Andrews, G. G., *Constitution in the Early French Revolution* (New York, 1927), *passim*.

[265] *Cf.* Bibliography, p. 461.

[266] Entitled: *Notice raisonnée et par ordre de matières des cahiers et instructions des bailliages et sénéchaussées*, MS, Arch. Nat. Ba 89.

[267] Among other works, Calonne's *De l'etat de la France présent et à venir* (London: 1790), used the cahiers extensively.

THE VALUE OF THE GENERAL CAHIERS

SUMMARY

The fact that the cahiers give us a picture of collective opinion, that a relatively complete series of opinions may be consulted, the possibility of comparison of opinion in 1789 with similar expressions at earlier periods of French history, and the actual use of the cahiers in 1789, make these documents significant sources. The present study presents many aids that should facilitate future consultation of the *general* cahiers.

V

CONCLUSIONS

THE GREAT French Revolution marked the beginning of a new era, not only for France, but also, in a measure, for all Europe. Ideas advanced in France during the Revolution became watchwords for liberal movements everywhere during the nineteenth century. A number of questions arise with respect to this historical crisis. Was a revolution inevitable? How long was it in preparation? What changes did the French masses desire? What were the dominating ideas? Was the later violence and radicalism foreshadowed on the eve of the first changes? One set of French sources enables us to answer these and many other questions—the *cahiers de doléances*.

A great many difficulties attending the use of these documents have resulted in neglect of them, or in a superficial utilization. If the aim is to consult rural opinion, the parish cahiers come nearer to furnishing a picture than any other contemporary records. Similarly, the cahiers of the lower clergy give some indication of opinion among the curates, monastic orders, chapters, and lesser ecclesiastics. The gild cahiers reflect the reforms demanded by gildsmen. If, however, one's chief interest is to discover the ideas, methods, and institutions that were to dominate the early days of the Revolution and, in some cases, to forecast the radical movements undertaken by the National Convention, the *general* cahiers are the best gauge. The purpose of the present study is to clarify ambiguities about this group of documents and to render them the reliable, useful sources which they should be.

Although six hundred and fifteen cahiers (not including colonial cahiers) were made in 1789, only five hundred and twenty-three texts can now be found. The loss of cahiers has left noticeable gaps, especially in the northeast, southeast, along the Spanish border, and in Brittany, yet the five hundred and twenty-three afford a fairly complete geographic and class expression of opinion.

A table on page 116 indicates where an original text of each general cahier has been preserved, where a reprint may be found, and in case the reprint is in the *Archives parlementaires*, what corrections are necessary in such texts to render them adequate substitutes for the original documents. In addition, thirty-four *general* cahiers, hitherto unknown outside of the archives where they have been preserved, are reprinted in the Appendix.

Not all of the general cahiers are of equal value as gauges of the opinion of the group which sponsored them. The great majority are reliable, but to those extant, seventy-seven (and the colonial cahiers) require some reservation, and twenty-five more should be seriously discounted. Information has been assembled about each electoral assembly and its cahier which will enable the reader to use the general cahiers with the proper perspective.

The cahiers form a special class of sources—unique in many ways—but their nature imposes certain limitations upon their use and at the same time offers numerous advantages. The general cahiers were the product of a great many influences—time, circumstances, prominent individuals and groups, eighteenth-century philosophy and its popularization by an extensive electoral propaganda. Nevertheless, the essential fact is that each general assembly adopted a cahier and, by its approval, signified that the text represented the collective will. Although the cahiers embodied no novel ideas, they are significant as the programs of reform uppermost in the minds of groups throughout France.

Despite limitations of similarity, brevity, lack of organization, fragmentary principles, monotony, the general cahiers have certain advantages. No other contemporary documents present so accurate a picture of popular opinion. Furthermore, the recommendations of the electorate, embodied in the general cahiers, led the deputies to adopt certain policies and consequently exerted a very perceptible influence upon the early course of the Revolution. Although rigid obedience to mandates was soon repudiated by the National Assembly, the ideas and methods advocated by the majority of general cahiers were reflected in the procedure and aims of the National Assembly in 1789.

Furthermore, the printing of many of the general cahiers of 1789 made possible the circulation of these expressions of collective opinion. There are many evidences that the cahiers were read in 1789, and that they thus contributed further to the spread of the enlightenment begun by eighteenth century philosophy and continued by the electoral pamphlets. The general cahiers were gauges of dominant opinion during the electoral period, and then were forces in the formulation and further development of public opinion. The fact that these documents may be compared with cahiers drawn up for previous States-Generals, even though one hundred and seventy-five years had elapsed since the last States-General had met, makes possible the identification of general trends in French history. The general *cahiers de doléances* of 1789 are necessary preludes to the Revolution—they make possible a résumé of its preparation and a prophecy of its achievements.

APPENDICES

COMPREHENSIVE TABLE OF GENERAL CAHIERS

THE CHART which follows aims to include in concise form, all necessary facts about the nature, validity, and places of consultation of all general cahiers of 1789. In the interest of brevity, and hence, of the convenience of such a table, much detail has been omitted. The result is, we hope, a clear tabulation, easy of consultation.

Column 1 contains a list of the general electoral districts (*bailliages, sénéchaussées, comtés, gouvernances,* etc.) where general cahiers were drafted, followed by the name of the *generality* to which each belonged. If a district belongs to the second type of convocation, the parenthesis contains first the center of reunion, and then the *generality*. There are 234 districts, including Corsica, and 5 colonies.

Column 2 states the classification of the convocation to which each district belonged.

Column 3 indicates whether Brette treated the given district in his four volumes, and whether the *D. I.* have a volume pertaining to it. This column is important. If Brette has summarized the convocation and given documentary descriptions of the cahiers, the reader should consult the pertinent volume without fail. Information in this table cannot attempt to be as complete as his analysis. Similarly, a specialized volume of the official *D. I.* series should be used. In cases where such treatment is lacking, an attempt has been made to make the comments in the final column of this table more complete.

Column 4 indicates the classes drafting general cahiers. The usual abbreviations of C (clergy), N (nobles), T (third estate), U (united orders), V (ville), or combinations of two letters have been used.

Column 5 indicates one place where the *procès-verbal* of the electoral assembly may be found.[1] No attempt has been made to show the presence of duplicates in other series of the National Archives, or in departmental archives. The best and most complete manuscript has been preferred.

Column 6 indicates where the mandate may be found. It usually appeared in the *procès-verbal* but was sometimes written into the cahier and rarely formed a separate third document. Not all districts differentiated the grant of power or mandate from the cahier, so that some blanks occur in this column.

[1] Not all p. v. MSS are complete. The best MS has been cited.

Column 7 indicates the type of mandate issued. G stands for a general mandate; S, for a special mandate; and I, for an imperative mandate. On the meaning of these three types, see *supra*, p. 39. The nature of the mandate is important for the interpretation of the cahier. It is regrettable that fuller detail cannot be given in the table.

Column 8 indicates districts which elected committees of correspondence (*supra*, p. 98). The class letter is repeated to indicate the adoption of such a measure.

Column 9 indicates the best manuscript text of the general cahiers. Original manuscripts in the series Ba or C at the National Archives have been preferred. When a text is lacking in one of these two series, but exists in the B III series, i.e., in the registers copied during the Revolution at the command of Camus, that copy has been listed. If for any reason no copy exists at the *Archives Nationales,* or the text in departmental archives is to be preferred, indication to that effect has been given. In each case, the manuscript text listed has been the basis of the verification of reprinted texts (*cf.* columns 11 and 12).

Column 10 indicates whether or not the cahier was printed in 1789. The call number of one printed text at the National Archives has been given, or if there is none there, the call number of a text at the *Bibliothèque Nationale* or elsewhere. Numbers in parentheses specify cases in which two or three editions were authorized. Where no number is given, only one edition was printed.

Column 11 indicates the inclusive pages where the text of a general cahier may be found in the *Archives parlementaires.* This defective publication should be used only with reference to this and the succeeding column. If a text of a general cahier has been reprinted in the official *D. I.* series, that text is preferred, and page references are supplied. If neither of these series contain the text of a general cahier, the book is listed in which a reprint may be found. If cahiers have remained in manuscript and are reprinted in the Appendix of this book, consult the table of contents for page references. Full titles of books may be found in the bibliography, *supra*, pp. 445 *et seq.*

Column 12 is an important column. Since the *Archives parlementaires* contain the only reprinted texts of the majority of general cahiers, care has been taken to verify these texts with the originals, and to list corrections or additions which are significant for the meaning of the cahier. These corrections form pp. 158-201 of this Appendix. Column 12 indicates whether such corrections should be consulted

114

when utilizing the *Archives parlementaires*. This is indicated by the repetition of the class letter in the column.

Column 13 indicates, by a letter "P" whether the preliminary cahiers of that order were given to the deputies along with the general cahiers.

Column 14 indicates how reliable each general cahier is as a gauge of opinion for the electoral assembly which adopted it. Those which may be trusted belong to group 1; those with some reservations, to group 2; and those with marked distrust, to group 3. The numeral is given in the column opposite the cahier. Even when a cahier has been lost, something has been learned from the *procès-verbal,* and a classification has been given. When the p. v. is missing, and no other information has been obtainable, a blank is left. *Cf. supra,* on the classification of the general cahiers on the basis of reliability, pp. 85 *et seq.*

Column 15 includes comments about the convocation, elections, or cahier which are vital for an interpretation of the cahiers. The items represent the minimum essentials, and indicate distinctive events or facts about the particular assembly or documents.

Although a chart of fifteen columns is necessarily complex, this chart assembles in one place the necessary facts for a consultation of the general cahiers of 1789.

District (1)	Convocation (2)	Brette or D.I. (3)	Class (4)	P.V. Text (5)	Mandate Text (6)	Mandate Type (7)	Committees (8)	Cahier MS Text (9)	Cahier FR Text (10)	Cahier Reprint (11)	AP Corrections (12)	Preliminary Cahiers (13)	Reliability (14)	Comments (15)
Agen(Bordeaux)	1	Brette, IV, 256 et seq.	C	Arch.Lot-et-Garonne, B 211; extract in 30 p.v.-Arch.Nat C 14/1.	30 p.v., C 14/1	I		B III 1, p.361	Ba9 (2)	AP, I, 675-79			1	Lieutenant general influential. Tumult. Protests. Cahier adopted by vote of 163 over 151.
			N	C 14/1 in 30p.v.-extract in Ba9 MS	cahier	I	N	B III 1, p.401	Ba9 (3)	AP, I, 679-86			1	
			T	extract in Ba9	30 p.v., C 14/1	I	T	B III 1, p.307	Ba9	AP, I, 686-91	T	P.	3	
Aix(Aix)	1		C	Ba9	p.v.	G		Ba9		AP, I, 692-93		P.	1	Long introductory speech by archbishop. Protest to king, seconded by C. and T. against future elections by district, rather than by whole sénéchaussée or pays. Unanimous adoption reported. Desired fairer representation for small towns.
			N	Ba9	Ba9	S		Ba9		AP, I, 693-95	N		1	
			T	Ba9	p.v. and cahier	I	T	Ba9		AP, I, 695-97	T	P.	1	
Alençon(Alençon)	1		C	Ba11	p.v.	G		Ba11	AD I 10	AP, I, 708-10	C	P.	1	Careful adoption. Pamphlets used. Careful discussion of cahier. Cabale not powerful enough to sway elections.
			N	Ba11	p.v.	I		Ba11		AP, I, 710-16	N		1	
			T	Ba11				Ba11, C 14/3		AP, I, 716-20	T		2	
Amiens(Amiens)	1	Brette, III, 70 et seq.	C	C 14/5	cahier			Ba12	Ba12, C 14/5	AP, I, 732-39			3	Hurried work. Complaint by curates and regular clergy. Authentication of text lacking. Peasants anxious to return home. Incomplete authentication of text.
			N	Printed with cahier	cahier	I		B III 4, p.113		AP, I, 739-44			1	
			T	Ba12	p.v.	G		Ba12		AP, I, 744-56			2	
Amont(Besançon)	1	D.I.	U	B III 5, B III 6,	N-cahier	I		Ba13		AP, I, 773-82			3	The elections of the bailliage of Amont were irregular. The recognition by the National Assembly of the first elections of the clergy and of the nobles validates the united cahier, with the supplement by the third estate, as the general cahier. (Cf.Brette,op.cit.,Vol.I,pp.193-98; Maréchal, La Révolution en Franche-Comté, pp.555 et seq.; Goddard and Abensour, D.I., op.cit.,Vol.I, Introduction).
			T	Ba13						Supplement-Goddard and Abensour, D.I., II, 538 et seq.				
Angers(Tours)	1	Brette,IV, 624 et seq.	C	Ba13	p.v.	G		Ba13		AP, II, 30-32			2	The volume of the D.I. does not give the general cahiers. See Le Moy, supra. Careful adoption; inadequate authentication of extant text.
			N	B III 7, or FR - AD I 9	cahier	I		C 14/8	C 14/8	AP, II, 32-38			1	
			T	FR with cahier	cahier	I	T	B III 7, p.547	C 14/8 (2)	AP, II, 38-45	T		2	Influential persons and literature. See introduction to Le Moy, op.cit.

1	2	3	4	5	6	7	8	9	10	11	12	13	14	15
Angoulême(Limoges)	1	D.I.and Brette, III,297 et seq.	C	C 14/7		I			Ba14	Boissonnade, D.I., 489 et seq.			1	The texts given in the AP are quite inaccurate. Be sure to use D.I. texts.
			N	Ba14	p.v.	G		Ba14	Ba14	Ibid, 498 et seq.			1	Ibid.
			T	C 14/7	p.v.			C 14/7	AD I 10	Ibid, 461 et seq.			2	Trouble between T. and seigniorial officers.
Annonay(Mont-pellier)	1		C	C 14/9	Arch. Ardèche	S		Arch.Ardèche		AP, II, 46-47			1	
			N	Arch.Ardèche B.145	cahier	I	N	Idem, Arch.Nat. B III 9, p.76	Ba14	AP, II, 47-49	N		1	
			T	C 14/9				Idem, Arch.Nat. B III, 9, p.142	Bib.Nat.Le24. 201	AP, II, 50-53	T	P	1	Careful adoption.
Arches and Charleville(Metz)	7		U	C 33/280				C 33/280		Unedited, cf. Appendix			1	The elections of this principality were exceptio sl. Cf. supra in chapter i. The cahier was adopted December 31, 1789. (Brette, op.cit., Vol.I, p.300).
Arles(sénéchaussée)(Aix)	1		C	Ba14	p.v.	G		Missing					1	No mention of adoption of a cahier in the p.v.
			N	Ba14	p.v.	G		Missing					1	Effort for joint cahier with C and N failed. Local claims of
			T	Ba14	p.v.	G		Missing				P.	1	communities added to general cahier.
Arles(ville)(Aix)	4		C	Ba14	p.v.	G		Arch.Comm. d'Arles	Arch.Bouches-du-Rhône	AP, II, 54-56			1	For the convocation for Arles(ville),see Brette, op.cit., Vol.I, pp.242 et seq.
			NT	Ba14	B III 10, p.851	I		B III 10, p.792		AP, II, 57-63	NT	P	1	
Armagnac(Auch)	1	Brette, IV,80 et seq.	C	Ba15	cahier	S		Ba15	Ba15	AP, II, 64-69			1	Careful adoption.
			N	Ba15	p.v.	G		Ba15		AP, II, 69-72			1	
			T	Extracts in 30 p.v., C 14/12	p.v.			Ba15		AP, II, 75-77			1	
Artois(Lille)	1		C	C 14/14	cahier	I		Arch.Pas de Caleis B.881	Arch.Comm. Arras	AP, II, 78-79	C		2	Curates powerful.
			N	C 14/13	cahier		N	B III 21, p.1	Ba15 (2)	AP, II, 79-85	N		1	Rejected memoire on privileges of Artois.
			T	C 14/13	p.v.	S			Bib.Nat.Le24. 293	AP, VI, 721-24	T		2	Protest against art.23 of cahier.
Auch(Auch)	1	Brette, IV, 69 et seq.	C	Ba16	cahier	I		Ba16	Voted to print; no example extant	AP, II, 91-94			1	Protest by chapter of Auch.
			N	C 15/14,B III 13	cahier	I		Ba16(extract)	Ba16	AP, II, 94-96			1	
			T	C 15/14	p.v.	I		Ba16	Ba16	AP, II, 96-99			1	
Auray(Vannes; Rennes)	6		T	Ba26	p.v., T, Vannes	I		Ba26	Arch.Morbihan	AP, II, 112-16	T		2	Violence and disorder.
Autun(Dijon)	1		C	Ba16	p.v.	G		Collection of M.Eugene Abord-Sibuet	The printed texts give the first half only.	Charmasse, A., 353 et seq.			1	The AP gives only the first part of the cahier. Talleyrand influential.
			N	B III 13,p.768				B III 13,p.760	Bib.Nat.Le24. 15	Ibid.,343 et seq.			1	AP text is inaccurate, but the inaccuracies are unimportant.
			T	C 15/15	C 15/15	G		Ba16		Ibid.,328 et seq.			1	Idem.

1	2	3	4	5	6	7	8	9	10	11	12	13	14	15
Auxerre(Dijon)	1		C	30/252bis	p.v.	S		B III 16,p-168	Ba16	AP, II, 108-12			2	Conflicts between ecclesiastical hierarchy; protest against presiding clergyman.
			N	30/252bis				B III 16,p.250	Ba16	AP, II, 114-19			1	Unanimous adoption reported.
			T	30/252bis	p.v.	S		B III 16,p.415	Ba16	AP, II, 120-25			1	
Aval(Besançon)	1		C	C 15/17	Collec-tion of M.Cerni-esson, Lonsle-Saunier	S	C	Ba17		AP, II, 137-39	C		1	
			N	Collection of M. Cernesson, Lons-le-Saunier	Idem	I		Collection of M. Cernesson	Bib.Nat.Le24. 22	AP, II, 139-43			1	The text given by the AP is not the general cahier, but the preliminary cahier of the principal bailliage of Aval.
			T	Idem, in 30 p.v.	cahier	I		Idem		Unedited, see Appendix	T	P	1	
Avesnes(Valenciennes)	1		C	Ba17	p.v.	G		B III 19,p.157	Ba17	AP, II, 146-49			2	Protest against arts. 9,37. Mémoires used.
			N	B III 19, p.883				B III 19,p.892	Voted to print	AP, II, 150-51			1	
			T	Ba17	p.v.	I		B III 19,p.180	Ba17	AP, II, 151-55	T	P	1	
Bailleul(Lille)	1		C	Ba18	p.v. and cahier	I	C	Ba18	Ba18	AP, II, 168-71	C		1	All three orders opposed the influence of Calonne, who by right, could have exerted considerable influence in this district.
			N	Ba18				B III 20,p.125	Ba18 (2)	AP, II, 171-73			1	Two lawyers influential.
			T	Ba18	p.v.	G		B III 20,p.153	Ba18	AP, II, 174-78	T	P	1	
Barcelonnette (Forcalquier;Aix)	2		C	Missing	p.v., C Forcal-quier	I		B III 66², p.927		AP, III, 365-66			1	Conflict between officers and city-delegates. Unanimous adoption except article on town privileges. The copy of the cahier in Arch.Nat. B III 662, pp.951 et seq. is incomplete as compared with that in Ba 41.
			N	Made none	Made none			Made none						
			T	30 p.v., Ba41	p.v.	G		Ba41		AP, III, 366-74			2	
Bar-le-duc (Bar-le-duc;Nancy)	2		C	30 p.v.,C 15/21¹	p.v.	G		Missing		La Révolution fran-caise,revue,1897, XXXII, 165 et seq.			1	Bar-le-duc was a center of the second type of con-vocation. The p.v. of the joint assemblies exist in Arch.Nat. C 15/20¹.
			N	Idem				Arch.Meuse						The assembly voted that one delegate from each commune should be present in the assembly, but the complete assembly should meet for the reading of the cahier and its adoption.
			T	B III 21,p.238				B III 21,p.133	Ba19	AP, II, 193-96			1	
Bar-sur-Seine (Dijon)	1	D.I.	C	Ba20	cahier	G		Ba20	C 15/21	Vernier,J.J., D.I., III, 445 et seq.			1	Unanimous adoption reported.
			N	Ba20	p.v.	I		B III 24,p.202	Ba20 (2)	Ibid., 460 et seq.			1	Idem.
			T	Ba20,PR	p.v.	I		C 15/21	Ba20 (2)	Ibid., 478 et seq.			1	The AP text will be more convenient for use, because of the method Vernier, editor of the D.I. volume, adopted for re-printing the text.
Bassigny-Barrois (Nancy)	7		U	Missing; held in December, 1789				B III 24,p.549;	Ba19(liasse for Bourmont)	AP, II, 196-98			3	This district was an exception to the regular convocation and belongs in class seven. See Brette, op.cit., Vol.I,pp.300-301. Authentication lacking in extant text.
								B III 21,p.648						

1	2	3	4	5	6	7	8	9	10	11	12	13	14	15
Bazas(Bordeaux)	1	Brette,IV,294 et seq.	C	Arch.Gironde	p.v.	I		Arch.Gironde		AP, II, 266-67			1	Authentication existing on original MS was not reprinted by AP. Texts in departmental archives are better than those at Arch.Nat.
			N	Idem	cahier	I		Idem	Ba20	AP, II, 267-68	N		1	Idem.
			T	C 15/23	p.v.	I		Idem	Voted to print	AP, VI, 494-96	T		1	Idem. Unanimous adoption reported.
Béarn(Auch)	3	Brette,III,204 et seq.	CN	C 16/24	cahier	I	CN	Arch.Basses-Pyrénées, C.826	Arch.Basses-Pyrénées C.1376	AP, VI, 497-500			1	Béarn belongs to the third type of convocation.
			cd	C 16/24	p.v.	S		Missing	Missing	AP, VI, 500-503			1	Cahier made after the elections, rather than before, as provided for in royal instructions.
			T	C 16/24	cahier	I		Arch.Basses-Pyrénées,C.826	Arch.Basses-Pyrénées,C.1376				1	T. opposed N. in the Provincial-Estates.
Beauvais(Paris)	1	Brette,III,352 et seq.	C	C 16/26	cahier	I		Ba20	Ba20 (2)	AP, II, 287-94	C		1	
			N	Ba20				Ba20		AP, II, 294-98	N		1	Pamphlets given to deputy.
			T	C 16/26				B III 28, p.351		AP, II, 298-309	T		1	
Belfort and Huningue(Strasbourg)	1		C	Ba20	p.v.	G		Ba20; Arch. Haut-Rhin C.1958	Ba20	AP, II, 310-15	C		1	Text from Arch.Haut-Rhin is better than texts at Arch.Nat.
			N	B III 27	p.v.	I		Missing					1	
			T	C 16/27	cahier	I		Ba20	Ba20	AP, II, 315-18	T		2	Disorder.
Bellême(Alençon)	1		C	B III 116	T.p.v.	I	C	Ba21	Arch.Orne	AP, V, 319-22	C		1	This bailliage is listed as "Perche" by the AP.
			N	Ba21	p.v.,	I		Ba21		AP, V, 323-25	N		1	Mémoires read aloud in assembly.
			T	Ba21	cahier	I	T	Ba21		AP, V, 325-29	T	P	2	Protests. Agriculture slighted.
Belley(Dijon)	1		C	C 16/28	30 p.v., Ba21	G	G	B III 30,p.121	Printed according to Recamier (op. cit. in Bibliography)	AP, II, 477-79			2	This district is sometimes listed as "Bugey et Valromey". Protest by curates. Bishop yielded.
			N	Lost. Account in Lex (of. Bibliography), p.27	Idem	I		B III 30,p.297	Ba21	AP, II, 479-85			1	
			T	Ba21	Idem	I		Lost	Printed according to Recamier	Recamier, E., op.cit. in Bibliography)			1	The printed text of cahier used by Recamier has been lost or is held by a private individual. Unanimous adoption after careful discussion of cahier.
Besançon(Besançon)	1		C	C 16/29	p.v.	I	I	Bib.Besançon 1534, no-261; Arch.Nat. B III 30, p.437		AP, II, 335-37	C		1	
			N	Extracts-Arch. Doubs,B.9501	Letters, B III 30, p.467	I		Arch.Doubs B.9501		AP, VI, 515-59	N		1	Protestant nobles caused trouble.
			T	C 16/29	p.v.	G		Idem and Arch. Nat. Ba21		AP, II, 537-43			1	The text of cahier in Arch.Doubs is incomplete.

1	2	3	4	5	6	7	8	9	10	11	12 13	14	15
Beziers (Montpellier)	1		C	C 16/30	p.v.	I		Ba21(two texts)		AP, II, 346 et seq. and unreprinted text Appendix		3	Trouble between bishops and curates. Two texts of the cahier exist, neither of which bears adequate authentication.
			N	C 16/30	p.v.	G						1	Protest against royal officers. Careful adoption. Officials impartial.
			T	30 p.v., C 16/30	p.v.	G				AP, II, 347-50		1	
Bigorre (Auch)	1	Brette,IV, 135 et seq.	C	B III 32	p.v.	I	C	C 16/31		AP, II, 350-54	C	2	Trouble over chairmanship of assembly. Protests.
			N	Missing	Action in National Assembly	I		Missing					Careful adoption. Nobles not possessing fiefs oppose art. 27.
			T	Ba80	p.v.	G	T	Ba80	Ba21	AP, II, 359-65	T	1	Barère may have been influential.
Bitche (Sarreguemines; Nancy)	2	Missing	C	Missing	30 p.v., Ba77	S		Ba77		AP, V, 692-93		2	Incomplete authentication.
			N	Missing	Idem	S		Missing					The p.v. is not clear as to whether the T. made a cahier, or failing in that, merely gave preliminary cahiers to the deputies.
			T	Missing	Idem	S		Missing					
Biamont (Nancy)	2		C	See Jerome, op. cit., p.110	p.v.	I		Missing but reprinted		Jérome, L, op. cit., p.114		1	The original text used by Jérome has disappeared.
			N	30 p.v., Ba57				Missing				1	
			T	Idem	C 21/110	G		Missing				1	There is some doubt as to whether the T. made a cahier. (See 30 p.v.)
Blois (Orléans)	1	D.I, and Brette, III, 425 et seq.	C	C 16/32		I		Ba22	Voted to print	Cauchie and Lesueur, D.I.,II,393 et seq.		1	Pamphlets read and given to deputy.
			N	C 16/32	cahier			Ba22		Ibid., 413 et seq.		1	Difficulties arose between bailliages of Blois and Romorantin (secondary). Electoral propaganda circulated.
			T	C 16/33				B III 33,p.559		Ibid., 447 et seq.			
Bordeaux (Bordeaux)	1	Brette,IV,237 et seq.	C	B III 34		I		B III 34,p.395		AP, II, 392-94	C	1	This district sometimes went by the name "Guienne". Protests against C. cahier.
			N	Ba22, PR	cahier	I	N	Ba22		AP, II, 394-97	N	3	Schism; withdrawal of part of N. assembly and protest.
			T	C 16/33		I		C 16/33		AP, II, 397-405	T P	2	Unanimous adoption reported. Difficulties between rural and urban delegates.
Boulay (Sarreguemines; Nancy)	1		C	B III 133	cahier	S		Ba77		AP, V, 693-94	C	1	Manuscript ends without signatures.
			N	B III 133	p.v.	S		Missing Arch.Moselle B 6.214		Annuaire de la Soc. hist.et arch. lorraine, 1904, XVI, 200 et seq.	T	1	
			T	B 6.214				B 6.214				1	
Boulogne-sur-mer (Amiens)	1	Brette, III, 120 et seq.	C	Ba23	cahier	I		Ba23		AP, II, 415-24	C	2	Authentication of text completely lacking.
			N	Ba23	p.v.	I		Ba23		AP, II, 424-31		1	Additions to cahier discussed and adopted.
			T	Ba23				Ba23		AP, II, 431-41	T	1	
Bourg-en-Bresse (Dijon)	1		U	Ba23; p.v. of separate orders; C-Ba23; N and T; C 16/35	C-Ba23; N-Ba23; T-30p.v.	S I S		Ba23	Bib.Nat.Le24. 214 (2)	AP, II, 452-64	U	1	Original text drafted in three columns, one for each order. Careful adoption.

1	2	3	4	5	6	7	8	9	10	11	12	13	14	15
Bourges(Bourges)	1	D.I and Bretto, III, 477 et seq.	C	C 16/36	p.v.	G		Arch.Cher		Cf. Gandilhon, D.I, p.755, and AP, VI, 512-14			2	Curates powerful.
			N	C 16/36(extract)	p.v.	I		B III 29,p.298		AP, II, 319-23			1	
			T	C 16/36	p.v.	S		Ba24	Ba24	AP, II, 325-25				Patriotic speech. Careful discussion.
Bourmont(Bar-le-duc; Nancy)	2		C	Ba19	30 p.v.	G		Arch.Haute-Marne		Unedited, see Appendix			1	Unanimous adoption reported.
			N	30 p.v., Ba19	cahier	I		Idem		Idem			2	Infra, see comment at end of cahier.
			T	Ba77	30 p.v.	G		Ba19		AP, II, 198-201			1	
Bouzonville(Sarreguemines; Nancy)	2		C	Ba77	p.v.	I		Ba77		AP, V, 694-98	C		1	
			N	Ba77	p.v.	S		Ba77		AP, V, 701-3			1	
			T	Ba77	p.v.	S		Ba77		AP, V, 703-7			1	
Brest(Rennes)	6		T	Ba25	p.v.	G		C 16/37 or Ba25	Bib.Nat.Le23.25	AP, II, 475-76 and 465-75	T		1	The general assembly of the sénéchaussée of Brest adhered to the cahier of the town of Brest, which is preserved in MS, Arch.Nat. Ba 25, and is given in the AP, Vol.II,pp.465 et seq. It should be read with the adherence. Unanimous adoption reported.
Briey(Bar-le-duc: Nancy)	2		C	30 p.v., B III 21	p.v.	G		Missing						
			N	Idem	p.v.	I		B III 21,p.402	Ba19	AP, II, 201-4			1	
			T	Idem	p.v.	I		C 15/20²	Ba19	AP, II, 204-14			1	
Brignoles(Toulon: Aix)	2		C	Missing	p.v.	S		Missing						
			N	Ba81	p.v.	I		Missing					1	
			T	Ba81	p.v.	I		Missing					1	
Bruyères(Mirecourt: Nancy)	2		CT	Ba53	cahier	I		B III 89,p.316	Ba53	AP, IV, 9-12			1	Approval of vote by head the only addition made to cahier submitted by committee.
			N	Ba53	cahier			Arch.Vosges	Voted to print	Unedited, see Appendix			1	
Caen(Caen)	1		C	C 17/38	p.v.	G		C 17/38	Ba28	AP, II, 486-88	C		1	Careful discussion. Unanimous adoption.
			N	C 17/38, PR	p.v.	I		Ba27		AP, II, 488-92	N	P	1	Careful adoption.
			T	C 17/38	p.v.	I		Arch.Calvados 16B6		AP, II, 492-95			1	Protests.
Cahors(Montauban)	1	D.I and Bretto, IV, 8 et seq.	C	Ba28	p.v.	I		Ba28	Ba28	AP, V, 483-88	N	P	2	This district is sometimes called Quercy. D.I. does not give general cahiers. Hurried composition of cahier. Pressed for time.
			N	Ba28	cahier	I		Ba28		AP, V, 488-90			1	Careful adoption.
			T	Ba28	C 23/150	S		Ba28		AP, V, 490-93			2	Unanimous adoption reported. Authentication weak.
Calais(Amiens)	1	Brette, III, 110 et seq.	C	C 17/39	p.v.	G		Museum of Arch. Nat. and also, B III 41,p.161 Idem, and B III 41,p.228 Idem and C 17/39	AD I 10	AP, II, 504-6	T		1	Power to increase or decrease powers of deputies given to a committee of correspondence.
			N	C 17/39	p.v.	I				AP, II, 506-10			1	Protests by two members.
			T	C 17/39						AP, II, 510-16 (inaccurate) See Loriquet (op.cit.in Appendix),II,515			1	

1	2	3	4	5	6	7	8	9	10	11	12	13	14	15
Cambrésis(Lille)	1		C	Ba29	p.v.	I		Missing					1	Careful discussion. Protest against the cahier, Arch.Nat. C 17/40.
			N	Ba29	p.v.	I		B III 41,p.270		AP, II, 517-19			1	The p.v. makes no mention of adoption of cahier.
			T	Ba29	p.v.	G		B III 41,p.309		AP, II, 519-23		P	1	
Carcassonne (Toulouse)	1		C	Ba29	p.v.	G		Arch.Hérault		Dom de Vic..., op. cit., XIV, 2558 et seq.			1	The cahier has two sections; part to which all agreed, and part to which there was dissent.
			N	Ba29	p.v.	I		B III 41,p.340	Ba29	AP, II, 527-31	N		1	A mémoire on commerce was read and given to deputy. Careful discussion, unanimous adoption.
			T	C 17/41	p.v.	G		Ba29		AP, II, 532-35	T		2	Authentication lacking.
Carhaix(Carhaix: Rennes)	6		T	Ba25	p.v.	S		Arch.Finistère		Unedited text in Appendix			1	Carhaix was a center of reunion of the sixth type of convocation. The text given by the AP is not the general cahier but is the text of the sénéchaussée of Carhaix alone.
Carignan(Sedan: Metz)	2		C	30 p.v., Ba78				Missing					1	
			NT	Idem				Missing					1	
Castellane(Draguignan: Aix)	2		C	Ba39 (in liasse for Draguignan)				Ba39, B III 63, p.688		AP, III, 272-73			1	Attention called by presiding clergyman to model instructions sent by General Agents of the Gallican Church. Cahier made by the assembly as a whole.
			N	See Mireur, F., op.cit., p.170				Missing					1	
			T	Ba39				Missing					2	Patriotic speeches. Protests.
Castelmoron d'Albert (Bordeaux)	1	Brette,IV,267 et seq.	C	Ba29	Ba29	I		Ba29		AP, II, 542-43			1	Unanimous adoption reported.
			N	Ba29	cahier	I		Ba29		AP, II, 543-45			1	
			T	Ba29	C 17/43²	I		Ba29		AP, II, 549, and 544-49	T		1	
Castelnaudary (Toulouse)	1		C	Ba30	p.v.	G		Ba30		AP, II, 552-53			1	
			N	Ba30	p.v.	I		Ba30		AP, II, 557-59			1	
			T	Ba30 and C 17/44	p.v.	S		Ba30		AP, II, 559-61	T		1	
Castres (Toulouse)	1		C	Ba30	p.v.	G		Ba30		AP, II, 562-63	C		1	Curates hurried. Committee authorised to sign cahier, but the whole assembly voted on the text.
			N	Ba30	p.v.	I		Ba30	Bib.Nat.Le24.229	AP, II, 565-68			1	Discussion of principles in assembly before committee began work.
			T	Ba30	p.v.	I		Ba30		AP, II, 569-71			1	Unanimous adoption.
Caudebec-en-Caux (Rouen)	1		C	B III 43	p.v.	G		Ba30	Printed according to Sanson, op. cit. in Bibliography Bib.Nat.Le24.35 (2)	AP, II, 573-75	C		1	
			M	B III 43	cahier	I			Printed according to Sanson, op. cit.	AP, II, 575-77	M			Careful adoption.
			T	C 17/46(extract)	p.v.	G		Ba30		AP, II, 577-81				Pamphlet received from Rouen called libelous and rejected.
Châlon-sur-Saône (Dijon)	1		C	C 17/48	C 17/48			Ba31		AP, II, 600-604	C		1	
			N	C 17/48	p.v.	S		Ba31		AP, II, 604-8	M		1	
			T	C 17/46		I		Ba31		AP, II, 608-13	E		1	

1	2	3	4	5	6	7	8	9	10	11	12	13	14	15
Châlons-sur-Marne (Châlons)	1	D.I. and Brette, III, 192 et seq.	C	Ba31	p.v.	G		C 14/47	Ba31 (2)	Laurent,G.,D.I.,821 et seq.			1	Hurried, but worked on a holiday to finish.
Charmes(Mirecourt: Nancy)	2		N	Ba31	C 17/47	S	G	B III 44,p.334	C 17/47 (2)	Ibid., 837 et seq.			1	Adopted cahier of N.Bordeaux with slight changes. Exact text unknown.
			T	Ba31	p.v.	G	I	B III 44,p.404	Ba31 (2)	Ibid., 845 et seq.			1	
Charolles(Dijon)	1		C	C 17/49	p.v.	I	C	Ba31		AP, II, 614-15			1	Unanimous adoption reported.
			N	Ba31	p.v.	I	N	Ba31		AP, II, 615-18			1	Long discussion. Swore secrecy on action of assembly.
			T	C 17/49	cahier	I	T	Ba31		AP, II, 618-22	T		1	
Chartres(Orléans)	1	Brette,III,436 et seq.	C	C 17/50	p.v.	I	C	B III 45,p.259	Ba31	AP, II, 623-26			1	Ambiguity as to whether cahier was adopted March 19 or 20.
			N	C 17/50	cahier	I	N	B III 45,p.288	Ba31	AP, II, 626-29			1	
			T	C 17/50	p.v.	I	T	B III 45,p.347		AP, II, 629-35	T		1	
Château-Salins (Sarreguemines: Nancy)	2		C	Ba77		I		Ba77		AP, V, 707-9	C		1	Project discussed and given to committee. Careful adoption.
			N	Ba77				Missing		Annuaire de la Soc. hist. et arch. lorraine, 1904, XVI, 220 et seq.			1	
			T	Ba77				Arch.Meurthe-et-Moselle					1	
Château-Thierry (Soissons)	1	Brette,III,154 et seq.	C	C 17/52	p.v.	S	N	Missing	Ba32	AP, II, 650-66	N		1	Patriotic speeches and action. Committee appointed to advise deputies on local demands left out of cahier.
			N	Ba32, PR				B III 46,p.146	Ba32 (2)	AP, II, 668-78			1	
			T	C 17/52		I		B III 46,p.668					1	
Châteauneuf-en-Thimerais(Alençon)	1		C	C 17/51	p.v.	I	C	Ba32	Ba32	AP, II, 638-40	N		1	The cahiers of the nobles and third estate are almost identical. Difference lies in demands relative to hunting (chasse) and dovecotes (colombiers).
			N	B III 45	cahier	I	N	B III 45,p.175		AP, II, 640-51			1	Idem.
			T	B III 45	cahier	I		C 17/51	Ba32	AP, II, 651-57			1	
Châtellerault (Tours)	1	Brette,IV,513 et seq.	C	C 17/53	p.v.	I	T	C 17/53		AP, II, 686-906	C		2	Adoption of cahier with protests.
			N	Ba32	p.v.	I		Missing		AP, II, 690-99			1	
			T	Ba32	p.v.	I		C 17/53					1	
Châtel-sur-Moselle(Mirecourt: Nancy)	2		C	Ba53	p.v.	G		Missing		Unedited text in Appendix			1	Cahier made by the entire assembly.
			N	Ba53	p.v.	S		Arch.Vosges		Idem	N		1	
			T	Ba53	p.v.	I		Arch.Vosges					1	
Châtillon-sur-Seine (Dijon)	1		C	Ba53	cahier	G		Ba53		AP, II, 700-702			1	Careful adoption.
			N	Ba53	cahier	I		Ba53		AP, II, 702-10	C		1	
			T	Ba53	p.v.	I		Ba53		AP, II, 710-19			1	
Chaumont-en-Bassigny(Châlons)	1	Brette,III,255 et seq.	C	Ba32	p.v.	I		Ba32	Ba32	AP, II, 720-23	C		2	Curates prominent. Protest by higher clergy. Question of authenticity. MS text in Arch.Nat. Ba53 is incomplete. Confusion. Interference by royal officers.
			N	Ba32	p.v.	I		Ba32		AP, II, 724-26	N		1	
			T	30 p.v., Ba32	p.v.	I	T	Ba32		AP, II, 726-29	T		3	

1	2	3	4	5	6	7	8	9	10	11	12	13	14	15
Chaumont-en-Vexin (Rouen)	1		C	Ba32				Missing	Ba32 Bib.Nat.Lc24. 50	AP, II, 730-32			1	
			N	Ba32	p.v.	I		B III 46,p.132		AP, II, 739-43			1	
			T	Ba32	p.v.	S							1	
Clermont-en-Beauvoisis (Soissons)	1	Brette,III,160 et seq.	C	C 17/57	p.v., new assembly	G		Arch.Oise	Ba32	AP, II, 744-48	C		1	
			N	Missing C 17/57	B III 48	I		B III 48,p.145 Arch.Oise		AP, II, 748-54 AP, II, 754-58	N T		1 1	
			T											
Clermont-à-Varennes(Verdun/Metz)	2		U	Ba84				Missing					2	Curates in a hurry.
Clermont Ferrand (Rion)	1	Brette,III,658 et seq.	C	Ba33	p.v.	I	C	Ba33	C 27/206 (2)	AP, II, 759-66	N		1	Abbé de Montesquiou influential.
			N	C 27/206	p.v.	I		B III 48,p.615	Ba22 (2)	AP, II, 766-69	N		1	
			T	Ba33	p.v.	I	T	B III 48,p.677		AP, II, 769-74	T		1	
Colmar and Schlestadt(Strasbourg)	1		C	Ba33, PR	p.v.	S		B III 49,p.116	Ba33 (2) Bib.Univ. Strasbourg Voted to print	AP, III, 3-7			1	Mémoires given to committee. Careful discussion.
			N	Ba33, PR	p.v.	I		Ba33		AP, III, 7-9			1	
			T	Ba33	p.v.	G		Ba33		AP, III, 9-12	T		1	Careful discussion.
Commercy(Bar-le-duc/Nancy)	2		C	Ba19	p.v.	G	G	Missing					2	The bailli gave specific instructions in the assembly of the three orders.
			N	Ba19	p.v.	G		Missing					2	Idem.
			T	Ba19	p.v.	G		Missing					2	Idem.
Comminges(Auch)	1	Brette,IV,106 et seq.	C	C 17/59	cahier	I		Missing	C 17/59 Ba56	AP, III, 21-26			2	Protest by gros-décimateurs.
			N	C 17/59, PR				B III 51,p.21, also p.362		AP, III, 26-28			2	Protests against the taille and franc-fief.
			T	C 17/59									1	
Condom(Bordeaux)	1	Brette,IV,305 et seq.	C	Ba33	p.v.	I		Ba33	AD I 11 (2)	AP, III, 33-36			1	Careful adoption.
			N	Ba33	cahier	I	N	Ba33		AP, III, 36-38			1	Petitions read before assembly. Careful adoption.
			T	30 p.v., C 28/212	p.v.	I				AP, III, 38-40			1	Parish cahiers read in assembly.
Corsica(corsica)	6		C	C 18/62[1]	p.v.	G		Missing of Archives of family Gaffori (in Italian)	Reprinted in Italian; for French translation, see Appendix.		T		1	The cahier (in Italian) has been reprinted by the Abbé Letteron in "Osservazioni storiche de l'Abbé Rossi," in Soc. des Sc. hist. et nat. de la Corse, Appendix 2, Bk. XIV, pp. 447 et seq. It seems to me that the term "cahier de reunion" in the p.v. of the T seems to indicate a joint cahier. This term would not be used of a cahier of the third estate alone. See supra,ch. 1, note 79.
			N	C 18/60 (in Italian); Ba34 (PR in French and Italian) C 18/62[1]	p.v.	G		Ba34		AP, III, 41-66			1	
Couserans(Auch)	5	Brette,IV,116 et seq.	C	Ba43	p.v.	S		Missing					1	The cahiers were lost in the fire of the archives of Hautes-Pyrénées.
			NT	Ba43	N p.v.	I	N	Missing					1	It would appear from the p.v. that the N and T made a cahier together. The p.v. of the nobles is not clear, but the use of the term "cahier de reunion" in the p.v. of the T seems to indicate a joint cahier. This term would not be used of a cahier of the third estate alone. See supra,ch. 1, note 79.

1	2	3	4	5	6	7	8	9	10	11	12	13	14	15
Coutances(Caen)	1	D.I.	C	C 18/62	p.v.		G	C 18/62		Bridrey,E., D.I.,467 et seq.			2	Protest by higher clergy.
			N	C 18/62	cahier (in PR)	I	I	C 18/62	Ba35	Ibid., 508 et seq.			1	Patriotic mémoires given to deputies.
			T	C 18/62	p.v.	I	I	Ba35		Ibid., 546 et seq.			1	Parish cahiers influential.
Crepy-en-Valois (Soissons)	1	Brette,III,144 et seq.	C	C 18/62			G	Ba35		AP, III, 73-74	C		1	Grain shortage reported. Duke of Orléans elected.
			N	Ba35	p.v.		I	Ba35	AD I 10	AP, III, 74-76			1	Representative of Duke of Orléans, de Limon, active.
			T	Ba35	p.v.			Ba35		AP, III, 76-79	T	P	1	
Darney(Mirecourt: Nancy)	2		C	Arch.Vosges Ba53	cahier		I	Missing Arch.Vosges B		Duhamel, op.cit., II, 356 et seq.			1 1	
			N	Ba53										
			T	30 p.v., Ba53				Missing					1	
Dauphiné(Grenoble)	3	Brette,I, on convocation	U	Ba74,PR; Ba75; MS	p.v. for Jan.9, 1789.		I	The original is missing,but a summary was given in the p.v.;Ba75, C 18/64	Ba74 (3)	AP, III, 80 et seq.	U		3	The p.v. of the Intermediate Commission of the Provincial-Estates is helpful, Arch.Isère, III C 4. The original of the cahier has disappeared. It is not among the Mounier papers (Mounier was secretary) as might be expected. Extant text is only a summary in the p.v.
Dax(Bordeaux)	1	Brette,IV,358 et seq.	C	C 18/65	p.v.		I	C 18/65		AP, III, 87-93			1	
			N	C 18/65	p.v. Ba36;AP, III,106-107	I	G	B III 57,p.609	Ba36 (2)	AP, III, 93-95			1	See Brette, op.cit., Vol.IV, p.361, on supplement. Document not found at Arch.Nat.
			T	C 18/65			G	B III 57,p.703	Ba36 (2)	AP, III, 95-98			2	Difficulty with lieutenant general.
Dieuze(Sarreguemines:Nancy)	2	D.I.	C	Ba77	p.v.		G	Ba77		Etienne,C.,D.I.,401 et seq.	C		1	
			N	Ba77	cahier		G	Arch.Meurthe-et-Moselle		Ibid.,405 et seq.			1	
			T	Ba77	p.v.	T	I	Idem		Ibid., 411 et seq.			1	
Digne(Forcalquier: Aix)	2		C	30 p.v., Ba41	p.v.,C, Forcalquier 30 p.v.		I	Ba41		AP, III, 336-40			1	
			N	Idem	30 p.v.		I	Ba41		AP, III, 346-47			1	
			T	Idem	30 p.v.	I	I	Ba41		AP, III, 348-56			1	
Dijon(Dijon)	1	D.I.	C	30 p.v. C 18/66 See also reprint in Guérin,A., Bull. d'histoire du diocèse de Dijon,1886,1887	cahier		I	Arch.Cote d'Or, C 3475; Bib. Dijon, Fonds Joigne	AD I 10	AP, III, 123-27	C		3	Trouble in assembly. Reservations to cahier. Authentication dubious.
			N	Bib.Mun.Dijon, Fonds Joigné, no.44,t.V.	p.v.		N	Ba37	Ba37 (2)	AP, III, 127-30			2	Project discussed. Vote by order adopted by majority of three only. Careful adoption.
			T	Ba37	p.v.		I	Ba37	Bib.Nat.Le24. 68	AP, III, 131-40	T		2	Cahier of Dijon (ville) used as guide. Protest against imperative mandate. Group of lawyers influential.
Dinan(Rennes)	6		T	Ba25	p.v.		G	Ba25		AP, III, 148-51			1	Cahier made by assembly.

1	2	3	4	5	6	7	8	9	10	11	12	13	14	15
Dix Villes Impér-iales(Strasbourg)	4		T	C 14/4 and B III 68. See also p.v. of each of ten cities,Ba45; B III 68	p.v.	G			Bib.Colmar (German text)	Unedited, see Appendix for French translation.		P.	1	
Dol(Rennes)	6	D.I. for Rennes	C^d	C 18/68^1	p.v.	G		C 18/68^1		Sée and Lessort, D.I. for Rennes, 299 et seq.			1	
Dôle(Besançon)	1		C	C 16/69	p.v.	G		B III 61,p.143		AP, III, 152-54			1	Bailli gave patriotic appeal. Long discussion.
			N	B III 61, with-out page number	cahier	G		Ba38	Ba38	AP, III, 154-60			1	Idem.
			T	C 16/69	p.v.	G		B III 61, without page number	C 18/69	AP, III, 160-66	T		1	Idem. Mémoire on Provincial-Estates given to deputies. Noisy assembly.
Dorat(Limoges)	1	Brette,III,611 et seq.	C	Ba38			N	B III 24,p.253	Ba38	AP, III, 675-76			1	This district is also known as "Larche-Masse."
			N	Ba38	cahier	I		B III 24,p.263		AP, III, 676-78			1	The extant text bears only the signatures of the committee.
			T	Ba38				Ba38		AP, III, 678-01	T		1	Unanimous adoption reported.
Douai(Lille)	1		C	B III 62	p.v.	I	C	B III 62,p.99	Ba38	AP, III, 174-75			1	Several mémoires given to deputy.
			N	Ba38	p.v.	I	N	B III 62,p.181	Ba38 (2)	AP, III, 175-79			2	Voted against inclusion of art.79 in cahier.
			T	Ba38	cahier	I	T	B III 62,p.216	Ba38	AP, III, 179-83	T		1	Careful adoption.
Dourdan(Orléans)	1	Brette,III,442 et seq.	C	C 16/71	p.v.	I		B III 63,p.69	Ba39	AP, III, 243-46		P.	1	
			N	Missing	New powers			B III 63,p.97	Ba39	AP, III, 246-50			1	
			T	C 16/71	p.v.	G		B III 63,p.173	Ba39	AP, III, 250-54			1	Unanimous adoption reported.
Draguignan(Drag-uignan:Aix)	2		C	Ba39	cahier			Ba39 for var-ious MSS		See Appendix for two certified texts.			3	The C. could not agree on a cahier. Hence, the preliminary cahiers were given to the deputies. Two of these texts only were certified by the registrar of the district.
			N	C 16/72				Missing	Bib.Nat.Le24. 215					Comte de la Clerc influential in drafting final text.
			T	30 p.v.,C 18/72	cahier	G		B III 63,p.169		AP, III, 255-64			1	Unanimous adoption recorded.
Epinal(Mirecourt: Nancy)	2		C	Ba53	p.v.	G	G	Missing						
			N	Ba53	p.v.	I	I	Missing					1	No adoption of cahier recorded.
			T	30 p.v., Ba53				Missing					1	
Etain(Bar-le-duc: Nancy)	2		C	Ba19				Arch.Meuse		Unedited text in Appendix.			1	
			K	Ba19	cahier	I		B III 22,p.131	Arch.Meuse	AP,II, 214-20			2	Tumult.
			T	Ba19				Arch.Meuse		Unedited text in Appendix.			2	Idem.
Étampes(Paris)	1	Brette,III,381 et seq.	C	Ba39	cahier	S		B III 64,p.247	Ba39	AP, III, 279-82			2	Protest against presiding clergyman.
			N	Ba39	p.v.	I	N	Missing					1	Mémoire on the constitution was read aloud and given to the deputies. Careful adoption.
			T	Ba39	p.v.	I	T	B III 64,p.347	Ba39	AP, III, 283-89	T		1	

1	2	3	4	5	6	7	8	9	10	11	12	13	14	15
Évreux(Rouen)	1		C	B III 64	p.v.	I	I	B III 64,p.222	Ba40	AP, III, 290-95	N		1	Slow adoption. Some articles held over and discussed, but finally adopted.
			N	Ba40, PR	Ba40	I	I	B III 64,p.310	Ba40	AP, III, 295-99	T		1	
			T	C 18/74	p.v.	I	I	C 18/74	Ba40	AP, III, 300-303	U		1	
Fénestrange(Sarre-guemines:Nancy)	2		U	Ba77, also p.v. for each order	cahier	I		Ba77		AP, V, 710-13			1	Preliminary cahiers read before committee began work.
Foix(Auch)	1	Brette,IV,158 et seq.	C	B III 100 (extract)				Missing			M		2	This district is also known as the sénéchaussée of Pamiers. The text given by the AP is not a cahier. Whatever text was adopted, the bishop overrode the assembly.
			N	Ba60	p.v.	I		Ba60	Arch.Ariège	AP, IV, 280-81			1	
			T	Ba60	p.v.		S	B III 100,p.367	Ba60 (2)	AP, IV, 281-85			1	
Forcalquier(For-calquier:Aix)	2		C	Missing	In re-union p.v., C 19/75	I		B III 66¹,p.255		AP, III, 324-28			2	Forcalquier was a center of reunion of the second type of convocation. The p.v. of these assemblies exist, Arch.Nat. Ba41. Authentication weak. Supplementary instructions given orally. The extant text was merely the draft by the committee. Voted to change articles so that provincial administration would be in hands of assembly of three orders, and that next convocation be by sénéchaussée.
			N	Idem	p.v.			B III 66¹,p.301		AP, III, 328-29			1	
			T	30 p.v., Ba41	p.v.	G		B III 66¹,p.311		AP, III, 329-36			2	
Forez(Lyon)	1	Brette,III,723 et seq.	C	Ba54	p.v.	G		B III 67,p.280	Ba54 (2)	AP, III, 362-83			1	Mémoires used. Careful discussion, before adoption. Disorder. Complaint by lieutenant general. Careful adoption.
			N	Ba54, PR	p.v.	I	I	B III 67,p.330	Ba54 (2)	AP, III, 383-85			1	
			T	Ba54	p.v.	I	I	B III 67,p.416	Ba54 (2)	AP, III, 385-87			1	
Fougères(Fougères: Rennes)	6		T	Ba25	p.v.	I		Missing			P		2	Protest to maintain privileges. The cahiers of the separate senechaussées were given the deputies, hence, Fougères served as a center of reunion.
Gex(Dijon)	1		C	C 19/76	C 19/78	I	I	Ba43		AP, III, 388-92	C		1	Conflict between French nobles and Genevan nobles holding fiefs, and hence eligible to assembly. Assembly prorogued. King allowed Genevans to take part. Plan for provincial organization read by one of committee. Added this to cahier, and also article on a gift of 6,000 livres.
			N	Ba43	p.v.	I	I	Ba43		AP, III, 392-94			1	
			T	Ba43	30 p.v., Ba43	I		Ba43		AP, III, 394-97	T		1	
Gien(Orléans)	1	Brette,III,447 et seq.	C	Ba43	p.v.	G		Ba43	Ba43	AP, III, 398-400	C		1	Long discussion of cahier. Oath irregular and late. Unanimous approval reported.
			N	C 19/79	p.v.	I	I	B III 66,p.108		AP, III, 400-406			1	
			T	Ba43	p.v.	I	I	B III 66,p.185		AP, III, 406-12			1	
Grasse(Draguignan: Aix)	2		C	Missing. See 30 p.v., Ba39. Cf. Mireur, op.cit., held no assembly				B III 63,p.431		AP, III, 267-68			2	Difficulty between bishop and curates. Too few members in assembly to make a cahier.
			N	Ba39	Made none Ba39			Made none Ba39		AP, III, 274-77			1	
			T											
Guadeloupe(colony)	7	Paris Gundeloupe	I T	C 30/247 C 30/247 and F III 159	cahier	I	T	B III 159,p.641		AP, VI, 235			2	The page for this colony was omitted, by error, in printing the Répertoire critique. As in the case of the other colonies, there was no royal convocation. The French colonists author-ized a committee in Paris, in February, 1789, to solicit.

1	2	3	4	5	6	7	8	9	10	11	12	13	14	15
Guadeloupe(colony) (continued)														representation. This committee elected deputies and these were admitted to the National Assembly provisionally on September 22, 1789. Primary assemblies were held in the colony in December, 1789, and the deputies to be sent to Paris took an oath in March, 1790. Finally, in July 27, 1790, the whole question was settled and part of the deputies elected in Paris, and part of those elected in the colony were admitted. There were three senechaussees in Guadeloupe, but only the documents for the final assembly have been preserved.
Guéret(Moulins)	1	Brette, III,549 et seq.	C / N / T	Ba44 / Ba44 / Ba44	p.v. / cahier / p.v.	G / I I / I I	Ba44 / C 19/81 N / Ba44	Ba44 / C 19/81 / Ba44		AP, III, 682-83 / AP, III, 684-05 / AP, III, 685-86			1 / 1 1 / 1 1	This district is also known as Haute Marche.
Haguenau(Strasbourg)	1		C / N / T	30 p.v., Ba45 / Idem / Idem	p.v. / p.v. / p.v.	G / G / G	Missing / Missing / Ba45	Missing / Missing / Ba45		AP, III, 416-20		P	2 / 1 / 2	Protest Authentication lacking.
Hédé(Fougères: Rennes)	6		T	Ba25	p.v.	G	Missing	Missing					1	
Hennebont(Rennes)	6		T	C 19/82	p.v.	G	Missing	Missing					1	The p.v. reports that changes were made on the margin of the cahier.
Hyères(Toulon:Aix)	2		C / N / T	Missing, see 30 p.v., Ba81 / Ba81 / 30 p.v., Ba81	p.v.	G	Missing / Missing / Missing	Missing / Missing / Missing					3 / 1	The deputies were given power to make the cahier. There was no adoption by the assembly. This was illegal. The p.v. states that all deputies signed who knew how to sign.
Ile de Bourbon et de France(colony)	7		C	C 43/388	p.v.	G	Missing	Missing					2	Our information about this colony has suffered because of loss of documents.
Jugon(St.Brieuc: Rennes)	6		T	C 24/242	p.v.	G	Missing	Missing					1	
Lamarche(Bar-le-duc:Nancy)	2		C / N / T	Ba19 / Ba19 / 30 p.v., Ba19	p.v. / New Powers / cahier	G / I / G	Ba19 / Missing / Arch.Vosges	Ba19 / Missing / Arch.Vosges		AP, II, 220-24 Dunhamel op.cit., II, 378 et seq.			1 / 1 / 2	Lieutenant general influential.
Langres(Châlons)	1	Brette,III,248 et seq.	U / F / T	Ba45 / Cf. 30 p.v., and B III 70,p.471 / Idem	B III 70,p.537	I	Missing / Supplement to U.cahier is missing / Supplement to U.cahier, in 30 p.v., Ba45	Missing / Supplement to U.cahier is missing / Supplement to U.cahier, in 30 p.v., Ba45		Unedited text in Appendix.			1 / 1	The texts which exist in XS and PR, reprinted by the AP, are not authentic. See Brette, op.cit., Vol. III, p. 248, on false texts.
Lannion(Morlaix: Rennes)	6			Ba26			Ba26	Ba26		AP, IV, 76-78			1	There are two texts in Arch.Nat. Ba26, which differ slightly in the endings.

1	2	3	4	5	6	7	8	9	10	11	12	13	14	15
La Rochelle(La Rochelle)	1	Brette,IV,398 et seq.	C	Missing, see 30 p.v., Ba73	30 p.v.	G		Missing						
			N	Missing, idem	Idem,also AP,III, p.478	I		C 23/138		AP, III, 471-78	N		1	
			T	Ba73	p.v.	G		C 23/138		AP, III, 479-86			1	Protest of many towns against art.36.
Lesneven(Rennes)	·6		T	C 19/64	p.v.	G		C 19/84		AP, III, 493-99	T		2	
Libourne(Bordeaux)	1	Brette,III,325 et seq.	C	Ba47	p.v.	S		B III 72,p.128	AD I 10	AP, III, 503-6			1	
			N	Ba47	New Powers	I		Ba47		AP, III, 506-7			1	
			T	Ba47	p.v.	I		B III 72,p.165		AP, III, 507-9			1	
Lille(Lille)	1		C	C 19/86	New Powers	I		B III 72,p.408	Ba46	AP, III, 522-26			1	Protest by two ecclesiastics.
			N	C 19/86				B III 72,p.466	Ba46 (2)	AP, III, 526-32			1	
			T	C 19/86	p.v.	S		B III 72,p.522	Ba46 (2)	AP, III, 532-35	T		1	Gild cahiers given to deputies.
Limoges(Limoges)	1	Brette,III,562 et seq.	C	C 19/87	p.v.	S		B III 73^1,p.309	Ba47 (2)	AP, III, 560-64			2	This district is also known as Haut-Limousin. It is possible that the secretary made changes in the text unauthorized. See Brette, op.cit., Vol.III, p.564.
			N	C 19/87	p.v.	G		B III 73^1,p.402	Ba47 (2)	AP, III, 564-70	N		1	
			T	C 19/87	p.v.	I		B III 73^1,p.477	Ba47 (2)	AP, III, 570-72			1	Parish cahiers read in assembly.
Limoux(Toulouse)	1		C	Arch.Herault C 879	p.v.	I		Ba47		Dom de Vic...,op.cit. XIV,2615 et seq.			1	The AP omitted this text.
			N	Ba47	cahier	I	N	Ba47		AP, III, 577-79			2	President gave plan for cahier at request of assembly.
			T	Ba47	cahier	I	T	Ba47		AP, III, 579-82	T		2	Lieutenant general active.
Lixheim(Sarreguemines:Nancy)	2		CN	Arch.Meurthe-et-Moselle	p.v.	I		Ba77		AP, V, 713-17			2	The Jews of this district drew up a Mémoire by royal permission. Powerful cabale.
			T	Idem	p.v.	G		Arch.Meurthe-et-Moselle		Unedited text in Appendix			1	
Longuyon(Bar-le-duc:Nancy)	2		C	Ba19	30 p.v., Ba19	S		Arch.Moselle, B 7698		Unedited text in Appendix.			1	Curates prominent.
			N	Ba19	Idem	S		Idem; also, Arch.Nat, C 15/202		Idem			1	
			T	Ba19	Idem	S				Idem			1	
Longwy(Metz:Metz)	2		C	Arch.Moselle, B 4191	30 p.v., Ba52	S		Arch.Moselle, B 4191, and Arch.Nat, B III 87,p.70	Voted to print	AP, III, 771-73	C		1	Guillaume probably drafted the cahier, but it was voted upon and accepted by the assembly.
			N	Idem	Idem	S		Arch.Moselle, B 4191		Unedited text in Appendix.			1	
			T	Idem	Idem	S		Arch.Moselle, B 4191, and Arch.Nat, C 15/202		Unedited text in Appendix.			1	

1	2	3	4	5	6	7	8	9	10	11	12	13	14	15
Loudun(Tours)	1	Brette,IV,680 et seq.	C	C 19/89	p.v.	G		B III 74,p.320	Be47	AP, III, 590-94	N		1	Assembly opposed the bailli.
			N	Be47	p.v.	I		Be47		AP, III, 594-96			1	Conflict between gildsmen and rural delegates.
			T	C 19/89	p.v.	S		Be47		AP, III, 596-98			3	
Lunéville(Nancy; Nancy)	2		C	See Jérome, op. cit. p.91	See Jérome, op. cit., p.106 cahier	I		Missing, but reprinted		Jérome, op.cit., p.97 et seq.			2	The original text used by Jérome has disappeared. The Abbé Grégoire and the secular clergy were influential.
			N	Missing; see 30 p.v., Ba57		I		B III 93,p.468	Ba57 (2)	AP, IV, 84-86			1	
			T	30 p.v., Ba57	p.v.	G		Missing					1	
Lyon(Lyon)	1	Brette,III,701 et seq.	C	C 19/90	cahier	G		C 19/90	Ba48	AP, III, 599-602	C		1	Careful adoption.
			N	Ba48, PR	p.v. and cahier	I	N	B III 76,p.164	Ba48 (2)	AP, III, 602-8			1	
			T	C 19/90, also	C 19/90	S		B III 76,p.349	Ba48 (2)	AP, III, 608-15	T		2	Quarrel between bailli and town. Authentication lacking.
			V	B III 76	p.v.	S		B III 76,p.421	Ba48 (2)	AP, III, 616-18			1	See Brette, op.cit., Vol.III, p.704, on this text and on false text given by AP, Vol.III, p.619.
Mâcon(Dijon)	1		C	C 19/92	p.v.	S		B III 77,p.290		AP, III, 621-23			1	
			N	B III 77	cahier	I		B III 77,p.317		AP, III, 625-28	T		1	Noisy assembly.
			T	C 19/92	B III 77,p.284	I		Ba49		AP, III, 628-34		•	2	
Mans,Le(Tours)	1	Brette,III,578 et seq.	C	Missing	p.v.	I		Ba49	AD I 10	AP, III, 636-40	C		2	Curates opposed other ecclesiastics.
			N	C 19/93	p.v.	G		C 19/93		AP, III, 640-42			1	
			T	C 19/93				Ba49		AP, III, 642-51			1	Unanimous adoption reported.
Nantes(Paris)	1	Brette,III,344 et seq.	C	C 19/94	p.v.	S		B III 80,p.237	Ba50	AP, III, 652-61			1	The curates of St.Croix revised the text drafted by the committee, and his text was adopted.
			N	B III 80,p.316, Bib.Nat.Le23. 231, PR	p.v.	G		B III 80,p.385	Ba50	AP, III, 661-66			1	President patriotic. Condorcet read Memoire, also other Mémoires read. Careful discussion of cahier.
			T	C 19/94	p.v.	G		B III 81,p.3	C 19/94	AP, III, 666-74	T		1	Isabeau de la Gastinière thanked for help.
Marches Communes (Poitiers)	1	Brette,IV,521 et seq.	U	30 p.v., Ba50, and elections of each order, B III 83.				B III 83,p.79		AP, III, 687-89			1	
Marseilles(Aix)	1	D.I.,	C	C 19/96	C 19/96	I		Ba50		Fournier,J.,D.I., 416 et seq.			2	Bishop prevailed.
			N	Missing		H		Ba50		Ibid., 408 et seq.			1	
			T	C 19/96	cahier	H	T	B III 82,p.504	Ba50	Ibid., 358 et seq.		P	1	
Martinique(colony)	7	Paris		Bib.Nat.Le23. 183, PR;Arch. Nat.C 32/270	cahier and p.v.	I		In p.v., PR and MS	See column 5	Unedited text in Appendix.				
Meaux(Paris)	1	Brette,III,338 et seq.	C	C 20/97	cahier	G		C 20/97	Ba51	AP, III, 721-25	C		1	Difficulties over choice of president.

1	2	3	4	5	6	7	8	9	10	11	12 13	14	15
Meaux(Paris) (continued)			N	Bib.Mun.Meaux, MSS	cahier		I	B III 83,p.429	Ba51	AP, III, 725-27		1	Protest against seigniorial justice.
			T	C 20/97	p.v.		S	C 20/97	Ba51	AP, III, 727-32	T	1	Additions to cahier on subject of currency.
Melun(Paris)	1	Brette,III,390 et seq.	C	Ba51	p.v.		I	B III 84,p.307	Ba51	AP, III, 733-39		1	Mémoire on capitaineries added, but is now missing. A necessary supplement for the cahier of the nobles is the Lettres de créances..., Bib.Nat. Le 25.78.
			N	Ba51;Bib.Nat. Le23.245, FR	cahier		S	Ba51	Ba51	AP, III, 739-43	N	1	
			T	C 20/98	B III 84,p.640		S	B III 84,p.609		AP, III, 743-50		1	Gouy d'Arsy influential. Advice given by him for cahier, but assembly adopted cahier. Careful exclusion of non-members from assembly.
Mende(Montpellier)	1		C	C 20/99	p.v.	G		Ba51		AP, III, 751-53		1	Two articles proposed by Marquis de Châteauneuf added. Long section of this cahier was omitted by the AP. Protest against article on the presidial.
			N	C 20/99, PR			I	Ba51		AP, III, 753-55, and see Appendix	N	1	
			T	C 20/99	p.v.	G		B III 85,p.497	Ba51	AP, III, 755-58		2	
Metz(Metz:Metz)	2		C	30 p.v., C 20/100	p.v.	S		B III 86,p.451	AD I 10	AP, III, 759-62	N	1	Metz was a center of reunion of second type of convocation.
			N	Idem / B III 86	cahier		I	B III 86,p.487 / B III 86,p.516	AD I 10 / C 20/101² (2)	AP, III, 762-65 / AP, III, 765-71	T	1	Preliminary cahiers used. Careful adoption. Unanimous adoption reported. The city of Metz was authorized to send deputies directly to the States-General by special concession (Brette,op.cit., Vol.I, p.227). These elections took place in April. The cahier given by the AP as of the city was the cahier made during the regular elections in March. There was also a supplementary election in October, 1789 (Lesprand, in Annuaire...).
			V	C 20/101²	p.v.		I	Ba52 / B III 86,p.625	Ba52	Annuaire de la Soc. hist. et arch. lorraine, 1903,XV, 192 et seq.		1	
Mirecourt(Mirecourt;Nancy)	2	D.I.	C	Arch.Vosges				Ba53		Martin,E., D.I.,258 et seq.		2	Mirecourt was a center of reunion of the second type of convocation. The p.v. for these assemblies exist, Arch.Nat., Ba53.
			N	Ba53	p.v.		I	B III 89,p.146		Ibid, 261 et seq.; M. Supplement,AP,IV, 2-6		1	Protest on taxation and provincial privileges.
			T	Ba53	p.v.		I	B III 89,p.181		Martin,E., D.I.,250 et seq.		1	
Mohon(Sedan:Metz)	2		U	Ba78	p.v.	I	I	U Ba78		AP, V, 729-30		1	
Montargis(Orleans)	1	Brette,III,452 et seq.	C	Ba53	cahier		I	B III 90,p.363	AD I 10	AP, IV, 17-20		1	Speech by bailli. Cahier of third estate read. Careful adoption.
			N	Ba53	p.v.		I	B III 90,p.451	AD I 10 (2)	AP, IV, 20-26		1	Cahier of third estate read in assembly.
			T	C 20/103	p.v.		I	B III 90,p.499, Ba53		AP, IV, 26-31		1	Hurry. Clergy and nobles acted too slowly for united cahier.
Mont-de-Marsan (Bordeaux)	1	Brette,IV,316 et seq.	C	Ba54	cahier		S	Ba54	Ba54	AP, IV, 32-33		1	
			N	Ba54	New powers		I	Missing				1	
			T	30 p.v., Ba54				Ba54	False text was printed	Unedited text in Appendix.		3	The text given by the AP is not a real cahier. Conflict. Cabale against lieutenant general. Second elections (Arch.Nat. AD I 10,C 20/104; Bib.Nat.Le24.107), are not reproduced from the real cahier.

1	2	3	4	5	6	7	8	9	10	11	12	13	14	15
Montfort l'Amaury (Paris)	1	Brette,III,386 et seq.	U	Ba54	p.v.	I	U	B III 91,p.192	Ba54	AP, IV, 37-43	U		1	Protest against the cahier by a lawyer who claimed that it was anticlerical.
Montpellier(Montpellier)	1		C	Ba54	p.v.	G		C 21/106		AP, IV, 44-45			2	Careful adoption. Extant text may be only the text adopted by the committee. Idem.
			N	Ba54, PR	p.v.	I		B III 92,p.427	Ba55	AP, IV, 45-49			1	
			T	Ba54				Ba55		AP, IV, 45-58			1	
Montreuil-sur-mer (Amiens)	1	Brette,III,104 et seq.	C	Missing; see 30 p.v. Ba56				Ba56		AP, IV, 59-61	C		1	
			N	C 21/107	p.v.	I		Ba56		AP, IV, 61-68			1	
			T	C 21/107	p.v.	G		Ba56		AP, IV, 68-71			1	
Morlaix(Morlaix; Rennes)	6		T	C 21/108				Ba26		AP, IV, 75 and 72 et seq.	T	P	1	The cahier of the town was adopted with additions.
Moulins(Moulins)	1	Brette,III,512 et seq.	C	C 21/109				B III 36,p.413	Ba56 (2)	AP, II, 442-44	C		2	This district is sometimes called "Bourbonnais." Authentication lacking. Careful adoption.
			N	C 21/109	New Powers	I		B III 36,p.513	Ba56	AP, II, 444-47			1	
			T	C 21/109				C 21/109	Ba56 (2)	AP, II, 447-49	T		1	
Mouzon(Sedan; Metz)	2		U	Ba78				Missing					1	Unanimous adoption reported. Mention of a text at Arch.Nat. in Revue historique ardennaise, 1889, p.197. No such text has been found.
Nancy(Nancy; Nancy)	2	D.I.	C	See Jerome op.cit., p.36				Missing, but reprinted		Jérome, op.cit., 56 et seq.			1	Nancy was a center of reunion of the second type of convocation. The p.v. of these assemblies are preserved in Arch.Nat. Ba57. Careful adoption. Idem. Additions and corrections of text before adoption.
			N	Ba57, PR				B III 93,p.283 and 293	AD I 10 (2)	AP, IV, 79-84			1	
			T	Ba57 (extract)				Arch.Meurthe-et-Moselle; also Bib.Mun. Nancy,no.851		AP, VI, 644-47, or Godfrin, J., D.I., p.487 et seq.	P		1	
Nantes(Rennes)	6		C[1]	C 21/111, also printed with cahier, Bib.Nat. Le24.249	p.v.	I	C		Bib.Nat.Le24. 249	Unedited text in Appendix			3	Curates hurried. Granted electors power to act for assembly. This was illegal.
			T	Ba26	p.v.	I	T	Ba26(with papers of Guerande)		For corrections of text in AP, IV, 94 et seq., see Appendix.			1	
Navarre(Auch)	3	Brette,IV,175 et seq.	U	Ba60				Arch.Nat.K692A		Bib.Nat. Le2.1161. Pages 263-322 of this publication give the cahier			1	The cahier for Navarre, whose convocation and procedure was exceptional (cf. supra, ch. i), was too long to reprint here. It covers about 100 pages of print. It is a description of the constitution of Navarre and of its relation to France, rather than a program of reform.
Nemours(Paris)	1	Brette,III,332 et seq.	C	C 21/12[1]	p.v.	I		B III 95,p.168	Bib.Nat.Le23. 222	AP, IV, 106-9			1	The Instructions of the Duke of Orléans were read in the assembly.

1	2	3	4	5	6	7	8	9	10	11	12	13	14	15
Nemours(Paris) (continued)			N	B III 95	Action in National Assembly p.v.	I		B III 95,p.213	Ba57 (2)	AP, IV, 109-12			1	The Duke de Noailles furnished a memorandum to serve as a basis for the cahier. The assembly added to this.
			T	C 21/112¹	p.v.	I	T	C 21/112²	Bib.Mat.Le24. 127 (2)	AP, IV, 112-215		T	3	Brette seems to have overlooked the original MS of the cahier. Influence of Dupont de Nemours.
Nérac(Bordeaux)	1	Brette,IV,277 et seq.	C	C 21/113	p.v.	I	C	B III 94,199 bis		AP, IV, 230-32			1	
			N	Ba57	C 21/113	I	B	B III 94, 215	Bib.Mat.Le24. 7	AP, I, 701-3	N		1	
			T	C 21/113				Ba57		AP, IV, 232-35			1	
Neufchateau(Mirecourt:Nancy)	2		C	Missing; see 30	30 p.v.,			Missing					1	
			N	P.v., Ba53	Ba53	I		Missing		Duhamel, op.cit. in Bibliography,II,323 et seq.			2	Protest against the octroi.
			T	Arch.Vosges	cahier	I	T	Arch.Vosges						
Nivernais(Moulins)	1	Brette,III,523 et seq.	C	B III 97	p.v.	I		B III 97,p.703		AP, IV, 246-52	C		1	
			N	C 22/115	cahier	I	B	B III 97,p.759	Ba58 (2)	AP, IV, 252-56			1	
			T	C 22/115	cahier	G	B	B III 97,p.797	Ba58 (2)	AP, IV, 256-61		T	1	
Nîmes(Montpellier)	1	D.I.	C	Ba57	cahier	G		C 21/114, Ba57	Ba57	Bligny-Bondurand, D.I., II,573 et seq.			1	Careful adoption.
			N	Ba57 (MS and also p.v. TR with cahier)	p.v.	I	N	Ba57		Ibid., 579 et seq.			1	Modified arts. 13, 14, 20-24.
			T	Ba57	p.v.	G		B III 96,p.669	Ba57 (2)	Ibid., 588 et seq.			1	Rabaut de St. Etienne influential. Careful adoption.
Nomény(Nancy; Nancy)	2		C	Jérome, op.cit. f.137	p.v.,op.cit.			Missing, but reprinted B III 95,p.609	Ba57	Jérome, op.cit., p.139 et seq.			1	The original used by Jérome has disappeared.
			N	Arch.Meurthe-et-Moselle						AP, IV, 87, art.1-88, art.10, and 92, art.11 to end.			1	The AP confused the texts of N. Nomény and U. Rozières. Note carefully correction. See Jérome, op.cit., p.144, note 1.
			T	Arch.Meurthe-et-Moselle	p.v., also C 21/110	G		Arch.Meurthe-et-Moselle		Unedited text in Appendix.				
Orange(Grenoble)	1		C	Ba59	p.v.	G		C 22/16	Ba59 (2)	AP, IV, 266-67			1	Careful discussion. Preliminary cahiers read aloud. Protests.
			N	Ba59	p.v.	G		Missing		AP, IV, 267-73			1	
			T	C 22/117	p.v.	I		B III 99,p.156					2	
Orléans(Orléans)	1	D.I. and Brette, III, 407 et seq.	C		p.v.	I	C	Arch.Loiret, B supp.141	Ba59 (2)	Bloch,C., D.I., II, 399 et seq.			1	Difficulty over presidency.
			N	C 22/117				B III 99,p.13 Arch.Loiret, B supp.139		Ibid., 422 et seq.			1	Cahier of town followed closely.
			T	C 22/117						Ibid., 399 and 287 et seq.			1	

1	2	3	4	5	6	7	8	9	10	11	12 13	14	15
Paris hors-les-murs (Paris)	1	D.I. and Brette, III,272 et seq.	C	22/120, PR	p.v.	G		B III 112,p-193	C 22/120	Chassin,C., D.I., IV, 393 et seq., and AP., V, 230 et seq.	C	1	Pamphlets read.
			N	C 22/120, PR	p.v.	I		B III 112,p-414	C 22/120 (3)	Chassin,IV,419 et seq.; AP,V, 235 et seq.		1	Mémoires influential. Petition for representation of St. Domingue presented, as well as others by Favras, Comte de Moreton-Chabrillant, etc. Petition in behalf of St. Domingue read.
			T	C 22/120				B III 112,p-508	C 22/120	Chassin,IV, 429 et seq; AP,V, 237 et seq.		1	
Paris-intra-muros (Paris)	4	Brette,III,317 et seq.	C	22/119, PR	cahier	S		B III 114,p-249	C 22/119	Chassin,C., D.I.,III, 305,et seq., AP, V, 263 et seq.	C	2	Elections carried on at the same time as composition of cahier. According to the royal instructions, the cahier should have been completed first.
			N	B III 114	cahier	I		B III 114,p-470	AD I 11 (2)	Chassin,III,321 et seq.,AP,V,271 et seq.		1	Patriotic mémoires read in assembly, and given to deputies to take to States-General.
			T	C 22/119				B III 114,p-669	AD I 11	Chassin,III,333 et seq.,AP,V,281 et seq.	T	1	Mémoires deposited at Hotel Le Ville used. Careful discussion.
			Mun.	Ba64, PR				Ba63	Ba64 (2)	Chassin,III,400 et seq.,AP,V,290 et seq.	M	1	Some question of influence of Abbé de Barmont.
Périgord (Bordeaux)	1	Brette,IV,336 et seq.	C	Ba66	p.v. and Bussière op.cit. Ba66	I	Missing	Missing	Ba66	AP, V, 338-41		2	See Bussière, op.cit., Vol.II, p-198. Although the cahier has been lost, this author describes its contents, deduced from the Compte-rendu a leurs commettants...
			N	Ba66	30 p.v., Ba66	I	N	B III 117,p-448	Ba66			1	
			T	30 p.v., Ba66	Supplement to cahier, Ba66,MS	G			AD I 11	AP, V, 342-44	T	3	Disorder. Letter of lieutenant general affirms that changes were made in cahier after its adoption.
Péronne (Amiens)	1	Brette,III,84 et seq.	C	C 22/123	p.v.	G		B III 118,p-411	Ba67 (2)	AP, V, 347-55	C	2	Curates in a hurry.
			N	Ba67, PR	p.v., also Bib.Nat. Le23.169	G / I		B III 118,p-559	Ba67 (2)	AP, V, 355-61	NT	1	Careful discussion. Parish cahiers read.
			T	C 22/123	cahier	I							
Perpignan (Perpignan)	1		C	C 22/124	p.v.	G / I	Missing	Missing B III 119,p-403	See note in Hyslop, Repertoire critique...p.581	AP, V, 368-73	N	1 / 1	Trouble over signing cahiers. Unanimous adoption reported.
			T	30 p.v., C 22/123	cahier	I		Ba67		AP, V, 373-77	T	3	Trouble between town delegates and country delegates. Direct accusation that cahier is not representative.
Plöermel (Rennes)	6		T	C 22/125	cahier	I	T	Arch.Morbihan, B3340	Ba26	AP, V, 378-85	T	1	Careful discussion.
Poitiers (Poitiers)	1	Brette,IV,463 et seq.	C	C 22/126	p.v.	G		C 22/126		AP, V, 389-94	C	3	Bishop of Lucon influential. Elections before making of cahier. This was illegal.
			N	30 p.v., Ba68	p.v.	I / N		Ba68	AD I 11	AP, V, 394-97		2	Mémoires on provincial assembly and renunciation of privileges read. Authentication lacking.
			T	C 22/126	p.v.	I		Ba68	Bib.Nat.Le24. 276	AP, V, 406-15	T	3	Protest against cahier as too radical.

1	2	3	4	5	6	7	8	9	10	11	12 13	14	15
Pondichéry (Colony)	7	Colony		C 42/366		I	C	C 42/368		AP, VI, 235-36		2	The cahier was accompanied by six Mémoires, which are preserved in MS, Arch.Nat. C 42/366. The six are entitled as follows: 1) Exposé abrégé de la position dans laquelle les citoyens des établissements français dans l'Inde...; 2) Mémoire pour demander des représentants à l'Assemblée nationale de France; 3) Mémoire sur les avantages et la nécessité du commerce dans l'Inde; 4) Mémoire pour demander protection pour le commerce et une exemption dans le cas où le commerce de l'Inde serait exploité par une compagnie nationale ou autre; 5) Mémoire au sujet de l'évacuation de Pondichéry; 6) Mémoire au sujet des alliances avec les princes de l'Inde. The seventh Mémoire, Réponse aux objections qu'il est possible que l'on fasse à la demande que forment les Français établis dans l'Inde is missing. There is also in this same series, a memorandum from the Malabres, both in their native language and in French translation.
Pont-à-Mousson (Bar-le-duc:Nancy)	2		C	Ba19	p.v.			Ba19	AD I 11	AP, II, 228		1	Careful adoption.
			N	Ba19	p.v.	I		Ba19	AD I 11	AP, II, 228-30	N	1	
			T	Ba19		I		Ba19	AD I 11	AP, II, 230-34		1	
Ponthieu (Amiens)	1	Brette,III,97 et seq.	C	C 22/127	Action in National Assembly				AD I 10	AP, V, 428-30	N	1	This district is sometimes called "Abbeville."
			N	C 22/127	p.v.	I		Ba9		AP, V, 430-36		1	
			T	C 22/127	p.v.	I		Ba9	AD I 10	AP, V, 435-44	T	1	Complaints against lieutenant general.
Provins (Paris)	1	Brette,III,326 et seq.	C	C 23/128	p.v. and cahier	S		B III 125,p.157	C 23/128	AP, V, 445-47	C	1	
			N	C 23/128; PR in 30 P.v.	cahier			B III 125,p.214	C 23/128	AP, V, 447-52	N	1	
			T	C 23/128	p.v.	G		C 23/128	C 23/128	AP, V, 452-55	T	1	Confusion.
Puy-en-Velay (Montpellier)	1		C	C 23/129	cahier	I		B III 125,p.291	Ba70	AP, V, 456-68		3	Bishop opposed to curates. Authentication incomplete.
			N	C 23/129	C 23/129	I		Missing		AP, V, 469-72	T	1	Disorder. Lieutenant general abused power. Authentication incomplete.
			T	30 p.v., C 23/129	cahier	I		Ba70	Ba70			3	
Quatre-Vallées (Auch)	5	Brette,IV,92 et seq.	T	Ba70				B III 126,p.98	B III 126,p.98	AP, III, 413-15		1	Patriotic speech, careful discussion.
Quesnoy (Valenciennes)	1		C	C 23/131	p.v.	G		Missing		AP, V, 503-507		2	Protest.
			N	Ba71, PR	cahier	S		B III 128,p.147	Ba71			1	Careful adoption.
			T	C 23/131	p.v.	I	T	Missing				1	Preliminary cahiers read.
Quimper (Rennes)	6	D.I.	C^R	C 23/132	p.v.	I		Missing		Savina and Bernard, D.I.,II,360 et seq.		1	The cahier given by the AP is the cahier of the sénéchaussée of Quimper and not the general cahier of Quimper and Concarneau united.
			T	AD I 9, PR	p.v.	I		Arch.Finistère				1	
Reims (Châlons)	1	D.I., and Brette,III,227 et seq.	C	Ba71	cahier	G		Ba71	Ba71	AP, V, 520-26	C	1	The volume of the D.I. does not give the general cahiers.
			N	Ba71	cahier	I		B III 129,p.269	Ba71	AP, V, 526-30		1	The members swore secrecy on activities of assembly.
			T	Ba71	C 23/133	S		B III 129,p.361	Ba71	AP, V, 530-55	T	1	

1	2	3	4	5	6	7	8	9	10	11	12	13	14	15
Remiremont(Mire-Court:Nancy)	2		U	Ba53, idem for p.v. of each order				Missing					1	
Rennes(Rennes)	6	D.I.	Cl	C 23/134, PR	New Powers cahier	I S	C T	B III 37,p.522	Bib.Nat.Lb24. 208 AD I 11	See and Lessort,D.I., IV, 287 et seq. Ibid., IV,239 et seq.			1	Lanjuinais influential.
Rhuys(Vannes:Rennes)	6		T	Missing	p.v., T, Vannes	I	T	Missing						
Riom(Riom)	1	Brette,III,638 et seq.	C N T	Ba72 Ba72, PR C 23/136, PR with 30 p.v.	cahier cahier	I I	C N T	Ba72 B III 14,p.638 B III 14,p.520	Ba72 (2) Ba72 (2)	AP, V, 561-63 AP, V, 565-68 AP, V, is a false text; see reprint in Appendix.	C		2 1 2	Bishop opposed arts. 27, 30, 45-47. Mémoires read aloud, including Instructions of Duke of Orléans. See Brette, op.cit., Vol.III, p.638, on text of cahier. Hurry for spring planting. Town dominant. Preliminary cahiers used. Duke of Orléans's Instructions read. Malouet influential.
Rivière-Verdun (Auch)	1	Brette,IV,127 et seq.	C N T	C 23/137 C 23/137 C 23/137	cahier p.v. p.v.	G I I	N	Ba85 Ba85 Ba85	Arch.Haute-Garonne	AP, V, 581-83 AP, V, 583-06 AP, V, 586-89	N T		1 1 1	Careful adoption.
Rochefort(La Rochelle)	5	Brette,IV,408 et seq.	T					C 23/138		AP, III, 486, and see supplement in Appendix.			1	
Rodez(Montauban)	1	Brette,IV,41 et seq.	C N T	Ba73 C 23/135 C 23/135	cahier p.v. cahier	G I G		Ba73 Ba73 Be73		AP, V, 551-54 AP, V, 555-57 AP, V, 557-59	C T		1 1 1	This is sometimes spelled "Rhodez." Authentication lacking for all three cahiers.
Rouen(Rouen)	1		C N T V	C 22/139 Ba76 C 23/139 Arch.Mun.Rouen, A 40	cahier cahier p.v.	S I G		B III 131, p.769 B III 13, p.901 Arch.Seine-Inférieure	Ba76 (2) Ba76 (2) Voted to print	AP, V, 590-94 AP, V, 594-97 See Appendix AP, V, 597-602	C N	P	1 2 2	Mémoires used. Careful discussion. Unanimous adoption. Protest. Elections before cahier was finished. Careful adoption. A carton containing a nearly complete collection of the cahiers of the grand bailliage of Rouen was discovered just recently. The cahier of the third estate, hitherto missing, will be published by M.Le Parquier, who has already edited several volumes of cahiers from Normandy. Due to the influence of Thouret, the cahier of the town of Rouen, the preliminary cahier, and the general cahier are very similar. A summary of the differences between the town cahier, which is reprinted in the Archives Parlementaires, Vol.V, pp.597-602, and the general cahier of the third estate is given in the Appendix of the present volume.
Rozières(Nancy: Nancy)	2		U	Ba57	p.v.	I	U	B III 93,p.579	Ba57	AP, IV, 91, arts. 1-10, and 88, art.11 to end	U		1	Cf. supra under "Roméry," on confusion of texts. Unanimous adoption.

1	2	3	4	5	6	7	8	9	10	11	12	13	14	15
Rustaing(Auch)	5	Brette,IV,144 et seq.	T	C 33/281	p.v.	I	T	Ba80		AP,II,366-72			1	Unanimous adoption.
St.Aubin-du-Cormier(Fougères: Rennes)	6		T	Ba25				Missing					1	
St.Brieuc(St. Brieuc:Rennes)	6	C	Ba25	p.v.			C 16/66²	Ba25 (2)	AP,V,627			1	The C. refused to send deputies, and drew up a declaration of protest.
			N	Ba25				Idem	Ba25 (2)	AP,V,627-29			1	Idem.
			Cl	Missing				Missing						
			T	Ba25	p.v.	I		Ba25	Voted to print	AP,V,629-32	T		1	Protests against method of convocation.
St.Dié(Mirecourt: Nancy)	2		C	Ba53	New Powers	I		Missing	Arch.Haut-Rhin	See unedited text in Appendix.			1	
			N	Ba53		I		Missing					1	
			T	Ba53	p.v.	I							1	
St.Domingue (colony)	7	D.I. [Paris] [Colony]	Colony	B III 135				C 86/15		Petition reprinted in Appendix			2	The request for admission to the National Assembly, reprinted as a near substitute for a cahier, exists in MS in Arch.Nat. C 86/15. The cahier must be supplemented by the other two documents: the reservations of the assembly of the West and a document on the assemblies. See D.I. volume.
				C 24/143		G			Arch.Nat.DXXV 13, liasse 122,piece 8	Maurel, B., D.I., 265-302			1	
St.Flour(Riom)	1	Brette,III,666 et seq.	C	C 24/144	p.v.	G		Missing					1	Full authentication is lacking. Text now mutilated.
			N	B III 136,p.167	p.v.	I		Arch.Aun.St. Flour		AP,VI,690-91			2	Idem. Bailli dictatorial. Unanimous adoption reported.
			T	C 24/144	p.v.	G		Idem;and Arch. Cantal, 4B.		AP,VI,691-95			3	
St.Jean d'Angely (La Rochelle)	1	Brette,IV,416 et seq.	C	C 24/141	C 24/141	S		C 24/141		AP,V,633-64			1	Mesnard does not indicate where he found the text which he reprints.
			N	Ba45		I		Missing		Reprint from MS by Mesnard,A., op.cit., 40 et seq. AP,XXXII,521-22			1	
			T	Ba45	cahier		T	Arch.Charente-Inferieure					1	
St.Malo(Rennes)	6	D.I.	Cl	C 24/145					Bib.Château de la Hanon-ais	Sée and Lessort,D.I. IV, 306 et seq.			1	
St.Mihiel(Bar-le-duc:Nancy)	2		C	Ba19	p.v.	G		Arch.Meuse	Ba19	Will be published soon in France			1	Publication of this text has been promised; probably in a regional publication.
			N	Ba19	Ba19	S		B III 23,p.585		AP,II,235-44	N		1	Unanimous adoption reported.
			T	Ba19	p.v.	S		Missing					1	

1	2	3	4	5	6	7	8	9	10	11	12 13	14	15
St.Pierre-le-Moutier(Moulins)	1	Brette,III,534 et seq.	C C 24/146	C 24/146	p.v.	G		Missing		AP, V, 635		1	Difficulty over presidency.
			N C 24/146	C 24/146	p.v.	G		Ba68	Ba68			3	Conflict with Bailli, who was accused of having substituted a text for the cahier adopted by the assembly. The document which we have contains only two articles and resembles a mandate rather than a cahier.
			T C 24/146	C 24/146	p.v.	S		B III 138,p.329		AP, V, 635-42		1	
St.Pol-de-Léon (Rennes)	6		C? Made none	Made none				Made none				1	Duchâtellier (Histoire de la Révolution dans les départements de l'ancienne Bretagne, Vol.I, pp.144-47), explains the p.v. and the fact that no cahier was made.
St.Quentin(Amiens)	1	Brette,III,128 et seq.	C Ba70	Ba70	p.v.	G		Ba70		AP, V, 647-52	C	2	Authentication lacking. Preliminary cahiers and pamphlets given committee. Unanimous adoption reported.
			N C 24/147	C 24/147	Ba70	S		B III 137,p.251	Ba70 (2)	AP, V, 652-53		1	Parish cahiers given to committee.
			T Ba70	Ba70	p.v.	G		Ba70	AD I 11 (2)	AP, V, 653-58	P	1	
Saintes(La Rochelle)	1	Brette,IV,428 et seq.	C C 24/140	C 24/140	cahier	S		Ba77	AD I 11	AP, V, 659-65		2	Mémoire given to committee. Careful adoption. Authentication lacking on extant text.
			N C 24/140	C 24/140	cahier	I		B III 139,p.366 et seq., and p.375	Ba77	AP, V, 665-69		2	Authenticity questioned.
			T C 24/140	C 24/140	Ba77	S		Ba77	Ba77	AP, V, 669-74	T	1	The cahiers of Ile d'Oleron and of Saintes (ville) are part of the general cahier.
Sarrebourg and Phalsbourg(Metz: Metz)	2		C Ba52	Ba52				B III 87,p.577		AP, III, 784-85		2	Reprint promised. Probably in learned review of northeastern department. The C. and N. met in advance of the general assembly and drew up a plan for the cahier. The cahiers adopted resemble this very closely.
			N Ba52	Ba52	cahier	I		Arch.Meurthe-et-Moselle Idem		To be published in France Idem		2	Idem.
			T Ba52	Ba52	cahier	I				See unedited text in Appendix.		1	
Sarreguemines (Sarreguemines: Nancy)	2		C Ba77	Ba77	p.v.	G		Ba77		AP, V, 689-90	C	1	Sarreguemines was a center of reunion of the second type of convocation. The p.v. of these assemblies is complete in Arch. Nat. B III 133.
			N Ba77	Ba77	New Powers	I		Ba77		AP, V, 690-92	N	1	
			T Ba77	Ba77	p.v.	I		Arch.Moselle, B 8.238		See unedited text in Appendix.		1	
Sarrelouis(Metz: Metz)	2		CN Ba52	Ba52	p.v.	G		B III 87,p.149-56		Unedited text in Appendix.		1	The cahier of the town, not the general cahier, exists in Arch.Sarrelouis, and was reprinted in Bull.de la Soc. des amis de la Sarre, 1925, pp.23-43.
			T Ba52	Ba52	p.v.	I		Missing				1	
Saumur(Tours)	1	Brette,IV,664 et seq.	C Ba78	Ba78	cahier	S		B III 140,p.329	AD I 11	AP, V, 718-20		1	Bailli makes speech. Unanimous adoption reported. Authentication incomplete.
			N Ba78	Ba78	cahier	I		B III 140,p.408	AD I 11	AP, V, 720-23		2	A text, Arch.Nat. Ba78, is incomplete, and the contemporary copy, B III 140, is more reliable.
			T B III 140,p.292	B III 140,p.292	cahier	I		B III 140,p.452	Ba78 (2)	AP, V, 725-26	T	1	

1	2	3	4	5	6	7	8	9	10	11	12 13	14	15
Sedan(Sedan:Metz)	2		C	Missing, see 30 p.v., Ba78				Missing					
			N	Idem				Missing B III 141,p.195	Ba78				
			T	Ba78	p.v.	I	T			AP, V, 727-28		1	Sedan was a center of reunion of the second type of convocation. The p.v. are in Arch.Nat. Ba78.
Semur-en-Auxois (Dijon)	1		C	Ba78	p.v.	G		Arch.Cote d'Or and Arch.Nat. B III 17,p.254 et seq.		AP, II, 126-28	C	1	Conflict between curates and higher clergy.
			N	Ba78	p.v.	I	I	Ba78		AP, II, 128-31	N	1	Mémoire on Provincial-Estates used.
			T	Ba78	p.v.	I	I	Ba78		AP, II, 131-33		1	
Senlis(Paris)	1	Brette,III,358 et seq.	C	Ba79	p.v.	G		Missing		AP, V, 734-36		2	The printed text, Bib.Nat.Lb39.1495, with a blank for the name of the bailliage is not the cahier. Protest against equal liability for taxation for all three orders, and against representation granted to clergy.
			N	Ba79	p.v.	I		B III 142, p.144	Ba79			1	
			T	Ba79	p.v.	I		B III 142, p.179	AD I 11 (2)	AP, V, 736-43;also, 743-47		1	Notice the supplement on provincial administration.
Sens(Paris)	1	Brette,III,374 et seq.; and D.I.	C	Ba79	p.v.			Ba79		Porée,C.,D.I., 787 et seq.		1	Unanimous adoption reported.
			N	Ba79	p.v.			B III 143, p.295 Ba79	AD I 11 (2)	Ibid.,801 et seq.		1	
			T	Ba79	p.v.					Ibid.,813 et seq.		1	
Sézanne(Chalons)	1	D.I. and Brette, III,219 et seq.	C	C 24/153	p.v.	G		C 24/153 or Ba79 p.248		Laurent,G., D.I.,464 et seq.		1	Preliminary cahiers read.
			N	C 24/153	B III 144,p.272	I		Ba79	Ba79	Ibid., 472 et seq.		1	
			T	C 24/153	p.v.	G		Arch.Revol. Sézanne		Ibid., 486 et seq.		1	Unanimous adoption reported.
Sisteron(Forcalquier:Aix)	2		C	Missing, see 30 p.v., Ba41	p.v., Forcalquier	I		B III 66^2, p.644		AP, III, 361-63		1	
			N	B III 66^2				B III 66^2, p.821		AP, III, 363-65		1	
			T	30 p.v., Ba41				Missing				1	Unanimous adoption. Cahier signed by those who knew how to sign.
Soissons(Soissons)	1	Brette,III,137 et seq.	C	C 24/154	p.v.	G		C 24/154		AP, V, 768-73		1	Careful adoption.
			N	C 24/154	p.v.	G		Missing, but reprinted		AP, VI, 696-700		1	Turbulent. The text has been lost, or mislaid, due to disruption of Arch.Aisne, during the German occupation of the Great War.
			T	30 p.v.,C 24/154								3	
Soule(Auch)	1	Brette,IV,152 et seq.	C	Ba80	p.v.	I	C	Ba80		AP, V, 774-76	C	1	Elections in June and July, 1789.
			N	Ba80	New Powers	I	N	Ba80		AP, V, 776-79		1	Idem. Questioned wisdom of sending deputy, because of expense. Vote to send one. Minority withdrew from assembly. Careful adoption.

1	2	3	4	5	6	7	8	9	10	11	12 13	14	15
Soule(Auch) (continued)			T	Ba80	p.v.	G		B III 145, p.290	Ba80	AP, V, 779-83		1	Idem. Asked for partial alienation of property.
Strasbourg (Strasbourg)	4		T	Ba80	p.v.	G		Arch.Mun.Strasbourg AA 2001	Reuss,R.,op.cit., I, 31-66		1	The cahier given by the AP is not the general cahier.
Tartas(Bordeaux)	1	Brette,IV,289 et seq.	C	C 24/156	p.v.	G		Made none	Bib.Nat.Le24.7	AP, I, 699-701		2	No proper verification possible, yet appears valid.
			N	Missing, see 30 p.v., C 24/156									
			T	C 24/156	p.v.	G		Arch.Comm.II[3]		AP, I, 704-7		1	The cahier was reprinted by Cauna (Armorial des Landes) before it was lost. Praise by assembly for royal officers.
Thiaucourt(Bar- le-duc:Nancy)	2		C	30 p.v.; C 15/202				Arch.Mun. Thiaucourt		Annales de l'Est, 1904, XVIII, 357 et seq		1	Preliminary cahiers read.
			N	Idem				Idem		Idem, 365 et seq.		1	
			T	Idem				Idem		Idem, 370 et seq.		1	
Thionville(Metz: Metz)	2		C	Ba52	p.v.	G		Ba52	Ba52	AP, III, 773-74		2	Protest against arts.6,16.
			N	Ba52				Ba52		AP, III, 774-76		1	Unanimous adoption reported.
			T	Ba52				Ba52		AP, III, 776 et seq. and Annuaire de la Soc.hist. et arch. lorraine, 1904, XVI, 90 et seq.		1	Adopted cahier of town with supplement.
Toul(Toul:Metz)	2		C	C 25/157	p.v.	G		B III 147, p.164	Ba81	AP, VI, 1-4	C	1	Toul was a center of reunion of the second type of convocation.
			N	30 p.v., C 24/157	p.v.	I		B III 147, p.205	Ba81	AP, VI, 4-8		1	The p.v. of these assemblies are in Arch.Nat. C 24/157.
			T	C 24/157	p.v.	G		B III 147, p.263	Ba81 (3)	AP, VI, 8-16	T	1	
Toulon(Toulon:Aix)	2		C	Ba81	p.v.	G		Missing		Unedited text in Appendix.		3	Toulon was a center of reunion of the second type of convocation. These p.v. are in Arch.Nat. Ba81. Withdrawals from assembly. Elections before cahier. Power to make cahier delegates. This was illegal.
			N	Ba81	p.v.	I	N	Missing				1	Whole assembly made cahier.
			T	Ba81	p.v.	G		Ba81					Whole assembly made cahier. The text given by the AP is the cahier of the town.
Toulouse(Toulouse)	1		C	C 24/159	p.v.	I		C 24/159	Br.Mus. R 40; Arch.Herault, C 879	AP, VI, 28-31		1	Careful adoption.
			N	B III 148,p.734	New Assembly C 24/159	I		Ba82	Bib.Nat.Le24. 253	AP, VI, 31-35	N	1	Careful adoption.
			T	C 24/159		S		B III 148, p.985	Ba82 (2)	AP, VI, 35-38	T	1	
Tours(Tours)	1	Brette,IV,537 et seq.	C	C 24/160	p.v.	G		Ba83	C 24/160 (2)	Faye,H.,op.cit. in Bibliography	N	3	The original of this cahier has been lost. The text cited is merely a summary of the articles, without authentication.
			N	C 24/160; AP, VI, 44				B III 150, p.475		AP, VI, 39-44		1	
			T	C 24/160				B III 150, p.363, Ba83		AP, VI, 52-54		3	Idem.

1	2	3	4	5	6	7	8	9	10	11	12	13	14	15
Tréguier (Rennes)	6	D.I. for Rennes	Cf	C 24/161				Ba26		Sée and Lessort, D.I., IV,312 et seq.			1	
Trévoux (Dijon)	1		C B III 151 N Ba83, PR T 30 p.v., C 25/162	B III 151 Ba83, PR C 25/162	p.v. p.v.	I T I T		Missing B III 151, p.157 B III 151, p.229	Ba83 Ba83	AP, VI, 65-68 AP, VI, 68-71			2 1 1	Text tampered with. Cahiers and mémoires read aloud. Unanimous adoption reported.
Troyes (Châlons)	1	D.I., and Brette,III, 235 et seq.	C C 25/163 N C 25/163 T C 25/163	Ba84 Ba84 Ba84	cahier	I		B III 151, p.319 B III 151, p.412 B III 151, p.465	AD I 11 Ba83 Ba83	Vernier,J.J.,D.I., III, 445 et seq. Ibid., 460 et seq. Ibid., 478 et seq.			2 1 1	Curates dominant. Protests.
Tulle (Limoges)	1	Brette,III,575 et seq.	C C 25/164 N Ba84 T C 25/164	Ba84 Ba84 Ba84	cahier	I		B III 73², p.119 B III 73², p.131 B III 73², p.189	Ba84 (2) Ba84 AD I 10	AP, III, 536-37 AP, III, 537-39 AP, III, 540-42	P	N	1 1 1	Tulle sometimes went by the name "Bas-Limousin." Unanimous adoption reported. Protest by an abbé. Cahier drawn up by Theatins given to deputy. Mémoire on privileges of Vicomte de Turenne added to cahier.
Uztaritz (Bordeaux)	1	Brette,IV,384 et seq.	C Ba84 T Ba84	Ba84 Ba84	cahier p.v.	I S		C 25/165	Bib.Mat.Le24. 256 Bib.Mun.Bay- onne (Reprint of 1874, orig- inal burned)	AP, III, 423-25 AP, III, 425-27 Text reprinted in Appendix.	P		1 1	This district is sometimes called "Labour." This cahier was reprinted in 1874. The copy at the Bib.Nat. La32.510 is missing. It seems wise to reprint the text. The original appeared in Basque and in French.
Valenciennes (Valenciennes)	4		T C 25/166	C 25/166	p.v.	G		B III 152, p.377	Ba84	AP, VI, 99-105	T	P	1	
Vannes (Vannes: Rennes)	6		Cf T Ba26	Missing Ba26	p.v.	I T		Missing B III 37, p.875	AD I 11, Ba26	AP, VI, 100-112	T		1	Mémoire on commerce added to cahier.
Vendôme (Orléans)	1	Brette,III,462 et seq.	C C 25/168 N Ba84 T Ba84	C 25/168 Ba84 Ba84	B III 152 cahier	G I		C 25/168 Ba84 Ba84	Ba84	AP, VI, 118-20 AP, VI, 120-22 AP, VI, 122-26	C	N	2 1 1	Authentication lacking. Mémoire of Société des Amis des Noirs read. Unanimous adoption reported.
Verdun (Verdun: Metz)	2		C Ba84 N Ba84 T Ba84	Ba84 Ba84 Ba84	p.v. p.v. p.v.	G I G		Ba84 B III 153, p.344 Arch.Meuse	Voted to print C 25/169 Arch.Meuse	AP, VI, 126-30 AP, VI, 130-33 La Revolution fran- çaise, revue, 1897, XXXII	C		1 1 1	Verdun was a center of reunion of the second type of convoca- tion. The p.v. of these assemblies are given in Arch.Nat. B III 153. Unanimous adoption recorded.

1	2	3	4	5	6	7	8	9	10	11	12	13	14	15
Vermandois(Soissons)	1	Brette,III,166 et seq.	C	Arch.Aisne				B III 154,p.299	Ba46	AP, VI, 134-37		P	2	This district is also called "Laon."
			N	Ba46, PR				B III 154,p.357	Ba46 (2)	AP, VI, 137-44			1	Curates against gros-décimateurs. A special section on military demands was added to the cahier, Bib.Nat. Le24.192.Arch.Nat. C 25/170.
			T	C 25/70	p.v.	G		B III 154,p.407	Ba46	AP, VI, 144-48			2	Turbulence. Unanimous adoption reported.
Vézelise(Nancy: Nancy)	2	D.I.	C	Ba57				Missing, but reprinted		Etienne,C., D.I.,448 et seq.			1	The original cahier of the clergy has disappeared.
			N	Ba57	p.v.	G		Missing					1	
			T	Ba57		G		Arch.Meurthe et Moselle		Ibid, 457 et seq.			1	
Vic(Toul:Metz)	2	D.I.	C	Ba81	p.v.	G		Ba81		AP, VI, 16-18	N		1	The volume of D.I. does not give the general cahiers.
			N	Ba81		G		Ba81		AP, VI, 16-19	T		1	
			T	Ba81	p.v.			Ba81		AP, VI, 20-22			1	
Villefranche-de-Beaujolais(Lyon)	1	Brette,III,712 et seq.	C	Ba85	p.v.	S		Ba85		AP, II, 279-81	C		1	Difficulty over president. Careful adoption.
			N	Ba85	p.v.	I		Ba85		AP, II, 281-82	N		1	
			T	30 p.v., Ba85	p.v.	S				AP, II, 282-86	T		1	
Villefranche-en-Rouergue(Montauban)	1	Brette,IV,52 et seq.	C	C 25/71				Missing					1	Protests.
			N	Ba85, PR with cahier	p.v.	I	N	Ba85	Ba85	AP, VI, 166-69			1	Careful adoption reported.
			T	C 25/71				B III 155,p.468	Ba85	AP, VI, 169-71			2	Changes in margin. Authentication lacking.
Villeneuve-de-Berg(Montpellier)	1		C	C 25/72				Arch.Hérault C 879, or Arch. Ardèche, B 142	Ba85	AP, VI, 702-6			1	Comte d'Antraigues influential.
			N	Ba85, PR	cahier	I		Ba85	Voted to print	AP, VI, 177-82	N		1	Unanimous adoption reported.
			T	C 25/72	cahier	I		Arch.Hérault,C 879 or Arch. Ardèche, B 142		AP, VI, 707-14	T		1	
Villers-Cotterets(Soissons)	1	Brette,III,149 et seq.	C	Ba86	New Powers	I		Ba86		AP, VI, 187-88	N		1	Authentication appearing on MS has not been reprinted by AP.
			N	Ba86	cahier	I		Ba86		AP, VI, 189-91			1	
			T	Ba86	p.v.	S		Ba86		AP, VI, 191-93			1	
Villers-la-Montagne(Bar-le-duc: Nancy)	2		U	p.v. of each order in Ba19				B III 23, p.859	Ba19	AP, II, 244-46			1	
Vitry-le-François(Châlons)	1	Brette,III,200 et seq.	C	Ba86	p.v.	S		C 25/174		AP, VI, 206-11	C		1	Authentication lacking.
			N	B III 157	p.v.	I		Arch.Mun.Vitry		AP, VI, 715-20			1	Instructions of Duke of Orléans given to committee.
			T	Ba86, in 30 p.v.				C 25/174		AP, VI, 211-21	T	P	2	

ALPHABETICAL LIST OF GENERAL CAHIERS OF 1789

Abbreviations: C—clergy; C¹—lower clergy; N—Nobles; T—third Estate; U—the three orders united; V—town; two letters together—the two orders united.

Letters in italics signify that the cahier is missing.

DISTRICTS IN FRANCE

Agen, C, N, T; Aix C, N, T; Alençon C, N, T; Amiens C, N, T; Amont U, T; Angers C, N, T; Angoulême C, N, T; Annonay C, N, T; Arches et Charleville U; Arles (*sénéchaussée*) *C, N, T;* Arles(ville) C, NT; Armagnac C, N, T; Artois C, N, T; Auch C, N, T; Auray T; Autun C, N, T; Auxerre C, N, T; Aval C, N, T; Avesnes C, N, T; Bailleul C, N, T; Bar-le-duc *C,* N, T; Bar-sur-Seine C, N, T; Barcelonnette C, T; Bassigny-Barrois U; Bazas C, N, T; Béarn CN, *C¹,* T; Beauvais C, N, T; Belfort C, *N,* T; Bellême C, N, T; Belley C, N, T; Besançon C, N, T; Beziers C, N, *T;* Bigorre C, *N,* T; Bitche C, *N, T;* Blamont C, *N, T;* Blois C, N, T; Bordeaux C, N, T; Boulay C, *N,* T; Boulogne-sur-Mer C, N, T; Bourg-en-Bresse U; Bourges C, N, T; Bourmont C, N, T; Bouzonville C, N, T; Brest T; Briey *C,* N, T; Brignoles *C, N, T;* Bruyères CT, N; Caen C, N, T; Cahors C, N, T; Calais C, N, T; Cambrésis *C,* N, T; Carcassonne C, N, T; Carhaix T; Carignan *C, NT;* Castellane C, *N, T;* Castelmoron d'Albret C, N, T; Castelnaudary C, N, T; Castres C, N, T; Caudebec-en-Caux C, N, T; Chalon-sur-Saône C, N, T; Châlons-sur-Marne C, N, T; Charmes *C, N, T;* Charolles C, N, T; Chartres C, N, T; Château-Salins C, *N,* T; Château-Thierry *C,* N, T; Châteauneuf-en-Thimerais C, N, T; Châtellerault C, *N,* T; Châtel-sur-Moselle *C,* N, T; Châtillon-sur-Seine C, N, T; Chaumont-en-Bassigny C, N, T; Chaumont-en-Vexin *C,* N. T; Clermont-en-Beauvoisis C, N, T; Clermont à Varennes *U;* Clermont Ferrand C, N, T; Colmar and Schlestadt C, N, T; Commercy *C, N, T;* Comminges *C,* N, T; Condom C, N, T; Corse *C,* N, T; Couserans *C, NT;* Coutances C, N, T; Crépy-en-Valois C, N, T; Darney *C, N, T;* Dauphiné U; Dax C, N, T; Dieuze C, N, T; Digne C, N, T; Dijon C, N, T; Dinan T; Dix Villes T; Dol C¹; Dôle C, N, T; Dorat C, N, T; Douai C, N, T; Dourdan C, N, T; Draguignan C, *N,* T; Epinal *C, N, T;* Etain C, N, T; Etampes C, *N,* T; Evreux C, N, T; Fénestrange U; Foix *C,* N, T; Forcalquier C, N, T; Forez C, N, T; Fougères *T;* Gex C, N, T; Gien C, N, T; Grasse C, T; Guéret C, N, T; Haguenau and Wissembourg *C, N,* T; Hédé *T;* Hennebont *T;* Hyères *C, N, T;* Jugon *T;* La Marche C, *N,* T; Langres U, *N,* T; Lannion T; La Rochelle *C,* N, T; Lesneven T; Libourne C, N, T; Lille C, N, T; Limoges C, N, T; Limoux C, N, T; Lixheim CN, T; Longuyon C, N, T; Longwy C, N, T; Loudun C, N, T; Lunéville C, N, *T;* Lyon C, N, T, V; Mâcon C, N, T; Mans C, N, T; Mantes C, N, T; Marches Communes U; Marseille C, N, T; Meaux C, N, T; Melun C, N, T; Mende C, N, T; Metz C, N, T, V; Mirecourt C, N, T; Mohon U; Montargis C, N, T; Mont-de-Marsan C, *N,* T; Montfort l'Amaury U; Montpellier C, N, T; Montreuil-sur-mer C, N, T; Morlaix T; Moulins C, N, T; Mouzon *U;* Nancy C, N, T; Nantes C¹, T; Navarre U; Nemours C, N, T; Nérac C, N, T; Neufchâteau *C, N,* T; Nivernais C, N, T; Nîmes C, N, T; Nomény C, N, T; Orange

ALPHABETICAL LIST OF GENERAL CAHIERS OF 1789

C, *N*, T; Orléans C, N, T; Paris *hors-les-murs* C, N, T; Paris *intra-muros* C, N, T, V; Périgord *C*, N, T; Péronne C, NT; Perpignan *C*, N, T; Ploërmel T; Poitiers C, N, T; Pont-à-Mousson C, N, T; Ponthieu C, N, T; Provins C, N, T; Puy-en-Velay C, *N*, T; Quatre-Vallées T; Quesnoy *C*, N, *T*; Quimper *C*¹, T; Reims C, N, T; Remiremont *U;* Rennes C¹, T; Rhuys *T;* Riom C, N, T; Rivière-Verdun C, N, T; Rochefort T; Rodez C, N, T; Rouen C, N, T, V; Rozières U; Rustaing U; St. Aubin-du-Cormier *T;* St. Brieuc High C, Low *C*, N, T; St. Dié *C, N,* T; Saintes C, N, T; St. Flour *C*, N, T; St. Jean d'Angely C, N, T; St. Malo C¹; St. Mihiel C, N, *T;* St. Pierre-le-Moutier *C*, N, T; (St. Pol de-Léon C¹ made none), St. Quentin C, N, T; Sarrebourg and Phalsbourg C, N, T; Sarreguemines C, N, T; Sarrelouis CN, *T;* Saumur C, N, T; Sedan *C, N,* T; Semur-en-Auxois C, N, T; Senlis *C*, N, T; Sens C, N, T; Sézanne C, N, T; Sisteron C, N, *T;* Soissons C, *N*, T; Soule C, N, T; Strasbourg T; Tartas N, T; Thiaucourt C, N, T; Thionville C, N, T; Toul, C, N, T; Toulon *C, N*, T; Toulouse C, N, T; Tours C, N, T; Tréguier C¹; Trévoux *C*, N, T; Troyes C, N, T; Tulle C, N, T; Ustaritz C, N, T; Valenciennes T; Vannes C¹, T; Vendôme C, N, T; Verdun C, N, T; Vermandois C, N, T; Vézelise C, *N*, T; Vic C, N, T; Villefranche-de-Beaujolais C, N, T; Villefranche-en-Rouergue *C*, N, T; Villeneuve-de-Berg C, N, T; Villers-Cotterets C, N, T; Villers-la-Montagne U; Vitry-le-François C, N, T.

COLONIES

Guadeloupe—Colony, *Paris;* Ile de France et Bourbon—*Colony;* Martinique—Paris; Pondichéry—Colony; St. Domingue—Colony; Paris—petition.

TOTALS

234 electoral districts (including Corsica) and 5 colonies.

General Cahiers of France and Corsica

Made 194 C, 182 N, 214 T, 17 U, 3 CN, 1 CT, 4 NT. 615
Lost 36 C, 28 N, 22 T, 4 U, 2 NT. 92
Extant 158 C, 154 N, 191 T, 14 U, 3 CN, 1 CT, 2 NT. 523

Colonial Cahiers

Made: 7. Lost: 2. Extant: 5.

LISTS OF GENERAL CAHIERS BY GENERALITY

	C	N	T	U	Total
Generality of Paris (35)					
Extant (33)	10	10	11	2	
Beauvais C, N, T; Etampes C, T; Mantes C, N, T; Meaux C, N. T.; Melun C, N, T; Montfort l'Amaury U; Nemours C, N, T; Paris *hors-les-murs* C, N, T; Paris *intra-muros* C, N, T, V;[1] Provins C, N, T; Senlis N, T; Sens C, N, T.					
Missing (2)	1	1			
Etampes N; Senlis C.					
					35
Generality of Orléans (21)					
Extant (21)	7	7	7		
Blois C, N, T; Chartres C, N, T; Dourdan C, N, T; Gien C, N, T; Montargis C, N, T; Orléans C, N, T; Vendôme C, N, T.					
					21
Generality of Bourges (3)					
Extant (3)	1	1	1		
Bourges C, N, T.					
					3
Generality of Moulins (12)					
Extant (11)	3	4	4		
Guéret C, N, T; Moulins C, N, T; Nivernais C, N, T; St. Pierre-le-Moutier N, T.					
Missing (1)	1				
St. Pierre-le-Moutier C.					
					12
Generality of Lyon (10)					
Extant (10)	3	3	4		
Forez C, N, T; Lyon C, N, T, V; Villefranche-de-Beaujolais C, N, T.					
					10
Generality of Riom (9)					
Extant (8)	2	3	3		
Clermont-Ferrand C, N, T; Riom C, N, T; St. Flour N, T.					
Missing (1)	1				
St. Flour C.					
					9
Generality of Montpellier (21)					
Extant (19)	7	6	6		
Annonay C, N, T; Beziers C, N; Mende C, N,					

[1] The cahier of the municipality of Paris has been counted among those of all three orders jointly.

145

	C	N	T	U	Total
T; Montpellier C, N, T; Nîmes C, N, T; Puy-en-Velay C, T; Villeneuve-de-Berg C, N, T.					
Missing (2)		I	I		
Beziers T; Puy-en-Velay N.					
					21
Generality of Toulouse (15)					
Extant (15)	5	5	5		
Carcassonne C, N, T; Castres C, N, T; Castel-naudary C, N, T; Limoux C, N, T; Toulouse C, N, T.					
					15
Generality of Perpignan (3)					
Extant (2)		I	I		
Perpignan N, T.					
Missing (1)	I				
Perpignan C.					
					3
Generality of Auch (29)					
Extant (23)	5	6	9	2U	
Armagnac C, N, T; Auch C, N, T; Béarn CN, T; Bigorre C, T; Comminges N, T; Foix N, T; Navarre U; Quatre-Vallées T; Rivière-Verdun C, N, T; Rustaing U; Soule C, N, T.				1CN	
Missing (6)	4	I		1NT	
Béarn C;[2] Bigorre N; Comminges C; Couserans C, NT; Foix C.					
					29
Generality of Bordeaux (35)					
Extant (33)	10	11	12		
Agen C, N, T; Bazas C, N, T; Bordeaux C, N, T; Castelmoron d'Albret C, N, T; Condom C, N, T; Dax C, N, T; Libourne C, N, T; Mont-de-Marsan C, T; Nérac C, N, T; Périgord N, T; Tartas N, T; Ustaritz C, N, T.					
Missing (2)		I	I		
Mont-de-Marsan N; Périgord C.					
					35
Generality of Montauban (9)					
Extant (8)	2	3	3		
Cahors C, N, T; Rodez C, N, T; Villefranche-en-Rouergue N, T.					
Missing (1)	I				
Villefranche-en-Rouergue C.					
					9
Generality of Limoges (12)					
Extant (12)	4	4	4		

[2] Lower clergy.

LISTS OF GENERAL CAHIERS BY GENERALITY

	C	N	T	U	Total
Angoulême C, N, T; Dorat C, N, T; Limoges C, N, T; Tulle C, N, T.					
					12
Generality of La Rochelle (10)					
Extant (9)	2	3	4		
La Rochelle N, T; Saintes C, N, T; St. Jean d'Angely C, N, T; Rochefort T.					
Missing (1)	1				
La Rochelle C.					
					10
Generality of Poitiers (7)					
Extant (6)	2	1	2	1U	
Chatellerault C, T; Marches Communes U; Poitiers C, N, T.					
Missing (1)		1			
Chatellerault N.					
					7
Generality of Tours (15)					
Extant (15)	5	5	5		
Angers C, N, T; Loudun C, N, T; Mans (le) C, N, T; Saumur C, N, T; Tours C, N, T.					
					15
Generality of Caen (6)					
Extant (6)	2	2	2		
Caen C, N, T; Coutances C, N, T.					
					6
Generality of Alençon (9)					
Extant (9)	3	3	3		
Alençon C, N, T; Châteauneuf-en-Thimerais C, N, T; Bellême C, N, T.					
					9
Generality of Rouen (13)					
Extant (12)	3	4	5		
Caudebec-en-Caux C, N, T; Chaumont-en-Vexin N, T; Evreux C, N, T; Rouen C, N, T, V.					
Missing (1)	1				
Chaumont-en-Vexin C.					
					13
Generality of Amiens (20)					
Extant (20)	7	6	6	1NT	
Amiens C, N, T; Boulogne-sur-Mer C, N, T; Calais C, N, T; Montreuil-sur-Mer C, N, T; Péronne C, NT; Ponthieu C, N, T; St. Quentin C, N, T.					
					20
Generality of Lille (12)					
Extant (12)	4	4	4		

	C	N	T	U	Total
Artois C, N, T; Bailleul C, N, T; Douai C, N, T; Lille C, N, T.					
					12

Generality of Soissons (18)

	C	N	T	U	Total
Extant (16)	5	5	6		

Château-Thierry N, T; Crépy-en-Valois C, N, T; Clermont-en-Beauvoisis C, N, T; Soissons C, T; Vermandois C, N, T; Villers-Cotterets C, N, T.

	C	N	T	U	Total
Missing (2)	1	1			

Château-Thierry C; Soissons N.

18

Generality of Châlons (21)

	C	N	T	U	Total
Extant (19)	6	6	7		

Châlons-sur-Marne C, N, T; Chaumont-en-Bassigny C, N, T; Langres T; Reims, C, N, T; Sézanne C, N, T; Troyes C, N, T; Vitry-le-François C, N, T.

	C	N	T	U	Total
Missing (2)			1	1U	

Langres U, N.

21

Generality of Dijon (37)

	C	N	T	U	Total
Extant (36)	11	12	12	1U	

Autun C, N, T; Auxerre C, N, T; Bar-sur-Seine C, N, T; Belley C, N, T; Bourg-en-Bresse U, Chalon-sur-Saône C, N, T; Charolles C, N, T; Châtillon-sur-Seine C, N, T; Dijon C, N, T; Gex C, N, T; Mâcon C, N, T; Semur-en-Auxois C, N, T; Trévoux N, T.

	C	N	T	U	Total
Missing (1)	1				

Trévoux C.

37

Generality of Besançon (11)

	C	N	T	U	Total
Extant (11)	3	3	4	1U	

Amont U, T; Aval C, N, T; Besançon C, N, T; Dôle C, N, T.

11

Generality of Grenoble (4)

	C	N	T	U	Total
Extant (3)	1		1	1U	

Dauphiné U, Orange C, T.

	C	N	T	U	Total
Missing (1)		1			

Orange N.

4

Generality of Aix (39)

	C	N	T	U	Total
Extant (24)	10	5	8	1NT	

Aix C, N, T; Arles(ville) C, NT; Barcelonnette C, T; Castellane C; Digne C, N, T; Draguignan

	C	N	T	U	Total
C, T; Forcalquier C, N, T; Grasse C, T; Marseilles C, N, T; Sisteron C, N; Toulon T.					
Missing (15)	4	6	5		
Arles (*sen.*) C, N, T; Brignoles C, N, T; Castellane N, T; Draguignan N; Hyères C, N, T; Sisteron T; Toulon C, N.					
					39

Generality of Rennes (29)

	C	N	T	U	Total
Extant (20)	6	1	13		

Auray T; Brest T; Carhaix T; Dinan T; Dol C;[3] Lannion T; Lesneven T; Morlaix T; Nantes C,[3] T; Ploërmel T; Quimper T; Rennes C,[3] T; St. Brieuc C, N, T; St. Malo C;[3] Tréguier C;[3] Vannes T.

	C	N	T	U	Total
Missing (9)	3		6		

Fougères T; Hédé T; Hennebont T; Jugon T; Quimper C;[3] Rhuys T; St. Aubin-du-Cormer T; St. Brieuc C;[3] Vannes C.[3]

					29

Generality of Valenciennes (10)

	C	N	T	U	Total
Extant (7)	1	3	3		

Avesnes C, N, T; Cambrésis N, T; Quesnoy N, Valenciennes V.

	C	N	T	U	Total
Missing (3)	2		1		

Cambrésis C; Quesenoy C, T.

					10

Generality of Nancy (93)

	C	N	T	U	Total
Extant (64)	19	18	21	4U 1CN 1CT	

Bar-le-duc N, T; Bassigny-Barrois U; Bitche C; Blamont C; Boulay C, T; Bourmont C, N, T; Bouzonville C, N, T; Briey N, T; Bruyères CT, N; Château-Salins C, N, T; Châtel-sur-Moselle N, T; Darney N; Dieuze C, N, T; Etain C, N, T; Fenestrange U; La Marche C, T; Lixheim CN, T; Lunéville C, N; Longuyon C, N, T; Mirecourt C, N, T; Nancy C, N, T; Nomény C, N, T; Neufchâteau T; Pont-à-Mousson C, N, T; Rozières U; St. Dié T; St. Mihiel C, N; Sarreguemines C, N, T; Thiaucourt C, N, T; Vézelise C, T; Villers-la-Montagne U.

	C	N	T	U	Total
Missing (29)	9	11	8	1U	

Bar-le-duc C; Bitche N, T; Blamont N, T; Boulay N; Briey C; Charmes C, N, T; Château-Salins N; Châtel-sur-Moselle C; Commercy C, N, T; Darney C, T; Epinal C, N, T; La

[3] Lower clergy.

	C	N	T	U	Total
Marche N; Lunéville T; Neufchâteau C, N; Remiremont U; St. Mihiel T; St. Dié C, N; Vézelise N.					93

Generality of Metz (33)

	C	N	T	U	
Extant (26)	7	7	9	2U 1CN	

Arches and Charleville U; Longwy C, N, T; Metz C, N, T, V; Mohon U; Sarrebourg and Phalsbourg C, N, T; Sedan T; Sarrelouis CN; Thionville C, N, T; Toul C, N, T; Verdun C, N, T; Vic C, N, T.

	C	N	T	U	
Missing (7)	2	1	1	2U 1NT	

Carignan C, NT; Clermont à Varennes U; Mouzon U; Sarrelouis T; Sedan C, N.

33

Generality of Strasbourg (11)

	C	N	T
Extant (8)	2	1	5

Belfort and Huningue C, T; Colmar and Schlestadt C, N, T; Haguenau and Wissembourg T; Dix Villes T; Strasbourg T.

	C	N
Missing (3)	1	2

Belfort and Huningue N; Haguenau and Wissembourg C, N.

11

Island of Corsica (3)

	N	T
Extant (2)	1	1

Corsica N, T.

	C
Missing (1)	1

Corsica C.

3

Total 615

Colonies (7)[4]

Extant (5)	5	

Guadeloupe—Colony; Martinque—Paris committee; Pondichéry; St. Domingue—Paris petition; Colony.

Missing (5)	2	

Guadeloupe—Paris committee; Ile de France et de Bourbon.

7

Extant—158C, 154N, 191T, 14U,[5] 3CN, 1CT, 2NT-523 general cahiers.
Missing—36C, 28N, 22T, 4U, 2NT-92 general cahiers.
Total made in 1789: 615 general cahiers; 7 colonial cahiers.

[4] Note the correction for the colony of St. Domingue of the number reported in Hyslop, B. *French Nationalism in 1789 according to the General Cahiers*, pp. 243-44.
[5] The cahier of the municipality of Paris has been counted with the united orders.

LIST OF GENERAL CAHIERS THAT WERE PRINTED, BY GENERALITY

Generality of Paris (35)[1] 27 printed: 7C, 10N, 8T, 2U
  Beauvais N; Etampes T; Mantes C, N, T; Meaux C, N, T; Melun C, N; Montfort l'Amaury U; Nemours C, N, T; Paris *hors-les-murs* C, N, T; Paris *intra-muros* C, N, T, V; Provins C, N, T; Senlis N, T; Sens N
Generality of Orléans (21) 12 printed: 4C, 7N, 1T
  Blois C, N; Chartres C, N; Dourdan C, N, T; Gien N; Montargis C, N; Orléans N; Vendôme N
Generality of Bourges (3) 1 printed: 1N
  Bourges N
Generality of Moulins (12) 6 printed: 1C, 2N, 3T
  Moulins C, N, T; Nivernais N, T; St. Pierre-le-Moutier T
Generality of Lyon (10) 7 printed: 2C, 2N, 3T
  Forez C, N, T; Lyon C, N, T, V
Generality of Riom (9) 4 printed: 2N, 2T
  Clermont Ferrand N, T; Riom N, T
Generality of Montpellier (21) 11 printed: 1C, 5N, 5T
  Annonay N, T; Beziers N; Mende T; Montpellier N; Nîmes N, T; Puy C, T; Villeneuve N, T
Generality of Toulouse (15) 5 printed: 1C, 3N, 1T
  Carcassonne N; Castres N; Toulouse C, N, T
Generality of Perpignan (3) 2 printed: 1N, 1T
  Perpignan N, T
Generality of Auch (29) 14 printed: 2C, 3N, 7T, 1U, 1CN
  Armagnac C; Auch C, N, T; Béarn CN, T; Bigorre T; Comminges N, T; Foix N, T; Navarre U; Rivière-Verdun T; Soule T
Generality of Bordeaux (35) 16 printed: 2C, 9N, 5T
  Agen C, N, T; Bazas N, T; Bordeaux N; Condom N; Dax N, T; Libourne C; Nérac N; Périgord N, T; Tartas N; Ustartiz N, T
Generality of Montauban (9) 4 printed: 1C, 2N, 1T
  Cahors C, N; Villefranche-en-Rouergue N, T
Generality of Limoges (12) 9 printed: 3C, 3N, 3T
  Angoulême C, N, T; Limoges C, N, T; Tulle C, N, T
Generality of La Rochelle (10) 2 printed: 1C, 1N
  Saintes C, N
Generality of Poitiers (7) 2 printed: 1N, 1T
  Poitiers N, T
Generality of Tours (15) 8 printed: 2C, 4N, 2T
  Angers N, T; Loudun C; Mans(le) N; Saumur C, N, T; Tours N
Generality of Caen (6) 1 printed: 1N
  Coutances N
Generality of Alençon (9) 4 printed: 3N, 1T
  Alençon N; Bellême N; Châteauneuf-en-Thimerais N, T

[1] The number in parentheses is the total number of general cahiers for the given *generality*.

GENERAL CAHIERS THAT WERE PRINTED

Generality of Rouen (13)   12 printed: 3C, 4N, 5T
  Caudebec C, N, T; Chaumont-en-Vexin N, T; Evreux C, N, T; Rouen C, N, T, V
Generality of Amiens (20)   9 printed: 2C, 3N, 3T, 1NT
  Amiens N; Calais T; Péronne C, NT; Ponthieu C, N, T; St. Quentin N, T
Generality of Lille (12)   11 printed: 3C, 4N, 4T
  Artois C, N, T; Bailleul N, T; Douai C, N, T; Lille C, N, T
Generality of Soissons (18)   7 printed: 1C, 4N, 2T
  Château-Thierry N, T; Clermont-en-Beauvoisis N; Crépy-en-Valois N; Vermandois C, N, T
Generality of Châlons (21)   10 printed: 2C, 5N, 3T
  Châlons-sur-Marne C, N, T; Chaumont-en-Bassigny N; Reims N, T; Sézanne N; Troyes C, N, T
Generality of Dijon (37)   18 printed: 5C, 7N, 5T, 1U
  Autun C, N; Auxerre C, N, T; Bar-sur-Seine C, N, T; Belley N, T; Bourg-en-Bresse U; Dijon C, N, T; Semur-en-Auxois N; Trévoux N, T
Generality of Besançon (11)   3 printed: 1C, 1N, 1T
  Aval N; Dôle C, T
Generality of Grenoble (4)   1 printed: 1U
  Dauphiné U
Generality of Aix (39)   3 printed: 2T, 1NT
  Arles NT; Draguignan T; Marseille T
Generality of Rennes (29)   11 printed: 4C, 1N, 6T
  Auray T; Brest T; Nantes C[1]; Ploërmel T; Rennes C[1], T; St. Brieuc C, N, T; St. Malo C[1]; Vannes T
Generality of Valenciennes (10)   7 printed: 1C, 3N, 3T
  Avesnes C, N, T; Cambrésis N, T; Quesnoy N; Valenciennes T
Generality of Nancy (93)   16 printed: 1C, 7N, 4T, 3U, 1CT
  Bar-le-duc T; Bassigny-Barrois U; Briey N, T; Bruyères CT, N; Lunéville N; Nancy N; Nomény N; Pont-à-Mousson C, N, T; Rozières U; St. Dié T; St. Mihiel N; Villers-la-Montagne U
Generality of Metz (33)   13 printed: 3C, 5N, 5T
  Longwy N; Metz C, N, T, V; Sedan T; Thionville N; Toul C, N, T; Verdun C, N, T
Generality of Strasbourg (11)   6 printed: 1C, 1N, 4T
  Belfort T; Colmar C, N, T; Dix Villes T; Strasbourg T
Corsica (3)   1 printed: 1T
  Corsica T
Colonies (7)   1 printed
  Martinique
Total.—263 general cahiers printed: 54 C, 105 N, 92 T, 8 U, 1 CN, 1 CT, 2 NT

EXPLANATION OF THE MAPS

THE OUTLINES for all three maps are adapted from a map (in two parts), showing all electoral districts, principal and secondary, in Brette, Armand, *Les Limites et les divisions territoriales de la France en 1789* (Paris, 1907). The lines of the subdivisions (i.e., the secondary *bailliages*), of principal *bailliages* have been omitted from the present maps in order to make clear the entire area represented by each general cahier. The final drafts of the maps are the able workmanship of Mr. T. R. Miller, architect and student of Columbia University.

MAP I. GENERAL ELECTORAL DISTRICTS OF 1789

This map was first given in the volume by the present author, *French Nationalism in 1789 according to the General Cahiers* (New York, Columbia University Press, 1934), but is a necessary accompaniment of the present study, and has, therefore, been reprinted. The explanation of the map is virtually a repetition of the comments printed in the volume cited (*loc. cit.*, pp. 247-48).

The aim of map I is twofold: first, to show the general electoral districts of 1789, and second, to show their grouping by *generalities*. A geographic disparity between the various districts is at once apparent, as for example, the contrast between Poitiers (which, in fact, had seven secondary *bailliages* attached to it), and any of the small districts of the northeast. The population was not necessarily equally disproportionate.

Large Roman numerals indicate the *generalities*. The number of each corresponds to the order in which the cahiers have been studied, and in which they should be read, unless special aims dictate a different classification.

Small Roman numerals refer to territories within the frontiers of France but subject to foreign jurisdictions. These were as follows:

I Avignon	VI Ville de Mulhouse
II Comtat Venaissin	VII Comté de Sarre-Verden
III Terre de Bidâche	VIII Principalité de Salm
IV Seigneurie de Mandeure	IX Comté de Sault
V Comté de Montbéliard	X Seigneurie de Montjoie

The names of all *bailliages* have been written on the area corresponding to them, but where the name was too long for the space, a

153

number has been substituted. The names of numbered districts may be checked with a complete numbered list, *infra*, for map III.

A few areas could not be shown on the map. The district of Bassigny-Barrois (seventh type of convocation), comprised the two districts of Bourmont and La Marche (184 and 197), and could not, therefore, be indicated separately. The boundaries of the dioceses of the lower clergy in Brittany (*generality* of Rennes) are not given, since the *sénéchaussée* lines have been indicated, but the diocesan center has been marked.

Map II. The Method of Convocation of 1789

The same outlines have been used as for Map I. The hatching indicates the areas convoked by each of the seven methods of convocation. The colonies and Corsica have not been indicated. Bassigny-Barrois (*supra*), should appear with double hatching, for its separate parts according to the second type of convocation, and for the whole, according to the seventh type of convocation. The indication of the latter fact has however, been omitted for the sake of clarity.

Map III. Districts for Which General Cahiers Are Missing

This map has a double purpose: to indicate districts where the general cahiers of one or more classes are missing, and, by means of the numbers on the electoral districts, to provide a key for the names of districts. Hatching of different kinds has been used to indicate the cahiers of the different classes. The geographic distribution of losses is at once clear.

Numbers were assigned to the electoral districts according to the order used throughout the present study, i.e., the districts were arranged alphabetically within *generalities,* and the *generalities* were arranged in the order indicated in map I. Thus, since the list began with the *generality* of Paris, Beauvais received number 1, Etampes, number 2, Mantes, number 3, etc., while the first district in order for the *generality* of Orléans, the *bailliage* of Blois, received the number of 13, and so on. The names of districts may be easily ascertained by consultation of the consecutive list of numbers, or by the map by *generalities,* no. I, on which the majority of names appear. An alphabetical list of districts, *supra,* pp. 145 *et seq.*, indicates the *generality* to which a *bailliage* belongs, and designates, therefore, in what part of France to look for a name. It has seemed desirable, however, for ready reference, to construct an alphabetical list of all the general districts with the corresponding numbers.

The ignorance and confusion of the royal councils for the convocation was such that it sometimes happened that all areas represented in a single general assembly were not contiguous (e.g., Autun, Riom, etc.). Where such has been the case, the number of the *bailliage* is printed on both areas.

KEY LIST OF NAMES FOR MAPS

Agen	56	Bordeaux	58	Chaumont-en-		Gex	129
Aix	139	Boulay	183	Vexin	93	Gien	16
Alençon	89	Boulogne-s-M.	97	Clermont-en-		Grasse	148
Amiens	96	Bourg-on-B.	124	Beauvoisis	109	Guéret	21
Amont	133	Bourges	20	Clermont à		Haguenau and	
Angers	82	Bourmont	184	Varennes	216	Wissembourg	231
Angouleme	71	Bouzonville	185	Clermont Ferrand	28	Hédé	159
Annonay	31	Brest	154	Colmar and		Hennebont	160
Arches and Char-		Briey	186	Schlestadt	229	Hyères	149
leville	214	Brignoles	143	Commercy	191	Jugon	161
Arles(sen.)	140	Bruyères,	187	Comminges	48	La Marche	197
Arles(ville)	141	Caen	87	Condom	60	Langres	115
Armagnac	44	Cahors	68	Couserans	49	Lannion	162
Artois	103	Calais	98	Coutances	88	La Rochelle	75
Auch	45	Cambrésis	177	Crépy-en-Valois	108	Lesneven	163
Auray	153	Carcassonne	38	Darney	192	Libourne	62
Autun	120	Carhaix	155	Dauphiné	137	Lille	106
Auxerre	121	Carignan	215	Dax	61	Limoges	73
Aval	134	Castellane	144	Dieuze	193	Limoux	41
Avesnes	176	Castelmoron	59	Digne	145	Lixheim	198
Bailleul	104	Castelnaudary	40	Dijon	128	Longuyon	199
Bar-le-duc	180	Castres	39	Dinan	156	Longwy	217
Bar-sur-Seine	122	Caudebec	92	Dix Villes	230	Loudun	83
Barcellonnette	142	Chalon-s-Saône	125	Dol (diocese)	157	Lunéville	200
Bassigny-Barrois¹		Châlons-s-Marne		Dôle	136	Lyon	26
184 and 197			113	Dorat	72	Mâcon	130
Bazas	57	Charmes	188	Douai	105	Mans	84
Béarn	46	Charolles	126	Dourdan	15	Mantes	3
Beauvais	1	Chartres	14	Draguignan	146	Marches Com-	
Belfort	228	Chateauneuf-en-		Epinal	194	munes	80
Bellême	90	Thimerais	91	Etain	195	Marseille	150
Belley	123	Château-Salins	189	Etampes	2	Meaux	4
Besançon	135	Château-Thierry	107	Evreux	94	Melun	5
Beziers	32	Chatellerault	79	Fénestrange	196	Mende	33
Bigorre	47	Châtel-s-Moselle	190	Foix	50	Metz	218
Bitche	181	Châtillon-s-Seine	127	Forcalquier	147	Mirecourt	201
Blamont	182	Chaumont-en-		Forez	25	Mohon	219
Blois	13	Bassigny	114	Fougères	158		

¹ Bassigny-Barrois was composed of the two sections of Bourmont and La Marche. Cf. *supra* p. 26 on the convocation.

KEY LIST OF NAMES FOR MAPS—Continued

NUMERICAL KEY TO MAP

Numerical Key to Map—Continued

Loudun	83	François	119	Fougères	158	Fénestrange	196
Mans (le)	84	Autun	120	Hédé	159	La Marche	197
Saumur	85	Auxerre	121	Hennebont	160	Lixheim	198
Tours	86	Bar-sur-Seine	122	Jugon	161	Longuyon	199
Caen	87	Belley	123	Lannion	162	Lunéville	200
Coutances	88	Bourg-en-Bresse	124	Lesneven	163	Mirecourt	201
Alençon	89	Chalon-sur-		Morlaix	164	Nancy	202
Bellême	90	Saône	125	Nantes	165	Neufchâteau	203
Châteauneuf-en-		Charolles	126	Ploërmel	166	Nomény	204
Thimerais	91	Châtillon-sur-		Quimper	167	Pont-à-Mousson	205
Caudebec	92	Seine	127	Rennes	168	Remiremont	206
Chaumont-en-		Dijon	128	Rhuys	169	Rozières	207
Vexin	93	Gex	129	St. Aubin-du-		St. Dié	208
Evreux	94	Mâcon	130	Cormier	170	St. Mihiel	209
Rouen	95	Semur-en-		St. Brieuc	171	Sarreguemines	210
Amiens	96	Auxois	131	St. Malo	172	Thiaucourt	211
Boulogne	97	Trévoux	132	St. Pol-de-Léon	173	Vézelise	212
Calais	98	Amont	133	Tréguier	174	Villers-la-	
Montreuil	99	Aval	134	Vannes	175	Montagne	213
Péronne	100	Besançon	135	Avesnes	176	Arches and	
Ponthieu	101	Dôle	136	Cambrésis	177	Charleville	214
St. Quentin	102	Dauphiné	137	Quesnoy	178	Carignan	215
Artois	103	Orange	138	Valenciennes	179	Clermont-à-	
Bailleul	104	Aix	139	Bar-le-duc	180	Varennes	216
Douai	105	Arles (sen.)	140	Bitche	181	Longwy	217
Lille	106	Arles(ville)	141	Blamont	182	Metz	218
Château-Thierry	107	Barcelonnette	142	Boulay	183	Mohon	219
Crépy-en-Valois	108	Brignoles	143	Bourmont	184	Mouzon	220
Clermont-en-		Castellane	144	Bassigny-Barrois		Sarrebourg and	
Beauvoisis	109	Digne	145	184 (also 197)		Phalsbourg	221
Soissons	110	Draguignan	146	Bouzonville	185	Sarrelouis	222
Vermandois	111	Forcalquier	147	Briey	186	Sedan	223
Villers-Cotterets	112	Grasse	148	Bruyères	187	Thionville	224
Châlons-sur-		Hyères	149	Charmes	188	Toul	225
Marne	113	Marseille	150	Château-Salins	189	Verdun	226
Chaumont-en-		Sisteron	151	Châtel-sur-		Vic	227
Bassigny	114	Toulon	152	Moselle	190	Belfort	228
Langres	115	Auray	153	Commercy	191	Colmar and	
Reims	116	Brest	153	Darney	192	Schlestadt	229
Sézanne	117	Carhaix	155	Dieuze	193	Dix Villes	230
Troyes	118	Dinan	156	Epinal	194	Haguenau and	
Vitry-le-		Dol	157	Etain	195	Wissembourg	231
						Strasbourg	232

RECTIFICATION FOR TEXTS REPRINTED IN THE ARCHIVES PARLEMENTAIRES

THE *Archives parlementaires* is the one publication which reprints the majority of the *general* cahiers. These volumes are, however, notoriously defective. Brette made a complete and scathing criticism, in which he scored eight points against the editors of the *Archives parlementaires* (Brette, *op. cit.*, Vol. I, Introduction, p. xciii). It is hardly necessary to repeat these criticisms. No attempt should be made to read all documents given in this publication, but, with the page references and the corrections that follow, the *Archives parlementaires* may be used as a valuable and adequate substitute for the original manuscripts.

Careful attention to the page references of general cahiers will eliminate the possibility of reading a false document, and will avoid long search for texts whose classification is faulty or ambiguous.

Two main faults were committed by the editors of the *Archives parlementaires* with respect to the texts themselves: omissions and errors affecting the meaning of the text, and omissions and errors affecting the authenticity of the text. In the first type may be included serious typographical errors, omission of words, phrases or passages, substitution of words and phrases for those in the original, changes in the form which destroy peculiarities of the original (e.g., omission of headings, embodiment of marginal notes in the main text, etc.). In the second type, are included differences of title, adoption, signatures, verification by royal officers, etc.

The present table of corrections aims primarily to list changes or additions necessary for the original meaning of the text. There are innumerable typographical errors, which the reader would readily detect,[1] and occasional substitutions of words which do not materially affect the sense of the phrase.[2] Such corrections have been omitted, as space is too valuable, and attention would be distracted from the really significant rectifications. Only the cahiers have been

[1] For example, "auucn" for "aucun," in T. Perpignan, AP, Vol. V, p. 374, col. 1; "eutendues" for "entendues" in T. Riom, AP, Vol. V, p. 571, col. 1, etc.

[2] For example, T. Annonay, art. 20, reads in the AP (Vol. II, p. 51): "Qu'on accorde à toutes les sénéchaussées et *en particulier* à celles d'Annonay et de Villeneuve-de-Berg . . ." The original gives *notament* in place of *en particulier*. The reader should recall that the editors of the *Archives parlementaires* modernized some of the spelling, and often inserted accents where none were given in the original texts.

mentioned for which important rectification is necessary. Corrections have been reprinted exactly as the passages appeared in the original texts. These cahiers have been referred to in the general chart, pp. 116 *et seq.*, col. 12.

The title, adoption, signing, and verification of a cahier are indispensable for determining the authenticity of a cahier, and for its classification as preliminary or general, but such information does not affect the meaning of the cahier (in so far as it is an authentic cahier). Consequently, differences in any of these documentary details have been cited, in order to further strengthen present conclusions on the reliability of the cahiers, but without indication of the exact differences. No effort has been made to indicate misspellings in the signatures reprinted. Such details might be interesting to genealogists, but are irrelevant to a significant use of the general cahiers as expressions of public opinion. Suffice it to say that the names have been checked with the original texts, and the names of officers and committeemen have been verified with the corresponding *procès-verbaux*.

The rectifications which follow are those necessary for the proper interpretation of the general cahiers involved.

AGEN

Third AP, Vol. I, p. 686.
> Page 690, col. 2, l. 66,[3] read the date as March 23.
> Corrected according to printed text, *Arch. Nat.* Ba 9.

AIX

Nobles AP, Vol. I, p. 693.
> Page 694, col. 2, l. 48, add: "que les contributions des provinces servent à payer dans les provinces mêmes, les dépenses de l'état."
> Corrected according to MS, *Arch. Nat.* Ba 9.

Third AP, Vol. I, p. 695.
> Page 696, col. 1, ll. 51–52, read: "le pays," instead of "la Provence."
> Page 696, col. 2, l. 14, insert: "Encaisser les rivières et ouvrir les canaux nécessaires."
> idem, l. 39, read: "Abolition de la milice forcée," instead of "obligation . . ."
> Corrected according to MS, *Arch. Nat.* Ba 9.

---

[3] Lines of the text of the cahier have been counted from the top of the page, but the title or subtitles have not been counted. Attention has been called to changes of individual words by underlining.

ALENÇON

Clergy AP, Vol. I, p. 708.

Page 710, col. 1, l. 62, add to art. 9: "et faire un nouveau tarif qui ôte tout l'arbitraire."

Corrected according to the MS, *Arch. Nat.* Ba 11.

Nobles AP, Vol. I, p. 710.

The list of signatures at the end differs from the original manuscript. The collation by Bremontier (greffier) should be added.

Corrected according to the MS, *Arch. Nat.* Ba 11.

Third AP, Vol. I, p. 716.

Page 717, col. 2, l. 29, insert after the word "souverain": "jusqu'à 300 de principal."

Page 718, col. 2, l. 66, read: "Que le droit de déport . . . "[3]

The original manuscript bears signatures at the end.

Corrected according to the MS, *Arch. Nat.* C 14/3.

ANNONAY

Nobles AP, Vol. II, p. 47.

Page 47, col. 1, l. 22, insert before "que la constitution": "qu'il n'ait été prononcé sur cet objet,".

Page 47, col. 1, l. 30, insert at end of article 1: "Lorsque les députés auront reçu cette assurance, la noblesse d'Annonay les autorise à voter sur les autres objets qui seront presentés aux Etats Généraux avec la réserve de ne consentir l'impôt que conditionellement à la réconstitution de son administration particulière, condition sans laquelle il serait impossible au peuple de Vivarais de porter aucun surcharge."

Page 47, col. 1, l. 56. From here to the end of this article is a citation in quotation marks from the "arrêt" referred to.

Page 47, col. 2, l. 36, add: "que les graces pécunaires."

The original bears original signatures.

Corrected according to MS, *Arch. Ardèche.* B 145.

Third AP, Vol. II, p. 50.

There is a difference in the title.

Page 50, col. 2, l. 12, add: "avec un effet rétroactif."

Page 52, col. 1, l. 28, add: "et de juges."

Page 52, col. 2, l. 51, read: "trousses, gellinage . . ." in place of "trouffes, genilage."

Page 52, col. 2, l. 69, add: "à Annonay."

Collation by the registrar, Chapuis, April 15, 1789.

Corrected according to MS, *Arch. Ardèche.* B 145.

TEXTS IN THE ARCHIVES PARLEMENTAIRES
ARLES (ville)
Clergy AP, Vol. II, p. 54.

The text was verified and pronounced correct with negligible changes, by M. Busquet, Archivist of the *Arch. Bouches-du-Rhône,* according to the original in the *Arch. Communales* of Arles.

Nobles-Third AP, Vol. II, p. 57.

Page 59, col. 2, l. 6, insert between "écclesiastiques" and "appliques": "Hors d'états de servir par le revenu des biens ecclésiastiques."

Page 60, col. 1, l. 37, read: "dans toute sa force."

Corrected according to MS copy, *Arch. Nat.* B III 10, p. 792.

ARTOIS
Clergy AP, Vol. II, p. 78.

Page 78, col. 1, l. 46, read, article 17: "Loi claire et précise . . ."

Corrected from reprinted text in Loriquet, *Cahiers de doléances . . . dans le Pas-de-Calais,* Vol. I, pp. 3 *et seq.*

Nobles AP, Vol. II, p. 79.

Page 79, col. 2, l. 59, read: "impots dont ils se composent."

Corrected according to reprinted text from Loriquet, *op. cit.,* Vol. I, pp. 10 *et seq.*

Third AP, Vol. VI, p. 721.

It was impossible to see the original, because it could not be sent to Paris since this cahier bears the original signature of Robespierre and the Departmental Archives consider the text too precious. Correct according to printed text, *Bib. Nat.* L°24.293.

AUCH
Third AP, Vol. II, p. 96.

The original has four pages of signatures at the end.

Correct according to MS, *Arch. Nat.* Ba 16.

AURAY
Third AP, Vol. VI, p. 112.

Page 115, col. 2, l. 34, read: "L'exécution absolue . . ." (Actually, the sense of the article seems to be "L'abolition," as the *Archives parlementaires* have given it, but the manuscript reads as in the correction.

Page 116, col. 2, l. 15, add: "Les mots leurs, leurs, les dignes, en intrelignes, aprouvés, le mot classe ne touches aussi aprouvé, deux mots rétires nuls."

Corrected according to MS, *Arch. Nat.* Ba 26.

AVAL
Clergy AP, Vol. II, p. 137.
Page 139, add at end of cahier:

"Petitions particulières des Messieurs les réguliers.

1. Messieurs les réguliers demandent à Sa Majesté et aux Etats Généraux de vouloir bien favoriser leurs désires sincères de se rendre utiles à l'église et à la patrie par l'enseignment.

2. La conservation de tous leurs droits, privileges, exemptions, immunities, pleines et entières accordées aux corps réguliers.

3. Que les hommes puissent faire d'émission de leur voeux à 18 ans et les femmes à 16.

4. Qu'au cas l'on supprime quelques uns de leurs maisons, les fonds et revenus des maisons supprimés soient transferés dans celles qui seront conservés et dans lesquelles on acquittera les fondations.

5. Que le lods de Commendes soit entre les mains des religieux, qui toutes charges de bénéfices prélevés, devront rendre compte aux états provinciaux pour les cédent, être employé soit en dotation des curés, soit pour recompenser les services rendus à l'église soit au soulagement des pauvres.

"Pour expedition à Messieurs les députés. Ardiet."

Corrected according to MS, *Arch. Nat.* Ba 17.

AVESNES
Third AP, Vol. II, p. 151.
Page 153, col. 2, l. 36, read: "payent les charbons etrangers."

Correct according to printed text, *Arch. Nat.* Ba 17.

BAILLEUL
Clergy AP, Vol. II, p. 168.
On the margin of the MS are numerous comments by the décimateurs on the articles of the cahier, given by the AP as footnotes.

Page 170, col. 2, l. 11, read: "Que les dépenses des départements . . ."

Page 170, col. 2, l. 60, read: "où il vient."

Correct according to MS, *Arch. Nat.* Ba 18.

Third AP, Vol. II, p. 174.
Page 174, col. 2, l. 57, read: "le droit de tuage . . ."

Page 175, col. 2, l. 6, read: "garnison."

Page 177, col. 2, l. 12, read: "puissent être partages et rendus rotures."

Page 177, col. 2, l. 62, add: "à charge d'être responsable des abus."

Corrected according to printed text, *Arch. Nat.* Ba 18.

BAZAS

Nobles AP, Vol. II, p. 267.

Page 268, col. 1, l. 52, insert after "criminelle": "de 1670."

Page 268, col. 2, l. 51, insert before "contre": "et protestera, conformement à l'energie de son caractère."

The original bears the signatures of the assembly.

Correct according to MS, *Arch. Gironde.*

Third AP, Vol. VI, p. 494.

Page 494, col. 2, l. 29, substitute for articles 16:

"Que l'édit concernant les hypotèques soit rectifié, que les contrats seront affichés au sénéchal du lieu du domicile du Créancier et aux portes de l'église paroissale où les objets vendus sont scitués pendant les délais déterminés par le même édit avant qu'il puisse être expèdié aucunes lettres de ratification, et que les oppositions dureront trente ans."

Page 495, col. 1, l. 14, read "renouvellement des baux."

Correct according to MS, *Arch. Gironde.*

BEARN

Clergy-Nobles AP, Vol. VI, p. 497.

Declared correct by M. Lorber, archivist of *Arch. Basses-Pyrénées,* according to MS, at those archives, C 826.

Third AP, Vol. VI, p. 500, *idem.*

BEAUVAIS

Clergy AP, Vol. II, p. 287.

Page 292, col. 2, l. 5, add: "Nous ne sommes pas encore débarassés aujourd'hui de la rancon du Roi Jean."

Correct according to MS, *Arch. Nat. Ba 20.*

Nobles AP, Vol. II, p. 294.

Page 295, col. 2, l. 14, insert:

"Que les Etats généraux s'occupent d'approfondir la situation active et passive du clergé.

"Que tous les biens du Clergé soient assujetti aux impots et charges publiques, que le recouvrement s'en fasse par les mêmes collecteurs et d'après un rôle commun à tous les contribuables.

"Que les baux des biens des gens de main morte ne puissent être à plus longue terme que neuf ans, et qu'il ne soient pas résolu par la mort ou retrait des bénéficiers.

"Qu'une loi précise fasse cesser les contestations rélatives aux dîmes, spécialement à celle des prairies artificielles. La Noblesse denonce aux Etats Généraux comme très abusifs le règlement qui ordonne que les deniers provenant de la

vente des bois en réserve appartenant aux communautés soient remise aux receveurs des domaines et bois, rien n'est plus difficile que de retirer cet argent et les frais en consomment toujours la plus grand partie."
Corrected according to MS, *Arch. Nat.* Ba 20.

Third AP, Vol. II, p. 299.

Page 303, col. 1, l. 28, read: "ni chemins ni l'arsis."
Corrected according to MS copy. *Arch. Nat.* B III 28, p. 351.

BELFORT AND HUNINGUE

Clergy AP, Vol. II, p. 310.

Page 310, col. 1, l. 40, insert after "naissance": "et autres recommendations."
Page 311, col. 1, l. 4, add: "dont le Régent ou Régente devra être assisté."
Page 311, col. 1, l. 45, read and add: "aux domaines du Roi."
Page 311, col. 1, l. 69, read the line: "avant d'être convaincu suppression du serment qu'on lui fait . . ."
Page 311, col. 2, l. 47, insert after "ordre": "de demander tous les renseignements, les mémoires désignés dans l'ouvrage qui sera joint pour cette raison à nos Cahiers de Doléances et de confronter . . ."
Page 311, col. 2, l. 48, add: "et le mémoire susdit."
Page 312, col. 2, l. 12, omit the word "bois," and line 13, omit the words "le reste."
Page 313, col. 1, l. 69, insert after "et": "à leur defaut."
Page 313, col. 2, l. 66, read: "Colmar et Molsheim."
Corrected according to MS, *Arch. Haut-Rhin.* C 1958.

Third AP, Vol. II, p. 315.

Page 315, col. 2, l. 52, add: "la tache qui lui aura été réglée."
Page 317, col. 1, l. 73, read: "Que la partie de Suntgau . . ."
Page 318, col. 1, l. 15, read: "à raison de leurs professions."
Correct according to MS, *Arch. Nat.* Ba 20.

BELLEME

Clergy AP, Vol. V, p. 319.

Page 322, col. 1, insert after l. 19: 4. "Réserver les forêts royales les soumettre à l'inspection des Etats provinciaux."
Variation in ending of cahier.
Corrected according to MS, *Arch. Nat.* C 22/121.

Nobles AP, Vol. V, p. 323.

Insert after title:
"En vertu des lettres de convocation qui ordonnent aux trois ordres du

bailliage du Perche d'élire leurs représentants aux Etats Libres et généraux du Royaume et de leur confier tous les pouvoirs et instructions qui seraient jugés nécessaires pour la restauration de l'état et prospérité particulière du bailliage du Perche, nous donnons le par ces présentes à notre député aux dits états qui doivent se tenir à Versailles le 27 avril 1789, les pouvoirs et instructions tels qu'ils suivent, lesquels objets et instructions ne pourront avoir leur plein et entier effet que pour un an à datter du jour de la première séance des états généraux."

The date at the end of the cahier should read: 8 avril 1789.

Corrected according to MS, *Arch. Nat.* Ba 21.

Third AP, Vol. V, p. 325.

Page 325, col. 2, l. 31, add to article 11: "conformement à l'article précédent."

The original bears signatures and collation by the secretary of the subdelegation, Blondel.

Corrected according to MS, *Arch. Nat.* Ba 21.

BESANÇON

Clergy AP, Vol. II, p. 333.

Page 334, col. 1, l. 16, there is written in the margin: "Déclaration du 14 mai 1724."

Page 334, col. 1, l. 23, insert after "substitue": "dans les quatre terres et dépendences."

Corrected according to MS, *Bib. Mun. de Besançon,* 1534, no. 261,[4] and *Arch. Nat.* B III 30, p. 427.

Nobles AP, Vol. VI, p. 515.

The parts in italics appear in the margin of the original.

Corrected according to MS, *Arch. Doubs.* B 9501.

BIGORRE

Clergy AP, Vol. II, p. 351.

Page 352, col. 1, l. 1, read: "ayant rang parmi les chanoines et habit de choeur."

The footnotes given by the *Archives parlementaires* appear as marginal notes on the original.

Page 353, col. 2, l. 9, beside this article 4 appears in the margin: "Cet article a été supprimé."

Page 354, col. 1, insert before the signatures: "La présent cahier de doléances a été arrêté et approuvé à la pluralité des suffrages et signé conformement au règlement par M. le Président, Messieurs les commissaires et M. le sécretaire."

Corrected according to MS, *Arch. Nat.* C 16/31.

[4] Article I of the text reprinted by Ricklin, P. ("Revendications du bailliage de Besançon in 1789" Dijon: 1910) from the Communal Deliberations, appears as a request for Catholicism for Franche-Comté, rather than for the whole of France.

Third AP, Vol. II, p. 359.

Page 361, col. 2, l. 26, read: "sabatines" instead of "sabalines."

Correct according to printed text, *Arch. Nat.* Ba 80.

BORDEAUX

Clergy AP, Vol. II, p. 392.

Page 393, col. 1, l. 20, insert after "spécialement": "par les abus dans l'administration de la justice et spécïalement . . ."

Corrected according to MS copy, *Arch. Nat.* B III 34, p. 395.

Nobles AP, Vol. II, p. 394.

Page 396, col. 2, l. 65, insert article 2, and renumber article 2 as article 3, with changes thereafter in the numbers.

Art. 2: "Que tous impots indirects, prorogés ou créés, seront simplifiés et tarifés de la manière la plus précise."

Correct according to MS, *Arch. Nat.* Ba 22.

Third AP, Vol. II, p. 397.

Page 399, col. 1, l. 24, read: "affaires" instead of "offrandes."

Page 401, col. 2, l. 72, insert the following paragraph:

"Qu'un droit qualiffié de premier tonneau de fret qui se perçoit à Bordeaux, sur les bâtiments destinés pour les colonies à raison de 26 livres 5 sols soit supprimé."

Page 402, col. 1, l. 65, insert the following paragraph:

"Que l'introduction des mouchoirs en couleur venus de l'Inde soit défendus, comme contraire à la prospérité des fabriques nationales."

Corrected according to MS, *Arch. Nat.* C 16/33.

BOULAY

Clergy AP, Vol. V, p. 693.

Page 693, col. 2, l. 33, the paragraph commencing "Le clergé, en se soumettant . . ." is a marginal note.

Correct according to MS, *Arch. Nat.* Ba 77.

Third Cf. text in *Annuaire de la Société historique et archaeologique lorraine*, 1904, Vol. XVI, p. 200.

Page 203, the last word of the first paragraph should read "provinciaux" in place of "généraux."

Corrected according to MS, *Arch. Moselle*, B 6.214.

BOULOGNE-SUR-MER

Clergy AP, Vol. II, p. 415.

Page 421, col. 2, l. 51, read "autres, et il y aurait une caisse . . ."

Correct according to MS, *Arch. Nat.* Ba 23.

BOURG-EN-BRESSE

United orders AP, Vol. II, p. 452.

There is an addition to the title, which explains the division of the cahier into three columns, one for each order, which arrangement was not retained by the *Archives parlementaires*. The original is much clearer than the reprint of the latter.

Page 455, col. 2, l. 31, add after "ordres" the word "réunis."

Page 459, col. 1, l. 1, omit the words in parenthesis and add: "sera d'occuper au travail ceux qui seront dans le cas."

Corrected according to MS, *Arch. Nat.* Ba 23.

BOUZONVILLE

Clergy AP, Vol. V, p. 694.

Page 696, col. 2, l. 25, add: "et des haras."

Next to articles 48 and 50, p. 698, was written on the margin: "Non admis à raison de notre non connaissance."

The cahier ends p. 698, col. 2; the supplement is not a valid addition.

Correct according to MS, *Arch. Nat.* Ba 77.

BREST

Third AP, Vol. II, p. 467.

Page 475, col. 2, l. 13, add: "au public."

Page 476, col. 1, last l., read: "Les dunes Gallois . . ."

Correct according to MS, *Arch. Nat.* C 16/37.

The cahier of the town of Brest, AP, Vol. II, p. 465, is also correct according to MS, *Arch. Nat.* Ba 25.

CAEN

Clergy AP, Vol. II, p. 486.

Page 487, col. 1, l. 17, read: "le droit de déport."

Page 488, col. 1, l. 60, add after "paroisses": "pour la rédaction du quel Sa Majesté sera supplié de prendre de conseils des universités et des principaux corps chargés de l'enseignement dans les états."

Corrected according to MS, *Arch. Nat.* C 17/38.

Nobles AP, Vol. II, p. 488.

Page 489, col. 2, add at end of art. 16: "Et les Etats généraux eux-mêmes seront dans cette salutaire impuissance à moins que la Majorité du Royaume, ne les ait chargés de pouvoirs à cet effet."

There are added signatures at the end of the original text.

Text corrected according to MS, *Arch. Nat.* Ba 27.

CAHORS

Nobles AP, Vol. V, p. 488.

There is a difference of title.

Page 488, col. 2, ll. 48–49, omit: "Que la périodicité . . . soit assurée."

Page 490, col. 2, l. 29, insert the paragraph:

"Les députés sont chargés de mettre sous les yeux de l'assemblée des Etats Généraux, les mémoires, qui leur seront réunis sur la gabelle, de controlle, la navigation du Lot, et autres objets intéressants."

The cahier ends with the name of the secretary and collation for the date of March 27, 1789.

Corrected according to MS, *Arch. Nat.* Ba 28.

CALAIS

Third AP, Vol. II, p. 510.

The AP has evidently reprinted this from one of the printed texts. A manuscript text, *Arch. Nat.* C 17/39 differs considerably from this. Although Loriquet (*cf.* Bibliography p. 454) has reprinted the text, this book is rare in this country. It has therefore seemed desirable to indicate the changes of text for the AP in order to make it conform to the manuscript.

Page 510, l. 45, read: "la plus égale" in place of "regulière."

Page 511, col. 1, l. 42, add: "Que le total en soit fixe à 10 millions"; last two lines, omit: "Ils demanderont que l'armée. . . ."

Page 511, col. 2, ll. 13–18, omit; "Ils demanderont . . . de la considération publique." Col. 2, l. 30, insert as an additional paragraph:

"Ils demanderont, en execution du voeu particulier de l'Ardésis que sa majesté daigne accorder à la ville d'Ardres, afin de l'indemniser des depenses de la construction d'un manège et l'écurie, les terreins de sa fortification intérieure et extérieure, pour aggrandir l'enceinte de la dite ville."

Page 511, col. 2, ll. 33-35, omit: "savoir . . . au denier 40"; col. 2, l. 41, read: "vente" instead of "rente"; col. 2, l. 55, add: "à conserver."

Page 512, col. 1, l. 10, add: "et que les gardes de côtes soient rétabli dans l'ancien régimè"; col. 1, ll. 17–27, omit: "Ils prendont . . . existence politique"; col. 1, ll. 56–59, omit, and substitute:

"D'ordonner pour prévenir les contestations entre les citoyens et les priseurs vendeurs; prévenir l'extension qu'ils donnent aux quatre deniers pour livre,— ensemble, celle sur la recette de leurs deniers, la suppression de leurs offices, de permettre pour donner à ses peuples le choix des personnes qu'ils honorent de leur confiance, à tous officiers publics de procéder aux ventes.

"De récréer dans le cas où la suppression ne seroit pas effectuée, quatre offices pour la ville de Calais, possédée par quatre personnes indépendantes.

"Que l'affranchissement soit particulièrrement ordonné pour les paroisses de March, de Lugnes et de Bremex, et de Pierre."

Add for this general section on taxes:

"Ils demanderont qu'il ne soit perçu, en cas de vente, que sur les deniers déboursés et non sur les capitaux des rentes surannées.

"Qu'ils ne puisse être exigé pour retraits consentir dans les délais préscrits par les coutumes.

"Qu'il ne puisse être demandé de *droits en sur* aux heritiers en collaterale, à moins qu'ils n'aient été constitué en demeure.

"Ils demanderont que les sols additionnels soient à jamais proscrits."

Page 512, col. 2, ll. 11–14, omit: "Que ces Etats . . . leur nomination."

Add to section on "Etats provinciaux":

"Que leur organization soit à l'instar de ceux de Dauphiné. Qu'ils soient absolument indépendant des Intendans.

"Que tous les emplois concernant l'assiette et perception de l'imposition soient à la nomination des Etats provinciaux.

"Que l'étendu des Etats soit réduite au taux qu'il est possible pour réunir les connaissances locales aux usages et intérêts particuliers."

Page 513, col. 1, l. 2, add: "Que celles établies soient conservées en éprouvant les modifications indiqueés par l'étendue et la population de paroisses"; col. 1, l. 3, omit: "Que les membres . . . élus"; col. 1, l. 10, add: "Ils demanderont que ces municipalités sous l'inspection de l'arrondissements, soit autorisé à faire les dépenses locales, dont les sommes réunies n'excéderont point celles à arbitrer par les Etats provinciaux." Add under the title "Répartition et verification . . .": "Ils demanderont que les contestations sur la répartition soient portées à l'assemblée d'arrondissements, ou les parties seront entendues contradictoirement et par appel à l'état provincial."

Page 513, col. 2, under the title "Suppression des tribunaux . . ." add: "Qu'aux juges ordinaires appartienne la connaissance de tout ce qui se traite à la perception des droits de controle aux intérêts des Fermes régies et administrations."

Page 514, col. 1, l. 33, read: "La liberté de la presse soit accordé"; col. 1, l. 39, read: "la garde bourgeoise." Add to section "Amelioration de la police":

Ils demanderont que les devoirs reciproques des domestiques et des maîtres soient solennellement déterminés. Que les mesureurs jurés des grains soient supprimés. Ils demanderont, sur la répresentation des habitans de Calais, que pour mettre fin aux monopoles des marchands, il soit, trois mois avant la vente des coupes fait une taxe des différents qualités de Bois.

"Que la police de Grueries soit confiée aux officiers municipaux."

Page 514, col. 1, l. 64, insert:

"Ils demanderont que les fermes actuelles soient conservées et qu'une étendue de cent meseurs ne puisse rester sans une habitation."

Page 515, col. 1, l. 25, omit "lors des échouements," and read: "par les amiraultés"; col. 1, ll. 29–30, omit "Qu'il soit fait . . . et métiers." Add to section on "Industrie":

"La suppression des droits de chef d'oeuvre et des réceptions des sindics et adjoints des communautés.

L'exécution des règlements relatifs aux communautes d'arts et metiers. L'exemption en faveur de veuves de tous droits pour continuer la profession suivie par leur mari.

La réduction en quart du droit de visite, chez les membres des communautés, et que l'arrêté des comptes soit fait gratuitement.

Ils demanderont selon le voeu particulier des Barbiers-Perruquiers la suppression du centième denier, ou au moins le payement en nom collectif de celui qui leur est imposé. Ils demanderont que les coronneurs, rouleurs, bateliers, et portefaire, suivant leurs demandes particulières soient affranchis du droits particuliers prélevé sur leurs salaires."

Page 15, col. 1, l. 52, add: "et rendu uniforme pour tout le royaume."

Page 515, col. 2, l. 4, read: "proroge à celui d'une année"; col. 2, l. 8, read: "est la source de la force de la Marine royale; qu'il . . ."; col. 2, ll. 57-62, omit: "Qu'en particulier . . . simple et général."

Page 516, col. 1, l. 23, read: "Que les droits d'entrée ne . . ."

Page 516, col. 1, l. 35, read: "bon d'une qualité nuisible à la santé"; col. 1, l. 40, add: "La rareté et la cherté des bois rend ce parti urgent et indispensable."

Page 516, col. 2, l. 10, add: "Ils observveront que les Parlements sont actuellement les seuls tribunaux supérieurs avoués par la Nation, et qu'il seroit dangereux d'ériger les grandes bailliages pour juger en dernier ressort au civil et au criminel."

There is slight variation of the ending, but it has the necessary marks of an authentic original.

Corrected according to MS, *Arch. Nat.* C 17/39.

CARCASSONNE

Nobles AP, Vol. II, p. 527.

Page 528, col. 1, add at end of art. 12, the following *motif:*

"Le droit de s'imposer dérive du droit de propriété: c'est de la violation de ce principe que sont résultés les maux qui affligent aujourd'hui la France, l'arbitraire introduit dans l'administration les atteints fréquentes que le despotisme ministériel a porté aux droits de la nation et des individus. La prospérité publique, la liberté des citoyens, reposent sur l'exécution rigoureuse de cette loi."

Page 529, col. 2, l. 38, the two paragraphs beginning "Les Etats de province ne doivent . . ." are the "motifs" of art. 27, and follow it.

Other slight variations in "motifs."

Correct according to printed text, *Arch. Nat.* Ba 29.

Third AP, Vol. II, p. 532.

Page 533, col. 1, l. 55, add at the end of the paragraph:

"Que les nouveaux titulaires des bénéfices écclesiastiques des prieurés et commanderies de l'ordre de Malte soyent tenus de s'en faire mettre en possession par acte public et que sur ces actes de prise de possession, le deux, droit de contrôle et de centième denier soyent perçus sur le capital du revenu des dits bénéfices, prieurés, et commanderies."

Correct according to MS, *Arch. Nat.* Ba 29.

TEXTS IN THE ARCHIVES PARLEMENTAIRES

CASTELMORON D'ALBRET

Third AP, Vol. II, p. 549.

The text is correct, but opposite arts. 15, 16, 18, and 19, in the margin appears "rejeté" with signatures, and beside art. 16, "admis" with signatures.

Page 548, col. 1, l. 48, read: "détresse" instead of "desserte."

Correct according to MS, *Arch. Nat.* Ba 29.

CASTELNAUDARY

Third AP, Vol. II, p. 559.

Add at the end of art. 1: "ou elles seront promulguées."

Corrected according to MS, *Arch. Nat.* Ba 30.

CASTRES

Clergy AP, Vol. II, p. 562.

The date, March 17, 1789, is inserted in the subtitle.

Corrected according to MS, *Arch. Nat.* Ba 30.

CAUDEBEC-EN-CAUX

Clergy AP, Vol. II, p. 573.

Page 575, col. 1, l. 10, add "sur chaque portion des décimateurs."

Corrected according to MS, *Arch. Nat.* Ba 30.

Nobles AP, Vol. II, p. 575.

Page 576, col. 1, insert before art. 4.

"Que le droit qu'à la nation de concourir avec le Roy à la législation soit rendu tellement constant qu'aucune loy ne puisse plus être regardée comme loy du royaume si elle n'a été consentie ou proposée par les états généraux que les formes de la proposition et du consentement soient entièrement fixées.

Qu'après avoir reçu leur sanction les lois soient enregistrées dans les états généraux pour être ensuite adressés aux états des provinces enregistrés, et par eux envoyées aux parlements qui seront spécialement chargés par la nation d'éveiller à leur exécution sans que les états provinciaux ni les parlements puissent les modifier ni les interpreter."

Page 577, col. 1, l. 28, insert the following paragraph:

"Qu'il soit reglé qu'à l'avenir on imprimera annuellement les états de recette et de dépense du tresor public."

Page 577, col. 2, add at the end of cahier:

"L'assemblée enjoint a ses députés de recevoir le compte qui sera rendu aux Etats-Généraux, des dettes du tresor royal, de discuter celle qui ont été contractée à un intérêt trop onereux et pour lesquelles les formes en usage n'ont pointe été rempliées, et seulement après cette discussion d'où il resultera que les dettes seront ou rembourses ou reduites à un juste taux, leur donne pouvoir de s'engager, avec les autres représentants de la nation et en son nom, au payment de la dette, de consentir les impôts qui seront jugés nécessaires pour l'acquitter et qui demeureront fixes jusqu'à son extinction. Leur enjoint d'examiner les comptes des sommes qui seront jugées nécessaires pour la depense annuelle des départements et leur donne pouvoir de voter après cet examen, la somme annuelle d'impositions qui y sera consacrée.

Enfin leur donne pouvoir de faire et consentir tout ce qui pourra procurer la gloire et le bonheur de la patrie, le rétablissement de l'ordre et la régénération du royaume, déclarant que pour les objets qui ne sont point contenus ou limites dans le Mandat ci-dessus, elle s'en rapporte aux vues patriotiques et au zèle de ses députés."

Corrected according to MS, *Arch. Nat.* Ba 30.

CHALON-SUR-SAONE

Clergy AP, Vol. II, p. 601.

Parts of arts. 2 and 8 were marginal comments, approved; also, art. 11.

Page 601, col. 1, marginal comment: "marchands défense de vendre aux roturiers domiciliés."

Corrected according to MS, *Arch. Nat.* Ba 31.

Third AP, Vol. II, p. 608.

Page 610, col. 1, art. 3, the MS, reads: "L'extinction stricte . . . "; although the sense of the article would seem to be "L'exécution . . ." as the AP gives it.

Corrected according to MS, *Arch. Nat.* Ba 31.

CHAROLLES

Third AP, Vol. II, p. 618.

Page 620, col. 2, insert at end of art. 14: "devant des députés nommés chacun en droit soi par leurs pairs."

Page 621, col. 1, add to article 1: "dans l'intervalle des tenues des Etats-généraux."

Corrected according to MS, *Arch. Nat.* Ba 31.

CHARTRES

Third AP, Vol. II, p. 629.

The date at the end should read: March 15, 1789.

Corrected according to MS, copy, *Arch. Nat.* B III 45, p. 347.

CHATEAU-SALINS

Clergy AP, Vol. V, p. 707.

Page 708, col. 1, l. 57, read: "et la réformation de la maîtrise . . ."

Corrected according to MS, *Arch. Nat.* Ba 77.

CHATEAU-THIERRY
Nobles AP, Vol. II, p. 658.

Page 662, col. 2, l. 12, read: "nécessité moins indispendieuse."
Corrected according to printed text, *Arch. Nat.* Ba 32.

CHATEAUNEUF-EN-THIMERAIS
Nobles AP, Vol. II, p. 640.

Page 640, col. 1, ll. 5–6, read: "patriotisme."
Corrected according to printed text, *Arch. Nat.* Ba 32.

Third AP, Vol. II, p. 651.

Variation in ending; certification added.
Correct according to MS, *Arch. Nat.* C 17/51.

CHATELLERAULT
Clergy AP, Vol. II, p. 686.

Signatures, and adoption March 31.
Corrected according to MS, *Arch. Nat.* C 17/53.

CHATILLON-SUR-SEINE
Nobles AP, Vol. II, p. 702.

Page 705, col. 1, l. 20, add: "que préalablement on ne lui présente et on ne lui remette copie duement signée de l'acte de dépôt fait de l'ordre du Roi."
Corrected according to MS, *Arch. Nat.* Ba 53.

CHAUMONT-EN-BASSIGNY
Clergy AP, Vol. II, p. 720.

Page 722, col. 2, add to article 38: "par ces brigades."
Negligible variations.
Corrected according to MS, *Arch. Nat.* Ba 32.

Nobles AP, Vol. II, p. 724.

Correct according to printed text, *Arch. Nat.* Ba 32.

The manuscript text in the same carton is incomplete, and differs in the introductory paragraph and in the ending. The latter appears to be the project of the commission, while the printed text is the final one adopted by the assembly.

Third AP, Vol. II, p. 726.

Difference of title, and the omission of the first paragraph.
Page 728, col. 2, addition of an article between art. 71 and 72, with change of numbers thereafter.

Art. 72. "Qu'il soit accordé des encouragements à l'agriculture et au commerce par des récompenses et distinctions honorables."
Correct according to MS, *Arch. Nat.* Ba 32.

CLERMONT EN BEAUVOISIS

Clergy AP, Vol. II, pp. 744–748.

It was impossible to see the original text. The reprinted text, given by Desjardin, G., *Le Beauvoisis, le Valois* . . . was used, and the AP found correct.

Nobles AP, Vol. II, p. 748.

Page 748, col. 2, l. 34, in place of the final phrase of art. 7, read: "supportent avec la plus exacte égalité les mêmes charges."

Page 750, col. 1, l. 8, add:

"enjoignant expressement à son député de protester hautement et publiquement, et de demander acte de sa protestation, si, par un événement impossible à présumer, la pluralité des voix emportait une opinion contraire à ces trois propositions."

Corrected according to the MS, *Arch. Nat.* C 17/57. Neither that text, nor the printed text Ba 32, give the "articles obligatoire" at the end.

Third AP, Vol. II, p. 754.

It was impossible to see the original. The text in Desjardins, *op. cit.* was used, and the AP found correct.

CLERMONT FERRAND

Nobles AP, Vol. II, p. 766.

There is a written certification by the deputy, the Comte de Montboissier, with the date of Oct. 7, 1789 on the printed copy.
Correct according to this text, *Arch. Nat.* C 27/206.

Third AP, Vol. II, p. 769.

Page 773, col. 1, l. 15, add to art. 4 the word "seulement."
Corrected according to printed text, *Arch. Nat.* Ba 33.

COLMAR AND SCHLESTADT

Third AP, Vol. III, p. 9.

Page 10, col. 2, l. 21, add to article 24: "dont le plan sera concerté par les représentans de la Province."

Page 11, col. 2, l. 54, read: "todfall," instead of "todfalt."

Page 11, col. 2, l. 58, insert an article between arts. 49 and 50 and renumber articles thereafter:

Art. 50. "Que les seigneurs ne pourront recevoir des étrangers pour bourgeois ou manans que du consentement des communautés."

Correct according to MS, *Arch. Nat.* Ba 33.

CORSICA

Third AP, Vol. III, p. 40.

Page 43, col. 1, l. 11, add: "avec distinction."

Page 45, col. 2, l. 11; add: "les capitaines et patrons pris parmi les Corses ou Français établis en Corse, lorsqu'ils devront être remplacés."

Corrected according to MS, *Arch. Nat.* Ba 34.

CREPY-EN-VALOIS

Clergy AP, Vol. III, p. 73.

Page 74, col. 1, l. 25, add: "ne contienne moins de quatre charues."

Correct according to MS, *Arch. Nat.* Ba 35.

Third AP, Vol. III, p. 76.

Page 76, col. 1, l. 24, add: "et de n'en proroger aucun sans la même condition."

Correct according to MS, *Arch. Nat.* Ba 35.

DAUPHINE

Estates AP, Vol. III, p. 80.

The cahier, or rather a summary of it is included in the p.v. of the Estates.

Page 80, col. 2, l. 22, add: "qui garantisse leurs droits et propriétés."

Page 80, col. 2, l. 31, insert after "subside": "ni qu'on fasse emprunt directement ou indirectement sans le consentement et le libre octroi des Etats-Généraux."

Page 80, col. 2, l. 36, add: "sans compromettre le droit sacre de la propriété, dont la nobilité des fonds fait partie en Dauphiné et qui doit être conservé."

Page 80, col. 2, l. 55, add: "dont l'époque sera toujours fixée avant le séparation des Etats-Généraux."

Page 81, col. 1, l. 2, add: "dont ils ne devront s'occuper qu'après avoir obtenu les règles fondamentales de la constitution, et dans le cas où le temps et les circonstances pourront le permettre."

These were the additions made to the cahier, according to a letter from the King's commissioners to Necker, Jan. 9, 1789, *cf. Arch. Nat.* Ba 75, but instead of adopting this particular wording, the last paragraph of the meeting of the Estates on January 9, 1789 was adopted. *Cf.* letter, Jan. 10, 1789, *Arch. Nat.* B III, p. 56, p. 325. *Cf.* the paragraph, AP, III, p. 83. The wording of the original full cahier must have expressed these same sentiments.

DIJON

Clergy AP, Vol. III, p. 123.

Page 124, col. 1, art. 10, is worded differently without changing the general sense, but with slightly more emphasis upon the provincial privileges.

Page 127, col. 2, l. 48, insert after "qui" in place of "peut être regardée": "qui ne doit être regardé que."

Corrected according to MS, *Arch. Côte d'Or.* C 3475.

Third AP, Vol. III, p. 131.

Page 133, col. 1, l. 2, add: "au quel effet il sera remis aux députés des mémoires particuliers."

Page 136, col. 1. There is a difference in the number of articles. Nos. 18 and 19 of the AP are no. 17. No. 17 of the AP is no. 19.

Add art. 18: "Qu'il sera pourvu par les Etats Généraux aux moyens de faire cesser les abus résultant des justices seigneuriales."

Variation in ending.

Corrected according to MS, *Arch. Nat.* Ba 37.

DOLE
Third AP, Vol. III, p. 160.

Page 166, col. 2, art. 17 is not combined with art. 18; it should read: "La suppression de l'école royale militaire." Art. 18 then follows.

Page 167, col. 1, l. 58, insert after "hypothèques": "et que les fonds vendus resteront affectés des hypothèques."

Corrected according to printed text, *Arch. Nat.* C 18/69.

DORAT (MARCHE-BASSE)
Third AP, Vol. III, p. 678.

Page 681, col. 1, l. 11, add: "MM. les députés donneront leur attention à ces deux points."

Corrected according to MS, *Arch. Nat.* Ba 38.

DOUAI
Third AP, Vol. III, p. 179.

Page 179, col. 2, l. 29. Insert after "propriétaires"—"de manière qu'aucune autorité, aucune puissance ne peut attenter à leur liberté, ni enlever la moindre partie de leurs droits, et propriétés."

Page 182, col. 1, add after art. 43, an art. 44, and change numbers of articles thereafter:

Art. 44. "Qu'il ne soit accordé, sans l'avis des Etats des provinces aucune permission d'exporter les matières premières qui servent à alimenter les fabriques du Royaume."

Page 183, col. 1, art. 57 bears the number 58; 58 is art. 60; and add art. 59: "Que les habitans des Seigneurs soient déchargés de toutes corvées personnelles-seigneuriales, reste barbare de l'ancienne servitude, dont l'honneur de l'humanité exige qu'on perde jusqu'au souvenir."

Corrected according to printed text, *Arch. Nat.* Ba 38.

ETAMPES
Third AP, Vol. III, p. 283.

Page 284, col. 2, add to art. 14: "eu égard aux délits."

Corrected according to printed text, *Arch. Nat.* Ba 39.

TEXTS IN THE ARCHIVES PARLEMENTAIRES

EVREUX

Nobles AP, Vol. III, p. 295.

Difference in title. A manuscript of the *Arch. Ardennes* ends with a certification by the Comte de Courcy, with date Mar. 28, 1789.

The AP text corresponds to the printed text, *Arch. Nat.* Ba 40.

Third AP, Vol. III, p. 300.

Page 301, col. 1, insert an article between arts. 29 and 30 and change the numbers of articles thereafter.

"Art. 30. "Que chaque province acquitte d'abord ses charges de ses propres fonds et que ce surplus soit versé directement à la caise nationale." Art. 31 as it appears in the AP is omitted.

Signatures and collation by registrar.

Corrected according to MS, *Arch. Nat.* C 18/74.

FENESTRANGE

United AP, Vol. V, p. 710.

Page 711, col. 2, l. 44, read: "pouvoir executif."
Corrected according to MS, *Arch. Nat.* Ba 77.

FOIX

Nobles AP, Vol. IV, p. 280.

In the margin opposite the beginning appears:

"Le Comté de Foix n'est venu domaine de la couronne que par sa réunion au Royaume de Navarre, et par l'avènement d'Henri IV au trône, et ce province était une propriété personnelle du bon Roy, dont il eut la jouissance comme héritier des comtes de Foix, nos anciens souverains."

Page 281, col. 2, l. 38, read: "semences" instead of "sommes."
Corrected according to MS, *Arch. Nat.* Ba 60.

GEX

Clergy AP, Vol. III, p. 388.

Collation by secretary of the assembly, with date March 19, 1789.
Corrected according to MS, *Arch. Nat.* Ba 43.

Third AP, Vol. III, p. 394.

Page 394, col. 2, l. 26, read: "payent point" instead of "parlent pas."
Page 394, col. 2, l. 72, read: "établirent un bailli à Gex."
Corrected according to MS, *Arch. Nat.* Ba 43.

GIEN

Clergy AP, Vol. III, p. 398.

Page 399, col. 2, l. 21, omit: "les plus essentiels"; and insert: "et des pauvres, les uns, parmi ces écclesiastiques les plus essentiels."

The word "admis" appears in the margin opposite p. 399, arts. 9 and 11, and p. 400, arts. 13, 16 and 19.

At the end add: "la présente expédition sans quelle puisse préjudicier aux droits du chapitre de Gien."

Corrected according to MS, *Arch. Nat.* Ba 43.

LA ROCHELLE

Nobles AP, Vol. III, p. 471.

Page 473, col. 2, l. 44, read: "francs" instead of "livres."

Page 474, col. 2, l. 7, read "présidiaux et bureaux de finances."

Correct according to MS, *Arch. Nat.* C 23/138.

LESNEVEN

Third AP, Vol. III, p. 493.

This is an example of a cahier in which the editors of the AP here modernized the spelling, and improved the grammar of the original MS.

Correct according to MS, *Arch. Nat.* C 19/84.

LILLE

Third AP, Vol. III, p. 532.

Page 535, col. 2, the paragraph: "Et par le procureur du Roi . . . dont acte." is omitted in the printed text.

Corrected according to printed text, *Arch. Nat.* Ba 46.

LIMOGES

Nobles AP, Vol. III, p. 564.

Page 565, col. 2, the statistics for the "domaines d'Angoumois affermés" should read:

"Part des propriétaires,	559 liv. moins de $51\frac{1}{4}\%$.
Part du Roi,	571 liv. plus de $48\frac{3}{4}\%$.
Total.	1,170 liv.

Page 566, col. 2, l. 52, insert after the word "Limoges": "(voyez les pages 221 et 306, Vol. I)."

Page 568, col. 1, art. 19, the printed text reads "puisque les Etats généraux peuvent régir . . ." However, "généraux" was crossed out, and "provinciaux" written in by hand. Addition at end of cahier.

Corrected according to printed text, *Arch. Nat.* Ba 47.

LIMOUX

Third AP, Vol. III, p. 579.

Page 581, col. 2, art. 21, omit: "La vénalité des charges abolie."

Page 582, col. 1, l. 43, read: "cantons de province."

Corrected according to MS, *Arch. Nat.* Ba 47.

LONGWY
Clergy AP, Vol. III, p. 771.

Page 772, col. 2, insert art. 16.

"Art. 16. Que toutes les charges des dîmes écclesastiques soient communes à tous les décimateurs, chacun à raison de sa portion de dîme."

Corrected according to MS, *Arch. Moselle.*

LOUDUN
Nobles AP, Vol. III, p. 594.

Certification by deputy, March 26, 1789.

Correct according to MS, *Arch. Nat.* Ba 47.

LYON
Clergy AP, Vol. III, p. 599.

Marginal titles sometimes omitted.

Page 602, col. 1, l. 54, read: "l'édit de 1768."

Corrected according to MS, *Arch. Nat.* C 19/90.

Third AP, Vol. III, p. 608.

Begins with a printed apology for the form and repetitions in the cahier, due to lack of time, and demand by country representatives that cahier be printed immediately.

Correct according to printed text, *Arch. Nat.* Ba 48.

MACON
Third AP, Vol. III, p. 628.

The title should read: "Cahier des voeux du tiers-état du bailliage de Mâcon."

Page 629, col. 1, l. 14, read: "Art. 13. Ampliation des présidiaux."

Page 631, col. 2, under the "Instructions sur les voeux particuliers du Mâconnais" insert:

"Instructions sur la constitution.

"Si l'administration des Etats est conforme à celle du Dauphiné, voir les modifications locales contenues au Projet imprimé par les commissaires de la ville de Mâcon le 28 janvier: voir aussi les projets qui seront addressés aux députés par les autres municipalités et communautés de la province."

Corrected according to MS, *Arch. Nat.* Ba 49.

MANS (LE)
Clergy AP, Vol. III, p. 636.

Read the date at end of cahier: le 30 mars, 1789.

Correct according to MS, *Arch. Nat.* Ba 49.

MANTES
Third AP, Vol. III, p. 666.

Page 666, col. 2, l. 66, read: "par tête et non par ordre."

Corrected according to printed text, *Arch. Nat.* AD I 10.

MEAUX

Clergy AP, Vol. III, p. 721.

Page 725, col. 1, add before the names of the signatures:

"*Bishop.*—L'assemblée charge son député de déclarer que son voeu est de voir résider les évêques en leurs diocèses, parceque leur présence est nécessaire au bien de la Religion, en conséquence le Roy sera très humblement supplié de rendre à leurs Eglises tous les Prélats retenus à la cour par un service qui semble étrangère à leurs fonctions et à leur caractère à l'exception toutesfois du Grand Aumonier que les lois de ce Royaume attachent particulièrement à la personne de Sa Majeste.

Dispenses.—Que pour assurer le repos des familles et pour y arguer les Frais qu'exige l'accord en cour de Rome pour le mariage à un dégré prohibé, les évêques soient rétablis dans leur ancien droit de dispenser jusqu'au dégré de cousin germain.

Commensalité de la maison du Roy. Que les chanoines commençaux de la maison du Roy en qualité d'ammoniers, chapelains, clercs, de chapelle ne puissent reclamer de privilèges pour être réputés présens à leur chapitre que ces deux titres soient déclarés incompatibles, le Roy pouvant sans doute trouver dans la sagesse de ses moyens et dans les biens Ecclesiastiques dont il est le distributeur de quoi fournis à la desserte de ses chapelles, sans enlever à leurs Eglises des Ministres qui y sont nécessaires pour l'exemple et pour la licence du culte divin.

Résidence.—Que tous écclesiastique pourvus de Bénéfices exigeant résidence soient tenus de résider effectivement, à l'exception des conseillers dans les cours de Parlement, qui seuls jouiront de l'exemption à raison des services qu'ils ont moyen de rendre à l'Eglise et dans cette exemption ne sont point compris les dignitaires, prébendes qui ont un service personnel à remplir.

Déport.—Que le droit de déport sur les curés vaccantes soit aboli comme un usage odieux qui prive une paroisse de son pasteur pendant un an pour la livrer à la desserte d'un mercenaire, au grand détriment des moeurs et de la Religion; et que les Exèques soient autorisés à dédomager par union de Bénéfices les archdiacres qui n'ont que ce droit pour dotation.

Monitoire. Que l'usage ou plutôt l'abus des monitoires soit détruit et réformé comme contraire à l'Esprit de l'Eglise, Esprit de douceur et de charité qui le porte plutôt à intercéder pour les coupables qu'à les faire de couvrir ou que si des raisons supérieurs n'en permettent pas l'entière abolition, ou ne les emplois du moins que pour les grands crimes, comme le meurtre et les crimes d'Etat.

Prévention.—Que la prévention en Cour de Rome étant une véritable plaie de l'Eglise surtout lorsqu'il s'agit des Benefices a charge d'ames, dont les ministres si precieux à l'Etat et à la Religion ne peuvent etre choisis avec trop de soin, il soit declaré et statué que pour les cures, les autres benefices, elle en sera admise qu'un mois apres la vacance.

Biens des Jésuits et autres ordres supprimés. Que les économes ou sequestres des biens des jésuites et autres ordres Religieux supprimés, soient forcés de rendre compte de leurs effets mobiliers et immeubles ensemble de leur gestion et administration afin qu'on connoisse l'employe qu'on a fait et celui qu'on pourra faire de ces biens à l'avenir.

Uniformité du culte.—Qu'il ni ait dans tout le Royaume qu'un bréviaire, qu'un Cathechisme, qu'un rituel et qu'un cérémonial afin que partout la doctrine, le culte, la manière de prier et de faire le service divin, soient les mêmes, ce qui aura lieu pour tous les ordres religieux.

Préséance.—Que pour éviter toutes les contestations, qui au grande scandale des peuples s'élèvent tous les jours entre les pasteurs et ministres des différents églises au sujet de rang et de la préséance il fait statué par une loi claire et précise sur les places, primauté et présidence entre les Evêques, abbés, réguliers et commendataires, les chapitres et leurs dignitaires, les curés et autres bénéficiers.

Edit des Protestants. Le Roy dans l'article premier de l'Edit du mois de novembre 1787, concernant les non-catholiques voulant et ordonnant que la religion catholique apostolique et Romaine contenu seule de jouir en France du culte public, que tout enseignement public soit interdit à tout non-Catholique désirant encore favoriser de tout son pouvoir les moyens d'instruction et de persuasion pour ramener tous ses sujets dans le sein de l'Eglise. Et n'annonçant d'autre but dans cette loi de donner un Etat civil qui en resultent.

Son député portera aux Etats Généraux le voeu de demander à sa Majesté que les dispositions de ce Edit ne s'étendent pas au dela de ce qui suffit pour assurer aux non-Catholiques le titre de citoyen, et la jouissance des effets civils. Conséquement à ces principes qui sont le résultat du Préambule et du premier article de l'Edit.

1. Toute culte public, toute assemblée à l'effet du culte, tout enseignement public, toute instruction, toute école seront expressement interdits aux non-Catholiques.

Et les procureurs du Roy tenus à cet effet de veiller à l'exécution de tout ce qui sera ordonné et défendu à cet egard.

2. L'article quatre du d.Edit sera supprimé en ce qu'il y est fait mention de Pasteurs d'une autre Religion que la Religion catholique loin de tolérer ces ministres, sous quelques habits qu'ils paroissent, loin d'en parler, d'en supposer, le nom de les ministres en sera pas même prononcé, et on continuera de les regarder comme exclus du Royaume.

3. Pour ce qui concerne le mariage des non-Catholiques il ne sera aucunement fait mention ni des curés, ni ces vicaires qui ne doivent y participer ni activement ni passivement les parties contractants seront renvoiées devant les seuls officiers de justice, tant pour faire la publication des bans que pour recevoir le déclaration des dites parties.

4. L'article 25 du d.Edit sera modifié de manière que les non-Catholiques n'auront pas la liberté de faire baptiser leurs enfants dans leur maison, mais qu'ils seront obligés de les faire porter à l'Eglise pour y être baptizé dans les 24 heures.

Pareillement les Enfants des non-Catholiques qui n'auront pas atteint l'age de raison seront inhumés dans le cimitière des paroisses avec les hommes de la sepulture ecclesiastique, l'article 27 l'insinue suffisamment.

Il serait même à souhaiter que sa Majesté ne regardat comme citoyens du Royaume, qui ceux qui par le Bapteme dont ils produiront les actes seroient devenus chrétiens.

Les curés non exclus des Bénéfices à la nomination du Roy.—Vu grand abus qui n'en paroit peut être pas un aujourd'huy parcequ'il datte de trop loin, c'est qu'un grand nombre d'écclesiastiques qui travaillent avec Edification dans le saint ministere et notamment les curés n'ont point départ aux bénéfices qui sont à la nomination du Roy: le seul titre de curé les en exclus, l'un nom ne peut, dit on, être inscrit sur la feuille comme si sa Majesté, qui par son amour atteint jusqu'au plus ignoré de ses sujets ne pouvoit atteindre par ses bienfaits jusqu'à des écclesiastiques et des Pasteurs épuisés par les travaux du Ministère.

Ce n'est pas que ces écclesiastiques, ces curés prétendent à l'opulence, à la fin de leur carrière une retraite honnête leur devient nécessaire et le plus souvent leurs évêques ne peuvent la leur procurer ou parcequ'ils n'ont pas de collation suffisante, ou parceque des sollicitations auxquelles ils croient ne pas pouvoir resister leur enlevent les Bénéfices et les Prébendes qu'ils conférent.

Sa Majeste sera doué très humblement et très respecteusement supplier d'ordonner que dans la distribution de ses Bénéfices il n'y ait plus d'exclusion pour les curés, que les Evêques pourront faire inscrire les noms de quelques uns des curés de leur diocèse sur la feuille des Bénéfices.

Conseil de conscience.—Comme le ministre de cette feuille ne peut avoir qu'une connoissance imparfaite du mérite de tous ceux qui peuvent prétendre aux faveurs de sa Majesté, il lui sera donné par sa Majesté un conseil composé de personnes sages éclairées faites par leur Etat ou par leurs Relations pour connoître les talens, les travaux et la conduite de ceux qu'il s'agira de récompenser.

Portions congrues.—La chambre du Clergé considérant que la déclaration du Roy de 1786 n'a pourvu que d'une manière insufisante à l'amélioration du sort des curés et des vicaires surtout dans les diocèses scitués à peu de distance de la capitale et notamment dans celui de Meaux, charge son député de solliciter aux Etats généraux, une loi qui ordonne—

1. Que dans tous les diocèses scitués en dela de la loire, il ne pourra y avoir de curés au dessous de 1500 livres dans les campagnes et au dessous de 1800 livres dans les villes.

2. Que la portion congrue des vicaires ne pourra être tant dans les villes que dans les campagnes au dessous de la moitié de celle des curés.

3. Que l'augmentation demandée sera fournie soit par les gros décimateurs soit en cas d'insuffisance des dismes par le moyen de réunion de bénéfices simples que les Evêques seront autorisés à opérer.

4. Que la prestation de la portion congrue sera payée en nature ou evaluée amiablement suivant le valeur des grains, si mieux n'aiment les gros décimateurs abandonner un fond qui représenteroit la portion congrue les curés autorisés à garder les fonds dont ils jouissent non chargés de fondation, estimation préalable faite de baux.

5. Qu'en dérogeant à l'article trois de la déclaration de 1786, il soit ordonné que dorénavant la portion congrue des vicaires soit payée par les gros décimateurs lors même que le curé ne seroit point à la portion congrue.

6. Que la portion congrue des vicaires soit supportée par tous les gros Décimateurs même par le curé s'il est décimateur pourvu qu'il luy reste toujours la somme de 1500 #.

7. Qu'en dérogeant à l'edit du Roy de 1768, il sera ordonné que dorénavant les curés qui ne sont point à portion congrue seront remis en possession de

toutes les dixmes novales sur les terres qui ont ete défrichées depuis 1768 qu'ils jouissent de toutes celles qui surviendront par la suite.

8. Que les Evêques seront tenus d'établir canoniquement tous les vicariats de leurs diocèses pour donner aux vicaires un titre en vertu du quel ils pourront légalement exiger le payment de la portion congrue.

Fonds pour la subsistance des Prêtres âgés et infirms et pour la dotation des Fabriques.—L'ordre du Clergé charge son député de demander aux Etats-Généraux l'exécution de la déclaration du Roy de 1786, en conséquence.

1. Qu'il soit fait dans chaque diocèse un fond suffisant pour pourvoir donner des pensions de retraites à des Prêtres âgés et infirmes.

Ainsy que pour augmenter la dotation des fabriques et que pour remplir cet objet les évêques soient autorisés à supprimer des bénéfices simples.

2. Qu'il soit fait une nouvelle loy pour rendre les unions plus faciles et moins dispenses et qui rende les procures moins longues en dispensant de la nécessité d'obtenir des lettres patentes préparatoires.

Bureau de charité.—Pour arrêter le progrès de la mendicité et même dans la vue de la detruire entierement, il sera établi dans toutes les paroisses un Bureau de charité, les fonds seront pris sur les propriétés au marc la livre de leurs impositions. Ce Bureau sera administré par les membres de la municipalité, et présidé par le curé.

Reform des abus par rapport aux gradués et aux septenaires.—Rien sans doute n'est plus respectable que les privileges des universités, rien de plus avantageux pour les sciences que de favoriser aux qui font leurs cours d'études dans ces universités qui s'y distinguent qui y prennent des degrés, ceux surtout qui se consacrent à l'enseignement et professent avec honneur, mais il s'est glissé tant d'abus rélativement aux gradués et surtout aux septenaires, qu'il est très intéressant de demander instamment une reforme à cet égard.

La Régale.—Quoique la Régale soit un droit auquel on ne doive donner aucun atteinte cependant comme ce droit est souvent la source des plus grands abus en ce que les Evêques sont quelquefois plusieurs années sans vouloir la fermer, et que par ce moyen ils suspendent l'effet de toutes les expectatives, et privent les titulaires de l'avantage des resignations et permutations. On demandera que la clôture de la Régale se fasse six mois après la prestation de serment entre les mains du Roy, lequel tems passe la Régale sera censée fermé et les titulaires parfaitment les maîtres de disposer de leurs bénéfices.

Restriction des droits des curés primitifs.—Comme les curés primitifs usent souvent de prétendus droits qui enchainent ceux des curés exerceant les fonctions du ministere, et qu'ils imposent à ceux-ci des servitudes d'autant plus humiliantes que ce sont quelquefois des abbesses qui les prétendent ces droits.

On demandera l'abolition de toutes ces servitudes, de manière que les curés seront tout à fait independant dans leurs fonctions curiales. Qu'en conséquence ils auront ce droit exclusif de célébrer dans leur Eglise les messes et paroisse de mariages d'enterrements et autres de dévotion publique et particulière, de présider généralement à tous les offices paroissiaux et de jouir de tous les droits attachés à leur qualité de curés.

Quant aux honneurs dus aux curés primitifs, ils ne leur seront rendus qu'en leur présens.

Maitres d'Ecoles.—Rien n'etant plus opposé au bon ordre et à la subordination qui doit regner dans les paroisses que de laisser aux habitants le choix de leur maître d'école sous le prétexte qu'ils le payent, que cette liberté de choisir ou de destituer à leur gré les maîtres d'école est la source d'une infinité de procès, ils seront dorènavant présentés à l'Evêque par les curés pour avoir l'approbation, sauf les droits des Ecolatres.

L'assemblée charge son député de demander que Messieurs les agents généraux du Clergé de France ayant comme par le passé leur entrée et séance à la chambre du Clergé aux Etats Généraux.

Tous lesquels pouvoirs et instructions ont été lus, approuvés et arrêtés en l'assemblée de l'ordre du Clergé du Bailliage de Meaux afin d'être présentés à l'assemblée des Etats Généraux du Royaume, par M. Barbou, curé d'Isle les Villenois, son député auquel l'ordre du Clergé donne pouvoir de remontrer, aviser, et faire pour la prospérité Générale du Royaume, la régénération de l'Etat et le bien de l'ordre du Clergé tout ce que les circonstances luy permetteront, déclarant l'assemblée que dans les cas non prévus et pour les objets non énoncés dans les mandats et pouvoirs cy-dessus elle s'en rapporte à sa prudence et au zele patriotique de son député. Déclare en outre l'assemblée qu'ayant prévu par son élection de ce jour le cas où le M. curé d'Isle les Villenois, son député, ne pourrait pas pour cause de maladie ou autre empêchment légitime porter son voeu aux Etats Généraux et en suivre les séances pendant toute la durée de l'assemblée d'ayant nommé pour suppléant la personne de M. De Rualleur, abbé commendataire de l'abbaye des Faronelle, lui donne pour le remplacer les mêmes pouvoirs que dessus.

Fait et arrêté à la chambre du Clergé du Bailliage de Meaux le 20 mars 1789 et signé au désir du Règlement de sa Majesté, ainsi signé:"

There are additional names over those given by the AP. Collation by Michet, with date April 16, 1789.

Corrected according to MS, *Arch. Nat.* C 20/97. The AP evidently used the printed text in Ba 51 which does not give these passages.

Third AP, Vol. III, p. 727.

Page 729, col. 2, l. 47, insert after "percevoir": "et de verser dans le tresor de l'Etat la portion des subsides, assignées par les Etats-Généraux.

Corrected according to MS, *Arch. Nat.* C 20/97.

MELUN

Nobles AP, Vol. III, p. 739.

Page 740, col. 1, add to art. 7: "dont les abilités produires la confiance des peuples, et les mettres à l'abri de toute variation dans les sentiments du succession du Seigneur-Roy."

Page 742, col. 1, l. 30, read: "sur la suppression de la vénalité."

Page 743, col. 1, l. 72, insert after "l'ordre militaires," the words "de St. Louis." There are slight variations of phrasing and the omission of a few unimportant phrases.

Corrected according to MS, *Arch. Nat.* Ba 51.

TEXTS IN THE ARCHIVES PARLEMENTAIRES

MENDE

Nobles AP, Vol. III, p. 753.

Cf. part omitted, *infra*, p. 365.

METZ

Nobles AP, Vol. III, p. 762.

Page 764, col. 1, l. 34, read: "plus de dix mille familles."
Corrected according to printed text, *Arch. Nat.* AD I 10.

Third AP, Vol. III, p. 764.

Page 766, col. 2, l. 66, insert after "patrimoine": "primitif."
Corrected according to printed text, *Arch. Nat.* Ba 52.

MONTFORT L'AMAURY

United AP, Vol. IV, p. 37.

Page 40, col. 1, l. 2, insert after line 2 the following: "Que la jurisdiction des eaux et forêts soit supprimée dans toute l'étendue du Royaume, et que la partie d'Administration qui lui est confié soit remise aux Etats provinciaux et le contentieux aux Juges ordinaires."
Page 41, col. 2, l. 51, read: "d'aliener le capital."
Corrected according to printed text, *Arch. Nat.* Ba 54.

MONTREUIL-SUR-MER

Clergy AP, Vol. IV, p. 59.

Page 59, col. 1, l. 18, read: "pour son départment."
Correct according to MS, *Arch. Nat.* Ba 56.

MORLAIX

Third AP, Vol. IV, pp. 72 et seq.

Page 75, col. 1, l. 46, add: "reversibles également sur les levées des gardes côtes, comme de toutes les autres milices qui devront être faites à prix d'argent."
Page 75, col. 2, l. 7, read: "sur le pied de l'apprécis."
Corrected according to MS, *Arch. Nat.* Ba 26.

MOULINS

Clergy AP, Vol. II, p. 442.

Addition of deputies' names at end of cahier.
Correct according to printed text, *Arch. Nat.* Ba 56.

Third AP, Vol. II, p. 447.

The AP follows the printed text of Ba 56. In the manuscript text, page 448, arts. 19, 20, and art. 11 of col. 1 were written in the margin and signed.

The MS text gives no date of acceptance, but ends with signatures and the name of the registrar.

Corrected according to MS, *Arch. Nat.* C 21/109.

NANTES

Third (AP, Vol. IV, p. 94.)

The cahier given by the AP Vol. IV, p. 94, is the cahier of the town of Nantes. The cahier adopted by the third estates of Nantes and Guérande, united (see illustrations, p. 36), differs so little from this text, that the changes necessary to represent the latter text will be indicated.

Title: "Cahier des doléances, remontrances et instructions de la ville et comté de Nantes, destiné à être porté aux Etats généraux convoqués à Versailles pour le 27 avril 1789."

There is a change in the numbering of the articles, with the result that the general cahier gives 184 articles.

Page 97, col. 1, insert art. 77: "Le droit de boisselage perçu par quelques curés de la province sera supprimé."

Page 97, col. 2, beside art. 100 was written in the margin: "Cet article demandé par le Commerce discuté, non arrêté."

Page 98, col. 2, l. 12, read "Tout droit de banc-étanche, boutallage . . ."

Page 100, col. 2, l. 26, read: "Les habitants de la ville et comté de Nantes . . ."
Various titles for articles are omitted. The signatures at the end of the cahier are different, although the date of adoption was the same. (This was correct according to the p. v.) Omit the verification by the secretary of the assembly of the town, Robert, and substitute, verification by registrar, Garnier, for April 30, followed by the verification by the king's councillor of the *sénéchaussée,* Bellabre, on May 1. The united cahier bears the official seals, and is written on the official paper. The text is a copy made by the registrar, as the signatures of the members of the assembly are copied.

Corrected according to MS, *Arch. Nat.* Ba 26.

NEMOURS

Third AP, Vol. IV, p. 112.

Page 116, col. 2, l. 4, read: "avaient rachetés."

Page 118, col. 1, the last of the paragraphs commencing line 45, and running to col. 2, l. 37, was an addition to the text, written in the margin, but approved.

Page 120, col. 2, l. 48, read: "de 61 villes, bourgs, et paroisses."

Page 121, col. 1, note (1), read: "Celles de Chevannes et d'Auxy ordonne en cas un peu près pareil."

Page 121, col. 2, ll. 58–59: read: "pour la plupart des jeunes gens."

Page 124, col. 1, ll. 18–19, read: "D'abord a-t-on dit, à 500 toises de distance; puis pour plus exactitude à 500 toises mesures à vol d'oiseau."

Page 124, col. 1, l. 43, read: "de la quotité et de l'âge . . ."

Page 124, col. 2, l. 39, read: "les bois à bruler, œuvrés et à ouvrer."

Page 125, col. 2, l. 62, read: "35 sous par delà."

Page 130, col. 2, l. 8, omit the "si."

Page 132, col. 2, ll. 48–51, omit the paragraph: "Ce droit est injuste . . . que l'on peut faire sur elle"; substitute:

"Ce droit est injuste en lui-même: car quelle raison y-a-t-il d'imposer des cuirs à un droit énorme plutôt qu'une autre marchandise."

"Il est excessif dans so proportion, car il est établi sur le pied 15% de la valeur totale de la marchandise ou de plus de 50% du profit que l'on peut faire sur elle."

Page 135, col. 2, ll. 63-69, omit the paragraph: "Les employes des gabelles . . . de les renvoyer à volonté"; substitute:

"Ils ne les font pas aussi souvent que le permet l'ordonnance dans le bailliage de Nemours, parceque les fermiers n'estiment pas qu'il leur soit avantageux d'entretenir un assez grand nombre de commis pour un exercise, mais il en font quelquefois, et ils sont toujours les maîtres de les renouveller à volonté."

Page 137, col. 1, last line, read: "reculee" instead of "retarde."

Page 139, col. 2, l. 32, read: "Pont-Thierry."

Page 143, col. 1, ll. 26-28, omit: "Il faut discuter . . . conduire l'exemple d'Angleterre."

Page 152, col. 1, l. 26, read: "Si pendant que la loterie . . ."

Page 153, col. 2, ll. 40–41, read: "les mechancetés que l'on croit convenable."

Page 153, col. 2, ll. 42–44, omit: "Cela pourrait se faire . . . mais, quoiqu'il en soit."

Page 159, col. 1, l. 10-col. 2, line 57, a long passage was written in, in very fine handwriting, extending from "Il faut ordonner . . . d'y pourvoir."

Page 160, col. 1, ll. 72–73, insert: "L'imposition directe est celle qui faible plus de bruit et qui choque davantage."

"C'est pour cet à même qu'elle est moins à craindre et plus conforme à la liberté: elle avertit de sa présence: elle éveille la réclamation, et celle ci lorsequ'elle est fondée, se faire toujours écouler du plus au moins par un gouvernement qui n'est ni insensé, ni cruel."

Page 160, col. 2, ll. 51–52, insert: "Cette idée doit faire trembler ceux qui se determinent à multiplier et à voiler les charges publiques."

Page 168, col. 1, ll. 70–72, omit: "Il veut que . . . être précipitée"; substitute: "Et tout ce que les égards, dus à la diversité des opinions, lui paraissent devoir éxiger, est que la déliberation décisive ne puisse être précipitée," etc.

Page 178, col. 1, l. 8, add "des citoyens."

Page 181, col. 2, l. 12, insert:

"Quelques autres observations ont été faites aussi rélativement aux hypothèques.

"Plusieurs personnes ont pensé qu'il serait très utile de les rendre toujours spéciales et jamais Générales, afin qu'on peut s'assurer dans chaque bailliage qu'aucun bien n'est engagé au delà de la valeur ce qui préviendrait les Banqueroutes, et garantiront d'une manière indubitable les droits des créanciers.

"On désirerait qu'indépendamment de l'imposition des contracts et actes translatifs de propriété au tableau des hypotiques pendant l'espace de deux mois, il fut donné plus de publicité à ses sortes d'actes avant l'obtension des lettres, de ratification en exigeant des publications et affiches dans la Paroisse de l'assiete des biens aux jours de Dimanches et de fêtes, dans ce temps intermédiaire des deux mois accordés pour l'exposition, ou pendant un plus long délai s'il eu nécessaire."

Page 187, col. 2, ll. 41–42, read: "beaucoup plus éclairées qu'il ne peut l'être."

Page 188, col. 2, ll. 54–56, substitute: "Le tiers-état du bailliage de Nemours ne se permettra point d'opinion arrêtée sur ces questions de droit."

Page 190, col. 1, l. 24, read: "Si l'on fait marcher de front . . ."

Page 190, col. 1, l. 49, read: "francs" instead of "livres."

Page 191, col. 2, ll. 41–43, omit: "Ses membres servaient . . . d'un zêle pur, civique, et actif."

Page 192, col. 1, ll. 63–64, omit: "Le tiers-état doit exposer . . . aurait à s'occuper."

Page 195, col. 1, ll. 7–68. These lines appear in fine handwriting inserted in the text, but signed.

Page 195, col. 2, ll. 56–57, omit: "mais sans déranger . . . des possesseurs actuels."

Page 196, col. 2, l. 72, insert after "gerbe": "Il y en a où, cumulé il est vrai avec la dîme, il emporte, non pas, il se fait porter la sixième gerbe."

Page 196, col. 2, l. 74, add: "Il le sont parceque leur terre est bonne. Nul pays de terre mediocre n'en pourrait supporter au tant."

Page 202, col. 1, l. 53, add: "pour les armaments maritimes."

Page 206 col. 2, l. 14, to p. 207, col. 1, line 11, appears in fine handwriting in the margin without signature.

Page 207, col. 2, l. 2, add: "Mais on ose tout contre les faibles, et rien contre les puissants."

Corrected according to MS, *Arch. Nat.* C 21/112.

NERAC

Nobles AP, Vol. I, p. 701.

Page 702, col. 1, l. 27, omit: "si."

Page 702, col. 1, l. 34, add: "Il nous est odieux, il pèse sur nous et sur le peuple, et à nos yeux, il est plus scandaleux et plus revoltant mille fois qu'aux yeux des autres ordres de la Nation."

Page 702, col. 1, l. 40, add: "et surtout de la prospérité nationale."

Page 702, col. 1, ll. 41–51, omit: "Que si nos regards . . . subjugué par conquérants"; substitute:

"Nous pensons enfin que notre ordre est méconnu dans ses principes et dans son existence, que mieux comme loin d'exciter l'envie, il la désarmerait; qu'il est dégradé, ruiné, anéanti, sans forme, sans ordonnances et sans organes, réduit enfin en pire état que s'il eut été subjugué par des conquérants."

Page 702, col. 2, ll. 29–31, omit: "nous demandons . . . et l'utilité"; substitute: "mais avant tout nous demandons que la besoin et l'utilité en soient constatés."

Page 702, col. 2, l. 64, add: "Le rapel au droit aux loix et à l'équité est la première économie politique."

Page 702, col. 2, l. 64, insert between "qui" and "par": "depuis quelques années."

Page 702, col. 2, ll. 67-70, omit: "Leur prodigieuse et subite . . . sans doute dévoilés"; substitute:

"Les méprises et les fauts de notre administration vont être reconnus. La Nation sans doute voudra les signaler, en portant un fanal perpetuel sur des écueils, dont nous serions heureux de pouvoir préserver les générations futures."

Page 703, omit col. 1, l. 48—col. 2, l. 25, substitute:

"remplis de cet espoir et convainçant que le plus urgent de nos besoins est de calmer la nation, en y rétablissant sur les bases antiques de la constitution, la liberté générale et individuelle des citoyens.

Convaincus enfin que la restauration des loix qui protègent nos propriétés générales et particulières classant les ordres sans les diviser les réunira dans un même voeu et dans un seul intérêt, pour ne tenir leur bonheur que de leur concorde et de leur harmonie; et après avoir unanimement établi ces principes fondamentaux de nos droits, de nos reclamations et de nos voeux, nous avons arrêté les articles suivants.

Art. 1. Notre député aux Etats-Généraux se conformera au droit constitutionnel de vôter par ordre et non par tête; nulle loi ne sera sensée revêtue du consentement de la nation qu'autant qu'elle aura réuni l'unanimité des trois ordres.

Art. 2. Il sera statué et reconnu solennellement par une charte authentique que la Nation seule a le droit d'accorder ou de refuser les subsides, de les suspendre ou de les prolonger pour un temps limité, d'en régler l'emploi, l'assiete, la repartition, et la perception, de faire et approuver les emprunts, si les malheurs de l'Etat forçaient à recourir à cette ressource funeste, et qui est illegale, inconstitutionelle et de nul effet.

Art. 3. Il sera pareillement reconnu que c'est à la Nation qu'appartient le droit imprescriptible d'établir de concert avec le Roi toutes loix nouvelles, bursales, générales, et permanentes, de corriger et de reformer les abus introduits dans toutes les parties du gouvernement.

Art. 4. La liberté générale et individuelle des citoyens sera reconnu pour être la base du contrat social de cette Monarchie. En conséquence, le voeu général de l'assemblée est pour la suppression totale des lettres de cachet, cependant elle croit devoir se référer sur cet objet à la sagesse des Etats-généraux.

Art. 5. Notre député demandera aussi l'abolition de toutes commissions particulières, evocations au conseil, et de tout droit de committimus, chacun devant être renvoyé par devant ses juges naturels afin que nul individus ne puisse être enlevé à la protection des loix, ni une seule contestation à leur connaissance.

Art. 6. Le retour périodique des états généraux sera fixé d'une manière irrevocable et dans les termes les plus prochains dèterminés dans l'assemblée générale. Le Ministre des finances sera tenu d'y rendre compte de l'emploi des deniers publics par pièces justificatives.

Art. 7. Si à l'époque qui aura été fixée pour la convocation des Etats Généraux, leur tenue était différée quelque fut la cause de ce retard, les subsides qui auraient été consentis par la Nation cesseront de plein droit d'être dus trois mois après la ditte époque, alors le corps de la nation, les états particuliers des provinces, et même les cours souveraines seront autorisées à poursuivre comme concussionaires, tous ceux qui oseraient s'ingérer à en continuer la perception avant qu'ils ayent été consentis de nouveau par l'Assemblée Nationale.

Art. 8. Il sera statué que toutes les lois générales faites de concert avec le roi dans le sein des états généraux, seront envoyées pendant le tenue même de l'assemblée tant au parlement de Paris, les princes et pairs y séants, qu'aux Parlements des provinces, pour y être enregistrées et placées sous la garde de ces cours souveraines, qui ne pourront se permettre d'y faire aucune modification, ni interpretation, mais qui seront désormais uniquement constitués pour l'exécution de l'ordre judiciare et chargés de veiller au maintient de la constitution; et elle en demeureront responsables envers la nation.

Art. 9. Il sera arrêté que toutes les loix de simple administration et police qui pourront être promulguées dans l'intervalle des tenues périodiques des états généraux, seront provisoirement adressées à l'enregistrement libre et à la vérification des cours mais elles n'auront de force, que jusqu'à la tenue prochaine des états généraux où elles auront besoin d'être rectifiées pour continuer d'être obligatoires.

Art. 10. Notre député demandera l'établissement, la restauration ou reformation des états particuliers qui devront être institués dans chaque province à l'unanimite du voeu des trois ordres.

Art. 11. Les ministres demeureront personnellement responsables envers la Nation de toutes leurs déprédations dans les finances ainsi que toutes les atteintes portées par eux aux droits tant nationaux que particuliers.

Art. 12. On établira la liberté indefinie de la Presse par l'abolition absolue de toute censure, à la charge par l'imprimeur d'apposer son nom à tous les ouvrages, et de repondre personnellement, lui ou l'auteur de tout ce que les écrits pourraient contenir de contraire à la religion, à l'ordre general, à l'honnêteté publique et à l'honneur des citoyens.

Tels sont les articles préliminaires constitutionnels sur lesquels nous enjoignons à notre député de faire statuer dans l'assemblée des états-généraux avant de voter sur aucune subside.

Et dans le cas ou notre dit député aux Etats-généraux ne pourrait parvenir à faire prononcer d'une manière positive sur les douze articles à dessus, nous lui ordonnons très expressement de protester en notre nom."

Articles secondaires

1. Notre depute ne votera les subsides qu'après l'obtention des articles ci-dessus.

2. Il exigera le tableau exact et détaillé de la situation des finances accompagne des pièces justificatives.

3. Il demandera uni vérification approfondie du montant du déficit de son origine et de ses accroissements successifs.

4. Un état très détaillé de toutes les pensions ou gratifications annuelles afin de pouvoir distinguer celles qui sont dues au mérite de celles qui sont le fruit de l'intrigue et de la faveur.

5. Un état motivé des dépenses de chaque département pour établir par tout la règle, la modération et l'économie convenable.

6. Il reclamera que les états généraux déterminent dans ses sagesse et de concert avec le roi, le régime le plus convenable pour la repartition et la perception des impôts d'en étendre la contribution sur les capitalistes et les créanciers de l'état.

7. Notre député devra demander qu'il soit statué sur les articles précédents avant de consentir les subsides qui seront jugés nécessaires pour subvenir aux besoins indispensables de l'état."

Observations

1. S'il est délibéré aux Etats-Généraux sur l'ascensement ou l'alienation du domaine et sur le retour des parties qui en sont engagés nous l'autorisons à voter en faveur de ce qui lui paraîtra le plus convenable aux intérêts de la nation.

2. Nous engageons notre député à voter pour l'établissement d'une constitution durable en faveur du corps militaire, et pour la réprobation d'une discipline avilissante faite pour des esclaves et non pour les français.

3. Il demandera que nul ne puissé être dépouillé d'un grade militaire que par le jugement d'un conseil de guerre.

4. Il fera ses efforts pour intérèsser la bonté de Sa Majesté à étendre sa justice et sa bienfaissance sur les braves soldats de ses armées.

5. Il réclamera la protection spéciale et les soins paternels de sa Majesté pour la perfection de l'éducation publique, et pour l'admission aux ecoles militaires des enfans de ces officiers que le mérite a élevé des derniers rangs de l'armée à la décoration de la Croix de Saint Louis.

6. L'assemblée demande qu'il soit dressé un tarif plus intelligible et plus simple que celui qui existe pour le controle et l'insinuation des actes.

7. Les vues du Régime actuel des corvées font desirer à l'assemblée la réalisation du voeu général pour qu'on emploie à la confection des chemins les troupes de sa Majesté. Les avantages qui en résulteraient sont universellement reconnus.

8. L'assemblée charge très expressement son député de supplier sa Majesté de vouloir bien ordonner l'exécution des titres rélatifs à l'exchange de l'Albret, et à la propriété incommutable de ce Duché. L'incertitude sur cet objet rend précaire la propriété du seigneur dominant d'une aussi grande étendue de territoire. Cette incertitude est très nuisible à tous les vassaux et censitaires de l'Albret en y rendant impossible toute espèce de traité avec le suzerain."

Conclusion

Dans le cas où l'on agiterait aux Etats généraux des questions qui n'auraient pas été prévues dans le présent cahier, nous enjoignons à notre député de se concerter avec les autres représentants de l'ordre de la Noblesse de la province et son voeu sera fixé par la pluralité des suffrages.

Enfin l'assemblée désirant concourir à la réforme des abus de toutes les parties de l'administration, supplie instamment et très respectieusement sa Majesté de réunir les citoyens les plus intègrés et les plus éclairés du royaume dans des comités particuliers de magistrature, de finance, guerre, marine, agriculture, commerce, arts, etc., pour y discuter toutes les améliorations dont ces départements sont susceptibles et en faire présenter les resultats à la prochaine assemblée nationale.

Fait et arrêté ce 5 avril, 1789 et dans l'assemblée des membres de l'ordre de la Noblesse des trois sénéchaussées de Nérac, Casteljaloux, et Castelmoron au Albret, tenues au dit Nérac, sénéchaussée principale. Signé,"

[Signed by the president, commissioners, two secretaries, and 61 members.]
Corrected according to MS copy, *Arch. Nat.* B III 94, p. 215.

NIVERNAIS

Clergy AP, Vol. IV, p. 246.

Page 247, col. 2, l. 44, read: "le service des autels."

Page 248, col. 1, l. 59, read: "protéger," instead of "proroger."

Corrected according to MS copy, *Arch. Nat.* B III, 92, p. 703.

Third AP, Vol. IV p. 256.

Page 260, col. 1, l. 19, add: "entière."

Corrected according to printed text *Arch. Nat.* Ba 58.

NOMENY

Nobles AP, Vol. IV, p. 87, art. 1—p. 88, art. 10; and p. 92, art. 11 to the end of the cahier.

Correct according to MS, copy, *Arch. Nat.* B III 93, p. 509.

PARIS *HORS-LES-MURS*

Cf. Chassin, C., *Les Elections et les cahiers de Paris en 1789.* The inconvenience of using these volumes without index, the fact that the texts as reprinted by Chassin differ slightly from the sources used, and the desire to make the cahiers of Paris easily available with those of the majority of general cahiers, leads to the presentation of the corrections for the texts given by the *Archives parlementaires.*

Clergy AP, Vol. V, p. 230.

Page 232, col. 1, l. 36, read: "rétablir le conseil de conscience . . ."

Page 234, col. 1, insert under "Police Civile," art. 5 (and call art. 5 of the AP art 6): "Que les loteries soient supprimées, comme contraires aux bonnes moeurs et à l'intérêt public."

Page 235, col. 1, l. 37, add: "en y faisont réfleurir toutes les vertus." Corrected according to printed text, *Arch. Nat.* C 22/120.

PARIS *INTRA-MUROS*
Cf. comment under Paris hors-les-murs

Clergy AP, Vol. V, p. 263.

Page 264, col. 2, l. 39, read: "l'exposition si commune . . ." Corrected according to printed text, *Arch. Nat.* C 22/119.

Third AP, Vol. V, p. 281.

Page 289, col. 2, next to last line, read: "et ceux des corps et des nations." Corrected according to printed text, *Arch. Nat.* C 22/119.

Municipality AP, Vol. V, p. 290.

Page 293, col. 1, l. 52, the following occurs as a footnote: "De ce nombre est celui du Ventillateur qui, par l'oubli de ses engagements, excité de la part du Public, les plaintes les plus fondées."

Addition at end, printed in by hand, "Pour expédition, Veytard." Corrected according to printed text, *Arch. Nat.* Ba 64.

PERONNE
Clergy AP, Vol. V, p. 347.

Page 353, col. 1, l. 51, read: "consommé" instead of "confirmé." Correct according to printed text, *Arch. Nat.* Ba 67.

Nobles-Third AP, Vol. V, p. 355.

Page 357, col. 2, l. 14, read: "Que les Etats provinciaux soient . . ." The word "généraux" was crossed out, and "provinciaux" written in. The error is obvious from the sense of the article.

Page 361, col. 2, l. 44, the date should read: "le 7 avril 1789." Corrected according to printed text, *Arch. Nat.* Ba 67.

PERPIGNAN
Nobles AP, Vol. V, p. 368.

The quoted passages, and also numerous other explanatory or philosophical phrases appear in the margin of the original text. Correct according to printed text, *Arch. Nat.* Ba 67.

Third AP, Vol. V, p. 373.

Add at end additional paragraph stating copy of cahier, in 21 articles, with date April 26. Corrected according to MS, *Arch. Nat.* Ba 67.

PLOËRMEL
Third AP, Vol. V, p. 378.

Difference of title.

Page 378, col. 1, l. 43, omit: "aux Etats généraux"; substitute: "au tiers-état."

Page 379, col. 2, l. 12, read: "Que le droit de *fumage*."

The cahier ends with the list of deputies and substitutes.

Corrected according to printed text, *Arch. Nat.* Ba 26.

POITIERS
Clergy AP, Vol. V, p. 389.

Add at end of cahier adoption by the assembly of the clergy with the date of March 27, 1789, followed by the signatures of the president, secretary, commissioners, and 31 members of the assembly.

Collation by the registrar, Puguet, without date.

Correct according to MS, *Arch. Nat.* C 22/126. The MS Ba 68 does not have this ending which is important for the authentication of the cahier.

Third AP, Vol. V, p. 406.

Slight difference of title, p. 406, omit the titles, "Préambule" and "Mandat impératif."

Page 410, col. 1, ll. 21-22, read: "des délibérations des paroisses en la justice royale."

Corrected according to MS, *Arch. Nat.* Ba. 68.

PONT-A-MOUSSON
Nobles AP, Vol. II, p. 228.

Add collation without date by registrar, Vistoo.

Corrected according to printed text, *Arch. Nat.* AD I 11.

PONTHIEU
Third AP, Vol. V, p. 436.

Page 440, col. 2, l. 49, add: "sur la confection du nouveau code civil et criminel."

Page 442, col. 2, l. 26, read: "parcage" instead of "pacage."

Omit the following passages:

Page 443, col. 2, ll. 26-45, the passage in italics and the article "Navigation."

Page 444, col. 1, ll. 40-43, "que l'obligation . . . s'il y a lieu."

Page 444, col. 2, ll. 30-38, "Le présent cahier . . . Clemenceau et Lavernier, avec paraphes."

Page 444, col. 2, ll. 42-44, "sauf les apostilles . . . la chose publique."

Corrected according to MS, *Arch. Nat.* Ba 9. The AP probably used the printed text in AD I 10.

PROVINS
Clergy AP, Vol. V, p. 445.

Page 445, col. 2, l. 29, add: Art. 8. "Nous supplions trés humblement le Roi de faire exécuter ses ordonnances sur la santification des Dimanches et des fêtes; enjoindre aux officiers de Police dans les villes et les campagnes d'y tenir la main, sous les peines les plus sévères. L'inexécution malheureuse des Loix, et le peu de soin des Juges, ont porté une atteinte considérable à la décence et la majesté du culte public, trop violé par les blasphèmes et la fréquentation des cabarets."

Corrected according to printed text, *Arch. Nat.* C 23/128.

Nobles AP, Vol. V, p. 447.

Slight variation in form of beginning of cahier.

Certification by registrar, Prive, with date March 26, 1789.

Corrected according to printed text, *Arch. Nat.* C 23/128.

Third AP, Vol. V, p. 452.

Page 453, col. 2, l. 58, insert between the words "royaume" and "et que le secret . . .": "Que les états soient suppliés de prendre en consideration la traite des nègres, de briser leurs fers, et de les faire jouir des droits sacrés des autres citoyens."

Page 454, col. 1, art. 44 is art. 45. Insert art. 44: "Que la tolérance religieuse soit consentie de manière qu'il n'y ait plus d'exception pour remplir des emplois civils sous telles modification que les états aviseront."

Collation by registrar, Privé, and certification by president, Crespin.

Corrected according to MS, *Arch. Nat.* C 23/138.

PUY-EN-VELAY
Third AP, Vol. V, p. 469.

Page 470, art. 47 is omitted in the MS original, but not in the printed text.

Page 470, col. 1, insert art. 84 (general change of numbers): "La navigation de la Loire jusques au lieu déconsolant paroisse de Cauzac, diocèse de Puy."

Art. 89 is art. 47 omitted with the following addition: "Les députés du Tiers Etat de la Sénéchaussée de Velay insisteront de tout leur pouvoir en l'assemblée nationale sur toutes les demandes et remontrances inserés dans le present cahier au quel effet tous pouvoirs généraux et suffisants leur seront donnés et conférés de proposer, remontrer, aviser, et consentir tout ce qui peut concerner les besoins de l'état, la réforme des abus, l'établissement d'un ordre fixe et durable dans toutes les parties de l'administration, la prospérité générale du Royaume, les biens et chacuns des sujets du roi promettant d'agréer et proposer tout ce que les députés auront fait, délibéré et signé.

Finalement les députés du pays et sénéchaussée du Velay seront tenus et obligés à leur retour des Etats Généraux de rendre compte de leur mission dans une assemblée de sénéchaussée qui sera convoquée à cet effet en cette ville du Puy.

Ainsi fait et arrêté par les commissaires du tiers Etat de la sénéchaussée du Velay le 3 avril 1789, les commissaires signés."

The names, together with this passage appear col. 2, of the AP.

Corrected according to MS, *Arch. Nat.* Ba 70.

REIMS

Clergy AP, Vol. V, p. 520.

Page 522, col. 1, l. 30, the following note appears in the margin: "Cet article doit être renvoyé à la partie II et placé au premier *à linea* de la dite page. Pierrard, sécretaire."

Page 524, col. 2, l. 18, this art. 2 is given in the margin, approved by secretary, with the following added at the end: "des deux autres ordres."

Corrected according to MS, *Arch. Nat.* Ba 71.

Third AP, Vol. V, p. 530.

Page 534, col. 1, l. 13, read: "des 21 juillet 1778 et 15 mai 1779."

Corrected according to printed text, *Arch. Nat.* Ba 71.

RIOM

Clergy AP, Vol. V, p. 561.

Page 561, col. 2, l. 57, add: "et soit pris à partie."

At the end, verification by the lieutenant general, without date.

Corrected according to MS, *Arch. Nat.* Ba 72.

RIVIERE-VERDUN

Nobles AP, Vol. V, p. 583.

Page 584, col. 2, l. 71, substitute: "national" for "naturel."

Corrected according to MS, *Arch. Nat.* Ba 85.

Third AP, Vol. V, p. 587.

Page 587, col. 1, l. 33, read: *"nul seigneur sans titre."*

Corrected according to MS, *Arch. Nat.* Ba 85.

ROCHEFORT

Third AP, Vol. III, p. 486, and add supplement from Appendix, p. 385.

At the end of the cashier are 41 signatures in addition to that of Griffon, the registrar.

Correct according to MS, *Arch. Nat.* C 23/138.

RODEZ

Clergy AP, Vol. V, p. 551.

Page 554, col. 1, l. 7, the word "l'état" was crossed out.

Page 554, col. 2, l. 33, read: "sans distinction d'ordre."
Corrected according to MS, *Arch. Nat.* Ba 73.

Third AP, Vol. V, p. 557.

Page 558, col. 2, l. 77, begin art. 61: Que le collège . . ."

Page 559, art. 62 is art. 63. Insert art. 62: "Que les communautés du bailliage de Millau tel qu'il doit être contribuent aux frais d'entretien du college royal de Millau."
Corrected according to MS, *Arch. Nat.* Ba 73.

ROUEN

Clergy AP, Vol. V, p. 590.

Page 593, col. 1, l. 15, read: "méchaniques" instead of "machines."
Corrected according to printed text, *Arch. Nat.* Ba 76.

Nobles AP, Vol. V, p. 594.

The printed text is followed by a statement of the charter of Normandy.
Correct according to printed text, *Arch. Nat.* Ba 76.

ROZIERES

United AP, Vol. IV, pp. 91-92, through art. 10; p. 88, art. 11 to end of cahier.

Negligible differences of single words.
Correct according to printed text, *Arch. Nat.* Ba 57.

ST. BRIEUC

Third AP, Vol. V, p. 629.

Page 629, col. 2, l. 57, read: "comme pour les rendre constitutuées."
The word "rentes" reproduced by the AP makes better sense.

Page 629, col. 2, l. 66, add: "chaque chambre composé de manière qu'elle soit mi-partie, sans déroger au surplus aux arrêtés pris en la ville de Rennes."
Minor differences, without change of meaning.
Corrected according to MS, *Arch. Nat.* Ba 25.

ST. MIHIEL

Nobles AP, Vol. II, p. 235.

Page 236, col. 1, l. 20, insert after "gouvernement": "dont il ne sera rien démembré pour être uni à l'autres gouvernements."
Corrected according to MS, *Arch. Nat.* B III 23, p. 585.

ST. QUENTIN

Clergy AP, Vol. V, p. 647.

Page 648, col. 1, l. 52, read: "entre tous les sujets de l'Etat."

Page 650, col. 1, l. 2, add: "dans toute la France."
Corrected according to MS, *Arch. Nat.* Ba 70.

SAINTES
Third AP, Vol. V, p. 669.

Page 670, col. 1, l. 27, read: "aucun nouvel impôt."

Page 671, col. 1, l. 52, read: "l'édit de 1771 . . ."

The cahier of the Ile d'Oléron and the cahier of the town of Saintes are an integral part of the text of the cahier of the third estate, instead of separate as given by the AP. The general cahier of the third estate, should therefore end on page 674, col. 2. There follows the "ne variétur" of the senechal and registrar.

Corrected according to MS copy, *Arch. Nat.* B III 139, pp. 488 *et seq.*

SARREGUEMINES
Clergy AP, Vol. V, p. 689.

Page 690, col. 2, l. 20, read: "ouvrages de la campagne chaument."

"Choment" as given by the AP would seem to give the better sense.

Correct according to MS, *Arch. Nat.* Ba 77.

Nobles AP, Vol. V, p. 690.

Page 692, col. 1, l. 44, add: "On peut citer à cet égard le règlement en vigueur dans la province d'Alsace avec les additions dont il pourrait être susceptible."

Corrected according to MS, *Arch. Nat.* Ba 77.

SAUMUR
Third AP, Vol. V, p. 723.

Variation in number of articles, etc.

Correct according to MS copy, *Arch Nat.* B III 140, p. 452. The MS, Ba 78 is less complete.

SEMUR-EN-AUXOIS
Clergy AP, Vol. II, p. 126.

Collation at end by president, Creusot, on April 1, 1789.

Correct according to MS, *Arch. Côte d'Or.*

Nobles AP, Vol. II, p. 128.

Page 129, col. 1, l. 34, add at end of art. 8: "pour ne durer que pendant l'intervalle d'une assemblée à celle suivante fixée par les dits Etats généraux."

Page 129, col. 2, l. 48, read: "en 1787."

Verification by commissioners, May 6, 1789, and certified by D'argenteuil, October, 1790.

Corrected according to MS, *Arch. Nat.* Ba 78.

SOULE

Clergy AP, Vol. V, p. 774.

"Ne variétur" at end.

Correct according to MS, *Arch. Nat.* Ba 80.

TOUL

Clergy AP, Vol. VI, p. 1.

Page 3, col. 2, l. 12, insert after "échanges": "et les contre échanges."

Correct according to printed text, *Arch. Nat.* Ba 81.

Third AP, Vol. VI, p. 8.

Page 9, col. 1, l. 18, add: "assemblée, sans qu'aucun corps, aucune province, aucun tribunal, aucune communauté puisse suppléer à cet égard le consentement de la Nation."

Corrected according to printed text, *Arch. Nat.* Ba 81.

TOULOUSE

Nobles AP, Vol. VI, p. 31.

Page 31, col. 2, l. 16, the original has a footnote to accompany the phrase ending with "troisième": "Ordonnance du mois de mars 1356. Ordonnance d'Orléans art. 135."

Correct according to MS, *Arch. Nat.* Ba 82.

Third AP, Vol. VI, p. 35.

At end, names of commissioners and members of assembly—36 names.

Corrected according to printed text, *Arch. Nat.* Ba 82.

TOURS

Nobles AP, Vol. VI, p. 39.

Page 40, col. 2, art. 10, as given is art. 10, item 2. Insert art. 10, item 1: "Les Etats-généraux prescriront, de concert avec le Roi, la forme qu'il conviendra donner aux assemblées nationales."

Corrected according to printed text, *Arch. Nat.* C 24/160.

TULLE

Nobles AP, Vol. III, p. 537.

Page 538, col. 1, l. 27, add: "Après l'obtention de ces articles fondamentaux, il sera permis à nos représentants de délibérer sur les subsides."

Corrected according to printed text, *Arch. Nat.* Ba 84.

VALENCIENNES (town)

Town AP, Vol. VI, p. 99.

Page 99, col. 2, l. 25, add: "L'une embrassera les objets communs à tout le Royaume. L'autre concernera les articles rélatifs aux intérêts particuliers de la ville de Valenciennes."

Page 100, col. 2, l. 20, read: "surabondance" instead of "abondance."
Page 104, col. 1, ll. 12–13, read: "francs" instead of "livres."
Corrected according to printed text, *Arch Nat.* Ba 84.

VANNES
Third AP, Vol. VI, p. 107.

Page 107, col. 1, l. 41, read: "de départager les voix."
Corrected according to printed text, *Arch. Nat.* Ba 26.

VENDOME
Clergy AP, Vol. VI, p. 118.

Page 119, col. 1, l. 61, add: "des finances."
Add at end, signatures, "ne variétur" on March 24, 1789 by Rochambeau.
There is a variation in the ending of C 25/168.
Correct according to MS, *Arch. Nat.* Ba 84.

Nobles AP, Vol. VI, p. 120.

Variation in title, and in ending.
Correct according to MS, *Arch. Nat.* Ba 84.

VERDUN
Clergy AP, Vol. VI, p. 126.

Page 130, col. 1, the "demande particulière" for the placing of customs lines at the frontier appears in one MS, and not in the other of *Arch. Nat.* Ba 84, both equally authentic.
Correct according to MS, *Arch. Nat.* Ba 84.

VIC
Nobles AP, Vol. VI, p. 18.

Page 19, col. 1, l. 30, read: "particulier" instead of "individu."
Corrected according to MS, *Arch. Nat.* Ba 81.

Third AP, Vol. VI, p. 20.

Page 20, col. 2, ll. 13-14, read: "soient diminués."
Corrected according to MS, *Arch. Nat.* Ba 81.

VILLEFRANCHE-DE-BEAUJOLAIS
Clergy AP, Vol. II, p. 279.

Page 280, col. 2, l. 14, read: "souveraines du royaume."
Slight variation of title.
Corrected according to MS, *Arch. Nat.* Ba 85.

Nobles AP, Vol. II, p. 281.

Page 282, col. 2, l. 11, read: "billets de congé."
Corrected according to MS, *Arch. Nat.* Ba 85.

TEXTS IN THE ARCHIVES PARLEMENTAIRES

Third AP, Vol. II, p. 282.

Page 284, col. 1, l. 16, add: "les dits règlements convenables."
Corrected according to MS, *Arch. Nat.* Ba 85.

VILLENEUVE-DE-BERG

Nobles AP, Vol. VI, p. 177.

Page 181, col. 2, l. 66, add to art. 43: "de Villeneuve-de-Berg et d'Annonay."
Page 182, col. 1, last l., the name should read: "M. de Moreton-Chabrillant . . ."
At the end, was the date April 3, 1789.
Corrected according to printed text, *Arch. Nat.* Ba 85.

Third AP, Vol. VI, p. 707.

Page 711, col. 1, l. 20, read: "réunis" instead of "remise."
Page 712, col. 1, next to last line, read the date: "1735," instead of "1755."
Corrected according to MS, *Arch. Ardèche.*

VILLERS-COTTERETS

Nobles AP, Vol. VI, p. 189.

Page 189, col. 1, l. 47, insert after "séparement": "dans chacun des dits ordres. Déclarons même que dans le cas ou en vertu de consentement donnés préalablement et séparement . . . "
Corrected according to MS, *Arch. Nat.* Ba 86.

VITRY-LE-FRANÇOIS

Clergy AP, Vol. VI, p. 206.

Page 207, col. 1, 37, add: "nationalle."
Corrected according to MS, *Arch. Nat.* C 25/174.

Third AP, Vol. VI, p. 211.

Page 213, col. 1, l. 34, insert after "territoriale": "en nature."
Page 214, col. 2, l. 42, add after "fermiers": "et aux entrepreneurs."
Page 219, col. 1, l. 55, add: "et moins dissuss."
Corrected according to MS, *Arch. Nat.* C 25/174.

UNEDITED TEXTS OF GENERAL CAHIERS

In the course of the author's research on *cahiers de doléances*, a number of unedited texts were discovered. As a study of the general cahiers should include the complete number of known texts, thirty-four texts are reprinted here. This still does not make available in printed form all of the known cahiers. The cahier of Navarre, which would require a hundred pages of print is so long that it would unduly enlarge the present volume. Since that district was exceptional, the cahier will some day be used for a specialized study of Navarre. A few cahiers have been reprinted in books which are now out of print and hard to get, but such texts have not been repeated here. Five cahiers, hitherto unedited, have not been given here because their publication is promised in the near future. They had not been reprinted, however, when this volume went to press. The five cahiers in question are: C, N, T, Sarrebourg and Phalsbourg, and C. St. Mihiel, while notations for the text of the cahier of T. Rouen have been included. These will probably appear in regional publications of the northeast of France. The cahier of the third estate of Rouen will be published by M. Le Parquier in the official series of volumes. With these exceptions, the publication of the following thirty-four texts makes all extant general cahiers available in printed form.

The same emphasis has been made in the reprinting of these texts as in the corrections for the *Archives Parlementaires;* the aim has been to make a reliable text available. There has been no intention to render unnecessary an integral study of single *bailliages* in the series of official volumes, under the *Documents inédits.* . . . For this reason, there has been no attempt to edit the documents, or to give the information about local institutions and conditions that would be useful for a detailed interpretation. Only the information from the *procès-verbaux* that bears upon the authenticity of the document, and upon influences in its composition have been given. In each case, the original cahier was verified in respect to officers, committee for its composition, date of adoption, title, verification by royal officers, etc., but the *procès-verbaux* contain too much irrelevant detail and are too repetitious to make it desirable to reprint them as well as the cahiers. The method here adopted, makes the texts available on the same footing with the *corrected* texts of the *Archives parlementaires*.

The complete list of signatures at the end of the cahiers has been omitted advisedly, for two reasons: first, the difficulty of correctly interpreting the original signatures would have entailed endless verification without commensurate importance (see illustration p. 86); and second, the meaning of the text is not affected by the signatures, whose chief value is for establishing the authenticity of a text. Hence, once a text has been declared authentic, the meaning of the cahier may be ascertained without reference to signatures. After handling the original documents of 1789 in the national collections and also in many departmental collections, the author should be competent to judge what is an authentic cahier and what is not, and also, to what group of cahiers a particular text belongs. The author was satisfied that the texts which follow are authentic. The reprinting of lists of insignificant signatures seemed an unnecessary addition to the length of the present book. This omission is likely to cause adverse comment in France, where the requirements of the official series are better known, and where the signatures might have a certain biographical or genealogical value. Anyone with such a motive for consulting the cahiers should see the original, in any case. The present reprinting aims to make available the text of the cahier as an expression of the opinion of the assembly which adopted it, and thus to make possible the consultation of public opinion for particular regions or for the whole of France. The subjective, rather than the objective, value of the general cahiers has prompted these reprints.

THE ORIGINAL SPELLING, ACCENTS AND PUNCTUATION OF THE TEXTS HAVE BEEN RETAINED, EVEN TO THE INCLUSION OF ERRORS AND INCONSISTENCIES. IN THIS WAY, THE REPRINT IS AN EXACT REPRODUCTION OF THE ORIGINAL.

NO. 1. ARCHES AND CHARLEVILLE

Reprinted from MS text: *Arch. Nat.* C33/280.
P.V.—MS, *ibid.* Committee for cahier chosen December 21, 1789; cahier adopted December 31, 1789. Signatures verified. Convocation, 7th type.

EXTRAIT DES FEUILLES ET
LIASSE DU GREFFE DE L'HOTEL DE VILLE
DE CHARLEVILLE

Nous tous habitants de Charleville assemblés, une entière et pleine adhesion aux arrets et decrets de l'assemblée nationale, des cœurs pleins d'amour et de respect pour un Roy citoyen, sont les premiers declarations que nous prions les augustes representants de la nation d'agreer, nous le faisons à la face du ciel temoin de leur sincerité de la ferme résolution où nous sommes de la soutenir de tout notre pouvoir et de la scelle de notre sang s'il le fallait.

Avant que d'entree dans les details interessants par leurs rapports avec le bien général comme le commerce, le nombre des individus, celui du faux-bourg villes et hameaux que composent la principauté et les établissements pour elever la Jeunesse, secourir les pauvres, les vieillards et faire travailler ses mendiants, avant dissous nom d'en faire un tableau tracé sur l'influence que notre ville peut avoir sur la prosperité de la nation, nous oserons temoigner nos regrets d'etre encore sans representants et notre désir d'en avoir un dans la formation nouvelle d'une constitution a laquelle nous venons de sacrifier la notre, ainsi les grands exemples attirent les grands actions et ce qui nous en a rendu capables, c'est qu'etre homme et citoyen, c'est etre français; voila les titres qui nous enhardissent a demander que M. Cochelet soit admis comme deputé pour qu'il ne soit pas que nous[1] . . . une seule pierre et l'édifice du bonheur publique que les lumières et la vertu des representans des français elevent sur les fondements inébranables de la justice et de la liberté.

Population de la villes, bourgs, et communes qui composent la principauté.—La principauté de Charleville contient environ 12,000 ames, dont plus de 9,000 pour la ville, et le surplus dans les 5 villages et hameaux de la ditte Principauté, composé de beaucoup de manoeuvriers, de cloutinets depende les laboureurs.

Situation de Charleville par rapport au Commerce.—Quatre grandes routes traversent cette ville et y aboutissent, la Riviere de Meuse baigne ses murs et tient lieu d'une 5e route d'autant plus avantageuse que depuis la hollande jusqu'au ports de cette ville qui est le plus spacieux et le plus commode qui se trouve sur son cours cette rivière porte dans tous les temps des batteaux de 120 pieds de longueur, quelle fécondite! quelle source de commerce par cette seule voie! Si sa navigation n'était point surchargée de péages multipliés.

Le marché de Charleville favorisé par sa situation.

Le marché de Charleville est le plus considerable qu'il y ait a trente lieues de rayons. Il alimente plus de 40,000 ames ce marché est si important par sa situation que lorsque les provinces voisines, manquants de grains, elles n'ont point d'autres ressources pour leur approvisionnement que le marché de cette ville.

Situation de Charlesville, pour un departement, un district et autres établissements plus favorables encore que pour le commerce.

Independement des quatres grandes routes, et de la Meuze, cette ville qui après Sedan est la plus peuplée du departement a établie l'emporte par

[1] Several illegible words.

le nombre de ses habitans et a tous égards sur Mezières, Rocroi, Givet, sur Rethel qui est à l'extremité ainsi que Givet, elle l'emporte sur Sedan même par sa position au centre par ses branches de Commerce, beaucoup plus multipliées qu'à Sedan, Rethel et Givet, tant en armes qu'en cloux, fer en bar, cuir tannés, huiles, marbres, charbons des terres, ardoises, cotton, bas au metier, peignes, orphevrerie, et toutes les relations commerciales de Charlesville qui y attirent beaucoup de monde par la certitude des reserves avantageux, la population, son marché, son port et sa situation qui semblent faire exprès pour être le point central d'un grand arrondissement, sollicitent pour Charleville un departement, un district, un bailliage ou au moins une jurisdiction consulaire.

Manufacture de Charleville.—Cette ville contient une manufacture d'armes a feu principallement destiné au service militaire qui est une des meilleures qu'il y ait en France, elle reunit la sureté, la solidité et la beauté du travail.

Une manufacture de cloux, la plus considerable qu'il y ait en France.

Une manufacture de cuirs dont la fabrication est preferable a celle des etrangers elle n'a pas de superieure et peut être d'égale en France.

Charleville réunissant encore avec ses manufactures beaucoup d'autres cy-dessus mentionnés; quelle ville renferme plus de commerce et de manufactures?

Observations particulier pour Charleville.—Le contrôle n'ayant jamais eu lieu a Charleville, on demande que si on l'y introduit par la faite, il ne puisse avoir un effect retroactifs, et que tous les actes, soit notariés où sous seing privés non contrôlés jusqu'au moment de l'introduction, puissent être produits dans tous les tribunaux et valables en Justice, et autrement sans etre assujetis a la formalité du contrôle, et que les mêmes actes soient de suite deposés aux archives de la ditte ville.

Cazernes.—Charleville à cause de la Constitution a toujours été chargé de la fourniture et l'entretien de la Cazerne. Solliciter la decharge de cette depense, auprès de l'assemblée soit auprès du ministre, on l'obtiendra et d'autant plus facilement qu'il est de tout justice que Charleville privé de ses privileges, et devenue tributaire de l'Etat comme les autres villes du Royaume, ne soit point traitee plus défavorablement que les autres villes du Royaume chez lesquelles cette depense est a la charge du Gouvernement.

Revenus de la ville.—L'assemblée nationale est priée de prendre en consideration que les revenus de la ville de Charleville, insuffisans deja, vont être diminuer du ¾ par les nouveaux arrangements.

Hotel de Dieu et Bureau de Charité.—On demande des secours pour l'hotel Dieu de cette ville, qui n'est doté que pour un nombre de lits insuffisants, vu la population actuelle, et un Bureau de charité qui a donné le premier exemple de la destruction de la mendicité en france, et dont presque tous les revenus consistent dans la contribution volontaire des habitants que leurs nouvelles charges mettront dans l'impuissance de faire les mêmes efforts.

College.—Le college de cette ville, fondé par les souverains de Charleville, possede un revenu suffisant, il est placé tres avantageusement et a un pensionnat nombreux et de vastes batiments, on pourra y donner tel genre d'éducation qui seroit adopté par l'assemblée nationale.

Maisons Religeuses.—Il y a une communauté de Capucines et de Recollets, a laquelle on donne le même interet que celui qu'ils ont merité de la nation.

Une maison d'education publique tenue par les frères des écoles chretiennes dont on demande l'augmentation.

La communauté des Religeuses Premontrés reformé du Calvaire est utile pour un village qui s'y forme depuis quelques temps.

La communauté des religeuses Carmelites et du Sepulchre ont chacun un pensionnat nombreux, elles n'ont que 200 de rents par tête, le surplus vient de leur travail, elles s'offrent l'une et l'autre a l'education gratuite des jeunes enfants de cette ville dont la population augmente tous les jours.

M. M. les Carmelites ont encore un pensionnat pour les veuves des militaires et des Dlles [demoiselles] dont l'education etant fini attendent un etablissement honnete, d'ailleurs elles sont toutes composées de citoyens françaises.

La communauté des filles seculieres de la providence à aussi un pensionnat nombreux, elle est uniquement consacrée a l'education publique et gratuit des jeunes enfants sans cloture et sans voeu.

La poste aux Lettres et Messageries.—La ville reclame contre l'injustice exercée envers elle en lui retirant depuis quelques années le messagerie dont elle était en possession des sa création. elle demande aussi qu'il soit établi a Charleville une direction de poste aux lettres qui est aujourd'hui regie que par commis soldé par le Directeur de Mezieres ou il n'y a pas de commune et dont le population est au plus le $\frac{1}{4}$ de celle de Charleville.

L'assemblée est suppliée de prendre en consideration les temoins justificatifs qui seront presentés a l'appui du present cahier et autres relatifs à la principauté.

Nous venons de vous presenter Messieurs l'exposé fidel de nos forces pour les employer selon vos voeux qui sont toujours les notres. Daignez vous frapper de cette idée, que c'est libre et soumise a vos decrets que nous presentons dans votre temps sacré. Ne nous jugez pas indigne de participer par notre deputé, aux oracles que vous rendrez pour la prosperité, la gloire et le bonheur d'un peuple qu'ils regenrent et de preparer avec vous, a la posterité reconnaissante, s'interessant et le premier spectacle de la fraternité de toutes les nations.

Fait et arrete en l'assemblée generale tenue dans la Salle des exercices du College et avant de clore le dit procès-verbal, malgré les observations faites par Monsieur Lhonte demande sur le choix general de sa personne pour se charger de porter le present cahier et memoire relatifs et autres necessaires pour faire connaitre de plus en plus la situation de Charleville et amplir l'adjonction avec Monsieur Cochelet pour parvenir a avoir une deputation, un departement, un district, et tout ce qui sera d'une utilité generale, pour la province, Monsieur Lhonte demande a annoncér qu'il ferait volontiers tous les sacrifices particuliers pour se rendre au voeu general de la commune et qu'un des moindres preuves qu'il pouvait donner de son[2] . . . de la Reconnaissance, etait de faire a ses frais toutes les depenses et avances necessaires pour remplir le voeu de tous les citoyens et declaré qu'il acceptait l'adjonction et a signé avec tous les habitant assemblés.

Fait et arreté en la ditte assemblée generale le 31 Decembre, 1789, 5 heure de relevee, Signe: [ten signatures].

Delivré par moi Greffier secretaire de l'hotel de ville de la ville soussigné.

Craucy.[3]

Nous consul, directeur et procureur syndic de la ville d'Arches et Charleville, certifiant que Monsieur Gailly,[4] qui a signé et delivré l'expedition des autres parts est greffier secretaire de l'hotel de ville du dit Charleville, que foÿ doit être ajoutée a sa signature tenu en jugement que dehors en temoin de quoi nous avons signé ces presents et a celles fait apposer le sceau de l'arme de cette ville.

Fait et donné en l'hotel de ville de Charleville le 12 Janvier 1790.

[four signatures]

NO. 2. THE THIRD ESTATE OF THE BAILLIAGE OF AVAL

Cahier and supplement reprinted from MS text owned by M. Cernesson, of Lons-le-Saunier, Jura. Original signatures. The text given by the *Archives parlementaires* Vol. II, pp. 143 *et seq.*, is the preliminary cahier of the third estate of the principal bailliage of Aval, without its secondary bailliages. P.V.-MS in p.v. of the three ordres, text owned by the same private individual. 32 members of the committee, cahier adopted April 14, signed by all members, local demands added, verification by registrar and procurator of king.

Convocation: 1st type, with secondary bailliages.

[3] This signature was very illegible, both here and at the end of the *procès-verbal*. From the name given by the consul, *cf. infra.*, it appears to be Gailly.

[4] *Cf.* note 3.

Chapitre 1. Constitution nationale

1. Qu'il soit reconnu que la France est une nation libre, que le royaume est une monarchie gouvernée par le roy, suivant les loix qui ne peuvent etre n'y détruites n'y changées, sans le consentement de la nation légalement assemblée.

2. Maintenir le pouvoir monarchique dans toute sa plentitude et reconnaitre la succession au throne dans l'auguste maison régnante, hereditaire de mâle en mâle, par ordre de primogeniture à l'exclusion des femmes et de leurs descendants.

3. La nation ne peut etre representée que par ses Etats generaux composés de Députés librement elus, dont la moitié sera choisie dans le Tiers état, l'autre dans les deux premiers ordres.

4. Les Etats generaux s'assembleront tous les trois ans au moins, et les suffrages y seront comptés par tête, dans une seule et meme chambre.

5. En cas de minorité du souverain les Etats generaux pourront seuls nommer un regent s'ils ne se trouvent pas assemblés pour lors, les députés aux derniers Etats generaux s'assembleront d'eux-mêmes, dans la ville où les derniers Etats auront été tenus.

6. Toutes loix générales seront consenties par les Etats Generaux. Tous impots, tous emprunts seront egalement consentis par les Etats generaux et ils la détermineront l'employ.

7. Toute perception d'impots cessera de plein droit à l'époque déterminée par l'assemblée nationale, jusqu'a ce qu'elle en ait consenti la continuation.

8. Demeuront abolis tout privilege, exemption quelconques, quelle que soit la cause, en fait d'impots des charges publiques, de maniere que les contributions soient toujours en raison des proprietés et facultés respectives; en consequence les fiefs seront dechargés de tout devoir et services particuliers, specialement du ban et de l'arriere ban.

9. Liberte individuelle des citoyens et de leur proprieté, liberté civile et politique; abolition des lettres de cachet.

10. Toutes les provinces du Royaume seront incessament constitués en corps d'états formés sur un plan général et sur le model des Etats generaux.

11. L'ordonnance qui exclut le Tiers des emplois militaires sera abolie à jamais et les membres du Tiers declarés habiles à toutes places ecclesiastiques, militaires et civiles.

12. Les Etats provinciaux seront établis, les gardiens et conservateurs de la charte nationale par les Etats Generaux, qui lors de la cloture, leur remettront les pouvoirs de la nation pour cet objet.

13. Avant que les députés aux Etats generaux puissent passer à une autre deliberation, il sera des articles ci-dessus dressé une charte; elle formera

à l'avenir la Constitution française elle sera remise dans une forme solennelle aux députés de chaque province, aux Etats generaux, pour être par eux déposés aux archives de leurs Etats particuliers, et y être promulguée ensuite enregistrée dans tous les tribunaux.

Chapitre 2. De la Justice

1. Abolition de la venalité de tous offices de judicature.

2. Suppression des parlements et autres cours sovereignes; des tribunaux d'exception et attribution quelconque, moienant le remboursement tel qu'il sera réglé aux Etats generaux. Création de nouvelles cours supérieures, dont la moitié au moins sera composée de juges de la classe du Tiers, les dites cours seront uniquement bornées aux fonctions de juges.

Les juges des cours superieures ne pourront être pris que parmi les officiers des bailliages qui auront exercé cinq ans, ou parmi les avocats qui auront dix ans d'exercice, la nomination aux dits offices sera faite par la loi sur la présentation qui lui sera fait de trois sujets, par les états provinciaux.

A l'égard des bailliages il sera pourvu au remplacement des juges et à leur remboursement de la maniére qui sera avisée par les Etats generaux de telle sorte que la nation puisse s'assurer que les places soient données au mérite, et qu'il n'y ait que deux dégrés de juridiction.

3. L'erection d'un bailliage roial dans la ville de St. Claude, sans entendre prejudices aux droits du bailliage seigneurial de Moirans, ni à ceux des bailliages royaux, composants le bailliage d'Aval.

4. Abolition des *mandat et veniat* de la part des cours superieures et de tous les droits de *committimus,* ainsi que toute commission en matière civile et criminelle, même des evocations au roi et en son conseil.

5. Il ne sera sous aucun pretexte accordé de dispense soit age, soit des qualités ci devant requises; et ne pourront tous les officiers des cours superieures, des bailliages et senechaussées même ceux des seigneurs, être destitués qu'en cas de forfaiture préalablement jugée.

6. Il sera incessament procedé à la réforme des codes civiles et criminelles, des coutumes et des ordonnances des eaux et forêts.

7. Des peines prononcés contre les coupables il ne résultera atteinte lache ou infames contre leur famille; et celles-infligées pour chaque espèce de délits, seront les mêmes pour tous les français et habitants du roïaume, sans distinction quelconque, sa Majesté demeuront supplier d'emploïer toute son autorité pour le maintien de cette loi.

8. Nul seigneur ne pourra amodier les droits de justice et sous les peines qui seront arbitrées aux Etats generaux. Nul agent des seigneurs ni leurs fermiers ne pourront etre leur procureur d'office et aucun officier des justices seigneuriales, même les gardes ne pourront assister aux deliberations des communautés.

9. Suppression de la mainmorte réelle et personnelle et de tous droits assimilés à la dite mainmorte, plutôt moïennant indemnité en ce qui concerne la mainmorte réelle et les droits réels y assimilés, sauf cependant la titre de St. Claude qui sera gratuitement affranchie suivant le consentiment du Mgr. l'eveque et celui de M. de Marneria inserés dans le procès-verbal d'ouverture de l'assemblée generale.

10. Sera demandée une loi generale pour l'abolition de toutes espèces de banalité, moienant l'indemnité contradictoirement réglée.

Chapitre 3. De l'église

1. Seront abrogées toutes annates, bulles, provisions, et dispenses de la cour de Rome, les dites provisions et dispenses réservées aux eveques dans leurs diocese.

2. Les bénéfices consistoriaux seront conférés de manière qu'il y en ait la moitié pour le clergé du Tiers état, sans que les pourvus de cette classe puissent être grévés de pensions plus fortes que les bénéfices nobles.

3. Sera tous les ans dressés un état de tous les bénéfices du royaume, de leurs revenus, des noms de leurs titulaires, comme aussi des pensions, soit sur les bénéfices, soit sur les oeconomats, et des noms des pensionnaires, le quel état sera imprimé et rendu public.

4. Seront supprimé les maisons religieuses peu nombreuses et réunies avec leurs revenus en maison principales dans les villes, pour s'occuper gratuitement de l'éducation de la jeunesse.

5. Il sera établi par les diocésains des curés ou vicaires en chef dans tous les villages éloignés de plus d'une demie lieue de l'église paroissiale, si la demande en est faite par les habitants: il sera fixé aux curés une portion congrue de 1200 livres aux vicaires domestiques de 350 L. et aux vicaires résidans de 700 L. à prendre les dites sommes sur les biens d'ancienne dotation dont ils jouissent deja; en cas d'insuffisance sur les dixmes, à défaut de dimes il y sera pourvu par la réunion des bénéfices de collation royale ou bénéfices simples, au moyen de quoi le casuel des curés sera supprimé, ainsi que tous droits qu'ils perçoivent sur leurs paroissens, coupes de feux, bichons, quartiers, gerbes et autres.

6. Toutes les dimes ecclesiastiques pourront être abonnées, et l'indemnité sera réglée contradictoirement.

7. Dans tous les lieux où il y aura des vicaires en chef, les habitants seront déchargés de toute contribution pour l'entretien et reconstitution de la mère église et du presbitère.

Chapitre 4. Des hopitaux et colleges

1. Auront les Etats de chaque province la surintendance et la police des hopitaux royaux, et les autres seront administré conformément à la declaration du Roi du 21 dec. 1698.

2. Former un revenu suffisant aux hopitaux des malades, enfants trouvés, et autres de cette espèce pour remplir l'objet de leur destination, et à cet effet réunir des bénéfices de nomination royale, et des bénéfices simples.

3. Les colleges établis, ou ceux à établir seront dotés proportionné au besoin sur les biens des cy-devant jesuites.

4. Il sera fait un règlement général pour la suppression de la mendicité, dont l'execution sera confiée aux Etats provinciaux.

Chapitre 5. Des Finances

1. Seront supprimé tous les receveurs generaux et particuliers des finances et seront établis des receveurs provinciaux qui seront chargés de la recette et de la dépense.

2. Pour la perception de l'impôt, il ne sera fait qu'un seul rôle qui comprendra les immeubles réels et fictifs et la taxation à faire à raison des biens meubles et de la faculte des contribuables.

3. Il sera fait en chaque province, des fonds pour les pensions destinées à tous les genres de services sans que les fonds d'un departement puissent être excédes, ou divertis à d'autre emplois.

4. Sera imprimé chaque année et rendu public l'etat des pensions, comme celui des finances et revenus du royaume, des dispenses, des charges, des dettes, et les fonds destinés a leur amortissement.

5. Sa Majesté sera suppliée de porter ses vues sur les pensions reversibles, pour supprimer la transmission s'il y a lieu.

6. Sera de meme supplié S.M. [Sa Majesté] d'ordonner le reduction, ou suppression de tous les emplois inutils, ou onereux à l'état, et de réduire dans les differentes branches d'administration, les emplois qui seront dans le cas d'être conservés à un taux modique et proportionné au travail.

7. Ne seront consenties aucunes rentes perpetuelles et pensions viagres aux Etats generaux qu'à la condition quelles seront soumises a une retenue proportionnée à l'impôt qui sera jetté sur les fonds.

8. Demeureront supprimé tous les droits compris sous le nom de droits reunis et notament les droits sur les cuirs à charge par les tanneurs et corroyeurs et autres sujets à la perception de ces droits de fournir aux Etats provinciaux l'equivalent du montant de la dte [la dite] perception actuelle suivant le reglement et la taxation qui sera faite dans chaque lieu par les contribuables; les droits sur les cartes et sur les objets de luxe seront conservés.

9. Les barriéres des fermes seront reculées par tout jusqu'aux frontieres du Royaume: l'interdiction limitrophe sera reduite au moindre espace possible, les habitans des frontieres seront dispensés des acquêtes a caution ainsi que de tous les les droits sur les objets d'industrie, de production territoriale et en aucun cas ils ne seront assujetis à l'ordonnance de 1687.

10. Les commissions pour l'approvisionnement des hopitaux de Paris occasionnant l'entrée en France d'une grande quantité de fromages qui ne

vont pas à cette destination, il sera établi un droit de 6 L. par chaque quintal de fromages étrangers, qui sera importé dans ce royaume, sans égard à la destination et sans exemption pour qui que ce soit.

11. Il sera procédé incessament à un nouveau tarif des droits de controle, de telle sorte que les droits perçus sur des bases fixes, invariables comme de tous sujets, le droit de percevoir sera proportionné à la valeur des actes, sauf les testaments partages et autres actes de familles pour lesquels il ne sera du qu'un simple controle.

12. Suppressions des sols pour livre des greffes, et des quatre deniers pour livre sur le produit des ventes mobilliaires ainsi que du sol pour livre qui frappe directement ou indirectement sur les objets de premiere nécessite.

13. Le pret à interêt au taux ordinaire sera autorisé dans toute l'étendue du royaume.

14. Seront les ministres de Sa Majesté responsables de leur conduite à la nation assemblée en Etats generaux.

15. Personne ne pourra obtenir des lettres de ratiffication sans au préalable avoir affichée relation exacte de son contrat, trois dimanches, de quinzaine en quinzaine à la Porte principale de l'église paroissiale du lieu de la situation des biens mis en purgation et les d. [les dites] affiches seront certiffiés par le curé du lieu, le tout sera ensuite enregistré au greffe de la justice locale et ne pourront être obtenue lettres de ratification qu'à vue du certifficat du greffier local, sans prejudice des formalités prescrittes par l'édit des hypothéques.

16. Il sera avisé par les Etats generaux aux moyens à prendre soit sur la vente soit sur sa conservation ou la regie des domaines du roy, ainsi que pour faire rentrer ceux qui ont été induement alienée.

Chapitre 6. De la Police Generale

1. Suppression de la censure et liberte de la presse, sauf l'administration des lois.

2. Uniformité de poids et mesures et de leur dénomination dans tous le royaume seront les poids et mesures portés dans les titres et terriers des seigneurs, reduits aux poids et mesures adoptés par les Etats generaux.

3. Abolition de tous droits de péage et roulage ou pontonnage appartenant aux roy dans tous le royaume.

4. Tous les proprietaires dont le terrein sera utile pour la confection des routtes et autres objets publics seront dédommagés aprés une estimation contradictoire et quand aux corvées des toutes, les Etats provinciaux regleront la manière dont elles seront faittes, d'aprés les memoires qui leur seront donnés.

5. Les Colombiers seront fermés pendant la tenue des semailles et cinq jours avant l'ouverture des moissons jusqu'après l'entière récolte des memes grains à peine d'amande.

6. La police generale des grains appartiendra aux Etats provinciaux ou

à la commission intermediaire et les d. [les dits] Etats seront tenus de veiller avec le plus grand soin, à tenir un juste equilibre et à pourvoir à ce que la province soit toujours suffisament approvisionnée.

7. Les salpetriers ne pourront faire aucune fouille dans les maisons et leur dependances que du consentiment des proprietaires et à charge de les dédommager.

8. Seront supprimés les droits attribués aux premier chirugien du Roy; ceux qui voudront exercer l'art de la chirurgie dans les campagnes, seront tenus de subir des examens et de se faire recevoir dans les formes prescrites pour les maîtrises des villes.

Chapitre 7. Du Militaire

1. Suppression des gouvernements dans toute la royaume des Etats-majors du deuxieme ordre, réduction dans les grands états majors, suppression des logements militaires qui se payent en argent à ceux qui n'ont qu'une résidence fictive.

2. Abolition du tirage de la milice saux aux communes à y pourvoir par les moyens que les Etats provinciaux jugeront les moins onereux.

Chapitre 8. De l'administration des Communes

1. Les officiers municipaux dans tout le royaume seront electifs, trienniaux et gratuits.

Chapitre 9. Intérêt particulier de la province

1. Si les autres provinces du royaume ne renoncent pas à leur privileges la Franche Comté sera conservée dans tous ceux dont elle jouit et doit jouir et dans tous les cas elle sera maintenue dans l'exemption des aides, du timbre des gabelles et tous autres.

2. Aucuns loix ou lettres patentes particuliers à la Franche Comté ne seront enregistrées, qu'auparavant elles n'aient éte envoyés aux Etats de la province pour y'être par eux consenties.

3. Les octrois de la Sône [The Saône] perçu au profit des Etats de Bourgogne sur les grains et autres marchandises embarqués en Franche Comté, seront et demeureront supprimés.

4. Le Roy sera supplié prenant égard à la rareté des bois dans cette province de permettre aux Etats provinciaux de supprimer les forges et fourneaux qu'ils jugeront inutiles ou prejudiciables.

5. Il sera pourvu à ce que les habitants des villes et des campagnes aient une quantité de sel,—proportionnée tant à leur besoins qu'à ceux de leur bétail et fromages, sans que la crainte des versement puisse y mettre obstacle, reservant aux Etats provinciaux d'en solliciter la livraison en grains pour les communautés qui le demanderont.

6. Les bois des villes, bourges et communautés de la province, affectés

à l'affouagement des salines, seront restitués aux villes, bourgs et communautés et régis comme ils étaient avant l'affectation et il sera declaré par la desaffection que tous les droits d'usages appartenants aux communautés et particuliers, seront rétablis suivant les titres et tels qu'ils existoient anterieurement.

7. Sera aboli le centieme denier de tous les offices dont la venalité ne sera pas supprimé.

8. L'administration des biens cy devant jesuites sera confiée aux Etats de la province qui se feront rendre compte des revenus des biens et de leur emploi par tous comptables.

9. Les dommages et interets pour mésus commis dans les fruits pendants, seront adjuges aux proprietaires de l'heritage a raison de tant par tête de bétail mésusant, si mieux n'aiment les proprietaires de l'héritage faire reconnaitre et taxer le délit conformément à l'ordonnance.

10. Les employes des fermes ne pourront être admis dans aucun cas a faire les fonctions de gardes de bois seront revoquées toutes commissions qui leur auront été données à ce sujet, les gardes des bois ne pourront avoir aucune part dans les amandes et confiscation prononcés sur leur rapport; les gardes demeureront sujets à toutes les charges de communautés.

11. Suppression des droits d'éminage, couponage et de tous autres établis sur les denrées de premiere nécessité, sauf a en indemniser les proprietaires. Sa Majesté sera suppliée d'en faire gratuitement la suppression pour ceux qui pourraient lui appartenir, et de pourvoir à l'indemnité des autres par la réunion de quelques benéfices pour les proprietaires qui en seraient susceptibles.

12. Le logement des troupes sera supporté par tous les habitans, sans exception ni distinction.

13. Seront verifiée et fixées les limites de la Franche Comté tant avec la Suisse qu'avec les provinces limitrophes du Royaume, et ce par deux commissaires, le premier nommé par le Roy, et le second par les Etats provinciaux.

14. Tous les seigneurs seront tenus de faire incessament délimiter leurs seigneuries, de faire afficher et publier les limites qui les circonscrivent à peine de nullité des rapport jusqu'aux d. [dites] affiches et publication.

15. Les deniers provenants de la vente du quart de réserve des bois appartenant aux communautés seront déposés entre les mains des personnes qui seront désignées par les Etats provinciaux pour en faire la remise sans délai et sans frais, moyennant décharge valable.

16. Il sera fait un réglement général pour prévenir et arrêter la contagion des episooties.

17. Les seigneurs seront assujettes à se conformer strictement à l'ordonnance des eaux et forêts pour la coupe de leurs bois à la revolution de 25 ans.

18. La prescription de 40 ans sera établie dans toute le royaume pour tout espèce de droits seigneuriaux ou particuliers de telle sorte qu'après le laps de temps à défaut de preuve que le droit ait été perçu ou exigé il demeurera éteint ou supprimé.

19. Les députés aux Etats generaux ne pourront recevoir aucuns bénéfice, grace don, ou pension, si ce n'est du consentement de la chambre à la quelle ils seront ou auront été attachés.

20. Et comme le present cahier general n'a pu comprendre tous les objets qui interessent chaque bailliage en particulier sera reunis aux députés qui seront choisis un cahier séparé d'instruction et des doléances locales de chacun des bailliages pour le faire valoir soit aux Etats generaux, soit aux Etats provinciaux.

Telles sont les doléances remontrances et plaintes que le bailliage d'Aval entend presenter aux Etats generaux et se sont tous les députés soussignés, avec nous, le d. [dit] procureur du roi et notre greffier et avons de plus cotté et paraphé le present cahier, le 14 avril 1789.

A instament les députés du bailliage de Pontarlier ont demandés de faire ajouter au present cahier les articles suivants.

1. Au cas de demande de l'abolition de la venalité des charges de judicature soit dans la tribunaux superieures soit dans les inferieures, seront accordé le prix des officiers ne sera remboursée qu'à mesure que la places vacqueront.

2. Le Tiers lot des bénéfices sera sequestré pour être employée à sa destination primitive.

3. Tout pourvu d'un benefice dont le revenu se portera a 10,000 L. ne pourra en posseder un autre.

4. Obligations aux seigneurs de donner a leur sujets aux frais de ceux ci copie de l'inventaire de leur titres et des titres communs qui seront demandés et les seigneurs bornés à se prevalloir des titres inventories avec suppression des droits de gardiennete et autre accordé aux seigneurs pour des motifs qui n'existent plus.

Voeu de l'assemblée du Tiers Etat du bailliage d'aval sous l'organization des Etats particuliers de la Franche Comté relativement à la lettre du 31 xbre [décembre] 1788 addressee aux gens du Tiers état de la province.

L'ordre du tiers adhere au plan formé par les notables de l'assemblée formée à Besançon les mois de novembre et decembre dernier sous la modification et restriction cy-apres.

1. Le clergé et la noblesse réunis n'auront qu'un nombre égal de députés a l'ordre du tiers et dans le nombre un quart restera au clergé et la distribution du nombre des députés qui sera accordé à la province sera fait sur les bazes ci-après.

2. Tous noble ayant la Noblesse acquise et transmissible pourra être electeur et eligible.

3. Les non nobles possesseurs de fief, lorsqu'ils auront renoncés à leur privilege, et les officiers des seigneurs lorsqu'ils seront rendus inamovibles, seront electeurs et eligible.

4. Il suffira d'être compris dans les rolles, pour pouvoir être electeur et eligible dans les Etats de la province.

5. Les corporations des villes seront representées par une député et non par leur sindic.

6. Sans égard a l'article 25, le nombre des députés du Tiers qui sera accordé à la province sera distribué entre les bailliages à raison de leur cottisations et population, la distribution dans les differentes bailliages sera faitte par cantons ou districts suivant quils en conviendront.

[Three hundred sixty-nine signatures.]

Le Michau d'Arçon.   Ardiet secretaire
pres. de l'ass. du tiers.
Coytier pro. du Roy[5]

SUPPLEMENT AU CAHIER GÉNÉRAL DOLÉANCES DU BAILLIAGE D'AVAL
Bailliage d'Arbois

Art. 1. La ville d'Arbois et la communauté de Montigny fondés en raisons particulières énnoncées dans un mémoire qui sera joint, insistent à l'abonnement de la dixme ecclesiastique demandée à l'article 6.

Art. 2. L'adjudication des ouvrages à faire pour la réconstruction de l'hôtel de ville d'Arbois, de l'hôtel Bailliagère, des prisons et de la halle, ayant été ordonnée par un arrêt du Conseil, l'adjudication ayant faite: on demande l'homologation de cette adjudication.

Art. 3. Il sera donné les ordres nécessaires pour qu'il soit payé au Receveur de la ville d'Arbois une somme de 24,000 ♯ qui lui a été accordée sur les Brevets de retenue de la provinice et 10,000 ♯ sur le domaine, pour subvenir à la reconstruction énnoncée en l'article précédent.

Art. 4. La Rue Mercière et le pont de faramand qui est à la suite et qui sert de communication à la routte de Lyon à Strasbourg, seront incessament réparés, et les fonds pour cette réparation seront pris sur le domaine.

Art. 5. Il sera construit un canal qui partira de la ville d'Arbois, pour communiquer à celui de Dole, et les fonds nécessaires à cette construction seront fournis par les provinces.

Art. 6. Sera recoquée l'edit des clotures, en ce qui concerne le bailliage d'Arbois et ceux des pays plats, et dans le cas ou laisseroit subsister cet édit, il sera défendu aux particuliers qui auront clos, de faire pâturer leur bétail ailleurs que dans leurs clôtures, (les . . .[6] exceptés) sans qu'ils puissent sous aucun pretexte profiter des paturages communs.

---

[5] Procureur du roi.
[6] An illegible word appeared here in the manuscript.

Art. 7. Ne pourront les seigneurs sous aucuns prétextes faire couper leurs bois avant la révolution de 25 ans.

Art. 8. Tous les prés sans distinction n'y privilége, seront, mis en ban de deux ans l'un.

Art. 9. Il sera libre a chacun de semer ses héritages, dans le temps, et de tels grains qu'il trouvera convenir sans être tenu d'observer l'ordre établi pour les prés.

Art. 10. Il sera fait un nouveau réglement concernant les harras, et lorsqu'il se trouvera plus de trente juments dans un arrondissement, le garde harras sera tenu d'y avoir un aide.

Art. 11. Les portions des Bois des communautés dont les seigneurs se sont emparés pour leur tenir lieu de triage seront rendues et restitués au dites communautés a vue de leurs titres.

Art. 12. Les cantonnements accordés aux communautés dans les Bois de leurs seigneurs seront augmentés, en raison de leur population actuelle.

Art. 13. Les communautés riveraines des forests du Roy pourront faire parcourir leur bétail, dans toutes l'étendue des dites forests lorsqu'elles seront défensables.

Art. 14 Les communautés qui ont alienés leurs forets, ou partie d'icelles, au profit du Roy ou des seigneurs seront autorisées a y rentrer, en remboursant le prix qu'elles en ont touchées.

Art. 15. Toutes redevances et tous droits tenants de l'ancienne feudalité, que les communautés payent a leurs seigneurs, en raison des services, auxquels les seigneurs ne sont plus assujettis seront supprimés.

Art. 16. Il en sera de même des corvées voitures et jours de charue; dont les communautés seront dispensés lorsque les seigneurs ne feront pas valoir leurs terres par eux mêmes.

Art. 17. Les successeurs de le beneficier seront obligées d'entretenir les beaux faits par leur devanciers et de dommander les fermiers des reparations utiles et necessaires qu'ils auront fait dans les batiments et fonds dependants du benefice.

Art. 18. Seront autorisé les états provinciaux a faire de nouveaux arrondissements des bailliages, sur les mémoires qui seront presentés par les justiciables.

Bailliage de Lons le Saunier

Art. 1. Attendu la rareté des bois, le peu d'interet que Sa Majesté retire de l'existence des salines, en comparaison des prejudices qu'éprouve sa province de Franche Comté la ville de Lons le Saunier demande qu'en provenant la désafectation des bois, on ordonne l'entière destruction et abolition de toutes les Salines de la province.

La ville et le bailliage d'Arbois se reunissent sur cet objet à la ville de Lons-le-Saunier pour faire prononcer sur cette destruction si necèssaire.

Art. 2. La ville de Lons-le-Saunier demande que les justiciables soient approchés de leurs juges et qu'a cet effet il soit formé de nouveaux arrondissements demande aussi la suppression des bailliages inutiles.

Bailliage de Salins

La ville et le bailliage de Salins demandent que les domaines du Roy soient assujettis à l'impôt.

Que la Saline de Choux dont l'établissement est dommageable à Sa Majesté soit supprimée que tout la formation des scels[7] soit concentrée, sans la saline de Salins, a laquelle il plaira au Roy d'affecter un partie suffisante de la forest de Choux.

Ils demandent la resiliation des assensements qui ont été faits des terriers dependants des forests du Roy affectés aux Salines de Salins qui ont été eparti le long des routes. Les dits assensements étant très prejudiciable aux villages qui y ont été conservés au droit de parcourir.

L'abolition des reglements faits pour la police des bois des Salines de Salins, par lequel certains communautés même des particuliers riveraines des forests du Roy, sont rendus responsables des délits qui se commettent dans les mêmes forests vis a vis de leur territoires ou de leurs domaines; qu'en conséquence l'exécution des jugements rendus par la réformation de Salins, soit interditte ou du moins suspendue provisoirement.

Que le Roy soit supplié d'ordonner la révision par devant les juges royaux ordinaires de toutes les décisions par lesquelles des terreins appartenans a des communautés, ou a des particuliers ont été réunis aux domaines et bois de Sa Majesté des droits d'usage acquis a titre onéreux ou de concession, ont été supprimés ou restrain, tandisque la communauté ou particuliers qui en ont été dépoüillés sont encore obligés de payer les redevances établies a ce sujet.

Suppression des scels[7] par pain de scel dont la perception a été établie pour fournir a de certaines dépenses qui n'ont plus lieu.

Suppression de touts privileges et exemptions à l'égard des octrois, à l'exception de ceux acquis aux hopitaux.

Le Canal commencé pour la navigation de la rivière du Doubs sera continué et toutes les provinces du royaume y contribueront.

La ville de Salins demande un nouvel arrondissement de bailliage, suppression de ceux qui sont inutiles et onereux.

Bailliage de Poligny

Demande la ville de Poligny de jouir du droit qu'elle a acquis de Sa Majesté de librement nommer ses officiers municipaux, dont elle n'a pu jouir jusqu'a présent malgré les réclamations reiterées faittes par des assemblées générales ou commissaires départi lesquelles jusqu'icy n'ont point eu de succés.

---

[7] This is evidently a misspelling; "sel" is intended.

art. 2. Demande la ditte ville a être réintegré dans la juridiction qu'elle avoit dans les bois communaux d'y apposer les assiettes et connoitre des délits qui s'y commettent.

art. 5.[8] Réduction dans les arrondissements des haras, de manière de manière qu'il n'y ait dans chaque arrondissement que trente juments et que les haras soient choisis de la plus belle et meilleur espèce et qu'à cette occasion les gages des gardes étalons, ainsy que leur rétribution soient augmentés.

art. 6. Que dans toutes les paroisses il soit établi des sages femmes instruites, auxquelles seront payés des gages. elles ne pourront être reçues qu'après avoir subi les examens suffisants.

art. 7. Que les gradués n'exercéants pas leur etat ou ne l'ayant pas exercé pendant dix ans soient assujettis aux charges locales.

art. 8. La renovation des seigneurs se fera de quarante ans a quarante ans.

Bailliage de Pontarlier

La ville de Pontarlier renouvelle au besoin les observations et protestations unises et contenus dans le procès-verbal de comparutions des députés de son bailliage en date du 26 mars 1789 paraphé par Mr. Maire Lieutenant General et signé de lui ainsy que de tout les dits députés lesquelles observations et protestations y ont étés rédigées dans les termes suivants.

Messieurs Antoine Alexis Robelot Lieutenant Criminel en ce Bailliage, Jean Baptiste Michaud de Doubs avocat en Parlement, Francois Joseph Gloriot ancien Secretaire de la ville de Pontarlier et Claude Minay ancien procureur du Roy de la Gruerie député de la ditte ville de Pontarlier, lesquels ont observés que pris egard a la quantité des feux de la ditte ville et de sa banlieu qui est de 750 feux ils ne sont pas en nombre suffisant pour la representer rélativement aux autres communautés du Bailliage et demandent un redressement a cet egard protestant que l'insuffisance actuel de leur nombre ne pourra tirer a conséquence pour l'avenir ainsy que contre toutes atteintes qui pourroient être donnés aux droits et aux privileges de la ditte ville a moins que ce ne soit pour l'interet general du Royaume et a l'instar de toutes les autres villes.

La ville de Pontarlier demande de plus que sa police soit maintenue dans le droit de faire des Reglements Relativement a ses marchés.

Voeux et doléances particuliers du tiers Etat du Bailliage de Pontarlier, que les deputés du Bailliage d'Aval sont chargés de presenter aux Etats Generaux

Indépendamment de l'augmentation de la quantité de sel le bailliage de Pontarlier demande qu'il lui soit livré en grain (l'experience ayant assuré que la réduction en pain nuit à la qualité) et que le dit Bailliage en soit

---

[8] There is some discrepancy in the numbering of the articles.

approvisionné dés l'automne pour l'hiver a Raison de d'interruption des chemins par les neiges.

Suppression des droits d'entrée et sortie sur les vaches que les habitants des frontieres louent a tant des Suisses pour la fabrication des fromages.

Suppression de l'établissement des haras les communautés libres de s'en choisir et dispenser de toutes inspections.

La liberté dans les marchés dans tous le Royaume sans aucun privilege ny distinctions pour tous citoyens.

Suppression de la vaine pâture au printemps sauf a chaque communauté a se regler pour celle d'automne.

Les Communautés déchargées de dixmes dues au Roy ou Sa Majesté tenue des Portions Congrües des desservants les paroisses dans lesquelles les dixmes sont dues, ainsy que de l'entretien de le choeurs et autres objets a la charge des décimateurs suivant les edits.

La ville de Pontarlier demande la restitution des Biens légués aux cidevant jesuites, de la ville et un suplément sur les autres biens de la Societé dans le Bailliage, pour fournir aux frais d'un collège en la dite ville dont il plaira a Sa Majesté d'autoriser l'établissement par Lettres Patentes.

Le Remboursement des finances que la ville a nantis successivement ensuite d'emprunt subsistant pour le office de receveur en titre de la ville, ou indemnité, convenable; cet objet qui a passé dans les trésors de Sa Majesté devant faire partie de la dette nationnale.

Les Etats Généraux priés de voir les titres d'affranchissements des communauté; de la seigneurie de Joux appartenant au Roy en conséquence; de les faire jouir de leurs privilèges, spècialement de l'exemption du droit de scel[9] sur les mutations des biens du douzième du prix, surtout pour échange, licitation, donnation et premier acte entre co-heritiers.

Defenses d'exiger dans les terres du domaine, un droit appellé d'ensaisinement, qui ne peut avoir lieu dans celles qui ne sont pas de l'ancien domaine de la Couronne, et la directe est générale!

Les habitants des seigneuries de Montbenoit, Ste. Marie, Rochejean et Chatelblanc que la dixme soit rendu a sa destination première, et employée aux dessertes et entretien des paroisses, et ou elles ne suffiroient pas, que le suplément soit pris sur les dixmes dans le surplus des seigneuries ou les abbés sont curés primitifs.

Les habitants de la terre de Mouthe d'être rétabli dans leur ancienne liberté et dans tous les droits dont ils justifieront par titres de 1296 a 1344; ceux de la Mouthe et de la propre paroisse du dit lieu entendent que la mere église soit conservée dans les droits qui luy sont acquis par titres.

Les habitants de la terre de St. Boin demandent la liberté de tenir des barques pour traverser le lac qui sépare leur village sans gêner ny entraver de la part de la ferme générale.

[9] "Scel" is correct here.

Liberté de commerce des bois de construction seulement de communauté à communauté, les ordonnances pour la sortie des Bois hors du Royaume, au surplus éxécutées.

Dans la répartition générale des impots fonciers du royaume; avoir égard de soulager la province de franche comté en ce qu'en une grande partie de la surface, surtout celle du jura étant occuppées par de très hautes montagnes garnies de rochers et coupées par des ravins et couvertes les trois quarts de l'année de neige; ne produit et en petite quantité, que des orges, avoine, mauvais foins et pâtis; lesquels fruits ont peine de parvenir a maturité, et sont souvent gêlés avant ce tems; que les seules ressources pour fournir aux impots, sont les bestiaux et fromages; que ces premiers y sont très sujets aux maladies episootiques et que les fromages coutent trop de fabrication; qu'au surplus plus de produit sur les bois puisque plusieurs cantons n'ont a ce moment pas de bois de chauffage.

Que l'article de l'ordonnance de 1680; sous le fait des aides que prescrit aux juges de recevoir les employés des fermes sans information de vie et moeurs soit abrogée.

[Seven signatures.]

Le Michau d'Arçon, president de l'assemblée du tiers état.

NO. 3. CLERGY OF THE SENECHAUSSEE OF BEZIERS

Cahier reprinted from MS text in 9 pages, *Arch. Nat.* Ba 21. Neither this text, nor that given by the *Archives parlementaires*, Vol. II, p. 346, of which the MS text exists in the same carton, have the requisite ending for proof of authenticity.

P.V.—MS, *Arch. Nat.* B III 31, C 16/30 (extract on elections.) There was trouble between the Bishop of Beziers and the curates in the assembly. According to the p.v., the cahier was adopted April 6, and covered six pages, signed by the president and the committee, minus four representatives of the chapters and chapelains, and was paragraphed by the registrar, Thouret.

The text given below is incomplete, and both texts of Ba 21 are probably incomplete copies. In view of the conflict between the bishop and curates, it is impossible to know which text was the authentic cahier. Both show the influence of the curates.

Convocation—1st type.

CAHIER DES DOLÉANCES DU CLERGÉ

La confiance honorable que le Roy daigne témoigner au clergé du second ordre de son Royaume dans le règlement qu'il a donnés pour les Élections des Députés du clergé à l'assemblée des États généraux, et le désir qu'il annonce d'une manière si touchante de pouvoir y être instruit des besoins de son peuple et des moyens de le soulager, sont des motifs trop nobles pour ne pas exiter [exciter] Son Zéle à repondre à ses Vues pleines de bontés, en portant au pied de son Trone son Voeu et sa reconnoissance et y faisant parler la vérité que Sa Majesté veut bien réclamer.

Le clergé de la Senéchaussée de Béziers demande à sa Majesté

1.—Le maintien et le seul culte public de la religion catholique et Romaine, de pourvoir à l'éducation chrétienne de la jeunesse pour l'établissement d'un ou deux corps réguliers Enseignant, l'un desquels seroit la congrégation des Bénédictins de Saint-Maure qui par leurs veilles et leurs travaux ont rendu des services importants à la religion et aux lettres, d'établir dans les séminaires des villes ou il y a université des professeurs de philosophie de théologie, sous lesquels on puisse prendre les grades et d'opposer une digue à ce torrent de mauvais livres qui entrainent la décadence de la religion, et qui ont jetté la nation dans l'état d'anarchie où elle se trouve, et que dans le cas ou l'offre des Bénédictins à cet égard seroit acceuillie les Ecclesiastiques actuellement chargés de l'enseignement dans lesd. colléges seront dédommagés par une pension alimentaire telle qu'il plaira à Sa Majesté de la fixer.

2.—L'exécution des ordonnances de l'Eglise et de l'Etat pour l'obtinence [l'abstinence] prescrite pendant le Saint temps du Carême et la Sanctification du Dimanche et des fêtes et qu'à cet effet il soit enjoint aux Magistrats de veiller à leur execution ainsi qu'au maintien dû bon ordre et du respect dû aux Lieux Saints.

3.—Qu'il soit déffendu aux non Catholiques de déquerir le ministère des prêtres pour tout ce qui concerne leur état civil et que le juge ne puisse recevoir la déclaration des protestans sans un certificat du curé attestant leur non Catholicité.

4.—Qu'il soit tenu des conciles nationaux et provinciaux ainsi que des Sinodes Diocésains pour le maintien de la discipline et la réformation des moeurs, et que tous les ordres du clergé y ayant la même séance qu'ils y avoient autrefois.

5.—Qu'il n'y ait dans tout le Royaume qu'un seul et même Rit, un seul et même Breviaire, un seul cathéchisme et uniformité d'Enseignement pour éviter la confusion contre laquelle on réclame depuis si longtemps.

6.—Le clergé offre de contribuer à toutes les charges quelconque en proportion de ses facultés de l'avis néanmoins de la chambre du clergé, des états généraux, mais supposé que toutes les possessions et les Dixmes ecclesiastiques soient soumises à la taille ou à toute autre imposition, il demande qu'il soit déchargé des décimes, que son Contingent aux charges publiques ne soit que dans la proportion de celui que suporteront les autres Citoyens, et que lorsqu'il sera question de faire la répartition de ces charges publiques il soit appelé tant dans l'ordre Séculier que régulier du Clergé un nombre suffisant des représentants, librement élus dans leurs corps, et par leur corps pour y soutenir leurs interêts respectifs.

7.—Le clergé demande pour les États de la province de Languedoc, une constitution nouvelle, et les membres librement Élus seront pris dans tous les ordres du Chapitre du clergé Séculier et régulier et notamment des curés.

8.—Il demande le retour périodique des États généraux ou[10] les Ministres de Sa Majesté seront tenus de rendre compte de leur administration.

9.—Il demande l'abolition des lettres de Cachet, et que Sa Majesté soit suppliée de faire vérifier les causes et les motifs de la détention de ceux qui en sont encore les victimes.

10.—Il demande la suppresion des gabelles, aides et traites et que le sel soit vendu marchand.

11.—Le Clergé supplie le Roy de modéré [moderer] les droits du controlle de donner un tarif clair et précis desdits droits, qu'il soit apportée d'être connu de tout le monde que l'attribution des questions Élevées sur cet objet soit au cours des Parlements et des aides, et que tout droit d'amortissement soit abrogé pour tout ce qui concerne le clergé Séculier et régulier relativement aux améliorations qu'il put faire dans les Batiments et Domaines.

12.—Il demande que sur tout les parages de la Méditerranee la peche et notamment celle appellée vulgairement au Boeuf soit libre comme trés nécessaire pour la Subsistance du pauvre peuple dont la plus grande partie n'a d'autre ressource pour vivre que la modicité du prix du poisson.

13.—Il demande la réformation du code civil et criminel et entre-autres la suppression de l'attribution au grand Conseil pour toutes les contestations que les abbés et autre privilégiés, ont droit d'y porter en vertu de la déclaration du Roy tant contre les ordres réguliers, qu'à l'égard de tous autres particuliers, et que toutes les causes seront deffinitivement jugées par les tribunaux de la province.

14.—Il demande que dans chaque Diocèse il soit établi une maison de charité ou[11] seront reçus gratuitement et sans la moindre recherche les enfants illégitimes aussi bien que ceux des indigens, et un autre pour les infirmes ainsi qu'un bureau de charité pour suprimer la mendicite et qu'on renouvelle l'Exécution des ordonnances contre toutes sortes de prostitution.

15.—La loy obtenue pour le ressort du parlement de Toulouse ne faisant que multiplier les procès bien loin de les éteindre, le clergé de la Sénéchaussée, demande une nouvelle déclaration qui relativement aux usages fixe à jamais la nature des fruits décimales dans le ressort dudit Parlement et qui ne rendent pas impossible au Décimateur le genre de preuve requise pour établir la possession de la dixme.

16.—Le clergé demande qu'on rende commune à tous les Établissements ecclésiastiques et notamment aux Collégiales la déclaration de premier Décembre 1769 qui réprime l'avidité des dévotutaires et rend irrévocables les

---

[10] This manuscript shows certain peculiarities, such as the omission of the accent on the French "where" and the erroneous infinitive form of verbs.

[11] Cf. note 10, infra.

unions faites depuis cent ans à l'exception des unions qui ont pour objet les curés.

17.—Il demande que la déclaration de 1721 qui assujetie la congrégation de france et les Bénédictins de Saint-Maur à obtenir des lettres d'attache de Sarrets d'enrégistrement et des déclarations des changements de Domicile aux greffes des Sénéchaussées et des officialités soit révoquée.

18.—Il demande une loy qui autorise les communautés du Royaume à transiger irrévocablement, et définitivement avec les chapitres ou autres possesseurs éclésiastiques les biens nobles surtout proies mus ou à mouvoir au Sujet de la nobilité des possessions.

19.—Il demande l'observation des anciens canons de l'Église contenant la résidence à la pluralité des bénéfices lorsqu'ils sont suffisants pour l'entretien honnête du titulaire.

20.—Il demande que les chapitres tant séculiers que réguliers soient autorisés à faire desservir par un de leurs membres les curés des paroisses dont ils sont fruits pressant que ceux de la congrégation de Saint-Maur et des citaux seront promus soient inamobibles comme les autres, pour obvier par là à l'insuffisance des congrues et au deffaut des sujets.

21.—Il demande que les curés soient réintégrer dans le droit de faire corps, de nommé [nommer] alternativement pour chaque Diocèse un agent général spécialement chargé de correspondre avec eux et porter leurs plaintes et leurs Voeux au pied du Trône, et qui ne leur soit donné pour adjoint et pour Vicaire aucun prêtre sans leur consentement tout comme aussi de révoquer les articles 10 et 11 de l'Édit de 1695.

22.—Il demande que tous les Vicaires qui seront jugés nécessaires dans les paroisses soient payés proportionnellement par tous les décimateurs dérogeant à cet égard à l'édit rendu sur la demande de la dernière assemblée du clergé, qu'il soit permis à tout curé de résigner son bénéfice, sous la réserve du tiers du revenu total du susdit Bénéfice comme on l'avoit pratiqué jusques icy, sans que cette réserve du tiers puisse être sujette à aucune Taxe.

23.—Il demande que lorsqu'un curé a raison de son âge ou de ses infirmités ne pourra plus servir son bénéfice, une pension honnête ne puisse jamais lui être refusée sur les biens Écclésiastiques du Diocèse ou il aura servi, et qu'après vingt ans de service ils jouissent des memes privileges que les gradués sur les bénéfices des Cathédrales.

24.—Il demande que les curés soient dottés suffisamment et relativement à l'étendue de leurs paroisses de manière à n'être plus dans la cas d'exiger un casuel toujours onéreux au peuple et avilissant pour ceux qui sont forcés de le demander.

25.—Le Clergé sollicite encore de la justice du Roy, que les curés de malte soient rendus inamovibles et que leur traitement soit pareille à celui des autres curés du Royaume.

26.—Vu la rareté des prêtres et les secours que l'église retire et peut retirer des corps religieux tant pour l'éducation de la jeunesse que pour les missions Etrangères aumoneries des troupes et services des paroisses le clergé demande la conservation des differents ordres et qu'il leur soit permis de recevoir les Voeux de ceux qui se présenteront à l'âge de dix huit ans.

27.—Il demande que dans chaque communauté il soit établi un conseil de prud'hommes qui jugent sur le champ définitivement et sans frais tous les petits procès occasionnés pour les partages des terres, fossés, limites, de puissance et autres objets minutieux qui ordinairement ruinent le pauvre peuple par les frais immences qu'ils occasionnent et l'avidité des gens d'affaires.

28.—Il demande que le partage des revenus des abbayes actuellement existants soient rendus irrévocables par une loy particulière de Sa Majesté, ce qui évitera des contestations ruineuses de soit pour les abbes, soit pour les chapitres Séculiers et réguliers.

29.—Le Clergé que pour assurer l'État des bénéfices, il soit, d'aprés l'article 9 de l'Édit de 1691, enjoint génerallement à tout patron et Collateurs de n'en passer les actes et titres que pardevant notaire à peine de nullité.

30.—Le corps des prébandés et Semy prébandés de la Sénéchaussée propriétaires ainsi que les chanoines de la manse commune supplient trés humblement Sa Majesté de les faire jouir du droit d'administrés leurs propriétés, droit dont ils eut été privés jusqu'à ce jour, en conséquence ils réclament contre l'abus qui les exclus de la gestion des affaires et demandent: 1.—à entrer par députés choisis parmi eux aux assemblées capitulaires en nombre égal à celui des chanoines lorsqu'il sagira du temporel. 2.—que les deux prevots nommé chaque année pour gérer les affaires, un soit pris parmi les chanoines et l'autre parmi les prébandés ou Semy prébandés et que tous les deux jouissent des mêmes prérogatives.

31.—Le clergé supplie Sa Majesté de trouver dans sa sagesse des moyens pour améliorer le sort de l'église de Lodeve et des autres de la même Sénéchaussée qui sont dans la détresse, ainsi que des couvents de religieuses qui par les soins qu'elle se donnent pour l'éducation de la jeunesse et leur vie vraiment chrétienne sont d'une grande utilités pour l'État et la religion.

32.—Il demande que le pauvre artisan qui n'a d'autre moyen pour subsister que son génie et son industrie puisse exister librement, et sans aucune gêne qui l'assujettisse à aucun droit d'entrée ni à aucun chef d'œuvre et en conséquence Sa Majesté sera très humblement suppliée de supprimer tout droit de Maitrise et de jurande et que pour les difficultés qui s'élévent entre eux ils seront renvoyés au Bureau du Conseil établi dans chaque paroisse comme il a été dit cy dessus article 27.

33.—La chambré du clergé aux états généraux suppliera le Roy de chercher et de prendre d'après sa sagesse tous les moyens les plus propres à procurer dans chaque paroisse un fonds pour la Subsistance des pauvres et l'entretien des fabriques.

34.—Qu'il soit pris dans chaque Diocèse les moyens les plus efficases pour connoitre les Capitalistes afin de les taxer relativement à leur fortune. [This text ends thus abruptly, without authentication.]

NO. 4. CLERGY OF THE BAILLIAGE OF BOURMONT

Cahier reprinted from MS text—*Arch. Haute-Marne,* B sans côte (copy supplied by M. Delessard, archivist.)
P.V.-MS, *Arch. Nat.* Ba19, B III 21. There were six on the committee for the cahier, which was adopted unanimously by the committee, March 18, and by the assembly March 20. The text was verified by the president and secretary of the assembly. Note that the cahier gives March 19 for the adoption. The difference may be a question of final adoption and signatures. Convocation—2d type, reunion at Bar-le-duc.

CAHIER DES PLAINTES, DOLÉANCES ET REMONTRANCES QUE L'ORDRE DU
CLERGÉ DU BAILLIAGE ROYAL DU BASSIGNY SCÉANT A BOURMONT,
CONVOQUÉ EN LA DITTE VILLE PAR ORDRE DU ROYS A
L'HONNEUR DE PRÉSENTER A SA MAJESTÉ ET
AUX ÉTATS GÉNÉRAUX DU ROYAUME

SIRE

supplie très humblement l'ordre du clergé du bailliage Royal du Bassigny scéant à Bourmont qu'il plaise à votre Majesté.

Article 1

Prendre en considération, que les moeurs, et la religion qui en est la base principalle, se trouvant attaquées dans leurs parties le clergé demande pour y remédier, que Sa Majesté rétablisse dans ses états la tenue des conciles provinciaux, et prohiber sous les plus grandes peines, cette foulle immense d'écrits impies et scandaleux qui se répandent de toute part, qu'en conséquence les imprimeurs et libraires soient surveillés de prêt, pour les empecher d'en imprimer ni débiter aucun, le luxe qui gagne même jusqu'au campagne étant une des sources de la dépravation des mœurs et des malheurs des peuples, Sa Majesté est suppliée d'y apporter un prompt et efficace reméde.

Article 2

Le voeu des peuples et de la plus grande et plus saine partie de la nation est de voir les ministres des sains autels dans l'honnête aisance que méritent leurs travaux, et les hautes fonctions dont ils sont honorés; en conséquence le dit clergé supplie Sa Majesté de vouloir ordonner que les portions congrues soient fixées au moins à quinze cent francs et les vicariats résidants érigés en cure et la pension augmentée pour ceux qui ne le seront point; cela mettra les uns et les autres à même d'exercer une honnête hospitalité et secourir les pauvres dont leurs paroisses abondent; renonceront volontiers à toute espèce de casuel non fixe que la pluspart ne percoivent que malgré eux, et par le besoin actuel qu'ils éprouvent il parait juste de faire attention aux pasteurs de grandes paroisses; le nombre de paroissiens augmentant celui des pauvres. Messieurs les curés Malthois demandent d'être traités comme tous leurs autres confrères.

Article 3

Supplie ledit clergé que Sa Majesté veuille bien ordonner que toutes les cures dépendantes des abbés soit en règle soit en commande, ainsi que de tous ordres et maisons religieuses des deux sexes, soient mises au concours, qui présentera trois sujets, dans le nombre desquels les patrons et nominateurs en choisiront un.

Messieurs les Réguliers, savoir, Révérendissime abbé de Morimond, représenté par dom Pointquarré, professeur en théologie de laditte abbeye, vénérable Louis le Nolt ministre de la Trinité de Bourmont, vénérable Francois Colier, religieux du même ordre tant en son nom qu'en celui de la maison de la Marche dudit ordre, vénérable J. Mathieu religieux prémontré, prieur de Crainvilliers, tant en son nom qu'en celui des vénérables religieux de l'abbaye de Flabémont même ordre, se sont opposés et protestés contre les demandes formées dans ledit article, ont demandé acte de leur protestation, ce qui leur a été accordé.

Article 4

L'éducation de la jeunesse, principallement dans les campagnes, Sa Majesté est suppliée d'y pourvoir en ordonnant qu'il soit assigné une honnête subsistance aux recteurs d'école; ces recteurs demandent une surveillance exacte, les curés seuls sont à même de juger de leurs moeurs et capacité; ils doivent par conséquent avoir une inspection directe sur eux et ne plus être contrariés par les cabales d'une populace capricieuse.

Article 5

Les fonds modiques dont jouissent la pluspart de nos fabriques, destinés à l'acquit de quelques obits, au luminaire, à l'entretient des ornements des autels, souvent employés à aider les paroissiens, dans les réparations et réeconstruction des églises et presbitères, au soulament[12] des pauvres et malades, ainsi qu'a l'instruction de la jeunesse se perdent souvent par les difficultés que des entraves nouvelles ont apporté aux remplacements. Sa Majesté est suppliée de faciliter les remplacements, et d'ordonner qu'ils soient fait sans frais, comme ci-devant; permettre aux fabriques et gens de mains mortes de remplacer les remboursement et de prêter ce qui provient des dots.

[12] Undoubtedly this should read "soulagement."

Article 6

Les presbytères batis à frais suffisans sont pour la plus part malsains, toutes les parties défectueuses par les mauvais matériaux qu'on y employe, l'on nous a chargé depuis quelques années non seulement des entretiens locatifs, mais de toutes réparations quelconques, exceptés les vilains fondoires, de la il arrive qu'à notre décés l'on nous oblige à remettre dans le meilleure état possible, ce qu'on nous a forcé dans la première construction à recevoir dans le plus mauvais. Suplions Sa Majesté d'ordonner que nous soyons déchargé des réparations usufrutières et rétablis dans nos anciens droits. Depuis quelques années l'on nous refuse des granges et écuries, de là ne pouvant loger les fruits de nos bénéfices, nous sommes obligé de les relaisser en argent, au dessous de leur valeur, ce qui nous met dans l'impossibilité de fournir des grains aux misérables dans les cas les plus urgents. Qu'il plaise à Sa Majesté ordonner que les règlements à cet egard établies et suivis de tems immémoriale dans le Barrois, abolis seulement depuis quelques tems, soient remis en vigeur.

Article 7

Les inventaires des curés soumis à la justice ordinaire devroient être fait et dressés par Messieurs les doyens ruraux, assistés de deux autres membres pris dans leur ordre, pour ce qui concerne les titres des fabriques et cures, copie desdits inventaires seroit envoyée dans les baillages et Messieurs les Officiers par ce moyen pouroient vérifier par l'inspection de l'inventaire précédent, s'il n'y a point eu de titres adhirés ou soustraits. Messieurs les doyens lors de la prise de possession, remetteroient tous les titres au nouveau titulaire ce qui leur épargneroit des frais considérables. Le clergé du Bassigny barrois supplie sa Majesté d'ordonner que les voeux ci-dessus exprimés soient rempli.

Article 8

Le Bassigny réclame avec justice un chapitre de chanoine qu'il devoit à la piété des anciens comte de Bar et de quantité de particuliers supprimé par un coup d'autoritié depuis quelques années, et les biens effectées aux chapitres de Poussey, le clergé joint ses réclamations et instances à celles du Bassigny avec d'autant plus de droits et interêts que ledit chapitre étoit chargé, par une place d'écolâtre, de l'instruction de la jeunesse.

Article 9

Le clergé réclame, ainsi que les deux autres ordres, le rétablissement des états provinciaux, qui faisoit la forme de la constitution du duché de Bar, lesquels ont été interrompues par le malheur des tems.

Article 10

La mouvance est un objet ruineux pour une partie du Bassigny. L'éloignement de la capitale, les longs séjours qu'on est obligé d'y faire à raison que le parlement de Paris est surchargé d'affaires, la longueur des procédures, les frais immenses quelles entrainent ruinent les familles dont la fortune paroissoit la mieux établie. La subzeraineté n'est plus nécessaire dès qu'il n'y a plus de vassaux.

Article 11

Le Clergé offre de contribuer aux impôts pécuniares selon ses facultés respectives et celle des deux autres ordres, mais sous le nom de don gratuit, pour un tems limité, se réservant la répartition et la recette, sans que ses offres puissent nuire en aucun cas à ses droits et privilèges et au condition que tout le clergé du royaume supportera les mêmes charges. N'entend ledit clergé entrer en aucune façon dans la liquidation du clergé de France. Ses représentans ne pourront consentir à aucune augmentation d'impôt ou établissement de nouveau, qu'au préalable le retour des États généraux n'ait été fixé et ne contribuer à l'acquit de la dette commune que jusqu'à son extinction vérifié par les états. Dans le bureau [bureau] écclésiastique tous les membres du clergé contribueront aux charges sans distinctions, n'auront que leur voix sous prépondérance aucune, même de la part de nos seigneurs nos evêques; tous ceux qui composeront le bureau seront élus et choisis à la pluralité des voix er par la voix du scrutin. La répartition sera fait en raison des revenus et des charges d'un chacun, information préalablement faite, déclaration juste sous peine de payer le double de l'objet recélé. Les membres dudit bureau ne pourront être en exercice que pendant trois ans; le bureau ne sera point fixé dans un seul endroit et pourra être transporté dans un autre aux désirs du plus grand nombre. Il sera oblige de faire dresser tous les trois ans un tableau et en envoyer copie sans réquisition à tous les bénéficiers dès le commencement de son exercise, mais au cas que l'on préféra l'impôt territorial à toute autre espèce notre ordre y donnera les mains à condition cependant qu'il sera perçu en argent et non en nature et que toute personne de quelque condition et état qu'il puisse être y soit soumise.

Article 12

Nous ne pouvons que louer les dispositions paternelles de sa Majesté qui se propose de réduire et fixer les dépenses de sa Maison, celle des bureau, extraordinaires et pensions.

Article 13

Sera reglée la proportion qui pourra être établie dans une caisse d'amortissement pour parvenir à la liquidation des dettes de l'État.

Article 14

Chaque receveur sera obligé de rendre conte à la nation, chacune dans leur département, des deniers versés dans leur caisse respectives.

Article 15

En cas de malversations, prevarications ou vexations des dits receveurs ou même des ministres ils en seront comptable envers la nation.

Article 16

Toutes lois nouvelles qui pourroient être proposées n'auront de force qu'autant qu'elles seront approuvées et acceptées par la nation; la liberté individuelle de tout sujets de l'État sera assurées par l'abolition des lettres clauses, lettres d'exil et tout autres espèces d'ordres arbitraires. Le clergé du second ordre voit avec douleur qu'il se trouve exclus depuis quelques tems des dignités ecclésiastiques ainsi que les chapitres que l'on a érigés en chapitres nobles. Nous ne pouvons consentir à aucune imposition que les abus n'ayent été réformés et les griefs redressés.

Article 17

L'objet des Gruries [grueries], une forme moins dispendieuse dans l'administration de la justice, les forges et usines, celui des sels et tabac, la ferme de chatrerie et riflerie, la marque des fers et cuirs, une répartition plus juste de la taile, le grand nombre d'exempts dans les villes à raison des charges de judicature et des emplois trop multipliés de la ferme, le nombre excessifs d'employés occupé uniquement à entretenir une guerre intestine dans le sein du royaume, la milice, les corvées sont des objets qui seront traités par le tiers état avec les lumières que nous lui connoissons et l'interêt qu'il doit y mettre. Le clergé interessé par état au soulagement des peuples accedera volontiers à ces motions du tiers pourvu cependant qu'elles soient faites avec la modération et la prudence convenable comme nous nous en flattons. Le clergé verroit avec peine et ne pourroit consentir que l'on enlevat à la noblesse les distinctions que ses services lui ont mérités.

Article 18

Nos representants ne pourront accepter aucun bénéfice, pension ou autres graces directes ou indirectes sans être réputés prévaricateurs et justement soupçonnés d'avoir trahit lâchement les intérests de leur ordre.

Article 19

Mettre en vigeur les loix canoniques qui déffendent la pluralité des bénéfices il est du plus grand intérêt des fidèles sujets de sa Majesté dans l'ordre ecclésiastique d'être traités en cour de Rome pour les resignations et autres bulles ainsi que les sujets des autres provinces et principallement comme la partie mouvante du Barrois.

Article 20

Nos représentants aux états généraux insisteront principallement à ce que dans les déliberations les voix soient prises par ordre et non par tête ce qui a toujours été pratiqué; ils insisteront même à ce que cela soit reglé et ordonné pour l'avenir.

Telles sont, Sire, les remonstrances que le clergé du baillage de Bourmont a l'honneur de présenter à Votre Majesté et aux États généraux lesquelles ont été agréés d'une voix unanime, après lecture faite, par tous les membres de l'assemblée qui supplient Votre Majesté de les acceuillir favorablement; faites et arrêtés dans la chambre destinée à son ordre et signés de tous les membres présens dans la séance de ce jour Jeudy dix neuf Mars mil sept cent quatre vingt neuf à cinq heure de relevé, sans préjudicier aux droits d'aucune des parties, conformement au réglement.

[Twenty-six signatures]
Pitory, curé de Soulaucourt, secrétaire de l'assemblée.

Je soussigné curé de Sommerécourt en ma qualité de procurer de Poussey déclare m'opposer au nom dudit chapitre à la demande faite par l'ordre du clergé au rétablissement du chapitre de Bourmont ce dont j'ay demandé acte. Pellegrin, procureur fondé du noble chapitre de Poussey. Pellegrin curé de Sommerécourt procureur fondé du chapitre de Poussey.

NO. 5. THE NOBLES OF THE BAILLIAGE OF BOURMONT

Cahier reprinted from MS text—*Arch. Haute-Marne,* B sans côte. (Copy supplied by M. Delessard, archivist.)
P.V.-MS, *Arch. Nat.* B III 21. There were four members of the commission. The cahier was adopted and signed by the president, secretary, and members on March 20. The cahier gives the date, March 18.
Convocation—2d type: reunion at Bar-le-duc.

CAHIER DES PLAINTES, DOLÉANCES ET
REMONSTRACES DE L'ORDRE DE LA NOBLESSE DU BASSIGNY SÉANT
À BOURMONT

Le duché de Bar dont le Baillage de Bassigny séant à Bourmont à toujours fait partie est une province séparée de la Lorraine; le duché à constamment joui de ses états particuliers jusqu'en l'année 1664.

Ces états étaient composés de l'ordre du clergé, de celui de la noblesse et du tiers-état; on y votait par ordre et non par tête. Ces prérogatives étaient fondées sur la raison qui ne permet pas qu'un ordre soit exposé à l'opression d'un autre.

La noblesse y a toujours joui de tous ses privilèges assurés par les cou-

231

tumes, les loix et les constitutions du pays stipulés et promis par le traité de cession de *1736*, les prises de possession de *1737* et *1766*.

Ce sont les mêmes privilèges que la noblesse du Bassigny réclamme et rassurée sur le coeur paternel du Roy, elle ne craint pas que sa Majesté et les Etats généraux veuillent altérer l'ancienne constitution du royaume: c'est dans cette confiance qu'elle a formé le cahier de ses plaintes, doléances et remontrances pour etre remis à M.M. les deputés aux Etats généraux qui seront priés, invités et requis de mettre aux pieds du Trône de sa Majesté et de faire valoir aux États généraux les différens voeux qu'il renferme.

Article 1

L'ordre de la noblesse s'en rapporte à tout ce qui sera fait par la nation dans les États généraux sur ce qui sera décidé relativement à l'administration des finances et aux abus entre autres toutes lettres clauses.

Article 2

Le rétablissement des Etats provinciaux du duché de Bar suivant son ancienne constitution, convoqués toutes les années au mois de mai, sans qu'il soit besoin de nouvelles lettres de convocation, et dans telle ville du duché qu'il plaira au Roy de l'ordonner.

Article 3

La conservation des privelèges, franchises et immunités de la noblesse assurée et promise par le traité de cession de *1736*.

Article 4

Le maintien de la forme constitutionnelle des délibérations aux Etats généraux qui ce sont toujours faites par ordre dans les monarchies et non par tête, usage commun en Allemagne et en Angleterre.

Article 5

De n'accorder aucun impot si ce n'est pour l'acquittement des dettes actueles de l'État jusqu'a leurs extinction.

Article 6

De demander le retour périodique des Etats Généraux, sans le consentement desquels aucun impôt ne poura être établi ny exigé.

Article 7

La suppression totale du Bureau des hipotèques [hypothèques].

Article 8

Le rétablissement du droit de sceau ainsi qu'il a été perçu de tout temps dans le Bassigny.

Article 9

La supression des droits de traite forene [forain], transite acquis et haut conduit et tous autres droits semblables ainsi que l'abus des privilèges accordés aux commis et employés des fermes.

Article 10

La suppression des huissiers priseurs.

Article 11

La suppression des hôtels de ville remplacés par un maire électif et changé tous les trois ans lequel sera tenu de rendre compte de son administration à la fin des dites trois année.

Article 12

Obliger les maîtres de forge de ne consommer dans leurs usines autres bois que ceux qui leur sont affectés.

Article 13

Que les impôts créés depuis *1615* soient déclarés nuls et illégament établis notament dans la province du Barrois.

Article 14

La réforme des abus dans l'administration de la justice.

Article 15

La supression des Intendans.

Article 16

L'abréviation des procédures.

Article 17

Qu'aucun sujet ne puisse être jugé par une commission ni par évocation. L'abus des évocations est prouvé par le mémoire cy joint.

Article 18

Des réglemens propres au rétablissement et maintien de la religion et des moeurs et à diminuer le luxe.

Article 19

Le maintien des traites et capitulations de chaque province à moins qu'il ne soit fait une chartre générale dans tout le Royaume.

Article 20

L'inspection et administration des travaux chemins établissemens publics et biens de communautés confiés à chaque province sans que les intendans puissent en prendre aucune connoissance s'il plait au roy de les conserver.

Article 21

Après avoir fixé la dépense de la maison du Roy, verifié les revenus de ses domaines, s'il ne suffisent pas, il sera par fourni jusqu'à concurrence nécessaire de la somme qui sera assignée sur un genre d'impôts dont l'emploi sera vérifié chaque année et rendu public par l'impression.

Article 22

L'examen et vérification des donations, échanges et concession des domaines depuis *1736*.

Article 23

Demanderont la supression des fermiers généraux avec établissement d'une caisse nationale.

Article 24

Que les denrées de première nécéssité soient affranchies de tous impôts.

Article 25

La vérification des titres et des causes des pensions accordées: la supression des uns et la réduction des autres.

Article 26 .

La résidence des Evêques dans leurs diocèses, celle des abbés et prieurs commandataires dans la province ou sont située leur bénéfice, neuf mois de l'année au moins sous peine de saisie de leur temporel et de l'emploi des revenus saisis au profit des hôpitaux atteliers et autres établissements publics.

Article 27

L'incompatibilité de plusieurs abbayes ou prieuriés en commande.

Article 28

La réduction des revenus excessif de quelques evêches et archevêchés à une somme qui sera jugée sufisante pour l'honnête entretien des prélats et l'emploi du surplus au profit du clergé du second ordre dont la portion congrue est trop modique.

Article 29

La liberté aux habitants du Bassigny barrois de faire des députations au Roy et le suplier d'agréer les mémoires qui lui seront presentés sans que les ministres puissent empêcher l'accès du thrône.

Article 30

La pleine liberté dans les déliberations des Etats Généraux.

Article 31

Que les cahiers des États généraux seront rendus publics par la voie de l'impression.

Article 32

Le rétablissement du chapitre de l'insigne église collégiale de Bourmont composée de treise [treize] prébandes sacerdotales suprimé en *1761* par authorité sans aucune forme légale, mais sur le simple prétexte de l'insufisance de ses revenus; tandis que chaque prébande valait au moins dix huit cent livres, celle du prevôt étant double independament des fonds affectés à la fabrique. En suprimant le chapitre et donnant ses biens à celui dames de Poussey le Roy s'est privé des nominations et collations de toutes les prébandes et les revenus de biens qui étaient un espèce de patrimoine pour tous les ordres du Bassigny Barrois, ont été transportés en Lorraine, quoique ces biens sont encor situés dans le même Bassigny et proviennent des comtes et ducs de Bar et des autres fondateurs particuliers de ce pays, ce qui est contraire au titre de fondation, dotation, à la constitution de la province et particulièrement au traité de Vienne de *1736*, au moyen duquel rétablissement nous demandons que l'un des chanoines soit curé, que l'église serve de paroisse, ce qui peut se faire avec d'autant moins d'inconvénient que le chapitre est curé primitif; et pour indemniser Mesdames de Poussey, sa Majesté est supliée de leurs accorder une pension sur des abbayes ou prieurés.

Article 33

L'encouragment de l'agriculture à l'effet de quoi notre deputé sera chargé d'un mémoire relatif à cet objet.

Article 34

Il est expressement deffendu aux députés aux généraux[13] de solliciter ou accepter directement pour eux, leurs parens, même pour tous étrangers, des pensions, bénéfices ou autre Grâces, sous peine d'être réputés traitres à la patrie.

Article 35

Donnons pouvoir à nos députés de représenter la province aux Etats Généraux aprés avoir vérifiés que les députés de toutes les autres provinces ont été librement élus.

[13] Undoubtedly the word "Etats" was omitted, and the phrase should read "aux Etats generaux."

Article 36

Ils ne pourront s'écarter dans les délibérations aux Etats Généraux, à peine de désaveu des principes contenus dans le présent cahier qui servira d'instruction et de pouvoir aux députés du Bassigny, pour proposer, remontrer, aviser et consentir tout ce qui peut concerner les besoins de l'État et la réforme des abus, en leur retirant leur pouvoir s'ils consentaient à l'anéantissement des privilèges de la noblesse et à déliberer par tête et non par ordre.

Article 37

Vu la précipitation avec laquelle ont été obligé de rédiger les pouvoirs, instructions et cahier, on se réserve d'envoyer de plus amples instructions aux députés pendant le séance des États Généraux pourquoi ils seront tenus d'informer exactement la commission qui sera établie pour cet effet à[14] . . . des objets importans qui pouraient être traités aux Etats Généraux et qui n'auraient pas été prévus par les pouvoirs, instructions et cahiers.

Lecture faite, ce travail a été aprouvé, arrêté définitivement et signé par M. le président, MM. les Commissaires et M. le secrétaire et tous les membres de la noblesse présens à la rédaction le 18 Mars 1789.[15]

[The signatures of the four committee men, eleven others, and]

de Fussey, président   Bernard de Crévechamp, secrétaire

NO. 6. THE NOBLES OF THE BAILLIAGE OF BRUYERES

Cahier reprinted from the MS text, *Arch. Vosges,* unclassified. Original signatures, verification.

P.V.-MS, *Arch. Nat.* Ba53. There were three members of the committee. After adding an article on the method of voting in the Estates General, the cahier was adopted by the assembly, March 23. The committee was authorized to print the cahier.

Convocation: 2d type, reunion at Mirecourt.

DOLÉANCES POUR L'ORDRE DE LA NOBLESSE
DU BAILLAGE DE BRUYÈRES EN LORRAINE

La dépradation des finances, la position malheureuse où L'état se trouve, alloient encore être aggravée par des Édits bursaux, présentée, a main armée, La Nation sortie de son assoupissement a porté ses Réclamations au pied du Trône.

Le Roy a permis a son peuple de lui proposer les moyens de réformer

[14] No name was filled in. A special substitute was elected, but the *procès-verbal* does not mention a committee for correspondence.

[15] The difference of date, in this case, plus this statement causes one to make reserves as to whether or not this was the final text adopted.

les abus, et de rafermir la confiance des citoyens en assurant la félicité publique. C'est pour répondre à ses vues bien faisantes que le député de la Noblesse du Baillage de Bruyeres sera chargé specialement de Voter.

1.—Pour la liberté individuelle, des Citoyens et la suppression des Lettres closes, ainsi que de la sureté de leurs Etats.

2.—Pour assurer les propriétés sans qu'on puisse y porter atteinte par des impôts qui ne seroient pas consentis par les Etats Généraux.

3.—Que tous les Domaines ascensés ou autrement allienés avant le traité de Vienne de 1737 tiendront Nature de biens patrimoniaux, sans avoir égard au sistême fiscal Etabli en france, relativement a L'inaliénation des Domaines de la Couronne, que led [le dit] traité Nous soit confirmé ainsi que les conditions, priviléges, immunité sur lesquels nous avons été cédé à la france.

On nous objecteroit en vain, qu'un Souverain n'étant qu'usufruitier ne peut alliéner ses Domaines; C'est une Loi en france qui ne peut regarder la Lorraine, que pour les alliénations faittes par le Roy depuis L'époque de 1737. Si les derniers Ducs de Lorraine, ancêtres de Notre Auguste Reine, n'avoient pu légalement alliénés des parties de leurs Domaines, ils n'auroient pû alliénés la Province, qui pourroit alors se soustraire à la Domination de Sa Majesté selon la volonté de la Nation, puisque le dernier Souverain seroit censé avoir fait cette cession contre les Lois. Enfin par le traité de 1737 Nous devons conserver tous nos privilèges et toutes nos possessions.

Le Duc Leopold à trouvé presque tout son pays abandonné et en friche, il à attiré beaucoup de Colons Étrangers en leur donnant des terres à défricher sur lesquelles ils ont bâtis, on ne peut les évincer avec justice puisqu'une jouissance passagère ne sauroit les indemnisés des travaux et des frais qu'ils ont faits, ainsi que du sacrifice de s'être expatriés, tous les habitants des montagnes sont dans le cas, on ne peut donc sans bouleverser, toute la province retirer les Domaines que ces Princes ont alliénés.

4.—Qu'aucune Loi Nouvelle n'aura de force exécutive qu'autant qu'elle sera sanctionnée par la Nation.

5.—Que les États Généraux seront rassemblés tous les trois ans.

6.—Qu'auqu'un [aucun] impôt ne pourra être prorogé au delà du terme fixé par sa perception que par les seuls Etats Généraux.

7.—Qu'eux seuls connoitront de la dette Nationale des charges et revenus de l'état, pour pouvoir juger des Retranchemens ou augmentations à faire sur chaque Département et déterminer les subsides.

8.—Que les dépenses de la Cour; celles des maisons des Princes et des Départements seront fixés et réglés invariablement.

9.—Que les Ministres des différents Départements seront comptables à la Nation de leurs administrations.

10.—Qu'il ne sera consentis aucun impôts, aucuns Emprunts qu'après l'acceptation des neuf articles précedents.

11.—Que le droit de répartir les subsides sur les différentes Provinces appartiendra aux Etats Généraux; Que graduellement cette répartition sera faitte sur les Baillages. Les trois ordres séparément se cottiseront eux-mêmes.

12.—Qu'il sera établi un Receveur dans chaque Province, pour porter directement les subsides au Trésor Royal: et que dans chaque Baillage, il sera choisi un Receveur particulier qui versera dans la caisse du premier aux moindres frais possibles.

13.—Que dans les Baillages, chaque ordre choisira ses asseyeurs et collecteurs, tant pour la répartition que pour la levée des subsides.

14.—Qu'il sera formé opposition à toute demande d'assanement [assaisissement] et d'aliénation des forêts de sa Majestée chargées de l'usage des habitans, de même qu'a tout nouvel établissement d'usine à feu.

15.—Qu'il sera demandé la diminution du prix du Sel.

16.—Demander la suppression des traites et foraines, sauf à indemniser le fisc, par une imposition pécuniaire proporsionée [proportionnée].

17.—Demander l'abolition de la Corvée en Nature, que l'imposition pécuniaire qui la remplacera, soit réglée par les Etats provinciaux et ne puisse être divertie n'y employée à d'autres usages, sous quelque pretexte que ce puisse être.

18.—Que les adjudications des constructions ou réparations des routes seront faitte par parties et au Rabais, pardevant des commissaires des trois ordres, et les deniers versés sans frais ses mains du Receveur dans celles des adjudicataires.

19.—Que la contribution de la Noblesse indépendante de celles des deux autres ordres, sera fixée par les états Provinciaux selon ses forces et facultés.

20.—Que les impôts seront bornés au tems de la libération de la dette publique, reconnue Nationale par les etats, sans se soustraire au besoin journalier et accidentel du Royaume.

21.—Que la Province de Lorraine ne sera tenue de contribuer à cette libération que depuis le traité de Vienne et sa réunion à la France en 1737.

22.—Qu'il ne sera porté aucune atteinte aux droits honorifiques et aux privilèges dont la Noblesse jouit; lesqu'els [lesquels] lui seront confirmés pour l'avenir.

23.—Que les Bulles et les dispenses, qui se donnent en Cour de Rome soient dorénavant données par les Evêques chaqu'un dans son Diocèse.

24.—Que les bénéficiers Eclésiastiques soient obliges à une résidence de Neuf mois par année dans les lieux de leurs bénéfices.

25.—Que de deux ou trois maisons de Religieux rentés; il n'en sera conservé qu'une dont le nombre des sujets sera fixé avec Cinq cents livres par tete et que le surplus de leur revenu, entrera dans la caisse d'amortissement de la dette publique, et que les Communautés de filles ne pourront plus recevoir de Dot, Vu qu'il est censé que depuis leurs établissemens elles ont été suffisament rentées.

238

26.—Qu'à la collation des bénéfices Royaux et consistoriaux en commande il sera réservé moitie du produit net du bénéfice que le titulaire sera obligé de verser annuellement dans la Caisse d'amortissement de la dette publique.

27.—Suppression de la ferme Générale l'orsqu'il [lorsqu'il] y aura des fonds pour la rembourser, rendre le tabac marchand, et en attendant cette suppression déffendre à ses employés d'user de voyes de fait, Cette dernière partie est de Rigueur.

28.—Demander que les Municipalités soient formées des trois ordres. Élus librement par eux pour assoir [asseoir] les charges de Ville.

29.—Pour un changement dans la constitution Militaire reconnue Mobile, étrangère au Caractere de la Nation et destructive d'une Émulation qui en est le plus puissant ressort.

Mobile est deslors décourageante par le caprice des Ministres de la Guerre, dont neuf depuis vingt ans n'ont fait que tracasser les troupes, soit dans leur formation, soit dans leur habillement,[16] [Nous avons vu donner successivement des habits verts, de Grands habits, de petits chapeaux, des grands chapeaux, à deux, à trois, à quatre cornes, des casques et d'après une ineptie révoltante du caractère français; proposer de faire des joquais, d'une infanterie inexpugnable en obligeant chaque individu de se faire couper les cheveux à Langlaise. Quand on a présenté à Sa Majesté un Soldat habillé en habit vert, elle s'est écrié, si c'est un habit, il est trop court; si c'est une veste, elle est trop longue.] soit par des coups de plats de sabre, ou autres, en horreur à la Nation, soit par les Manoeuvres impracticables, selon que l'inexpérience des Ministres était entrainée par de jeunes ambitieux et des flateurs, qui sans avoir jamais vu bruler une amorce, avoient pour perspective de faire un chemin rapide en présentant leur enthousiasme et leurs rêves pour des idées Lumineuses et en arrachant des ordonnances qui devastent journellement les corps par la désertion, et qui découragent les anciens officiers au point de leur faire préférer une retraite prématurée à la douleur de servir d'instrument à l'avilissement de la Nation pour laqu'elle il seroit à craindre après un laps de temps très court de voir les troupes composés de gens tirés de la Lie du Peuple.

Autrefois les Capitaines, l'Âme des Régiments dont ils tenoient en mains les forces et les Ressorts, Viellisoient dans leur état; ils devenoient les instituteurs et les modèles des jeunes officiers, qui apprenoient sous eux à respecter leur chef, à se plier sous le joug de la discipline, et de la subordination. Pourquoi? C'est qu'alors les grades honorables, devenoient l'appanage des longs services. Une Lieutenance Colonelle à rang d'ancienneté dans son corps, et une Lieutenance du Roy pour but faisoient dévorer les fatigues et les dégouts inséparables d'une obéisance toujours passive et nôtre armée composée de pareils vétérans devenoient une Ecolle de valeur et d'héroisme, Aujourd'Huy, tout est changé, le Capitaine quelque soit sa valeur, ses bles-

---

[16] The passage in brackets appeared as a footnote in the original MS.

sures, son expérience, ses talents et ses longs services; s'il manque de fortune et d'une protection qui le suit, se voit condamné à trainer son existence dans les grades subalternes, et ne soupire plus qu'après le moment de sa retraite, L'amour de la Patrie s'éteignant dans des âmes que l'on révolte en cherchant sans cesse à les rabaisser: Les récompenses honorables ne devroient être dans notre constitution Militaire que le prix des services signalés, L'orsque cette Morale vraiement guerrière se trouvoit en activité, Nos troupes étoient une pépinière de héros. Le soldat devenant Officier et l'Officier pouvant devenir général: on voioit à la tête de Nos Légions, Les Catinats, les Faberts et les Cheverts. Maintenant qu'on semble avoir élevé une Barriére insurmontable entre le simple Officier et les premiers grades, les anciens Capitaines se retirent. Une jeunesse sans frein, sans discipline et souvent sans Moeurs, forme la tête de Nos Régiments. Plus de surveillans qui imposent à de jeunes Adolescens; Lesquels n'apportent de nos Écolles Militaires qu'un gout éffrené des plaisirs, de la dépense et de l'insubordination. C'est à cette jeunesse éffeminée qui n'a pour titre qu Sa Naissance, ses Richesses, et les faveurs de la Cour qu'on prodigue les premiers honneurs.

Un autre abus trop toléré dans Notre Militaire, c'est l'impunité qui autorise dans les officers supérieurs, les punitions souvent excessives et presque toujours arbitraires. La discipline doit être sévère, la Subordination absoluë, mais si une loi Nationale rendoit l'officier superieur comptable et responsable de sa sévèrité déplacée, L'impétuosité ou la prise qui L'entraine au dela des bornes, seroit arrété par la crainte du Blame et de la réprimande.

Notre Député doit donc s'occuper aux Etats Généraux de solliciter Sa Majesté pour obtenir une constitution fixe, immuable et fondée sur le Caractère Nationale d'après un nombre déterminé de Princes du Sang, de Maréchaux de France, et de Lieutenant Généraux, patriotes et françois, qui formeront entre eux un Conseil de la Guerre dans lequel aucun Ministre ne pourra entrer, s'il n'est au moins Lieutenant Général, étant de Notoriété publique, qu'il y a beaucoup de nos Maréchaux de Camp qui n'ont jamais vû tirer un coup de fusil.

30.—Qu'il sera opiné par tête, ainsi qu'il a été déliberé par 200 membres du Clergé, 300 de la Noblesse, et 350 du Tiers etat assemblés à Nancy le 21 dernier, cet article à passé à notre assemblée de quatorze voix contre huit.

31.—La Réformation des abus dans les Maitrises des Eaux et forêts dans les Recettes et la perception des impôts.

32.—La Réformation de L'abus des lettres d'Etat, de surcéances et commitimus du grand Sceau, et Evocations, s'en rapportant pour les exceptions à la décision des Etats Généraux.

33.—Suppression de toutes les Lotteries et nottament de celles connue sous le titre de Lotterie Royale de France, comme dangereuse, usuriaire, cause de vol Domestique, et la ruine de plusieurs familles et d'un grande nombre de suicide.

34.—La suppression des droits de Mairie et de vouëte établis sur les quatre jurations de Laval, La Chapelle, Jussarupt, et Frembemenil, qui forment un Canton très considérable dans le Ressort du Baillage de Bruyères, comme une charge très onéreuse, qui gène l'agriculture et ôte l'emulation d'elever le bettail.

Tels sont les pouvoirs et les Instructions que la Noblesse du Baillage de Bruyères a cru devoir donner à son Député et pour en garentir l'autenticité, Nous Membres convoqués à l'assemblée de la Noblesse dudit Baillage avons signé ce 23 Mars 1789: Le Comte de Giverni, Bailli.

[Twenty-one signatures.]

Gerboulet secrétaire de l'ordre de la Noblesse.

Le présent cahier a été cotté et paraphe par nous Dieudonné Gabriel de Humbert, Comte de Giverni, Bailli de Bruyères le dit jour vingt-trois Mars 1789, il continent quatre feuillets. Le Comte de Giverni.

NO. 7. THE THIRD ESTATE OF THE SENECHAUSSEE OF CARHAIX

Cahier reprinted from the MS text, *Arch. Finistère,* original signatures of commission, deputies and senechal.

P.V.—MS, *Arch. Nat. Ba 25.* The assembly of Carhaix united with the *sénéchaussées* of Chateaulin, Châteauneuf du Faou, Gourin and Quimperlé, chose 12 for the committee, and adopted the cahier April 9.

Convocation: 6th type; Brittany.

PLAINTES, DOLÉANCES ET REMONTRANCES DE L'UNIVERSALITÉ DES RESSORTS OU JURIDICTIONS DE CHATEAULIN, CHATEAUNEUF, CARHAIX, GOURIN ET QUIMPERLÉ REPRESENTÉS PAR LEURS ÉLECTEURS EN L'ASSEMBLÉE TENUE EN CETTE VILLE LE SEPT DE CE MOIS AUX TERMES DE L'ARTICLE QUATRE DU REGLEMENT DU 24 JANVIER DERNIER ET DE L'ARTICLE 4 DU RÉGLEMENT DU 16 MARS SUIVANT, À LA RÉDACTION ET RÉDUCTION DESQUELLES À ÉTÉ VACQUÉ PAR NOUS—VINCENT SAMUEL BILLETTE, ANNE-JACQUES-BERNARD-FRANÇOIS-CARQUET, URBAIN-MARIE DE LEISSEGUES DE LEGERVILLE, JEAN MARIE LE GOLIAS, FRANÇOIS-JUILLIEN LE LEDAN, SAMSON BIENVENU, JEAN-FRANÇOIS LE CORNEC, FRANÇOIS-MARIE-ALLAIN DE LAUNAY, JEAN-MAURICE-RÉNÉ-MARIE FOUEFF DE MONTALEMBERT, ET LAURENT CAURAUT—COMMISSAIRES NOMMÉS À LA SÉANCE DE L'ASSEMBLÉE DUDIT JOUR, COMME SUIT.

SIRE

Le Voeu Général et unamine de plus de cent mille de vos fideles Sujets sous le Ressort des Sénéchaussées de Chateaulin, Chateauneuf, Carhaix, Gourin, et Quimperlé, représentés par leurs 28 Electeurs, assemblés de votre ordre à Carhaix, est qu'il ne soit porté aucune atteinte au culte de notre Religion.

2.—Que les droits, franchises et immunités de la province Soient conservés dans leur intégrité, Sauf le redressement des Griefs de L'ordre du Tiers état, Tendant à ce que les députés du Tiers aux Etats de la province soient en nombre égal à ceux des deux ordres privilègiés, ainsi que vous avez bien voulu, Sire, l'admettre pour les Etats Généraux.

Qu'on opine par têtes;

Que les membres du Tiers soient admis à tous les emplois et offices, ecclésiastiques, civils et militaires, et que toutes Loix ou usages à ce contraire soient abolies;

Que la moitié des charges du parlement soit occupée par des membres du Tiers;

Que le président aux états de la province soit de l'ordre du Tiers et de son choix, que l'une des places de procureur Général Sindic soit occupée par un membre du tiers, et celle de Greffier alternativement même dès la prochaine Tenue d'Etat, que le nombre des commissaires soit égal dans toutes commissions et députations à celui des deux autres ordres réunis et aux mêmes ordres honneurs et émolumens; que les dits députés ne puissent être à l'avenir ni nobles ni annoblis, ni Subdélégués et qu'ils ne puissent être choisis parmi les juges, procureurs fiscaux, officiers, ni agens des Seigneurs;

Que la répartition des impositions soit pour tous les ordres en raison de leurs facultés, qu'il n'y ait pour chaque espece d'impots qu'un même Rolle et que s'il est necessaire de Créer de nouveaux impots ce soit de préférence sur les objets de Luxe;

Que tous les dons pensions et gratifications soient Supprimées, que les appointemens du Trésorier des états soient réduits, que les établissements purement à l'avantage de la noblesse soient à sa seule charge et que les Tables, emploi inutiles, frais de Baptêmes et obsèques soient aussi supprimés; Que l'ouverture et l'entretien des Grandes routes ne soient plus à la charge du Tiers Etat, Mais que la dépense en soit faite par le Trésor public, ces routes étant utiles à tous;

Que le Tirage au Sort pour la milice, gardes côtes et matelots et tous autres enrollemens forcés soient Suprimés, sauf à les remplacer par des levées a prix d'argent, et au cas que ladite supression n'ait pas lieu, que les Valets Domestiques du clergé et de la noblesse ne soient plus exemptés du Tirage au Sort;

Que le Logement des Troupes, le transport de leurs Bagages et les fournitures aux casernes soient à la charge des Trois Ordres.

3.—Que les jurisdictions Seigneuriales soient réunis aux Sénéchaussées Royales, qu'au cas que la réunion n'ait pas lieu, les juges inferieurs soient chargés d'instruire et parfaire jusqu'à sentence définitive inclusivement les procédures criminelles dont les Seigneurs Suporteront les frais.

4.—Que les batards soient a la charge des Seigneurs ayant droit de Batardise.

5.—Que les Sieges Royaux soient maintenus et conservés dans leurs Villes actuelles, qu'il n'y ait plus que deux dégrés de jurisdictions, et que les Sièges Royaux puissent juger en dernier Ressort les affaires où le principal n'excédera pas 200 #. Deux cens livres.

6.—Que la Législation civile et Criminelle soit reformée et que provisoirement il soit enjoint à tous juges de juger dans six mois les procés appointés en état de recevoir judgement à peine de prise à partie et de tous dépens dommages et intérets.

7.—Que les peines afflictives soient les mêmes pour tous les ordres de l'état et de la Societé.

8.—Que la Venalité des offices de judicatures soit Supprimée et que les Juges soient électifs par les justicables à la pluralité des voix Votants par têtes.

9.—Que les frais de Saisies réelles soient Simplifiés et rendus moins ruineux.

10.—Que le droit de Committimus soit aboli.

11.—Que les offices de procureurs et de consignataires et de Notaires et Contrôleurs, soient declarés incompatibles.

12.—Qu'il soit établis des auditoires decents et des prisons Salubres dans tous les Siéges et que le pain des prisonniers soit augmenté.

13.—Qu'il soit fait un fond pour procurer des réparations aux accusés par le Ministère public et renvoyés d'accusation.

14.—Que L'Economat soit Suprimé et qu'il soit enjoint de rendre ses Comptes dans Trois mois.

15.—Que les revenus des abbés commandataires et prieurés sans charges d'ames, soient attribués, Vaccation avenante, à des établissements utiles et propre à écarter la mendicité.

16.—Que les appointemens des Gouverneurs de province soient suprimés ainsi que ceux de Chateaux et places où il y a état major.

17.—Que le Corps pastoral depute aux Etats de la province comme aux états généraux, et qu'il soit fait sur les grands Bénéfices une pension de 400 # aux Simples prêtres desservants ou infirmes.

18.—Qu'il soit fait un nouveau régime pour les municipalités qu'il en soit établi de nouvelles, principalement à Chateaulin, Le faou, Chateauneuf et Rostrenen et Callac, et en attendant, que les villes qui sont privées de cet avantage puissent envoyer des Deputés aux municipalités Voisines pour concourir à toutes délibérations et y être eligibles.

19.—Que les droits sur les cuirs et tous autres objets de premiere nécessité, soient réduits;

20.—Que les juges ordinaires de police soient autorisés suivant Leur prudence et l'exigence des cas, à arreter toute exportation des Grains même de province à province.

21.—Que les mesures, poids et autres, soient uniformes dans toute la province et aient la même denomination.

22.—Que les droits de chasse, fuies et colombier soient Suprimés.

23.—Que le franc-fief soit egalement suprimé comme le droit le plus onéreux et le plus humiliant à l'ordre du Tiers.

24.—Que les droits de Contrôle, Scélé, insinuation, et autres de même nature principalement pour les inventaires des Biens des mineurs, Soient notablement Moderés, qu'il en soit fait un nouveau Tarif qui les fixe invariablement, avec attribution aux juges royaux ordinaires pour toute matiere contentieuse relative a tous droits de regie.

25.—Que les Trois Sols pour livre sur les épices, Vaccations des juges, et sur les Vaccations des huissiers et Sergens royaux soient suprimés, et que leurs salaires leur soit payés dans les procédures criminelles.

26.—Que le centieme denier sur les offices Royaux, soit Suprimés, et que les juges soient payés pour les procedures criminelles.

27.—Que pour tous actes, Contrats et Sentences il soit permis de se servir de papier Timbré et que les Sentences même définitives soient seulement d'une Ecriture Transomptée.

28.—Que les douanes, Traittes Vives, mortes et Barrieres soient reculées aux frontieres du Royaume.

29.—Que la Banalité des fours et moulins soit Supprimée et convertie au argent.

30.—Que les fermiers généraux soient suprimés, les droits mis en régie, et que pour en diminuer les frais le nombre des régisseurs soit Tellement réglé et établi que les deniers des Contribuables soient immédiatement versés dans la caisse de la province et de celle-ci dans le Trésor nationnal qui sera distingué et établi pour cet effet.

31.—Que le nombre des ingénieurs des ponts-et-chaussées Soient réduit ainsi que leurs appointemens.

32.—Que les réparations et réedifications des ponts-et-chaussées situés sur les Terreins des Seigneurs soient faites à leurs frais.

33.—Qu'il soit établi un second college dans l'evêché de Quimper soit à Carhaix ou à Quimperlé qui jouissoit de cet avantage il y a soixante ans.

34.—Que le retour des Etats généraux soit fixé de Trois ans en Trois ans, Sauf à les assembler extraordinairement suivant l'exigence des cas.

35.—Que le plan sage établi par le ministre, qui jouit de la confiance du prince et qui en est si digne, de rendre de deux ans en deux ans, un compte imprimé à la nation de l'emploi des finances et de la Balance de la dépense et des revenus de l'Etat soit suivi; et qu'au Surplus les ministres seront comptables aux etats-généraux des fonds qui leur seront confiés et qu'en cas de renvoi, il ne leur soit accordé aucune pension.

36.—Que l'impot ne sera consenti qu'après avoir vérifié et réglé les dépenses de l'Etat et ne durera que jusqu'à la prochaine Tenue des états généraux en sorte que cette Tenue venant a ne pas avoir lieu tout impôt cesseroit.

37.—Que le Domaine congéable, et le droit de Quevaise soient convertis en peage ou cens avec faculté aux colons de disposer des Bois existants lors du convertissement, sur le pied de l'évaluation qui en sera faite, et en evenement que le convertissement n'ait pas lieu que les colons soient autorisés à disposer des Bois nécessaires pour se Loger Commodément et se construire de granges pour la conservation de leurs grains, que dans le même cas pour l'encouragement de la plantation et conservation des Bois, les colons soient Licentiés à rembourser à leurs Seigneurs la moitié des Bois fonciers pour en recevoir à leur Tour le remboursement en cas de congement, en même nature que leurs édifices et Superfices.

Que les colons soient pareillement autorisés à payer leurs redevances en grains, especes ou en argent suivant l'appreci et que dans tous le cas les frais de congement soient Suportés par les Congédiants.

Le present cahier de charges, doléances et remontrances arrété par nous Commissaires Sus-dits Sous nos Seings en la chambre du Conseil du Siege de la Sénéchaussée royale de Carhaix, ce jour 9 Avril 1789, en interligne aux, le droit, aprouvés, huit mots raturés nuls.

Carquet, Le Cornec.

[Eight signatures.]

Lecture faite publiquement approuvé par nous Soussignés électeurs.

[Eleven signatures.]

NO. 8. THE NOBLES OF THE BAILLIAGE OF CHATEL-SUR-MOSELLE

Cahier reprinted from MS text—*Arch. Vosges* (unclassified), unsigned, dated.
P.V.—*MS. Arch. Nat. Ba* 53. One member with the president and secretary were chosen to make the cahier. There is no mention of the adoption of the cahier. The assembly began March 10. The deputies took an oath not to exceed their instructions.
Convocation—2d type; reunion at Mirecourt.

CAHIER DE PLAINTES, DOLÉANCES, ET REMONTRANCES DE MESSIEURS DE LA NOBLESSE DU BAILLIAGE DE CHÂTEL SUR MOZELLE FAIT EN EXÉCUTION DES LETTRES, ET RÈGLEMENT DU ROY DU 24E JANVIER ET 7E FEVRIER DERNIER PAR MONSIEUR LOUIS JOSEPH DE GAUDEL CHEVALIER SEIGNEUR DE NOMESCY, ANCIEN SOUS-LIEUTENANT À LA SUITTE DU RÉGIMENT DE DAUPHIN CAVALERIE, ET MONSIEUR DIEUDONNÉ HENRY JOSEPH COSSERAT DE ROUVEROIS ECUYER SEIGNEUR DU DIT FIEF ET DUDIT CHÂTEL, LIEUTENANT GÉNÉRAL, CIVIL, ET CRIMINEL AU DIT BAILLAGE, TOUS DEUX NOMMÉS COMMISSAIRES À CET EFFET.

La Noblesse Lorraine est connüe de toutte L'europpe par son inviolable attachement, Son parfait dévouement à Ses Souverains; La Noblesse du Baillage de Châtel ose esperer que Sa Majesté ne doutte nullement des mêmes dispositions de sa part; et de son entiere soumission aux volontés de son maitre actüel, jusqu'à sacrifier La derniere goutte de son sang pour en donner des preuves à Sa Majesté.

1.—Conservation des droits privilèges et prerogations de la Noblesse et de La Lorraine

En conséquence La Noblesse du baillage de Châtel à l'honneur de très humblement, très respectueusement Supplier Sa Majesté de vouloir bien lui conserver ses droits privilèges et prérogations, ainsy qu'à la Province de Lorraine conformément au traitté de cession.

2.—Fixité et rapprochement de tenüe des états généraux

Qu'il plaise à Sa Majesté fixer une époque périodique et rapprochée pour la tenüe des états généraux du royaume, parce qu'il paroit naturellement impossible que dans une seule, on puisse remédier aux maux qui pésent sur le Cöeur du meilleur des Monarques:

Les abus introduits dans L'administration des finances, ne paroissant pouvoir s'opérer que par l'économie dans leur perception et qu'en Rendant les ministres de Sa Majesté responsables des fonds qui leur sont confiés par leur Départemens.

3.—Rétablissement des états provinciaux

De rendre à la Lorraine ses états provinciaux formés selon leur ancienne constitution; pénétrée de la confiance la plus respectueuse en la justice de Sa Majesté, cette même Noblesse ose attendre de sa bonté vraiment röyale, que cette province sera traittée aussy favorablement que d'autres de ses états qui en ont obtenus l'établissement, sans avoir encore jouis jusqu'alors de ces avantages si prétieu.[17]

4.—Consentement à supporter une partie de L'impôt à établir

Les mêmes trés fidels, trés soumis Sujets de Sa Majesté convaincus de ses vues bienfaisantes; et quelle ne leur demandera jamais rien que dans les plus pressants besoins de l'État, sont trés disposes à supporter une partie de l'impôt qui sera jugé nécessaire par les états généraux pour y subvenir; espérants qu'il plaira à Sa Majesté ordonner qu'il sera réparti sur son

[17] Probably "precieux."

ordre, par son ordre, proportionement au nombre et aux facultés de ceux qui le composent: et considérer que lors de la réunion de cette province au royaume elle a déja acquitter ses dettes particulieres.

5.—Suppressions des Maitrises, leurs opérations gruriales rendues aux baillages, et moyens de rembourser les finances des officiers des maitrises

La réclamation général de toutte la province portant sur L'administration confiée aux maitrises, Les mêmes de la Noblesse ont l'honneur d'exposer très respectueusement à Sa Majesté que les opérations gruriales sont à présent couteuses des deux tiers sans que les forêts en soient plus ménagées, que faitte par les officiers des hauttes justices et qu'elles ne le seroient par ceux des baillages auxquels les intéréts de Sa Majesté et ceux de tous les sujets sembleroient indiquer de les Rendre: Le rapprochement des préposés à la Conservation des forêts devant nécessairement procurer un meilleur effet; en chargeant les baillages du remboursement des finances des maitrises.

6.—Suppression des offices de jurés priseurs et moyen de rembourser leurs finances

La suppression des offices de jurés priseurs présente un avantage si sensibles à tous les sujets de Sa Majesté dans la province de Lorraine, que Messieurs la Noblesse du baillage de Châtel mettent au pied du trône leur très instante et respectueuse supplique pour qu'il plaise à Sa Majesté L'accorder: mais comme ils seroient désespérés que les finances de Sa Majesté puissent en souffrir la moindre diminution, ils osent présumer que la province se chargeroit de rembourser par baillage, et dans un espace de tems suffisant le montant du prix de ces offices.

7.—Abolitions des lettres de Cachet moyens d'y suppléer

Intimement persuadés que le Coeur de Sa Majesté est toujours sensiblement painé [peiné], lorsqu'il est nécessaire d'employer la force d'une Lettre de cachet contre aucun de ses Sujets, La même Noblesse à l'honneur de lui réprésenter le plus profond respect que Sa Majesté pourroit alléger son esprit de justice en remettant à ses tribunaux souverains les pouvoirs de faire arretter et détenir quiconque auroit eu le malheur par ses crimmes ou sa mauvaise conduite d'encourir ou s'attirer l'indignation de Sa Majesté; l'établissement d'une chambre surêtté dans ces tribunaux previendroit le déshonneur des familles.

8.—Suppression des Municipalités des villes élection des officiers de police, et moyen de rembourser les anciens pour[18]

---

[18] Unfinished in original.

La formation des municipalités des villes leur paroit onéreuse, parce qu'elle payent sur les deniers communaux la rente de la finance des charges de police; que d'ailleurs on se plaint que cette police n'est pas des mieux administrée; il seroit possible qu'elle l'a soit par l'élection des personnes employées à la faire; en choisissant les plus prudents, les plus notables, et les plus instruits dans ces villes; (qui sont ceux qui pouroient se refuser à veiller au bon ordre, à la sûreté de ses Concitoyens, etc. . . .) mais le remboursement, des finances pouroit devenir un obstacle à ce changement désiré: ces mêmes villes ne pouroient-elles être authorisés à faire une aliénation quelconque de partie de leur fonds, ou de leurs revenus pour y suffir.

9.—Sel à rendre marchand, et dédommagement pour les finances de Sa Majesté

Le Sel étant un objet de première nécessité, il est du plus grand interet pour tous les sujets de Sa Majesté qu'il soit rendu au prix le plus modique possible, et qu'il soit de la meilleure qualité, parce qu'il est (pour ainsy dire) Le nerf et la force des habitans de campagnes, et le soutien et le restaurateur du bétail propre à l'agriculture et autres; surtout dans le voisinage des Vosges, ou les fourrages aigres ne fournissent que peu de substance; sa chéreté empêche conséquament qu'on fasse beaucoup de nouris ainsy Messieurs de la Noblesse du même baillage ont l'honneur de trés humblement supplier Sa Majesté de le rendre marchand; et pour que ses finances n'en soient point alterées, on pouroit bien payer sur le Sel ce qui leur revient, avant sa sortie des salinnes.

10.—Confirmation d'aliénation des biens domaniaux en Lorraine

Sa Majesté est aussy trés humblement suppliée par les mêmes de sa Noblesse d'authoriser les états généraux à confirmer irrévocablement toutes aliénations faitte des biens domaniaux scituées dans la province de Lorraine.

Fait et arrêté le 10 Mars 1789, sous le Seing de tous les Membres de la noblesse du baillage de Châtel sur Mozelle comparants.

NO. 9. THE THIRD OF THE BAILLIAGE OF CHATEL-SUR-MOSELLE

Cahier reprinted from the MS text—*Arch. Vosges* (unclassified) original signatures.
P.V.-MS, *Arch. Nat.* Ba53. The *proces-verbal* gives no information on the committee or adoption, which may have been March 11, before the elections began.
Convocation—2d type, reunion at Mirecourt.

UNEDITED TEXTS OF GENERAL CAHIERS

BAILLAGE DU CHÂTEL SUR MOZELLE

Cejourd'huy dix Mars mil sept Cent quatre vingt neuf Nous Soussigné Députés du Tiers-État de la ville de Châtel-sur-Mozelle, et des communautés de Nomecy, Bouxurulles, Labeuville, Hadigny, les Verrières d'ouraine, Badmeul, Padoux, Saint Genest, Ortoucourt, Passoncourt, Rehamcourt, Hailleuville, Dommard aux Bon, St. Boin, Boiville, Laure et Montrey, St. Remy-aux-Bon, Saint German, Villacourt, Langley, Portieux et Mouville, Composans le ressort du Bailliage de laditte Ville avec la Communauté de fréson qui a fait déffaut, avons procédé à la rédaction des pouvoirs que les Députés de l'ordre du Tiers-État dudit Baillage seront tenus de porter à l'assemblée générale convoquée en la Ville de Mirecourt pour le trente et un du courant et après mures délibérations avons enjoint auxdits Dèputés de n'entrer en aucun examen d'administration ou de besoin de l'État de n'acquieser ni même de faire espérer aucun secours d'impôt que les états n'y ayent donné leur consentement sous la Sanction de Sa Majesté et qu'elle n'ait rendu une déclaration qui assure irrévocablement la nation.

1.—Qu'en aucun cas la liberté individuelle ou de propriété du Citoyen de quel ordre il soit ne sera génée qu'en vertu des dispositions des loix rédigées par les états généraux et régistrée d'aprés leurs ordres et réquisitions des Etats particuliers des provinces dans les greffes des tribunaux de chacune de ces provinces, qu'aucune lettre de Cachet, aucun ordre ministeriel ne pourra arrêter, détenir, emprisonner, exiler les citoyens que dans les cas ou la loi l'ordonneroit, ou la police l'exigeroit ils seront toujours rémis dans les vingt-quatre heures, entre les mains de leurs juges naturels et territoriaux sans qu'il puisse y avoir déclinatoire ou deni de justice, commissions particulières, évocation au Conseil.

2.—Qu'aucune Loi en fait d'administration générale, faits de justice civil et Criminel ne sera admise et n'aura force d'Exécution qu'elle n'ait été consentie par la nation assemblée en états Généraux et revetue de la Sanction du Souverain et de la publicité.

3.—Que les États Généraux dont les Membres seront élus librement par tous les Électeurs choisis dans tous les Cantons de la province seront assemblés de droit tous les trois ans au vingt sept Avril sans qu'il soit besoin d'autre convocation hors le cas ou les circonstances exigeroient que cette époque fut rapprochée, que les assemblées préliminaires d'élection suivront la même marche qu'en la présente année.

4.—Que les Etats Généraux pourront seuls consentir et répartir entre les provinces l'impôt général qui sera pour les besoins généraux de l'Etat, Entretien de la maison de Sa Majesté, guerre, marine; verser dans les caisses de leurs départemens que ce Consentement sera limité à un mois au delà de l'époque triennale de réunion des États Généraux à Versailles, qu'à cet instant l'impôt cessera de droit sans qu'aucune autre autorité que celle des États Généraux librement formés puisse en prolonger la perception à peine contre les infracteurs d'être poursuivis comme concussionaire par les tribunaux des provinces sur la réquisition de leurs États particuliers et jugé définitivement par les États Généraux qu'il n'y aura qu'un impôt Général et assis sans distinction d'ordre sur le produit net des propriétés de fonds territoriaux ou d'industrie.

5.—Que les Ministres dans tous les temps et à toutes époques seront comptables à la nation de l'emploi des deniers qui leur auront été confiés, et en cas de malversation pourront être décrété et jugés par les Etats Généraux qui seuls pourront leur donné une décharge valable d'après la révision de leur Compte.

Et que les emprunts suivront la même régle.

6.—Qu'en fait d'administration intérieure consentement aux réglements locaux, Répartition de l'impôt Général, détermination, levée et distribution des sommes particulieres que le besoin ou amélioration locale des provinces exigeront. Elles ne seront soumises qu'à leurs états particuliers, formée par des Elections libre et triennale de tous leurs Cantons et assemblées annuellement au premier Janvier; assemblées toujours en activité par leur commission intermédiaire et secondaire qui leur rendront des comptes annuels que dans les cas de plaintes des peuples elles seront portée et soumises aux Etats Généraux; qu'au moyen de cette administration des Etats provinciaux les intendants, fermes, régies, Maitrises et toutes entraves de cette espéce disparaitront.

7.—Que la réforme des Loix pénales et judiciares seront déterminées par états Généraux mais que les changements, dans les tribunaux ne pourront se faire que sur la demande des états provinciaux aux états Généraux que le tribunal suprème de chaque province chargé du maintien des loix ou Contentieux, ou de police, ou de délits pourra d'après les ordres des Etats Généraux et réquisition des États provinciaux veiller au maintien de loix de simple administration, prononcée par l'une ou l'autre assemblée Nationale sans qu'il puissent en aucun cas étendre ou restreindre les dispositions des loix ou ordonnance dont l'exécution lui aura été confiée.

8.—Lesdits Députés demanderont le rétablissement des États provinciaux en Lorraine qui seront composés de députation de tous les Baillages dans lesquels il y aura autant de représentans du Tiers État que dans les deux autres ordres réunis.

9.—Qu'avant d'avoir obtenu une déclaration conforme aux huit articles précédens et sa publication les Députés aux États Généraux ne pourront s'occuper du deficit National, des moyens d'y remédier, des secours, emprunts ou autres objets qui pourraient leur faire perdre de vüe que le premier pas vers le bien est d'avoir une Constitution Nationale sous peine d'être désavoué par leurs Comettans et d'être déchus de fait de tous les pouvoirs que leur province leur confie leur donnant au surplus aux conditions cy dessus tous pouvoirs généraux et suffisant pour proposer, Remonter, aviser et consentir tout ce qui peut concerner les besoins de l'État dans la réforme des abus, l'établissement d'un ordre fixe et durable dans toutes les parties de l'administration, la prospérité générale du Royaume, et le bien de tous les Sujets de Sa Majesté.

10.—Chargeons lesdits Députés de demander que toutes les contributions pécuniaire de même que l'entretien des ponts et chaussées et chemin communaux soient à la charge des trois ordres et répartis sur chaque individu qui les composent à proportion de leurs facultés au moyen de quoi tous privileges d'exemption accordées aux emplois et à certaine ville demeureront supprimés.

11.—La suppression des Colombiers à la réserve de ceux des Seigneurs hauts justiciers mais à charge que le nombre des boulins sera trés modique et que les pigeons seront retenus dans tous les temps de semaille et moissons.

12.—La suppression des jurés priseurs, des tribunaux d'attribution et la réunion des maitrises des eaux et forets aux baillage, enfin la suppression des receveurs particuliers des finances.

13.—D'aviser aux moÿens de soutenir le prix des biens dans l'état actuel tant en accordant aux propriétaires le regain de leur pré sans les astreindre à la cloture qu'en leur accordant les fruits champêtres des arbres qui se trouvent dans leurs héritages, en diminuant le prix du Sel si nécéssaire à la santé du bétail, et en accordant aux sujets tant du Roy que des Seigneurs la faculté de racheter les Cens, Corvées, bannalités, sous indemnités et en rendant la perception de la dixme uniforme dans la province, et en fixant la quotité au vingt quatrième pour les vignes.

14.—De demander la suppression des gages du parlement de Nancy en rétablissant les epices comme aussi tous droits de passage péage et autres impots qui genent le Commerce et l'industrie ainsy que la décharge des permissions des Carosses.

15.—Demander la suppression du haras de Rozières auquel il sera substitué des étalons qui seront nourris dans quelques communautés de chaque Baillage.

16.—De rechercher la cause de l'augmentation rapide du prix du fer et d'aviser aux moyens d'y remédier et d'empecher tout monopole.

17.—Au surplus lesdits Députés se concerteront aves les Députés du Royaume et ceux de la province pour opérer le plus grand général et particulier et prendront dans tous les Cahiers des Communautés de ce baillage les instructions nécessaires pour parvenir à ce but et leur faire obtenir leurs demandes notament demander l'expulsion des juifs de cette province.

Faite et arretté en l'auditoire du Baillage Royal de Châtel-sur Mozelle les ans et jours avant dits et tous députés présens ont signé:

[Forty-five signatures.][19]

[19] The cahier does not appear to have been signed by either the president Rouverois, or the secretary, Guerin, of the assembly.

UNEDITED TEXTS OF GENERAL CAHIERS

NO. 10. THE NOBLES OF THE ISLAND OF CORSICA[20]

The original cahier was in Italian, the text of which is in the family archives of the Gaffori or of the Gregori family, of Corsica.[21] The Italian text has been reprinted in the bulletin of the *Société des Sciences historiques et naturelles de la Corse*, Jan.-June, 1897, by the Abbé Letteron, 2d Appendix, pp. 447-69. The translation here was made by the translation service of the *Bibliothèque Nationale*.
P.V.-MS, extracts *Arch. Nat.* B III 52 in French.
    MS, full, *ibid.*, C18/60 in Italian
    PR, full, *ibid.*, Ba 34 in Italian and French, s.l.n.d., in 4°, 153p.
There were seven members of the committee including the secretary of the assembly. From the p.v. of the third estate, we learn of trouble in the assembly of the nobles over two parties among them, and of reconciliation toward the head of the Superior Council (M. Gautier) of Corsica. It was voted to print the cahier and *procès-verbal*. The cahier was probably adopted June 7. (Note difference with date at end of cahier.)
Convocation: 6th type.

CAHIER DES DEMANDES, DOLÉANCES, ET REPRÉSENTATIONS DE L'ORDRE DE LA NOBLESSE DE L'ÎLE DE CORSE, ARRÊTÉ PAR L'ASSEMBLÉE GÉNÉRALE DE CET ORDRE CONVOQUÉ À BASTIA LE 18 MAI 1789

Si les disgrâces acharnées qui ont désolé la Corse durant plusieurs siècles ont détruit ou assoupi les sources de la perfection dont elle est capable, les heureuses révolutions dont elle fut le theâtre en peu de temps l'ont sortie de cette léthargie où elle languissait abattue et elles lui ont préparé les moyens d'être rendue à la félicité à laquelle toute Nation est naturellement destinée.

Passée sous la domination du plus juste et du plus puissant des rois elle a éprouvé les influences salutaires d'une législation parfaite; le bon ordre a succédé à l'anarchie et à l'arbitraire, et la violence s'est dissipée devant la vénérable Majesté des lois.

Admise à l'auguste Assemblée des Etats-Généraux de l'Empire français, elle s'est vue protégée et considérée à l'égal des autres Provinces célèbres de ce Royaume. Toutes les formes qui assureront la constitution de cette Monarchie la concernent en tant que la partie qui concourt à la former.

Elle sent l'étendue de sa reconnaissance et rassemble ses sentiments

[20] Corsica became French by the Treaty of Compiègne in 1768. It was to be administered by France until the costs of the war had been repaid to Genoa. The Paoli faction fought against French dominion, but the strength of French control was shown in the inclusion of Corsica in the convocation, and the elections held.

[21] The Abbé Letteron gives the Gaffori family archives as his source. The archivist for Corsica gave the Gregori family, in a letter to the Minister of Public Instruction, during the inquiry on the cahiers (1931).

les plus vifs pour la prouver au pied du trône puissant qui la protège et de la généreuse Nation qui l'accueille.

Heureuse si elle pouvait contribuer par ses richesses au rétablissement des finances de l'Etat, jusqu'à offrir son courage et son sang pour la défendre.

Les conséquences d'une guerre désolatrice, les principes faux d'un gouvernement destructeur, font encore sentir leur effet en la tenant dans l'impossibilité d'avoir cette gloire.

Les bases de la Constitution générale qu'elle attend, les moyens qu'elle propose développent les germes concentrés en elle-même de sa régéneration, et elle pourra se transformer en peu de temps en une Province utile à l'Etat par le secours de ses finances dans la mesure même où sa situation la rend nécessaire dans le système politique, et se féliciter du double avantage qu'elle obtiendra dans la balance du pouvoir.

Pour y parvenir la facilité et la rapidité qu'elle désire, les Députés demanderont:

Que pour assurer d'une façon plus inviolable à la Province de Corse la fortune d'être devenue française, cette province soit incorporée expressément à la Couronne et fasse partie intégrante de cette Monarchie dont elle ne puisse être séparée ni aliénée sans le consentement des Etats-Généraux.

Que les Etats-Généraux travaillent à fixer la Constitution de la Monarchie et que les principes déterminés et établis à cet effet soient rendus publics.

Que lesdits Etats-Généraux soient périodiquement convoqués tous les trois ans et que les députés de la Province de Corse y assistent en un nombre proportionnel à l'étendue de sa population.

Que les Etats provinciaux de Corse jouissent de la liberté des droits et des privilèges dont jouiront les Etats-généraux des autres parties du Royaume et qu'ils travaillent à régler les demandes des différentes juridictions, paroisses ou communes.

Que tous ceux qui seront placés à la tête de quelque partie de l'administration soient responsables devant la Nation de la violation des lois ou des prévarications auxquelles ils auraient pu être mêlés, devant les Etatsgénéraux qui désigneront les tribunaux par lesquels ils devront être jugés s'il y a lieu.

Que tous les impôts, droits ou autres taxes soient établis par les Etatsgénéraux, sans que les Intendants des Provinces puissent les augmenter, les diminuer, ou les modifier ou en imposer de nouveaux.

Que les Etats-Généraux prennent les moyens nécessaires pour modérer la rigueur des lois criminelles, que celles-ci soient précises et que la procédure civile soit réduite à une forme plus simple pour rendre plus facile le jugement des procès qui sont le fléau de la société.

Que les coupables aient la facilité de se faire défendre par un avocat.

Que la confiscation des biens ne dure pas plus que la vie du condamné.

253

Que soit abolie la peine de mort, sauf pour les délits de lèse-majesté divine et humaine du premier degré, et convertie en une autre peine afflictive et infamante.

Que les condamnés à temps aux galères ne subissent pas l'ignominie de la marque.

Que soit supprimée la peine du blâme.

Que l'exil ne comporte pas d'infamie, sauf dans le cas où le délit a été prémédité.

Que les avertissements, amendes et arrêts portant la mention "fuori di Corte" dans les délits qui par nature ne sont pas infamants, n'entraînent aucune flétrissure et que ceux qui les auront soufferts jouissent de tous les privilèges civiques, selon la qualité de leur naissance.

Que l'infamie des peines criminelles de toute nature ne rejaillisse en aucun cas sur les descendants, ascendants ou collatéraux du condamné.

Que les décrets de peine de corps soient décidés avec l'avis concordant des deux membres qui composent le tribunal inférieur, et dans le cas où ils ne seraient pas d'accord, qu'ils soient obligés de se faire assister par le premier gradué impartial du Tribunal.

Que la peine de la question soit entièrement abolie ainsi que la formalité de la sellette.

Que la liberté individuelle soit inviolable, que personne ne puisse en être privée, sauf par ordre du Juge et selon les lois de l'Etat et que les lettres de cachet ou ordres supérieurs soient abolis.

Que les propriétés ne puissent être violées, pas même sous prétexte de bien public, et qu'en cas de nécessité le propriétaire en soit avisé et indemnisé d'avance au plus haut prix.

Que soit établie l'administration provinciale, devant se composer d'un nombre suffisant de membres à choisir à chaque réunion d'Etats, dans la forme observée pour l'élection des Douze Gentilshommes.

Que la dite Commission soit chargée de l'exécution des lois de l'administration du commerce, de la subsistance, de l'économie politique, de la culture et de l'administration des gabelles, et que cette Commission ait à rendre des comptes à chaque réunion des dites Assemblées provinciales.

Qu'il soit permis d'avoir à Paris un orateur à choisir à chaque session des Etats-Provinciaux, orateur qui soit chargé de s'occuper auprès de Sa Majesté et du Ministère, des questions qui ont trait à l'intérêt de la Province et de chaque particulier, ceci à cause de la difficulté qu'ont les Corses de faire parvenir leurs demandes et leurs doléances au pied du Trône.

Que soient diminués les droits excessifs d'importation et d'exportation spécialement sur les objets de première et nécessaire consommation, augmentés pour l'étranger jusqu'à trente pour cent, celà étant un obstacle évident aux progrès d'un commerce naissant, et que les droits ainsi modifiés soient fixes et connus, afin de ne souffrir ni de changements ni de décisions arbitraires.

Que les peines de ceux qui sont surpris en délit de contravention soient diminuées et restreintes à la seule confiscation des marchandises prises en contravention.

Qu'on ne permette pas l'extraction des produits maritimes ou terrestres de l'île avant que le pays n'en soit pourvu; à tel effet les Officiers Municipaux constateront si les denrées sont nécessaires ou si elles peuvent être enlevées sans inconvénient et ils se tiendront en rapport avec la commission intermédiaire pour faire sentir les besoins de chaque juridiction particulier.

Que de l'imposition territoriale du vingtième, soit réduite la semence qui ayant déjà supporté cette retenue dans la récolte antérieure est soumise à un double impôt vu l'exigence répétée des années successives.

Que quiconque établira en Corse des manufactures de quelque espèce qu'elles soient, puisse être exempt du droit d'exportation pendant un certain nombre d'années, afin de stimuler par cette franchise l'initiative des entrepreneurs pour d'autres établissements analogues.

Que les communes et les particuliers qui ont été dépouillés de leurs propriétés sans aucune formalité de jugement ordinaire et par simples ordonnances de M. l'Intendant qui a uni les dits biens aux domaines sans tenir compte des titres et des possessions de longue date et le plus souvent sans entendre les parties intéressées, que ces communes et ces particuliers soient remis en possession des dits terrains et ne puissent en être privés que par les dispositions générales des lois et des tribunaux ordinaires.

Que les concessionnaires des Domaines de Sa Majesté soient tenus dans une période à fixer, à remplir les obligations auxquelles ils se sont assujettis dans les lettres de leurs concessions et, en cas de manquement qu'ils demeurent déchus de leur droit; que les dites propriétés soient concédées, moyennant une redevance qu'on fixera, aux Individus des communes qui les mettront en valeur.

Que les procès domaniaux ressortissent directement aux Tribunaux ordinaires, sans intervention judiciaire de la part de l'intendant et que ces procès soient jugés selon les règles communes de la Jurisprudence et sans privilège.

Que les lettres qu'on confie aux guichets de la porte soient inviolables et conservées avec plus de soin qu'il n'est pratiqué actuellement.

Que soient rétablies en Corse les salines qui, d'après le témoignage de l'histoire, produisaient un sel parfait et abondant, constation répétée dans les quelques essais imparfaits des paysans dans les ruines des anciennes salines.

Que Sa Majesté ait dans la distribution des emplois des égards particuliers pour ses sujets Corses, ceux-si se flattent de s'en être rendus dignes en toute occasion.

Ceci est le moyen le plus efficace de régénérer le pays sans aucune subside extraordinaire, par l'emploi utile que le Corse fait de l'argent qu'il gagne, à la difference des Français de France qui visent à une épargne qu'ils remportent en France, ou à des dépenses de luxe dans des objets que la Corse ne fournit pas actuellement; qu'il y ait l'égalité de traitement entre les employés Corses et les employés Français.

Que le Clergé Corse jouisse de tous les privilèges de l'Eglise gallicane à laquelle il entend généralement être assimilé.

Que les bénéfices ecclésiastiques, y compris les évêchés, soient attribués au clergé Corse, cette espérance stimulera chacun à s'en rendre digne autant que l'exclusion tendrait à lui enlever tout espoir et à le maintenir dans un état de médiocrité humiliante.

Que les évêques soient autorisés à accorder les dispenses de mariages afin d'empêcher les versements d'argent en Cour de Rome et de prévenir les difficultés qui souvent obligent à vivre en état d'inceste, contre les lois de la Religion et de l'Etat.

Qu'un des évêques de Corse ait le titre de Métropolitain et exerce la juridiction attachée à cette charge.

Qu'il y ait une règle générale pour le paiement de la dîme; que celle-ci soit proportionnée à la stricte nécessité qu'exige le traitement des Ecclésiastiques auquel elle est liée, et que dans ce but soit nommée députation des trois ordres pour s'occuper de la formation de ce nouveau plan pour le faire adopter et confirmer par Sa Majesté, s'il y a lieu, tout en conservant les privilèges d'exemption à ceux qui paient cette dîme.

Que le revenu libre des évêchés en Corse soit réduit à 12,000 lires et que l'excédent soit employé à suppléer à la portion congrue des curés dont beaucoup de ceux-ci manquent; donc, qu'on établisse dans chaque diocèse une commission pour gérer les rentes de l'évêché et en faire la distribution, avec l'obligation d'une vérification annuelle des comptes devant la Procureur du Roi.

Que soit établie à Corte une Université et à cet effet Sa Majesté est suppliée de délivrer des lettres patentes; que la première assemblée des Etats provinciaux travaille à déterminer les fonds pour son entretien suppliant en même temps Sa Majesté d'abandonner à cet établissement le revenu du marquisat de Marbeuf.

Que soient établies dans les cités de Bastia et d'Ajaccio deux écoles navales, afin de perfectionner les talents corses en cette partie vers laquelle ils se sentent attirés par un courage dont ils ont donné les preuves convaincantes dans les campagnes qu'ils ont faites sur les vaisseaux du Roi.

Que soit activé le travail de législation qui donne aux propriétes une règle plus conforme aux coutumes et à la situation du pays.

Que l'édit du Roi sur les abus champêtres, promis depuis longtemps, soit publié et avec autant de rapidité que possible afin de remédier aux inconvénients qui se manifestent actuellement.

Que Sa Majesté se complaise à proroger le droit d'exemption de l'impôt territorial, pour les terrains qui seront défrichés ou déséchés, en amplifiant les dispositions de l'arrêt de son Conseil d'Etat publié à cet effet.

Que l'impôt des deux vingtièmes sur le revenue des maisons louées soit modifié et réduit au vingtième sur le pied de l'imposition territoriale, étant contraire à l'agrandissement des villes et lourd au locataire qui en ressent le plus grand poids par l'augmentation des locations; d'autant plus que les frais des logements militaires auxquels il est destiné n'absorbent pas le produit du dit impôt à cause des casernes royales qu'on a élevées dans tous les postes de l'Ile.

Que les gentilshommes jouissent sans restriction de tous les droits qui découlent de leur naissance et que le port d'armes en ce qui les concerne soit libre.

Que dans les jugements criminels les juges ordinaires soient assistés d'un nombre égal de pairs qui auront voix délibérative.

Que le Tribunal des Juntes étant purement pénal, n'ait aucune puissance de juridiction sur les gentilshommes.

Que la forme d'élection soit modifiée, qu'on réduise à deux les élus; ceux-ci le seront à la pluralité des suffrages et en cas de mort que celui qui aura obtenu le plus de voix après l'élu lui succède.

Que la peine de la roue, de la potence, de la marque et de la galère, dans le cas où la peine de mort continuerait à exister, soit convertie en décapitation, en prison perpétuelle ou en exil et qu'il soit exprimé que l'ignominie ne rejaillisse pas sur la famille du condamné, et que les sentences ne puissent être exécutées qu'après l'approbation de Sa Majesté.

Que les actes municipaux soient exempts de la formalité du contrôle et que ceux de l'instruction devant les Juges Royaux en soient aussi dispensés, exception faite pour les demandes d'introduction et les sentences définitives qui y seront soumises.

Que les actes des notaires, privés de cette formalité des dits notaires conservent par grâce spéciale toute leur valeur, afin de ne pas jeter le trouble dans les familles du pays. Que dans les livres des anciens notaires les formalités extérieures, venant soit du Chancellier soit du greffier, et faisant défaut, soient cependant accomplies selon les dispositions qu'elles contiennent.

Qu'aucun sujet ne puisse entrer dans la magistrature avant d'avoir exercé l'office d'avocat au moins six ans et d'avoir remporté en sa faveur les suffrages favorables de l'opinion publique; cette mesure empêchera qu'il y ait des juges ignorants—comme il s'en est trouvé en certaines juridictions de Corse, véritables fléaux et éléments destructeurs de ces juridictions.

Que les procès sur lesquels sera prononcé le "délibéré" soient jugés par les Juges inférieurs dans le délai de deux mois, et par ceux de la Cour souveraine dans celui de quatre mois à partir du jour de la réunion générale

257

des pièces, et que toute autre condition imposée à la mise en état du procès soit considérée de droit comme un motif à la prise à partie sans autre restriction.

Que les marins corses aient la libre pêche des coraux dans les mers du Levant, sans que la Compagnie dite d'Afrique puisse nécessairement les contraindre à travailler dans les lieux de ses propres établissements. Ces difficultés ont détruit une branche du commerce qui maintenait l'opulence dans le pays et qui, rendue à son ancien lustre, est capable de lui procurer les ressources les plus importantes et d'être une des causes principales de sa richesse.

Que les emplois soient répartis d'une facon distributive, sans en accumuler plusieurs sur un même sujet comme cela se pratique souvent, afin de stimuler chacun à les mériter avec l'espérance de pouvoir les obtenir, et que les charges ne puissent être transmises ou résignées de père en fils, à moins que ceux-ci ne les aient méritées par leur travaux ou par un service particulier.

Qu'en toutes les assemblées provinciales, les ordres travaillent séparément et que chacun procède à délibérer de son côté pour ce qui le regarde.

Qu'en chaque juridiction il y ait deux assesseurs qui aient voix délibérative et que le siège formant trois avis se plie à la décision des deux qui se trouveraient d'accord.

Que Sa Majesté soit suppliée d'augmenter le nombre de ses soldats en Corse; ce moyen pourra servir à faciliter la consommation des denrées, à l'encouragement des arts et à faire circuler un argent considérable qui employé insensiblement à la culture aidera au relèvement du pays.

Que le régiment provincial Corse soit porté au nombre de deux bataillons complets, que le Régiment Royal Corse soit remis sur le pied de sa formation première et que le colonel soit pris parmi les Officers Corses.

Que Sa Majesté intéresse son activité puissante à rendre aux Corses le droit d'envoyer au Collège "del Bene" à Gênes les douze élèves que les Corses ont le droit d'y entretenir d'après les faveurs à eux accordées par le dit Collège qui leur conférant ce droit spécial non comme sujets de la République, mais comme invités par le Fondateur de la dite organisation.

Que les Iles de la Maddalena, Caprera er Santo Stefano, étant dépendances de l'Ile de Corse soient réunies à la dite Ile à cet effet, le député sera muni des documents nécessaires pour prouver la justice de cette demande et mettre Sa Majesté en état de faire valoir son autorité royale pour recouvrer cette partie de son territoire.

Que l'administration des biens de l'Economat et de l'Instruction publique, soit unie à celle des trésoriers particuliers des provinces, les sujets du pays étant pleins d'expérience et capables d'en tirer de plus grands avantages.

Que soit continué et accéléré le travail des rues royales et des ponts, travail qui se trouve assez peu avancé en regard de l'attente des Corses et les intentions paternelles de Sa Majesté et que l'administration des fonds qui se dispensent pour ces travaux soit autrement gérée et que le nouveau mode prévienne et empêche les abus notoires qui se commettent à cet égard.

Que personne ne puisse être admis à la charge de notaire sans un examen préalable et rigoureux en ce qui regarde les devoirs de son Etat et que autant les dits notaires que les chanceliers des Juridictions royales donnent par mesure de sécurité six mille lires ou une indemnité de dommages et d'intérêts en faveur des parties lésées.

Que la juridiction de Corte qui est une des plus étendues de l'Ile, ait trois Députations à l'Assemblée générale de la Province pour les Etats-Généraux comme Ajaccio, Bastia, Porta, Calvi et Balagna, ayant déjà un nombre de représentants égal à celui des provinces sus-dites pour la députation à l'Assemblée des Etats particuliers de Corse.

Que les officiers Corses retirés reçoivent leurs pensions sur la caisse militaire, qui circule dans l'Ile, afin de ne pas faire attendre à ces vieux serviteurs du Roi ce peu de soutien que la munificence royale et leurs mérites leur ont procuré, et que ces officiers soient admis aux places de l'Etat-major de Corse.

Que le grain et l'orge distribués en Corse en 1787 pour lutter contre la famine ayant été de très mauvaise qualité et incapables de germer une fois semés, les populations qui ont été obligées de s'en procurer soient indemnisées de leurs pertes.

Que la noblesse de Corse soit réintégrée dans ses droits féodaux, en la possession desquels elle était au temps du gouvernement de la République de Gênes [Genoa] et que le Commandant en chef de la Province soit autorisé à recevoir au nom de Sa Majesté le serment des Seigneurs féodataires.

Les Députés de la Juridiction de Bastia supplient spécialement Sa Majesté qu'elle veuille bien renouveler les Officiers Municipaux de la dite cité, rendre à l'avenir l'élection triennale et comme pour toutes les autres cités et communes de l'île, avec l'obligation pour les sujets qui sont actuellement en fonction, de rendre un compte exact de leur gestion et administration, cela étant la répétition des votes et des demandes de tous les ordres et classes de la dite commune.

Que dans les cités de Bastia, Ajaccio, Calvi et Corté, pour prévenir les tumultes et les confusions produits par les assemblées nombreuses du Peuple lors des délibérations sur l'élection des Officiers Municipaux et aussi dans l'intérêt de la commune soit établi un Conseil de Quarante composé de la façon suivante: le Tiers-Etat se réunira et élira 25 sujets choisis au sein de la cité parmi les syndics des Corporations des différents Arts et Métiers; parmi la Noblesse de son côté, 15 autres sujets pris dans son ordre et tous réunis ils formeront le Conseil des Quarante. Les membres de ce Conseil qui disparaîtraient seraient remplacés par d'autres choisis dans les différents ordres auxquels ils appartiendraient. Ce Conseil réuni délibérera sur tous les intérêts de la commune et la représentera dans toutes les occasions ordinaires et tous les Officiers municipaux de cette cité seront au nombre de cinq parmi lesquels un aura le titre de "Maire" et sera choisi dans l'ordre de la Noblesse, séparément, et les quatre autres dans les deux ordres réunis et indistinctement.

Le dit Conseil aura la faculté d'élire les dits officiers municipaux dans la forme sus-énoncée comme aussi quatre syndics parmi lesquels un sera obligatoirement noble. Ce sont ces Syndics qui procéderont à la vérification des comptes des Officiers municipaux sortis de charge et qui constateront l'état de l'Administration et le mode selon lequel celle-ci passera aux mains des nouveaux officiers nommés.

Les sujets convaincus de malversations ou d'abus seront déclarés privés de voix active ou passive ou pour toujours ou temporairement en proportion de leur manquement, sauf à recourir devant la Cour souveraine de l'Ile pour ceux qui se trouveraient lésés par ce jugement.

La cité de Bastia, n'offrant qu'un port petit et peu sûr, le commerce en souffre et cela empêche l'agrandissement de cette capitale; les vaisseaux qui viennent du Levant ne pouvant se réfugier dans le dit port à cause de la situation actuelle où il se trouve sont obligés de se réfugier à Livourne et d'emporter ainsi des bénéfices dans un pays étranger. La députation de la dite Juridiction supplie le Souverain d'avoir la munificence de donner des ordres pour qu'on y établisse un port qui offrant un refuge aux vaisseaux d'important tonnage, équilibrerait les dépenses avec les droits qu'on exigerait sur les marchandises introduites dans le commerce.

Que la ville de Bastia fasse paroisse à elle seule, indépendamment des villages de Lota, Cardo et Pietrabugno; cela à cause de sa population et pour être considérée comme la capitale de la Province.

Que soit construite une route praticable, du nouveau port de Macinajo à celui de Bastia, afin de donner libre champ au commerce.

Que les Officiers Municipaux aient le droit de fixer la taxe des vivres, en égard au temps et aux circonstances; l'ordre tout entier a approuvé cette demande comme générale pour toute l'Ile.

Que le tiers de la gabelle du vin et du lard, qu'on exige dans la cité de Bastia, soit adjugé au profit de la dite cité, ceci étant un droit originairement établi au profit de ladite commune.

Que soient construits des établissements pour les eaux minérales de Fiumorbo, en suivant le plan adopté par l'Assemblée des Etats de 1775, afin de rendre profitable ce don précieux de la nature destiné à la conservation de l'humanité affligée.

Que soit abolie et supprimée la charge d'Inspecteur des Collèges de

Corse, dont est pourvu M. l'abbé Germanes, charge inutile: 1°) vu la suppression de la plupart des Collèges; 2°) parce que cette charge est inutile de par sa nature même;—et que les trois mille lires attachées à cet emploi soient employées au traitement d'un professeur de philosophie à Ajaccio et de droit civil et canonique à Bastia.

Que soient renvoyés les Pères Doctrinaires qui sont chargés de l'éducation publique à Bastia, vu le peu de profit que retirent les élèves de leur enseignement, vu l'impéritie desdits Pères, et que ceux-ci soient remplacés par autant de sujets corses, parmi lesquels Sa Majesté est suppliée de comprendre MM. les abbés Colombani et Marinetti, anciens professeurs qui se sont distingués par leur zèle et leur capacité.

Les députés des Juridictions d'Ajaccio, Vico, Sartène et Bonifacio composant le district d'outre-monts ne peuvent se dispenser dans le présent livret les voeux et les sentiments de l'ordre de leurs Juridictions, dont ils sont spécialement chargés, et de prier humblement Sa Majesté et les Etats-Généraux de vouloir établir à Ajaccio, comme en la ville principale dudit district, un Présidial ou quelque autre Tribunal composé d'un nombre suffisant de Juges, qui reçoive les appels desdites Juridictions et les juge définitivement et en dernière instance jusqu'à la somme de trois mille lires. Cet établissement est d'une évidente nécessité. La Cour souveraine se trouve éloignée, les routes très mauvaises et dangereuses, les monts qu'on doit traverser converts de neige en hiver, les appels multipliés, les dépenses excessives, l'expédition des affaires trainant en longueur, de sorte que les populations desdites quatre Juridictions qui forment à peu près la moitié de l'Ile souffrent pour ce seul motif de la destruction d'une partie de leurs ressources.

Les dits députés présentent également leurs humbles et respectueuses doléances au pied du Trône et de l'auguste assemblée des Etats-Généraux au sujet de l'exclusive presque générale dont souffrent les habitants de leurs Juridictions quant aux emplois que les Corses ont la fortune d'occuper. Leurs Juridictions supportent les charges de l'Etat au-delà du tiers, les sujets qui s'y trouvent se flattent ouvertement de réunir les qualités nécessaires à l'exercice de n'importe quelle charge, et cependant ils tolèrent depuis longtemps un oubli humiliant et ils se voient préférer ceux qui, près du centre le plus important de la Province, ont la chance de comparaître plus souvent devant les chefs de l'Administration.

Les exemples répétés ne leur permettent pas d'alimenter leurs espérances avec l'idée grâces futures, sans une loi positive, ils demandent respectueusement qu'il soit établi que le tiers des emplois et des charges de toute sorte soit attribué aux sujets desdites quatre Juridictions d'outre-monts, et que les premières promotions leur soient réservées pour les indemniser des pertes subies jusqu'alors.

La cité d'Ajaccio manque d'eau et cette privation empêche qu'elle puisse s'agrandir; les députés de cette Juridiction demandent des secours du Roi pour mettre en oeuvre toutes les possibilités de fournir cet élément si nécessaire à la vie et ils demandent aussi que la gérance de l'argent à employer soit réglée par les députés de la commune.

Que Sa Majesté se plaise à faire intervenir son pouvoir royal, par son Conseil d'Etat, dans la solution du différend qui existe depuis longtemps entre la Commune et l'évêché d'Ajaccio, pour les réparations de l'église. La Cour souveraine de l'Ile les ayant déclarés à la charge du prélat, celui-ci a obtenu qu'il fut fait défense à l'exécution de cet arrêt, et la dite église se délabre journellement au scandale et au préjudice des habitants du Diocèse.

Que soit établie une Commission des trois ordres dans ladite Cité d'Ajaccio pour rétablir le Séminaire du Diocèse qui est abandonné depuis l'époque où l'évêque actuel a été intronisé.

Les revenus de cette organisation sont inconnus. Il n'y a pas de procureurs ou ceux-ci sont arbitrairement nommés, les bibliothèques sont détruites, et une oeuvre qui était une source de vertu et de sainteté dans le clergé se voit démentie dans les fins mêmes de sa véritable institution. Que ladite Commission soit autorisée à faire valoir les droits dudit Séminaire en un état conforme aux principes mêmes de son institution.

Que soit supprimé le droit de péage au passage du fleuve de la Gravona dont jouit M. Stefanopoli, concessionaire du domaine de la Confina, la Province d'Ajaccio s'offrant d'y maintenir le bac ou ponton exigé dans les lettres patentes en faveur de M. Stefanopoli qui ne remplit pas ses obligations, ne disposant que d'un bateau peu sûr. Ce droit est lourd par sa nature pour les passages et il est arbitraire en ce sens qu'il devient sans cesse plus élevé.

Que Sa Majesté, confirmant le privilège dont jouissent les étrangers et indigènes qui viennent habiter dans ladite cité, par exemption de la dîme ecclésiastique se complaise aussi à déclarer que ledit mot "indigène" soit aussi interprêté en faveur des Corses des villages qui viennent habiter dans ladite Cité, afin d'éviter les procès qui naissent souvent à ce sujet.

Que les habitants de ladite Cité soient autorisés à transformer en vignes ou en jardins n'importe quelle partie des terres communales, cela étant conforme au droit, au temps de la République de Gênes, et sous les modes et conditions contenus dans ledit privilège.

Que les Nobles de ladite Juridiction d'Ajaccio soient maintenus dans leurs droits féodaux ou autrement réintégrés, et en particulier les feudataires de Bozi et Locari qui avaient le plus grand nombre de vassaux, selon les voeux contenus dans le cahier particulier des doléances de ladite Juridiction et selon les mémoires qu'ils se réservent de donner à ce sujet.

Que le port d'Ajaccio soit déclaré port franc pour quelque temps, étant propre par son étendue et sa situation à recevoir n'importe quel vaisseau et cela étant le seul moyen d'accroître en Corse le commerce et l'agriculture.

Que les charges qui dépendront de l'élection de l'Assemblée des Etats soient réparties entre les sujets des différentes juridictions, à mesure qu'ils supporteront les dépenses de la Province.

Les députés de la Juridiction de Sartène supplient Sa Majesté que ladite Sartène—comme étant l'endroit le plus important—soit declarée Cité, s'étant rendue considérable par son extension qui chaque jour progresse.

Qu'il y soit établi un Collège pour l'éducation de la jeunesse jusqu'à la classe de Rhétorique et les professeurs seront entretenus avec le revenu du quart des dîmes et du produit des terrains appartenant au Séminaire d'Ajaccio et situés dans la même Juridiction, revenus qui se trouvent être encaissés depuis longtemps par Monseigneur l'évêque d'Ajaccio sans qu'il les ait consacrés à quelque usage utile pour le bien public; ce nouvel établissement rendrait des services à toute la dite Juridiction qui pourrait en profiter facilement pour la situation du lieu.

La Juridiction de Sartène souhaite qu'il plaise à Sa Majesté que le nombre des Députés de la Province soit de trois nobles, trois du Tiers-Etat et deux du clergé aux Etats Ordinaires de l'Ile de Corse, que l'on choisisse parmi les Députés de la Province d'Ajaccio qui, bien que égale par le nombre de ceux de la Noblesse et de ceux des Pièves, envoie à l'Assemblée Nationale des Etats cinq députés Nobles, cinq du Tiers-Etat et trois du clergé, tandis que la Province de Sartène envoie seulement deux députés du Clergeé, deux de la Noblesse et deux du Tiers-Etat, Juridiction à laquelle s'opposent les Députés de la Juridiction d'Ajaccio, comme à une organisation injuste contre les droits de la même juridiction, accordés par Sa Majesté, eu égard à sa population, supérieure de beaucoup à celle de Sartène.

La Juridiction de Sartène demande également que, après la mot de Mgr. l'Evêque il plaise à Sa Majesté d'accorder que cet évêché soit séparé de la Juridiction de Sartène et qu'il en soit constitué et formé un nouveau dont la résidence soit dans la cité de Sartène; que ce nouvel évêché soit remplacé et agrandi par la paroisse de Carbini qui est située dans la Juridiction de Sartène et qui appartient présentement á l'évêque d'Aléria, et par la cité et le district de Bonifacio qui aujourd'hui se trouvent dépendre de l'archevêche de Gênes, ces Juridictions réunies fournissant une dîme suffisante pour fonder et entretenir avec un certain décor un nouvel évêché sans porter de tort à l'évêché d'Ajaccio.

Que les terrains des Particuliers qui se trouvent compris dans le cercle appartenant au Domaine de la région de Bruno à celle de Solenzara dans le territoire de Bonifacio, lequel cercle a été fixé sans préjudice des dits biens particuliers, soient laissés aux Propriétaires qui en jouissent et dans le cas où l'Inspecteur des Domaines prétendrait y avoir droit, Sa Majesté est suppliée d'y mettre ordre au moins qu'il leur soit permis seulement de se prévaloir de leurs droits devant les tribunaux de justice ordinaire.

263

Que la dite Cité de Bonifacio soit séparée quant à la juridiction ecclésiastique de l'archevêché de Génes dont elle depend et incorporée à l'évêché d'Ajaccio.

Que soient supprimées les confréries de la dite cité, et que leur revenu serve à l'entretien des Professeurs pour l'instruction des élèves du Pays.

Que la dite Cité de Bonifacio soit admise particulièrement à avoir une députation aux Etats de la Province séparée de celle de Sartène et qu'elle soit déclarée Capitale de la Province.

Que soit établi dans le Fiumorbo un tribunal royal, vu la séparation de celui de Cervione dont il dépend actuellement, et que les trois fleuves qu'on doit traverser soient pourvus de ponts; qu'il y ait au moins un magistrat qui juge jusqu'à mille lires et instruise les procédures criminelles pour en rendre compte ensuite au dit tribunal de Cervione; cette mesure préviendra les délits qui demeurent impunis dans cette région, parce que le tribunal ne peut agir avec l'activité et l'énergie nécessaires et elle mettra les justicables dans la possibilité d'obtenir plus promptement la justice qu'ils souhaitent en vain depuis longtemps; et aussi que les députation de la province d'Aléria soient semblables à celles de Corte et de Sartène autant pour les Etats du Pays que dans la convocation de l'Assemblée pour les Etats-Généraux.

La députation de la noblesse de Calvi demande que les Officiers de justice du dit Tribunal soient déplacés, vu les étroites alliances et les parentés qui existent entre eux, ce qui occasionnent des abus manifestes dans l'administration de la justice et que soit etabli un nouveau tribunal royal en Balagna, séparé de celui de Calvi. La dite députation demande encore que le député qui sera élu attire spécialement l'attention de M. le Garde des Sceaux sur la demande faite à ce sujet, telle quelle, elle devienne insérée au procès-verbal de la Noblesse de Calvi afin qu'il en soit remis copie.

Que soient conservés les Officiers des Bois et Forêts en donnant cependant et dorénavant de tels emplois de préférence aux Corses, parce qu'ils ont une plus grande expérience dans la connaissance de tout ce qui est nécessaire à la conservation et l'augmentation des dits Bois.

Que soit changée la forme d'élection des Officiers Municipaux des villages et qu'elle soit réduite au mode suivant: que les communes qui comptent jusqu'à 50 feux élisent 12 notables, de 50 à 100 feux 15, de 100 à 200 feux 20, celles qui en comptent davantage devant en élire 30. Ces notables qui seront pris dans le Tiers-Etat, qu'ils sachent lire et écrire et qu'ils payent au moins 15 lires d'impôts sur le revenu de leurs biens; ils s'assembleront unis aux nobles de l'endroit qui seront réputés nobles de droit et ils éliront les officiers municipaux à la pluralité des suffrages et ceux qui l'auront emportée seront confirmés de plein droit, exception faite des Députés de la Juridiction de Sartène, lesquels ne pourraient adhérer à la condition que les notables à élire soient choisis parmi les habitants qui sont en état de payer au moins 15 francs d'impôts, attendu que dans la dite Province se trouvent quelques communes champêtres composées de pasteurs et de campagnards lesquels ne pourraient absolument pas être compris dans la règle générale sans un inconvénient manifeste, condition à laquelle par conséquent, ils s'opposent et pour le reste, s'unissent à tous les autres.

Que l'on évalue les besoins de la Nation et que l'on réduise les dépenses au strict nécessaire; à cette demande s'unissent tous les autres Députés, à l'exclusion de MM. de Arrighi, Giambattistimo De Susini, Frederico De Susini, Beneditti, qui allèguent que cette demande a été discutée à l'Assemblée des Etats Ordinaires de Corse qui ont décidé que les prochains Etats régleront cette question qui les regarde spécialement.

La Province de Bastia à laquelle s'unissent celles de Calvi, Nebbio, Capocorso, La Porta, Aleria et un député de Corte, les autres déclarant ne pas pouvoir se joindre à moins que le Chancelier ne commît des manquements qui méritassent la privation de l'emploi qui lui a été donné par le Roi par des lettres patentes à vie pour cette charge, la Province de Bastia donc demande que le Chancelier des Etats soit nommé par ces Etats eux-mêmes et puisse être par eux révoqué, s'ils le jugent nécessaire.

La Province de Cap Corse fournit des marins dans la dernière guerre des bâtiments du Roi, au nombre d'environ trois cents qui tous dit-on n'ont pas reçu leur quote-part du butin. La dite Province a environ cent cinquante bâtiments entre petits et grands qui payent et prennent tous les ans le passeport. Sa Majesté est priée de bien vouloir établir en cette province un Commissaire de la Marine qui soit du pays.

La Province de Bonifacio demande que les terres domaniales après qu'il sera reconnu qu'elles appartiennent au Roi, soient données en concession d'une façon répartie aux Nobles de ladite Province qui sont en situation de les mettre en valeur.

La Province de Calvi demande l'établissement d'un port à Ile Rousse, ce pays étant le lieu le plus favorable au commerce de la Province.

La Province de Sartène ne pouvant plus supporter les vols continuels de bestiaux qui se commettent journellement parmi les habitants et les bergers, vols qui bien souvent occasionnent la ruine des familles, prie Sa Majesté de bien vouloir confirmer le chapitre du Statut criminel de Corse relativement au vol; ce chapitre serait, s'il était approuvé, l'unique moyen pour prévenir les abus du vol. A cette demande adhèrent les députés de Nebbio, Aleria, Vico, Corte, Bonifacio, La Porta, et Calvi.

Enfin l'Ordre présente unis ses voeux les plus fervents au coeur paternel du Roi, à l'auguste Assemblée des Etats Généraux et à toute la Nation française, afin qu'il leur plaise de continuer les secours que la munificence royale a prêtés jusqu'à ce jour à la Corse et qu'elle ne pourrait supprimer sans détruire les moyens qui peuvent aider au renouvellement du Pays. La Corse avec le temps aura la fortune de se trouver accrue dans ses richesses et de concourir à supporter les charges de l'Etat en raison de ses progrès dans l'agriculture, dans le commerce, et dans les manufactures que la bonté du Souverain et la forme nouvelle de l'administration peuvent établir chez elle.

Le présent cahier de doléances a été arrêté et clos par Nous Ignazio Morelli, Paolo Battista Cattanes, Pietro Paolo Cuneo d'Ornano, Carl' Andrea Pozzodiborgo, Giambattista De Susini, Francesco Saverio De Frediani et Pasquale Negroni, Commissaires Députés à la rédaction dudit cahier, en vertu de la délibération de l'ordre du vingt neuf mai échu.

Ce jour, cinq juin, 1789. Neuf lignes et trente et un mots rayés, approuvés comme nuls.

[Eight signatures.][22]

(Toutes ces signatures sont autographes.)

Et le présent cahier de doléances présenté à l'Assemblée de l'Ordre à été par celui-ci reçu et signé pour être remis au Député et présenté à l'Assemblée des Etats-Généraux, en exécution du réglement de Sa Majesté, publié en Corse pour la tenue desdits Etats-Généraux.

Ce jour 6 juin, 1789.

[Sixteen signatures, including]
Baccheciampe, président, and Pozzodiborgo, secrétaire

NO. 11. THE TEN IMPERIAL CITIES: DIX VILLES IMPERIALES

Cahier reprinted from printed text, *Bibl. Colmar, Haut-Rhin,* s.l.n.d. in-8°, 30 pages. This text was a translation into German of the original in French. In the German text, the title appears as "Klagepunkte der zehen Reichsstädte der königlichen Landvogten Haguenau. . . ." The original French text has been lost. It has seemed advisable to reprint a text in French, rather than the German text. The translation into French with some corrections, was made by Mme. Totem, of Paris.

P.V.-MS, *Arch. Nat.* C14/4. There were five on the committee to make the cahier. It was voted March 31, and copies of the p.v. were given to the deputies with the cahier.

Convocation: 4th type.

DOLÉANCES OU CHEFS D'ACCUSATION

des dix villes impériales du gouvernement royal de Haguenau, rendus à l'assemblée tenue à Schlestadt, à la suite de la circulaire royale pour la prochaine assemblée, concernant le décret du 7 fevrier, 1789, et celui du 24 janvier précédent. Ordonnance de M. le gouverneur général, Maréchal de Stainville, sous la présidence de M. le Sous-gouverneur Depons, chevalier, brigadier des armées royales, et des commandants de la ville de Haguenau.

---

[22] These signatures are of six commissioners, the president and secretary.

266

Les dix villes impériales, pleines de respect, de fidélité et d'amour pour la personne sacrée du meilleur et du plus grand des monarques, comme de la plus tendre confiance en sa bonté paternelle, avec laquelle il leur a consenti un privilège particulier dans son ordonnance concernant l'Alsace, se jettent au pied du trône pour prier Sa Majesté, qui répand ses bienfaits sur tous ses sujets et leur a permis de lui représenter leurs griefs, plaintes et réclamations, et de les entendre avec bienveillance et favorablement.

Art. 1. Les députés desdites villes prient Sa Majesté de maintenir et confirmer leurs droits, libertés, privilèges et statuts. Ces droits ayant été confirmés par les traités de paix de Munster et Risswick, que les dites villes soient maintenues sous la protection de leurs chefs, comme elles l'étaient, sous les rois précédents, avant leur réunion à la couronne de France.

Art. 2. Etant donné le désordre des finances de la nation, les états du royaume s'étant rassemblés pour leur rétablissement, lesdits députés assurant Sa Majesté que villes impériales, désireuses de venir en aide à la patrie, collaboreront de toutes leurs forces au relèvement du bien-être de la nation et à la réorganisation des finances, dans l'espoir que la noblesse et le clergé animés du même désir, renonceront à leurs privilèges et libertés, et par conséquent se soumettront volontairement aux mêmes formes d'impôts que ceux qui sont répartis sur chaque habitant du royaume, proportionnellement à la fortune, et aux biens mobiliers et aux dîmes ainsi qu'aux redevances et aux prestations.[23]

Art. 3. Les dits députés demanderont que toutes charges collectives, sérieusement établies, quelles qu'elles soient, abolies par un édit permanent avec le conseil et l'adhésion de l'assemblée du royaume, ne seront désormais changeés qu'avec le consentement de ladite assemblée.

Art. 4. Que l'assemblée du royaume fasse établir des relevés exacts et détaillés de toutes les dettes d'Etat, ainsi que des revenus et dépenses annuelles de la couronne, afin de pouvoir, après examen, déterminer sérieusement aussi bien le montant des impôts annuels que le temps nécessaire à l'augmentation des dits impôts, jusqu'à l'extinction de la Dette nationale.

Art. 5. La base financière ainsi déterminée devra être supportée par les trois ordres, par rapport à leurs biens particuliers et sans distinctions d'aucune sorte de privilèges, libertés et exemptions; de même si des biens, dîmes, redevances, fonds et autres cens qui feront partie de cette base, se trouvaient entre les mains de propriétaires étrangers; et dans ce cas, princes étrangers, nobles, communautés temporelles ou spirituelles, ne pourront être exonérés de contribuer pour leur part au plan susdit, même si des traités généraux ou particuliers les y autorisaient. Leur part, qui devra être néanmoins fixée par le registre de ladite base viendra en déduction du

---

[23] The German text reads "je nach Proportion des Vermögens und der eigenthumlichen Besitzungen, Zehnden, auch Grundzinse und Gulten eines jeden, gelegt und verteilt werden soll."

trésor royal et sera considérée comme argent comptant; bien entendu dans la répartition de ladite base pour chaque province, il sera tenu compte des circonstances de tous genres ainsi que de la variété des fonds et du sol.

Art. 6. Toute autre taxe consentie et désignée par les états généraux, sera soumise à la même mesure dans les trois ordres sans distinction, par rapport à leurs biens; pour cela, il ne devra exister aucun abonnement ni bail pour une certaine somme; par conséquent, il y aura pour chaque ville ou commune un registre unique, qui devra comprendre les impôts des trois ordres ainsi que des étrangers.

Art. 7. Les sommes consenties par les états généraux pour le bien général de l'Etat, seront utilisées selon leur affectation propre; et afin d'entretenir la confiance générale de la nation, les comptes seront imprimés et rendus publics.

Art. 8. Afin que la province d'Alsace soit légalement représentée, nous prierons Sa Majesté de révoquer l'assemblée provinciale instituée par l'édit du mois de juin 1787, et de la remplacer par des états provinciaux qui devront être composées d'un nombre de députés du tiers-état égal à celui des députations des deux autres ordres réunis, et tous ces députés seront élus par leurs ordres; il est entendu que nul, à quel que titre qu'il appartienne, ne doit participer à l'élection s'il est encore député, et que les voix seront comptées par tête et non par ordre.

Art. 9. Les états provinciaux auront à s'occuper sous l'autorité royale, de la complète administration, qui était auparavant attribuée aux Intendants.

Art. 10. La commission intermédiaire des états provinciaux devra consister en trois membres du clergé, trois de la noblesse et six du tiers état, parmi lesquels sera désigné réciproquement un président dans les deux premiers ordres, un syndic de la noblesse, un syndic du tiers, et un secrétaire; tous seront choisis par les Ordres réunis. Parmi les six députés du tiers état, il y aura toujours un député des Dix Villes Impériales, afin que Sa Majesté permette aux dites Villes d'envoyer deux députés aux assemblées nationales, sur les vingt-quatre députés pour toute l'Alsace.

Art. 11. Les députés solliciteront de Sa Majesté que soit révoqué toute ordonnance ou décret excluant le tiers de l'armée et de l'accès aux places d'honneur dans le service de la guerre; car quelques décrets sont injurieux pour l'Ordre le plus nombreux de la nation et préjudiciables à l'état, particulièrement à l'Alsace. Car cette province est spécialement désignée à l'accès des hauts grades militaires par les membres de sa bourgeoisie.

Art. 12. Ils solliciteront également de Sa Majesté que nul ordre, abbaye, chapitre, institution spirituelle doué de rentes et occupé par des gens du tiers état, ne puisse supprimer ses revenus pour les transférer aux corps nobiliaires; ni les abbayes jouissant de pensions au-dessus du tiers de leurs rentes, déduction faite de l'entretien de leurs maisons, les aumônes de fondation et d'usage, pour en charger les placements royaux, redevances et charges, car par ces suppressions, dépossédant le tiers état des places qui lui étaient consacrées par les fondateurs et à cause des pensions exagérées dont sont chargées les abbayes, les aumônes dont se nourrissent les pauvres du pays leur seront retirées.

Pour décréter de plus que les pensions dont pourront être chargées les abbayes, seront toutes désignées pour l'accroissement de la portion des curés, qui sont besogneux pour la plupart; ou pour adoucir la vie à quelques autres en instituant des fondations utiles pour les gens du commun; ou pour diminuer le nombre des mendiants, qui sont un grand fléau pour la campagne; ou simplement en les laissant aux abbayes, si celles-ci viennent elles-mêmes en aide aux prêtres, ou se rendent utiles à l'éducation de la jeunesse; les autres ordres pourront prendre part également à ladite éducation. Elles serviront de même à aider aux cloîtres d'hommes et de femmes, lorsque ceux-ci n'acceptent que des membres pauvres.

Art. 13. Lesdites Dix Villes attendent de la justice de Sa Majesté la constitution du code civil de même que criminel pour abréger les formalités et rendre les procédures moins coûteuses; elles souhaitent également que les coutumes, dans les provinces où elles ne sont pas encore consignées, soient rédigées et imprimées dans les dialectes utilisés par le peuple, et éditées en volumes qui seront approuvés par l'autorité, lus, proclamés et appliqués dans les villages.

Art. 14. Le Roi sera invité à abolir l'usage des lettres cachetées et secrètes et ordonner que chacun de ses sujets qui sera emprisonné sur son ordre ou celui du tribunal, sera remis entre les mains de son juge compétent sans autres frais que ceux de son arrestation ou de son transport.

Art. 15. On désire la liberté de la presse, mais de telle sorte que, sans priver la nation des enseignements utiles dont la pensée peut-être rendue publique par l'impression, elle ne donne pas motif à insultes envers la religion, Sa Majesté royale, les ordonnances du gouvernement. Pour prévenir ces abus, l'auteur sera tenu de présenter son ouvrage avec sa signature, et l'imprimeur devra imprimer ce nom sur le livre.

Art. 16. Il ne sera accordé aucun privilège exclusif nuisible au commerce et à l'industrie.

Art. 17. On demande que les séminaires et les cloîtres soient autorisés à placer l'excédant de leur argent parmi les paysans, afin que l'usage se répande d'encourager l'agriculture et de retarder la ruine du peuple qui est en général dévalisé par l'usure des juifs.

Art. 18. Que la vie, l'honneur, la liberté puissent être assurés pour toujours à tous les habitants; que leurs biens particuliers soient invulnérables, et que nul puisse en être privé en vue de l'intérêt général, sans en être dédommagé d'après les rapports d'experts.

Art. 19. Il sera permis aux députés de faire la proposition que chaque ville ou commune ait à pourvoir à la perception et au recouvrement de ses fonds royaux; et que les percepteurs ou receveurs soient tenus de livrer ces fonds royaux; et que les percepteurs ou receveurs soient tenus de livrer ces fonds avec le moins de frais possibles, soit dans la caisse du pays, ou au trésor royal; faute de quoi les receveurs généraux, particuliers et autres seront congédiés après restitution de leurs finances mal gérées.

Art. 20. Que tous les quartiers concédés jusqu'à présent aux officiers supérieurs, qui se sont multipliés à l'excès, ainsi que les inspecteurs des hôpitaux et des apothicaires soient supprimés; de même que seront licenciées les pensions après la mort de ceux qui en jouissaient, tant en province que dans les villes et communes, sans qu'ils puissent être concédés à nouveau sous aucun prétexte; que les pensions constituées sur les biens patrimoniaux de quelqu'une des Dix Villes soient examinées et immédiatement supprimées s'il se trouve qu'elles ne soient pas maintenues à l'une ou l'autre des Dix Villes, pour une raison légitime.

Art. 21. Que désormais la construction des casernes, annexes pour officiers, et autres bâtiments militaires de même que la livraison des lits, du bois, et de la lumière, soit à la charge de la ville, vu que les villes fortifiées et les forteresses sont à la charge générale de la nation et des frontières; pendant que les logements de soldats devront être supportés par chacun, sans distinction de situation.

Art. 22. Les dits députés exigeront la suppression du recrutement des milices, lorsque celui-ci est contraire à la liberté des habitants; et au nom des Dix Villes, excepté de celles qui ne sont pas soumises au recrutement des milices, ils proposeront une taxe proportionnelle applicable à ceux qui prennent part au service militaire et dont l'éducation sera faite dans les dépôts déterminés; ou bien ils demanderont l'établissement de milices provinciales, afin que soient évités les grands frais auxquels on était assujetti jusqu'ici. On doit représenter à Sa Majesté qu'un homme contraint au service militaire ne fait pas un bon homme de guerre.

Art. 23. En conséquence de ce que la province d'Alsace a acquis la propriété de l'intendance du haut Conseil royal et en assume les charges, Sa Majesté devra désormais disposer de ces places, lorsqu'elles seront vacantes, en faveur des trois Alsaciens qui lui seront proposés par les Etats provinciaux. Enfin, il sera interdit à l'avenir de financer une charge royale ou seigneuriale.

Art. 24. La province d'Alsace sera maintenue dans son état de province étrangère, et aucun sujet Alsacien ne pourra être ôté de sa juridiction, excepté pour un délit; en conséquence, toutes évocations générales ou particulières, seront abolies, ainsique le "committimus," etc.

Art. 25. Comme l'agrandissement des barrières devait être proposé, Sa Majesté sera invitée à en exclure l'Alsace, car sa ruine serait inévitable en ce qui concerne la prospérité de son commerce et de sa situation.

Art. 26. Comme les champs de trèfles et autres prairies artificielles agrémentent l'agriculture, procurent aux paysans la nourriture pour leur bétail et augmentent l'engrais, lesdits champs seront exempts de taxe, car ces impôts paraissent extraordinaires, et leur levée, selon les diverses manières dont elle est opérée, est aussi pénible pour les seigneurs qui en ont le droit, qu'elle est gênante et coûteuse pour le paysan, au surplus, le défrichement des biens communaux qui sera la suite obligatoire du placement des fonds, dédommagera largement les seigneurs de l'abolition de cet impôt.

Art. 27. La mendicité doit être interdite et chaque communauté et presbytère seront tenus de pourvoir à l'entretien de leurs pauvres, malades ou en santé.

Art. 28. Les députés tiendront à la suppression des loteries, lorsqu'elles seront pour le peuple une occasion de ruine.

Art. 29. Ils solliciteront également, que le clergé soient tenus d'instituer une caisse de leurs revenus, pour l'amortissement de leurs dettes, sans que pour cela on puisse leur demander un minimum; mais chaque membre du clergé devra y contribuer d'après ses rentes.

Art. 30. En conséquence, dans chaque ville ou communauté dorénavant, les corvées ordinaires seront dévolues à ceux qui offrent le moins, et payées par les trois ordres, sans distinction.

Art. 31. Parceque l'Alsace est chargée du très grand entretien des quais, digues, éperons et fascines sur le Rhin, elle sera exempte à l'avenir de toute contribution extérieure, pour l'achèvement des canaux.

Art. 32. Les Juifs résidant dans les villes du royaume seront inscrits pour les taxes comme les autres contribuables, dans les registres appartenant aux dites villes, et leurs parts relevées dans cesdits registres seront réunies et remises aux percepteurs; les dix villes demandent à l'unanimité que le nombre desdits Juifs soit réglementé de façon précise par les lettres impériales; et ils devront se conformer ponctuellement aux ordonnances passées concernant le commerce et les prêts d'argent des Juifs sous peine d'expulsion le leurs habitations.

Art. 33. L'ordonnance concernant les fosses de salpètre devra être établie de façon à gêner le moins possible le peuple, qui doit en supporter la contrainte prolongée.

Art. 34. Vu que les villes du royaume rétribuent leurs juges, elles demandent que la justice soit rendue gratuitement à leurs habitants.

Art. 35. Le droit forestier et l'administration des fôrets devront être rendus à ces dites villes, qui en ont été dépouillées, contrairement à leurs statuts primitifs.

Art. 36. Celles des Dix Villes comprenant une garnison, se plaignent collectivement que depuis quelque temps les garnisons se procurent elles-mêmes au dehors, marchandises, travailleurs de toutes sortes, approvisionnements; ce qui désorganise le commerce, fait languir les travailleurs et enlève aux habitants un bénéfice qui leur était auparavant un moyen de les distraire de leurs griefs.

271

Art. 37. Attendu que diverses taxes et impôts permettaient à ces villes d'augmenter leurs revenus; ces taxes étant précisément placées sur les moyens d'existence les plus indispensables, qui deviennent pour cette raison difficiles à acquérir par le peuple, Sa Majesté sera priée d'abolir peu à peu celles qui, après examen, n'auront pas été établies de façon ferme, soit par des lettres patentes stipulées ou par des lettres impériales.

Art. 38. L'Alsace doit désormais, comme autrefois, être libérée des papiers timbrés et du contrôle, et le demeurer; ainsi qu'elle en a été exonérée par l'arrêt de l'an 1694.

Art. 39. Il sera permis aux propriétaires de dégager avec le capital doublé, les redevances foncières attachées à leurs biens, en vue des taxes annuelles, les cloîtres et fondations religieuses seront autorisées à admettre cet amortissement, quand on le leur offrira.

Doléances particulières des Dix Villes Impériales

Parceque les dix villes impériales présentent devant le trône des doléances particulières, et des propositions, aussi bien sur le trop grand nombre de magistrats que sur l'administration trop onéreuse de leurs revenus patrimoniaux, lesdites villes prient Sa Majesté d'accueillir favorablement chacun de ces griefs surtout dans leur opinion sur les sujets de leurs requêtes; mais avant de s'engager dans le détail, lesdites villes supplient à nouveau très humblement Sa Majesté de bien vouloir les maintenir dans leurs droits, libertés, et privilèges légués par leurs pères et dont elles jouissent depuis le seizième siècle sous la protection de leurs gouverneurs (préfets) sans que la nouvelle organisation qui appartiendra à chacune des dites villes (s'il plaît à Sa Majesté de l'ordonner ainsi) qui sera uniforme pour toutes, ne porte aucun préjudice auxdits droits et privilèges. Car les villes, par les nouvelles ordonnances qu'elles prennent la liberté de proposer, ne cherchent rien autre que plus de promptitude dans l'administration de la justice, une constitution mieux organisée et une administration plus sûre et plus ferme. Ce sont tous des moyens consolants pour le bien-être de chacun que Sa Majesté leur assurera gracieusement, par cette présentation à l'Assemblée des états généraux.

Ville de Colmar

Les députés, au nom de cette ville; demanderont à Sa Majesté de permettre à la bourgeoisie de choisir comme autrefois, parmi les concitoyens, qui sont nés Français et dont le savoir et l'honnêteté sont suffisamment reconnus, une magistrature perpétuelle, comprenant en un officier royal[24] 4 bourgmestres gradués, 4 conseillers; une administration du fisc inamovible et un greffier de ville; lesquels magistrats devront administrer la haute, moyenne et basse justice, ainsi que la police, dans la ville de Colmar

---

[24] The German reads : "königlichen Prator."

et ses dépendances, comme autrefois; et devront défendre toute régie des revenus de la ville.

L'administration devra nommer, à l'exclusion de tous autres, un officier royal et huit échevins qui seront choisis par la bourgeoisie parmi les 48 échevins des dix corporations réduites à quatre, et un secrétaire-régisseur. Ceux-ci composercnt une chambre administrative qui devra siéger dans les états provinciaux.

Les dix corporations de Colmar seront réduites à quatre; par exemple, la première comprendra les lauboureurs, vignerons et jardiniers; l'organisation de tout ce ressort devra, comme autrefois, demeurer confiée à cette corporation. La deuxième englobera les bûcherons, bouchers et bottiers; la troisième les tisserands, tailleurs et boulangers; et la quatrième les tailleurs. Chacune de ces corporations aura dix échevins; elle comprendra un conseiller qui sera changé tous les ans pour le jour d'assemblée des maîtres.

La chambre administrative s'occupera de la répartition des taxes, de la régie de tous et de chacun des revenus de la ville, ainsi que de ceux de l'hôpital.

La nomination et le salaire, aussi bien des magistrats que des membres de la Chambre administrative seront fixés par les 48 échevins, dans la mesure des revenus de la ville.

Les comptes seront déposés trois mois par an, au bout d'un an, dans la Chambre administrative en présence d'un député de chaque corporation, et à chacun de ces députés seront remise l'ouverture et la clôture du compte, afin qu'il en fasse un rapport à sa corporation. En l'bsence de l'officier royal, l'échevin le plus âgé présidera toute assemblée de la Chambre administrative.

Cette Chambre ainsi organisée se fera donner les comptes de l'administration des anciens magistrats depuis 1770; il y sera recherché les attributions de l'argent perçu; il sera aussi procédé à une enquête exacte de l'utilisation de tous les biens communaux; et comme les chefs de la magistrature se sont appropriés ces biens par M.M. les intendants, contrairement à l'arrêt du Conseil d'Etat du 28 novembre 1721, et sans le consentement et au préjudice de la bourgeoisie, ils seront rendus à cet ordre qui en prendra de nouveau possession.

Pour ne pas mettre les familles dans l'embarras, ni léser les personnes en fonction depuis six ans, les bourgeois de la ville de Colmar offrent de laisser à chacun des maires un paiement de 840 francs, et de 100 francs à chacun des Conseillers (membres du Conseil) qui seront relevés de leurs fonctions à la suite de l'ordonnance ci-dessus. Ils jouiront de cette solde leur vie durant, selon l'article du 28 nov. 1721 par la liquidation-arrêt.

Comme les Corps de métier de Colmar font partie par moitié de l'une ou l'autre religion, la même méthode sera appliquée dans les deux religions, à l'exception de l'officier royal, du secrétaire d'Etat et du secrétaire-régisseur de la Chambre administrative.

Nota: Le député soussigné, de Colmar, a protesté à Schlestadt et exigé que les postes de secrétaire d'Etat et de secrétaire-régisseur de la Chambre administrative organisée à Colmar, ainsie que tous les fonctions municipales de cette ville soient partagées parmi les membres des deux religions, conformément à l'alternative admise en l'année 1680.

Signé Lebs, fils.

Traduit sur l'original françois, à Colmar ce 14 avril 1789.

Signé Beck, avec parafe.

Les six maisons des corporations abolies seront vendues, et l'argent qu'on en retirera sera utilisé de la manière ordinaire, après acquittement préalable des dettes éventuelles desdites corporations.

Tous les autres officiants et employés de la ville de son ressort seront nommés par les 48 échevins des corporations qui représentent la bourgeoisie, et pour cette nomination, on prendra en considération la vertu, l'habileté et l'honnêteté des personnes.

Personne ne sera libéré des taxes seigneuriales, quelles qu'elles puissent être; la mainmorte, qui est une servitude, devra être irrévocablement supprimé.[25]

Deux parents ne pourront être admis ensemble ni dans la magistrature ni dans la Chambre administrative, d'après la défense de l'ordonnance; et si un tel cas se présente réellement, un des deux sera destitué. La bourgeoisie prie en dernier lieu, Sa Majesté de considérer dans Sa sagesse combien fréquemment le choix libre de magistrats d'après de prétendus brevets souvent captés, a causé de scandales; pour remédier à ce désagrément, Sa grandeur sera priée de vouloir bien que nul brevet ne sera désormais, valable, moyennant quoi le choix de ce droit si cher pourra être effectué dans sa pleine liberté; tout ceci sans préjudice du droit de Sa Majesté en ce qui concerne la nomination des préteurs royaux.

Ville de Haguenau

La ville de Haguenau désire une magistrature qui, en mesure réduite, comprendra un officier royal nommé par Sa Majesté; deux bourgmestres gradués, et quatre conseillers, les six élus par les 50 députés choisis par la bourgeoisie partagée en 25 corporations, ainsiqu'un fisc inamovible et un secrétaire d'Etat. Cette magistrature devra, comme autrefois, exercer la haute, moyenne et basse justice ainsi que la police dans la ville de Haguenau et son ressort; par contre, l'administration des revenus de la ville lui sera complètement interdite.

En ce qui concerne l'administration des revenus municipaux, on choisira en forme de municipalité, huit échevins parmi les 50 députés de la bourgeoisie ou deux députés de chacune des 25 corporations, sous la présidence

[25] The German reads: "der sogennante Todtenfall, als welcher eine Abgabe ist, die nach der Leibligenschaft reicht, soll unwiderruflich abgestellt werden."

de l'officier royal, et en son absence, du plus ancien échevin; puis un greffier et un administrateur; cet ensemble constituera la municipalité ou chambre administrative et devra siéger parmi les états provinciaux. Cette chambre s'occupera de la répartition des dépenses, de l'administration des revenus de la ville et communaux, ainsi que de ceux des forêts en commun avec Sa Majesté, des presbytères de Saint-Georges et de l'Hôpital civil (Hôtel-Dieu).

La nomination et la solde des magistrats comme des membres de la Chambre administrative seront fixées par les 50 députés des 25 corporations, d'après les revenus de la ville.

Le rendement des comptes se fera dans les mêmes conditions que pour la ville de Colmar; et dès que la Chambre administrative sera constituée, elle devra procéder immédiatement à la recherche des biens communaux et leur emploi, afin que ceux-ci puissent être rendus et restitués sans distinction à la municipalité.

La solde des employés supprimés par la présente ordonnance sera la même que celle qu'ils recevaient et sera maintenue leur vie durant. La nomination de tous les autres employés appartient à la ville, sera également attribuée aux 50 députés des 25 corporations, qui dans ce cas, ne tiendront compte d'aucune recommandation, mais du mérite, des talents et de l'honnêteté; ils prendront aussi en considération qu'ils ne devront pas nommer des personnes apparentées à des magistrats, selon les clauses de défense du décret. Ce choix doit être libre, et Sa Majesté sera humblement priée de maintenir ce droit à la ville de Haguenau, qui s'associe ainsi à la même demande de la ville de Colmar. Nul ne jouira de quelque revenu de la ville, mais ceux-ci seront adjugés au plus offrant, et la plus forte somme sera déposée dans la caisse de la ville.

Sa Majesté sera également priée d'autoriser à parler du contenu du mémoire concernant la bourgeoisie de Haguenau, et envoyé à la Cour soit par les Etats provinciaux, soit par un commissaire spécial, attendu que la discussion de tous les cas qu'il présente est sollicitée uniquement par la bourgeoisie.

La ville requiert de plus que pour l'instruction de sa nombreuse jeunesse aux revenus des bourses taxées des Molsheimer-Collegii, soient ajoutées les rentes de tous les biens des ex-Jésuites, donnés à ladite ville, sous cette condition.

Ville de Schlestadt

Les députés demandent au nom de la bourgeoisie de Schlestadt, que dans ladite ville puisse être instituée une muncipalité conforme à l'ordonnance royale concernant les administrations provinciales; que la gérance des revenus de la ville ainsi que de l'hôpital, ne soit confiée qu'à cette seule municipalité; qu'en conséquence la magistrature devra se contenter des droits invoqués par le droit, et que l'administration des revenus municipaux

275

sera placée sous le contrôle des Etats provinciaux. Sur ces trois requêtes, les deux députés qui ne font pas partie d'une corporation, ainsi que les officiers municipaux qui en font partie, remarqueront que la municipalité existant dans cette ville depuis bien longtemps, qui a été instituée d'après les anciennes lois de la ville, approuvée par l'autorité supérieure et sanctionnée par les traités de paix, doit être une municipalité d'autant plus loyale que les membres dont elle se compose, sont les vrais représentants de la ville, puisqu'ils ont été nommés par la bourgeoisie. A ce point de vue exclusif, la magistrature de Schlestadt sera la municipalité la plus parfaite qui puisse exister, et à laquelle puisse être confiée l'administration des revenus de la ville ainsi que ceux de l'hôpital. De plus, si Sa Majesté voulait ordonner le relèvement des Etats provinciaux, on se soumettrait à ceux-ci comme à toute autre autorité légitime.

Les bourgeois de ladite ville demandent que les membres de la magistrature soient choisis par la bourgeoisie, ses employés ne seront nommés que pour trois ans, sauf ceux qui seront maintenus par un nouveau choix. A ceci, les deux députés et les officiers municipaux répondront que les places dans la magistrature sont reconnues par l'autorité royale comme fonctionnaires à vie et que les membres actuels exigent et ont accepté cette perspective; c'est pourquoi ils demandent à Sa Majesté et aux Etats généraux de rejeter une motion contraire au droit commun de la province comme aux intérêts privés.

Ils demandent que le secrétaire de la ville et l'intendant soient à l'avenir nommés de la même manière que précédemment; que la solde des magistrats soit estimée en argent et que nulles clauses, nulle attribution de lois, nul événement imprévu ne se produise. A ce sujet, lesdits deux députés et les officiers municipaux remarquent que les attributions de bois des lieux les plus élevés sont préciséis par l'arrêt du Conseil d'Etat royal du 25 octobre, 1733; d'après cela, on est en droit d'espérer qui nul changement ne s'y produira; et en ce qui concerne les accidences que ne peuvent consister en rien autre que dans le salaire de soins particuliers, on croit qu'ils sont d'autant moins chers qu'ils consistent en très peu de chose.

Ils demandent que la chasse soit affectée au bénéfice des revenus municipaux; que le bois abattu en forêt soit tenu en provision, en partie pour être réparti pour un prix minime dans la bourgeoisie, et en partie pour venir en aide aux pauvres dans les hivers rigoureux; l'attribution du bois à brûler qui est donnée aux magistrats et aux fonctionnaires sera abolie; cette attribution sera taxée en argent aux magistrats; mais à ceux qui en ont joui sans être au service de la ville, elle sera retirée, et la ville en sera dispensée. Sa Majesté sera priée de décréter le nécessaire pour organiser l'administration des forêts selon les réglements prescrits par les Etats généraux d'après les conditions locales. Pour ce qui concerne les biens communaux, ils seront affectés aux besoins de toute la bourgeoisie, ce que les députés ont également demandé.

Ils requièrent que le collège qui était à Schlestadt jusqu'au moment de la dissolution de l'ordre des Jésuites, y soit de nouveau réinstallé; et que par conséquent si les 3000 francs qui sont consacrés aux bourses établies en taxes au Molsheimer-Collegii pour les enfants de Schlestadt, ne sont plus suffisants pour suffire aux frais du collège réinstallé, les sommes séquestrées provenant des revenus de l'ordre dont il est question précédemment devront être d'autant plus consacrées à ce but, que les Jésuites subvenaient aux dépenses et à l'instruction. Quant à la requête, que Schlestadt soit isolée des autres villes du gouvernment de Haguenau, et être placée sur le pied du reste des villes de province, les deux députés ont signifié aux habitants ne faisant pas partie des corporations, à M. Hermann, député des . . .[26], et aux fonctionnaires municipaux, que cette requête est directement opposée aux intérêts des habitants de Schlestadt; car quelques-uns ont été trouvés mêlés à une foule innombrable de gens qui donnent leur voix dans les districts réunis de Colmar et Schlestadt; dans la circonstance actuelle de la convocation des Etats généraux; et qui en revanche ont obtenu par la protection de M. le Gouverneur général l'avantage inappréciable de délibérer seuls et paisiblement sur l'intérêt général; que la séparation demandée est également contraire au droit du fief du gouverneur, celui-ci ayant promis solennellement la conservation de ce droit à la ville, et réciproquement; et qu'enfin elle est opposée aux traités de paix qui ont ratifié les constitutions des villes imposées.

Finalement, Sa Majesté est invitée au nom de la ville de Schlestadt de maintenir la religion catholique à l'exclusion de toute autre et de retirer tous et chaque décret pouvant autoriser la libre pratique de toute autre religion dans les villes de la province et du royaume.

Ville de Kaysersperg

Les députés demandent que dans les villes du royaume, la magistrature soit de nouveau placée sur le pied de sa première investiture; et que dans lesdites villes les municipalités soient rétablies. Les bourgmestres de Kaysersperg devront être gradués; le droit forestier et l'administration des forêts seront rendus à la ville et confiés à la municipalité réinstituée; de même que les punitions encourues pour délits forestiers seront abandonnées et abolies. L'abbaye de Marbach sera réinstallée. On demande également qu'il soit interdit à chacun de remplir deux ou plusieurs fonctions qui ne peuvent pas être réunies; et comme ce cas se présente précisément dans la magistrature de Kaysersperg, on requiert que cette interdiction-ci soit créée. Enfin, chaque fils de bourgeois, dans la 20e. année de son âge, sera admis et affirmé dans son droit de citoyen de la ville de Kaysersperg, gratuitement et sans aucun frais.

[26] The word "Schirmverwandten" appears in the German version.

UNEDITED TEXTS OF GENERAL CAHIERS

Ville de Rossheim

Les députés demandent au nom de cette ville, que la ville conserve ses privilèges et sa constitution par choix libre, en ce qui concerne les places de magistrats et tous autres fonctionnaires, comme auparavant; que les huit maîtres de corporations de la ville de Rossheim qui participent à l'avenir, à ce choix, selon leurs statuts, soient élus par la bourgeoisie à l'exclusion de la magistrature et qu'ils conservent ce poste pendant trois ans; à la réserve d'y être maintenus pendant trois autres années s'ils ont bien rempli leurs fonctions; par contre, que toutes les ordonnances et décrets passés seront considérés comme s'ils n'avaient jamais existé; que les revenus patrimoniaux de la ville de Rossheim soient administrés désormais par la magistrature, de concert avec les huit maîtres de corporations sans lesquels les magistrats ne pourront prescrire aucune nouvelle dépense; les comptes seront rendus, désormais en présence desdits maîtres de corporations, et les peines pour délits forestiers seront remises sans formalités et sans frais, par les magistrats.

Sa Majesté sera instamment priée d'ordonner que toute réclamation de la bourgeoisie, qui aura été instruite par un commissaire après avoir entendu les deux parties, sera traitée sans délai; et dès que le bien-fondé de cette plainte déposée par la bourgeoisie aura été établi, le compte en sera rendu, car le repos des habitants dépend de la discussion du procès. Les coupes de bois dans les forêts seront interdites et l'exploitation des forêts sera rendu aux bourgeois, comme auparavant.

Rossheim demande aussi que les pensions attribuées à des gens n'ayant rendu aucun service à la ville et qui sont à la charge de celle-ci, soient abolies; ainsi que les pensions non motivées qui donnent lieu à des coupes de bois, sont cause de la dévastation des forêts et de la ruine des habitants d'une ville, auxquels tout commerce est enlevé. De même, tout ce qui est contraire à l'arrêté des liquidations de l'année 1717, sera anéanti et supprimé.

Les bourgeois requièrent que les ordonnances contre deux magistrats qui sont apparentés dans un degré interdit, soient exécutées dès que l'un d'eux est élu, ou tous les deux, qui sont en contradiction avec les statuts, et qu'ils seront destitués; enfin, que les comptes des forêts et de l'hôpital, qui n'ont pas été remis depuis 15 ou 16 ans, soient examinés en présence des huit maitres de corporations.

Ils demandent que les comptes municipaux déposés depuis la commission de M. Kolb soient de nouveau examinés; que le greffier municipal soit tenu d'acquitter les sommes arriérées et autres finances qui n'ont pas été payées depuis 30 ans; que la dotation pour St. Jean et St. Martin, ainsi que toute autre soient abolies; et que l'administration de la magistrature concernant les ornements sacrés de la cure de St. Stephan qui a été adjugée pour 23,000 francs à l'insu de la bourgeoisie, alors qu'elle était proposée pour un minimum de 10,000 francs, soit examinée par un commissaire.

Ville de Oberehenheim

Parceque les magistrats se sont appropriés l'administration des revenus de la ville sans la coöpération de la bourgeoisie, et que pour cette raison, les finances municipales sont en mauvais état, les députés demandent, au nom de cette ville, que pour ramener le bon ordre, les revenus municipaux et la police forestière (puisque les forêts sont la seule propriété de la ville), soient administrés par la magistrature, en s'adjoignant les représentants du Tiers Etat; que, selon les statuts, le choix de tous fonctionnaires municipaux soit fait par la bourgeoisie et doit être libre; que la bourgeoisie abolira les délits forestiers en présence des maîtres de corporations; que les pensions qui sont à la charge de la ville, soient supprimées; et Sa Majesté sera priée de n'en plus établir aucune; ainsi que d'ordonner que les procès concernant des causes très importantes et faites par l'intendance, soient jugés au plus tôt; que toute élection contraire aux statuts et aux privilèges de la bourgeoisie soit réduite à néant; et que la commune soit autorisée à élire ces fonctionnaires par choix libre; les habitants de la ville de Oberehnheim qui compte 1100 feux, demandent que pour favoriser leur unique commerce, qui consiste en vins, il soit établi une voie de communication de Niederehnheim à Erstein.

Ville de Wissembourg

Les députés représentent à Sa Majesté, au nom de la bourgeoisie de cette ville, de proposer la réduction de sa magistrature; elle devra consister désormais en un officier royal, deux bourgmestres, dont l'un catholique, et l'autre de la Confession d'Augsbourg, et six conseillers, également de l'une et l'autre religion par moitié; ils seront élus par les députés des huit corporations dont chacune ne donnera qu'une voix. De plus, un fisc inamovible et un greffier municipal, tous deux catholiques et choisis de la même manière. Leur solde sera attribuée à chacun selon son rang et en proportion des biens et des revenus de la ville; elle sera fixée par lesdits députés. Chaque bourgmestre, dont la place est supprimée jouira pendant sa vie d'une solde de 600 francs; les conseillers déposés jouiront également de leurs traitements leur vie durant et en même temps conserveront le titre honorifique de leur fonction, sans qu'ils aient toutefois la préférence, au cas où l'une ou l'autre des situations deviendrait vacante. Dans ce cas, les huit députés de corporations choisiront les sujets aptes à remplir le poste, et le présenteront aux six Conseillers, qui nommeront le plus capable d'entre eux; il prêtera alors serment à l'officier royal et au bourgmestre. Ce magistrat ainsi nommé devra exercer la haute, moyenne et basse justice, ainsi que la police.

Pour ce qui concerne l'administration des revenus de la ville, de l'hôpital, et des autres biens municipaux, les six Conseillers seuls en seront chargés; ils feront aussi la répartition des deniers royaux, et autres charges pesant sur leur ville, soit pour les besoins de l'Etat, ou ceux de la province, ou aussi pour ceux de la ville elle-même ou des Etats provinciaux, auxquels elle doit participer pour ce qui touche à son administration. Tous les comptes seront laissés à l'intendant-trésorier; à cette fin, les députés de corporations devront proposer deux sujets capables, parmi lesquels les six conseillers en choisiront un. Les six Conseillers devront être et rester les directeurs des huit corporations, et changeront tous les trois ans; bien entendu que chacun des deux plus anciens conseillers devra diriger deux corporations. Les six Conseillers disposeront de tout autre emploi de la ville, aussi bien ceux qui se rapportent à l'administration de la justice et des revenus municipaux, que les places de prêtres et autres.

Les députés devront solliciter le rappel du décret qui se rapporte à la juridiction des forêts et dont est chargé M. l'Intendant; car cette juridiction revient de par la loi à la ville, en communauté avec M. l'Evêque de Speier. Car ces forêts étant l'unique propriété et l'unique ressource de la ville de Wissembourg, et les dommages qui s'y sont produits depuis le susdit décret étant demeurés impunis, les députés devront insister pour que le procès intenté à ce sujet par l'intendance depuis longtemps déjà, arrive à sa fin.

Ils demanderont que les impôts sur la viande, le pain et le sel, en particulier les impôts au quarteron[27] à Wissembourg, et les douze sous sur chaque sac de fruits, soient abrogés; car ces taxes sont d'autant plus insupportables qu'elles s'exercent sur des choses inévitablement nécessaires; ils représenteront brièvement combien sont mal gérés les revenus de la ville et de l'hôpital, auquel on est redevable avec les impôts de 20,000 francs depuis plus de 60 ans; que l'évêque n'a pas encore été installé officiellement, bien que ses lettres patentes l'y autorisent; que les magistrats interviennent dans la ferme de la ville, qu'ils demandent des contributions excessives sur le bois à brûler; que les biens de la ville sont aliénés sous les yeux de tous; que la répartition de l'argent royal aussi bien que seigneurial est défectueuse, car les revenus municipaux ne s'en chargent que d'une partie, et il s'ensuit que la bourgeoisie est trop surchargée; les biens communaux devront être labourés et seront utilisés pour les besoins de la ville. Ils devront enfin représenter combien les bourgeois appartenant à la Confession d'Augsbourg sont injustement tenus de payer douze livres pour leur admission dans la ville, et dix-huit francs quand ils amènent une femme étrangère au pays. On est prêt à faire la preuve de toutes ces doléances devant un commissaire, que Sa Majesté est instamment priée de nommer.

[27] The German reads: "Vierlingssteuer."

Ville de Landau

Les griefs principaux que la ville présente, consistent en ce que leur zèle pour le service du roi les a chargés peu à peu d'une dette de 150,000 tt.[28] qui s'est accrue des quatre sièges qu'elle a eus à supporter dans ce siècle. Que l'honneur d'être une place forte de la frontière et le point capital de défense du royaume leur coûte très cher, car les bâtiments militaires qui reviennent à 300,000 tt. depuis cinquante ans, et leurs frais de matériel, indemnités de logement, cadeaux d'argent, et autres charges militaires s'élèvent annuellement à 25,000 tt. de plus, chacun connaît la perte réelle qui atteint les meilleurs propriétaires de fonds par les forts, redoutes et autres travaux de fortifications.

Il est vrai que la ville semble avoir une sorte de dédommagement par la présence de la garnison; mais sans raison, car chacun sait combien peu il est possible de gagner avec les garnisons, puisque celles-ci se procurent elles-mêmes tout le nécessaire, ainsi que les travailleurs de toutes sortes. Pour obtenir une indemnisation équitable et rétablir ainsi peu à peu les finances municipales, la ville attend du roi la libération de toutes les dépenses que nécessite l'organisation militaire, telles que bois de chauffage et lumière pour corps de garde, équipages, indemnités de logement qui doivent être payés aux officiers d'état-major et aux autres officiers résidant dans la place, impôts d'habitation, des magasins, et autres bâtiments.

La situation de la ville de Landau qui se trouve à moitié sur le territoire étranger est précisément ce qui entrave son commerce et la vente de ses produits; les nombreux octrois qui l'environnent, dont il existe trois sur la seule route de Wissembourg, retardent et affaiblissent toute circulation; d'où il résulte que différents commerçants et toutes sortes de travailleurs se sont installés dans les environs, et par là enlèvent aux habitants de Landau un très honorable bénéfice dont profitent les étrangers ne dépendant pas de la ville. Cet état de choses est d'autant plus mauvais que les taxes d'entrée et de sortie de la ville qui étaient doublées et même triplées, sont exigées avec sévérité par les employés d'octroi et de manière confuse et exorbitante. Elles empêchent les étrangers d'apporter les choses indispensables et nécessaires à la vie, et rendent la nourriture très chère dans l'intérieur de la ville. Afin d'empêcher cette situation fâcheuse, la ville supplie Sa Majesté de vouloir bien consentir la libre entrée et sortie de toutes sortes de marchandises au-dessous de . . .[29] et d'ordonner que le registre de douane institué pour les circonstances actuelles soit de nouveau

---

[28] The abbreviation, tt., may stand for teston, a silver coin of Lorraine or it may be the teston tournois, an almost obsolete French coin worth 10 sous. On coinage in Lorraine, see *Mémoires de la Soc. d'arch. Lorraine* . . . 1883, Vol. XI, pp. 1-106, and Vol. XII, 1884, pp. 1-43.

[29] The original German uses the word "Viertelszentner."

laissé à la connaissance de chacun et rédigé de manière plus détaillée afin que les affaires ne soient plus retardées, car les étrangers pourraient être exposés à de telles exactions qui empêcheraient les importations, seule ressource pour cette ville frontière qui, en considération de sa situation mérite d'être protégée.

En présence des commissaires désignés, ce mémoire ainsi composé a été lu à haute voix en assemblée publique; et après lecture faite, les deux députés de la ville de Schlestadt ont remarqué que le temps ne leur avait pas permis de rédiger leurs doléances comme ils l'auraient désiré; c'est pourquoi ils se proposent, avec le consentement de M.le Président, de présenter aux députés nommés pour la réunion des Etats généraux, un supplément de doléances et des indications spéciales concernant l'intérêt de leur bourgeoisie. Les députés d'Oberehenheim annoncent qu'ils solliciteront de Sa Majesté la réduction des magistrats et une nomination pour trois années. Ceux de Wissembourg ont dit qu'ils se rangeaient aux doléances de la ville de Landau, concernant la surcharge des douanes royales aussi bien que seigneuriales; et tous les députés, d'un commun accord se sont réservés de choisir au nom de leurs villes, les députés qui assisteront à l'Assemblée des Etats généraux et de leur remettre les rapports et les instructions selon leurs droits et organisations particuliers; tous les députés présents ont signé immédiatement. Fait à Schlestadt, le 31 mars 1789.

Et lesdits députés ont également fait la remarque suivante que l'ordre soit maintenu aussi bien dans la disposition du procès-verbal que dans les doléances présentes; également dans les affaires ultérieures de l'Assemblée présente; cet ordre ne doit être défavorable en rien aux séances régulières réglées par les traités et sera observé également par la Diète de l'empire. Les députés, en voulant prouver obéissance qu'ils doivent en tout, au mandat de leurs respectables chefs, n'ont pas cru devoir accentuer leurs requêtes; et le présent mémoire est tenu comme acceptable selon le décret des députés rassemblés.

Dans l'original, ont signé. Eggerlé, député de la ville de Colmar et commissaire; Debs, député de Colmar; Weiss, député de Haguenau et commissaire; Ignace Rädel, député de Haguenau; Stall, député de Schlestadt; Lohmuller, député de Schlestadt; Meyer, député de Kaysersperg; Franx Dietrich, député d'Oberehenheim; Hummel, député d'Oberehenheim; Kayser, député de Rossheim; Antoine Mercian, député de Rossheim; Bernard, député de Wissembourg et commissaire; Louis Esser, député de Wissembourg; Schattenmann, député de Landau et commissaire; Hurt, député de Landau et commissaire.

Que le mémoire ci-dessus semble avoir été traduit fidèlement de français en allemand; il a été signé Beck, avec parafe, avocat et interprète près le Haut Conseil royal, le 11 avril 1789.

Visé le même jour et transcrit dans le registre du bureau. Signé, Beck, syndic, avec parafe.

Plus loin, il est remarqué au procès-verbal: que, étant donné que les envoyés de la ville de Munster n'ont pas rempli leurs fonctions avec une autorité suffisante, ils ont été exclus de cette assemblée, et qu'à cause de leur non-comparution, la même mesure a été prise contre les députés de la ville de Thuringheim.

Fait à la mairie de Schlestadt, le 26 mars 1789.

NO. 12. THE CLERGY OF THE SENECHAUSSEE OF DRAGUIGNAN

P.V.-MS, *Arch. Nat.* Ba39 (*cf.* also Mireur, *Procès-verbaux des élections ... des sénéchaussées de Draguignan, Grasse, et Castellane,* 1891)

According to the p.v. the committee could not agree upon a text that would be a compilation of the preliminary cahiers. There was trouble between the Bishop of Glandèves, the Bishop of Frejus, and the curates. In the end the assembly adopted the cahier of the Bishop of Frejus with the understanding that the other preliminary cahiers be given the deputies. For a list of these cahiers, *cf.* Hyslop, B., *D.I., Repertoire critique des cahiers de doléances de 1789.*

Two cahiers are reprinted here, the text of the cahier of the Bishop of Frejus, and a text signed by the prior Manuel, which text is given because it alone of the other cahiers had received the verification of the lieutenant general of the *bailliage.* Both are defective in spelling, accents, and punctuation. The original MS texts are at the *Arch. Nat.* Ba39, original signatures. The *Archives Parlementaires* give one of the preliminary cahiers, Vol. III, p. 264.

Convocation: second type, reunion at Draguignan.

CAHIER DE DOLÉANCES
Religion

Le clerge doit demander a Sa Majesté la permission de tenir des conciles provinciaux dans le cas ou les assemblees generales du Clerge seraient supprimées a fin de s'occuper dans ces conciles des moyens de conserver la foi ou de maintenir la discipline ecclesiastique.

Mauvais Livres

Sa Majesté sera très humblement suppliée de prendre dans son conseil des mesures efficaces pour empecher l'introduction et les droits des livres contraires a la religion ou aux bonnes moeurs.

Colleges et petites écoles

Le Clerge doit se plaindre de ce que dans plusieurs colleges les bonnes etudes sont negligées, et la connaissance des verités de la religion presqu' abbandonée ce qui provient du peu d'autorité que l'édit de 1763 donne aux evêques sur les regens et la discipline des colleges. Il doit demander que les evêques ayent le droit de choisir les regents et de veiller sur la manière d'enseigner, et que nul ne puisse s'ingerer a tenir des écoles sans l'approbation de l'evêque et des curés.

Sanctification des Dimanches et Fetes

Demander que les anciennes loix concernant la sanctification des saints jours de dimanches et de fettes [fêtes] soient renouvellées, et qu'en consequence il soit enjoint aux officiers de police de veiller: 1) a ce que les oeuvres serviles cessent ces jours là. 2) a ce que tout divertissement public cesse absolument pendant le service divin de la paroisse le matin et le soir. 3) a ce que les cabarets soient exactement fermé pendant le même temps.

Parraines et marraines

Demander qu'il soit ordonné par une loi generalle qu'on n'admettra plus a l'avenir qu'un parrain ou une marraine au bateme, c'est-a-dire un parrain pour un garçon et une marraine pour une fille, conformement au voeu du consile de Trente et pour le même motif qu'en de diminuer autant qu'il est possible les empechements des marriages qui viennent de la compaternite.

Marriages

Demander que les marriages soient toujours publiés dans le lieu d'origine; qu'il soit tenu registre des publications, et que pour conserver dans les paroisses, la connaissance des actes de marriage, il soit ordonné que les parties qui se marieront hors de la paroisse où ils sont domiciliés seront tenues dans le mois de rapporter extrait de leur marriage, et de la faire enregistrer sur le registre de la paroisse ou ils sont domiciliés.

MM. les Agents Généraux

Demander que M.M. les Agents Généraux du Clerge soient appellés en cette qualité aux états généraux pour y porter les doléances dont ils ont connaissance par la place qu'ils occupent.

Objets de doléances temporel
Prévention

Le droit de prévention que le pape exerce au prejudice des patrons ecclesiastiques, a souvent excite des reclamations. Il est odieux en soi et nuisible a l'eglise, odieux en ce qu'il prive les patrons ecclesiastiques de leur droit, vainement le concile de latran leur a donne six mois pour nommer aux benefices vacants, s'ils peuvent être prevenus par le pape ou par ses officiers. Ce droit nuit essentielement a l'eglise en ce qu'il assure un benefice vacant a celui qui la demande le premier, qu'elle que soient d'ailleurs ses qualités.

Cet abus est bien plus grand en provence et en dauphiné qu'ailleurs a cause de la proximité de la vice legation d'Avignon.

Il en resulte cependant un avantage en ce que les benefices sont remplis sans delai.

Pour conserver cet avantage sans injustice et sans inconvenient on doit *demander que le pape ou son vice-legat ne pourront prevenir les collateurs ordinaires qu'un mois après la vacance des benefices.*

Patrons protestant

Par la declaration du 16 decembre 1656, article 5, il était ordonné que lorsqu'un patronage appartient a un seigneur qui fait profession de la R. P. R.[30] l'evêque devait conferer librement en cas de vacance sans prejudice du droit de la terre après l'empechement cessé. Il en a craindre qu'une jurisprudence contraire en est difficile et les evêques ne peuvent prononcer la suppression des places de vicaires inutiles, sans l'exposer a voir reformer leur jugement parcequ'il n'y a point de loi qui fixe quel nombre de paroissien est necessaire pour l'etablissement d'un ou d'un plus grand nombre de vicaires.

Pensions aux prêtres agés ou infirmes

Cette meme declaration ordonne encore qu'il sera pris de moyens pour assurer des pensions aux anciens pretres que leurs infirmités ou leur grand age contraignent a quitter les fonctions du ministere ce ne peut être encore qu'en unissant des benefices au diocese, il faut donc demander:

1.—Qu'il soit uni à chaque diocese des benefices simples jusqu'à la concurrence d'un revenu determiné pour ce revenu être regi et employé par le bureau diocesain.

2.—Qu'il soit rendu une declaration qui simplifie le plus qu'il sera possible les formalités pour les unions, et qui fixe le nombre d'habitans necessaire dans une paroisse pour avoir un ou plusieurs vicaires.

3.—Qu'il soit permis dans chaque diocese de reunir dans les memes lettres patentes et la meme procedure toutes les unions a faire.

Le clerge doit s'occuper en meme temps du sort des titulaires des eglises principales dont le revenu n'est pas suffisant.

Economats

Dans l'assemblée prochaine des états généraux le Clerge renouvellera sans doute la demande de la suppression des économats qui sont très onereux au clerge, qui par leur établissement auroient l'avantage de procurer la reparation des benefices mais qui dans le fait ne remplissent point cet objet, il n'en resulte ordinairement que du trouble dans la famille

[30] The protestant religion—Calvinism. The French words are "religion pretendue réformée."

du beneficier mort et un retardement de jouissance sans fin pour des établissements utiles fondés sur sa succession.

On a proposé de suppléer a leur defaut en chargeant les bureaux diocesain de veiller a l'entretien des biens et des titres des benefices. Ce moyen ne parait plus absolument assuré à cause de l'ascendant que les plus riches beneficiers peuvent avoir sur les membres du bureau diocesain.

On peut parer a cet inconvenience en nommant dans chaque province ecclesiastique des commissaires pris dans chaque diocese qui tout les ans visiteront les biens d'un diocese autre que celui où ils sont domicilés.

Alienation des biens d'eglise

L'alienation des biens d'église est un abus trop multiplié et trop pernicieux pour qu'on ne s'occupe pas des moyens d'y remedier. Ces moyens sont de demander au Roi:

1.—Qu'il lui plaise n'accorder que trés difficilement des lettres patentes pour des alienations ou des echanges.

2.—Qu'aucune alienation, echange ou bail emphiteotique ne puissent être fait sans le concours de l'evêque et du bureau diocesain, et dans le cas où il s'agirait des biens dependant de la manse episcopale sans le concours du chapitre de la cathedrale *et vice versa*.

3.—Qu'aucune alienation ne puisse être faite argent comptant, à moins d'une utilité evidente de l'emploi de la somme comptée, et qu'en cas de prestation annuelle, cette prestation ne soit jamais stipulée en argent, mais en denrées, qui soient appreciables tous les 10 ans d'après l'evaluation commune.

4.—Et comme il arrive que pour faciliter une alienation on suscite des litiges qu'on termine ensuite par une transaction dans laquelle les biens ecclesiastiques sont sacrifiés, Sa Majesté sera en même temps suppliée d'accorder aux successeurs la faculté de recourir d'une transaction pendant 30 ans a compter de la mort de celui qui a fait l'alienation et pendant les 3 premieres années de la possession du second successeur.

Dîmes

A l'égard des dimes on doit demander qu'il soit pris des moyens pour assurer les droits des decimateurs sans être vexatoires pour le peuple.

Droits Domaniaux

La perception des droits domaniaux est une source intarissable de plaintes non seulement par la facilité que les administrateurs ont d'obtenir des decisions nouvelles contraires aux precedentes, mais aussi par l'ignorance où sont toutes les particuliers au sujet de ces lois et plus encore par l'attribution des contestation a des tribunaux ou peu connus ou peu accessible.

Le clerge doit demander 1.—que la connaissance des contestations soit devolu aux cours souveraines. 2.—Que tout comme les particuliers sont soumis a un droit plus fort lorsqu'ils ont contrevenu aux ordonnances, les regisseurs soient obligés aussi à une peine lorsqu'il ont perçu au dela de ce qui est dû, au lieu qu'ils sont soumis seulement a restituer. 3.—Que toutes les nouvelles ordonnances ou decisions n'auront force de loi qu'en vertu des lettres patentes dument verifiées et suffisament publiée pour être connues.

Titres Clericaux

On demandera encore a ce sujet que les titres clericaux constitués par la desamparation [desemparation] d'un fonds, et en ligne directe tout seulement soient exempt du centieme denier a l'instar des donation par contract de marriage, jusqu'à la concurrence de la somme exigée dans chaque diocese pour les titres clericaux.

Em. Fr. evêque de Frejus

[Signatures of 3 curates and 3 other
clerical delegates.]

Paraphé ne varietur Draguignan, 6 avril 1789.

Lombard Paradin.

DOLÉANCES ET INSTRUCTIONS A REMETTRE AUX DEPUTÉS QUI SERONT ÉLUS
DANS L'ORDRE DU CLERGÉ ASSEMBLÉ À DRAGUIGNAN LE 27 MARS 1789.

Avant propos

L'assemblée dans sa seance du 28 Mars à nommé des commissaires pour indiquer ses doléances, lesquels commissaires ont dû s'occuper de ce travail dans la journée du lendemain Dimanche 29. lesdits redacteurs ayant déclaré dans la seance du lundy 30 n'avoir pû achever leur commission, le seigneur eveque de Frejus président l'assemblée declara vouloir terminé l'assemblée par la présente séance qui n'etoit pourtant que la troisieme, il se contenta de faire lire quelques observations particulieres qu'il avoit fait inserré d'avance dans le procès verbal, et malgré toutes réclamations ou contraires, il fit procéder à la nomination des électeurs, il fut cependant arretté que tous et chacun des deliberans feroient leurs doléances particulieres, pour toutes ses doléances etre unies au verbal sans rédaction avant de la seule voye qui m'a été donnée pour exprimer mon voeu aux états généraux du royaume, je soussigné déclare ce qui suit, et je vote.

1.—Pour qu'auxd. [aux dits] états généraux les suffrages soient recueillis non par ordre mais par tête.

2.—Si auxd. états généraux il est présenté quelques reglements concernant l'administration, les deputés de mon ordre suivront les lumieres de leur conscience dans leurs suffrages mais dans le cas, qu'après avoir fait tout leur possible pour s'instruire, leurs propre lumieres et les instructions puisées dans les lumieres d'autruy[31] les laissent encore dans l'indécision

---

[31] It was not clear whether this should read "d'autruy" or "d'autres."

et l'incertitude, ils rangeront leur opinion du coté de celle du ministre des finances qui jusqu'à ce jour a si bien mérité la confiance de la nation.

3.—Lesds [les dits]. Deputés feront la motion de demander humblement au Roy, l'établissement d'une loy qui fixe la convocation des états du royaume a une période fixe, et qui tout a chaque changement de régne, dans la forme qui luy a plû de les convoquer actuellement.

4.—Que si dans les inter-états il plait au Roy dans sa sagesse de promulguer une loy nouvelle ou déclaration, la verification de cette loy sera confiée aux états provinciaux en attendant la sanction des états généraux.

5.—Qu'il soit promulgué une loy qui exige l'adhésion aux quatre fameux articles du clergé de France assemblé en 1682 avant d'etre admis aux ordres sacrés d'etre pouvû [pourvu] de benefice quelconque, et que l'office de gregoire y sera supprimé de tous les bréviaires en usage dans l'étendue de la domination française.

6.—Lesd. [aux dits] Deputés uniront les réclamations et doléances à celles qui porteront vraisemblablement tous les ordres de l'Etat contre l'abus des lettres dites de Cachet.

7.—Ils rappelleront avec amertume le triste souvenir des troubles qui ont agité l'eglise et l'état pendant plus d'un siecle à l'occasion des disputes Theoligiques, et ils demanderont avec instance qu'il soit ordonné un corps d'enseignement et de doctrine redigé avec toute l'attention que mérite une pareille entreprise, pour lad. [la dite] doctrine etre enseignée, à l'exclusion de toute autre dans toutes les universités, tous les Seminaires et tous les colléges.

8.—Ils demanderont que dans toutes les villes, qui ont un arrondissement, il soit établi un cours d'accouchement, à la fin d'y former des sages femmes, destineés à etre répandues dans les villages et les campagnes; lesquelles sages-femmes ne pourront exercer leur ministère qu'après avoir subi le plus rigoureux examen, elles seront gagées par les communautés, sous l'inspection des curés et des consuls; non seulement elles iront gratuitement au secours des pauvres femmes en travail, mais elles les soigneront avec soin, et toujours gratuitement tant que leur personne aupres de la malade paroitra utile et nécessaire, le tout aux dépens de la communauté si la femme en couche est reconnue n'avoir pas des moyens par elle même.

9.—Ils remontreront les inconveniens qui peuvent résulter du privilege dont jouissent les seigneurs eveques de conferer les bénéfices par un acte déposé simplement dans les registres de leur secretariat et ils demanderont que cette collation soit faite par acte public avec notaire, controllé le même jour.

10.—Ils demanderont que la 2e ordre du clergé de chaque diocèse pris dans toutes les classes soit authorisé à s'assembler annuellement sous les yeux Seigneur eveque a l'effet d'y agiter les affaires qui leur sont communes, et de proceder a l'election libre de deux sindics chargés de veiller à la conversation de leurs droits.

Si mieux n'aiment les seigneurs eveques assemblés tous les ans leur sinode conformément aux saints canons.

11.—Ils demanderont le redressement du tort fait à 2e classe de leur ordre dans les assemblées générales du clergé, le 2e ordre n'y est point representé, amoins qu'on ne veuille donner le nom de son représentant à un phantome de deputé pris aux choix des seigneurs evêques par tour de vicars, et dans la classe de ceux qui ont des prétentions aux graces, ce sont néanmoins ces deputés qui conjointement avec les prélats deliberont les dons gratuits faits au Roy, et que tous les autres objets qui interressent l'ordre entier du clergé.

Lesd [les dits] Deputés demanderont donc que la 2e classe soit représentée dans ces assemblées générales par deux deputés; élus librement au nombre de deux dans les dioceses auxquels la députation appartiendra, de plus ils demanderont que l'agence générale du clerge soit confiée a trois individus dont l'un pris dans la premiere classe, Le second dans la classe des chanoines, et le troisieme dans la classe des bénéficiers.

12.—Ils demanderont le redressement du tort fait a leur classe dans la levée et la répartition des decimes, et qu'en consequence il soit établi dans chaque diocese un bureau légal qui commencera ses fonctions par se faire rendre un compte exact et détaillé de l'administration actuelle depuis dix ans, ce bureau dont les membres seront pris dans toutes les classes des contribuables et elus par les contribuables mêmes tous les cinq ans établira des regles fixes et connües de tout le monde par la maniere dont il sera procédé a la répartition, il nommera un trésorier ou receveur qui rendra ses compte tous les ans au bureau assemblé de plus il sera donné tous les ans un tableau de situation de l'etat de la caisse, et ce tableau sera rendu public par l'impression.

13.—Les cures à simple congrüe seront exemptées de l'imposition des décimes, parce que la portion congrüe ne pouvant être regardée que comme une pension alimentaire, doit être exempte de toute charge.

14.—Lesd. Deputes releveront avec force et respect l'injure faite a la 2e classe de leur ordre par le peu d'inffluence qui luy est donné dans la manière avec laquelle sont traitées les matières les plus graves comme la relorme des rituels, des bréviares, des cathechismes et autres livres de même nature, à la confection desquels il ne sauroit pourtant être porté trop de circonspection, et ils demanderont que, dans le cas que le voeu qu'ils forment pour la confection d'un rituel, d'un breviaire, d'un cathéchisme commun a toute l'eglise gallicane ne soit point exaucé, toutes les fois qu'il s'agira dans un diocèse d'un changement à faire dans les livres cy dessus enoncés, le seigneur eveque soit tenu non seulement de prendre l'avis de son chapitre, des églises collegiales, et de tous ses curés, mais qu'il fasse part du changement projeté à tous les parties de son diocese séculiers et réguliers, afin que tous ces avis particuliers puissent etre ensuite puisament pesés dans un sinode libre que nul peut donner la sanction ou de changement.

15.—Lesd. Deputes releveront le tort fait aux droits divins et imprescriptibles des curés par les seigneurs evêques en les privant du choix de leurs cooperateurs, et il sera demandé que les curés rentrent pleinement dans ce droit naturel qui inflüe si fort à la conversation du bon ordre dans les paroisses, que les vicaires une fois établis sur une paroisse ne puissent en etre tirés que du consentement des curés, ou selon les règles de droit.

16.—Lesd. Deputes releveront le tort fait a la 2e classe de leur ordre par l'abus que tout de leurs pouvoirs les seigneurs evêques en interdisent l'exercise des fonctions sacrées du ministére . . . des pretres qui n'ont souvent contre eux que des delations sourdes et calomnieuses, ces interdits arbitraires sont une des plus grandes playes de l'eglise de france, non seulement ils compromettent l'honneur des pretres en donnant lieu aux peuples de soupçonner leurs doctrines ou leurs moeurs; mais ils empechent un grand nombre d'enfants de famille, effrayés de ces vexations d'entrer dans l'état ecclésiastique.

Ils releveront encore l'abus de cet usage contraire au droit commun, et tout recemment etabli par la pluspart des ordinaires de ne confier l'administration des sacremens aux pretres qui leur sont subordonnés que pour un an, après lequel terme leurs pouvoirs cessent et sont coupés être nuls c'est la reforme de ces abus qui exitera la réclamation desd. Deputés, à cet effet ils supliront humblement le Roy de vouloir bien retirer et rendre nulles nombre de ses déclarations prejudices à la religion, et tendantes à affaiblir les droits de la 2e classe de son clerge qui implore une protection contre les exemptions et vexations qu'il eprouve de la part de la première classe, que par un effet de sa justice et de sa pieté la hierarchie ecclesiastique soit rétablie dans son intégrité, afin que les seigneurs eveques, premiers pasteurs de leurs dioceses mais non pasteurs uniques ne puissent interdire les saintes fonctions des ministres aux pretres, qu'ils ont une fois trouvé dignes de leur confiance, qu'après les avoir charitablement pourvus des plaintes formées contre eux, qu'après que ceux-cy auront eu le moyen de produire leurs deffences et qu'ils auront ensuite été trouvés indignes de l'exercice des saintes fonctions des ministres.

Le tout afin que la condition des ecclésiastiques ne soit pas pire que celle des autres citoyens, qui, sous la protection des loix, sont assurés de conserver leur état, et de jouir des privileges qui y sont attachés, tant qu'ils en remplissent les devoirs avec fidélité.

17.—Lesd. Députés représenteront les inconvénients qui résultent tant de l'évocation d'un grand nombre d'affaires ecclésiastiques au grand conseil, ou à ia grand-chambre du parlement de Paris, en ce qui concerne la régale, que de tous autres privileges tendans à decliner les jurisdictions locales, tous ces privileges sont abusifs puisqu'ils ne tendent qu'à mettre les armes dans la main du plus fort contre le plus faible, ils feront sentir combien il est ruineux pour les habitans de notre province et de toutes les autres provinces, éloignées du centre du Royaume de se transporter a grands frais a deux cens [cent] lieues de leur domicile pour défendre leurs droits.

Ils demanderont donc la revocation de tous ces privileges et autres s'il en a, a l'exception des privileges attachés en la personne des commencaux de la maison du Roy, lesquels n'auront lieu cependant que pour le temps de leur service, et ils feront tous leurs efforts pour obtenir que tous les sujets du Roy et les ecclèsiastiques en particulier ne puissent etre obliges de comparaitre que devant les tribunaux ordinaires et locales au moins qu'il ne plaise au Roy d'ordonné qu'il soit crée dans chaque paroisse ecclésiastique un tribunal presidé par un des seigneurs eveques de lad. province nommé a cet effet par Sa Majesté, et composé de douze docteurs en droit canon, lesquels ne seront admis qu'apres le plus scrupuleux examen de leur science et vertu ... ce tribunal provincial connaitrait de toutes les affaires purement ecclèsiastiques et ne serait assemblé que pour un temps limité après les quinzaines de paques et de Noël.

18.—Leds. Deputés feront la motion de suplier humblement le Roy d'ordonner dans chaque diocèse l'établissement d'un fonds destiné au soulagement des pauvres curés et autres ecclesiastiques—qui affaiblis par l'age et les infirmités, ne soupirent après avoir travaillé a la sanctification de leurs terres, qu'a n'avoir plus à travailler qu'à leur propre sanctification, et qu'il soit en conséquence ordonné d'assemblée en chaque diocèse un sinode à la fin de pourvoir a cette dette de justice et de charité il semble que la suppression d'une multitude de benefices simples à collation ecclesiastiques parait plus que suffisante pour fournir les fonds necessaires à cet établissement.

19.—Enfin comme il parait que tous les voeux de la nation ramenée aux sentimens de justice et d'equité tendant une repartition égale et proportionelle de toutes les charges de l'état entre les trois ordres du clergé, de la noblesse et du tiers-etat, lesd. Deputés feront observer que si l'ordre du clergé consent a partager tout le poids des impots avec le reste de la Nation, il parait aussi qu'il est de toute justice que la Nation se charge de la dette du clergé, pour la partie qui en differentes epoques n'a été empruntée que pour fournir aux puissans besoins de l'etat.

Tels sont les voeux et sentimens a Draguignan ce premier Avril mil sept cent quatre vingt neuf.

Maurel, prieur
Paragraphé ne Varietur Draguignan
6 Avril 1789.
Lombard Parady[32]

[32] The lieutenant general for Draguignan.

NO. 13. THE CLERGY OF THE BAILLIAGES OF ETAIN

Cahier reprinted from MS text—*Arch. Meuse* (unclassified), original signatures.
P.V.-MS, *Arch. Nat.* Ba 19. There were four members of the committee. The cahier was adopted before the elections, which began March 26. Convocation: 2d type; reunion at Bar-le-duc.

L'ORDRE DU CLERGE DU BAILLIAGE D'ETAIN

Plaintes, Doléances, et Remontrances du Clergé du Bailliage d'Étain assemblé aux termes de la Convocation donnée à Versailles, le 24 Janvier, de la présente année, 1789, et suivant l'ordonnance de Monsieur le Lieutenant-Général audit Bailliage, rendue en conséquence, le deux du mois de Mars de la dite année.

Paragraphe 1

Le premier devoir d'un corps ecclésiastique, c'est de s'occuper de la Religion en général.

Le clergé du Bailliage d'Étain désire avant toutes choses:

1.—Que toutes les loix faites en faveur de la Religion et des bonnes moeurs soient maintenus et protégées: que la Police la plus exacte soit établie dans toutes les Paroisses, afin d'éviter les désordres, la ruine des familles, souvent occasionnées par la fréquentation des Cabarets.

2.—Que la Liberté excessive de la presse soit réprimée, et que les anciennes ordonnances y relatives soient exécutées, Les campagnes commencent a être infectées du poison contenu dans les mauvais Livres qui portent avec eux la corruption des moeurs, la perte de la foi et le renversement de l'ordre dans la Société.

Paragraphe 2

Nous allons ensuite exprimer nos Voeux pour le bien général du Royaume, celui des provinces, et particulièrement celui du Tiers état dont les intérêts nous serons toujours aussi chers que les notres.

1.—Que l'assemblée des États-Généraux veuille bien s'occuper d'abord de la forme et de la constitution des assemblées Nationales, et en fixer le retour périodique au terme qu'elle jugera le plus convenable.

2.—Qu'elle assure la propriété et la liberté de tout Citoyen, de manière qu'aucun Sujet du Roy ne puisse être privé de sa Liberté, qu'en vertu des Loix protectrices du repos public.

3.—Que les États-Généraux s'occupent de la grandeur du déficit et des dettes de l'État, ainsi que des moyens de les réparer: que pour y parvenir, tous les sujets du Roi, Ecclésiastiques, Nobles, Privilégiés, Roturiers, sans aucune exception, payent à l'avenir leur cotte part de toutes les Impositions pécuniaires, en raison de leurs forces et facultés; et qu'aucun impôt ne soit établi, qu'il n'ait été voulu et consenti par les États Généraux légalement convoqués en assemblée.

4.—Qu'on simplifie la perception des impôts, ruineuse pour le peuple, onéreuse et inutile à L'État.

5.—Qu'il y ait révision et réduction des Pensions, et, qu'à l'avenir, elles ne puissent être accordée qu'au seul mérite, sans faveur ni distinction d'état.

6.—Que toutes les Provinces du Royaume, et notamment celle de Lorraine-Barrois, ayent leurs États-Provinciaux; que l'organisation en soit formée par les États Généraux, et que les Ordres y jouissent, dans les Déliberations, des mêmes avantages que dans les États Généraux.

7.—Que les États Généraux veuillent bien, après avoir établi et consolidé les Provinces, en Pays d'états, rappeler à ceux qui composeront leurs assemblées le Désintéressement et la générosite qui doivent les animer; et combien il est important de les rendre les moins dispendieuses possible.

8.—Que pour ce qui regarde la justice, il paroit bien essentiel de travailler à un nouveau Code Civil et criminel, clair, précis, et s'il étoit possible, commun à toutes les Provinces; de Simplifier les formes de la Justice, d'en diminuer les frais, d'en accélérer les jugements, et de supplier le Roi de renoncer aux droits qui lui reviennent des Jugements. Quant à l'inamovibilite des Magistrats, à l'age et aux qualités requises pour entrer dans la Magistrature, on s'en rapporte à la Sagesse et à la Prudence des États Généraux.

9.—Qu'il paroitroit utile au bien public et en particulier, d'établir une Justice dans chaque Lieu, qui empêcheroit les injustices et les vols si communs dans les Campagnes: Le plan à suivre, pour y réussir pourroit être que le Sindic de la Communauté ou Municipalité seroit, dans les matières du fait, Le premier juge, et auroit deux Elus pour adjoint: les Délinquents seroient cités pardevant eux, verbalement, par le doyen de la Communauté, sur la plainte que la partie laizée auroit formée; l'un et l'autre déduiroit contradictoirement leurs raisons; les faits seroient verifiés sur place, et à temps: On jugeroit aussi des anticipations qui se font si souvent sur les biens communs et particuliers: et le tout mûrement examiné, on jugeroit ce que de droit, et toujours la restitution de la chose usurpée; ce qui S'opéreroit sans frais, ou à moindres frais possibles, et sans écritures, excepté l'inscription du Jugement au Greffe de la justice locale; lequel Jugement, en cas d'appel, le Juge ultérieur se feroit représenter. Delà résulteroit plusieurs avantages.

1.—Le pauvre obtiendroit sur place une justice que son indigence ne lui permet pas d'aller chercher ailleurs: 2.—le Délinquant seroit surveillé et souvent prévenu, perdroit toutes ses ressources de Chicanes, et craindroit de se voir mal-noté au Greffe de son Lieu. 3.—Les Juges locaux seroient obligés d'insérer dans leur Jugement les motifs qui les auroient déterminés à le rendre et si le Sindic se trouvoit parent ou allié d'une des parties, il lui seroit ordonné de préférer la justice à toute considération, ou seroit supplée par un autre membre de la même justice. 4.—Le Juge de l'appel verroit, dans le premier jugement, la pensée des gens de la justice du lieu, qui sont plus à même que personne de connoitre les délits et la vie rapace de certains pertubateurs des Paroisses, qui, par leurs menaces, en imposant effronté- ment à ceux qu'ils vexent. 5.—Les officiers établis pour rendre et faire rendre la justice dans les sièges Royaux, ne seroient occupés qu'a des affaires dignes de leurs soins et de leur Ministère.

10.—Qu'il soit établi dans chaque ville du Royaume des Magasins à proportion de l'étendue de leur arrondissement; et qu'il soit pourvu par le Roi, conjointement avec les états de chaque Province aux moyens d'ap- provisiomens, ces Magasins dans les années d'abondance, pour le bled [blé] en être distribué aux pauvres, au prix le plus modique possible, dans les années de disette et de chéreté; pour facilité aussi le Laboureur qui, dans les circonstances fâcheuses, se trouvant dénué de Bled, pour- roit se pourvoir de la quantité qui lui seroit nécéssaire; à charge par lui de remplacer la même quantité qu'il auroit perçue; à charge encore par lui d'être muni pour en obtenir, d'une attestation signée de la Justice locale et du curé, qui constateroit son besoin.

11.—Que le mendicité source d'une infinité de désordres soit prohibée dans les campagnes; et que les biens, tels que partie des Dimes qui ont été données pour le soulagement des pauvres, soient versés dans une caisse par- ticulière, et que la distribution s'en fasse par les principaux des Lieux, sous la surveillance des Curés.

12.—Qu'il est intérréssant de rompre toutes les entraves qui gênent le Commerce dans l'intérieur du Royaume qu'en conséquence il faudroit sup- primer tous les droits d'aides, de Traites-foraines, de Transits, et notam- ment ceux du Verdunois et du Pays-Messin; Droits qui rendent les Pro- vinces étrangères les unes aux autres.

13.—Que le Sel étant une denrée de première nécéssité pour les hommes, si utile pour les animaux; il seroit à désirer qu'il fut rendu commerçable, ainsi que le tabac.

14.—Que le cuir étant d'un besoin absolu à tous les hommes et surtout aux Cultivateurs, tant pour eux que pour les harnois, il est nécéssaire de l'exempter de Marque et de tout impôt afin d'en diminuer le prix excessif et inoui jusques à present; Ces impôts faisant un tort considérable au peuple, sans apporter aucun soulagement à l'Etat.

15.—Qu'il soit avisé de nouveaux moyens plus simples et moins coûteux, pour la conservation et administration des Bois, qu'il soit reglé que le Bois de charbon aura un Etalon fixe et certain et que le surplus des Coupes sera mis en bois marchand et en bois d'oeuvre.

16.—Qu'il est d'une nécessité urgente de réduire les forges et usines à feu vu la pénurie des bois qu'elles causent. Cet article n'échappera pas, sans doute au zéle et à la vigilance de nos représentans aux Etats Généraux ils observeront que, quoique le fer soit une branche de commerce, propre à amener du Numéraire en france, il ne sert souvent qu'à grossir la fortune d'un citoyen, tandis que mille autres en souffrent.

17.—Que les clos devenant nuisibles à l'agriculture, en ce qu'ils enlèvent aux Communautés le parcours libre et commun, il paroit essentiel qu'il soit dérogés, par une Loi générale, aux privilèges qui, jusqu'à présent les ont autorisés.

18.—Que les Curés qui voyent de plus près ce qui est préjudiciable aux campagnes regardent comme tels la trop grande quantité de Colombiers; pour un, plus grand bien, et sans déroger au respect du à toute propriété, ne pourroit on pas en diminuer le nombre, vû les dommages inappreciables causés par tant de pigeons, surtout dans les tems de semence et de récolte.

19.—Que dans les Lieux où le Roi est Seigneur, les amendes de ses fermiers se perçoivent au Profit des fabriques locales, tandis que celles des admodiateurs ou fermiers des autres Seigneurs, tournent uniquement au Profit de leurs Maitres ce qui ne peut qu'autoriser les délits qui se commettent dans les Campagnes; En conséquence il seroit à désirer que les Seigneurs, conformement à l'exemple du Souverain, fissent le même emploi des amendes prononcées contre leurs ádmodiateurs et fermiers.

Paragraphe 3

Peu de mots vont former les doléances du Clergé du Bailliage d'Étain. Sa Majesté et les États Généraux sont très humblement Suppliés:

1.—De conserver aux Curés la confiance si precieuse à leur coeur, dont Sa Majesté daigne les honorer dans la circonstance présente.

2.—Que leurs droits et Priviléges soient reconnus dans la tenuë des États libres et généraux, ou ils doivent être admis comme Electeurs et Éligibles, toujours dans leur Classe, pour les représenter soit aux Etats Généraux, Provinciaux, ou autres assemblées du Clergé qui auront lieu à l'avenir.

3.—Qu'il soit pourvu aux besoins des Curés et Vicaires Portionnaires qui relativement à la misère présenté, sont reduits dans une condition au dessous de leur Etats, et sont veritablement à plaindre.

4.—Que le droit commun soit la Base et la Règle pour tous les autres Curés.

5.—Que dans le cas ou des Curés opteroient la portion congrue, Les Terres attacheés à leur Cure leur restent, à moins que l'on ne prouve pas bons et vallables Titres, que lesdites Terres ont été données pour dotation de leur Bénéfice.

6.—Qu'à l'avenir tous Curés, Vicaires autres Écclésiastiques puissent, sans aucun Titre de Nobless, obtenir et posséder des Prébendes de Cathédrales, et autres Chapitres.

7.—Que les Ecclésiastiques Seculiers et Reguliers ayent la liberté de faire des Échanges de biens amortis avec d'autres biens amortis sans être obligés de payer aucun droit d'amortissement ni Centieme denier à raison de ces Échanges.

8.—Que les Curés possédées par des Réguliers, et qui ne leur ont été accordées dans les tems, qu'à cause de la pénurie de Prêtres Séculiers, retournent à leur première destinantion à la mort de Chaque Titulaire actuel.

9.—Que le droit de Déport dans les Archidiacres se prévalent pour priver les Curés entrants des premiers fruits de leur Cure, soit annulle; le même bénéfice ne pouvant appartenir à deux Titulaires à la fois.

10.—Que la portion des Impôts à acquitter par le Clergé pour subvenir aux besoins de l'État, lui soit assignée particulièrement.

11.—Que la somme totale pour la province relativement au Clergé, soit divisée par Bailliage dans les États Provinciaux.

12.—Que les biens Écclésiastiques et tous les Bénéfices dépendant desdits Bailliages, soit que les Titulaires y aient le Chef de leur résidence ou non, soient imposés par un bureau qui y sera établi, sans frais, à la pluralité des suffrages, composé des Curés et autres Écclésiastiques y ayant droit.

13.—Qu'afin de connoître l'État des contributions données d'après l'abonnement de 1756, et soldé jusqu'à présent, les Receveurs des Décimes cydevant réparties sur la partie Lorraine du Diocèse de Verdun, soient tenus de rendre compte par devant les Curés choisis à cet effet par leurs confrères et autres Écclésiatiques qui y auroient intérêt; afin de combler le Déficit, s'il y en a, ou récupérer le Bon qui pourroit en résulter.

14.[33]—Que le Clerge Lorrain soit charger de payer ses dettes, s'il en a, sans pouvoir être forcé d'entrer dans celles contractées par les Clergé françois.

15.—Que pour tout ce qui regarde en général les abus à retrancher, soit dans l'église, soit dans l'Etat; pour tout ce qui peut avoir trait à régéneration du Royaume; enfin, ce qui auroit du rapport aux bonnes moeurs, au bien public et à l'avantage particulier de cette Province, on s'en rapporte à la prudence, à la Sagesse, aux lumières et à la probité de tous ceux qui composeront les Etats Généraux.

Le présent cahier rédigé par M.M.Joly curé de Bouvigny, Collignon Curé de Norois-le-Sec, Bigeat[34] Curé de Sareid, et Toussaint Curé de Gondrecourt, Commissaires nommés à cet effet par l'assemblée du Clergé du Bailliage d'Étain, à été arrêté définitivement, tant par lesdits Commissaires, par nous Jean-Baptiste Claude Achille Marquis de Nettancourt Chevalier Seigneur de Nubécourt, Wandlainville, et autres lieux, Bailli d'épée audit Bailliage, président l'assemblée des trois Ordres, et par M. Creite Curé d'Étain, Président de l'assemblée du Clergé, et par Monsieur Bléhée Sec-

---

[33] The handwriting beginning with article 14 differs from the rest of the text.

[34] In the p.v. this name would appear to be Bigeard, and the signature at the end of the cahiers Bigear.

retaire dudit Clergé à Étain en la Salle du balcon de l'hotel de Ville à nous designée, le 26 mars, 1789, fait double, et lecture faite, approuvé, avant Signatures la rature et le surcharge qui se trouvent à la dixième ligne de la quatrième page; approuvé aussi le changement d'écriture qui se trouve aux deux dernières pages.

Creitte, president, . . . [twenty-three signatures, plus]
Bléhée Cure de Misible secretaire de l'ordre.

NO. 14. THE THIRD ESTATE OF THE BAILLIAGE OF ETAIN

Cahier reprinted from MS text—*Arch. Meuse,* original signatures.
P.V.-MS, *Arch. Nat.* Ba. 19. There were 9 members for the committee. The cahier was adopted before the election began March 25. The assembly was tumultuous and disorderly.
Convocation: 2d type, reunion at Bar-le-duc.

CAHIER DES PLAINTES, DOLÉANCES ET REMONTRANCES DU TIERS-ÉTAT DU BAILLAGE D'ÉTAIN POUR ESTRE PORTÉ A L'ASSEMBLÉE QUI SE TIENDRA A BAR LE 31 MARS PRÉSENT DU MOIS ET FAITES A SA MAJESTÉ DANS LES ETATS GÉNÉRAUX QUI SE TIENDRONT A VERSAILLES, LE 27 AVRIL PROCHAIN

Nos Maux sont Grands, ils sont connus; et puisque la bonté de Sa Majesté veut, pour y rémedier, en chercher la source, on la trouvera dans les objets sur lesquels vont tomber les demandes cy-aprés, que chargeons les députés qui nous représenteront aux Etats Généraux de faire pour nous, avec la confiance qu'ils les appuyeront de tout leur Pouvoir, et quelles seront favorablement Ecoutées par notre bon Roy.

Ils demanderont donc, au nom du Baillage D'Étain

Article 1

Qu'il soit procédé d'abord, à la redaction des Loix Constitutionnelles.

2.—Que la tenue des Etats Généraux soit renouvellée à des Epoques périodiques qui seront déterminées.

3.—Quaux Etats Généraux le Tiers-Etat ne puisse être représenté que par des membres de son ordre.

4.—Que les Suffrages n'y soient pris par tête qu'autant que les députés du Tiers-Etat seroient en plus Grand nombre que ceux du clergé et de la Noblesse réunis, mais qu'en cas qu'on vôte par ordre, l'avis du Tiers-Etat fasse seul Balance, et qu'appuyé de celui d'un des deux autres, il fasse décision.

5.—Qu'il soit accordée des Etats Particuliers à cette Province.

6.—Que la Noblesse désormais, ne soit accordée qu'au mérite distingué et non à l'argent, et en conséquence que les offices qui ennoblissent demeurent supprimés à mesure qu'ils viendront à vaquer, sans que les Titulaires actuels puissent les résigner.

7.—Que Toutes Loix qui excluent le Tiers-Etat de quelques Emplois ou dignitées Ecclesiastiques, civiles et militaires soient supprimées, comme injustes et injurieuses; sauf à Sa Majesté dans la distribution à donner la préférence aux nobles, quand elle jugera à propos.

8.—Qu'on admette les gens du Tiers-Etat, en tel nombre qu'il plaira à Sa Majesté, non seulement dans toutes les parties de l'Administration, afin de veiller à la conservation de ses droits mais encore dans tous les Tribunaux Supérieurs.

9.—Que toutes corvées personnelles envers les Seigneurs soient supprimés ou au moins rachetées.

10.—Que le tirage de la Milice soit supprimé.

11.—Qu'aucune lettre de cachet ne puisse être accordé, que sur une déliberation de famille.

12.—Qu'en tout autre cas, tout citoien arrêté soit remis dans les vingt-quatre heures aux juges ordinaires.

13.—Qu'il ne soit fait aucune imposition n'y Etabli aucune nouvel impôt sans le consentement des Etats-Généraux.

14.—Que les Ministres soient tenus de rendre compte, de leur Gestion à Sa Majesté dans les Etats Généraux.

15.—Que toutes les pensions soient vérifiées et moderées si l'Echet.

16.—Qu'aucune pension ou gratification nouvelle ne soit accordé sans le consentement des Etats-Généraux.

17.—Que la presse soit libre.

18.—Que les impositions de toutes espèces qui ne tombe que sur le Tiers, comme subvention, Pont et chaussée, Tailles d'exploitation, industrie, imposition representative des Corvées, bien moins supportable que cette charge en nature etc., etc., soient supprimés.

19.—Que toutes autres impositions qui ne tombent pas égallement sur la Généralité des personnes des Trois Ordres sans distinction, et sur les biens de toutes espèces sans exception, comme vingtieme etc. soient supprimés.

20.—Que les impôts deguisés, qui ne tombent que sur le Tiers, comme les droits de franc-fief etc., soient supprimés.

21.—Que les impôts connus, et déguisés, sous quelque nom que ce soit, qui mettent des entraves au commerce, et désolent surtout le Peuple, comme ceux compris dans la ferme Générale, la vente exclusive du Sel, et du Tabac, les Traites foraines etc. Les droits en régie; sur les papiers, poudres, amidon, marque des Cuirs, marques des fers, cinque sols pour Livres sur les Octrois des Villes, accessoires etc. . . . les Droits Dommaniaux administrés, Gallage, Coupelle, Encanage, faciente de Bievre, Riflerie, Chatrerie, Les Parchemins et Papiers, Timbres, le Sceau, le contrôle, sauf seulement une rétribution modique et innaviable [unidentified word] pour le Salaire de ces dernières formalités sur les actes qui en sont susceptibles sans égard au nombre n'y à la valeur des objets y énoncés, etc. Les droits d'amortissement au moins pour les échanges avec les gens de main morte etc., même les droits de Péage, ou Transit qui ont este accordés à la sollicitation imprudente de quelques Villes ou Cantons; comme ceux sur le vin dans le Verdunois en Pays Messin etc., soient supprimés.

22.—Que les Bannalités de Moulins, fours et Pressoirs soient supprimés ou au moins Rachetés.

23.—Qu'il soit fait un réglement Général, uniforme relativement à la quotité et Perception des Dixmes tant Grosses que Menues, qui sont une source intarissable de Procès dans le Royaume.

24.—Que le Collombiers [les colombiers] soient supprimés, ou au moins leur nombre excessif modérés et les Pigeons renfermés pendant les semailles et moissons.

25.—Que les haras, qui ne reussissent pas dans cette province soient supprimés.

26.—Qu'il soit fait une vérification générale de tous les droits, perçus ou prétendus, au nom des Seigneurs sur leurs Vassaux, qui en sont accablés, comme terrages, Cens, Rentes, etc. afin de ne laisser subsister que ceux qui auront esté reconnu Légitimes, et que tous les autres soient supprimés.

27.—Qu'il soit établi une Chancellerie Ecclesiastique en France.

28.—Que sous prétexte d'annates, ou autres droits, il ne soit plus envoyer d'argent en cours de Rôme.

29.—Que le droit de Déport ou autres semblables qui dépouille les Curés d'une partie de leur subsistance pendant la première année de leur exercice, soit supprimés.

30.—Que l'ordre du Clergé prenne les arrangements nécessaires pour faire disparoitre la disproportion qui se trouve entre les Revenus des Bénéfices de la même nature, et qu'après avoir suffisamment pourvus chacun d'eux suivant les besoins et la dignité de leur Etat, s'il se trouve quelques choses de superflu, il soit appliqué aux besoins de L'état, de manière cependant, qu'aucuns des Curés du Royaume n'aye moins de douze cent Livres de revenus; et qu'il y'en ait dans tous les villages qui en sont susceptibles; au moien de quoi toutes les rétributions sur les Paroisses supprimées.

31.—Que les revenus des commandes et Bénéfices vacant, sans charge Dame [d'ame], soient mis en Sequestre dans chaque province, jusqu'au payement des dettes de l'État.

22.—Qu'en cas de suppression de quelques maisons Religieuses, le revenue en soit mis en séquestre jusqu'à la même Epoque, sauf ensuite à en remettre les Bien en communs; à l'effet de quoy on s'occupera de l'examen et distinction de celles qui sont vraiment utiles et de celles qui ne le sont pas.

33.—Que toutes les contributions nécessaires pour fournir aux charges de toutes espèces du Royaume soient imposés sur toutes les personnes des

Trois Ordres sans distinction, en proportion de leurs forces et facultés, et sur tous les Biens immeubles sans exception.

34.—Qu'il ne soit établi des impôts que sur les objets de luxe dans l'intérieur du Royaume.

35.—Que les Officiers Municipaux soient supprimés et les officiers rendus Électifs et Triannaux.

36.—Que les seuls habitans des Communautés des paroisses soient admis dans les assemblées et délibérations des affaire communalles.

37.—Qu'il soit pourvus par les États provinciaux à la Recette et à l'emploi; des Bois et biens des Communautés, de facon à produire des interêts aux dittes communautés.

38.—Qu'il soit avisé aux moyens de favoriser et faire fleurir L'agriculture à l'effet de quoy réduire l'extention de Ledit des clôtures aux Prairies artificielles.

39.—Que les anciennes et nouvelles maitrises d'arts et métiers soient supprimées.

40.—Que tous privilèges exclusifs en matière D'industrie et de Commerce soient supprimés.

41.—Que les salines soient supprimées.

42.—Que le nombre de forges soit réduit.

43.—Que tous ceux des offices civils, Militaires, et de finances qui sont couteux et peu utiles soient supprimés.

44.—Que les Offices qui sont notoirement à charge au peuple sans aucune utilité, comme ceux des jurés priseurs, Vendeurs soient supprimés.

45.—Qu'il soit fait une grande Réforme dans L'Administration des Eaux et forets.

46.—Que les Grand Maitres et Maitrises soient supprimés et les choses rétablies sur l'ancien pied.

47.—Que les justices Seigneurialles soient supprimées; afin que la justice soit administrée aux fidéles sujets du Roy, par les Officiers de Sa Majesté ou en tout cas, que les justices Seigneurialles ne soient conservées qu'à condition que les Seigneurs auront des officiers innamovibles et résident sur place, qui ne pourront avoir entrée dans les Municipalités et que les amendes de Misus contre les Seigneurs et leurs amodiateurs soient appliquées aux fabriques.

48.—Que ceux des Tribunaux D'attribution ou d'exception, qui ne seront pas trouvés d'une utilité évidente soient supprimés; ainsi que les Privilèges de Committimus et autres semblables.

49.—Qu'il n'y ait qu'un Poid et sous une seule dénomination, pour tout le Royaume.

50.—Que toutes les mesures d'étendue et de contenance seront réduites à une seule de chacque espèce et sous une même dénomination dans tout le Royaume ou au moins dans la Province.

51.—Que les différentes coutumes soient réduite en une seule dans le Royaume, s'il est possible, ou au moins dans la province.

52.—Qu'il soit fait un code de droit général pour tout le Royaume.

53.—Qu'il n'y ait en toutes affaires que deux degrés de juridiction.

54.—Que les formes des procédures civille soient simplifiées et abbreviées.

55.—Que le code criminel soit réformé et les procédures rendues publiques, au moins après L'instruction et avant le jugement avec Liberté à tout accusé de se déffendre alors, par Ministère d'avocat.

56.—Que la Vénalité des offices de judicature soit supprimée; à l'effet de quoy les offices de Bailliages et d'autres sièges de judicature en finance, aussi supprimés.

57.—Que la justice soit administrée gratuitement sauf à faire un Traitement convenable aux officiers de judicature.

58.—Que les Procureurs soient supprimés, mais en même tems tous les droits qui se perçoivent sur eux et par eux.

59.—Qu'il soit fait une Taxe ou réglement détaillé des droits et vacations des Notaires avec défense à eux Loutre [l'outre] passer.

60.—Que les finances de tous les Offices qui tomberont dans le cas de la suppression soient exactement remboursé.

Le présent cahier Rédigé par les Sieurs Richard Rollin, Sindicq des avocats, Lieutenant de Mair, Lieutenant de Police, Louis Gabriel chappes de La Genvière[35] avocat au Parlement, Jean Baptiste Beguinet aussi avocat au Parlement exerçant au Bailliage, Député de la Ville d'Étain, Jean Francois Waltriny[36] amodiateur Député, Damel, Pierre Robert Laboureux, Député de Beyonvaux, Jean Drols amodiateur Député de Bouligny, Jacques Harmand amodiateur Député de hondelancourt, et Dominique Benoit de la Pierre, maitre en chirurgie, Député de Saint Jean Lez-Bury, Commissaires nommés à cet effet par l'assemblée du Tiers-État du Bailliage d'Etain a este arrêté définitivement en la ditte assemblée et Signé tant par les dits Commissaires, Par nous Jean Maucourble Seigneur de Gommery Conseiller du Roy, Lieutenant Général Civil et Criminel audit Bailliage Présidant la ditte assemblée et par M. Henry Beguinet Greffier en chef du Bailliage, Secrétaire du Tiers-Etat, que par tous les membres présents, à Etain en la Grande Salle d'audience dudit Bailliage le 25 Mars 1789 aprés Lecture faite. *fait double, dont le présent Signé comme dit est,* restera au Greffe de ce Bailliage et l'autre signé seulement des Commissaires du président et du Greffier sera mis en main à Monsieur le Bailly pour estre remis aux Députés qui seront Élus.

[Ninety-nine signatures, ending with Marcourble and Beguinet.]

[35] This would appear to be "Henvier" in the p.v. and in the signatures below.
[36] This appears as Watriny in the signatures.

NO. 15. THE THIRD ESTATE OF THE BAILLIAGE OF LANGRES

Cf. Brette, *op.cit.,* Vol. III, pp. 248-49. The supplement to the cahier of the three ordres united exists in MS, *Arch. Nat.* Ba 45, from which this text is reprinted.

P.V.—MS, *Arch. Nat.* B III 70. *Cf.* Brette, *op. cit, supra.* There were to be 18 members for the committee to make the joint cahier, and 6 for the supplement. There are 11 signatures of the committee at the end of the reprinted text.

Convocation: 1st type.

PETITIONS PARTICULIERES DU TIERS-ETAT DU BAILLIAGE DE LANGRES

1.—Les interêts du Tiers-Etat sont aussi sacrés et plus étendus que ceux des deux premiers ordres, il desire que les deliberations ne puissent être prises dans les Etats Generaux que par tête de maniere que, soit que l'assemblee generale se divise en bureaux que soient formés de membres du tiers état en nombre égal a ceux du Clergé et de la noblesse rèunis, soit que chaque ordre se retire dans sa chambre pour discutter l'objet proposé, la decision ne puisse être portée que par les trois ordres et a la pluralité des suffrages qui seront pris et comptes par tête.

2.—Que la régeneration du bonheur public et les ordres de la nation ayent pour baze une loi inviolable et constitutionelle qui soit désormais a l'abri de toute atteinte par la Sanction qu'elle recevra de Sa Majesté dans les Etats Generaux, et si claire qu'aucun des ordres ne puisse l'enfreindre ni s'y soustraire.

3.—Que les Etats Generaux statueront sur une composition d'Etats provinciaux pour la Champagne, dans la forme qu'ils jugeront la plus propre a la bonne administration de la province, de façon cependant que le Tiers Etat y ait une représentation égalle a celle des deux premiers ordres réunis et composés de membres choisis librement, dans la même forme que les deputés aux Etats Generaux, que la repartition, assiette et levée des impots ne se passent que par les Etats provinciaux.

4.—Que les Etats Generaux solliciteront auprès de Sa Majesté une loi qui supprime celle qui en accordant a l'ordre de la Noblesse le privilege exclusif d'obtenir les grades militaires, jette une espece de meprise sur le Tiers Etat qui s'est toujours signalé par son attachement a ses Souverains et son devouement au soutien de l'Etat, en consequence que toute personne de famille vivant noblement dans le tiers etat aura droit d'entrer au service en qualité d'officier et d'exercer toutes autres places tant ecclesiastiques que civiles.

Impots

1.—Que les aides et gabelles soient supprimées, les barrieres interieures raportées aux frontières extremes du Royaume.

2.—Que l'impôt presse également sur tous les ordres et sur toutes les provinces, qu'il n'y ait d'impot particuliere, de charge particulieres pour aucun ordre, pour aucune province, de sorte qu'il n'y ait dans toute l'etendue du Royaume au profit d'aucuns ordres, province, ville, corps, compagnies, communauté, paroisse ou particulier, aucun privilege pecuniaire relatif a l'impôt, lequel privilege serait inconstitutionnel.

3.—Que la formalite du controle absolument necessaire pour parer a une multitude d'inconveniens et d'abus, en ussuront la datte des actes soit rendue commune et de la même indispensabilité dans toutes les parties du Royaume, avec abolition absolue de tout privilege et de toutes exceptions a cet égard. Que la loi sur le mode d'accomplissement de cette formalité soit également une et la même comme fondée en même raison pour toutes les parties du Royaume sans aucunes sortes d'exceptions. Que le tarif des controles, insinuations, centieme denier et aucunes parties domaniales fiscales soit reformés. Que les droits soient fixés a raison des sommes énoncées aux actes et non sur la qualité des contractans que ce tarif soit uniforme pour tout le royaume, clair et non susceptible de modifications et extensions arbitraires, de maniere qu'il ne puisse être perçû aucun autre droit et sans une loi sanctionnée, que la connoissance de l'execution et des contestations que naitront au sujet du nouveau tarif, soit attribuée aux tribunaux de l'impôt, enfin que les droits domaniaux ne puissent a l'avenir être donnés à ferme ou à engagement mais soient toujours regis au Nom du Roi a l'effet de quoi Votre Majesté rentrera dans ceux de ses droits qui sont actuellement affermés ou engagés.

4.—Que le papier et parchemin timbrés deviennent communs a tout le Royaume ou qu'ils soient supprimés.

5.—Que l'imposition representative de la Corvée ne sera portée dans chaque élection qu'a la somme que coute l'entretien des routes des dites elections et sera supportée par les trois ordres. Que l'état des adjudications des routes ainsi que celui des impositions soit rendu public annuellement par la voie de l'impression. Que l'entretien des routes soit adjugé par detail et par des atteliers de peu d'etendue pour en multiplier le nombre, procurer aux habitants des Champagnes des travaux utiles pour l'arriere saison et éviter l'abus des adjudications de douze ou quinze lieues d'étendue faites a des entrepreneurs qui ne peuvent y travailler par eux mêmes et qui font un benefice considerable sur le prix, retrocession sans aucun avantage pour l'etat.

Droits Onereux et Observations

L'adoucissement ou la suppression des impots ne suffirait pas au soulagement de vos peuples, il existe encore plusieurs droits injustes et vexatoires dont les tiers etat est plus specialement accablé.

1.—Le sort des proprietés relativement aux contributions ne devant plus dependre aucunement des qualités ou distinctions personnelles de ceux qui les possedent, l'objet et les conditions primitives des fiefs n'ayant plus la même realité dans l'etat actuel de la monarchie, le droit de franc fief parait deplacé, on ne lui connait d'autre origine qu'une perception toujours forcée, arbitraire, sans mesure et sans principes; ce droit s'il était conservé serait odieux puisque dans l'asservissement des fonds il opererait en quelque sorte celui des personnes, qu'il soit donc aboli, comme devenu inconstitutionnel autant qu'il fut injuste.

2.—Les droits établis par les édits burseaux et contre les dispositions soit des coutumes soit des titres des Seigneuries sur des contracts d'ailleurs favorables et utiles a l'agriculture comme le sont des echanges de fonds, ces droits, dit si[37] doivent être entierement supprimés dans toutes les directes de Votre Majesté qui sont les seuls qui ayent été conservés dans la province de Champagne; sauf les indemnités au profit des engagistes ou des fermiers. Les d. droits degenerent evidemment en un impot d'autant plus injuste et illegale qu'il ne paye que sur une tres petite portion de vos sujets dont la condition ne doit pas être pire pour s'etre trouvés dans la directe de Votre Majesté.

3.—Les droits de Guet et de Garde n'ont été etablis que par des conventions et des abonnements pour les services qui se faisaient dans les chateaux forts, ils etaient comme le prix de la protection qu'ils assûraient aux personnes et aux biens des habitants circonvoisins, dés lors jamais ils n'ont été de veritables droits de directe fondés sur la conception des fonds. Ils auraient dûs cesser avec les services de Garde et la destruction des chateaux comme l'effet avec sa cause. Touttes levées et perceptions de ces pretendus droits doivent êtré defendus a peine de concussion.

4.—Les trois ordres de votre bailliage, Sire, demandent à Votre Majesté qu'il n'existe plus de trace de la servitude qui a accablé pendant tant de siecles vôtre province de Champagne; depuis longtemps il est vrai la main morte a cessé d'appuyer son joug odieux sur les habitants de ce report. L'etablissement des communes que le peuple dût aux Bontés paternelles de vos prédécesseurs, commença ce Glorieux ouvrage dans les bonnes villes. L'exemple des Rois, l'interêt éclairé des Grands Vassaux, et successivement celui de presques tous les Seigneurs leur prescrivit ce que l'humanité plus éclairés et la force de la nation jointe a la vôtre commandera bientôt imperieusement a quelques seigneurs isolés, qui a l'appui de coutumes barbares tiennent encore le français, attaché a la Glébe, comme l'animal compagnon de ses travaux.

Mais les Corvées, les bannalités et quelqu'autres servitudes personnelles qui remontent a cette triste origine, dégradent encore dans presque tout votre empire cette portion si utile des cultivateurs qui font la principale richesse de votre Etat.—D'un autre coté ces differents droits sont devenus un patrimoine legitime pour les proprietaires, et la crainte de

[37] "Dit si" makes no sense, but should probably be "dits ainsi."

donner la plus legere atteinte aux principes sacrés de la proprieté, nous aurait fait hésiter de vous proposer nos voeux a cet egard, s'il ne se trouvait pas un moyen determinant de concilier l'interêt du proprietaire avec le principe de la liberté. Que les communautés et les particuliers soient donc autorisés par une loi generale a faire le rachat de tous ceux de ces droits qui se trouveront suffisament etablis et justifiés. Ces transactions se feront bientôt de gré a gré; si Votre Majesté elle même daigne dans ses domaines donner l'exemple de ce nouveau genre de sacrifices. L'exemple des Rois est plus puissant encore que leur volonté; et votre noblesse genereuse se ferait un devoir de s'y conformer.

5.—Dans le nombre des droits inherents aux fiefs, il en est qui sont plus honorifiques que profitables ou qui participent de l'une et l'autre de ces qualités également respectables dès qu'ils tiennent a la proprieté, on ne peut y toucher qu'avec la plus grande circonspection, mais ils peuvent être reglés par la haute police, et dans quelle main peut elle resider plus efficacement que dans l'assemblée auguste qui va s'ouvrir, presidée par le Chef Suprême de la nation.

Toutes les campagnes du bailliage n'expriment qu'un seul voeu pour que les colombiers et volieres soient fermes dans le temps des semailles quand les grains sont verses et pendant les recoltes. A ce voeu unanime les trois ordres en joindront un autre celui de restraindre le droit de colombiers et de volieres.

Que chaque Seigneur tant justicier ne puisse avoir qu'un colombier dans chaque seigneurie; qu'il soit determiné quel nombre de boulains il pourra contenir. Qu'aucun particulier ne puisse avoir une voliere ou fuye, qu'il ne possède sur le territoire de la paroisse au moins le double d'arpents de terre que la loi exige actuellement, et qu'il soit decidé si dans la supputerition [supputation] en comprendra les prez, vignes et bois.

6.—Le regime de la milice est infiniment onereux a la classe la plus malheureuse, prejudiciable a l'agriculture, contraire a la liberté individuelle et asservissant les personnes contre le droit naturel, qu'il soit supprimé a perpetuité, et remplacé par une contribution supportée par les trois ordres.

7.—Le regime relatif aux recettes des domaines et bois, est onereux au public, qu'il soit changé, que les fonds provenants des ventes des quarts de reserve soient versés directment entre les mains des adjudicataires des reparations dans les termes portés par les adjudications et le surplus a constitution de rente au profit des communautés ou au rachat des droits onereux a l'agriculture.

8.—Les charges fiscalles sont un veritable impôt par un produit considerable pour une finance mediocre, suprimer les recettes generales et particulieres des finances qui seront faittes par les municipalites des villes a apointemens fixes qui seront chargées des frais de recouvrement et de versement au tresor royal.

9.—Les officiers des maitrises des eaux et forêts ne pouvant veiller a la conservation des bois a cause de l'étendue de leur report qui est trop considerable et ne pouvant s'occuper des affaires contentieuses qui sont portées par devant eux, l'administration de la justice ne pouvant se concilier avec l'inspection qui leurs est confiée, qu'ils soient supprimés.—Les contestations dont la connaissance leur est attribuée, renvoyées aux juges ordinaires, et l'inspection et l'administration des bois et forêts, confiées a des personnes preposées par les Etats provinciaux.

10.—Le dixieme prelevé sur les ventes des quarts de reserve appartenants aux communautes laiques et ecclesiastiques sous le pretexte de subvenir aux besoins des communautes relligieuses, est contraire au droit de proprieté, qu'il soit supprimé!

11.—Les officiers de receveur des consignations etablis prés des sieges des provinces n'étant entre les mains des pourvus qu'un instrument de vexation pour la facilité qu'ils leur donnent d'obliger sans aucune necessité pour le public et presques toujours au detriment des créanciers et des debiteurs, les acquereurs ou redevables, a faire, sans necessité et contre le gré de toutes les parties interessées des depots entre leurs mains, et ce qui est plus revoltant encore de leur payer des droits des consignations pour des sommes qui ne peuvent ni ne doivent entrer dans leur caisse, qu'ils soient suprimés sauf aux tribunaux a ordonner que les sommes pour lesquelles il y aura litige seront consignées entre les mains des greffiers de chaque justice ou des notaires, dans le cas ou cette consignation sera jugée necessaire.

12.—Les offices de jurés crieurs et priseurs sont onereux au public, qu'ils soient supprimés.

13.—La multiplicite des usines occasionnent une consommation de Bois infiniment superieure a leur reproduction, il en est resulté une disette presque generale et une cherété si excessive, qu'il est impossible au peuple de s'enprocurer; comme c'est une chose de premiere necessité tant pour le chaufage que pour la construction des habitations, que le nombre en soit diminué, et en consequence que toutes les forges, fournaux, verreries et autres usines qui n'ont point des bois pour leur attonage, soient suprimés. Les reglements relatifs a la grosseur des bois qui peuvent être convertie en charbon, soient executtés sans des peines graves, et qu'il soit accordé des primes d'encouragement a ceux qui repeupleront les brossailles et replanteront des bois.

14.—Les comptes des sindics seront visés sans frais etants debattus et arrêtés avant d'etre presentés a la vision.

15.—Que pour repartir l'impot avec èquité il soit pris des sages mesures pour établir entre les cultivateurs et proprietaires d'une part et les capitalistes de l'autre, un equilibre sans lequel l'imposition surcharge l'agriculture et les travaux de la campagne.

16.—Que pour la repartition des impositions il ne soit fait dans chaque paroisse qu'un seul rôle, dans lequel seront comprises les proprietés, possessions et facultés des trois ordres.

17.—Que dans la repartition de l'impot sur chaque province il soit observé que la partie qu'en a supporté jusqu'a ce jour la champagne excedoit les bornes d'une juste proportion, tant relativement a son ètendue jusqu'ici exagerée, qu'a sa population et aux faibles responses du sol de l'industrie et du commerce de cette portion du royaume. Il est prouvé que cette province quoique d'un cinquieme seulement plus considerable que la franche comté paye six cinquièmes de plus. Que le sel et le tabac y forment un objet de six millions et demi de plus, et que quoique la champagne contienne six cent mille ames de moins que la generalité de Bordeaux province Maritime ou le commerce est plus florissant, cependant les contributions de ces deux provinces sont a peu prés les mêmes.

18.—Que sa Majesté soit suppliée d'abroger l'édit des clotures en ce qui concerne la faculté accordée par cette loy de faire des clos dans les prairies, ce qui est nuisible au paturage et produit souvent des infractions et des proces dispendieux, la faculté devant être néanmoins réservée aux cultivateurs de clore les terreins isolés et ceux adjacents aux batiments.

19.—Que l'édit qui en donnant des encouragements à L'agriculture a favorisé les defrichements, a souvent servi de palliatif a des usurpations sur les biens patrimoniaux des communautés et sur les chemins vicinaux, qu'il a aussi donné lieu a une foule de proces, que d'ailleurs celles des temps qu'il importait de remettre en valeur lors de la sanction de cette loi, ont été cultivées depuis cette loi a reçû jusqu'a ce jour toute l'execution dont l'interêt personnel des cultivateurs la rendait susceptible. Le surplus des terreins incultivés sert au paturage dont il est important de ne pas resserer l'etendûe, en consequence l'interêt public sollicite en ce moment, l'abrogation de cette loi.

20.—Que Sa Majesté soit suppliée d'abolir le regime des haras ou étalons, il est notorieté que cet établissement occasionne une depense d'environ 130,000 livres pour les campagnes et fait le bien de quelques individus seulement. L'interet particulier suffirait pour engager les cultivateurs a se procurer de belles especes de chevaux sans les entraves que presente le Regime des haras. Quoique cet établissement ait paru utile dans le principe, il n'en est pas moins vrai qu'on ne doit aujourd'huy le considerer que comme une surcharge, et qu'on a presqu'aucune eleve de ces haras.

21.—Que sa Majesté soit suppliée de permettre aux Communautés d'habitans le paturage dans les bois défensables de ses domaines.

22.—Que l'agriculture soit encouragée par des prix en argent pour le cultivateur dont la recolte serait jugée la plus belle de sa paroisse.

23.—Que les ordonnances qui defendent de chasser dans les grains et vignes soient renouvellées.

307

24.—Que les communautés ne soient plus garantés des arbres plantés routes qui traversent le territoire.

25.—Que le casuel de necessité onereux surtout a la classe la plus nombreuse et la plus indigente soit supprimé, et qu'en indemnité la portion congrue des curés et vicaires soit augmentée afinqu'ils puissent suivre leur esprit de bienfaisance envers les pauvres et les infirmes de leurs paroisses. Qu'en consequence tous les decimateurs ecclesiastiques de chaque paroisse soient tenus de contribuer aux portions congrues proportionellement a la quotité des dîmes qu'ils percoivent dans chaque paroisse.

Qu'il sera établi un bureau de conciliation dans chaque ville de bailliage, ou les parties puissent se presenter pour éviter des discussions juridiques.

Commerce

Le commerce est le nerf de l'etat, on doit donc le proteger et encourager les manufactures du royaume, dans la combinaison des impots, on doit suprimer toutes les entraves qui on gèneraient le circulation, c'est au commerce qu'il importe surtout que le prêt legal soit autorisé, que les poids et mesures de surface et de capacité, soient uniformes, il est ègalement de son interêt que les especes monoyées soient les mêmes et de la mème valeur dans tout le royaume sans distinction d'argent de Lorraine, franc barrois et autres et que le mot livre numeraire ou franc ne puisse desormais recevoir d'autre exception que celle de 20 sols tournois.

On recommande aux Etats Generaux d'examiner scrupuleusement les causes de la stagnation et de la decadence du commerce national, surtout de soumettre a une nouvelle revision le dernier traité de commerce avec l'Angleterre évidemment désavantageux, parcequ'il a été fait sans consulter les differentes chambres du commerce des principales villes du royaume.

Le seul moyen de faire fleurir le commerce de la France est de favoriser le libre passage des productions nationales à l'etranger en diminuant les droits a la sortie et en augmentant au contraire les droits d'entrée sur les natures premières que nous possedons sans avoir recours a l'etrangere.

Notamment, d'abroger les droits qui se percoivent sur les cuirs tannés ou corroyés dans les differentes fabriques du royaume, et ordonner qu'en remplacement les tanneurs payeront annuellement les $\frac{3}{4}$ de ce qu'ils rendent à la Regie.

D'accorder sur le même pied un abonnement aux orphevres sauf l'inspection en regie en leur maison commune.

La communauté des orfevres de Langres desirerait encore qu'on mit sous les yeux de sa Majesté et des Etats Generaux, que le sureté publique, et le bien general demandent l'Egalité du titre des matières d'or et d'argent dans tout le royaume ainsi qu'une expresse prohibition de tous ouvrages doublés et plaqués, parceque la difference dans l'un et l'autre entraine des inconvenients, des abus et des pertes pour toutes les personnes qui achetent de ces sortes d'ouvrages; tel croit avoir acheté de l'argent au titre de Paris, qui n'a souvent que de l'argent d'Allemagne, de Lorraine, ou autre titre inferieur.

Ils demandent aussi de n'être plus astreints a aller prèter serment tous les ans par devant M.M. les officiers de la Monnoye de Troyes eloigné de 30 lieues, ce qui necessite des voyages onereux par la perte du temps et les frais, il serait plus avantageux qu'ils puissent prèter serment dans leur ville par devant tel juge qu'il plairait et Sa Majesté de nommer .

La communauté des epiciers se plaint de ce qu'elle paye un vingtieme a raison des offices dont elle a payé la finance sans qu'elle en touche aucune interêt ni produit.

Qu'elle paye encore une industrie annuelle d'une somme exhorbitante qui ne se repartit qu'entre 12 maitres tandis qu'il y a dans la ville une centaine de marchands forains qui font le meme commerce sans contribuer a cette industrie.

La jurisdiction consulaire a de tout temps été regardée comme l'établissement le plus utile au commerce, elle maintient son activité dans les traites, remises et payements, elle arrête les effets de la mauvaise foi.

En consequence, on demande qu'il plaise a Sa Majesté revoquer sa declaration du 7 Avril 1759, et ordonner que sans acceptation des reports des bailliages et senechaussées il soit libre en toute matiere consulaire de traduire le debiteur devant la jurisdiction la plus prochaine de son domicile ou du lieu indiqué pour la livraison ou pour le payement au choix de creancier.

Maintenir les juges et consuls dans la connaissance exclusive de toutes les matières dont la competence leur est attribuée par les édits de creation, loix et reglements intervenus depuis.

Rendre aux tribunaux consulaires la connaissance des faillites et ban queroutes, cessions et homologations des contrats d'atermoyements et deliberations passées entre commercans et leurs créanciers.

Supprimer le droit de présentation en defendant que les contrôleurs exigent dans les jurisdictions consulaires en venant en personne aux audiences et ne permettant pas aux debiteurs malheureux de plaider leurs causes et d'implorer un delai, s'il n'a prealablement acquitté ce droit fiscal onereux et inutile. Comme aussi supprimer toutes les autres perceptions fiscales sur les défauts et sentences émanées de cette jurisdiction et de diminuer en general tous les frais qui nuisent à la celerité des jugemens.

Supprimer enfin les privileges attachés a ces asiles ouverts aux banqueroutiers frauduleux ou ils portent la depouille de leurs creanciers.

Le Tiers Etat chargera en consequence ses députés d'aviser aux moyens les plus efficaces pour y parvenir. Ils auront aussi principalement en vue la sainteté du culte et des moeurs publiques la reforme de l'education nationale, la consolidation de la dette publique, la fixité, l'emploi et la durée determinée de l'impôt désastreux des gabelles, de celui des aides et de celui des traites dans l'interieure du Royaume et le remplacement du produit net de ces impositions en une contribution moins onereuse pour le peuple, d'une assiette plus facile et d'une perception moins dispendieuse.

Les deputés renouvellent aux pieds du Trône l'hommage de vénération d'amour et de reconnaissance de tous leur commetans envers Sa Majesté, ils la suplieront très humblement d'agréer l'expression des sentimens de piété filiale dont ses sujets sont penetrés et les sacrifices qu'ils sont prêts à faire pour le bonheur de son regne et la prosperité de la nation. Enfin ils oseront exprimer les voeux ardens qu'ils forment pour la conservation des jours precieux de Sa Majesté. Signez à la minute

[Eleven signatures (Commissioners).]

Collationné par nous greffier en chef soussigné ce 16 Avril 1789. Josse.

NO. 16. THE THIRD ESTATE OF LIXHEIM

Cahier reprinted from MS text, *Arch. Meurthe-et-Moselle*, B, no. 40, liasse 31. Original signatures of commissioners, verification by secretary.
P.V.—MS copy in *Arch. Nat.* B III 134, in the p.v. of the three orders. The third estate thought it to their own advantage to make a separate cahier. They adopted their cahier March 20.
Convocation: 2d type. Reunion at Sarreguemines.

PROCÈS VERBAL DE RÉDUCTION DES CAHIERS EN UN SEUL, DES VILLES, VILLAGES, ET COMMUNAUTÉS DU RESSORT DU BAILLIAGE DE LIXHEIM

CAHIER DE PLAINTES DOLÉANCES ET PÉTITIONS DU TIERS ETAT DU RESSORT DU BAILLIAGE DE LIXHEIM POUR METTRE SOUS LES YEUX DU ROI ET DES ETATS GÉNÉRAUX

1.—Que la liberté individuelle de tout Citoyen français soit protégé laquelle ne puisse lui être enlevé qu'après avoir été jugé Légalement par ses juges Naturels.

2.—Que nulle Loi tendante a priver le Citoyen français de la Liberté, de la vie, de l'honneur et de ses propriétés ne puisse avoir lieu qu'apres avoir été Librement proposé et Consenti par les Etats Généraux.

3.—Que les Loix civiles et criminelles seront repondües, les formes inutiles et dispendieuses au civil supprimées, et celles qui dans l'instruction au Criminel tendante à faciliter la justification de l'accusé soient augmentées.

4.—Que désormais la justice soit administrée gratuitement; mais que sa Majesté sera supliée de rembourser les finances et de Stipendier les juges et officiers, ce que seront tenus de faire également les hauts justiciers, et que dans le cas ou il plairoit au Roi où aux Etats Généraux de laisser aux Seigneurs les droits de haute justice dont les frais sont plus onéreux au public que ceux des justices Royalles il leur plaire permettre à leurs Vassaux de pouvoir franchir ce dégré de justice.

5.—Que le Bailliage de fenetrange qui n'est eloigné de celui de Lixheim que de deux lieues et demie soit reuni à cedite, attendu que le Bailliage de fénétrange à été beaucoup mutilé depuis quelque temps, que la charge de Lieutenant Général est vacante, qu'il n'y reste plus pour tous officiers que le Procureur du Roi et le Greffier, qu'il n'y à aucun avocat plaidant, que le Domaine d'ailleur de ce qui reste de la Baronnie de fenetrange est alliené actuellement à M. le Duc de Polignac, et enfin parce que la pluspart des Villages qui restent du Ressort du Bailliage de fénétrange sont enlevés dans le Ressort du Bailliage de Lixheim, et trés aportée de cette Ville.

6.—Que tous les tribunaux d'attribution seront supprimés et notament ceux qui ont été crées pour juges en dernier ressort dans le Royaume, les Matières fiscalles de même que les Matieres des Eaux et forets, comme trop onéreuses au public par leur trop grand éloignement, supprimer aussi les Intendances.

7.—Que l'usage établit en Lorraine de faire des inventaires à la mort de l'un des conjoints lorqu'il y à des Enfants Mineurs soit restraint au seul cas ou le Survivant convoleroit en secondes noces, où qu'il y auroit des enfants de deux lits où de conventions Matrimonialles par lesquelles il seroit établis communautées de meubles, et enfin où Les Parents des Mineurs ne jugeroient pas le survivant capable d'administrer la succession du premourant.

8.—Que l'Edit portant création d'huissiers jurés priseurs aux Inventaires et aux ventes, sera Revoqué comme trop à charge au public.

9.—Que les familles juives quoi que circoncrites en Lorraine seront res-traintes par un Réglement sévêre, les Usures, et les fraudes que cette nation perverse commet tous les jours, se font avec tant de précaution et de ruses qu'on à peine à les convaincre, Il est trés nécessaire pour y porter remede de remettre en vigueur les Dispositions de l'Edit du 30 Xre [Décembre] 1728, plutot encore étendre en Lorraine les Lettres Patentes donnée pour L'alsace le 10 Juillet 1784, attendu qu'ils sont la vraye cause des Emigrations et du Dépérissement de l'agriculture.

10.—Que la loi qui deffend aux hopiteaux et aux fabriques de replacer les fonds remboursés soit Révoquée ce sont des Etablissements respectables au regard de la piétie des fondateurs, et recommandables par les secours qu'ils donnent aux besoins de l'humanité, les fabriques dans les campagnes ont le merite des hopiteaux dans les Villes. L'excédent de ce qui est necessaire pour le service Divin doit être employé au soulagement des pauvres.

11.—Que l'édit qui a autorisé les clos et clotures soit Revoqué.

12.—Que les droits de Chatrerie seront abolis comme contraire à la Liberté, que chacun soit libre de faire chatrer comme bon lui semble, que l'exercise de chatreurs en titre est trop onéreux.

13.—Que l'Etablissement des haras dans la Province soit aboli, après une infinité d'epreuves et de dépenses qui n'ont servis qu'à enrichir les Administrateurs au Dépend des Communautés, l'objet à toujours été manqué.

14.—Que la Gabelle ou l'impot sur les Sels soit supprimé et le Sel rendu marchand et exempt de toutes Prohibitions. Il n'est personne qui ne connoisse L'odieux de cet impot, ses suittes funestes, et son influence désastreuse sur les Bestiaux et l'agriculture.

15.—Que les Impots sur les cuirs ainsi que la marque des fers, et les Impots sur les papiers, Amidon, huiles et savon soient supprimés; il sera infiniment plus avantageux au peuple et à l'Etat de reporter par ampliation le produit net de ces Impôts sur quelques autres subsides.

16.—Que pour jamais la foraine et tous droits de transis d'un Lieu, où d'une province à l'autre soit aboli, et que les Domaines soient alliénés en détail dans chacun des chefs-Lieux, Les recettes particulieres des finances supprimées, comme ruineuses pour le Public par leurs éloignement et mauvaises administrations.

17.—Que le tarif général que les états Généraux jugeront nécessaires d'établir soit par un motif de politique soit pour le bien général de l'Etat, soit porté aux frontières du Royaume, qu'il soit des plus modérés pour les matieres première et de première nécessité.

18.—Que les Usines à feux qui ne pourront se procurer leurs alimentations de leurs propres productions seront supprimées ou restraintes dans leur étendue et Exploitation jusqu'à la concurrence des productions venant de leurs propriétés.

19.—Que le droit de contrat établi sur ventes soit réduit au quart dans tout le Royaume et étendu proportionnellement sur toutes les sommes quelconques, le peuple en sera soulagé et le Gouvernement trouvera les mêmes fonds que cette partie de finance a produit jusqu'à présent, au détriment du pauvre en faveur du Riche.

20.—Que toutes les Impositions pécuniaires que les Etats Généraux jugeront devoir consentir seront supportés également par tous les individus du Royaume, soit du clergé, soit de la Noblesse, et du Tiers-Etat, et la Répartition faite suivant les Richesses les forces et facultés de chaque individu.

21.—Que les Etats Généraux supplieront Sa Majesté d'établir en la Province de Lorraine des Etats pour son administration particuliere, au choix de la Province.

22.—Attendu que la Dixme de Pomme de terre est par elle même une Dixme Insolide, que le fruit fait la principale nourriture des pauvres gens, et qu'elle n'est point en usage en france ou demande que la Lorraine en soit affranchie.

23.—Et que les Impositions a venir seront administrées et réparties par les Etats provinciaux.

24.—Que la vaine pature établie par la Loi Muncipale, sera restrainte, quant aux prairies jusqu'à la seconde récolte qui ne pourra excéder le temps de la St. Mathieu.

25.—Que les offices Municipaux crées en finances ou commission à défaut de finances, soient supprimées, que tous les préposés des villes et Bourgs seront Elus et leurs Exercises Triennalles aux choix des communautés, et la police des dittes villes et Bourgs rendus aux tribunaux ordinaires.

Fait et arretté par nous Nicolas Ricatte Président, François Thouvenin, Nicolas Antoine Lacombe, Louis Tourneur, Joseph Holtz, Joeseph Chatou et Michel Malte, et Jean, francois Bouvert Commissaires nommés du consentement et en présence des Députés remis en la même chambre le 20 Mars 1789, avons signé avec notre Sécretaire

[Ten signatures.]

Cotté et paraphé par premier et dernier feuillet aprés avoir été arretté en l'assembleé Générale de l'ordre suivant qu'il en conte par le procés verbal General de la réunion des trois ordres, et élection de Députés du tiers Etat et présentation de serments de ceux des dits trois Ordres, Par nous Président du tiers Etat assisté du procureur du Roi a signe avec nous et notre Sécretaire le jour et au susdit

Ricalte   Thouvenin

Bourgel,

Secretaire.

NO. 17. THE CLERGY OF THE BAILLIAGE OF LONGUYON

Cahier MS, *Arch. Moselle* B7698 (copy verified by secretary.)
P.V.-MS (of elections), *Arch. Nat.* Ba19, and also in p.v. of 3 orders (*ibid.*).
The cahier was voted March 26. The curates predominated in the assembly.
Convocation: 2d type, reunion at Bar-le-duc.

Les Commissaires de l'ordre du Clergé au nombre de cinq, presidés par Monsieur le Doyen de la Chrétienneté de Longuyon curé de Grand-failly, et chargés de rédiger le cahier des demandes plaintes et Doléances selon l'invitation qui en est faite par la lettre du Roy à tous les ordres de son Royaume, demandent et se plaignent comme s'ensuit.

1.—Que l'assemblée des Etats Généraux de la Nation soit tenue périodiquement et à epoque fixe.

2.—Le rétablissement des états provinciaux sous la forme et l'organisation qui seront jugés les plus convenables; qu'en conséquence la répartition général des impôts quelconques soit confiée aux dits états et qu'ils ayent le droit de connoitre de décider de toutes les contestations qui pourront s'élever à ce sujet.

3.—L'éxécution jugée nécéssaire et attendue depuis longtemps du projet d'une réforme dans l'administration de la justice de manière qu'elle se rende avec plus de celerité et moins de frais.

4.—Le sel et le tabac vendus marchands.

5.—La suppression du droit de *faciente* sur les bierres, cidre et autres boissons fabriquées dans la province, iten [item] de la forraine, de manière que le Commerce soit libre dans tout le royaume.

6.—La suppression des Huissiers priseurs comme trop à charge à toutes les classes de Citoyens.

7.—La suppression ou du moins une meilleure organisation des Maitrises, puisqu'il est évident qu'ils ont manqué le but de leur institutions; l'abolition des tranchées qui divisent les coupes, et ces tranchées remplacées par des bornes; que les deniers provenant de la vente des bois des Communautés soient déposes dans le coffre de leur Municipalité pour être employés à leurs besoins, quand aux deniers qui sont actuellement entre les mains des receveurs, qu'ils soient obligées d'en rendre compte exact et vigoureux,

8.—La suppression d'une partie des bouches à feu de la province, nouvelle cause de la pénurie des bois de chauffage ce qui le porte à un prix si excessif que l'humanité en gémis; que les bouches à feu ne puissent jouir que de la souille et que la haute futaye soit venue au public.

9.—Que les Chefs des Communautés soient tenus de communiquer aux cūrés les Édits, arrêts et ordonnances concernant l'Administration publique.

10.—Qu'il soit donné un moyen sur de faire observer les réglements de police touchant les cabarets.

11.—Qu'il soit pourvus à la subsistance des Curés à portion congrue à qui l'âge et les infirmités ne permettent plus de faire leurs fonctions; et que les places des Cathédrales et Collègiales puissent devenir des retraites pour les anciens Curés.

12.—Qu'il soit permis aux fabriques de placer sur toutes sortes de personnes indistinctement l'argent des fondations qui leur seront remboursées.

13.—Que l'arrêt du Roy qui ordonne de renouveller tous les Trente ans les titres passés au profit des fabriques soit révoqué.

14.—Que les terres des religieux Bernardins et autres privilégiés payent la dixme commes les autres terres au profit des pauvres sur tous Malades et Cadues qui habiteront les lieux ou ces terres sont situées.

15.—Que la portion congrue des Curés sont augmentée.

16.—Le Clergé demandant que les lettres d'enoblissement accordées à différents chapitres soient révoquées, qu'en conséquence chaque ecclesiastique sans distinction puisse aspirer à devenir membres de ces chapitres.

17.—Qu'un cas que l'on juge à propos de conserver au clergé ses anciennes formes, le clergé Lorrain demande d'être toujours séparé du clergé de France, et qu'il puisse former dans sa province une chambre écclésiastique composée de membres pris dans son ordre choisis par ses pairs.

314

18.—Le rétablissement des droits et privilèges dont on joint de tems immémorial les quatre décanats Wallons.

19.—Que les bénéfices dans l'étendue du royaume ne soient conferés qu'à des Nationaux: que l'Administration ne soit plus aussy facile à accorder des lettres de Naturalité, a moins qu'on n'etablisse entre les Nationaux et les Etrangers une exacte réciprocité de manière que les françois jouissent chez les étrangers des mêmes facilités dont ces étrangers jouissent en France.

20.—Qu'il soit etabli un Séminaire dans la partie françoise ou Lorraine du Diocese de Treves; que les revenus des cy-devant jésuites dont jouit aujourd'hui le Séminaire de Trêves soient employés à la nourriture et entretien des sujets de la province qui habiteront ce nouveau Séminaire; et si ce nouvel établissement n'a pas lieu, qu'il soit du moins réglé par le Roy, que douze séminaristes nés sujets françois soient reçus gratis dans le Séminaire actuel qui existe à Trêves.

21.—La suppression des abbaÿes en commande au profit de l'Etat et celle des prieurés occupés par des Religieux, dont il sera formée une caisse qui servira à fournir à la subsistance des curés à portion congrue; et des vicaires à qui l'âge et les infirmités ne permettent plus de faire leurs fonctions.

22.—Enfin que les Ministres de l'Administration des finances soient obligés de rendre compte à la Nation assemblée en Etats Généraux.

Telles sont les demandes, plaintes, et doléances que portent avec une respectueuse confiance aux pieds du Trône, le clergé ressortissant du Bailliage de Longuyon remises es [en] mains de Monsieur Philippe Laurent Doyen rural, curé de Grand-failly son député, lui donnant plein pouvoir de proposer, remontrer, aviser, et consentir tout ce qui peut concerner le bien de l'État, la réforme des abus, l'établissement d'un ordre fixe et durable dans toutes les parties de l'administration, la prospérite générale du Royaume et le bien de tous, et chacun des sujets du Roy, arrêté et signé par les Membres dudit clergé, présents et fondés de pouvoir pour les absents, en la salle de l'hotel de ville de Longuyon, le 23 Mars, à midi, 1789. Signés:

[Sixteen signatures.]

L. Bertrand curé de Pierrepont fondé de procuration pour Monsieur Lorrette Curé de Ham. L. Bertrand Curé de Pierrepont, secrétaire f. frémiot ch. R. Curé de Mouillompont.

Pour copie collationnée et conforme à l'original donnée par nous secrétaire de l'ordre du clergé soussigné à Pierrepont ce 25 Mars, 1789.

L. Bertrand
Curé de Pierrepont
secrétaire.

315

NO. 18. THE NOBLES OF THE BAILLIAGE OF LONGUYON

Cahier reprinted from the MS text, *Arch. Moselle*—B7698. The cahier displays careless recording or ignorance of good grammatical form. P.V.-MS (election), *Arch. Nat.* Ba19. The cahier was adopted March 26. Convocation: 2d type, reunion at Bar-le-duc.

La Noblesse résidente dans l'arrondissement du Bailliage de Longuyon, s'étant assemblée conformement aux lettres de Sa Majesté daté du 7 février 1789.[38]

La Cour pleine de respect, et de devouement, pour son Souverain qui daigne appeler aujourd'huy près de son auguste personne tous les ordres de l'Etat pour y porter sans crainte, non seulement leurs Voeux, mais encore se servir de leurs lumieres pour concourir et faire plus surement le Bonheur de tous ses Sujets, Pénétrée de reconnoissance pour les vues bienfaisante de sa Majesté, et animé d'un zèle patriotique, la noblesse après avoir murement deliberé sur les abus qui se sont glisés dans toutes les Branches du corps de l'Etat et sur les réformes indispensables à y opérer m'est au pied du Trône ses Voeux et Doléances cy apres enoncées.

1.—Sa Majesté sera humblement suppliée d'accorder des Etats particuliers à la province de Lorraine et Barrois, de decider que les Etats auront seul le Droit de repartir les Subsides d'en faire faire la levée de connoitre défi-nitivement et en dernier resort de toutes les contestations qui pourroient naitre à ce sujet qu'à eux seul appartiendra l'administration Général de la province et qu'eux seul s'occuperont des objets relatifs à L'agriculture, au Commerce et a la Police, en un mot de tous les objets projets, qu'ils juge-ront propres à amener la province à L'Etat de prospérité, dont elle peut être susceptible.

2.—Il est d'une très grande importance de laisser jouir à la Noblesse des distinctions honorables qui en la placant au dessus du peuple lui don-nent une influence sur lui, par un respect et les differences qu'il a tou-jours pour ceux qu'il voit honorer, distinguer par l'opinion publique et par l'autorité convenable qui lui est confié pour maintenir l'ordre intérieur dans les campagnes dont dépend la tranquillité et la félicité publique.

3.—Oter toutes Considerations aux nobles et aux Seigneurs dans leurs terres vous verrez le peuple arrogant indésiplinable [indisciplinable] et méprisant les mêmes ordres qu'ils ont respecté, sous un autre point de vue la Noblesse et les Seigneurs d'apres ses réflections faites par un desir sincere du bien général demandent qu'il ne soit porté aucune atteinte aux prosperité fiefs justice leur rentes et autres que la justice Locale puisse juger définitivement des Contestations entre les Particuliers jusqu'à la concur-rence de cinquante Livres. Qu'elle soit autorisée à faire toute espèce de tutelle Curatel, invantaires, et rentes sur papier timbré fourni par les in-

[38] This cahier had no formal title.

téréssés aux moindres frais possibles que tous les droits dont les Seigneurs ont jouit ou du jouir qui ont été altérés ou perdues par les tems et circonstance soient rétablies clairment déterminés et proportionnés aux possessions relatives qui les leurs donnant entre eux pour éviter tous sujets de contestations.

4.—Que toutes les loix seront proposées et délibérées et sanctionnées par les états généraux pour être ensuite promulgées au nom du Monarque que les Etats Généraux auront en retour périodique t'el qu'il aviseront pour les plus grands avantages de la Nation que tous les subsides qui seront accordés par la Nation cesseront de plein droit si les États généraux ne sont pas convoqués aux époques fixées sauf à sa Majesté de les assembler dans d'autres tems suivant les circonstances et les besoins de l'État.

5.—Que tout Citoyen ne pourra être jugé par les loix et les Magistrats que toute lettres de Cachet seront supprimées.

6.—Que les Ministres soient contables aux États généraux de l'administration des finances comme le seul moyen d'en prévenir les dépradations.

7.—Que tout privileges Pecuniere soient suprimés et qu'il ne soit établis aucun subsides sans être réparti sur tous les ordres indistinctement.

8.—Que les tribunaux d'exception commissions, soient supprimés ainsi que les privileges exclusives des huissiers priseurs et marc d'or nouvellement établis dans la province sur les terres Seigneurialles et en un mot que les formes judiciares soient simplifiées et les frais réduits que la liberté indéfinies de la presse soit autorisée.

9.—L'Administration des Maitrises des eaux et forets et vicieuse dans toutes les parties par tout on se recrie sur les abus sans nombre se sont glisés à l'ombre de cette administration, les Bois sont ruinés et dans peu il est à craindre qu'ils deviennent si rare que le prix n'en soit plus à la portée du plus grand nombre, augmentant tous les ans il est plus que tems de s'en plaindre de demander la réforme de ces Compagnies et que l'Administration des Bois soient remises comme elle étoit à l'époque ou on la leur confie, l'Administration étoit bonne puisque à cet époque les Bois étoient superbe et bien conservé.

10.—Outre la réforme des Maitrises, L'Administration des forges bouches à feu est très nécessaire dans cette province étant une cause principale de la rareté des Bois cette grande consommation des[39] exige une suppression de moitié de ses Usines.

11.—Que tous les droits ou impots quelconques tel que gabel, ferme du tabac, forene [forain] conduits, facientes, encavage de Bière, et ceux connus particulièrement dans cette province sous le nom audacieux de Chatrerie et riflerie soient supprimés.

12.—Que Sa Majesté sera trés humblement supplié de prendre en Con-

[39] There was no space for a word in the original manuscript. It would appear that it should be "bois."

sidération les réclamations de tous les ordres de l'état contre le concordat entre Francois Ier et Louis X.

13.—Que les fruits de Régale seul de tous les biens en commande qui viendront à vaquer dans la suite en un mot tout l'argent que l'on envoie à Rome pour Bul [Bulle], Bref, etc., soit applique à la Libération à l'Etat et au soulagement du peuple le plus pure maxime l'Église promettant d'aliéner les choses saintes pour secourir les pauvres et obvier aux encaux present et imprévus que l'on fasse donc une ressource de toutes ces richesses accumulées et conservé en differents lieux pour le nom de Trésor et qui ne servent qu'à l'attentation et la curiosité.

14.—Que toutes charges annoblissante à prix d'argent soient supprimés et que la noblesse ne soient accordé desormais qu'a des personnes qui l'auront merité par des services utiles ou de tosent [unidentified word] essentielles.

15.—La multiplicité des Bailliages et prévotes royales ou Bailliages dans cette province est trop considérable, il seroit nécessaire d'en diminuer le nombre pour la tranquillité public et le repos de citoyens et surtout que l'on reprime l'avidité des procureurs qui sont les fleaux de l'humanité; qu'il soit expressement défendus sous peine d'amende considérable à aucun procureur ou gradue de se charger d'aucune affaire sans une consultation de trois avocats les plus instruits du siècle.

16.—L'Émigration continuel qui se fait par la desertion des troupes de Sa Majesté ce remplacement qui y est nécessaire de peupler les campagnes et met le cultivateur dans la gêne et ce fait languir par le manque de bras.

17.—Qu'il soit établi dans la province un tribunal héraldique compose de Gentilshommes pour juger definitement de tous les preuves de noblesse.

18.—Que les Deputés s'occuperont d'abord à constater la dette nationale qu'ils ne pourront consentir à aucun subsides que la Constitution soit preablement etablis et que tous les articles cy dessus n'ayant été proposés aux etats Généraux et fournir à leur delibération après laquelle il pourront seulement accorder des secours proportionnés aux besoins réels de l'État et selon les facultés de la province.

[Four signatures]
Chomet de Bellemont[40]
Le Baron de Reumont.[41]

NO. 19. THE THIRD ESTATE OF THE BAILLIAGE OF LONGUYON

Cahier reprinted from MS text, *Arch. Moselle*, B7698, also *Arch. Nat.* C15/20. There are very slight differences of text. The latter text is given here.

P.V.-MS, *Arch. Nat.* Ba19 (election) and in p.v. of the three orders. There

[40] Secretary of the Assembly.
[41] President of the Assembly.

were 8 members of the committee, but all withdrew except Guilliaume, who was charged to make the cahier. It was signed by only one or two of the committee. The cahier was unanimously adopted by the assembly March 26. The assembly split into factions over the elections.

Convocation: 2d type, reunion at Bar-le-duc.

CAHIER DES DOLÉANCES, PLAINTES, ET RÉCLAMATIONS DU TIERS-ETAT DU BAILLIAGE DE LONGUYON

Tout ce que les francois ont toujours souhaité avec le plus d'ardeur, reçoit aujourd'hui son entier accomplissement, nous désirons un Roy qui ne voulant gouverner que par les Loix, un Souverain épris de l'amour sévère de la justice, désireux de nous procurer des jours de tranquillité, de douceur, et de paix, nous le possedons, la Nation s'assemble, jour heureux pour nous! Jour encore plus consolant pour nôtre Souverain, il y connoitra plus particulièrement L'amour de son peuple, tout lui dira que si le Trône étoit encore, Electif, ce serait lui que nos Voeux y appeleroient, que nous l'avons toujours aimé toujours chéri, qu'aux milieu des maux et des attentats multipliés contre la liberté publique et particulière qui nous arrachoient des pleurs de désespoir, nous le portions dans nos Coeurs nous l'admirons en silence.

C'est pour remedier à ces maux pour recompenser notre amour, que la bonté autant que sa justice nous permet de lui présenter nos doléances et nos reclamations, Le tiers-état du Bailliage de Longuyon va exposer les siennes avec la confiance que des enfants ont à leur Père, en conséquence le Seigneur Roy, est trés humblement supplié d'agréer premierement: Que l'assemblée générale avant de rien écouter, d'accorder aucun impôt, de prendre aucun arrangement sur la dette publique, prononce et decide définitivement, que les Voix seront comptés par tête et non par ordre, avec cette reserve que si le tiers vient se trouver en opposition avec l'un des deux premiers ordres ou tous les deux ensemble, il puisse se retirer à part pour déliberer sur les questions proposées et voter avec plus de liberté que les Riches et puissants ne craignent rien du tiers, il ne tend point à une égalité absolue, tout ce qu'il demande, c'est que les égards et le respect pour les Loix et devant les Loix soient égaux pour tous.

Qu'en suite l'assemblée sollicite de sa bienveillance et de sa justice une loi sous le nom de contrat ou d'acte social entre le Souverain et son peuple, qui deviendra pour l'avenir la Sauvegarde de la liberté personnelle de tous les Citoyens, de la prospérité générale et particulière, l'appui du Trône et surtout la préservatif contre le retour de ces évènement désastreux qui oppriment en ce moment le Roy et la Nation.

Que le premier point de cette loi, prononce l'abolition des Lettres de Cachet qui ne sont que des jouissances de Ministres et repugnent au coeur du Souverain qui est trop élevé pour avoir une injure personnelle à venger;

319

si cela pouvoit arriver elles seroient inutiles, le Souverain trouveroit dans chaque françois un Vengeur.

Que cependant pour la conservation de l'honneur et du repos des familles, il poura en être decernées sur les demandes expresses des familles et ensuitte des deliberations par elles prises dans des assemblées judiciairement convoquées.

Que si dans les tems d'orage et de sédition, le gouvernement se trouvoit forcé à faire arreter un sujet, la personne arretée de quelle qualité elle puisse être et sous quel prétexte se soit, ne puisse être emprisonnée plus de 24 heures, sans la faire comparoitre devant les juges naturels pour constater le délit et prononcer sur la saisie de la personne.

Ce n'est que sous la sauvegarde de cet article que ceux qui dans les états et la Nation auront osé dire la verité demeureront dans leur patrie et continueront de l'eclairer.

Qu'il ne sera établi aucunne loi, sans l'authorité du Prince et le consentement des représentants du peuple réunis dans des assemblées nationales fréquentes et périodiques.

Qu'il ne soit fait aucun emprunt directe ou indirecte, établi aucun impôt, accordé aucun subside, sans le libre consentement des états généraux, ni pour un temps illimité, mais seulement jusqu'au retour périodique des états généraux qui sera fixé par eux-mêmes, que ce terme arrivé sera celui de la perception, si la concession n'en est renouvellée, ou la continuation solennellement accordée par l'assemblée Nationale.

Que la Liberté de la presse, comme étant le plus sur rempart qu'on puisse opposer aux abus en les faisant connoitre est le plus sur moyen d'assurer la liberté nationale, d'étendre les lumières, de donner de l'essort au génie et aux vertus: sera accordé par tout le Royaume.

Qu'il sera posé autour des propriétés une enceinte, que nulle autorité ne puisse franchir ni renverser, de sorte que le si bon ordre, la sagesse du gouvernement, le bien de l'état exigeoit des changemens; des supressions de certaines charges ou emplois en finance, la gloire de la France exige en même tems que les Titulaires de ces emplois supprimés n'en soient pas les victimes que le prix en soit au moins remboursé suivant l'évaluation juste et modérée qui en sera faite.

Que la vénalité des charges de judicature d'administration publique sera entierement abolie; L'importance de cet article n'a pas besoin de commentaire, et si les circonstances actuelles résistent à donner à cet article de la loi un effet présent du moins qu'elle soit prononcée et assurée pour les tems heureux auxquels la Nation et les Provinces auront acquis par des Retranchemens utiles et une sage economie, des ressources et des fonds qui en assurent le remboursement et l'indemnité légitime.

Que tous les françois sans aucune distinction auront le droit et l'espérance de parvenir à toutes les charges de l'État, à tous les grades, et à toutes les dignités Militaires et écclésiastiques.

Qu'étant d'une maxime sage en politique d'empêcher l'argent de sortir du Royaume, si non par le commerce qui nous le rapporte, et d'avoir des ressources toujours prêtes pour subvenir aux besoins imprévus, les annates seront suprimées, toutes les commandes et tous les Bénéfices sans charge d'âme qui viendront à vaquer seront mis en economat et Les Revenus employés à la liberation de la dette de l'Etat.

Que le bonheur des peuples dependant en partie d'une juste répartition des impôts d'une sage économie dans la perception et dans l'usage des biens des réformes qui ne manquent jamais de se trouver dans un pays d'un peu d'étendue, les provinces seront erigés en pays d'état, et leurs assemblées fixées à une même époque dans toute l'étendue du Royaume; c'est par ce moyen que les différentes provinces pourront s'accorder dans leurs demandes respectives, tout aura été examiné et discuté dans leurs assemblées, et l'on apportera à L'auguste assemblée de la Nation que des tableaux exact qui faciliteront la décision.

Telle doit être en partie cette loi fondamentalle du bonheur de la France; comme elle est de toute sociétée et l'assemblée nationale est suppliée de ne point se séparer ni d'accorder à rien qu'elle n'ait été consentie par le Roy et rendue publique: Après avoir ainsi pourvu à la prospérite générale, à la Liberté publique et individuelle, à la sureté des propriétés: il faut remedier au desordre des finances, remplir le Vuide [vide], effrayant du Trésor Royal; la dette publique est énorme, outre cela la gloire de la Couronne la sureté de l'État exigent des dépenses annuelles et considérables; il faut y satisfaire, il faut payer, c'est le cri général du peuple Lorrain dont le Tiers État du Bailliage de Longuyon fait partie, il le veut il est prêt ce Tiers-état, à faire tous les sacrifices, et ceux de ses membres qui par leurs charges jouissent des privileges pécuniaires y renoncent volontiers et en donnent ici leurs déclarations.

En récompense ce tiers-etat ose t'il trop demandé? lorsqu'il ne demande que la tranquillité dans ses maisons, dans son commerce, dans ses voyages. et pour l'obtenir, il sollicite du Coeur patriotique du Souverain et des représentants de la Nation; L'abolition entière de tous les impôts qui existent, de l'industrie qui dégrade l'homme, anéantit les arts et tue le mérite, de la corvée personnelle, des droits de franc-fief, de centième de denier, de la chancellerie, des traites et foraines, de la Marque des cuirs, de la Gabelle, de la Chatrerie, enfin de tous ces droits odieux compris sous le nom de Régie et de ferme qui entretiennent dans l'état un corps perfide qui le devore, et qui ne produisant que trop souvent la Ruine entière des particuliers, le trouble dans les familles, la honte et l'ignonoinie [ignominie] attachée à la peine de la contravention.

Qu'en place de ces droits Ruineux pour le peuple sans être pour plus du tiers de ce qu'ils produisent d'aucun profit pour l'état, il soit fixé et établi deux impôts uniques, la taille réelle et la taille personnelle.

Que le produit de ces deux impôts serve en premier lieu à satisfaire aux charges annuelles et aux besoins de l'État, prévus ou non prévus, que ces charges et besoins satisfaits, l'excédent du produit de ces deux impôts soit réglé dans une caisse d'amortissement pour éteindre chaque année la dette publique de sorte que les impôts devant diminuer progressivement à mesure de la diminution de la dette publique, de sorte que les impots devant diminuer progressivement à mesure de la diminution de la dette publique, le peuple y verra un soulagement prochain et cette espérance le consolera.

Mais comme les dettes et les besoins de l'État sont les dettes et les besoins de tous les Citoyens ensemble et de chacun d'eux en particulier il faut et l'on demande que tous les biens sans distinction de propriétaires, ainsi que les personnes sans distinction d'ordre et de rang, soient assujetis à ces deux impôts, en conséquence, que les privilégiés d'exemption accordés à certaines villes soient abolis.

Le point le plus important semble déjà etre decidé le clergé abandonne ses anciennes prétentions, la noblesse renonce à ces priviléges et les parlements autre classe noble ont manifesté la même intention. Le Tiers-état n'avoit aucun sacrifice à faire puisqu'il les faisoit tous à la fois, ainsi plus de distinction pour les Biens, ils sont tous roturier comme ils l'étoient en sortant du Cahos.

Que l'on ne dise pas qu'au lieu de décharger le peuple, on veut ici le contraire, on se tromperoit volontairement, n'est-ce pas du peuple que vient l'argent, que tous les droits dont on demande la suppression, produisent; et ou seroit le mal? si au lieu de payer de dix de vingt enfin d'autant de manière différentes qu'il y a d'impôts différents, on satisfait aux besoins de l'état par deux impôts uniques et de facile perception.

Loing [Loin] que ces deux impôts puissent être jamais regardés par le peuple comme une surcharge, il y trouvera au contraire un avantage sensible, parce que la masse commune se trouvant augmentée par l'abolition des privileges cela doit diminuer d'autant ses charges, qu'il y retrouvera cette première Liberté essence de l'homme en éloignant de lui ces insectes dévorants de la Régie et de la ferme, il ni [n'y] aura plus de Commis, conséquemment plus d'exacteurs, plus d'inquietude, plus de chaines, plus de galère, mots affreux et qui font frémir.

Du moins si tel pouvoit être le sort du peuple, qu'il ne lui reste que des cabanes et du chaume, il lui restera au moins la douce consolation de pouvoir vivre à l'abri du pouvoir absolu et de la voracité des Commis qui troublent son sommeil et l'inquiétent à son réveil.

Mais il est loin d'être réduit à cet etat, il ne le craint pas la bonté, la justice du Roy, les lumieres, la prudence et les vertus patriotiques de ses Ministres le Rassurent. La Nation en offrant de combler le Vide effrayant du Trésor publique et d'alléger le poids de la dette dont elle se rendra caution aux conditions prérapellées ne peut elle pas espérer d'avoir le droit de décider la grande question des domaines, c'est elle qui leur a attachée l'inamovibilité, L'imprescribilité, ne peut-elle pas les leur ôter? et les joindre aux ressources que chaque province peut rassembler aux economies qu'elle peut faire avec sagesse. Ici nait un nouvel ordre de demander et de réclamation de la part du Tiers-état du Bailliage de Longuyon, il demande donc ler.

Le rétablissement des états gé[42] provinciaux de la Lorraine, la province a d'autant plus de droits de les réclamer que sous le gouvernement de ses princes elle a toujours jouit du droit précieux de s'assembler, droit qui n'a pas été aboli mais seulement interrompu.

Que les états de la province soient formés sur le plan des états généraux actuels, en conséquence que le tiers y ait autant de représentans que les deux autres ordres réunis, et que les voix y soient comptées par tête et non par ordre.

Qu'ils aient seuls le droit de dresser l'assiette de la répartition des impôts, de fixer la manière d'en faire la levée, qu'ils ayent seuls l'administration intérieure de la province, et le droit de désigner et déterminer les fonctions relatives à cette administration, de nommer ceux qui doivent les remplir et y surveiller et autoriser les communautés pour tout ce qui peut les conserner.

Que les états généraux ayant consenti l'aliénation des domaines de la couronne, les Etats provinciaux soient authorisés et les alienés dans chaque province respective, ou à les Régir et administrer, à charge d'en verser le produit dans le trésor public.

La réformation des loix civiles et Criminelles afin que celle-la ne présentent plus qu'une législation claire et précise, une procédure simple uniforme et moins dispencieuse, et que celles cy soient plus conformes aux moeurs et au caractere de la nation française, peuple le plus doux de l'univers, et dont les Loix criminelles par un contrast effrayant ne présentent partout que la mort, l'humanité demande qu'il soit donné des déffenseurs à l'accusé que toutes les charges lui soient communiquées après l'instruction de la procédure.

L'abolition des lettres de repis et de survivances presque toujours sollicités par des débiteurs de mauvaise foi, en laissant aux juges ordinaires seuls le droit d'accorder des sursis dans des cas prévus par la loi contradictoirement avec les créanciers, c'est le moyen le plus assuré de concilier l'interêt particulier avec l'intérêt général.

La suppression des droits de transit et de peage établis sur les vins de la Lorraine en traversant le pays messin et le Verdunois.

La réformation des abus erronnés qui se sont glissés dans l'administration des bois qui sont devenus de premiere nécessité, la dégradation est à son comble, et on en connoit cinq causes principales.

---

[42] Evidently by mistake, the writer started to put "généraux."

Le premier vient des sols pour Livres accordés aux officiers de maitrises, ce qui fait qu'on ne ménage aucunement les anciennes reserves parce que plus l'on vend plus l'interet est satisfait.

La seconde est la multiplicité des forges établies surtout dans cette partie Septentrionale de la Lorraine, dans le ressort seul du Bailliage de Longuyon et à une lieüe de distance de cette ville, il se trouve trois forges avec chacune un fourneau et un autre fourneau appartenant à l'abbaye Dorval, qui passe tous ses fers dans les pays étrangers.

La troisième des privileges accordés sous de vains pretextes à des forges situées dans les provinces Etrangères de s'approvisionner dans la Lorraine de bois et charbons necessaires au roulement de ces usines. La quatrième des tranchées multipliées à l'excés sous prétexte de diviser les coupes, tranchées qui coûtent des frais aux communautés par les visittes et les reconnoissances quelles exigent des officiers de la Maitrise, qui leur en- levent une forte partie de leurs bois, qui enfin, sans être par elles mêmes d'aucune utilité donnent un plus libre accés au pillage par la facilité qu'elle procurent de transporter les bois coupés en délit.

Le cinquième la modicité des gages accordés aux gardes des bois du Roi et des Communautés, les gardes n'étant pas responsables des délits et ne trouvant pas dans leurs gages le moyen de se subsister, négligent de veiller à la conservation des bois qui leur sont confiés.

Ce n'est qu'en remediant particulièrement aux abus qui découlent de ces cinq causes que les bois et forêts se conserveront se régéneront, aussi l'on demande avec instance à Sa Majesté en suppliée d'ordonner que les gages des gardes de bois seront fixés à L'avenir à la somme de 200 t. à prendre sur le produit des bois et qu'à ce moyen ils seront responsables des délits.

Que les forges et fourneaux seront reduits à un certain nombre suivant la possibilité et l'état actuel des bois.

Que les priviléges accordés à des forges étrangères seront retirés. Que les sols pour Livres du prix des ventes seront ôtés aux officiers des maitrises, sauf à regler leurs honoraires par argent et par vacation.

Qu'il sera fait deffense expresse sous des peines rigoureuses à quelque personne ce puisse être de transporter les bois et charbons hors du Royaume.

Enfin qu'il n'y aura plus de tranchées dans les bois[43] et que les forges ne pourront s'approvisionner que dans les bois du Roi et des seigneurs, de sorte que les bois des Communautés leur restent en entier tant pour leurs affouage que pour les besoins de construction et réparation des maisons particulières et des édifices publiques, et que les proprietaires des forges et usines ne pourront convertir en charbons aucun bois de futaye.

Le Souverain en est outre instament supplié d'ordonner, que la prestation représentative de la corvée continuera à se payer en argent en laissant ce-

---

[43] Difference of texts between *Arch. Nat.* C15/20 text and *Arch. Moselle* text.

pendant aux états provinciaux le droit de faire adjuger dans chaque communauté la quantité des toises qui leur aura été fixée, et le prix supporté par les trois ordres. Que les fonds precédens de la vente des bois communaux seront déposés dans chaque communauté en un trêsor destiné à cet effet lequel sera par elle garanti, quelles y puiseront pour leurs dépenses usuelles sur l'exposition qu'elles en feront et en vertu d'une authorisation, de ceux désignés pour cela par les états de la province quelles seront encore authorisées à les employer à des choses d'utilité publique et évidente, comme à l'établissement de magasin des Bleds pour subvenir au secours des malheureux dans des tems de disette, ou en faire des prêts pour cinq ans aux plus lesquels seront assurés par des actes autentiques et pour lesquels sa Majesté sera suppliée de faire remise de tous droits bursaux que les laboureurs qui auront besoin d'avances ou qui auront eprouvé des pertes naissantes des calamités publiques y auront la préférence et que ces prêts leur seront faits à deux et demi pour cent.

Que le prélat chargé de la feuille des bénéfices et autres collateurs ne pourrons en conférer à ceux qui en sont dejà pourvus de suffisans pour les nourrir et soutenir la dignité de leur état et les bénéficiers déjà suffisament pourvus en accepter aucun autre sous peine pour les collateurs d'être privés de leur droit et les bénéficiers de leur bénéfice? ce point n'a pas besoin d'explication c'est la loi de l'église.

Que tous les curés qui viendront à vaquer seront mises au concours, et ne seront donnés qu'au mérite, c'est le moyen le plus propre de porter à la vertu ceux qui se distinguent au Saint Ministère des autels.

Que les prêtes réguliers rentreront dans le couvent de l'ordre dont ils ont juré de suivre la règle, et leurs curés données aux prêtes séculiers par la voie du Concours; Le bon ordre la religion exigent cette réforme.

Qu'à l'avenir les constructions, réparations des presbitères des églises et clochers seront au compte et à la charge des gros Décimateurs seuls autres que les curés chargés du soin des âmes, et s'il se trouvent que ceux-cy soient seuls Décimateurs, que l'argent de leur obligation se prendera sur la masse du produit des commandes et des autres bénéfices dont on na demandé que les revenus fussent mis en économat, c'est par là que les dixmes rentreront dans leur première destination.

Que les chasses domaniales seront laissées à Bail, comme les pêches par les états de la province, et le produit verser dans la caisse d'amortissement destinée à éteindre la dette publique.

Le Tiers état se jette au pied du Trône de son Roi, et se confiant en sa bonté paternelle, il ose encore lui demander avec instance la suppression des Colombiers, et voliers; ou la réduction à un seul dans chaque communauté; avec déffense aux propriétaires de qu'elle qualité ils puissent être de lacher leurs pigeons dans les tems des semailles et des moissons.

L'exemption de la dixme et du terrage pour tous les fruits et grains de la terre qui se coupent et se mangent en vert: pour tous les légumes pomme de terre et autres qui se plantent et se receuillent soit en versaine, soit dans les jardins et enclos.

L'abolition entière de la banalité des fours, moulins, et pressoirs.

La suppression des huissiers priseurs.

Les maux affreux qui découlent particulièrement de ces quatre derniers objets de réclamation de la part du tiers état toucheront sans doute le Coeur paternel du Souverain, le laboureur, l'artisan occupé à semer à recolter voit avec douleur les pigeons dévorer une partie de ces sueurs et de son travail dont ils s'engraissent pour venir ensuite orner la table du Riche. Tous gémissent de se voir privés par la Dixme et le terrage d'une part considérable de ces fruits, de ces légumes semés et plantés uniquement pour les besoins de l'agriculture qui demande d'être encouragée plus que jamais, et pour la nourriture des individus pauvres et malheureux qui ne trouvent que dans ces fruits et légumes le moyen de substenter leurs famille indigente et de satisfaire aux charges publiques, de voir leur bleds et leurs pates perdus en partie pour eux, parce que la loi rendue en faveur de la banalité devient dans les mains de ceux à qui elle appartient une verge de fer et leur donne tout droit de vexer impunément, en moulant et cuisant à leur gré, se plaindre ce seroit s'exposer à être encore plus maltraité.

Les huissiers priseurs ne grèvent pas moins sensiblement le peuple, Leurs vocations Exorbitantes et exigées sans aucun ménagement sans parler d'autres inconvenients qui résultent de leur établissements sont une surcharge cruelle et affligente, elles n'enlèvent que trop souvent à la veuve et à l'orphelin le peu qui leur reste, ces êtres malheureux ont à pleurer en même tems et la perte de leurs mari, de leur père, mère et parent et la perte du bien qu'ils pouvoient en espérer.

Fait et arrêté en l'assemblée générale du tiers-état du Bailliage de Longuyon, en présence de tous les deputés des villes et Communautés dudit bailliage, qui ont signé à Longuyon cejourd'huy 26 Mars 1789.

Jenot,   Petitjean,   Guillaume[44]

Lib,   Mangin[45]

[Fifty-six signatures.]

NO. 20. THE NOBLES OF THE BAILLIAGE OF LONGWY

Cahier reprinted from MS text, *Arch. Moselle* B4191.

P.V.-MS, *Arch. Moselle* B4191. There was a committee, and the cahier was adopted March 23.

Convocation: 2d type, reunion at Metz.

> L'intention du Roy étant pleinement démontrée par la seule convocation des états généraux, dans une sage proportion des trois ordres qui les composent.
>
> L'ordre de la noblesse du baillage de longwy:

[44] Evidently the "Guillaume" charged with the making of the cahier.
[45] The secretary of the assembly.

Pénétrée d'amour, de reconnaissance, et animée du plus grand zèle à concourir aux vues bienfaisantes de sa Majesté.

Demande

1.—Que l'assemblée des états généraux se renouvelle dans des tems fixés et périodiques.

2.—Que les Ministres soient comptables aux états généraux de l'administration des finances comme le seul moyen d'en prévenir la dépradation.

3.—Que les provinces soient érigées en états provinciaux dont la forme et l'organization sera réglée d'aprés les états généraux.

4.—Que dans chaque province il y ayt un tribunal heraldique composé d'un nombre suffisant de gentils hommes pour juger deffinitivement des preuves de noblesse, et autorise a en donner les attestations nécessaires pour être admis aux états.

5.—Que toutes les charges anoblissantes à prix d'argent qui diminuent le mérite réel de la noblesse, en les rendant trop multipliées soient supprimées, et que la noblesse ne soit plus donnée qu'à ceux qui l'auront véritablement mérité par des services rendus, ou talents essentiels.

6.—La liberté de la presse comme le seul rempart qu'on puisse opposer aux abus, en les faisant connaitre, mais a la charge aux imprimeurs de se conformer aux réglements qui pourront être fait, comme d'opposer leurs noms à tous leurs ouvrages et de répondre personellement de tout ce qui pourrait être contraire à la religion, à l'ordre, et à l'honnetété publique.

7.—La liberté individuelle aux français, d'aller et de venir, et de vivre ou ils voudront dans l'intérieur du Royaume.

8.—Que cette partie de la noblesse la moins aisée, et la plus particulièrement vouée à l'état militaire comme le seul quelle puisse embrasser ne soit plus exposée à être plusieurs années à la fuitte des régiments, avant d'obtenir de l'employ, ce qui les constituent dans des dépenses auxquelles ils ne peuvent fournir et qui les en éloigne nécessairement.

9.—Que tous ceux qui embrassent la deffence du Roy et de la Patrie, ne soient plus bornées dans leur embition [ambition] et émulation que ceux qui n'ont ni protection ni recommandation, s'ils en ont, leur talents puissent parvenir aux grades les plus distingués.

10.—Comme un moyen de bonification qui peut s'étendre à d'autres partis, que dans l'assemblée des états généraux on fasse un examen scrupuleux des grâces pécuniaires si multipliés et sans nul proportion la plus part données à l'intrigue, aux sollicitations, et la faveur plutôt que sur des justes titres pour les obtenir, ce qui diminue le mérite et la valeur des derniers.

11.—Que tous les bénéfices simples, à charge d'âmes, canonicats, abbayes, prieurés réguliers ou en commande, à la nomination du Roy, soient donnés avec plus de justice et d'égalite, particuliérement au mérite sans distinction d'état et non accumulées sur une même tête, pour fournir à un luxe contraire aux maximes de l'église.

327

12.—Que les sujets des pays étrangers ou il n'y a pas de réciprocité soient exclu des bénéfices qui sont en france et qui doivent être dévolue de droit aux fidèles sujets du Roy.

13.—Qu'il y ayt une loix fondamentale et constitutionnelle qui régle les droits du monarque et ceux de la nation que l'un des droits de cette loix en ce qui concerne les sujets, prononce l'abolition des lettres de cachets, comme contraire à la liberté des citoyens et aux loix qui prononcent seules des peines, que cependant pour l'honneur et le repos des familles, il puisse en être, décernée sur leur demande, en suite de délibération convoquée judiciairement, avec liberté aux accusés de se procurer un défenseur et se demander la preuve des faits qu'on leurs imputent.

14.—Que tout citoyen ne puisse être arrêté et détenu dans les prisons, plus de quatre vingt heures, sans être remise en liberté en fournissant caution, hors les cas de délits qui mériteraient peine corporelle; qu'alors ils soient livrés aux juges naturels qui pourront toujours les revendiquer.

15.—Comme le bonheur des peuples dépend des loix c'est pourquoy on demande que la procédure civile et criminelle soit examinée et reformée par des juristes consuls les plus sages et les plus éclairés, que les tribunaux d'exception et de commission ne soient plus connus, que les priviléges exclusives soient supprimés, qu'il en soit de même des huissiers priseurs si à charge au public, en un mot que toutes les formes judiciaires soient simplifiés et moins onéreuses.

16.—Que toutes les propriétés soient respectées et assurées, que le propriétaire ainsy que le cultivateur ne puissent être contrariés dans son industrie en aucune manière.

17.—Que la Nation assemblée par les représentants ayt seule le droit d'accorder des impôts des subsides, de faire des emprunts, qui ne pourront dans aucun cas être prorogés, que jusqu'au rétour périodique des états généraux, qui auront seul le droit d'en consentir le renouvellement et la continuation, et si par des circonstances imprévues la ditte assemblée n'avait pas lieu, dans l'instant tous impots cesseront de droits.

18.—Que le nombre des impôts soit réduit à un réel et personnel, dont la répartition sera réglée indistinctement et proportionnellement par les états provinciaux, qui feront charges d'en rendre la perception simple, facile, et moins onereuse, de manière que les deniers qui en proviendront soient versés sans frais dans les coffres du Roy.

19.—Qu'il soit étably une caisse d'amortissement pour servir à l'acquittement de la dette publique et successivement au remboursement de toutes les charges en finances en commençant par les plus à charges et onéreuses.

20.—Que les fruits de la regalle et des bénéfices en commande qui viendront à vacquer entrent dans la caisse d'amortissement ainsy que les retenues qui peuvent être faittes sur les gros bénéfices, dont ceux qui en seront pourvus à l'avenir, seront encore trop heureux de les obtenir à la condition d'une réduction de la moitié du revenu qui peut y être attaché.

21.—Que tout ce qui se paye à Rome comme annates, frais de dispences et autre soient supprimés, et versés dans la caisse d'amortissement à la décharge du peuple.

22.—Que le Commerce n'éprouve plus d'entraves dans l'interieur du Royaume, que les droits de traites foraines marque de cuire et généralement tout ce qui est compris sous la dénomination odieuse de fermes et régies, soient suprimées.

23.—Qu'on facilite l'exportation comme le seul moyen d'attirer l'argent de l'étranger, qu'on cherche à donner une nouvelle activité à l'agriculture et aux arts et aux manufactures de tous genres.

24.—Qu'il soit permis aux capitalistes de pretter par obligation à terme, portant intérêt ainsi qu'il se pratique en lorraine ce qui ferait un trés grand avantage pour les commerçants et les particuliers qui ne veuillent pas alliener leurs fonds dans l'espérance d'acquisition qui leur conviennent, et qui autrement garderaient un argent qui ne rapporterait rien.

25.—Qu'il n'y ait plus de gabelle, que le sel et le tabac soit marchand, le prix plus moderé, alors il se fera une plus grande consommation du premier, les cultivateurs pouvant en donner à leurs bestiaux, le prix de ces deux objets étant aussi plus raproché de l'étranger, plus de contrebande, ce qui conserverait au Roy beaucoup de sujet, qui en encourant la peine qui est une cause de désolation pour les familles par le préjugé qui y est attaché et tout ce qu'il en coute aux malheureux pour le racheter.

26.—Ni ayant plus le même nombre d'hommes employés dans les fermes combien de bons sujets qui ne quitteront plus le militaire dans l'espérance d'une place qui leur était quelquefois promise avant le temps de leur congé absolu, combien aussi de bras utiles rendus à l'agriculture et d'individus au commerce dont ils pourront s'occuper.

27.—De changer l'administration des bois, de la rendre uniforme dans tout le royaume, que les frais de marque et délivrance qui sont exorbitans, soient modéré, qu'on apporte plus de soins à leurs conservations, que les parties connues sous la dénomination de clair chêne ou l'on coupe toujours sans remplacer, et autres susceptibles de l'être soient replantés, qu'on établisse des gardes en nombre suffisant et salariés de maniere à être responsables des délits dont il ni auraient pas de rapports faits, et qu'ils soient toujours dans la crainte de leur révocation.

28.—Si la pénurie des bois commence à se faire sentir, si on ne peut en modéré la consommation que par la suppression des bouches à feu, que les forges et autres usines de cette nature, possédées par de riches abbayes considerées comme un objet de dissipation et de commerce qui n'est pas fait pour ceux qui sont par état vouée à la priere et à la meditation, soient interdits et supprimes de préférence à toutes autres.

29.—Que les deniers provenant des ventes de bois communaux ne soient plus déposés dans la caisse des receveurs généraux ou elle si consomme à la longue, mais dans les coffres des municipalités, avec la liberté aux communautés de les placer en rentes constituées à terme ou autrement s'ils n'ont pas dans l'instant occasion de les employer.

30.—S'il reste peu de bois susceptible d'être employé dans les constructions de bàtiments qu'il soit déffendu d'en couper pour tout autres usages comme l'abus s'en est introduit.

31.—La corvée en nature ayant été convertie en deniers par des motifs de compassiont pour le peuple donnant aujourd'hui occasion à des reclamations vives et générales, on demande que la construction et entretien des routes soient de nouveau distribuées par tâches aux communautés avec liberté de les faire eux-mêmes, ou à prix d'argent; que les villes, bourgs, et villages qui en devient affranchis par des priviléges, ou leurs grands éloignements des routes, contribuent à leurs constructions par un impôt pécuniaire et leger tel qu'il pourra être réglé par les états provinciaux aussi dans le cas de nouvelle construction qu'a l'exemple des romains, on y employé le militaire au moyen d'une augmentation de solde, ce qui leur serait trés avantageux, et d'une grande économie, par la difference du payement des ouvriers qui y sont ordinairement employés.

32.—Les bannalitées de fours et moulin considérés comme une gêne, les sujets du roy demandent qu'il leur soient permis de se racheter de cette servitude et de rompre leurs chaines, aussi que les seigneurs puissent egalement renoncer à ce droit.

33.—On demande qu'il y ait une uniformité générale dans le royaume pour toutes espèces de poids et mesures, soit pour les liquides aunages et arpentages des terres.

34.—On demande la confirmation des anciens priviléges de la ville de longwy, à la faveur desquels les bourgeois s'y sont établis, ils sont d'autant plus susceptibles de cette grâce que depuis nombre d'années la population diminue, que le commerce y languit, et que le plus sur moyen de lui rendre son ancien état, serait que dans les temps ou l'exportation des grains serait permise, elle n'ait son effet qu'autant qu'ils soient achetés sur les marchés de la frontière comme de cette ville, alors les étrangers qui y viendraient soit par leurs consommations ou achats de marchandises de toutes espèces pourraient ranimer le commerce qui est tout ce que peuvent désiré les habitants, il serait également avantageux que les foires qui se tiennent dans différents tems de l'année soient de plus longue durée, il est donc à désirer qu'il plaise au roy d'accorder six jours de plus à chacune des foires d'hiver et seulement trois à celle d'été qui ferait tomber celles qui se tiennent dans le pays étranger à une lieue de la frontière dans le pays de Luxembourg qui n'ont été établie que pour nuire au commerce de cette ville.

35.—Les députés aux états généraux s'occuperont à faire constater la dette nationale, et ils ne consentiront à aucune subsides que la constitution ne soit prealablement établie, que tous les articles y dessus énoncés n'ayant été proposés et soumis aux représentants de la nation après laquelle délibera-tion ils pourront accorder seulement des secours proportionnés aux cir-constances et besoins réels de l'état et toujours de manière à ce qu'il ne pésent pas trop sur les fidéles sujets du roy.

Fait, clos, et arrété en l'assemblée de la Noblesse du baillage de longwy le 23 mars 1789.

[Six signatures and the secretary (illegible).]

NO. 21. THE THIRD ESTATE OF THE BAILLIAGE OF LONGWY

Cahier reprinted from MS text, *Arch. Moselle* B4191. The date of adoption is correct. By the title, one would be led to suppose that this was the cahier of the town.

P.V.-MS, *Arch. Moselle* B4191, and parts in p.v. of three orders. The Third Estate did not approve of the cahier of the Clergy and refused to unite with them. There was a committee, and the cahier was adopted March 23. Convocation: 2d type, reunion at Metz.

DOLÉANCES ET REMONTRANCES DES HABITANS
DE LA VILLE ET BANLIEÜE DE LONGWY

Les habitans de la Ville et Banlieue de Longwy, pleins de zèle, d'amour et de Reconnoissance envers leur Souverain qui a daigné manifester à tous ses sujets en les rassemblant prés de luy, les intentions bienfaisantes dont son Coeur paternel est animé, ont crû devoir y répondre en luy offrant l'Énumération sincère, de tous les Maux et Surchage sous lesquelles ils gémissent, et aussi les moyens d'adoucir leur sort; mais ils ne se dissimulent point en même tems, que les besoins urgents de l'État exigent des secours promts et efficace: Ils supplient donc un Roy si digne de l'être, d'agréer le Voeu et la promesse qu'ils apportent à ses pieds, d'y concourir unanimenent et d'y coopérer selon leurs facultés.

Ils esperent Meriter par cette Marque Indubitable de leur attachement, que leurs justes Réclamations seront Écoutées.

1.—Priviléges et franchises de la ville de Longwy:

Longwy, et son ancienne prevôté appartenoit aux Ducs de Bar avant de passer sous la Domination francoise; Les habitans jouissoient alors de toutes especes de franchises et suivant un chartre du 16 janvier 1589, Dé-posée au Greffe de L'hotel de Ville, la Noblesse et le Tiers-État contri-buoient egalement aux charges publiques.

Par le traité de paix conclu a Nimegue en 1679, Longwy fut cédé à la France; Louis XIV, fit démolir la ville peu de tems après, et la fit rebatir sur la Montagne voisine.

Par des lettres patentes donnés à Versailles en 1684, au mois de Dé-cembre, Registrée en parlement le trois Fevrier suivant et dont un exemplaire est jointe au présent; Sa Majesté accorda aux habitans les privilèges, exemption et franchise cy énoncée sous la foi desquels la ville ne tarda pas à être peuplée.

Toutes les fois que les fermiers ont entrepris d'anticiper sur les privilèges, la justice du Roy est venue au secours des habitans.

Par un arrêt de son Conseil du 30 Novembre 1700, elle a déchargé les particuliers Etrangers établis à Longwy de prendre des lettres de naturalité. Par un autre decret du 8 Juillet 1704 Sa Majesté a déclaré que son intention etoit, que les villes de Longwy et Sarrelouis fussent exemptes de tout droit et affaire extraordinaire.

Par autre du 18 Decembre 1708 les officiers du Bailliage de Lonwy,[46] ont été déchargés des augmentations de gages, pour lesquels ils avoient été employés dans les roles arretés au Conseil. Par autre du 3 Xbre [décembre], 1709, les memes habitans ont été dechargés du payement des droits de centième denier et Insinuations Laïques.

Par lettres patentes données à Paris au mois de Juin 1716 régistrée au Parlement le 15 Xbre [décembre] suivant, tous le privilèges accordés par celles de 1684 ont été confirmés.

Que infinité d'autre Loix émanée depuis du Souverain, ont consacré les privilèges, qui ont été reconnus, tout recemment encore, par l'arrêt du Conseil du 19 Septembre 1780, revetus de lettres patentes données à Versailles le 15 Novembre suivant, Registres au Parlement le 11 Decembre aussy suivant portant prorogation des foires de Lonwy.

On devrait croire d'aprés de Semblables titres, que la ville de Longwy n'a point à se plaindre et qu'elle a jouit paisiblement jusqu'a ce jour, de ces franchises et privilèges.

Mais quels titres auroient pu contenir l'avidité des fermiers; leurs entreprises sur la ville de Longwy ont été formée par degrées; tentée par un sistême révoltant; Appuier par un concert artificieux et consommé par des Manoeuvres repréhensibles; il faut pour saisir l'ensemble en parcourir le détail.

En 1769 les Regisseurs se sont fait autoriser à percevoir un droit exorbitant sur les bestiaux entrant dans la ville pour la consommation. Dans un autre tems, ils ont introduit les droits sur la Marque des cuirs; dans un autre encore, ils ont fait imposer les papiers et Cartons. Les Regisseurs ont aussy entrepris differentes fois, d'établir les droits sur la marque des fers on vouloit encore y étendre la ferme de la vente exclusive du tabac si ces tentatives odieuses sont toujours demeurées sans effet, elles n'en n'ont pas moins affaiblis les Moyens de la ville, par le nombre de procès ruineux qu'elle s'est Vu forcée de soutenir, pour faire reprimer les attentats de la ferme et de la régie; encore la sagacité financiere est-elle parvenuë à

---

[46] The MS is inconsistent in the spelling of Longwy, sometimes spelling it with the g, and sometimes without.

mettre des entraves au Commerce, par l'établissement de Bureaux, tant pour faire les déclarations des fers venant de l'étranger, que pour la perception d'un droit de quarante cinq sols par livre de tabac qui entre dans la ville.

Les revenus patrimoniaux de la Ville, déduction faite des cens et vingtième dont ils sont chargés envers le Roy, et des frais d'entretient, ne montent pas a 1000 d. par an, on concluera donc aisément, que les charges personnelles à la Ville, excédent de beaucoup cette modique somme; aussi les Officiers Municipaux, ont ils été obligés de restreindre eux-mêmes, les privilèges des habitans, en demandant des octrois.

Jusqu'en 1772, L'octroi de la Ville de Longwy, consistoit en un droit sur les grains; les habitans en étoient affranchis, le produit de ces octroi n'étoit grevé que du 6e au profit de sa Majesté.

Un surcroit de charges, à force de solliciter à la même époque la conversion de ces Octroi, en un droit d'entrée sur toutes espéces de Marchandises; L'arret du Conseil qui en autorise la perception, a grevé une partie des habitans en exceptant l'autre; aussy le parlement la t'il jamais Sanctionné; mais la Ville n'en a pas moins perçu L'octroi.

Quoi qu'il en soit, cette ressource allarmante n'a pu suffire à l'acquittement des charges les régisseurs S-çus[47] bientot s'appropier plus des trois quarts de l'Octroi aujourd'hui même qu'il ne subsiste plus n'osent-ils pas prétendre que les accessoires multipliés de la régie sont indépendans du principal doivent continuer d'être perçues.

Les Maux que la Ferme et la Régie ont causés à la Ville de Longwy ne sont pas les seuls dont les habitans ont à se plaindre ils énoncent à regret qu'au lieu de trouver quelqu'avantages à posséder dans leur enceinte des officiers établis au gouvernement de la place, ces mêmes officiers leur ont fait subir le Joug de l'imposition la plus accablante.

Tandis que la Municipalité cherchant à remplir ses charges s'adressoit au Conseil pour obtenir une prorogation de ses Octrois, les officiers d'état-Major exposoient au même conseil que les revenus de la ville excédant les dittes charges, ils demandoient en conséquence qu'elle fut tenue de leur payer un homme de 1.200 d. par année tant pour leur logement que pour Ostencils, il est à observer qu'ils étoient alors et sont encore Logés dans les batiments du Roy.

Cependant par arret du Conseil du 18 Novembre 1755 cette somme leur fut accordée sur ce simple et faux exposé sans avoir entendu la Ville et contrairement aux lettres patentes de 1684 lesquelles entre autre, dispositions déchargent pour toujours les habitans de Longwy de logement des gens de guerre tant de garnison ordinaire qu'extraordinaire de subsistance et contributions pour ceux des étapes et impositions tant en argent fourrages qu'autrement.

Rien de si abusif que les autre charges Militaires, qui se sont accrües

[47] Unidentified: "Ci-ceux"?

successivement et dont on a encore grévé la Ville sans aucun titres valables on exige sans avoir égard à la situation des finances de la Ville et au prejudice de ses privileges:

1. 480 d.[48] à titre du sucre d'Étrennes aux Officiers de l'État-Major.
2. 200 d. pour le logement du Commissaire des Guerres, il en a un en nature dans les pavillons du Roy et ne réside pas.
3. 50 d. pour celui du Commissaire d'artillerie il réside à Metz.
4. 150 d. pour celui du Directeur du Génie il reside egallement à Metz.
5. 20 d. pour celui du Lieutenant de Maréchaussée, il réside à Montmédy.
6. 100 d. pour celui du Directeur D'Artillerie il en a un en Nature dans les pavillons, et reside à Mezières.
7. 36 d. pour celui de la Blancherie des troupes.
8. 250 d. pour celui du subdélegue de Monsieur L'Intendant.
9. 150 d. pour la cotte part de l'entretien des Bureaux de l'Intendant.

Toutes les sommes réunies montent à 2.636
Les cens et vingtième, affectée sur les biens patrimoniaux à 3.189
Les sols pour livres pris dans les Octrois au profit de la régie
   à environ 3.400
                                                 9.225

Les dépenses personnelles à la ville en égard a ses charges considerables et malgré les soins économiques des officiers-municipaux montent à environ 8.000

     Total des charges annuelles 17.225
La recette consistant uniquement dans les revenus patrimoniaux et les Octrois montent au plus à 12.000

Partant la dépense excéde annuellement la recette environ 5.225

Ce tableau effrayant fait connoitre suffisament la justice et la Nécessité des plaintes de la ville de Longwy depuis l'établissement des charges extraordinaires, et les entreprises des fermiers sur les privileges de la Ville, le commerce est tombé dans un langeure [langueur] absolue, la ville est réduite au quart des habitants et les maisons ont perdues les trois quarts de leur valeur; examinons maintenant le motif qui a peuplé Lonwy dans le principe et qui a rendu pendant quelques tems la ville après fleurissante. Il est évident que ce sont les priviléges accordés a la Ville en 1684, tant

[48] "Deniers," but from the table which follows, the figures must refer to "livres."

qu'ils ont été respectés Longwy sembloit s'accroître chaque jour, aussitôt qu'on n'y a porté atteinte la Ville s'est dépeuplée, le Commerce s'est anéanti, et la plus affreuse misére s'est rapidement étendue sur le peu d'habitants qui lui restoit.

Les priviléges de Longwy n'étoient donc pas du nombre de ceux à la révocation desquels la nécessité des circonstances pouvoit forcer, et il n'y a d'autres moyens d'y ramener des habitants qu'en les faisant Revivre dans toute leur Etendue.

Cette vérite reconnuë la ville ne peut recouvrer ses priviléges qu'en la soustrayant d'une manière absolue à toutes especes d'impots extraordinaire, il faudroit donc la mettre à l'abri de toutes les entreprises financieres et Militaires, écarter de son enceinte tous les Bureaux de Régie, abolir tous les Octrois Municipaux dont les trois quarts ont fait la proye des fermiers en ruinant le commerce et le Citoyen, Renoncer de la part de Sa Majesté au Cens éxorbitant effecté sur les biens patrimoniaux et permettre à la ville de faire mettre en coupe réglée, de vingt-cinq ans environ deux cent quatre vingt arpents de bois faisant partie de son patrimoine.

En retranchant de ses besoins actuels et personnels la ville trouveroit à force d'économie de quoi satisfaire ses charges.

Ces revenus patrimoniaux dégage de tous Cens et impositions montroient à environ six mille Livres, elle feroit en sorte que ïa dépense n'excédat pas plus la recette, mais il faut établir à cet effet son administration sur une baze solide.

A cet égard le Voeu général des citoyens et à l'exemple du grand Ministre, qui ranime dans ce moment la confiance publique, les officiers Municipaux publient les Comptes annuels du Receveur pour être fournis à l'examen. Et à la censure de tous les individus qui prennent part à la chose commune.

Il n'est pas moins intéressant pour le bon ordre et la Gestion des affaires Municipales de supprimer les offices de Maire, de Receveur, de Greffier, et d'établir une forme d'Élection de tous les Officiers Municipaux qui previenne les cabales et assure un juste choix.

L'éxécution de ces projets rétabliront à Lonwy, le bon ordre et la prospérite; D'aigne Sa Majesté S'y arrêter sa justice suprême rassure d'avance les habitans, et sa bonté leur fait espérer un reméde aussy prompt qu'efficace.

Article 2. Impositions

Il est un principe certain baze de tout immuable appliquable egallement aux plus interets comme aux plus médiocres parce qu'il est fondé sur la justice et sur la vérite, C'est la proportion entre la recette et la dépense.

On se croit donc fondé à réclamer contre l'imposition de la Capitation qui loin d'être proportionnée à l'amoindrissement des moyens de subsistance des citoyens asemblé au contraire s'accroître pour chaque particulier à mesure de la diminution de leurs facultés on peut démontrer par la Comparaison des quottes des habitans de même états des Villes principales de la province que celles de Lonwy s'élévent à peu prés d'un tiers de plus de capitation quoique les Ressources qu'allimentent ici le commerce et l'industrie et conséquemment les Bénéfices soient infiniment moindres par ces raisons la même l'égalité de quotter sur cet objet seroit encore disproportionnée.

Les habitans de cette ville ont été chaque année imposés à la Capitulation sans doute selon les besoins de l'état, ils ont trouvé la contribution d'autant plus considérable et plus grévante que les privilegiés qui par leur aisance auroiennt pû les alleger d'une partie de cet impôt portoient ailleurs leurs contributions, il paroit étrange que les Consommateurs d'une Cité payent leurs quottes des impositions publiques dans un lieu éloigné de leur domiciles, il seroit donc de toute équité d'obliger les Contribuables de supporter em commun le poid d'un imposition prelevée sur le lieu qu'ils ont choisis pour leur Résidence.

Le Capitation et Subvention se percoivent sur les gens de la campagne soit en taxes personnelles soit en perceptions sur les terres, prés, vignes, chauviers, etc.

On observera que les Subventions devient d'autant plus onéreuse aux Communautés que le propriétaire non domicile ne Contribue à la somme imposée sur le Village ou qu'affermant ses possessions son fermier ne paye que moitié de cette taille l'autre est répartie sur tous les autres habitans.

On conclura donc qu'il est injuste que la propriétaire quoique non domicilié ne soulage point la communaute en raison du bien qu'il posséde dans le village imposé, On observera encore que cette subvention semble repartie en proportion de la force de la population d'une paroisse et qu'elle devrait l'etre en raison des terres formant le bais et dépendante de la Communauté; Le Voeu des habitans de la campagne serai donc.

1.—Que lad. [la dite] subvention soit repartie et divisée en tailles de proprieté sur les Biens réels, et en taille d'exploitation pour les simples cultivateurs.

2.—Que la taxe personnelle soit divisée en quottes egalles relatives aux Biens Communaux partagés entre les habitans et en taxation particulière et proportionnée tant à l'aisance qu'a la profession du Contribuable. Il existe un autre imposition intitulé en premier lieu Subsistance des Mandians cette dénomination fut ensuite convertie en celle d'accessoire a la capitation et à la Subvention, elle existe d'autant plus les réclamations du peuple que sa déstination luy est inconnue, il désireroit ou d'en être affranchi ou d'être instruit du Motif qui fait établir cette taxation.

La prestation en argent de la corvée vient encore exciter les Murmures du tiers ordre, il ne plaint point de partager aves les gens de la campagne le pénible fardeau de l'entretien des routes, mais il croit juste de reclamer que personne ne puisse être exempt de cette contribution que le clergé que la Noblesse dont les facultés sont généralement au dessus de celles des contribuables soient egallement astreints à cette surcharge d'autant qu'il leur paroit contradictoire que ceux qui contribuent égallement à la defection des Routes, soient absolument exempt des frais relatifs à leur entretien.

Le Voeu des habitants tant des villes, que des Campagnes seroit qu'on laissat à chaque Communaute le soin d'entretenir la portion de chaussée proportionnée à sa force qu'on évaluat par un tarif le prix de la Toise à entretenir sauf les accidents particuliers et imprévus et qu'on versat dans la Caisse de chaque Communauté les sommes à ce destinée laquelle seroit employée dans les tems morts par les dittes communautés et deviendroit par ce moyen non une charge mais un soulagement qui procureroit une subsistance assurée à tous les malheureux.

On estime qu'il seroit avantageux et economique pour l'État d'employer à l'exemple des Romains les Troupes aux Contributions des nouvelles routes.

On ne doit point obmettre la répartition des Vingtièmes sur les Maisons, cet impot terrible qui vient grever les proprietaires, On estime que le deperissement et la Vétusté des Maisons diminue de prix et de valeur soit par la dépopulation, soit par les ravages du tems, on doit porter sur ces objets la même attention que sur les autres c'est à dire les imposer en raison de leur réele et actuelle.

Il est à observer que l'on s'est permis de donner sur les biens de campagne une extention condamnable et criminelle à cet impot déjà si pezant, on a compris dans l'évaluation et la taxation desdits biens les maisons cy attachés, Innovation d'autant plus injuste qu'il paroit de toute équité que la demeure de celui qui cultive un bien déjà grévé soit affranchit d'un impot que ledit bien ne payeroit point s'il n'étoit pas cultivé.

Le peuple se plaint encore d'une autre imposition connue sous le Nom d'Industrie, il desireroit plus d'equité dans cette Contribution qui selon même sa Dénomination doit etre proportionné au Commerce et à la Situation de celui qui y est astreint, or il est à observer que cet impôt ne devant porter absoluement que sur ceux qui exercent un quelque Commerce ou profession on doit le proportionné surtout au Bénéfice qu'on Suppose resulter desdittes professions que dans une ville sans aucuns débouché, il ne peut résulter que peu d'activité dans le Commerce si l'on fait attention que quantité de Marchands sont Etablis dans les Campagnes voisines, et que d'autres forains viennent encore enlever une grande partie des ventes devolues aux habitans, les ressources des habitans de cette ville sont aussy diminuée par une cause qui s'est fait sentir généralement, mais qui influe plus particulierement sur ceux qui n'ont pas le choix des moyens; On a attaché chaque Régiment des ouvriers de tous les genres, des Magasins de toutes espéces, cette observation ne paroitra point injuste s'y [si] l'on considère qu'elle est formée par ceux dont les Contributions servent à l'entretien des troupes.

On ne peut s'empecher d'ajouter encore que cette imposition nommée industrie, semble odieuse et faite pour énerver le commerce et l'activé [l'activité] puisqu'elle porte sure un Baze absolument arbitraire.

Les habitans des villes et des campagnes se plaignent amérement des droits imposés sur les denrées de première néccéssité, ils observent que ce sont principalement les objets d'une consommation journalière et indispensable qui sont grévés des droits les plus exorbitans, ils désirent unanimant que les Cuirs, les fers, les étoffes et Lainerie grossières soient exempt de toute rétribution.

On insiste plus particulièrement pour la suppression des droits sur les Cuirs d'une nécessité absolue est d'une consommation considerable surtout pour les gens à la campagne dont le genre de travail en absorbe une grande quantité soit pour leurs chaussures soit pour les harnois de leurs chevaux; Il seroit bien important que le sel soit rendu libre surtout dans une province limitrophe de L'étranger où les habitans ont sans cesse sous les yeux la difference du prix de la même denrée, il en résulteroit un bien inapréciable les campagnes ne se verroient plus enlever leurs habitans pour raison de contrebande et le nombre des Bestiaux s'augmenteroit le sel étant absolument Nécéssaire à leur santé.

Les Cures ont observé que la pluspart des épidémies qui désolent les campagnes n'ont souvent d'autres causes que la pauvrete du paisant [paysan] qui le mettant hors d'état de se procurer du sel rend insalubre sa nourriture laquelle ne consiste pour la plus grande partie qu'en Légumes grossiers.

Le Commerce du tabac ne devroit-il pas éprouver la même faveur? Si l'on ajoute à la Masse des Differentes impositions qu'on D'énuméree celle de Localité comme droits sur les papiers et cartons perçus seulement dans quelques Villes et notamment dans celles cy ceux dénommés pied fourchu Octrois acquis, etc. . . . .

On sera sans doute convaincu que cette Masse de Contributions excéde infiniment les facultés de ceux qui y sont assujétis, On concluera donc qu'il est de toute équité de diminuer leurs charges ou d'augmenter leurs moyens de subsistance soit en formant des établissements utile soit en doublant la Garnison, ce qui ne présente aucune difficulté puisque les Casernes sont en grand nombre en bon état et qu'elles ont suffit lorsqu'elle étoit plus considerable que celle qu'on désire obtenir.

On préféreroit un regiment de Cavalerie à un autre d'Infanterie parceque les engrais pour les terres étant insuffisant ce moyen suppléeroit aux besoins de l'Agriculture, en augmenteroit les produits, et conséquemment ameneroit l'abondance.

Les habitans observent encore que leurs moyens de subsistes ont été successivement réduits soit par l'échange fait avec L'Autriche qui a enlevés les Villages Nourrissiers du pays et restreint l'arrondissement soit par la diminution de la garnison soit enfin par la Mort du Gouverneur, en Residence dont les appointements considérables étoient dépensés sur les lieux; Ce n'est qu'en augmentant les Consommateurs qu'on régénérera ce Commerce et L'Industrie, l'on multiplira les moyens d'amélioration par la plus abondante circulation du Numéraire.

Tous les Citoyens de la Ville et de la Campagne osent donc espérer que l'on cherchera tous les moyens de les alleger des charges et impositions diverses qui gênent, Énervent et découragent le commerce et L'Industrie, ils leurs sembleroit avantageux à tous d'adopter le projet de l'impot unique présenté par un Bon Citoyen, il simplifieroit la perfection en détruisant les entraves subviendroit plus facilement aux besoins de l'état et consequemment rempliroit le but proposé qui est le Voeu de tous les bons francois.

Article 3. Impositions concernant les Actes

L'impot sur les actes s'étant éléves pour Longwy et sa Banlieue à un degré excessif porte une gêne trés préjudiciable dans le Commerce des immeubles on le voit encore doubler par les fermiers où leurs préposes qui enflent les droits exigibles en interprétant toujours à leurs avantage les Dispositions les moins équivoques de la Loi; les Commis, qui veillent sans cesse à la Bonification et extensions des droits de la ferme, percoivent le plus souvent sauf à restituer, la restitution n'en est pas poursuivie, Tantôt parce que l'objet est modique, tantot parce qu'on est éffrayé des suites que peut avoir un procés, il en résulte que les abus à force de se multiplier acquierent une sorte d'autorité qui n'en impose pas moins aux employés eux mêmes qu'aux Contribuables.

Outre les droits de contrôle insinuations et les Sols pour livres que les fermiers font percevoir à Longwy, en étendant abusivement ces droits à des cas non prévus par la Loi; ils y prélevent encore un droit ancien sous le nom de Tabellionnage qui est le Centième denier du prix des immeubles aliénés.

Ce droit fut establi en Lorraine et dans l'ancienne prévoté de Longwy, chose dont la Ville étoit autrefois une dépendance; il n'étoit autre chose qu'un droit de relief et de reconnaissance dû au Souverain à cause du changement de propriétaire ,aussi ne le percevoit-on que dans les cas de ventes ou d'aliénation par donnation entre vifs et Testamentaire et parce qu'il n'y avoit alors aucun autre droits établis.

Ce droit sous un nom different est le même que celui du centième denier des insinuations laïques; ce fut à raison de cette paritée et de la double perception au profit du Roy d'un même droit de centieme denier à chaque mutation de propriété que Sa Majesté, par arret de Conseil du 3 Décembre 1709, ayant reconnue qu'en effet ces droits ne differoient que de Nom, avait déchargé les habitans de Longwy de celui d'insinuation Laïque.

Les mêmes habitans n'ont pas profité longtemps des justes dispositions de cet arret: La ferme encouragée par l'inertie la Timidité et l'ignorance des Contribuables a su non seulement faire revivre le droit d'insinuation mais, a étendue avec une sorte d'affectation ce droit ainsy que celui de Tabellionage a des cas ou ils ne peuvent être dûs; On citeroit une foule d'abus à ce sujet: en voici quelques exemples frappans.

Un artisan de la Ville recoit de sa ferme par contrat de Mariage une somme de 600 qu'elle se constitue pour tous ses droits, il ne se fait aucune constitution du Chef du futur parcequ'il ne possede aucuns biens; Les Commis exigent vingt livres de Controle non compris les dix sols pour livres suivant le qualité du futur, tandis qu'ils ne devroient le controlle que sur le pied de six cent livres, ce qui produiroit cinq livres cinq sols seulement.

Supposons qu'un heritage de valeur de 800, appartienne à quatre propriétaires, chacun un quart: le premier vend son quart à un tiers moyennant 200 d.,[49] cette vente donne lieu aux droits suivants.

Controlle	2 d.	5 S.[50]	
Insinuation	3 "		
2 sols par livres	1 "		8 d.[49] 5 S.[50]
Tabellionage	2 "		

Non compris le scel, le papier, le parchemin, les frais de minutes et l'expédition.

Que le même acquereur achete le second quart moyennant pareille somme de deux cent livres: pêu un abus des plus crians les Commis étendent leur perception sur le premier quart, en sorte qu'ils percoivent les droits sur le pied de 400 d.[49]

Savoir			
Controlle	3 d.[49]	15 S.[50]	
Insinuation	6 "		15 d. 15 S.
2 Sols par livres	2 "		
Tabellionage	4 "		
D'autre part			24 d.

Que le même aquereur achete le troisième quart pour le même prix on percoit sur le prix de 600 d. faisant les trois quarts réunis de la valeur entière.

Controlle	5 d.	5 S.	
Insinuation	9 "		
2 Sols par livres	3 "		23 d. 5 S.[50]
Tabellionage	6 "		

Enfin l'achat du dernier quart engendre suivant les Commis une perception sur la valeur entiere de l'immeuble ce qui fait.

Controlle	6 d.	15 S.	
Insinuation	12 "		
2 Sols par livres	4 "		30 d. 15 S.[50]
Tabellionage	8 "		
		Total	78 d.[49] 15 S.[50]

[49] This evidently should read "livre" and not "denier."
[50] "sou," the old form was "sol." There are 20 sous in a pound (livre).

En sorte qu'y compris les Scel, papier, parchemin, les frais de minutes et expédition des quatre actes L'acquereur se trouve avoir payé plus de deux cent livres de frais pour un héritage huit cent livres.

Si L'acquéreur ne pays pas comptant le vendeur l'assujétis ordinairement à lui fournir une seconde grosse en forme pour pouvoir à deffaut de payement exercer des poursuites dans ce cas les Commis percoivent deux fois le droit de Tabellionage et le percevroient sur autant de grosse du même acte qui tombroit sous leurs mains, il leur est même arrive de le prélever deux fois sur la même grosse.

Dans le principe le droit de Tabellionage ne ce percevroit que sur le prix des ventes, Donnations entre vifs ou Testamentaire; les fermiers l'ont insensiblement étendu sur toutes especes de contrats; ils les percoivent sur les obligations; constitution, partages, Baux, Contrats de Mariage et généralement sur tous les actes que les parties contractantes sont dans le cas de faire mettre à exécution.

Les fermiers non contens de la perception exorbitante et abusive des droits établis a Longwy au préjudice des franchises de la ville ont produit et reproduit en differens tems un nouveau genre d'impot sur les immeubles: C'est le Droit d'ensaisonnement méconnu de tous tems dans la dite Ville et sa Banlieue: ce nouveau fantôme présenté avec emphase par les fermiers nés à imposés que quelques habitans timides dont les Commis ont tiré quelque parti les gens censés s'y sont soustrait la ferme s'est tue; mais ne renouvellera t'el [t-elle] pas tôt ou tard cette pretention?

Il résulte de toutes ces vexations que les Mutations de propriétés sont devenus presqu'impratiquable et que les contractans s'addressent rarement à un Officier public dans la crainte d'être écrasé de Droite trés souvent arbitraires, la pluspart des Conventions se redigent sous signature privées et, si les Jurisprudence du parlement de Metz les à constamment tolérées, cette maniere de contracter n'a pas moins donnée lieu a des difficultés sans nombre, soit qu'il fut question de prouver une parente, un Droit, un don, une propriété, soit que la rédaction en fut vicieuse obscure equivoque illegale.

On estime qu'en ne touchant aux droits de Controlle, Insinuation et deux sols pour livres qu'autant que la régle seroit générale pour le Royaume ou pour la province, les habitans de Longwy et sa Banlieue trouveroient déjà un Soulagement dans une perception mieux ordonnée de ces mêmes droits; il seroit donc à désirer qu'on s'occupât d'un réglement qui, en ainversant [renversant?] les abus encore de la perception actuelle, prévint ceux que les fausses interprétations des fermiers introduisent journellement.

Ce réglement tel clair et tel Sage il fut, ne mettroit qu'un frein léger à la cupidite si la connaissance des Contestations entre les fermiers et les contribuables, n'étoit attribuée aux juges Royaux des Lieux ou les bureaux sont établis, pour les juges sur simples Memoires et sans frais.

Le droit de centième denier des insinuations Laïques restant en vigueur à

Longwy, il semble juste de supprimer le même droit anciennement établi sous le nom de Tabellionage; cette réclamation est d'autant mieux fondée que Sa Majesté a reconnu d'avance par l'arrêt de son Conseil cy devant l'injustice de la perception de ce double droit; il Blesse évidemment ses interêts puisque les Contribuables trouvent moyen de cy soustaire en contractant à l'ombre du mistere et Sous Signature privées; il nuit également aux interêts de ces fidèles sujets, il les éloigne des formes prescrites pour contracter légalement il les expose par la à des recherches et à des procés ruineux.

Depuis la création des droits de contrôlle et d'insinuation nombre de Lieux ou le tabellionage était établi comme à Longwy en n'ont été déchargés sur le fondement que ces droits étoient réprésentaifs du Tabellionage; la ville de Longwy doit elle être plus surchargée que ne le sont toutes les provinces du royaume et n'ont-ils pas lieu de se plaindre que les Lorrains anciens frères des habitans contractent à moitié moins de frais sous la même Domination.

En supposant que le Tabellionage fait au droit Domanial ainsy que le prétendent les fermiers cette considération ne peut plus suffire en autoriser la perception, au moyen du droit équivalent résultant de l'insinuation de ces deux droits, il ne peut sans doute en subsister qu'un seul; ils appartiennent également au Roy, donc il n'y a plus de différence; Or celuy qui conviendroit de supprimer, c'est le Droit dont Sa Majeste tire le moins d'avantage, celui qui n'est pas généralement perçu en un mot c'est le Tabellionage, ce droit enfin supprimé la cause da la rareté des actes publics cessera, les familles seront en sureté, les droits de controlle et d'insinuation se multiplieront, la ferme y gagnera, et, la gêne disparue, Sa Majesté rétablira la prospérité dans le commerce des immeubles.

Améliorations
Article 1. Administration de la Justice

Un crie général dénonce les dépradations de la justice; on craint de traduire ou d'être traduit dans les tribunaux comme on craint de passer dans une route dangereuse; chacun redoute comme un fléau l'entrée des officiers de justice dans sa maison, ou d'être obligé d'avoir recours à leur ministère pour la discussion ou pour l'arrangement de ses affaires.

Ces sentiments injurieux sont-ils donc fondés? est-ce donc la justice qui est toujours coupable des excés qu'on lui attribue? non, cherchons ailleurs les causes d'un pareil soulévement.

La législation, objet si essentiel à la félicité des peuples, est de toutes les parties d'administration celle dont on se soit des moins occupé en france; nos loix sont perdues dans la confusion: on ne les connait le plus souvent que par les jugements et lors qu'on est plus à tems de les suivre.

Par une espèce de fatalité, elles donnent lieu à des interprétations presque toujours Equivoques; ces interprétations enfantent une infinité de questions, ces questions, des procés, et ces procés des arrets, qui, souvent contraire les uns des autres, ne font qu'augmenter l'embarras, de la vient que dans presque toutes les affaires, chaque partie presente pour eguide [guide], une foule de flambeaux differens, de leur choc, et de leur multitude nait d'obscurité; est-il question de prononcer? Les juges gémissent eux mêmes de l'incertitude de leurs décisions.

C'est ainsy qu'en poursuivant un droit qui parait être évident, on s'engage dans un Labirinthe dont la loi elle même semble avoir formée les détours.

A prendre la pluspart de nos loix en particulier, il n'en est guére qui n'irrite le mal en voulant le guérir; l'appareil de leurs formalités est effrayant par leurs immensités, ruineux par les impots exorbitants dont tous les actes de procédures sont grevé.

La lenteur d'un débiteur force t'elle un creancier, qui a des engagements à remplir, à se pourvoir en justice? sa demande n'étant pas contestée, les frais qu'il est obligé de faire pour obtenir un simple jugement de condamnation excédent le plus souvent la somme principale; L'objet de la demande ne seroit-il que de six livres, la condemnation engendre plus de vingt livres de frais au malheureux débiteur.

Si la demande est contestée, les frais qu'entrainent les preuves, le serment Décisoir, ou la vérification d'écriture, passent souvent deux cent livres tant par les droits de Scel, control émolumens et autres droits de Greffe réunis que par les formalités inutiles dont dépent la validite de la produce.

Par qu'el abus encore, exige-t-on l'affirmation du créancier non fondée en titre, lorsque le débiteur fait deffaut, cette formalité entraine seule pour plus de quinze livres de frais.

Sagit-il de la discussion des biens du Débiteur, point de fin; et chaque jour voit eclore des volumes d'ecritures sous la main praticienne; il est rare que le bien suffise, qu'il serve même à l'acquittement des dettes, des formalites aussy barbares que désastreuses, imaginés dans des tems de grossierté, en absorbant le plus souvent le prix; tel est le fruit que produit ordinairement les décrets forcés ou Saisies réeles.

Les adjudications volontaires sont à peu prés dans le même cas; elles sont en usage lorsqu'une héritage est indivis et ne peut être partagé, elles sont de rigueur dans les cas d'absence ou de minorité d'aucun des propriétaires; ce but de la loi est excellent puisqu'il prévient quelquefois la fraude; mais combien cette précaution coute t'elle aux parties? il en résulte des pilles énormes d'écritures chargées d'autant de Sentences que de publications, d'autant de répétitions que d'Actes, dont les frais monstreux emportent souvent la majeure partie du prix principal.

Un autre objet digne d'occuper sérieusement le législateur c'est le retrait Lignages, un amas de formalités l'environne, l'Omission de la plus légere suffit pour faire Déchoir le retraiant, pourquoi tendre autant de pieges?

pourquoi charger les actes d'une infinité de clauses, conditions, renonciations, reserves et protestations, tandis que le but est presque toujours de se mettre à couvert des règles les plus générales pourquoi exprimer ici plus que partout et ailleurs ce qui seroit mieux entendu sans en faire mention.

La confusion dans les proprietes de campagne; est une source abondante de procés; le déffaut de demarcation de chaque heritage enhardi la cupidité, le voisin prend sur son voisin, les anticipations donnent lieu à des demandes en trouble, la conplainte est suivie d'enquetes, de vues et descentes de lieux et d'autres formalités qui ne tendent le plus souvent qu'a égarer la religion du juge, et à faire pour vingt fois plus de frais que la valeur du terrain en contestation.

Ces exemples pris au hasard dans la foule de ceux qui se présentent chaque jour, ne donnent que des faibles idées d'une dépradation que le malheur des tems semble avoir mis au dessus des loix.

Un père a sacrifié son repos, sa Santé à des Veilles pour soutenir une famille nombreuse, il meurt et laisse quelques biens, fruits de ses Sueurs, Ses enfants son mineurs ou absents, la veuve déja trop accablée est saisie tout à coup et sans ménagement par l'appareil effrayant de la justice qui vient veiller à la conservation des biens en les mettant sous son Sceau respectable; rien de plus admirable que cette formalité; mais sy ce Sceau consume tout ce qu'il touche, le remede devient pire que le mal incertain qu'il previent, joignons à cela les frais qu'entrainent les nominations de tuteur curateur, levée de Scellé, inventaire, briseé, vente, . . . il ne paroitra plus étonnant que cette surcharge de formalités cause la Ruine de la veuve et de l'orphelin.

Ce qui n'expose pas moins la justice aux reproches du Citoyen, ce sont les partages de succession; malheur aux héritiers diviser d'interest; une foule de formalités sont misses en oeuvres, le mineur, l'absent ne peuvent les éviter; il en résultent des procédures longues et immenses qui assez souvent font passer le fond de l'héritage dans les mains de la justice. Mais ce qui vient de mettre recemment le comble à la misère du peuple, c'est l'établissement d'un juré priseur à Longwy, avant cette époque la confiance du Citoyen étoit au moins libre, il avoit le double avantage de choisir parmi les hyussiers ordinaires et de traiter avec celui qui lui convenait le plus; ce nouvel établissement blesse donc ce que nous avons de plus cher; mais les plaintes seroient moins amères, s'il ne faisait qu'enchainer la confiance; il produit bien d'autres maux; les droits exorbiteurs attribués aux jurés priseurs sont encore et le plus souvent doubles arbitrairement et sous le prétexte de peines extraordinaires, ce genre d'impot gréve d'autant plus qu'il pése particulierement sur la classe indigente; Réduits par leur peu de moyens, les laboureurs, les artisans, sont souvent forcés de vendre leur chétive mobilier, soit pour acquitter leurs dettes et conserver leurs crédits, soit pour se substanter dans des tems difficiles, où bien une mort prématurée enleve un pere à ses enfants; rien ne peut alors les soustraire à cette révoltante contribution, le jure [juré] priseur enlève la majeure partie de leur mince héritage.

Les emprunts sauvent chez d'autres peuples des dangers de la poursuite et facilitent le commerce, cette ressource nous manque, la loy n'ayant pas suffisamment pourvue à la facilité et à la sureté des prets par l'établissement du Tableau des hipotéques, lequel ne sert qu'à purger les immeubles; pourquoi encore condamne t'elle comme usuraires les intérests qu'une convention libre introduit dans les obligations ne résulte t'il pas plus de mal que de bien d'une pareille gêne.

Enfin quels abus n'entraine pas tous les jours la vénalité des charges de judicature; elle cause les plus grands maux, degrade et avilit la Magistrature en écrasant le peuple.

Idées de Reforme

Rendre la justice est sans doute un des plus beaux attributs de la Royauté, rien ne peut égaler d'apres cela L'interet qu'a Sa Majesté d'établir des loix simples et puissantes, loix qui n'eussent qu'un même but: le bien public et le repos des particuliers.

Nous ne pouvons qu'a cet égard former des désirs, c'est aux grands hommes à remplir une tache aussy pénible, notre but est d'indiquer les moyens de prevenir les desordres que nous venons de tracer.

On ne peut et il seroit dangereux de soustraire un debiteur à la poursuite, mais on peut en simplifiant, éviter sa ruine à quoi sert t'il de présenter requeste au juge pour avoir permission d'assigner, comme cela est d'usage dans le ressort? cette formalité ne tend qu'a faire monter les frais d'assignation à une pistole tandis qu'un simple emploit suffiroit et ne couteroit au plus que trente sols y compris le contrôl? mais la sentence est ce qu'il y a de plus onéreux, elle est grevée de plusieurs impôts connus sous les noms, démoluments, Scel, control de Dépens, droits sur les parchemins dont on sert pour l'expédier et pour que la condamnation soit modique, ces différents droits excède le principal; il est donc essentiel de les retrancher; il semble d'ailleurs qu'un acte aussi respectable devroit être exempt d'impôt.

N'éviteroit t'on pas aussy des frais bien frustatoirs aux débiteurs en dispensant les créanciers sans titre, d'affirmer lorsque la sentence est par déffaut; qu'el inconvénient il y auroit t'il enfin à recevoir les affirmations à L'audience et sans frais l'orsqu'il y a contestation.

Pour étouffer le germe des discussions; il faudrait prévoir par ou degorge le mal et l'empecher, cet art est reserver aux grands génies, Nous observons seulement qu'il paroit très essentiel d'admettre plus de rigueur dans l'exécution des engagements écrits, qu'aucune allégation entre majeurs ne pût y porter atteinte l'orsqu'ils se font entendre.

La demande n'étant pas fondée en titre, la mauvaise foi triompheroit moins souvent et le demandeur éviteroit bien des frais si la loy assujettissait le deffendeur à subir un interrogatoire dans le principe de l'affaire audiance tenant et sans frais; il ne seroit pas moins essentiel d'abreger les délais et d'attribuer aux juges Royaux de première instance la connoissance en dernier ressort des demandes en payement des sommes au dessous de cent livres en fixant néanmoins un nombre suffisant de juges.

Les poursuites de decrets sont investies de formalités dont la pluspart prepare leur inutilité en ouvrant elle même une porte à qui veut se dérober; elle ruine et font languir le débiteur et le créancier; ne suffirait-il pas, la Sentence obtenue ou munit d'un titre exécutoir; de faire au simple commandement de payer dans un délai honnete, de faire ensuite procéder à l'étude d'un nottaire à la diligence du créancier et la vente des immeubles le debiteur présent ou appelé et après trois publications de quinzaine en quinzaine; cette forme simple n'auroit d'autre inconvénient que de ne pas purger, mais les lettres de ratification y suppliroient.

Ne pourroit-on pas adopter une règle à peu prés semblable dans les cas de licitation et lorsqu'il sagit de la vente des biens de mineurs ou absens; les biens peuvent être licités en l'étude d'un notaire comme à l'audience, il en résulteroit autant d'avantages et les frais seroient épargnés; que seroit-il besoin alors de faire ordonner la licitation en justice; un simple exploit d'assignation a comparois en l'étude du Nottaire ne mettroit-il pas le proprietaire refusant en demeure de veiller à l'intérêt de sa chose; en cas de contestation sur la division ou la nécéssite de vendre les parties ne pourroient elles pas avant tout faire visiter l'immeuble par un ou plusieurs experts convenus et en cas de difficultés d'absence ou de minorité en faire nommer d'office au moyen d'un mot de requête présenté au juge? un simple avis de parents ne suffirait-il pas pour autoriser la vente de biens des mineurs ou absents en observant toujours les publications.

Le retrait n'a été introduit que pour conserver les biens dans les familles de ceux qui les acquis; ce préjugé semble gener la liberté du commerce; on dirait que les coutumes qui autorisent le retrait l'ont elle même regardé comme peu favorable; elles l'ont environnée de formalités si sévères, que l'action demeure le plus souvent sans effet, d'après cela ou le retrait est odieux ou ne l'est pas; il faut l'abolir s'il l'est; s'il ne l'est pas, il faut le dégager des épines qui le rendre impracticable et le présenter dans l'appareil simple de la raison, combien de discussion n'éviteroit-on pas.

La Loy naturelle nous apprend que les propriétés doivent être respectées; quand elle sont envahies la loy civile prescrit la complainte, ny auroit-il pas moyen de rendre cette action moins frequent? il seroit nécéssaire à la sureté, des familles et à la paix de la Société de régler par des limites les héritages de campagnes; ce moyen simple peut être éxecuté en autorisant les communautés d'habitans à procéder à un arpentage et à un abonnement général de tous les héritages Scitues sur leurs Bancs, parties présentes ou appelées et en leur assignant pour Base les possessions avouées de chaque propriétaire; L'ordre ainsi établi dans les propriétés on pourroit le maintenir en assujetissant les mêmes communautés à faire tous les deux ou trois ans le recollement des bornes et à remplacer celles enlevées qu'il seroit alors le temeraire qui prendrait sur son voisin.

L'apposition où la levée d'un scellé sont des fonctions purement méchaniques, elles consistent dans l'action d'apposer un cachet sur les bornes de plusieurs bandes de papier pour empécher d'ouvrir les portes, coffres ou armoires et de reconnoitre en les levant si les empreintes du cachet n'ont pas été effacées ou alterées; le proces verbal n'est autre chose que le Récit fidel de cette opération, il est donc loissible de n'y employer qu'une seule personne; cette formalité devenue très dispencieuse pour l'assistance du corps entier de la justice, n'en seroit pas moins bien rempli; l'homme du Roy dans les villes, les Sindics dans les campagnes s'en acquitteroient avec soin, mais pour prévenir l'effet d'un zele trop excessif, il seroit intéréssant de limiter les cas où elle serait vraiment du bien publique, il parait souverainement inutile d'en faire usage lorsqu'au decés a'un père de famille il peut être procéde sur le champ même à la tutelle des mineurs et le public forme des Voeux pour en être affranchi dans ce cas.

Les successions parviendroient plus surement à leur destination si on retranchait les formes qui les perpetuent; la Loy liquide les droits de chaque héritier, le partage, étant calqué sur ses Dispositions, ne devrait souffrir aucun retard dans son exécution pour cause D'abscense où de minorité d'aucune des parties interressées; parce que leurs intérets seroient suffisamment à couvert défendus par des tuteurs; pour dire mieux, jamais il ne devrait y avoir de partage judiciaire on n'en verrait guére si la jurisprudence faisait supporter les frais à celui qui y auroit donné lieu.

Avant l'établissement du juré priseur les huissiers ordinaires prisoient et vendoient, les choses n'en alloient que mieux, son ministère est donc inutile, mais il a acheté le droit d'être à charge au public, il convient de la désintéresser et qu'el est le Citoyen qui refuserait d'y contribuer? le Voeu des habitans de Longwy doit paroitre d'autant plus fondé, que toutes parts il s'est élevé des plaintes contre les jurés priseurs et que leur établissement met la confiance publique dans une espéce d'esclavage.

La facilité des emprunts est nécessaire à l'interet du commerce; on trouverait maintes bourses ouvertes si comme en Lorraine, il étoit permis de prêter à intérests sur obligation ou sur billets obligatoires, un tuteur ne seroit plus dans le cas d'alliener les fonds de son pupille pour leurs faire porter interests, le pupille auroit l'avantage de trouver ses fonds en Especes à sa majorité, il seroit donc à désirer qu'une semblable disposition fut adopté dans toute la France, un second moyen de faciliter les emprunts est de procurer la sureté des créanciers; dans l'état actuel de la jurisprudence on hésite de preter, qu'elle sureté a t'on dans le fait; un hypotèque sur le bien de l'emprunteur mais ce bien n'est-il pas déjà grevé; il est impossible de le savoir; mais qu'el seroit le moyen de s'en assurer! le voici; un régistre établi dans chaque lieu contenant par lettres alphabétiques les noms de tous les propriétaires; la designation de leurs héritages et la mention de toutes les hypotèques dont ils seroient grevés; ce registre seroit un guide bien sur pour les presteurs; il produit le plus grand bien chez les peuples qui s'en servant, il aimerait notre commerce, il viviefirait la circulation si nécessaire dans l'état.

La vénalité dans les charges est devenue plus onéreuse aux peuples qu'aux ministres même de la justice, parce qu'elle pèse indirectement sur lui; Si Sa Majesté jugeait t'elle même ses sujets; elle ferrait gratuitement; ceux à qui elle confie l'exercice de son autorité devroient être dans le même cas; il seroit à désirer que les charges devinssent inaccessibles à la venalité, que chaque province fut chargée de l'entretien de ces officiers de justice, et qu'on admit aux charges que des hommes doues de talents et de capacité, des hommes animée du bien public, des hommes enfin dont le désinterressement, la douceur, la franchise et l'humanité captiveroient, le respect et L'amour du peuple; c'est un Voeu qu'ont formés tous les grands princes qui ont gouvernés les hommes pourquoi ne nous seroit-il pas permis d'en espérer l'exécution puisque nous avons la consolation de sentir que la datte des états généraux va devenir une epoque memorable, par laqu'elle on marquera désormais le tems ou la Règle a Succédé à la license, l'ordre à la confusion, la Lumière à l'obscurité.

Article 2. Agrandissements du Ressort

On réclame généralement contre le Droit de forraine qui se perçoit en Lorraine tant à l'entrée qu'a la sortie de toutes les Marchandises et objets de consommation parcequ'il aporte des obstacles et des entrâves au commerce et à la circulation.

Ces entraves nuisent particulièrement à la province des Evechés et la ville de Longwy par sa position en ressent plus singulierement encore les effets; Suivant le traitté de Paris de 1718, son territoir ne comprend que huit hameaux scitués à une demie lieu de circonference les qu'els ne suffisent point au approvisionnements necessaire à la consommation des habitans, La Lorraine qui environne de toutes parts la banlieue de Longwy devient donc leur unique ressource.

Toutes les marchandises que la ville et son territoire tirent de l'intérieur du[51] sont assujetis non seulement à ces droits de foraine perçus en Lorraine mais encore au payage établi dans les differentes provinces sous diverses dénominations, elles varient suivant la destination des Dittes Marchandises lesquelles dans tous les cas sont soumises à des visites résultantes du Dépôt qui doit en être fait dans les Doüanes établies dans l'interieur du Royaume cette gene ne peut être que la formation graduelle du Royaume, cependant

[51] There was no space in the MS, but obviously a word has been omitted. The word may have been "royaume" or "pays."

cette formation bien établie des Droits d'entrée ou de sortie d'une province à l'autre, n'auroient ils pas dût être abolis en même tems que la réunion s'est opérée.

Si l'on considère les frais énormes que nécessite la perception de ces différens droits presque tous supportes par le peuple il s'en suivra qu'ils ne sont point réellement avantageux à L'Etat, une libre circulation dans le royaume seroit elle point preferable? et le reculement des Barrieres aux frontières ne rempliroit-il pas le but.

Si ces justes reclamations étoient acceuillies on éviteroit les Vexations multipliées qu'entrainent les contrevantions le peuple seroit allegé des amendes trop souvent arbitraires exigée par les Traitans, il est à observer que par la situation du Territoir de chaque paroisse ces entraves se renouvelle continuellement il est impossible de parcourir cinq Lieues sans être astreint à prendre des acquits.

La ville de Longwy et sa prevoté fut composée lors du traité de Riswik en 1797; du Ban de Bazeilles de la haute justice d'audun le Roman,[52] et des Bailliages de Longuyon et villes la Montagne, à l'époque du traité de Paris la ville et la prevoté furent restrainte au ressort actuel, et enfin le siege de la prevoté fut reunie au Bailliage en 1737, ce fut lors du traité de Paris que la Lorraine recouvris les possessions dont on avait diminué son arrondissement.

La ville de Longwy n'auroit-elle donc point de droits à réclamer le ressort qui luy fut jadis attribué et la province des evêches ne pourroit-elle point compenser les sacrifices demandes à la Lorraine par l'abbandon du Toulois et du Bailliage de Vic dont les relations avec cette province sont plus faciles et plus prochaines, d'ailleurs la Lorraine étant passée sous la Domination française les raisons qui ont motivés cette division ne peuvent plus subsister et semblent au contraire militer en faveur de cette Réclamation.

Si l'on ajoute à ces considérations les avantages résultans d'un ressort plus étendu. 1.—il dispenseroit les sujets françois et Lorrains exposés par des relations de commerce à des contestations journalières de la nécessité d'obtenir des pareatis, 2.—ils préviendroient les conflits de juridictions dont les suites entrainent ordinairement la ruine des parties, 3.—enfin il faciliteroit les moyens d'augmenter le nombre des juges si nécessaire à la bonne administration de la justice, on conclura donc que cette reunion produiroit non seulement la prosperité de la ville mais le bien même de tout l'arrondissement.

Il ne seroit pas moins essentiel au bon ordre de rendre aux justices royales la connoissance des affaires qui se portent dans les hautes justices, si l'on considère que les sieges ne sont que des restes de la Barbarie féodale, que les praticiens y commettent journellement des vexations outrées et qu'or-

---

[52] "Audun-le-Roman," a town southeast from Longwy, in the direction of Metz.

dinairement il y a peu de choix dans les officiers qui y distribuent la justice on conviendra qu'il résulteroit le plus grand bien de leur suppression, que ce ne seroit priver les Seigneurs haut justiciers que d'un droit honorifique purement chimérique et qui paroit contrarier l'autorité directe du prince sur ses sujets, Lesquels gagneroient à ce moyen un degré de juridiction et ne seroient plus exposés à être victime de la cupidité et de l'Ignorance.

Article 3. Agriculture

Les prairies artificielles étant d'un grand secours méritent et sollicitent des Encouragemens on désireroit donc que toutes les terres destinées à cet objet soient exemptes de Dixmes et de Droits de terrages. elles devroient encore par leur utilité être respectée et non sujette, à la vaine pature. On fait la même reclamation relativement aux terreins destinés à produire des pommes de terre.

Les Communautés réclament le droit de vaine pâture dans les clos autorisés par l'État du Roy du Mois de May 1768, objet acceuillit par le Gouvernement et qui Demanderoit des exceptions dans les lieux ou une trop grande quantité de terrein jouit de cet avantage.

Pour établir l'equilibre entre les proprietaires des prez sujets à faire versaine et les habitants des Communautés ou sont situés ces pres, il conviendroit que ces derniers, respectassent la propriété des premiers en leur laissant une récolte dont ils ne jouissent pas par un abus qu'on croit nécéssaire de supprimer: Le Roy ayant fait espérer par l'Édit concernant les d'éffrichemens des communes de pouvoir à la prorogation du tems limité pour leurs exemption de Dixmes et de droits de terrage les communautés se croyent fondée à solliciter lad. prorogation n'ayant pas été suffisament indemniser jusqu'à ce jour des peines et travaux occasionnés par lesdits d'effrichemens [defrichements].

Les Communautés réclament encore contre l'inéxécution de l'ordonnance concernant les Colombiers qui oblige les propriétaires de les fermes pendant un certain tems de l'année.

L'agriculture étant la Baze de la prospérité publique cet art si util demande et exige la protection particuliere du Gouvernement.

Les Communautés des campagnes réclament donc avec Espoir de Succés que les bras necessaire à leurs travaux ne leur soient point arrachés par la Milice et que le Conducteur principal de chaque charrue soit exempté du sort qui peut le ravir aux champs qu'il cultive.

Le peuple réclament généralement contre la Banalité des Moulins qui oblige chaque Citoyen de Servir sous peine d'un double droit de Mouture d'un Meunier qui ne mériteroit pas sa confiance, on estime que l'abolition de ce droit établiroit une concurrence nécéssaire entre les Meuniers qui seroit tout à l'avantage du bien public.

On ne croit point superflu d'ajouter un Voeu formé par la pluralité des

Communautés qui toutes semble connoitre le prix d'instruction, quelques unes se plaignent de n'avoir pas même un Vicaire en résidence et d'être privées des Secours Spirituelles, elles désirent avec instance qu'il leur soit accordé soit sur les dixmes, ou autrement une somme sufisante au payement d'un Maitre d'école capable d'enseigner la jeunesse, les gages qui leur sont maintenant attribués étant une charge pour les Communautés elles ont été forcées de les restreindre en raison de leur peu de moyens et conséquemment n'ont pû espérer de fixer par un si Mince Salaire un homme en état de remplir ce but.

L'Edit du mois de May 1768, concernant les d'éffrichemens a souffert dans les campagnes des interprétations onéreuses aux Communautés.

Des particuliers domicilés et non domicilés se sont emparés sous ce prétexte et sans aucunes formalités de différens cantons, places Vagues et aisances de Communauté plusieurs d'entre eux aprés s'être appropriés ces différens terreins par une simple ligne de Démarcation et sans les avoir d'éffriché [défriché], se sont arogés le Droit de les Louer, et ont conséquement éludés la clause expresse qui ne les leurs accordé que pour les cultivés.

On observe que cette Liberté favorable aux d'éffrichemens a fait naitre une foule d'abus et d'inconvénients. On estime donc qu'il seroit juste, ou de restituer ces terreins aux Communautés, ou d'astreindre lesdits terreins à une redevance envers elles qui les Indemnisera de leur privation.

Article 4. Commerce

Le Commerce étant la Baze de la Richesse de l'État doit sans doute mériter l'attention particulière du Souverain de toute la Nation.

Les Commercans ayant entr'eux des rapports immédiats et pouvant être regardés comme anneaux de la chaine générale il en resulte que le commerce particulier d'une ville doit attendre les mêmes encouragemens de la sollicitude du gouvernement.

Les Marchands et Négocians de la ville de Longwy ayant observés que les forains viennent dans le courant de l'année leur enlever les ressources qui peuvent vivifier leur Commerce ils désireroient qu'on daigne remédier à ces abus qui leur deviennent si préjudiciables, ils pensent donc qu'en accordant deux jours de franchise aux quatre foires fixées a Longwy à differentes époques, on pourrait alors empêcher les Colporteurs en d'autre tems de l'année.

Les dittes foires ont lieu la première aux Rois, la seconde aux Cendres, la troisieme à la Saint-Jean, la quatrieme enfin le jour de la Saint-Barthélemy, les deux premieres sont en grande réputation pour les chevaux que les Marchands Liégois y aménent, ces chevaux arrivant de la hollande de la frise [Friesland], et des frontières de prusse, il est évident qu'ils ne peuvent être rendus précisément le jour de la foire, ils sont obligés au contraire de séjourner quelques jours pour reposer leurs chevaux et les mettre en état d'être vendus, si donc on daignoit accorder huit jours de franchise pour chacune des deux premières foires, et trois jours pour chacunes des deux derniers cette ditte franchise rempliroit le Voeu des Commercants il en résulteroit une consommation plus considérable par le séjour des Marchands dans la ville et la dépense des Conducteurs des chevaux qui s'arretent maintenant à Aubange gros village du Duché de Luxembourg situé à une Lieue de la ville tourneroit toute à l'avantage des habitans.

Les habitans de la ville de Longwy et surtout les Commercans sollicitent depuis trés longtemps une chaussée qui conduisent directement à Verdun en passant par Rehon, Catry, Peuville, Arrancy, l'abbaÿe de Chatillon, Maugienne et Ozenne.

Monsieur le Marquis de Mezières ancien gouverneur de Longwy et le corps Municipal ont présenté en différens tems des Mémoires pour prouver 1.—Que la ville de Longwy sert depuis longtemps d'entrepôt aux Vins qu'on tire de la Bourgogne et du Barrois pour être ensuite exportés par la Route D'arlon dans le Duché de Luxembourg, le Braban, la flandre Autrichienne le pays de Liege et même la hollande 2.—que les charrois de ces Vins est souvent fort difficile les voitures étant obligées de parcourir quatre lieues de paÿs dont les chemins sont impracticables quatre mois de l'année précisement dans le seul moment ou les cultivateurs dégagés des soins de leur état peuvent s'occuper des transports dont ils tirent les moyens de payer les impositions royales, 3.—que la Banlieue de cette ville étant trés Circonscrite elle tire la plus grand partie de ses subsistance de la Woivre paÿs Riche et faisant partie du Verdunois.

Si donc au lieu de la conduire directement par les villages cy-dessus dénommés on la faisait passer à Longuyon ainsy qu'il est projetté on ouvriroit à ce coin de la frontière un déboucheé dont L'Etranger tireroit tout l'avantage en construisant luy même une chaussée d'Arlon à Virton et de Virton à Ruette sur son territoir d'ou il n'y a que deux lieues de distance de Longuyon, ils éviteroient par ce moyen le passage de la ville de Longwy, Virton deviendroit donc alors un Entrepôt considérable et un des principaux Marché du Duché de Luxembourg et le Commerce de cette ville seroit absolument ruiné.

Pour éviter ce désastre il conviendroit de mettre en vigeur L'arret du Conseil qui ordonne la construction de la chaussée demandée abandonner totalement le Morceau construit de Longuyon à Tellancourt et permettre même aux villages des environs d'en prendre les pierres à mesure qu'ils en auroient besoin pour la construction ou réparations de leurs Batimens.

Des considérations particulieres détaillée dans le Mémoire de feu Monsieur le Marquis de Mezieres et dans deux autres de la Muncipalité de Longwy de Janvier 1778, et de Novembre 1779 ont jusqu'icy retardés l'execution de cette Chaussée.

Article 5. Etablissement des Marchés de grains
sur les frontières . . .

La production principale des Evechés et de la Lorraine est en bled elle suffiroit dans certaines récoltes à la consommation des habitans de l'une et de l'autre province pendant deux années.

L'abondance des grains devient quelques fois embarrasante pour le cultivateur particulièrement pour ceux dont les redevances sont en argent et à terme; il est donc alors forcé ou de vendre à trop bas prix ou d'exporter; On observe que c'est seulement dans ces cas d'abondance ou l'exportation est permise qu'il faudroit recourir à un moyen qui concilia les interets des cultivateurs avec ceux du peuple des frontieres.

On se persuade qu'il seroit possible d'établir dans les années abondantes le Marché des grains dans les villes frontières en permettant aux Etrangers d'y venir acheter et en interdissant aux cultivateurs la Liberté de l'exporter eux mêmes sans qu'au préalable ils se fussent présentés aux Marchés des dittes Villes.

On ne peut douter des avantages resultants d'un semblable établissemens. 1.—Il diminueroit les frais de transport auxquels les cultivateurs exportans sont exposés soit par la longeure des voyages soit par l'obligation ou ils sont trés souvent de Louer des emplacemens pour déposer leurs grains quand ils n'ont pas vendu; 2.—il attireroit les étrangers et les dépenses des acheteurs tourneroient au profit des francois lesquels jusqu'à ce jour ont laissé dans les Marchés impériaux une partie du prix des denrées exportées. 3.—Enfin il rendroit au commerce l'activité en fournissant de nouveaux consommateurs et augmenteroit donc l'aisance des habitans et ces villes frontières deviendroient fleurissantes et conséquemment plus importantes.

Article 6. Réclamation des habitans de la partie
francoise du Diocese de Trêves

On s'éléve généralement contre un abus introduit dans le paÿs lequel deviendroit trés préjudiciable à tous ceux qui se d'estiment [destinent] à l'État écclésiastiques. Le Diocèse de Trêves s'étend sur cent soixante et douze paroisses francoise tant en Lorraine que dans le Clermontois la plus de Nominations de ces Cures appartenantes à des collateurs étrangers, ils y nomment au préjudice des francois par la facilité d'obtenir en france des Lettres de Naturalisations ce qui n'est aucunement compensé puisqu'on peut jouir du même avantage en Allemagne.

On espère donc de la justice du Roy qu'il n'accordera a l'avenir aucune lettres de Naturalisation aux Ecclesiastiques Etrangers et qu'il daignera conserver à ses Sujets la certitude de posseder des Bénéfices existant et situé dans sa domination. Cette partie francoise et Lorraine dépendante de L'Archéveché de Trêves, n'ayant dans son arrondissement ny Instituteur n'y Colleges, n'y Seminaires forme le Voeu de n'être point d'aller au loin chercher les Secours dont elle est privée à cet égard.

Les fonds étant la Baze de ces établissemens on espère qu'en indiquant les moyens simples de s'en procurer sans être à charge à l'Etat ces réclamations auront tout le succés qu'elles peuvent attendre.

Le Bénéfice situé en France à Ukange pres de Thyonville attaché au Séminaire de Treves ceux aussy en dépendant des Maisons de Marienthal et du Saint-Esprit supprimes dans le duché de Luxembourg semblent indiquer luy même l'usage auquel on doit les employer.

On estiment que ces objets seroient suffisans pour établir un College et un Séminaire à Longwy, centre de l'arrondissement francois ce qui est prouvé par l'érection du siege de l'officialité en 1783.

Il en résulteroit pour les jeunes francois qui se d'estinnent à la pretise, L'avange[53] inapreciable de recevoir des instructions conformes aux Lois, usages et doctrines du Royaume dans lequel ils doivent les pratiquer, les suivre, et les propager.

Article 7. Etablissement relatif à
l'instruction de la Jeunesse

Les habitans de la ville de Longwy intimement convaincus de la tendre sollicitude qui daigne acceuillir les justes réclamations de tous les Citoyens, osent espérer que le moyen qu'ils présentent d'améliorer leurs enceinte sera recu favorablement.

Lors de la deffection des jésuites, ils laissent des biens tres considérables; ils en possedoient dans ce paÿs dont une partie située aux environs de cette ville fut assignée au College de Verdun l'autre à Ukange prés de Thyonville appartenante aux Jésuites de Trêves fut dévolue au Domaine Royal.

L'Electeur de Trêves désirant attirer dans ses États les revenus de cette dernière portion exposat que son Diocese s'étendant sur partie de la province françoise il avoit droit de réclamer la jouissance d'un bénéfice situé en France et devenu vaccant que d'ailleurs il le destinoit à alimenter un Séminaire à Trêves que les habitans de la partie françoise de son Diocèse qui se Destineroient à l'État Ecclesiastique pourroient profiter de cet avantage.

L'Archevêque de Treves obtint l'objet de sa demande et on luy accordat environ dix mille livres de rente annuelle sous la condition expresse que deux sujets francoise seroient reçus gratuitement et à perpetuité dans led. Séminaire.

On doute que cette condition ay [ait] été remplie mais on ne peut ignorer, l'influence des préjuges Nationaux les prétextes n'ont pas manqués à ceux dont les disposition étoient peu favorable aux candidats françois on les

---

[53] "avantage."

dégouta souvent en leur faisant subir les examens les plus rigoureux on éluda presque toujours ainsy la clause formelle qui avoit été la Base de l'abandon annuel de cette comme de dix mille Livres.

Il est facile de prouver qu'il est possible de mieux employer une somme destinée à une bonne Oeuvre; il est constant que L'abandon Special de cette somme annuelle fut fait pour produire le bien et l'avantage de la province françoise quel autre motif en pût Déterminer le gouvernement à un semblable sacrifice? nous avons fait voir plus haut comment cette intention avoit été remplie mais quand il ne seroit pas douteux que la province ay jouit de l'avantage qui a motivé cet abandon quand même il seroit avéré que deux sujets francois ont jusqu'a ce jour profité de l'exécution de cette *expresse* condition pourroit-on comparer un si mince résultat avec la certitude de contribuer au bien d'une ville entière et devroient-ils balancer les avantages indubitables et certains qui Naitroient infailliblement de L'emploi mieux ordonné de laditte somme.

Si donc on daigne acceuillir ces justes réclamations cette somme qui chaque anneé enrichit les Etrangers sera accordée a la ville de Longwy et circulera dans le paÿs qui la produit, elle y sera employée à la fondation et à l'établissement d'un Collège sufisant pour la construction et l'entretien, ces fonds perdus pour la province serviront à ramener l'activité et à Ranimer l'industrie dans une ville apauvrie et découragée, en attirant les Etrangers en augmentant les Consommations on multipliera les besoins on vivifiera le commerce et Conséquemment ce Collège procurera aux habitans de Nouveaux moyens de Subsistance.

Pourroit-il ne pas prospérer sous les yeux d'un Prélat que l'érection d'un officialité fixa dans notre ville en 1783, sans doute il protégera un si util projet, il ne daignera point d'acquérir sur notre reconnoissance les droits qu'il a déjà à notre vénération, son exemple sa Surveillance sont de sur du Succés de cet établissement.

Mais il est sans doute un bien plus désirable encore au dessus de toute richesses et que rien au monde ne sauroit remplacer nous le devront à l'execution de ce projet, c'est l'instruction de la jeunesse.

Nous ne craignons pas de l'avouer, il n'existe dans cette ville aucuns secours pour l'éducation des enfants livrés, à eux mêmes des l'age le plus tendre en proie à l'oisiveté et à la dissipation, ils parviennent à l'âge de raison sans avoir aucune notion n'y du bien n'y du Mal, le mésaire des habitans ne leur permettant aucun sacrifice ils ne peuvent les faire instruire ailleurs, ils viellissent donc dans l'ignorance et meurent emportant le regret de n'avoir put remplir qu'imparfaitement les devoirs de Citoyen ils laissent il est vrai au Roy de bons et fidèles sujets mais L'Instruction en auroit fait des hommes.

Les Communautés du ressort réclament des Maitres d'Ecole plus instruite, il faut en conséquence augmenter leurs salaires, on pourroit charger le Collège de cet augmentation il pourroit encore influer sur le choix des sujets ainsy cet établissement rempliroit par ce moyen le Voeu de la ville et de la Campagne.

Article 8. Rareté des Bois

Le bois étant une matière de premiere nécessité il a paru indispensable d'attirer l'attention du gouvernement sur cet Objet.

Le peuple désire qu'on remédie à la Disette cruelle dont il est menacé à cet égard on tachera d'en Developer la cause affin qu'il luy soit permis d'espérer en la faisant cesser ils deviennent moins chers et moins rares dans un pays qui la quantité de bois dont il est entouré devoit s'attendre à une abondance permanente.

Le Tableau anexé aux présentes Doléances offre L'Enumération des bois qui alimente Longwy et ses environs on y établit la quantité d'arpents qu'ils contiennent celles qu'on doit exploiter annuellement et la quantité de cordes de bois qu'ils produisent en opposant à cette quantité celle provenant de l'Évaluation approchée de la consommation annuelle de la ville et de la campagne, avec celles des forges qui l'avoisinne et dont le travail s'entretient sur les bois de l'arrondissement pris pour base, on sera convaincu qu'il n'y a aucune proportion entre la recette et la dépense.

C'est en ayant une connoissance exacte des bois qui fournissent à la consommation du pays qu'on pourra en régler les coupes et leur donner le tems nécéssaire pour recroitre, ce seroit le moyen de proportionner la dépense à la recette sans doute c'étoit la le but de l'Etablissement des Maitrises mais les Gruries Voisines ne s'accordant point entre elles leurs opérations se sont souvent croisés d'ailleurs les attributions de leurs droits leur étant alloués d'aprés la plus valuë des adjudications, il etoit important pour elle que le prix des bois fut élevé.

On réclame généralement contre l'indifference des Maitrises relativement à la conservation des bois ce qui peut avoir pour la suite les conséquences les plus dangereuses, on leur a en vain denoncé plusieurs fois les débits et dégradation des bois commis par une classe de gens que la Misére a Malheureusement multipliés, les rapports faits aux dittes Maitrises sont demeurées sans effet toutes les fois que les Délinquans n'avoient pas de quoi payer l'amende. Na.[54]

Na. On croit devoir cependant attribuer aussy à l'humanité la conduite des maitrises qui sans doute trouvoient cruel de sevir contre des gens qui n'ont pas de pain, ne seroit-il point à propos d'observer pourquoi l'on a mis une différence entre les pauvres de la ville et ceux de la campagne auxquels on accordent annuellement du bois, en affouage peut être un sacrifice de ce genre arrêtroient ces dépradations journalières que la cherté excessive du bois nécessite.

Il existe encore des réclamations générales de la part des Communautés

[54] This mark signifies "nota."

TABLEAU APPROXIMATIF DE LA QUANTITE DE BOIS

Dont les exploitations alimentent les six fourneaux qui avoisinent Longwy et doivent aussi fournir a la consommation journaliere des villes et villages compris dans cet arrondissement jusqu'a Rechicourt au Midy, jusqu'a Ottange et Fontoye a L'Est, Marville et St. Laurent a l'ouest et le Duche de Luxembourg au Nord.

NOMS DES BOIS DES VILLAGES QU'ILS AVOISINENT	TOISES QUARR ES DE LEUR SURFACE	REDUCTION EN ARPENTS DE PARIS	COUPES REGLEES QU'ILS DOIVENT PRODUIRE PAR 25 ANS OU PAR ANNEE	EVALUATION DES CORDES DE BOIS MESURE DE BAR ESTIMEES À 35 PAR ARPENT
Mont St. Martin, Cône, Cussigny, etc.	1,250,000	930	37	1,295
St. Pancre, Flaucourt et Cône	1,800,000	1,339	54	1,890
de Grand Cour	1,530,000	1,138	46	1,610
Entre Arondelet et Grenoy	3,000,000	2,000	80	2,800
de Flabenville près la Prelle	500,000	372	15	425
de Colmey	280,000	208	8	280
Entre Vivier, Chapy et Longuyon	1,440,000	1,071	43	1,505
Entre Fermont et Montigny sur Chiere	400,000	297	12	420
de Cumont aux Convers	750,000	558	22	770
de Cossemont et la Grand-ville	280,000	208	8	280
de Tirmont près St. Quentin	490,000	364	14	490
de Lexy, Cutri, Rehon, Chenieres	2,000,000	1,500	60	2,100
de Xay, vulgairement, de Chat	180,000	134	5	175
de Longlaville	480,000	357	14	490
de Tiercelet	660,000	491	20	700
de But près Villerupt	1,400,000	1,042	42	1,470
de Romelange entre Audun le tiche et Ottange	2,500,000	1,875	75	2,625
de la grande Rimont entre Crûne et Filiere	3,120,000	2,322	93	3,255
de Nundekail	720,000	536	21	735
Entre Filiere et Villaumontois	510,000	380	15	425
de Morfontaine	750,000	558	22	770
Le Moine près Bouren	960,000	715	28	980
de Selémont et Herserange jusque Bouren et Tiercelet	5,400,000	4,018	161	5,635
de Baslieu au Chemin de Filiere	1,750,000	1,302	53	1,855
	32,180,000	23,715	948	33,180

contre les droits exorbitans perçus par les Officiers de Maitrises on ne peut se dissimuler que ce ne soit unes des causes de l'augmentation excessive du prix des bois.

Ceux en affouage accordés aux habitans des Campagnes étant grévés des frais de la Marque des coupes annuelles exigées par les Gruries cet avantage devient presque nulle pour eux.

Il en est de même des quarts en réserve que la perception desdits frais reduit à un tel point qu'il ne peuvent sufire à leur destination, on estime que les droits dévolus aux Maitrises absorbent au moins le dixième du produit.

On se plaint généralement encore quelles adjudications d'ouvrages deferées aux Maitrises sont toujours faites au Dessus de leur Valeur et que les Deniers résultans de ces adjudications étant versées dans la caisse d'un receveur y laissent toujours une bonne partie du principal.

Les Communautés se plaignent aussy d'être frustré du droit de faire ses réserves relatives et utiles à leur situation.

La suppression absolue des Maitrises semble être le résultat des inconvénients sans nombre qui n'aisent de leur administration le voeu général

OBSERVATIONS	NOMS DES BOIS DES VILLAGES QU'ILS VOISINENT	TOISES QUARRÉES DE LEUR SURFACE	REDUCTION EN ARPENTS DE PARIS	COUPES REGLEÉS QU'ILS DOIVENT PRODUIRE PAR 25 ANS OU PAR ANNEE	EVALUATION DES CORDES DE BOIS MESURE DE BAR ESTIMEES À 35 PAR ARPENT
On ne peut repondre de la precision des mesures des bois dénommés dans ce tableau, mais afin de prévenir les erreurs qui auraient pû se glisser dans les reductions ainsi que les obmissions involontaires on a augmenté de 50 arpents ceux resultants des coupes supposés annuelles que l'on porte à 1400 arpens au lieu de 1350. C'est à dire qu' on augmente le fond de 1250.	Cy contre Notre Dame des hermites et Pierrepont	32,180,000	23,715	948	33,180
	de Beuville	600,000	447	18	630
	de Martinfontaine à	200,000	150	6	210
	Puisieux de Sorbet, D'Arrancy et	1,440,000	1,071	43	1,505
	Rouvroy	2,000,000	1,500	60	2,100
	de Wassermont	1,440,000	1,071	43	1,505
	3 petits bois près de Remenoncour	270,000	201	8	280
On s'est servi de la corde de Bar qui est la mesure usitées dans ce pays et l'on s'est contenté pour abréger ce travail d'indiquer sa proportion avec celle de Roy. Elle est établie cy apres.	de Hoüecour pres Nouillonpont	400,000	297	12	420
	d'Olliers	950,000	707	28	980
	de Han devant Pierrepont	660,000	491	20	700
	de Mercy le Bas	360,000	268	10	350
	Le Chanois pres de Baudresy	660,000	491	20	700
La corde de Roy contient 128 pieds cubes de bois. Celle de Bar 73 pieds aussi cubes.	Mercy Le Haut	200,000	150	6	210
	de la petite Rimont	2,340,000	1,741	69	2,405
	de Beuvillers	480,000	357	14	490
On estime généralement que 10 cordes mesure de Bar forment exactement 6 cords de Roy.	de Boulange et Goudrange	720,000	536	22	770
	Petite Moyenvre et un autre au dessus de Fontoy	440,000	327	13	455
	de Bazonville	180,000	134	5	175
	de Sancy	260,000	119	5	175
	TOTAL GENERAL	45,780,000	33,773	1,350	47,250
	Ajoute pour compenser les erreurs	1,679,400	1,250	50	1,750
	TOTAL APPROXIMATIF des bois a exploiter dans l'arrondissement pris pour baze	47,459,400	35,023	1,400	49,000

ne laisse aucun doute sur celle qu'on estime devoir être préferé c'est de conférer aux Municipalités le soin de l'Exploitation des Bois elles seront toujours alors interessée à la conservation et à l'Entretien d'un objet si important.

On pourroit attribuer aux juridictions royales les plus prochaines la connoissance des délits et dégradations relatives aux bois.

On doit ajouter qu'une des causes de la Diminution sensible des bois c'est la Négligence qu'on apporte à les répeuplés, il existe au centre et aux Lizières des terreins considérables dénués d'arbres ce tort ne doit-il point encore être imputé aux Maitrises? On désire qu'il soit étably comme en Allemagne des pépinières remplies de sujets ou l'on puissent prendre chaque année de quoi recruter les Bois en augmentait les salaire des Gardes on pourroit les chargés de ce soin on verroit bientot alors les forets se repeupler et nous aurions la satisfaction de mettre nos Neveux[55] à l'abry de l'affreuse disette donc nous sommes menacés.

[55] This means posterity, not simply "nephews."

Il y a quatre Lieües à la ronde autour de Longwy tant en Lorraine que dans l'abanlieue [la banlieue] six fourneaux allimentant chacun deux forges, on estime à sept mille cordes environ Mesure de Bas la Consommation annuelle d'un fourneau pour qu'il N'éprouve n'y retard n'y chaumage. N^a.

N^a.—Les Registres de la marque des fers sont un moyen certain de s'assurer de la consommation réelle de chaque forge on évalue à seize mille cordes Mesure de Bar, la quantite consomme pour un Million de fers.

Or les dittes forges s'approvisionnent sur les differentes adjudications de Bois de L'arrondissement et leur interet étant d'éviter le chaumage on doit conclure qu'elles font de grands sacrifices pour y parvenir et qu'elle influent nécessairement sur le prix des bois destinés à la Consommation des particuliers.

Il seroit a désirer que les Maitres de Forges et leurs facteurs fussent restreint à ne s'approvisionner qu'aprés que la consommation des particuliers auroit été assurée car n'attendant point leur principal interret de la vente des bois qu'ils achétent et se contenant d'assurer le travail de leurs usines on doit conclure que nul adjudication ne peut soufrir la Concurrence, il est encore à observer que n'ayant consequemment point de Concurrurent ayant converti en charbon la plus grande partie des bois qu'ils ont accaparés, Ils deviennent les Maitres du prix de celuy qui leur reste.

La forge D'herserange située à une demie Lieue de Longwy est celle qui influe le plus particulierement, sur le prix du bois qui se consomme dans la ville et Banlieüe parce que n'ayant aucuns bois en propriete elle est obligée pour allimenter son travail d'accaparer ceux mis en adjudication qui sont à sa portée, c'est à dire ceux d'estinés [destinés] à la consommation de la ville et des environs.

Ladite forge absorbe anuellement depuis six ans qu'elle est affirmée, environ douze mille Cordes de Bois, Mesure de Bar, les Baillieurs ne l'ayant que pour un tems limité ont taché d'en tirer tout le parti possible sans doubler le travail et conséquemment la Consommation.

Lorsque le propriétaire Seigneur de la sauvage autre forge dans le Luxembourg faisoit valoir par luymême cette usine il consommoit à peine quatre mille Cordes de bois par an ayant à luy assez de bois pour allimenter cette forge dans cette proportion elle n'influoit point alors sur la vente publique la corde de Bois Mesure de Bar valoit à cette époque de sept à huit Livres l'une elle est maintenant à quatorze Livres c'est a dire à vingt quatre Livres environ Mesure de Roy.

On ne peut donc attribuer qu'à la forge D'herserange ou à la maniére dont elle est administrée aux augmentations Subtile et excessive du prix du bois puisque cet exaucement datte précisément de l'époque ou les Baillieurs ont fait leurs approvisionnemens. On estime qu'il n'y a point de tems a perdre pour restreindre cette terrible Délapidation soit en fixant la consommation en bois de lad. forge aux taux anciens du propriétaire, soit en la luy faisant exploiter pour son compte puisqu'il possede des bois sufisant pour l'allimenter soit enfin en l'astraignant à consommer une certaine quantité de charbon de terre.

Évaluation au plus bas des consommations annuelles tant de la ville et de l'arrondissement pris pour Base que des forges qu'y sont situés.

Environ cent villages non compris les fermes ou Maisons particulières estimées à soixante feux. L'un évaluer a quatre Cordes par feu par villages,

280 Cordes et pour cent villages cy	2,800 cordes
Consommation des villes haut et basse de Longwy la garnison comprise cy	5,000
On doit évaluer aussy separément les villes ou bourgs de Longuyon et villiers la Montagne qui ont chacun un Bailliage ensemble à 750 feux cy	4,000
Évaluation modérée de la consommation annuelle des six fourneaux de Villancey, Longuyon, Lopinieux, Herserange, Villerupt et hottange allimentant chacun deux forges à raison de 7,000 corde par fourneaux cy	42,000 cordes
Total de la consommation de l'arrondissement pris pour Base cy	75,000 cordes

Résultats

La recette présentée par le tableau est de cy	49,000
La Dépense résultante de l'évaluation cy dessus cy	75,000
Partant excédant de dépense cy	26,000

Le résultat de ce tableau sera sans doute effrayant pour l'administration, il présente une consommation de plus de moitié en sus de ce qu'on devroit esploiter annuellement qu'on ajoute à cette apercu les dépradations journalières et les non valeur des Bois dégarnis on se hatera sans doute de s'occuper des moyens de prévenir la disette certains de cette matière de première nécessité dont il seroit facile de calculer l'époque si l'on n'en restraint la consommation.

On estime qu'il est d'une absolue nécessité de diminuer le nombre des forges ou de limité la quantité de bois qu'elles doivent consommer, dans le premier cas on observera que plusieurs forges existantes dans le païs appartiennent à des Moines et il semble que n'étant point par leur état destinées à des Spéculations lucratives, ils devront supporter de préférence la rigeure d'une suppression.

On croit encore d'une nécessité indispensible de faire régler irrévocablement pour l'avenir à vingt-cinq ans les coupes annuelles des bois: Peut être s'opposera on à de si justes reclamations et attribuera t'on l'excédent de consommation demontré à l'importation des bois Etrangers, mais il est aisé de prouver la futilité de cette objection.

1.—Le Duché de Luxembourg recèle sur cette frontière une quantité de forges au moins égales à celles de France.

2.—S'il étoit vrai que les secours titres de L'Etranger eussent été suffisans jamais on auroit accaparé les Bois destinés à la consommation des habitans, et le prix du bois seroit infailliblement resté de même, Si les secours susdits eussent été proportionnés à nos besoins.

On ne peut d'ailliurs Statuer sur une ressource aussi précaire d'autant que le Souverain peut d'un instant à l'autre promulguer sur cet objet la même déffense D'importation pratiquée pour toutes les autres denrées de consommation.

Mais en supposant qu'il soit toujours libre d'importer les Bois, sans doute on ne pourra compter sur ceux qui avoisinnent les Usines lesquelles comme nous l'avons énoncé sont trés Multipliés, il faudra donc restraindre ce Secours à quelques excédents de Communauté, mais réduisons encore cette ressource à ces justes valeurs.

Il y a une déffense promulguée pour empêcher l'exportation des bois et charbons mais on y a dérogé en faveur de la forge de Berchiwé situé dans le Luxembourg, sous le prétexte qu'elle fournit du fer à la Manufacture des fusils de Charleville.

Maintenant qu'on balance avec la quantité de bois qu'il est impossible d'importer de l'Étranger cette exception en faveur de Berchiwé, il sera prouve évidemment que si ce Secours n'est pas nul du moins il ne peut être que trés Médiocre.

Doléances concernant le Bien Général

Le tiers ordre demande en outre:

1.—Que la puissance Législative réside essentiellement dans la Nation qu'on ne puisse porter et annuller aucune Loy n'y Impositions que dans l'assemblée des états Généraux dont le retour périodique sera déterminée des époques fixes et qu'en conséquence il ne doit fait aucun emprunt directe ou indirecte sans le libre consentement desdits états Généraux.

2.—Que le Roy, Les Ministres les Tribunaux et aucuns des sujets du Souverain ne puissent violer impunément les loix nationales.

3.—Que les Ministres soient garans et comptables envers la Nation des fonds qui seront attribues à leur département.

4.—Que l'abolition des lettres de Cachet et de tout ordre Supérieur tendant à Oter la Liberté du Citoyen soient acordée qu'aucuns des Citoyens ne puisse etre arreté par Ordre des Commandans des places sans etre livré à l'instant même, à l'Officier de police.

5.—L'établissement des états provinciaux pour les Évêchés dont les Membres soient électifs dans la forme prescrite, pour les Etats Généraux qu'ils ayent seuls le droit de répartir les impositions et de connoitre des contestations y relatives, qu'ils ayent encore la connoissance et L'administration des Constructions et entretiens des Routes Ensemble la connoissance de toutes les affaires des Communautés.

6.—Qu'il soit étably dans la province des Evêchés et dans toutes les autres une caisse d'amortissement destinée a l'acquittement des Dettes de l'état, et que les Membres des Etats provinciaux soient responsables des fonds qui seront versés.

7.—Que l'égalité de la répartition de tous impots et subsides soit désormais étably entre les trois ordres en raison de leurs biens et facultés et sans distinction de Rôle.

8.—Que lesdits trois ordres ayent également le droit de posséder toutes charges dans l'état civil Militaire et Ecclésiastiques et que les mêmes charges ne puissent être accordées qu'au mérite personnel.

9.—Que tous les genres de propriété soient garantis de Maniere qu'on n'y puisse porter atteinte et que les possesseurs soient toujours assurés d'une indemnité effective juste et proportionnée dans le cas ou le bien public exigeroit quelques changemens qui leur soient préjudiciables.

10.—Que le droit de franc fief soit aboli comme étant encore une marque de servitude et une distinction avillissante.

11.—Qu'il n'y ayt qu'une seule loi, un seul poid, et une seule Mesure.

12.—Qu'il soit fait une révision des pensions et que toutes celles accordées à l'intrigue à la faveur et non au Mérite soient supprimées.

13.—Que les bénéfices soient attenus à résidence.

14.—Qu'on permette tous échanges entre les Mainsmortables et les Laïques sans etre assujetis aux droits d'amortissemens qu'il soit même permis aux Mainsmortables de placer leurs espèces à constitution de rente ou obligations portant interets qu'ils soient en conséquence dispenser de verser les fonds destinés à cet effet au Trésor Royale sans néanmoins par lesdits Mainmortables pouvoir acquérir aucun immeubles.

15.—Qu'on jouisse dans tout le Royaume de la Liberté indéfinie de la presse sous les modifications néantmoins que les états généraux jugeront convenables.

Tels sont les Voeux que le tiers-ordre de la ville et de la Banlieue de Longwy apportent aux pieds de Sa Majesté.

Fait clos, approuvé et arrêté en assemblée dudit tiers-ordre à Longwy le vingt trois Mars 1789, et lecture faite nous avons signé:

[Twenty-three signatures.]

Bernard.[56]

NO. 22. THE COLONY OF MARTINIQUE

Cahier reprinted from the p.v., *Arch. Nat.* C32/270. The cahier appears in the p.v. without formal end.

[56] This is probably a M. Bernard, lawyer, mentioned in the p.v. of the three orders, who cooperated in making the cahier (*Cf.* 30 p.v. *Arch. Nat.* Ba 52, in list of members present). There was a Sr. Charles Bernard, mayor and lieutenant-general of the police of Longwy, also. Neither was secretary of the assembly.

P.V.-*ibid.* There were 6 members of the committee, with 3 substitutes added. After some observations had been made, the cahier was adopted by the Paris committee August 17, 1789.

Convocation: 7th type.

TENEUR DU CAHIER À REMETTRE AUX DÉPUTÉS DE LA MARTINIQUE

Le Voeu de l'assemblée nationale de la Martinique, en autorisant les concitoyens à nommer pour cette colonie des députés à l'assemblée nationale, à été de faire acte de François dans cette grande et solennelle occasion, et d'offrir à Sa Majesté le tribut de reconnoissance que lui doivent tous les peuples soumis à son empire, pour les nouveaux biens dont il les fait jouir, en les reintégrant dans l'état de francs; de faire hommage à la nation des produits de cette colonie et de ses influences dans les prospérités de l'État, et de réclamer la part qui lui appartient dans les avantages de la constitution qui va régénérer toutes les parties de la Monarchie.

Les Députés de la Martinique, lorsqu'ils seront agréés par l'assemblée nationale, s'y présenteront sous deux caractères; comme françois et comme colons.

Comme François, les Electeurs qui les auront nommés, ne peuvent que s'en rapporter à leur conscience et à leurs lumières, quant aux voeux qu'ils croiront devoir porter sur tous les objets qui seront à traiter et à régler dans l'assemblée nationale, relativement à la Constitution générale de la France.

Ils sont néanmoins spécialement chargés de demander, comme l'ont fait tous les autres françois, le droit de ne pouvoir être imposés que de leur consentement, la responsabilité des Ministres et autres agens civils et militaires de l'autorité; la permanence ou périodicité de l'assemblée nationale, avec changement des personnes; la sanction législative et le pouvoir exécutif en entier réunis dans les mains du Roi.

Article 1.—Comme colons, ils soumettront à l'assemblée nationale le plan d'une assemblée coloniale qui rectifiera l'organisation de celle maintenant existante à la Martinique, et se rapprochera, autant que les permettront les relations locales, des états provinciaux qui doivent faire partie de la constitution du Royaume.

Article 2.—Ils demanderont l'abolition des lois anciennes, et que l'etablissement de nouvelles lois, qui seront particulières aux colonies, ne puissent y avoir lieu qu'aprés avoir été communiquées à l'assemblée coloniale, qui adressera à ses députés à l'assemblée nationale les observations et changemens dont l'assemblée coloniale les aura jugées susceptibles.

Article 3.—Il est, en conséquence, spécialement recommandé à ses Députés, lorsqu'il sera fait quelques propositions qui intéresseront la colonie, de demander un délai suffisant pour en faire part à l'assemblée coloniale, et se procurer les instructions et autorisations spéciales sur les objets proposés; et lorsqu'elles leur seront parvenues, ils solliciteront la formation d'un comité composé pour moitié des Députés des colonies, à l'effet d'y discuter préalablement les questions qui seront soumises à la discussion de l'assemblée nationale.

Article 4.—Ils exposeront à l'assemblée nationale les motifs tirés de la nature des colonies, et de celle de l'impôt, qui, pour le plus grand bien de la France elle même, doivent éloigner de la colonie, tout impôt direct; la modicité des fortunes dans les isles du vert, les fléaux auxquels sont plus fréquement exposées ces isles, et la moindre fécondité de leur sol leur rend plus particulièrement applicable ce principe général sur les colonies.

Article 5.—Ils demanderont outre l'introduction libre les objets deja permis, celle de tous comestibles quelconques, sous la condition de ne payer qu'en sirops, taffias, lettres de change ou marchandises importées de France; les autres denrées manufacturées dans la colonie demeurant ainsi réservées au commerce nationale; et cette introduction, exempte de tous droits, aura lieu dans les ports du Fort-Royal, de Saint-Pierre, de la Trinité et du Marin.

Article 6.—La tolérance religieuse la plus absolue, même les marriages entre personnes de communions et sectes différentes, auront lieu dans cette colonie.

Article 7.—Les députés demanderont la suppression absolue du droit d'aubaine, également contraire au droit des gens et à l'objet particulier des colonies, et ils réclameront, en faveur des bâtards, la faculté de succéder à leurs mêres.

Article 8.—Comme il n'y a point de distinction d'ordre dans la colonie (quant aux objets d'intérêt généraux) les Députés de la colonie demanderont a être placés parmi ceux des communes.

Article 9.—Les Députés demanderont, d'apres la conformité qui doit exister sur ce point, entre les lois du Royaume et celles des colonies, que les administrateurs n'ayent plus de séance dans les tribunaux de la Martinique, si ce n'est le jour de leur réception qu'ils y auront entrée, et y prendront la place qu'ils y ont maintenant, mais sans voix ni fonctions.

Article 10.—Ils demanderont aussi la suppression du Tribunal appelé Tribunal du gouvernement, et que les matières qui y sont portées, soient renvoyées aux tribunaux de justice.

Article 11.—Ils réclameront aussi pour que les demandes en cassation, et que toutes les autres suites des jugemens rendus par le conseil supérieur de la Martinique, soient portées en France dans les tribunaux qui seront chargés de prononcer en pareil cas sur les jugemens des cours souveraines du Royaume.

L'assemblée attend avec confiance du zele et du patriotisme de ses députés, qu'ils feront bien connoître à l'assemblée nationale l'importance propre à la Martinique dans la masse des intérêts généraux et réciproques des provinces continentales du royaume, et de ses possessions situés au delà des mers.

364

Cette colonie ne peut offrir à la nation un tribunal annuel de richesses comparable à celui de Saint Domingue; elle influe cependant au moins pour un cinquième activement et passivement dans les 70 millions qui, suivant l'exposé du Ministre des finances rendu aux voeux de la nation, forme la prépondérance de la France dans la balance du commerce, mais elle a plus qu'aucune de nos isles l'avantage de procurer aux produits du sol et des fabriques françoises, un débit important chez les Espagnols et autres Étrangers.

On n'a pu voir sans étonnement d'ailleurs, dans la guerre dernière, combien l'industrie particulièrement propre à la Martinique, habitée par des propriétaires, la rendue promptement et constament abondante en moyens secourables de tout genre pour les armeés de terre et de mer. On peut toujours attendre autant de ses moyens en semblables circonstances; d'ailleurs, indépendament des facilités que présentent ses ports et ses anses, situés au vent de l'isle, pour la réception des secours de France, elle seule possède un bassin sûr pour le dépôt des forces navales, un arsenal où peuvent être sûrement déposés tous les objets des besoins à prevoir en temps de guerre. Dans cette colonie seule est une fortresse de première importance; elle a deux hopitaux considérables, bien situés, et qui rassemblent toutes les ressources et les convenances les plus propres à multiplier les effets secourables de tels établissements placés à l'entrée du golfe du Mexique au milieu des isles de cet archipel, plus au vent que presque toutes celles que la France y possède, elle semble désignée par la nature pour être le point d'appui de leur dépense commune.

Suivi de: Projet d'une nouvelle ordonnance pour la constitution de l'Assemblée coloniale de la Martinique, [in 40 articles.]

NO. 23. THE NOBLES OF THE SÉNÉCHAUSSÉE OF MENDE

The *Archives parlementaires,* Vol. III, pp. 753-55 gives two documents, entitled respectively *"Cahier de doleances plaintes et remontrances de l'ordre de la noblesse du pays de Gevaudan,"* and *"Cahier d'instructions et mandats illimités donnés au député de l'ordre de la noblesse de la sénéchaussée de Gévaudan."* Both documents carry the same signatures although they have been so transcribed by the *Archives Parlementaires* as to be scarcely recognizable and within an error in the date of the second part (error in AP, Vol. III, p. 755, should reach March 31). In the same carton at the *Arch. Nat.*, Ba51, there exist several incomplete texts of the cahier. The complete text includes the document reprinted here.

P.V.-MS, *Arch. Nat.* Ba51—There were fourteen committeemen. The nobles added two articles proposed by the Marquis du Châteauneuf. The cahier was voted on March 30, but finally adopted on March 31.

Convocation, 1st type.

POUVOIR LIMITÉS AU DÉPUTÉ

L'an 1789 et le 30 Mars avant midi, en vertu des lettres du Roy portant convocation des Etats Généraux du Royaume à Versailles le 27 Avril prochain en datte du 24 Janvier d'en passé en présence de nous Lieutenant Général du Sénéchal du pays de Gévaudan, sont comparu M. M. les gentilhommes de la dite senechaussée de Gevaudan, lesquels ont élu pour comparoitre et assister en laditte assemblée des Etats Généraux tant et puissant Seigneur Messire Jean Joseph de Chateauneuf de Randon, Marquis d'apcher, auquel dit élu les dits gentilhommes donnent les pouvoirs et instruction qui suivent.

Considérant que les ministres du Roy pale résultat de son conseil du 27 8bre [octobre], 1788 ont avoué au nom de sa Majesté les droits incontestables de la nation en declarant; 1.—Que la volonté est non seulement de ratifier la promesse qu'elle a faite de ne mettre aucune impôt sans le consentement des Etats généraux, mais encore de n'en proroge aucun sans cette condition.

2.—D'assurer le retour successif des Etats Generaux en les consultants sur l'intervalle qu'il faudrait mettre entre leurs Epoques de leur convocation et en y ecoutant favorablement les representations qui lui seront faites pour donner à ces dispositions une stabilité durable.

3.—Que sa Majesté impatiente de recevoir l'avis des Etats Generaux sur la mesure de liberté qui convient d'accorder à la presse et à la publicité des ouvrages relatifs à l'administration au gouvernement, et à tout autre objet public.

4.—Que sa Majesté veut prevenir de la manière la plus efficace que les désordres que l'incomodité ou l'incapacité de ses ministres pourront introduire dans les finances en concertant avec les Etats généraux les moyens les plus propres d'atteindre à ce but.

5.—Que sa Majesté veut que dans le nombre des dépenses dont elle assure la fixité on ne distingue pas même celles qui tiennent plus particulierement à sa personne.

6.—Que sa Majesté veut aller au devant du voeu legitime de Ses Sujets en invitant des Etats Generaux a examiner eux mêmes la grande question qui s'est elevée sur les lettres de cachet.

7.—Que Sa Majesté préfére avec raison aux conseils passagers des ministres des délibérations durables des Etats Généraux de son Royaume.

8.—Que sa Majesté a formé le projet de donner des Etats provinciaux dans le Sein des Etats Generaux et de former un lien durable entre la legislation particuliere de chaque province, et de la legislation generale de son Royaume.

Et attendu qu'il est indispensable pour la sureté de tous les individus qui forment la nation que leurs droits soient en ce moment etablis sur des bazes inébranlables, les gentilshommes de la senechaussée de Gevaudan, chargent leur deputé de declarer aux Etats Generaux que la volonté de ses commettans est que les Etats Generaux statuent dans la forme la plus autantiques [authentique].

1.—Que le Royaume soit reconstitué et soumis aux regles d'une vraye monarchie, ou le prince a seul le pouvoir executif, et la nation avec lui l'autorité legislative.

2.—Que les Etats generaux seront rassemblés avec periodes raprochés tels qui seront fixés par les d. Etats Generaux.

3.—Que la liberté de chaque citoyen sera garantie par une loy qui prescrivent a jamais l'odieux regime de lettres de cachet et les ordres arbitraires declara infames ceux qui en seront les parteurs quand cette loy sera prononcée, dans le cas ou un Ministre voudroit surprendre la religion de Sa Majesté pour en rétabli l'usage.

4.—Que l'on fixera invariablement les depenses de chaque departement que tous les ministres seront responsables de leur gestion relativement aux finances et que l'on remettra toute personne employée dans le service public de quelque qualité et condition quelle soit au tribunal de la nation sur le requisition.

5.—Que l'impot sera egalement reparti par les commissaires et sous les mêmes formes dans tous les ordres sans aucune exemption ni privilege pecuniaire et personnel dans toute l'etendue du Royaume et qu'on s'occupera à des moyens de le simplifier et de diminuer les frais de perception.

6.—Que nul emprunt ne sera désormais valable qu'il n'ait été consenti par les Etats Generaux.

7.—Qu'aucun impot ne sera à l'avenir mis ou prorogé sans le consentement des Etats Generaux du Royaume et en consequence que toutes impositions mises ou prorogées par le gouvernement, sans cette condition ou accordée hors des Etats Generaux par une ou plusieurs provinces, une ou plusieurs villes, une ou plusieurs communautés soient nulles illégales et qui sera deffendu sous peine de concussion de les repartir assoir et lever.

8.—Que les domaines du Roy seront alienés ou leur administration soumise avec regles plus Economiques qu'ils seront cizaliés pour être mis a la portée d'un grand nombre d'acquereurs que tous les marchés anterieurs seront revisée afin que l'on puisse revenir sur ceux qui ont été honnereux a l'Etat pour le produit des dites ventes, améliorations, et revisions d'être employés a l'acquittement de la dette nationale.

9.—Que le regime abusives, état actuel de languedoc, sera supprimé et par voye de suite celui des Etats particuliers du pays de Gevaudan, et qu'il sera substitué une nouvelle forme d'Etat constitutionnelle, représentative dont les membres soient librement elus par leur pairs et soumise aux regles du plan général qui sera adopté par la nation assemblée aux Etats Generaux.

10.—Que tous les comptes du gouvernement, et des Etats provinciaux et particuliers seront rendus publics annuellement par le voie de l'impression, afin que l'entiere administration soit connue de toute la nation.

11.—Que les interets des dette provinciales du Languedoc et particulieres de ses dioceses seront payées sur les impositions generales de la ditte Province en deduction de ce qui en parviendra dans les coffres du Roy, en y comprenant les fonds des Emprunts pour lesquels la province a preté son credit au Roy et que ces interets continueront a etre payés dans la ville de Montpellier pour la commodité et Sureté des preteurs.

12.—Qu'il ne sera porté aucune atteinte aux droits et prerogations des Etats Generaux qu'ils seront constitués a leur prochaine assemblée et que dans le cas ou cette loy seroit enfrainte toutes les provinces rentreront dans leurs anciens droits, privilèges, immunités et prerogatives auxquelles il pourroit avoir été derogé en faveur du bien public, et non autrement la present regle etant expresse et de rigeur de Languedoc.

A ces conditions les gentilshommes de la senechaussée du Gevaudan donnent pouvoir à leur deputé de sanctionner la dette contractée par le gouvernement après en avoir constate toutes les parties et après avoir veriffié les titres sur lesquelles elle est etablie, ils lui prescrivent de consentir tous les impots qui seront jugés necessaires pour mettre le revenu de l'Etat appoint de ses besoins réels, sous les reserve expresse que tout impot sera limité pour la durée, au terme fixé pour le retour des Etats Generaux lui en joignant les dits gentilshommes, si les douze articles cydessus ne sont pas sanctionnés de protester contre tout ce qui pourra être deliberé dans l'assemblée de contraire aux propriétés et avantages de ses commettans. Fait clos et arrêté par nous commissaire president et secrétaire soussignés à Mende ce 31 Mars 1789.

Signés.

et le dit enregistrement fait par le dit Vachin per,[57] mon dit Sieur de Randan de Mirandol a retiré les dits verbaux, cahiers de doleances et autres pieces pour etre deposées devers le greffe de M. le senechal Royal de Gevaudan le tout fait en presence du Sieur Joseph Randan et de Jean Francois Vialard[58] per de Mende signes avec nous dit Sieur de Mirandol de ce requis et nous Vachin per avocat de la ville de Mende.

NOS. 24. THE THIRD ESTATE OF THE SENECHAUSSEE OF MONT-DE-MARSAN

The text given by the *Archives parlementaires,* Vol. IV, p. 33 is false. *Cf.* Brette *op. cit.,* Vol. IV, p. 319-20. The text reprinted here is the one described by Brette.

[57] This name was unidentified, probably the procurator of the king. The abbreviation "per" may stand for "procurator."

[58] A. Vialard signed the cahier of the Third Estate, but this was neither the lieutenant-general, registrar, nor the president for the nobles.

P.V.—MS, *Arch. Nat.* Ba54, *cf.* Brette, *ibid.,* Vol. IV, p. 317.
Convocation: 1st type.

CAHIER GENERAL DES DOLÉANCES DU TIERS ÉTAT DE MARSAN,
TURSAN ET GABARDAZ, 22 AVRIL 1789

Articles Preliminaires

Les Députés du Tiers-état seront reçus à presenter leurs cahiers de la meme maniere que les deux premiers ordres.

Les membres des états généraux seront reconnus et déclarés personnes inviolables et ne pourront répondre dans aucun cas de ce qu'ils auront fait proposé ou dit dans les états généraux si ce n'est aux états généraux eux-mêmes.

1.—Les députés du Tiers aux états généraux ne pourront déliberer que dans une assemblée commune de tous les répresentants du Royaume et où les suffrages seront comptés par tête et non par ordre.

2.—La forme de délibérer étant fixée les deputés s'occuperont de régler invariablement les droits du prince et ceux de la nation.

3.—Ils demanderont qu'on fixe la pluralité des suffrages qui determinera la loi.

4.—Les états généraux s'assembleront à des époques périodiques qu'ils determineront eux mêmes.

5.—Il sera reconnu par un acte authentique que la nation seule a le droit d'accorder ou de refuser les subsides d'en régler l'étendue, l'assiette, la repartition, la durée, d'ouvrir des emprunt et que toute autre manière d'imposer ou d'emprunter est nulle, illégale, inconstitutionelle, et de nul effet.

6.—Les loix qui auront été déliberées par les états généraux seront enrégistrées sans delai ni remontrance préalable dans le cours qui seront chargées d'en maintenir l'exécution.

7.—Les reglements sur l'administration de la justice, de la police et du commerce emanés du Conseil durant l'intervalle d'une assemblée à l'autre, seront vérifiés et enregistrés par la cour provisoirement.

8.—L'état des tribunaux, les offices de judicature, les emplois civils et militaires, ainsi que les pensions seront inamovibles en sorte qu'aucun changement ne pourra y être fait, ni aucun titulaire dépouillé que pour forfaiture préalablement jugée par juges competents ou par suppression arrettés par les états généraux.

9.—Le conseil des parties ne connaîtra que de la cassation des arrêts et jugements en dernier ressort sans que dans aucun cas il puisse retenir les causes et y faire droit.

10.—Les évocations, attribution et commissaires n'auront plus lieu en matière civile et criminelle, toute instance sera portée devant les juges commis par la loi.

11.—Tout droit de committimus sera aboli.

12.—Les Etats Généraux nommeront des commissaires pour la redaction d'un code civil et criminel.

13.—Les lettres de cachet et autres ordres arbitraires seront supprimés et les personnes actuellement detenus seront renvoyée par devant leurs juges naturels.

14.—Les charges municipales seront, dans tout le Royaume rendue à la nomination des villes et communautés.

15.—La pressa sera libre, à la charge par l'imprimeur d'apposer son nom aux ouvrages.

16.—Les articles ci-dessus préalablement arretés et enrégistrés, les états généraux approfondiront les causes et le montant du déficit, feront dans la dépense les réductions les plus rigoureuses et délibereront ensuite sur les subsides de nécessité absolu qui seront supportés par les trois ordres sans distinction ni privilège.

17.—Les états généraux ne continueront les subsides et n'en accorderont de nouveaux que pour l'intervalle d'une assemblée à l'autre.

18.—A l'expiration de cet intervalle, toute levée de deniers, à quelque titre et sous quelque dénomination qu'elle ait été établie, cessera de plein droit et à peine de concussion.

19.—Toute espèce de subsides de taxes même pour la confection des routes sera supportée également par les trois ordres au *prorata* des revenus et des facultés de chaque contribuable.

20.—Tous les biens de quelque nature qu'il soient seront assujettis aux mêmes taxes sans distinction ni privilège.

21.—Il n'y aura pour les trois ordres et les biens à eux appartenans qu'un même rôle pour chaque nature d'impositions.

22.—Les comptes détaillés de recette et de dépense seront rendus publics tous les ans par la voie de l'impression.

23.—Le montant des nouvelles taxes à la charge des privilégiés dans tout le Royaume sera également rendu public dans l'année qui suivra celle de leur établissement.

24.—Les fonds nécessaires à chaque departement seront fixés et chaque departement seront fixés, et chaque ministre demeurera responsable des dissipations qui auront eu lieu dans le sien.

25.—Le montant des pensions sera determiné à une somme fixe et la liste en sera aussi publiée tous les ans avec les motifs qui les auront determinés.

26.—La dette de l'État sera consolidée.

27.—Les bureaux des traites et foraines seront portés sur les frontières.

28.—La contrabande sera reputée dèlit ordinaire et la preuve en sera reçu par temoins.

29.—Les péages de terre et d'eau pour raison desquels ceux qui les perçoivent ne sont assujetis à aucun entretien ou charge seront supprimés.

30.—L'arbitraire sera banni de la distribution des billets des classes pour la marine et il sera fait une ordonnance particulièrement à cet effet.

31.—Les poids et mesures seront rendus uniformes dans tout le Royaume.

32.—Les droits de franc fiefs seront supprimés.

33.—Les emphiteotes auront la faculté de se rachetter des corvées banalités et autres servitudes seigneurialles fondées, en titre, en indemnisant le seigneur suivant la fixation qui sera faite par les états généraux.

34.—Les arrerages de ces protestations seigneuriales ainsi que des rentes secondes seront sujets à la prescription de cinq ans.

35.—Le droit de prelation ne sera plus accordé par sa Majesté sur les héritages et dependants de la censive.

36.—Le droit de prelation ne sera plus cèssible et les seigneurs n'auront la faculté du rétrait que pour eux seuls et pendant six mois.

37.—Il sera rédigé un tarif qui fixera d'une manière claire et détaillée le perception des droits de contrôlles.

38.—Aucuns papiers royaux circulants, aucuns officiers, ou commission de quelque nature qu'ils soient ne pourront être établis et crées que par la nation asemblée.

39.—Il sera établi dans chaque province des états particuliers dont la constitution soit regulière parfaitement réprésentative et convienne également à toutes les provinces ou les deliberations soient prises en commun et les suffrages comptés par tête et sans distinction, d'ordre ni de privilège.

40.—Il sera demandé aux états généraux que l'ordre du clergé nomme des commissaires pour la redaction d'un catechisme pour tout le royaume sans qu'il puisse y être fait aucun changement lorsqu'il aura reçu la sanction.

41.—La Jurisdiction écclésiastique sera irrevocablement fixée.

42.—Les annates et autres rétributions de la chancellerie romaine seront supprimés.

43.—L'intérêt du prêt à jour sera autorisé au taux de l'ordonnance.

44.—La portion congrue des curés et des vicaires sera augmentée et portée au taux que les états généraux détermineront.

45.—Vacance arrivant les annexes qui exigent la résidence ordinaire d'un vicaire par rapport à leur situation ou à leur étendue seront désunis de leur matrices et pourvues d'un curé lorsque leurs revenus suffiront à son entretien.

46.—Les particuliers pourront racheter des gens de mainmorte les rentes chargera et fondations obituaires de la manière qu'elle sera fixée par les états généraux.

47.—Les évêques et abbés royaux seront tenus de resider dans leurs dioceses et dans leurs abbayes sous les peines portées par les états généraux.

48.—Nos députés demanderont le maintien des privileges des états de

Marsan avec plainte de ce qu'ils ont été meconnus dans l'envoi des lettres de convocation.

49.—En conséquence et vu la nature et la sterilité de son sol qui ne lui permettent point de s'unir à aucune administration voisine il lui en sera accordé une propre et locale et en païr d'état aux trois ordres.

50.—Les statuts des villes et communautés du Marsan seront rétablis.

51.—Les émoluments des charges municipales seront aboli, et l'exercise s'en faira gratuitement et pour deux ans seulement.

52.—Il sera permis à chaque ville et communauté d'établir une caisse applicable à des indemnités ainsi qu'au soulagement des pauvres et contribuables.

53.—Les fonds de cette caisse ainsi que leur emploi seront réglé annuellement dans les assemblées générales desdittes villes et communautés.

54.—L'emploi des revenus patrimoniaux et les comptes qui y sont relatifs seront examinés et reçus par les conseils des villes et communautés sans que les commissaires de parties puissent em prendre connaisance ni disposer des dites revenus.

55.—Les lettres patentes qui fixeront l'abonnement des impositions seront adressées aux états et enregistrées dans les cours sur la demande du procureur sindic des états.

56.—Les états généraux sont prié de prendre en consideration la sterilité notoire du pays de Marsan, la progression excessive dans laquelle les impôts et le droit de consommation s'y sont multipliés et accrus tandis que le produit des terres et les ressources y ont dechû d'une manière très sensible.

57.—Les états de Marsan seront autorisés à déterminer les chemins, ponts et chaussées dans leur arrondisement ainsi qu'a fixer, répartir et employer ce qu'ils jugeront convenable de lever.

58.—Toutes les villes du Marsan qui ont été dépouillée du francaleu seront rétablis dans ce droit, et celles qui en jouissent seront maintenues.

59.—Les communaux et vacants ne seront plus accensés par le domaine au mépris d'un droit d'usage que le pays de Marsan paye annuellement, quoique l'uzance [usance] de Marsan art. 2 des herbages, les réserves aux habitants sans tribut.

60.—Afin de prevenir les contestations qui peuvent naitre des lettres patentes du 29 Avril 1768, concernant le défrichements, les exemptions accordées seront nominement attribuées au pays de Marsan comme etant un pays de landes en friche, sterile, renfermée dans les limites portés par la loi, et ne contenant aucune paroisse en pleine culture; en consequence tout espece de défrichements y jouira de l'exemption de la dîme pendant 20 ans et des autres faveurs énoncées dans les dittes lettres patentes.

61.—Les temps de l'exemption expiré, les curés percevront la dime de ces défrichements à raison de 51 conformément aux dittes lettres patentes.

62.—Les dimes seront payées, distraction faite des semences.

63.—La premier qui est un droit insolite et exhorbitant de la dîme sera supprimée ainsi que tous autres droits perçus sur les propriétaires outre la dîme.

64.—Toute espèce de casuel sera supprimé dans les campagnes.

65.—Les scholanier [unidentified] dont les titulaires chargés des l'instruction de la jeunesse ne remplissent aucune de leurs fonctions seront supprimées, vacance arrivant et les états de Marsan aviseront à l'emploi et à la partition eu égard au besoin et à la situation des lieux.

66.—Les cultivateurs à raison du défaut des bras ne seront assujetis à la milice et aux classes qu'à l'âge de 20 ans revolus.

67.—Les contrats de mariage, les contrats de faisance et les testaments des journalliers et des colons qui n'auront point de propriété foncière ne seront point assujetis dans aucun cas qu'au payement des 10 sols pour tout droit de controlle et d'insinuation.

68.—Les journaliers et colons en minorité seront dispensés de se faire pourvoir d'un curateur pour leur mariage, et l'assistance de six principaux parents au contract de mariage, à défaut de parents de six voisins et amis tiendra lieu pourvoyance.

69.—Il sera nommé des commissaires pour rédiger l'usance de Marsan et lui assurer force de loi.

70.—Le sénéchal connaîtra en première instance, des matières qui sont attribuées aux juges d'exception tant au civil qu'au criminel.

71.—La connaisance des contestations sur les droits de controlle sera egalement attribuée au sénéchal pour être jugée sur simple mémoire et sans frais.

72.—Le senechal jugera en dernier ressort au nombre de cinq juges les causes qui n'excéderont pas 500 livres.

73.—Les causes qui excéderont la somme de 500 livres, seront portées par appel au parlement, et non au présidial.

74.—Le sénéchal tiendra des audiences populaires ou se décideront en dernier ressort et sans frais les affaires qui n'excéderont pas la somme de 50 livres, il en sera uzé de même par les juges royaux ordinaires jusqu'à concurrence de 30 livres.

75.—Les justices seigneuriales seront éxercées par des gradués et à defaut les causes seront dévolus au sénéchal.

76.—Toutes les causes qui regardent les seigneurs ne pourront être jugées par leurs juges.

77.—Les notaires qui seront pourrvu à l'avenir seront gradués.

78.—Il sera établi des brigades de maréchaussée dans les villes de Roquefort, Villeneuve, et Gabarret.

79.—Les députés des états de Marsan, ne pourront accepter du Gouverne-

ment pour eux-mêmes ni pour leurs enfants place, charge, pension, gratification, lettres de noblesse, ni aucune grâce quelconque, durant les trois années
qui sécouleront depuis la cloture des états généraux sous peine d'infamie.

Fait et arrêté en l'assemblée générale du Tiers-état par nous commissaire soussignés pour être déposé au greffe du sénéchal et en être expédie
copies collationées aux députés le 22 Avril, 1769.

Ainsi signé:

[Eight signatures of committee], Dunogué, lieutenant général.

Collationné

Lamaison   Greff.

NO. 25. THE LOWER CLERGY OF THE DIOCESE OF NANTES

Cahier reprinted from text, printed with *procès-verbal*, *Bib. Nat.* Le24.249.
The cahier occupies pp. 26-36 of this text. Although from the numbered
pages, one would judge that pages 33 and 34 were missing, it is an error
of printing, for p. 35 seems to continue the article interrupted on p. 32,
and no articles are missing.

P.V.-*idem*. The members of the assembly were in a hurry to return to their
parishes, and chose electors to act for the assembly. The nineteen commissioners, with the president and secretary, who were thus chosen, were also
to serve as a committee of correspondence with the deputies. Their signatures were printed at the end of the cahier. Whereas the assembly of the
clergy was held April 3 and 4, the cahier was not ready until April 20.
There are also MS copies of the p.v., *Arch. Nat.* C21/111, and B III 39,
pp. 570 *et seq.*

Convocation: 6th type: Brittany.

DEMANDES ET REMONTRANCES DE L'ASSEMBLÉE DIOCÉSAINE
DE NANTES, POUR LES ETATS-GÉNÉRAUX DE 1789

L'ASSEMBLÉE diocésaine de Nantes, pour seconder les vues bienfaisantes du Souverain, & répondre à la confiance dont il a bien voulu
l'honorer, en l'invitant à concourir avec lui à la régénération de l'Etat,
& au bonheur commun de ses Sujets, recommande à ses Députés aux Etats-
généraux, le plus grand zele pour le bien public, & la plus grande énergie
pour l'opérer. Elle les charge, avant tout, de porter à Sa Majesté le juste
tribut de son respect, de son amour, de sa reconnoissance, & des voeux
ardents qu'elle adresse au ciel pour la gloire, la prospérité & la durée de
son regne.

L'Assemblée n'a pu voir sans la plus vive douleur, la séparation du Clergé
Bretagne, dont elle auroit desiré la réunion & la représentation dans un
même lieu, conjointement avec les autres Ordres, & elle ne cessera de sou-
pirer après un régénération heureuse, qui, fixant de concert les droits respectifs de chaque Ordre, puisse ramener surement la paix & la concorde dans

la province. Occupée, selon l'intention du Roi, de l'examen important des réformes à faire dans l'Etat, pour en guérir radicalement les maux & en assurer à jamais le bonheur, elle a arrêté unanimement de demander:

1. Que la protection du Roi & de la Nation soit continuée à la Religion catholique apostolique & romaine, la seule vraie, dominante dans le royaume, & que le concours de l'autorité appuie efficacement le zele du Clergé.

2. Qu'il soit pres des mesures pour réprimer la licence de la presse & de la librairie, & pour arrêter les progrès effrayans de l'irréligion, du luxe & de la dépravation des moeurs.

3. Que les lois constitutives du Royaume soient invariablement fixées, & que les codes civils & criminels soient utilement réformés.

4. Que la liberté individuelle de tout Citoyen soit sacrée, & qu'on ne puisse y attenter sans formes légales.

5. Qu'il soit pris des mesures promptes & efficaces, pour détruire dans tout le Royaume, la mendicité qui corrompt les moeurs & produit des désordres de toute espece.

6. Qu'il soit fondé dans les Paroisses des bureaux & ateliers de charité.

7. Qu'il soit établi des Ecoles dans les Campagnes, & des Pédagogies dans les Bourges & petites Villes, pour préparer seulement la jeunesse à l'enseignement public des Colléges patentes.

8. Qu'il soit avisé aux moyens de prévenir la cherté du pain, presque toujours occasionnée par le monopole des Villes & des Campagnes.

9. Que les impôts ne soient consentis que pour un temps limité, et qu'ils ne puissent être prorogés, ni augmentés que par la Nation légalement assemblée.

10. Que la perception des impôts soit simplifiée, & qu'ils soient tous également répartis sur les trois Ordres de l'Etat, à raison des facultés respectives de chaque Citoyen; ce qui suppose nécessairement que les décimes du Clergé seront totalement supprimées, & que la dette qu'il a contractée jusqu'ici pour les besoins du Royaume, soit réputée nationale.

11. Que pour le soulagement des Peuples, les frais de Corvées, Tirage de Milices, de Voitures, de Casernement, de Patrouilles, etc., etc., soient supportés proportionnellement par les trois Ordres, au moyen de contributions pécuniaires.

12. Que les Citoyens de tous les Ordres puissent également prétendre à toutes les charges & emplois civils & militaires, & à toutes les dignités de l'Eglise.

13. Que dans tous les Tribunaux royaux & dans les Municipalités il y ait toujours un nombre proportionnel des Membres des trois Ordres, pour que chaque Citoyen puisse être défendu & jugé par ses pairs, suivant la constitution du Royaume.

14. Que les droits respectifs des Seigneurs & des vassaux sur les Communes, soient enfin réglés invariablement.

375

15. Que les droits, privilégés & franchises de la Province de Bretagne, soient conservés dans leur entier, sauf les droits respectifs que les Ordres du Clergé & du Tiers-Etat sont fondés à réclamer pour leur légitime représentation aux Etats, & à toutes les députations & commissions qui en dérivent.

16. Que les Recteurs, Bénéficiers séculiers & réguliers, & Communautés rentées, soient admis par députation en nombre suffisant, aux Etats de la Province, comme aux Etats-généraux, pour y soutenir leurs intérêts; qu'ils jouissent du même droit aux Assemblées générales, provinciales, diocésaines, & aux chambres syndicales du Clergé, & que tous les Députés à ces Assemblées soient élus toutes les fois qu'il s'agira de les former, & tous les trois ans pour les chambres syndicales.

17. Qu'à l'avenir la distinction du haut & bas Clergé n'ait plus lieu, & que l'Ordre de l'Eglise dans chaque Diocese comprenne tous les Prêtres & autres Ecclésiastiques[59] tant séculiers que réguliers, présidé par l'Evêque leur Supérieur dans la Hiérarchie.

18. Que la prochaine Assemblée-générale du Clergé soit invitée à faire rédiger incessamment un Catéchisme pour être seul enseigné dans tous le Royaume, un recueil de toutes les lois Ecclésiastiques, actuellement en vigueur en France, & un Corps de Théologie dogmatique & morale, pour tous les Séminaires: que des Députés de chaque Diocese soient admis à la composition & à la revision des ces ouvrages précieux, qui établiront l'uniformité de doctrine, de discipline & de rits dans toute l'Eglise gallicane, & que pour prévenir l'altération du texte sacré, toutes les nouvelles éditions & traductions de l'Ecriture sainte, soient soumises à l'examen du même Tribunal.

19. Que les loix ecclésiastiques & civils, concernant les Conciles nationaux, provinciaux, & les Synodes, soient remises en vigueur.

20. Que les loix canoniques qui proscrivent la pluralité des bénéfices, soient mises en exécution, & que tout possesseur de bénéfices ne portant pas l'habit écclésiastique, ou exerçant une profession vraiment laïque, en soit privé.

21. Que pour remédier efficacement à la multiplicité scandaleuse des Monitoires, les Officiaux soient seuls Juges des cas pour lesquels il est nécessaire d'en décerner, & qu'ils ne puissent y être contraints par aucune autorité séculiere.

22. Que toutes les dixmes, s'il est possible, retournent à leur destination primitive, en indemnisant néanmoins les décimateurs par union de bénéfices; l'intention de l'Assemblée étant de ne consentir à l'alienation d'aucune propriété, sans indemnité foncière.

23. Que l'on s'occupe incessamment du retrait de l'article de l'Edit de 1768; qui appelle tous les décimateurs indistinctement au partage des

[59] The "l" was omitted in the printed text, obviously as a typographical error.

dixmes novales, dont les Curés, avant cette époque, avoient à si juste titre la perception exclusive; & sur-tout du paiement provisoire d'une nouvelle augmentation portée à un taux convenable pour les Recteurs & les Vicaires.

24. Que pour parvenir à la suppression du casuel forcé des Paroisses, qui seroit l'objet des voeux de l'Assemblée, il soit pourvu suffisamment, par union de bénéfices, à la dotation des Cures de Villes, & a l'amélioration de celles de Campagne qui sont trop modiques, en simplifiant pour les réunions, les formalités d'usage, onéreuses par leurs lenteurs & leurs frais excessifs.

25. Que les Recteurs de la Province de Bretagne soient déchargés des grosses réparations de leurs Presbyteres, comme dans le grand nombre des Provinces du Royaume, & que les propriétaires des dixmes inféodées, soient assujettis proportionnellement avec tous les autres décimateurs, aux réparations du Choeur & Cancel.

26. Que toutes les dispenses ecclésiastiques soient gratuites, ou du moins que l'aumône donnée par les Impétrants, soit renvoyée aux pauvres de leur Paroisse.

27. Que les droits de contrôle & d'amortissement relatifs aux réédifications & améliorations des bâtiments des Bénéficiers & Gens de mainmorte, soient supprimés; & que le droit d'indemnité pour tout bénéfice ne puisse plus être exigé, quarante ans après l'érection; le Seigneur étant censé en avoir reçu le paiement, ou fait la remise.

28. Que tous les baux à ferme des biens ecclésiastiques puissent être passés sous signatures privées, ou que tous ceux de biens laïques le soient par devant Notaires.

29. Que tous les Notaires indistinctement soient habiles & autorisés à rapporter tous actes concernant les biens ecclésiastiques, même les prises de possessions quelconques.

30. Qu'il soit pris des moyens suffisants pour assurer une retraite honnéte aux Ecclésiastiques affoiblis par l'âge ou les infirmités.

31. Qu'un des Agents généraux du Clergé, soit nécessairement choisi parmi les Ecclésiastiques non Nobles.

32. Que si les décimes subsistent, on rende public, chaque année par la voie de l'impression,[60] le tableaux de la masse d'imposition affectée au Diocese, de tous les imposés & de la contribution de chacun d'eux.

33. Que pour remédier aux inconvenients trop multipliés, relativement aux Cures desservies par des Prêtres séculiers, dans les Eglises régulieres, lesdites Eglises soient dans le suite desservies par un Religieux de leur Ordre, sauf les droits des Nominateurs & Collateurs actuels desdites Cures.

34. Que les Religieux, Religieuses & tous Gens de main-morte, ayent la permission de colloquer les dots, épargnes & remboursements sur les Corps & Particuliers indistinctement.

[60] This is the point where the number of the printed text skips from page 32 to page 35. See *supra,* p. 374.

377

35. Qu'il soit avisé aux moyens de pourvoir à l'honnête subsistance des Religieux-Mendiants de l'un & de l'autre sexe.

Telles sont les principales demandes & remontrances que l'amour du bien public a inspirées à l'Assemblée diocésaine de Nantes, Convaincue de leur justice, elle charge, avec confiance, ses Députés de les présenter aux Etats-généraux. Puisse le Roi des Rois qui veille sur la destinée des Empires en assurer le succès!

Signe Lebreton de Gaubert, Docteur en Théologie, Recteur de Saint-Similien, *Président;* Faugaret, Docteur en Théologie, Recteur d'Arton, *Secretaire;* Binot, Prêtre-Bénéficier, *Secretaire;* Saint-Blancard, Religieux Minime, *Secretaire;* Garnier, Docteur en Théologie, Recteur de Teillé, *Secrétaire* & *Commissaire,* Lefeuvre, Docteur en Théologie, Recteur du Saint-Nicolas, *Commissaire;* Odéa, Recteur du Bignon, *Commissaire;* Genevois, Recteur de la Chevroliere, *Commissaire;* Chevalier, Recteur de Saint-Lumine-de-Coutais, *Commissaire;* Samson, Recteur du Pont-Saint-Martin, *Commissaire;* Moyon, Recteur de Saint-André-des-Eaux, *Commissaire;* Chatelier, Recteur de Cordemais, *Commissaire;* Blouin, Recteur de Saint-Julien de Concelles, *Commissaire;* Simon, Recteur de la Bernardiere, *Commissaire;* Hervé de la Bauche, Recteur de Couffé, *Commissaire;* Bodiguel, Prieur-Recteur de Bonnoeuvre, *Commissaire;* Darbefeuil, Prêtre, Bénéficier, *Commissaire;* Marsac, Prêtre, Bénéficier, *Commissaire;* Villeneuve, Prêtre, Bénéficier, *Commissaire;* Robert, Prêtre, Bénéficier, *Commissaire;* Latyl, Supérieur de la Maison de l'Oratoire, Recteur de l'Université, *Commissaire;* Vanin, Prieur des Bernardins de Villeneuve, *Commissaire;* Mauri, Prieur des Dominicain, *Commissaire.*

Fin.

NO. 26. THE THIRD ESTATE OF THE BAILLIAGE OF NOMENY

Cahier reprinted from MS text—*Arch. Meurthe-et-Moselle,* B sans cote. (Copy of signed original supplied by M. Pierre Marot, Archivist.) The P.V. of the Arch. Meurthe-et-Moselle, was not seen, but certain facts were checked with the 3 O.p.v., *Arch. Nat.* Ba57. The cahier was adopted before March 18, when elections began. Convocation: 2d type: reunion at Nancy.

CAHIER DES REMONTRANCES, PLAINTES ET DOLÉANCES, MOYENS ET AVIS, DES DÉPUTÉS DU TIERS ÉTAT DE LA VILLE DE NOMENY ET DE CEUX DES COMMUNAUTÉES DU BAILLIAGE DE LA DITTE VILLE, RÉDIGÉ PARDEVANT MONSIEUR LE LIEUTENANT GÉNÉRAL PRÉSIDENT

Cejourd'huy seize mars, 1789, les membres composant l'ordre du tier Etat du bailliage de Nomeny, assemblée en exécution de lettre de Sa Majesté, pour concourir à la redaction du cahier des remontrance, plainte et reclamation qui doit être porté par la voix de leur députée à l'assemblée des Etats généraux, convoqué à Versaille le 27 avril prochain et pour conférer leur pouvoir auxdits députées, déclarent qu'ils sont pénétrées de la plus respectueuse reconoissances pour leurs auguste souverain qui par sa bonté paternal veut bien appeler et consulter son peuple, pour mettre fin aux maux de l'état et préparer le retour à la félicité public.

Pour arriver a ce but si désiré et sans blesser la foi plaine et entier qui este dub[61] à Sa Majesté, l'assemblé recomande expressement a ses deputées ce qui suit:

1. Aussitôt que les état généraux seront assemblée lesdits députées demanderont que la liberté individuel des citoyens soit maintenus et qu'en consequence il ne poura y être portée aucune atteinte par les lettres de cachet.

Art. 2. Qu'il soit ordonné et réglé que dans les délibérations aux Etat généraux on opinera par tete et non par ordre.

Art. 3. Qu'il soit établie en principe et loi fondamental que tout sujet du roy quelqu'ordre qu'il soit sera tenus de contribuer selon ses faculté aux impots librement consentis de la nation.

Art. 4. Que l'on vende a la province de Lorraine ses anciens etat provincieaux, dont les membres librement élus, seront chargées de la repartition et perception des impots consentis par les etat généraux, qui auront l'inspection et adminstration des traveaux, chemin et etablisement public, et des biens des communautées, sans que les intendants puissent en prendre conoissance; les dits étant provinciaux au surplus seront organisées par les états généreaux.

Art. 5. Que le retour périodique de etats généreaux soit fixé par la nation et que la duré des impots qui y seront consentis soit determinée de manière cependant qu'il ne puisse outre passé l'époque du retour du dit états.

Art. 6. Qu'il soit procédé à la vérification de la dette national, à la fixation de sa quotité et la recherche de ses causes et a celle des moyens d'y pourvoir.

Art. 7. Qu'il soit introduit l'economie la plus rigoureuse dans les departements de la guerre, la marine, les affaires etrangeres, la maison du roy, etc. En conséquence fixe, les sommes qui leurs doivent etres affectées et déterminée celles qui pouront etre accordées pour pension, vérifié toutes celles qui existent, suprimer celles qui ont été accordées abusivement et reduire les autres au dessus de douze cents livres.

Art. 8. Que les ministres devienne contable envers la nation de l'emploie des fonds affectées aux services de leurs department respectif.

Art. 9. Que l'on examine tous les impots qui existent, directe ou indirecte et qui se sont accumulées sans avoir recue de la nation l'assemsion

---

[61] There are many peculiarities of spelling and apparent errors in this text. The archivist of Meurthe-et-Moselle furnished a typed copy, supposedly exact, but I could not verify it with the original.

nécessaire, l'assemblée entend, que ses deputée aux etats genereaux incisteront au tant qu'il sera possible a ce qu'il soit statué sur les articles cy-dessus avant de consentir aucune impots.

Art. 10. Qu'il soit fait un retranchement dans les gouvernements militaire et etat-major et consuprime toutes les places et office inutiles qui ne servent qu'a augmenter la surcharge du peuple.

Art. 11. Demander de diminuer la subvention dont le fardeau s'est accrut sans mesure et ordonnées que cette subventions sera rapportée par les sujets des trois ordres.

Art. 12. Supprimer les fermiers genereaux et tous leurs agents qui forment une armée très nombreuses qui par les frais de regie absorbent un partie des revenus de l'état, si l'on ne peut y parvenir a la destruction de la ferme general debarasée cette province des entraves, multiplier des traits de foraine et faire en sorte que les Lorrains et leurs voisins puissent s'entre communiquer sans redoute les gardes, sans payer des acquits, sans craindre des amendes, confiscations, procets, etc. . . .

Art. 13. Supprimer les droits sur la marque des cuirs et tous ceux exercées par la regie general.

Art. 14. Changer l'administrations des eaux et forets, adopter en consequence une regie économique et revoier le contencieux aux officiers des bailliages.

Art. 15. Faire de nouvelle loi relativement à la partie des controlle seaux et autres, afin d'en rendre la perception plus clair et moins arbitrer, abolir et eteindre les droits de franc fiefs impot prejudiciable au propriété de la noblesse, faire pareillement une loi plus et moins enbarrassé pour la conservation des ypoteques [hypotèques].

Art. 16. Supprimer une foule de charge qui ne servent qu'a vexer et ruiner le peuple notament les huissiers prisseurs.

Art. 17. Supprimer les salines de Moyen Vic et Chateau Salins, fixer le nombre des poiles de celle de Dieuze et empecher la vente du sel à l'étranger, la grande consomation de bois que font ces salines celle occasionnées par le luxe et la mauvaise administrations des forets entreneroit a coup sur la ruine de la province de Lorraine et des evechées.

Art. 18. Proscrire le tirage de la milice et laisser aux etats provinciaux le soin d'y suppléer.

Art. 19. Faire supporter l'impôt representatif de la corvée par tous les sujets des trois ordres dans la proportion de leurs propriété.

Art. 20. Supprimer le municipalité et les faires remplacer par des elus qui pourront etre changés tous les trois ans.

Art. 21. Demander qu'il ne sorte aucun argent du royaume pour sa cour de Rome pour dispenser bulle en conséquence l'on pourra établir un conseil eclesiastique chargé de maintenir les loix relatif a ses objets.

Art. 22. Que les denrées de premiere nécessité soient affranchis de tous impôts notament les bleds des droits de coupes ou autres qui se percoivent dans beaucoup de ville.

Art. 23. Demander la reformation des loix civil et de la justice criminel en degagent les procedures de toutes les formalités lentes et embrouillées et fixant la durée des procés. Interdire a tous praticiens non gradué la faculté de postuler dans les hautes justices, l'expérience ne prouve que trop que leur ignorance et leur aridité? font la ruine de nos campagnes. Ordonner qu'à l'avenir tous les procureurs et notaire seront gradué dans les universitées et que les ecoles de droits seront surveillées et assujettis a des examens plus rigoureux.

Art. 24. Révoquer les commitimus et toute les juridictions privilegié qui ne servent qu'a vexer les pauvres habitans des campagnes en les eloignant de leurs foyers et en multipliant les frais.

Art. 25. Abroger la loi des clotures; malgré tout ce qui a été dit en sa faveur, l'experience nous prouve qu'il est infiniment pernicieux à la Société et au commerce puisque depuis qu'il est en vigeur le nombre de bétail a beaucoup diminuer dela l'excessif chereté dans le prix de la viande, du suif et des cuirs.

Art. 26. Qu'il soit fait des changement a la loi relative au droit de parcour et au partage des comunes s'en raporter pour les changements aux etats provinciaux qui les determineront suivant que les localitées l'exigeront.

Faire en sorte que les seigneurs a qui appartient le droit de tier deniers soit tenus de contribuer aux depense de comunautés dans la proportion de ce tiers.

Art. 27.[62] Demander la residence des eveques dans leurs diocese, celles des abbées et prieurs comandataire dans la province ou sont situées leurs benefices, pendant neuf mois de l'anné sous peines d'être saisis de leurs temporelle et de l'emploit de leur revenus, aux hopitaux attellier de charite et autres etablissement public.

Art. 28. Vérifier les revenus des différentes communautées religieuse en appliquer le supperflu a des etablissements utile pension et autre recompense.

Art. 29. Proscrire la pruralitée des benefices sur la meme tete et soustraire de ceux qui sont considerable une partie des revenus, soit pour l'appliquer au profit du clergé du second ordre ou a des etablissement public, soit a des recompenses militaires et aux agriculteurs et fabriquant qui auront supportées des pertes.

Art. 30. Supprimer le casuel non fixe des cures et leurs accorder en conséquence une indemnité, les retributions qu'il percoivent pour mariage, bateme et enterrement, excite beaucoup de declamation contre eux ce qui diminue l'estime le respect qui leurs sont dub.

Art. 31. Demander pour la facilité du comerce l'unité des poids, aulne et mesures du moins dans chaque province.

[62] "Nota renvoye a l'article 41," in margin.

Art. 32. La liberté de la presse a la condition que l'auteurs signera sa minutte qu'il remttra à l'imprimeur ce dont ce dernier sera garant.

Art. 33. Que l'exportation des bleds hors le royaume n'aura lieu que pour l'agrement des etats provinciaux.

Art. 34. Supprimer toute les bannalitées.

Art. 35. Faire une loi relative aux abus de la trop grande multiplicité des colombiers dans cette province.

Art. 36. Que tous les cens et droits seigneuriaux puisse être racheté, laisser en conséquence aux états provinciaux le soin d'en faire les evaluations.

Art. 37. Que tous invidus [individus] du tiers etat soit apte a toute les place militaire judiciaire et eclesiastique et autre s'il en est digne, la noblesse aura sa preference a égalité de mérite.

Art. 38. Que la noblesse ne puisse plus l'acquérir par aucune charge mais quel devienne la recompense de ceux qui auront bien mérité de la patrie.

Art. 39. Demander de faire rentrer a l'agriculture les vignes qui ont été planté de puis trente ans et qui sont susceptible d'etre cultivé par la charue les plantations infinie qui ont eut lieu nuise beaucoup au comerce des bled, diminue cette denré si rare et si precieuse et entreine beaucoup d'abus.

Art. 40. Qu'il soit expressement deffendus a tous deputées aux états genereaux de solliciter ni accepter aucune grace de la cour pour eux ou pour les leurs sous peine d'etre reputé traite a la patrie.

Art. 41. Demander que les seigneurs doresnavant ne puisse jouir que d'une double portion dans les partages des communes, soit terres ou prez et qu'il seront assujettis aux charges de communautées à raison de cette double portion.

Art. 42. Demander que toutes les amendes des mesus champetre encourus par les fermiers des seigneurs ne soit plus applicaple aux profit de ses derniers, mais à la fabrique du lieu.

Ce sont les remontrances, plaintes et doléances, moyens et avis des députées du tiers état du bailliage de Nomeny, redigé a l'assemblé général; tenus en salle de l'Hotel de ville dudit Nomeny, les ans et jour avant dits et ont tous les députées signé avec nous et notre greffier.

[Thirty-two signatures]

Fourier de Bacourt[63]   Colombe[64]

NO. 27. THE THIRD ESTATE OF THE SENECHAUSSEE OF AUVERGNE AT RIOM

Cf. Brette, *op. cit.*, Vol. III, pp. 638-40. The necessary supplement to the texts given by the *Archives Parlementaires*, Vol. V, pp. 570-74, is given

---

[63] Lieutenant general, presiding officer.
[64] Secretary.

here, reprinted from the MS text—*Arch. Nat.* Ba72. *Cf.* also—Mége, F., "La dernière année de la province d'Auvergne," in *Mém. de l'Acad. des Sciences, Belles-lettres, et Arts de Clermont-Ferrand,* 1904. P.V.-MS, *Arch. Nat.* B III 14. *Cf.* Brette, *ibid.,* pp. 636 *et seq.* Convocation: 1st type.

Approuvé par l'assemblée générale du Tiers-État de la Sénéchaussée d'Auvergne pour servir de cahier général d'instructions et pouvoirs aux députés aux Etats Généraux, le 12 Mars 1789, Signés Dufraisse, Lieutenant Général, et Président du Tiers Etat, Malouet Président de la Commission.

[Sixty-four signatures]

Sen suit le supplément annexé audit Cahier.

Impôt

La province d'Auvergne dans son ancienne et nouvelle enclave, y compris le pays des Combraille, et la partie qui a été démembré pour former l'élection de Gannat, étant Redimée des petites et grandes Gabelles et de tout droit sur les consommations, l'uscerpation de ces genres d'impots qui pesent sur différentes parties de la Province doit être Reprimée ainsy que celle du surhaussement de prix de dix sous par livre dans les pays abonnés qui ont Traiter avec le fermier à un prix fixe.

2.—Il sera défendu au fermier et à ses préposés entre possesseurs de délivrer et fournir aux debitants ni au public aucun tabac en poudre.

3.—Que les Seigneurs haut justiciers ne puissent plus à l'avenir accorder des provisions de juges et procureurs d'office à leurs régisseurs et fermiers.

4.—Qu'il soit crée dans la province le plustot possible une Cour superieure de justice.

5.—Qu'il soit établi dans les Paroisses un Bureau de conciliation composé de Curé, du Syndic, et de deux notables habitants, lesquels jugeront gratuitement et sans appel sur un simple avertissement signé du Greffier, toutes les affaires légères comme dommages de Bestiaux et autres dont l'objet n'excéderoit pas la somme de trente livres une fois payée.

6.—Que les gardes des Seigneurs soient tenus de se faire assister de deux Témoins pour que leurs procès-verbaux fasse foi en justice.

7.—Qu'il soit permis aux habitants des communautés qui le demanderont de partager leurs communaux, à raison de leurs propriétés respectives, sans néanmoins qu'il soit loisible à aucune personne de défricher les Bois.

8.—Qu'on procure le défrichement des marais dont le mauvais air infecte les campagnes, fait périr les habitants et endommager les Récoltes.

L'assemblée après être convenue du petit nombre d'articles rédigés en supplément au cahier général, auroit beaucoup d'autres observations locales et intéressantes à faire et chacun de Messieurs les Commissaires pour remplir les Voeux de leurs comans [commettants] et exposer les articles principaux de leurs doléances, mais il a été reconnu unanimement par l'assemblée que chacun des griefs et demandes détaillés dans les Cahiers des différentes municipalités se trouvoient rélatifs aux principes Législatifs proposé dans le cahier général, en sorte que si les ds. principes sont adoptés par les Etats Généraux comme nous, de vous l'exposer le meilleur adon [unidentified word] qui en résultera opperera touts les redressements pers. Et néanmoins l'assemblée se réserve le droit de faire parvenir à ses représentants Généraux tous les mémoirs relatif à un intérêt commun et local lorsqu'elle croira que l'enpron [unidentified word] des affaires Généralles du Royaume permettre de s'occuper des affaires pus [unidentified word] de chaque province.

A l'effet de quoy l'assemblée a arrêté de nommer dix Sindics du Département qui entreront en correspondance avec les dix représentants.

Fait et arrêté le 13 Mars 1789,
et ont signés, Dufraisse Lieutenant Général, President, Malouet,[65]
[Eighty-two signatures.]

S'en suit autre supplément annexé aud. Cahier de doléance.

Les députés de la Chatellenie Royalle d'usson et nonette demandent qu'à la suite de l'article 16 de la législation il soit ajouté.

Sans que les supérieurs puissent dépouiller les inférieurs sous prètexte de prévention si ce n'est dans les cas prévus par les ordonnances.

2

Qu'à la suite de l'article 8 de l'addition réglée par Commissaire il soit ajouté . . . et qu'on exempte de tout impôts tous mauvais terrains qui des Communes ou des particuliers semeront ou planteront en Bois jusqu'à la première coupe.

3

Ils penseroient qu'il seroit utile d'établir dans la province, un ou plusieurs grenier de charité pour soutenir en faveur des pauvres les Denrées de première nécessité à un prix médiocre et pour en prévenir la disette.

4

Ils demandent la Réunion à justice d'usson et nonette des parties qui auront été démanbrées [demembrées] ou engagées,
[Eight signatures.]

Nous soussignés Greffier de l'assemblée du Tiers État, de la Sénéchaussée d'Auvergne certiffions que le cahier de doléances de laditte Sénéchaussée cy dessus imprimé, et les deux supplements cy joint sont Sincères et véritables et conforme à L'original; En conséquence avons délivré une expédition en forme du tout à Mre. Dufraisse Duchey Lieutenant-Général président de laditte assemblée.

FAMON.

[65] The secretary of the assembly.

384

NO. 28. THE THIRD ESTATE OF THE SIEGE ROYAL OF ROCHEFORT-
SUR-MER

Secondary of the *sénéchaussée* of La Rochelle

Cf. Brette, *op. cit.*, Vol. IV, pp. 401 and 408. By a royal order in council
of March 28, 1789, the cahier of Rochefort was to be annexed to that of
the principal *sénéchaussée* (La Rochelle). The cahier was reprinted by
the *Archives Parlementaires,* Vol. III, p. 486, without the text which follows.
This is reprinted from the MS text, *Arch. Nat.* C23/138.
P.V.-MS, *Arch. Nat.* B III 71. *Cf.* Brette, *ibid.*, Vol. IV, p. 407.
Convocation: 5th type. *Cf.* Brette, Vol. I, pp. 132-34.

PÉTITION PARTICULIÈRE DE LA VILLE DE ROCHEFORT

Art. 1er

L'importance de la ville de Rochefort est trop bien connue par celle de
son port, le seul existant et praticable de Brest à Toulon, pour qu'en la
nommant on ne doive pas espérer de fixer l'attention du gouvernement et
des Etats Généraux.

Cette ville (Sittuée dans un climat tempéré, à portée de la plus part
des choses nécessaire à la marine et des bois de la première qualité, Environnée d'un sol trés fertile et en jouissant d'un ciel aussi beau qu'en aucun
autre lieu de ce Royaume) est entourée de Marais qui infectent l'air et qui
par la quantité prodigieuse d'hommes que les maladies qui en resultent
enlèvent à L'Etat, Rendent presque nuls tous les avantages de sa position.

Ce vice n'est point de ceux qu'il est impossible de corriger ni même
de détruire entièrement, il ne faut que le vouloir bien fermement et le succés
en est certain, déjà depuis quelques années le gouvernement s'en est occupé
et a même dépensé dans cette intention des sommes assez considérables,
desja l'on commence à ressentir de bons effets de cette première tentative, et
quoi qu'ils soient encore faibles, ils donnent au moins les plus grandes espérances pour la réussite de ce que l'on pourra tenter à l'avenir, et font
voir que ce n'est pas se hazarder que d'assurer que ce Vice local peut être
entièrement détruit.

A ce qui est fait il est indispensable d'ajouter beaucoup plus; et il le
seroit probablement encore d'apporter des changemens à la marche que
l'on a suivie jusques ici. L'objet est d'une assez grande conséquence pour que
le Gouvernement ne néglige rien de ce qui peut en assurer le succés, et
l'on estime que le plus sur moyen seroit, avant de mettre la main à l'oeuvre,
de réunir sur cela les opinions des plus habiles gens du Royaume et de donner la préférence dans l'exécution à celle qui réunira le plus d'avantages
aux yeux d'une Compagnie éclairée comme L'academie. Mais pour mettre
les gens de l'art en État d'établir leur opinion avec connaissance de cause,
il paroit nécessaire de faire graver et distribuer la carte de ces marais, qui
vient d'être levée, sur laquelle on tracera les travaux faits, et à laquelle

encore on ajoutera des nivellemens tendant à faire connoitre les hauteurs au dessus des eaux de la Rivière prise à Basse mer, des différents plateaux et bas fonds des marais et celles des travaux faits, les dits nivellemens exprimés sur cette carte comme le sont les sondes sur les cartes marines, il seroit encore utile de joindre à cette carte un memoire rendant compte de la qualité du sol et de l'intention des travaux faits ou projettés.

Art. 2e

Ce n'est pas assez pour la Salubrité de la ville de dessecher parfaitement les marais qui l'environnent, elle renferme dans son sein des causes d'insalubrité qu'il est d'autant plus important de détruire que plus les foyers d'infection sont voisins et plus ils sont nuisibles.

Les pentes des rües, dont plusieurs sont très foibles, sont mal réglées; les pavés, à la charge de la Communauté qui manque de fonds pour les Entretenir, sont dans un état de dégradation tel qu'a chaque pas sont des flaques d'eaux croupissantes, Remplies d'immondices que le même défaut de moyens empêche d'enlever soigneusement, et qui dans les rües fort larges Bordées de maisons peu élevées, sont tenues en fermatation du matin au soir par l'ardeur du soleil et font respirer sans cesse un air d'autant plus corrompu que le sang des Boucheries et charcuteries, et les eaux des Tanneries (tous établissemens épars dans la ville) viennent se réunir aux immondices. Au tour des Remparts sont des parties de fossé d'enceinte produisant la même infection.

Pour que la ville puisse jouir du bon effet que l'on doit attendre d'un désséchement extérieur bien entendu, il est necessaire de fournir à sa Communauté les moyens de rétablir les pavés sur des pentes plus régulières; de profiter de la machine à feu que la Marine a fait établir pour se procurer une quantité d'eau de rivière suffisante aux Besoins du public, qui manque généralement d'eau bonne à Boire tant dans la Ville que dans le faubourg et à laver les Ruisseaux, de faire les changemens convenables aux fossés d'enceinte; de porter la Tuerie générale sur le bord de la rivière à Coté de celles des vivres dans le lieu qui lui est assigné par le Ministre; Enfin d'établir des tanneries et ca dans le lieu le plus reculé de la Ville, et le plus à portée de la rivière, et de mettre a exécution l'arrêt qui ordonne la Translation des Cimetières hors des Villes.

Les mêmes attentions doivent être apportées dans le pavement et le nétoyement du faubourg, et afin de s'assurer d'une surveillance exacte à cet egard, et de pourvoir à la Sureté de cette dependance considérable de la Ville, il convient d'y établir un Commissaire à demeure et une patrouille tirée du faubourg même.

Art. 3e

Pendant longtemps la ville de Rochefort a eu des Revenus capables de couvrir ses dépenses, et elle pouvoit Subvenir aux frais de l'entretien des pavés et du nétoyement des Ruës, elle ne renfermoit alors dans ses murs d'autres troupes que celles de la marine et n'avoit d'autres charges à cet égard que les fournitures de leurs casernement.

Le Gouvernement ayant jugé qu'il était contraire à la conservation des hommes de mettre trois soldats à coucher dans un seul Lit, et réduit ce nombre à deux, la ville s'est trouvée contrainte d'augmenter de moitié les fournitures du Casernement, et dés lors la dépense s'est trouvée supérieure à la Recette.

Pour parer à toute surprise de la part de nos Ennemis, le gouvernement a jugé convenable encore de cantonner des troupes de terre à portée du port et de tenir depuis plusieurs années un Regiment en garnison dans la Ville même; mais cette ville étant en majeure peuplée d'individus tenants à la marine et exempts du Logement, il ne résulte l'impossibilité d'établir ce logement en nature à moins d'écraser la petite portion d'habitans qui s'y trouve sujette; ensorte que la commune, dont les dépenses excédoient desjà les moyens, s'est vuë forcée d'ajouter encore à ses charges celle énorme du casernement et des fournitures de ces nouvelles troupes, ce qui à tellement grossi sa dette que maintenant elle se trouve sans ressource et hors d'état de faire face plus longtemps à toutes ses dépenses: il est donc autant de l'interet du gouvernement que de celui de la ville de Remédier à ce manque de moyens, tant en déchargeant cette dernière des fournitures de casernement des troupes de la marine, qu'en lui procurant pour la troupe de terre, des Casernes plus nécessaires ici que partout ailleurs, et en lui accordant des moyens capables de maintenir la balance entre ses recettes et ses dépenses, et d'amortir graduellement la dette actuelle.

Art. 4e

Cette ville, tres nouvelle, n'a été formée dans le principe que relativement à la marine Royale; cependant l'activité du Commerce, qu'on ne peut trop encourager, y a nécessité un port particulier; mais comme toute origine est petite ce port manque de toutes les commodités propres à favoriser dans les mouvemens l'économie inséparable du commerce, comme de Calles, quays, chaussées etc. qui lui deviennent de plus en plus indispensables à mesure qu'il s'étend, et il convient de lui donner en cela toutes les facilités qui peuvent accélérer son extention.

La prompte expédition dans les affaires du commerce ne concourrant pas moins à lui assurer une existence durable que la liberté, et cette prompte expédition ne pouvant s'attendre d'une justice Royalle qui se doit à tous également, il conviendroit donc encore de lui donner une Cour consulaire, Justice, prise dans ses pairs, plus prompte et plus appropriée à ses besoins dont elle s'occupe uniquement.

Art. 5e

La même cause qui prive le commerce des choses les plus utiles à son Extention, prive aussi la Ville des établissemens publics dont les plus petites villes anciennes sont toutes pourvues, Son église paroissialle est une grange, ce monument peu décent et mal Sain, est encore infiniment trop resserré Relativement à la population qui, L'air devenu plus salubre, s'accroitra probablement beaucoup.

Lors de la fondation de la Ville la necessité d'une Eglise convenable fut tellement reconnuë que Louis XIV en y appelant des prêtres de la mission leur promit des revenus de L'abbaye de St. Jean Dangely [D'Angely] pour subvenir à la dépense qu'elle occasionneroit, et leur donna l'emplacement sur lequel elle doit être batie.

On demande donc, qu'en conséquence de cette promesse les Revenus d'une abbaye soient affectés à l'édification d'une Eglise et d'un Seminaire également promis auxdits prêtres chargés de fournir des aumoniers sur les Vaisseaux et qu'aprés avoir rempli cet objet ils soient employés, tant à faire un traitement suffisant auxdits prêtres (ce qui Déchargera d'autant le Trésor Royal) qu'a venir au secours de l'établissement bien précieux de l'hopital des Orphelines, dont les moyens à la charge de la caisse de la marine sont trop precaires et trop bornés, et le mettre en état de donner, non seulement la nourriture et l'éducation aux orphelines (pour la plus part filles de Marins mort au service du Roy) mais encore d'avoir dans une partie du jardin de l'ancien hopital des salles particulières et secrettes affectées au soulagement et à la guérison de quantité de femmes honnêtes qui, par l'incontinence de leurs maris, se trouvent atteintes de maux Vénériens (plus communs dans les ports de Mer qu'ailleurs) qu'elles communiquent à leurs enfants et dont elles périssent le plus souvent faute de moyens de se faire traiter.

Art. 6e Isle d'aix

Cette isle est tellement utile au port de Rochefort et d'un si grand interêt à la deffense de sa Rade que sa pétition particulière y doit nécessairement être liée, ses habitans, composant environ 40 feux, n'ont avec la grande terre aucune communiquation régulière, en sorte que ce n'est que fort rarement et moyennant 6 tt.[66] pour l'aller et autant pour le Retour qu'ils peuvent se procurer un passage; il est facile de concevoir combien ce prix énorme doit paroitre onéreux à des hommes aussi peu fortunés, et combien, tant par cette Raison que par l'incertitude du retour, leurs relations avec le continent doivent être genées: Cependant il existe à fourras aux ordres du Commandant un Bateau destiné au passage dans l'isle lequel est payé aux frais du Roy sur le pied de 6tt. par jour et reste dans une inaction prés qu'absolue. Si lors de ses voyages fort rares, Ce Bateau passe quelques habitans, ce n'est qu'autant que ceux-ci payent leur passage trés chèrement, ne seroit-il pas raisonnable, et l'humanité ne devroit-elle pas porter à ordonner que ce Bateau, payé pour être mis en action, fit un voyage dans L'isle chaque jour ou il y auroit possibilité et en passat les habitans et leurs effets gratuitement ou moyennant une légère rétribution? Ce Bateau,

---

[66] See p. 281, note 28. Here, tt. probably refers to the *teston tournois*.

Ramené tous les soirs à fourras, seroit toujours aux ordres du Commandant et il n'en pourrait resulter aucun inconvénient pour le service du Roy.

Ces malheureux habitans ainsi abandonnés se trouvent privés de tout secours, et pour surcroit de misère ils sont souvent exposés à mourir de faim faute d'un moulin pour moudre leur grain. il en existoit un appartenant au Roy, dont ils se servoient, les Ennemis l'ont détruit dans une descente; la Tour de ce moulin est cependant encore entière et avec peu de frais on le pourroit rétablir, ce que l'on sollicite avec tout l'empressement qu'inspire L'humanité.

Fait et arrêté à Rochefort par les Députés du Tiers-Etat de la Ville et du Baillage de Rochefort en éxécution du dernier article du Cayer de doléances dudit Baillage le 12 Mars 1789. Signé. [Fourteen signatures.]

Collationné

Dumar.

Chaye greffier.

NO. 29. THE THIRD ESTATE OF THE BAILLIAGE OF ROUEN

The manuscript cahier of the third estate of the grand *bailliage* of Rouen had been lost until a liasse of documents was found recently in the *Archives Seine-Inférieure*. Efforts to find the text had been unavailing (see Hyslop, B., *La Révolution française*, January, 1932, pp. 42 *et seq.*, "Le Cahier général du tiers état du grand bailliage de Rouen," in which article it is shown that the text did not exist at London). Inasmuch as Thouret had been very influential in Normandy, and there was little difference between the cahier of the town of Rouen and that of the *bailliage*, it was assumed that the cahier of the grand *bailliage* would also show his influence and hence bear resemblances to the two preliminary cahiers. The discovery of the real text supports this assumption.

M. Le Parquier, a savant of Rouen, who has published many works on the cahiers intends to publish the text along with the parish cahiers of the *bailliage* which were found in the same liasse. He was kind enough to go over the text and to point out differences from the cahier of the town, which is reprinted in the *Archives Parlementaires*, Vol. V, 597-602. The following summary of the changes involved may be useful until the whole text is published by M. Le Parquier in the official series of volumes. The manuscript bore all evidences of authenticity.

The text of the cahier of the town of Rouen (AP, Vol. V, pp. 597-602) may be used, with the following changes and additions:

Page 597, col. 2, art. 12, l. 1, insert after "Etats-généraux," the phrase "et ceux des assemblées graduelles."

Page 598, col. 1, art. 19, l. 2, insert after "successives," the phrase "de cinq an en cinq an."

Column 2, insert after art. 22 a new article forbidding the establishment of an intermediate commission.

Column 2, insert after art. 24 a new article asking for Provincial-Estates for Normandie like that of the Dauphiné, in which the orders are to be united and the vote by head.

Page 599, col. 1, insert after art. 29 a new article describing representation in the Provincial-Estates, and providing for graduated assemblies by municipalities and districts.

Insert after art. 34 a new article providing for a provincial referendum to the Provincial-Estates of all laws pertaining to the province issued between meetings of the States-General, or if not that, providing for approval by the States-General at its next meeting.

Insert after art. 37 a new article asking for the formation of a commission to reform commercial law, to be formed of one third lawyers and two thirds merchants.

Column 2, art 38, the last two words should read "Etats-provinciaux" instead of "Etats-généraux," and a phrase should be added asking for reform of the courts with respect to vacancies.

Insert after art. 39 a new article calling for reform of the jurisdiction of a *bailliage,* equality in elections, graduated elections, with representation of the third estate equal to that of the clergy and nobles to-gether.

Insert after art. 40 a new article calling for free election of municipal officers.

Insert after art. 41 a new article asking for the establishment of justices of the peace in rural districts. Details of term of office and salary are given.

Insert after art. 45 an article relative to "consignations aux cartrôleurs et receveurs." A second new article discusses the jurisdiction of the Comté d'Eu, which was subject to the Parlement of Paris, but asks to be placed under the Parlement of Normandy.

Page 600, col. 1, under art. 52, add 9°: "Le droit en gros."

Insert after art. 52 a new article discussing taxation which can only be established by the States-General. The cahier asks for two taxes, one territorial, and one personal. The Provincial-Estates should have the power to suggest means of assessment and collection.

Page 601, col. 1, insert after art. 63 an article asking for suppression of the *octroi* and substitution of a personal tax.

Insert after art. 67 an article asking for verification of the domains.

Page 601, col. 2, insert after art. 74 a new article asking that the age when monastic vows may be taken be set at 30 for men and 25 for women.

Insert after art. 76 a new article providing for payment of repairs and reconstruction of presbyteries from the dîme, and asking for suppression of the "droit de déport."

Insert in the section on agriculture (art. 78-83) several new articles. One asks for free sale, both internal and foreign, of "eaux de vie" and cider. A second asks for reform of the Caisse de Poissy. A third asks that no rabbits may be kept except in pens, and that anyone be allowed to kill wild ones. The next article protests against guardians of hunting preserves carrying guns. A fifth article provides for ransoming the *corvée* and the *banalité*. A sixth article provides for taking over communal lands.

Page 602, col. 1, insert after art. 87 an article on the building of roads and on indemnity to those having property from which stone and sand are taken.

Column 2, insert after art. 95, sec. 2, several articles. An article calls for improvement of provisioning royal vessels. Another demands abolition of the slave trade and improvement of their lot. An article calls for the suppression of machinery for carding and weaving cotton and wool (the wording is more forceful than in the town cahier). An article would limit grants to help manufactures to cases recommended by the Provincial-Estates. An article asks for prohibition of the export of rabbit skins, old rags and other things for making paper. An article asks for reform of education, the provision for schools in parishes, a uniform, graduated system, and the teaching of civic duties. Another article asks that the status of non-Catholics be legalized and mixed marriages be permitted. A further article asks that the preliminary cahiers be annexed to the general cahier, and a final article expresses patriotism toward Louis XVI much as the cahier of the town does.

The signatures, date of adoption, and verification differ, but conform to the requirements of the general cahier as indicated in the procès-verbal.

NO. 30. THE THIRD ESTATE OF THE BAILLIAGE OF SARREGUEMINES

Cahier reprinted from MS text, *Arch. Moselle* B8238, original signatures. P.V.-MS, *Arch. Nat.* B III 133 (date March 18), Ba77. There were six members of the committee. When the cahier was discussed in the assembly, it was read in French, and then interpreted in German. The cahier was adopted March 22.

Convocation: 2d type; reunion at Sarreguemines.

DOLÉANCES ET PROPOSITIONS DU TIERS ETAT DU BAILLIAGE DE LA VILLE DE SARREGUEMINES

Les Députés aux Etats Généraux demandent:

1.—Que les Etats provinciaux soient établis en Lorraine d'après l'organisation de la Province, qui sera indiqué et que l'administration confiée à l'assemblée Provinciale leur soit attribuée ainsy que la répartition des impositions.

2.—Qu'il soit procédé à la rédaction du Code Civil annoncé et promis; qu'il plaise à sa Majesté interdire par le même code à tout juges de recevoir aucun soliciteur; de leur enjoindre de prononcer sur les demandes portées devant eux dans le délai de six Mois pour les causes d'audiences, et dans l'année pour celles appointées, à peine de tous dépens dommages intérets.

3.—Qu'il soit également procédé à la rédaction du Code Criminel promis et annoncé; que les procédures soient instruites publiquement; que les accusés ayent des Conseils, et que les crimes soient punis sans acceptations de personnes.

4.—Que le tiers-Etat soit admis dans tous les tribunaux Souverains; qu'il forme la moitie des juges; que le même ordre soit observé dans la division des chambres, et que les juges tires de cet ordre, soient présentés par les Etats provinciaux.

5.—Que l'ordonnance du Commerce pour la france soit rendu commune à la Lorraine, et que la peine contre les falcificateurs de lettres de change et fabrications de fausses soit augmentées, ces voleurs aussy dangereux se multiplient journellement.

6.—Que dans le cas où il soit procedé à la refonte des sièges Royaux, sur la demande des habitants de la campagne, Les Maires et gens de justices soient authorisés à connaitre de toutes demandes au dessous de la somme ou valeur de vingt quatre Livres, sans aucune rétribution que celle de 5 sols pour le Sergent par chaque assignation et que les droits de centième denier et industries sur les offices soient supprimés.

7.—Que tous droits de haute justice sur la demande Générale des Vassaux, pour l'Exercise civil et Criminel soient supprimés.

8.—Que les offices des jurés soient abolis, aux offres de contribuer au remboursement de leurs finances, et que la forme suivie en france, pour la confection des inventaires, lorsqu'ils sont indispensable, soit renduë commune à la Lorraine.

9.—Que l'édit du Duc Léopold du 30 Decembre 1728, concernant les actes qui se passent avec les juifs reprenne vigueur, et qu'il y soit ajouté que toutes stipulations et conventions, mêmes passées pardevant Notaires, avec eux, soient de nulle valeur si les conventions contenus aux actes n'ont pas été faites et arretées avant leurs rédaction, en présence d'un officier de justice ou de Police du Lieu, en présence duquel aussy, outre celle de deux Notaires, où d'un seul et de deux témoins, l'acte sera rédigé de l'aveu de cet officier qui le fournira avec les parties.

10.—Que les juifs fixés par les ordonnances de Lorraine à 180 familles, et ceux résidents dans les Etats en vertu de Brevets obtenus postérieurement, soient réduits au nombre actuel, à charge par ces derniers d'Exercer les professions pour lesquelles ils se sont pourvûs de Brevêts, à peine d'etre déchus du bénéfice desdits brevets, et d'etre expulsés, que par la même Loi, il soit rendu un nouveau réglément pour arrêter les ravages de l'usure.

11.—Qu'attendu qu'il n'y à point de tarif pour les Notaires en Lorraine, il en soit demander un pour prévenir les abus commettent aucuns de ces officiers répandus dans les campagnes.

12.—Que pour exciter l'émulation du tiers-Etat ses membres puissent être admis aux grands bénéfices, offices, charges et emplois Ecclésiastiques, civils, et militaires.

13.—Que les commandes soient supprimées à l'avenir au profit de la Province.

14.—Que les pensions des Curés, administrateurs, et Vicaires, ayant

charge d'âme, soient de nouveau reglées uniformément et proportionellement par les Etats Généraux.

15.—Que les Maitres et Maitresses d'école et autres desservants les Eglises,
soient à la décharge de la communauté, payés sur les biens de l'Eglise;
qu'il soit également pourvû à l'instruction de la jeunesse dans les campagnes.

16—Qu'il ne soit plus accordé de lettres de naturalisation aux sujets
Etrangers pour posseder des bénéfices en france.

17.—Qu'il soit défendu à toutes communautés Religieuses d'hommes et
de filles de recevoir des dots, de ceux et celles qui font profession dans leur
ordres, sauf à se faire payer une pension modique pour les années de novi-
ciat.

18.—Que le nombre des Soldats Provinciaux fixé pour la Province, la
liste en soit envoyée à ses Etats, qui en feront la distribution entre les villes
et les villages, commettront des Commissaires pour proceder au tirage, lors
duquel il sera permis à tout sujet qui y sera soumis, de se faire substituer
un autre convenable pour le tirage, et que nul domestique de la Noblesse,
du clergé, et des privilégies du tiers Etat en soit Exempt; qu'il soit même
permis par une répartition sur tous les sujets au sort de payer une somme
pour le recrutement des hommes à fournir.

19.—Que la Bannalités des moulins, jours et pressoirs Bans vins et corvées Seigneuriales; ainsy que la bannalité convertie en argent, dont les
Seigneurs sont aujourd'huy plus qu'indemnisés soient supprimés sur la demande Générale; les habitants de la campagne, que les Domaines de Sa
Majesté soient allienés avec les droits qui en dépendent.

20.—Que toutes concessions gratuites des chasses soient révoquées et
qu'elles soient relaissées à des censitaires pour leur vie naturelle durante
seulement; que la multiplication du gros gibier étant nuisible à l'agriculture
il soit enjoint à tout proprietaire ou censitaire de droit de chasse de ne
point entretenir une trop grande quantité à peine de tous dommages intérets.

21.—Qu'il soit nommé les Commissaires pris également dans les deux
ordres, de la Province pour examiner sur les mémoires qui leur seront
fournis, et la représentation des pieces originales, les échanges engagement
et alliénations des Domaines faits par sa Majesté et son prédécesseur Roy,
notament ceux désastreux des haras de Saralbe et Villervald, Velferding,
et Frauemberg et en etre demandé la nullité s'il échét.

22.—Qu'en procédant à ladite verification, les droits dont les communautés échangées se trouvent grèvées soient également vérifiées.

23.—Qu'en interprettant et ajoutant à l'Edit du mois de Mars 1767,
tous les heritages soient déclarés clos de plein droit, chaque proprietaire
autorisé à jouir de son immeuble à son gré, le parcours aboli sur les preys
[prés] avant la second faulx et sur les terres lorsqu'elles seront chargées
de grains ou légumes, ou converties en prairies artificielles, que la conver-
tion [conversion] des terres en susdites prairies artificielles soient en-

couragées et qu'il soit permis à tous proprietaires de disposer ainsy que bon lui semblera des fruits et arbres percrus dans les terres arrables.

24.—Que la Province soit dechargée de son contribution à l'entretient de l'école du géni [génie] à Paris et qu'il soit permis aux etats Provinciaux de pourvoir dans la province à la nomination des ingénieurs ainsy qu'à l'instruction des élèves.

25.—Que la nomination des directeurs des postes soit attribués aux Etats provinciaux et que les Bureaux soient plus multipliés.

26.—Que les affectations de forêts à toutes les usines à feux soient modérées et celles cy devant destinées au service du public aujourd'hui affectée à celui des Salines et autres usines à feux soient de nouveaux rendue au service du public et toutes autres de leurs anciennes affectations les plus éloignées des Salines, que le nombre des dites Salines soit restraint et que le Dons des 416 Muids de sel—accordés à la maison de Nassau ainsy que les dix mille livres payés annuellement pour avoir renoncé à la faculté d'établir des Salines dans leur Principauté soient revoquées, sauf à ladite maison d'établir telles Salines elle jugera à propos.

27.—Que l'universite établie à Pont-a-Mousson, transférée à Nancy soit rétablie à Pont-a-Mousson ainsy que la chaire de droit coutumier.

28.—Que la Maréchaussée soit augmentée d'un nombre égal de gens à pieds par des soldats retirés avec pension qui sera augmentée.

29.—Que l'égalite des poids et mesures soit établit dans toute la france.

30.—Que la défense du port d'armes soit levée et icelui à toutes personnes indiquées par les officiers de Police.

31.—Qu'il soit procédé à un nouveau réglement pour l'administration des Eaux et forêts, même à la Suppression des maitrises sur la demande de toutes les communautés, parce qu'il est généralement reconnu que les foretiers qu'ils établissent sont d'ordinaire de malhonnêtes gens, qui par leur conduite ajoutent à la misère publique par leurs moyens, les forêts très deffensables, souvent ne sont point jugées telles pour avoir quelques raisons d'accorder la permission d'y user de la pâture, ou si cette permission est accordée pour rançonner le pauvre habitant, ce qui est d'autant plus oppressif que l'on sçait qu'on ne peut se passer de ces patures.

32.—Que la suppression de la Gabelle soit accordée parce qu'elle est un obstacle à la multiplication des troupeaux, et aux élèves que les sujets ont le plus grand besoin de faire pour pouvoir fournir au soutient de leur —famille et leur donner le moyen de payer les impots: La gabelle le plus désastreux de tous est une des principales cause de leur misère, que celui sur les cuirs et peaux et autres objets sujets à prohibition ainsy que toutes commission extraordinaires soient demandées par les Etats généraux et qu'il soit par eux pourvus aux remplacemens des droits ainsy supprimés, pour éviter une foûle d'assassinats.

33.—Que lesdits Etats Généraux dans le cas que l'impôt Territorial serait admis réglent également ses répartitions levées et versements sur les trois ordres.

34.—Que les Etats Généraux soient mis en état par la Communication des pieces originales de pénétrer dans toutes les parties du déficit.

Qu'il ne soit accordé de pensions n'y gratifications aux militaires que pour des services signalés et bien constatés et aucune retraite avec pension qu'à ceux qui sont hors d'état de continuer leur service, que les memes pensions soient déterminées pour tous les grades des différens corps, et que les motifs des pensions soient rendus public. Que toutes les pensions accordées cy devant aux militaires soient revisées à l'assemblée des Etats Généraux, celles surprises et non mérités supprimées et celles réduites au tau[x] qui sera fixé pour celles à donner à l'avenir.

Que toutes les autres pensions accordées jusqu'à ce jour soient également revisées et celles non méritées réduites à un tau[x] légitimes.

Que les fortifications des plans dans l'intérieur du Royaume soient abandonnées et les Etats Majors Supprimés.

Que la Loterie Royale soit supprimée et qu'en aucuns temps elle ne puisse être rétablie, n'y aucune autre semblable.

Qu'il ne soit plus accordé subsides aux Princes étrangers qu'autant qu'ils seront reconnûs indispensables par les Etats Généraux qui en fixeront le tau[x].

Que la recette des bois soit supprimée à l'égard des Communautés, que les parts à elles avenantes soient versées dans leur caisse communalle, à charge par les officiers locaux d'être responsables de l'employ des deniers.

Que pour encourager les manufactures nationales, l'administration des habillemens militaire soient supprimés, et qu'il soit libre aux Régiments de traiter avec tels fabriquant que bon leur semblera.

Que le droit de Colombier des plus nuisibles à l'agriculture soit supprimé, en tous cas que l'exercice de ce droit soit borné par un nouveau Réglement.

Que le droit du tiers déniers n'étant pas un droit univoque de hautes justices, le droit soit supprimé.

Que les corvées accordées et Exercées durement par les Engagistes des domaines des haras de Sarabbe et Villervald sur une forte partie des communautés de la Lorraine Allemande distantes de huit et dix Lieuës desdits haras dans les temps les plus précieux et aussy que toutes corvées seigneurialles soient supprimées en faveur de l'agriculture: qu'en sa faveur encore, tous droits de dixième dénier à percevoir sur le produit des ventes faites par des sujets de sa Majesté et que la perception de ce droit soit bornée aux sujets Etrangers qui n'usent point de réciprocités.

Qu'il soit procédé à un réglement à raison du payement des frais de proies communaux pour éviter une répartition sur les Contribuables de memes frais qu'une demande ou deffense légitime auront occasionnées.

Que les barrieres soient reculées jusqu'aux extremes frontieres; et qu'il soit établi un tarif modique pour l'entrée des matieres premieres et necessaire, et la sortie de celles non nécessaires, et que ledit tarif soit publié en chaque bureau et traduit en allemand.

Qu'il soit procédé à un nouveau réglement pour les honoraires des curés et pretres desservants les paroisses, et que ce réglement soit rendu public.

Que les Edits et ordonnances dans la Lorraine Allemande soient traduites en allemand et énoncées dans cet idiome aux campagnes.

Que les décimateurs soient sur la demande des campagnes, généralement attenus à la fourniture ses Betes males, beaucoup d'entre eux, sy refusent et voulant s'en exempter.

Que la dixme de pomme de terre le jachera [jachère] et toute mêmes dixme sur les jardins, soient abolies.

Les Députés aux Etats Généraux feront connaitre toute la misère, ou le tiers état du Bailliage de Sarreguemines est réduit par les impositions Royales portés à l'excés et que l'on à d'autant plus de peine d'acquitter cette année que le plus grand nombre des habitans sans pain et sans travail par la rigueur de la saison, l'hyver se faisant encore sentir au 21 Mars, les impossitions y compris le prix du Sel qu'on levera et non compris les droits Seigneuriaux qui sont aussi multipliés qu'accablants dans cette partie de la Lorraine se montant à plus de 21.5000⚖ argent du Royaume, c'est au dela de la valeur du produit du sol pendant l'année 1788 des quatre lieuës quarrées que le Bailliage de sarreguemines occupe et toute sa ressource est dans l'esperance de la recolte prochaine, n'ayant qu'un petit commerce mercantil: aussi les Députés doivent-ils solliciter une reduction pour la suite les membres des deux premiers ordres qui habitent les campagnes sont les témoins de cette calamité générale, et des ravages occasionnés par la grêle l'été dernier et qui fait souffrir tant de familles du tiers, et le tiers attend de leur humanité qu'ils appuyeront ses justes reclamations.

Fait et arreté par nous, Commissaires rédacteurs choisis à la pluralité des voix par les Députés des Villes Bourgs et villages formant le ressort du Bailliage de Sarreguemines le 22 Mars 1789.

[Seven signatures.[67]]

Le present cahier à été par nous Lieutenant Général du Bailliage de Sarreguemines, arreté, cotté, et paraffé par premiere et derniere pages, au nombre de dix pages celle-ci comprise, après que Lecture et interprétation en à été donnée par le ministére de Me. Michel-Vaulont, et interpretté juré en notre siège, à tous les députés des villes, bourg, paroisses et communautés de campagne assemblés cejourd'huy, formantes les députations de notre ressort, et après avoir en leur présence approuve la rature de la quatrieme ligne de l'article trente trois et l'ajouté de ces mots, sur les trois ordres, la rature des sixieme, septieme et huitieme lignes de l'article trente unieme, La rature des dix neufvieme et vingtieme lignes de la page d'autre part, et le changement d'ecriture commenceant par les mots, que les bar-

---

[67] The six commissioners and president of assembly.

rieres soient reculées, etc. Ordonnons, que le présent sera déposé au greffe de notre Siège, et joints aux minuttes des proces verbaux pour y avoir recours le cas échéant: fait à Sarreguemines le 22 mars 1789. quatre heures de relevée, et avons signé, avec l'interprette et notre greffier commis après lecture et interprétation faite.

[One signature.]

Serva
greffier commise.

NO. 31. THE CLERGY AND NOBLES OF THE BAILLIAGE OF SARRELOUIS

Cahier reprinted from MS text, *Arch. Nat.* B III 87, pp. 149-56. This is a copy in the registers made during the revolution at the order of Camus, the head of the archives. All other texts have disappeared.
P.V.—MS (elections), *Arch. Nat.* Ba52. The cahier was adopted March 9.
Convocation: 2d type, reunion at Metz.

9 MARS 1789

EXTRAIT DU PROCÈS-VERBAL DE LA RÉDUCTION
DES CAHIERS DU CLERGÉ ET DE LA NOBLESSE EN UN SEUL

Cejourd'hui 9 Mars 1789, en vertu de l'ordonnance de Monsieur le Bailly, l'ordre du clergé et de la Noblesse réunis sous la présidence, de nous Jean—Pierre Comte de Lambertye, Seigneur de Cosme, Birring, Bitteting et autres lieux, chevalier de l'Ordre Royal et Militaire de Saint Louis Commandant pour le Roi au gouvernement de Sarrelouis, Bailly-d'épée au Baillage de Sarrelouis de cette ville.

Il a été unaniment délibéré que Sa Majesté seroit suppliée; De mettre la province en Pays d'Etats.

D'ordonner que les impôts ne pourront jamais être établis que par les Etats généraux dont le retour périodique, sera fixé tous les trois ou quatre ans, qu'il ne pourra rien être ajouté auxdits impôts sous la dénomination de sols pour Livres ou tous autres ni même rien changé à la forme, de leur perception sans le consentement de ces États.

D'ordonner que l'on s'occupera des moyens de simplifier, les fillieres de la perception.

De supprimer les fermes générales et nommément les Chambres de Reims et autres dont cette ville ressent dans le moment la funeste influence dans persécution d'un de leurs compatriotes.

De supprimer les droits reunis sous une dénomination quelconque.

De permettre la libre circulation dans l'intérieur du Royaume.

De convertir toutes les impositions et droits répartis proportionnellement sur tous les individus tant au réel qu'au personnel, en deux, Savoir:

Sur les propriétés foncières.

397

L'autre sous la forme de Capitation, imposée sur l'industrie et la portion tant libre qu'apparente des fortunes.

D'ordonner la simplification dans les formes judiciaires, la promptitude et l'ordre dans l'administration de la Justice, une fixation authentique dans les rétributions dues à ses Ministres et Agens.

De supprimer les offices d'huissiers—Priseurs de Chatrents Rifleurs, en un mot les priviléges exclusifs aussi nuisible à l'industrie que vexatoires pour les particuliers.

Le clergé et la Noblesse confiant dans la Justice de Sa Majesté ne se permettent pas de doute qu'elle puisse jamais toucher à la proprieté des droits—Seigneuriaux qui sont les prix des concessions faites antérieurement, c'est quelque fois le seul revenu des individus.

Le Clergé consentans à supporter les mêmes impositions que la Noblesse, ne doute pas non plus qu'on ne lui accorde, les priviléges et avantages dont jouiront les Séculiers; qu'en conséquence ils auront la liberté d'emprunter, preter des fonds, d'amodier librement ses terres et que les dixmes ne seront pas plus chargées que celles des Particuliers, et que cette grâce s'étendra également sur les biens des fabriques.

Le Clergé ose espérer qu'il plaire au Roi supprimer les abbayes Commandataires, et Commandes quelconques qui ruinent les Communautés, par les discussions qu'elles font naitre, détériorent les Biens par l'abandon où ils les laissent, et privent la Province de leurs revenus.

Quant aux circonstances absolument locales, le Clergé et la Noblesse réunis ne peuvent que cerciorer Sa Majesté de la profonde misère des habitans de cette Ville, exposée dans le Cahier de leurs doléances de ce jour.

Fait et arrêté en l'assemblée desdits Ordres présidé par mondit Sieur Comte de Lambertye, A Sarrelouis ce neuf Mars 1789. Signé à la minute.

[Eighteen signatures, 12 nobles, 6 clergy.]

Pour extrait collationné
Bettramin.[68]

NO. 32. THE THIRD ESTATE OF THE BAILLIAGE OF ST. DIE

Cahier reprinted from printed text, *Arch. Haut-Rhin,* C1615—s.l.n.d. in 4°, 32 p.

P.V.—MS (election), *Arch. Nat.* Ba53. The cahier must have been adopted before March 23, when the elections began.

Convocation: 2d type; reunion at Mirecourt.

CAHIER DES DOLÉANCES, PLAINTES, REMONTRANCES ET DEMANDES DU TIERS-ÉTAT DU BAILLIAGE ROYAL DE ST. DIEZ EN LORRAINE, À PORTER À L'ASSEMBLÉE DES ETATS-GÉNÉRAUX DU ROYAUME, CONVOQUÉS PAR SA MAJESTÉ POUR LE 27 AVRIL 1789

[68] The local registrar.

Les Députés réprésentants le Tiers-Etat dudit bailliage, soussignés, sur la rapport qui leur a été fait par leurs Commissaires nommés dans l'assemblée du dix-septième du présent mois, des doléances, plaintes, remontrances et demandes de toutes les communautés du ressort dudit bailliage.

Convaincus qu'il est indispenable pour le repos de la Nation et le bien général du royaume, que ses droits soient établis sur des bases inébranables, après y avoir mûrement délibéré.

Ont arrêté de charger leurs Députés aux Etats-Généraux (lesquels députés, ils regardent, d'après les principes de la Constitution du royaume, comme leurs mandataires, leurs fondés de pouvoirs et les organes de leurs volontés,) d'insister de tous leurs efforts pour que les points suivants soient érigés en loix fondamentales, préalablement à toutes autres délibérations.

1.—Que les représentants du Tiers-État aux Etats-Généraux, soient toujours au moins en nombre égal aux représentants de deux premiers ordres réunis: et qu'il y soit délibéré par têtes et non par ordres sur tous les objets qui y seront traités, discutés et réglés.

2.—Que la liberté individuelle des citoyens de tous ordres soit assurée à jamais par l'abolition de toutes lettres closes, lettres de cachet, lettres d'exil et toutes autres espèces d'ordres arbitraires; qu'aucun citoyen ne puisse être enlevé à ses juges naturels; qu'il ne soit plus accordé de commissions particulières, de lettres d'évocation au conseil, de lettres de surséances ou toutes autres lettres dont l'objet seroit d'arrêter ou suspendre l'exécution des lois; que toutes celles qui ont été accordées jusqu'ici demeurent nulles et sans effet; et que le secret de la poste ne puisse être violé à l'avenir dans aucun cas, ni sous aucun pretexte.

3.—Que la nation seule ait droit de s'imposer et d'accorder des subsides, d'en régler l'étendue, l'emploi, la durée et d'en faire le département entre les diverses provinces du royaume; qu'elle seule ait droit d'ouvrir des emprunts pour les besoins de l'État, et que toute autre manière d'imposer ou d'emprunter, soit illégale, inconstitutionelle et de nul effet.

4.—Que non seulement aucune loi bursale, mais encore aucune autre loi générale et permanente quelconque, ne soit établie à l'avenir qu'au sein des Etats-généraux, et par le concours mutuel de l'autorité du roi et du consentement de la nation; que ces loix portant dans le préambule, ces mots; de l'avis et consentement des Etats du Royaume . . . soient pendant la tenue même de l'Assemblée Nationale, adressées aux premiers tribunaux des provinces pour y être inscrites sur leurs régistres et placées sous leur garde, lesquelles ne pourront se permettre d'y faire aucune modification.

5.—Que le retour périodique et régulier des Etats-généraux soit fixé irrevocablement au terme de quatre ou cinq ans au plus, pour prendre en considération l'Etat du royaume; examiner la situation des finances, l'emploi des subsides accordés pendant la tenue précédente; en décider la continuation ou la suppression, l'augmentation ou la diminution; faire les réformes, les améliorations nécessaires dans toutes les branches de l'économie politique; à l'effet de quoi l'époque et la forme de convocation seront déterminées par la loi pour pouvoir s'assembler, sans qu'il soit besoin d'autre convocation, et sans qu'il puisse y être apporté aucun obstacle, sauf les convocations extraordinaires que Sa Majesté croiroit devoir faire dans l'intervalle d'une assemblée à l'autre.

6.—Qu'il soit établi des Etats-provinciaux, dans toutes les provinces, composés et organisés comme les Etats généraux, et d'une manière uniforme, s'il est possible, avec cette différence que les Etats-provinciaux auront seuls une commission intermédiaire, toujours subsistante, pendant le temps qu'ils ne seront point assemblés, ainsi que les Procureurs-généraux, syndics spécialement chargés de veiller au maintien des droits de provinces et de leurs concitoyens.

7.—Que tous impôts distinctifs entre les trois ordres soient supprimés, pour leur en être substitués d'autres, si les besoins de l'état l'exigent, et la répartition en être faite dans les provinces, (sans égard aux privileges ou exemptions ci'devant accordés, qui seront abolis pour toujours,) sur les mêmes principes et les mêmes bases pour tous les ordres, dans la proportion des propriétés mobilaires et immobilaires des citoyens de quelque classe, rang et condition qu'ils soient, dans toutes les communautés, en préférant les impots qui péseront sur les propriétés, qui atteindront plus facilement les facultés de tout genre, et qui présenteront le moins d'embarras et de frais dans la perception, d'après le département des Etats-généraux entre toutes les provinces, et des Etats-provinciaux entre les diverses communautés de chaque province.

8.—Que les loix, (autres que les loix générales et permanentes, ou bursales) c'est-à-dire, les simples loix d'administration et de police à faire pendant l'absence des Etats-généraux, soient provisoirement adressées aux Etats-provinciaux, lesquels seront chargés, dans les provinces, de toutes les parties de l'administration, sans exception, ou à leurs commissions intermédiaires, qui les feront remettre aux procureurs-généraux des premiers tribunaux des provinces pour les faire enrégistrer avec les modifications qui auront été déliberées par lesdits Etats-provinciaux ou leurs commissions intermédiaires et cependant les dites loix n'auront force que jusqu' à la tenue des Etats-généraux où elles auront de force que jusqu'a la tenue des Etats-generaux, où elles auront besoin d'être ratifées pour continuer à être obligatoires.

9.—Que les ministres soient responables de leur gestion aux Etat-généraux; d'une assemblée à l'autre.

10.—Que le Tiers-état soit capable de posséder tous bénéfices, tous offices, tous emplois civils et militaires; et que les membres de cet ordre, pour être jugés par leurs pairs dans tous les tribunaux, y soient au moins en nombre égal avec les membres de l'ordre de la noblesse.

11.—Que la liberté indéfinie de la presse soit établie, par la suppression de la censure, à la charge par les imprimeurs de signer tous les exemplaires des ouvrages qu'ils auront imprimés, et de répondre solidairement avec les auteurs de tout ce qui s'y trouvera de repréhensible contre la religion et les bonnes moeurs.

Ces grands objets traités et réglés par les Etats-généraux, comme points fondamentaux de la Constitution du royaume, et dans le cas ou il seroit accordé des subsides par l'assemblée nationale.

Le dits Sieurs Députés, en se réunissant à cet égard aux autres députés des divers bailliages des Duchés de Lorraine et de Bar, sont chargés de repré-senter au Roi et aux Etats-généraux dans l'intéret particulier de la province.

1.—Qu'elle est étrangère à la dette nationale, pour tout ce qui est antérieur au traité de cession et à sa réunion au royaume; que cette considération est d'autant plus puissante, que les dettes de la province à cette epoque, tout ce qui restoit à payer de celles qui avoient été contractées par ses anciens souveraines, en un mot, toutes ces dettes particuliers sont demeurées à sa charge et ont été acquittées par elle successivement, sans que les autres provinces du royaume y contribuassent, d'où il résulte qu'elle ne doit elle-même contribuer qu'aux dettes qui ont été faites depuis la cession et dans la proportion de ses forces et facultés comparées avec celles des autres provinces du royaume.

2.—Que la province n'ayant point profité jusqu'ici des fonds de l'Etat destinés à l'encouragement de l'agriculture et du commerce, comme divers autres objets d'utilité particuliers à quelques provinces, seulement il seroit juste de les distraire de la masse générale des impositions du royaume, sauf aux provinces à y pourvoir chacune pour ce qui les concerne, par les moyens indiqués dans les Etats-provinciaux qui y sont ou seront établis.

3.—Qu'il conviendroit de supprimer la Ferme générale, toutes les régies et recettes actuelles, pour en remettre la direction aux Etats-provinciaux, en abolissent les impôts les plus onéreux aux peuples, comme l'impôt sur les cuirs, qui anéantit les tanneries du royaume, et porte chez l'étranger avec l'industrie nationale, le bénéfice immense de la fabrication des cuirs, sup-primer les douanes, la foraine et toutes autres espèces de droits établis entre les provinces d'Alsace, de Lorraine et des Trois-Evêchés, comme autour de la Principauté de Salm entre d'Alsace et la Lorraine, qui, sans être d'une grande ressource à l'Etat, détruisent néanmoins le commerce de ces trois provinces et ruinent chaque année un grand nombre de citoyens, exposés à des contraventions qu'ils ignorent, en passant d'un lieu à l'autre; le droit de châtrerie du produit d'environ quinze ou dix-huit cents livres seulement, et qui tient dans une gêne continuelle les habitants des campagnes, et plusieurs autres impôts qui éteignent l'industrie.

4.—Qu'il conviendroit également de supprimer l'impôt destiné à l'entretien des pépinieres et haras de la province, établissements dispendieux et sans aucune sorte d'utilité jusqu'à présente, plusieurs autres impôts portés au second brevet de la taille, connus en Lorraine sous le nom de ponts et chaussées et autres impositions accessoires, dont plusieurs ne sont pas moins inutiles que les haras et pépinières, et d'autres sans objet, et dont le produit détourné de sa destination primitive, est appliqué à des depense que la province ne devroit point supporter, dont il resulte qu'il ne faut qu'un seul impot à repartir sur les propriétés mobiliaires et immobiliaires.

5.—De supprimer les gages du Parlement et retablir les choses sur l'ancien pied, à cet égard.

6.—De supprimer les Etats-majors de toutes les villes ouvertes et qui ne peuvent être considérées comme des villes de guerre, ou forteresses nécessaires à la sûreté des frontiéres; de réduire même le nombre des officiers qui composent l'Etat-Major des villes de guerre, et le gouvernement militaire des provinces, et de comprendre pour tous dans leurs appointemens, ainsi que pour la maréchaussée le logement dont on surcharge les provinces.

7.—De supprimer les milices, sauf à fournir de la part des communautés en temps de guerre un nombre de recrues, proportionés à leur population, sous la direction des états-provinciaux, toute la dépense à supporter par les trois ordres.

8.—De supprimer dans tous les départments les graces, gratifications et pensions inutiles; réduire celles qui pourroient paroitre exorbitantes, après en avoir connu les motifs, et n'en accorder à l'avenir qu'a ceux qui les auroient mérité par leurs services.

9.—De supprimer pour toujours, par une loi faite aux Etats-généraux, pour la rendre irréfragable, la vénalité des charges, offices et emplois quelconques, dans tous les départements, pour ne les accorder qu'au merite, et spécialement les offices de judicature, auxquels il seroit pourvu par Sa Majesté sur la présentation à lui faite des personnes les plus dignes, choisies par le voie d'élection, de la manière qui paroîtroit la plus sûre, pour atteindre le but que l'on se propose; le remboursement des finances pour les offices héréditaires, à faire par les provinces chacune pour ce qui les concerne à mesure des vacances d'une année à l'autre, en remettant aux provinces les gages qu'elles paient aux titulaires.

10. De réformer la justice civile et criminelle dans toutes les parties qui en sont susceptibles, à l'effet de quoi il seroit établi des commissions dans toutes les provinces, pour éclairer l'administration sur le point important, par la discussion des plans divers qui pourroient leur être adressés par les bons citoyens, en corrigeant, sur l'avis des Etats-provinciaux, les arrondissements défectueux des sièges actuellement subsistants, surtout en Lorraine, où les bailliages ont été multipliés sans mesure dans la vue bursale d'y multiplier les finances.

11.—De commencer la réforme de la justice, par la suppression des justices seigneuriales et des notaires seigneuriaux, sous la réserve, en faveur des seigneurs, de la juridiction de Police, de la juridiction tutélaire, des plaids-annaux, et de tous droits utiles et honorifiques dans leurs seigneuries.

Il seroit procédé à la confection des inventaires dans les terres du Roi et celles des vassaux, soit en ligne directe ou collatérale, par un seul officier assisté du greffier de chaque lieu, même dans les coutumes qui auroient une disposition contraire; les vacations réduites dans les sièges royaux, en les rendant uniformes dans toutes les juridictions, n'entendant cependant pas les habitants du Val-de-Liepvre déroger à leur coutume de l'an 1586, confirmee en 1662, qui sera suivi sans égard à l'arrêt de 1781, non plus qu'à l'ordonnance de 1707.

Les juges royaux, dans le lieu de l'établissement du siège, le Maire, ou autre premier officier des lieux dans chaque communauté, dans les terres du Roi, ou des vassaux, à l'assistances des elus de l'assemblée municipale, seroient autorisés à juger, sans requête, sur citations verbales toutes répétitions de dûs, les premiers, jusqu'a concurrence de 100 livres; les maires, jusqu'à concurrence de 24 livres seulement, et sans autres frais que de 20 sols pour tout, dont 10 aux juges et elus, 5 aux huissiers et sergents pour la citation verbale, et 5 aux greffiers pour la rédaction du jugement; à l'effet de quoi les greffiers auroient un régistre, cotté et paraffé par le premier juge royal du ressort, sans qu'il fût nécessaire d'expédier le jugement pour le mettre à execution sur les meubles et effets du débiteur, ce qui se feroit également sans forme jusqu'à concurrence des 24 livres; les jugements rendus dans les communautés de la campagne seroient sans effets, au bout de six mois, sauf à se pourvoir de nouveau.

Les enchères pour vente de biens des mineurs pourroient être faites par devant le maire, ou autre premier officier des communautés, après affiches et publication en la maniére accoutumée par les sergents des communautés, sans être obligés de se servir du ministère des huissiers des sièges royaux pour obvier aux frais, à la charge d'en passer contrat dans la quinzaine par devant notaire.

L'émancipation seroit fixée à 20 ans pour tous ceux qui la demanderoient, et qui en seroient jugés dignes par les juges tutelaires en assemblée de famille, sans qu'il fut nécessaire de se pourvoir en lettres; mais il seroit fait un réglement particulier pour les enfants de famille qui auroient encore leurs pères et mères, si ceux-ci avoient manqué à leurs créanciers, pour les garantir des fraudes qui sont dans ce cas-là la suite des émancipations.

Il en seroit fait un autre sur les banqueroutes et séparation de biens entre gens mariés devenues beaucoup trop fréquentes.

Pour prévenir les inconvénients des lettres de ratification, dont il seroit d'ailleurs nécessaire de modérer les droits, il seroit important d'insérer dans le contrat et l'affiche, de qui le vendeur tenoit le bien par lui vendu, et de faire publier l'affiche dans le lieu de son domicile, à l'issue de la messe de paroisse, par le premier sergent des lieux et qui la feroit insinuer sur le champ au greffe de la communauté, le tout un mois au moins avant l'obtention des lettres, dont il seroit donné certificat par le maire et greffier.

Les jurés priseurs qui ruinent les villes et les campagnes seroient supprimés, ainsi que les quatres deniers pour livres.

Les formes de la procédure seroient rendues plus simples et plus faciles, et les droits de justice réduits et fixés par un tarif général.

Mais dans la réforme de la procédure criminelle, il seroit de la plus grande importance de rechercher les moyens de concilier l'intérêt de la société qui exige des peines contres les coupables, avec l'honneur des familles, que ces peines flétrissent dans l'opinion publique, par l'effet d'un injuste préjugé.

12.—De supprimer les grands-maîtres des eaux et forêts et les maîtrises particulières, en attribuant les fonctions des premiers aux Etats-provinciaux, qui commettroient des officiers particuliers pour l'administration des forets dans chaque arrondissement, et les anciens officiers seroient préférés; mais ils ne pourroient exiger les remboursement de leurs offices qu'en cessant leurs fonctions, sauf à leur payer l'intérêt de leurs finances au delà des gages qui leur seroient attribués par les états-provinciaux.

Il ne pourroit être fait aucune vente extraordinaire, soit dans les forêts communales des villes et communautés de la campagne, soit même dans les forêts du Roi et celles des seigneurs, sur lesquelles les communautés auroient des droits d'usage, que de l'agrément des états-provinciaux, après avoir consulté les communautés dans une assemblée générale.

13.—De supprimer les sièges de municipalité et de police, en rendant aux villes le droit d'élire leurs officiers et l'administration de leurs biens et revenus, sous l'autorité et l'unique surveillance des Etats-provinciaux.

Elles feroient de même et sous la même autorité, ainsi que les communautés de la campagne, l'enchère au rabais des portions de routes qui pourroient leur être distribuées dans chaque district, dans une proportion équitable, sauf à répartir ensuite sur les trois ordres le prix de l'enchère, comme toutes autres impositions.

Enfin il seroit pourvu, par les Etats-provinciaux, aux indemnités qui sont ou pourroient être dues aux communautés en particulier, dont les terreins ont été employés à la construction des routes.

14.—Pour remédier aux abus de la fréquentation des cabarets, d'accorder aux officiers municipaux dans les villes, aux assemblées municipales dans les campagnes, le droit de régler, selon leur prudence, le nombre des cabarets, en obligeant les particuliers qui en auront obtenu la permission de tenir des enseignes et de suivre les ordonnances, à peine d'être privés du droit de tenir cabaret, sur les plaintes qui seroient portées contre'eux, sans que les officiers soient tenus de motiver leur résolution à cet égard, ni d'en rendre compte aux tribunaux supérieurs.

15.—Pour la sureté du commerce, et garantir les peuples des usures des juifs, de les obliger à prendre de leurs débiteurs, à peine de nullité, des réconnoissances de leurs créances par devant notaires, dans le domicle des débiteurs, s'il y en a; et dans les lieux ou il n'y en auroit pas, de les faire certifier en présence des débiteurs par deux officiers des lieux non-suspects.

Il seroit également utile et important de leur interdire tout commerce de biens immeubles, et de leur faire défense de rien acheter ou vendre les jours de fêtes et de dimanches; il en seroit de même dans tous les cas pour les Anabaptistes.

16.—De supprimer dans les villes les maîtrises d'arts et métiers, sauf l'indemnité des finances, s'il y a lieu.

17.—De supprimer sans aucune exception tous droits sur le commerce des grains et farines, notamment le droit de coupel, sauf l'indemnité qui pourroit être due à quelques propriétaires, d'après l'avis des Etats-provinciaux, qui jugeront seuls, ou leurs commissions intermédiaires, des motifs qui s'opposeroient à leur exportation, et des moyens à prendre pour prévenir le monopole et les accaparements.

18.—De déclarer le sel et le tabac marchands, avec la liberté de planter du tabac, en tout cas en modérer le prix, jusqu'au moment où l'état des finances permettra d'en faire des objets de commerce, comme ils l'étoient anciennement.

19.—De supprimer l'usage des plaques aux voitures, comme un entrave inutile et une surcharge dans les campagnes, dont les habitants sont exposés, sans le savoir, à des reprises et des contraventions, en passant avec leurs charrettes d'un village à l'autre.

20.—De réduire le nombre des usines à feux de la province, sur l'avis des Etats-provinciaux.

21.—D'y rendre uniformes les poids et mesures, s'il est possible.

22.—De supprimer la bannalité des moulins et pressoirs, sauf l'indemnité, s'il y a lieu; en tout cas, rendre la bannalité uniforme et la fixer aux taux le plus de la province.

23.—De restreindre le droit de colombier, et d'obliger les seigneurs à les tenir fermes dans le temps des semailles et des recoltes.

24.—De fixer l'ouverture de la chasse, dans la province, au premier septembre.

25.—De déclarer rachetables toutes les rentes et redevances domaniales et seigneuriales, droits de reliefs et ménanties, et tous cens et autres droits seigneuriaux en deniers ou en grains, vins et autres denrées, au denier vingt, pour les rentes, cens et droits en argent; et pour les autres, sur l'estimation qui en seroit faite au moment du rachat, aussi au denier vingt, ou tel autre prix qui seroit réglé par la loi; et cependant supprimer, sans indemnité, toutes les redevances injustes de leur nature, par connoissance acquise des motifs qui les ont fait établir; notamment dans le ressort du bailliage, les rentes et redevances dues au château de Beauregard et de Spitzemberg et à la traisonnerie d'Anould.

26.—De confirmer pour toujours les anciennes alienations du domaine, et surtout celles qui ont été faites dans les montagnes de Vosges, où il se trouve une multitude d'acensements accordés de siècles en siècles, dans la vue d'y défricher et mettre en valeur des terres froides et ingrates, sans produit jusqu'alors, et qui exigent des travaux continuels; et en tout cas, dispenser les censitaires de prendre des arrêts de subrogation aux mutations, sauf à les déclarer au greffe de chaque communauté sur un registre à ce destiné, et qui seroit paraffé par le premier officier du bailliage.

27.—De faire défense de baraquer dans les campagnes, sans le consentement des seigneurs et des communautés, même sur son propre terrein, à moins qu'on en ait assez pour une ferme, et qu'il n'y ait d'ailleurs aucuns inconvénients pour le public, et de faire démolir toutes celles qui existent actuellement, s'il échet.

28.—D'ordonner l'exécution des réglements, qui défendent de planter de la vigne dans la plaine, du moins pour les terres propres au labourage.

29.—D'autoriser à prendre de l'eau dans les rivières et ruisseaux pour l'arrosement des prés, sans être exposés à des rapports de pêche et à ouvrir des roies d'arrosement où il seroit nécessaire, pour faire de nouveaux prés ou mettre en valeur les anciens, à la charge d'indemniser préalablement les propriétaires des terreins ou les roies doivent passer, et de reparer chaque fois tout le dommage qui pourroit en résulter; et cependant, en cas d'oppositions pour inconvénients majeurs, il y seroit statué par les Etats-provinciaux sur les mémoires des parties de d'après les renseignements qui seroient pris sur les lieux.

30.—De faire un réglement qui assure et restitue aux villes et communautés de la campagne la propriété de leurs biens communaux et previenne d'une manière efficace les anticipations qui s'y commettent journellement, ainsi que sur les chemin.

31.—De fonder dans la province deux maisons de réclusions gratuites, d'ajouter au fond de l'hôpital des enfants trouvés de Nancy et d'accorder des secours à divers hôpitaux et autres maisons de la province, le tout à prendre sur les biens ecclésiastiques reguliers.

32.—De permettre à tous les établissement de charité, comme aux fabriques des paroisses, de constituer et reconstituer leurs fonds qui dépérissent sensiblement dans l'administration actuelle.

33.—De régler la prestation de la grosse dixme d'une manière uniforme dans la province au taux le plus bas et d'y supprimer toutes espèces de menues dixmes et la dixme de pommes de terre, surtout dans les montagnes de Vosges et particulièrement dans le val de St. Diez, une sorte de dixme personnelle, connue sou le nom d'imal, que les habitans payent à la maison, en grains, ou gerbes de seigle et d'avoine quand bien même ils n'en receuilleroient pas, plus ou moins fortes selon les lieux et que les curés sont obligés d'aller chercher eux-mêmes chez leurs paroissiens de porte en porte, d'un manière humiliante, laquelle ne doit son origine qu'à une offrande volontaire des peuples, à leurs desservants amovibles, pour les fixer plus surement près d'eux dans les siécles d'ignorance ou le relâchement de la discipline de l'Eglise autorisoit par l'usage, le Chapitre de St. Diez seul gros décimateur dans presque tout le val, à mettre en enchère au rabais de la desserte des paroisses, sauf en cas de suppression à indemniser les curés de la perte qu'ils souffriront, sur le produit de la grosse dîme destinée de sa nature à cette desserte, comme à toutes les dépenses relatives au culte divin.

34.—De supprimer également le casuel forcé des curés, sauf à leur en faire aussi l'indemnité sur la grosse dime; de supprimer également les frais de dispenses percus par les evêques.

35.—Pour prévenir tous procès sur les obligations respectives des paroisses et des décimateurs, de déterminer leurs charges d'une manière précise, par un réglement qui mettroit à la charge des décimateurs, dans toute la province, le choeur et la nef des églises paroissiales, annexes et succursales, sans distinction, toutes les fournitures nécessaires au service divin et les presbytères, dont l'entretien demeureroit aux curés; comme l'entretien des vitraux, de la nef aux paroisses qui seroient par tout chargées des tours, cimetières et maisons d'écoles, à moins qu'elles n'eussent, sur ces trois points et tous autres, un titre formel ou possession immémoriale; toutes constructions ou reconstructions, soit à la charge des paroisses, soit à la charge des décimateurs, renvoyées aux Etats-provinciaux qui ordonneroient les plans et devis, ainsi que les adjudications des ouvrages, après avoir oui les parties intéressées par mémoire.

36.—D'appliquer la succession des curés réguliers aux pauvres de leurs paroisses, à l'exclusion des monastères, déduction faite des charges, si mieux l'on aime les séculariser.

37.—De supprimer la pluralité des benefices et obliger les beneficiers à résidance, comme à contribuer à l'aumône publique dans tous les lieux où ils ont du bien.

38.—De supprimer les notaires apostoliques, pour en réunir les fonctions aux offices des notaires royaux.

39.—De supprimer toute espèce de loteries dans l'Etat, pour le maintien des moeurs publiques, qu'elles intéressent essentiellement, et le repos des familles, dont elles causent la ruine.

40.—Enfin, d'établir une commission dont l'objet soit de remédier aux vices de l'enseignement et de l'education publique, et de prévenir les maux qui peuvent être la suite du dépérissement des bonnes études.

OBJETS PARTICULIERS

Aux Communautés des Villes et de la Campagne, dont elles ont demandé l'insertion au present cahier.

Ville de St. Diez. Robache, les Raids, les trois villes et Gratain

Opposition aux ventes et nettoiement qui restent à faire dans leurs bois communaux, en exécution d'un arrêt obtenu au Conseil sans leur agrément et participation; et comme le tiers denier se perçoit au montant de la moitié du prix de ces ventes, le réduire au tiers, ainsi que pour tous autres objets, suivant le droit commun.

Rétablissement du droit de pêche appartenant à la ville dans la rivière de Meurthe.

Restitution des biens communaux vendus ou acensés par le Chapitre de la Cathédrale de ladite ville, ainsi que de ceux réunis à aucun des biens dépendants de son domaine.

Les Meme Communautes, de Robache, les Raids et Gratain

Demandent le rétablissement de leurs anciens droits d'usage sur la forêt de la Goutte au Chapitre de St. Diez, et la reconstruction d'un moulin à Robache par ce Chapite.

Ville de Raon-L'Etappe

La réintégration dans ses anciens droits de parcours dans les forêts de l'Evêche de Metz, au ban de Neuf-maison et autres bans joignant de la Gruerie de Baccarat.

Ville de St. Hyppolitte

1.—L'abolition absolue des bureaux et péages qui y sont établis; cette ville enclavée en quelque sorte dans la province d'Alsace, n'ayant d'issue du côté de la Lorraine, que par les montagnes de Vosges inaccessibles presque en tous temps, ne peut conséquemment s'approvisionner qu'en Alsace; mais ces bureaux et péages l'assujetissent à des droits onéreux et sans nombre, sur toutes espèces de denrées, même les plus nécessaires à la vie; entraves qui lui enlevent jusqu'au dernier germe de commerce, et l'empêchent même d'établir des foires et marchés qui vivifient les villes; de-là la nécessité d'abolir ces bureaux.

2.—Ce voeu est d'autant plus just, que le petit village de Tanviller, voisin de St. Hyppolitte, a obtenu cette faveur, quoiqu'il n'ait pas eu de motifs aussi puissants.

3.—Le rétablissement de ses anciens droits et privilèges, notamment le droit de gourmage, qui lui a été enlevé sans motifs dans le siècle présent.

4.—L'exemption du tiers denier sur ses biens patrimoniaux, dont cette ville a été déchargée par ses anciens Ducs, au moyen d'une redevance de deux cents dix livres, cours de Lorraine, qui se paie encore aujourd'hui au-delà du tiers denier.

5.—La décharge des cens en vins, dans les années stériles, et la nomination d'un commissaire, pour vérifier la lésion que cette ville éprouve dans le partage des forêts qui étoient communes entr'elle et les communautés d'Aerchwiller, Bergheim, Alsace.

Tanviler

Établissement d'un regrat, en cas que la liberté du commerce du sel ne seroit pas accordée.

La reintegration dans ses anciens droits d'usage sur les forêts seigneuriales, dont les habitants sont privés, quoiqu'ils paient exactement la redevance convenue anciennement et fixée à neuf livres de France par chaque ménage.

Ville de Sainte-Marie-Aux-Mines

La suppression des acquits de paie, établis depuis deux ou trois ans dans cette ville, sur les marchandises de toutes espèces qui passent de Strasbourg à Paris. Ce nouvel impôt inventé par la Ferme générale et perçu sans l'autorité d'aucune loi connue, a totalement enlevé à la route de communication entre ces villes par Ste. Marie, Vizembach et Gemaingotte, le roulage qui vivifioit et formoit seul la fortune des bourgeois et habitants de ces lieux, placés aux pieds des Montagnes les plus arides des Vosges, pour le reporter sur les routes de communication entre ces deux capitales, par Saverne et Schirmeck qui sont exemptes de cet impôt.

Liberté de demander un commissaire, pour procéder aux Inventaires conjointement avec le procureur du Roi, duquel ils ont a se plaindre journellement.

Rétablissement de la Prévôté Bailliagère, ainsi qu'elle existoit avant l'edit de création des bailliages, du mois de juin 1751.

Sur quoi il a été protesté au contraire par les habitants du Val-de-Liepvre, qui demandent la confirmation de leurs coutumes dans l'article qui les concerne ci-après.

Val-de-Liepvre

Compose des Communautes de Liepvre, Ste. Croix, Lallemand-Rombach et ce qui en depend

La confirmation en tous points de ses anciennes coutumes de l'an 1586, approuvées par Lettres-patentes du Duc Charles de Lorraine, du 12 novembre 1662, et enrégistrées en la cour souveraine de cette province le 17 du même mois au dit an, sans égard à l'enrégistrement de ladite cour du 11 août 1781, non plus qu'à l'Ordonnance de Lorraine de 1707, qui ne peut avoir aucune force de loi dans le Val-de-Liepvre.

Sur quoi il a été protesté au contraire, par les bourgeois de Ste. Marie-aux-Mines.

Le rétablissement 1. de son ancienne justice.

Liepvre

2.—De ses marchés et de ses trois foires franches, établis par Lettres-patentes du Duc Léopold, du 28 octobre 1711, savoir; la première le 11 mars, la seconde le 26 juillet, et la troisième le 22 octobre de chaque année.

3.—De ses anciens droits sur la forêt de Chalmont, et autres du Prieuré de Liepvre réunie au Chapitre de la Primatiale Cathédrale de Nancy, ainsi que sur celle de l'Avantcelle appartenante au Chapitre des 24 comtes de Strasbourg.

Protesté au contraire par les bourgeois de Ste. Marie-aux-Mines, sur le rétablissement de la justice et des foires et marches à Liepvre.

4.—La liberté du droit de pâturage et autres dans la forêt d'Hinderwaldt, accordés au village de Liepvre par l'article 24 du Traité de Paris de 1718, conformément à la sentence arbitrale, datée du mercredi après le dimanche de Jubilate de l'année 1516.

5.—Défenses aux bourgeois de Ste. Hippolite, Orschvviller et Bergheim de troubler, gèner en façon quelconque les habitans de Liepvre dans l'exercise de ce droit, en mettant en reserve partie de cette forêt, comme Bergheim l'a fait les années dernières, sans observer aucun ordre de gruerie et sans en donner avis auxdits habitants, ce qui leur a occasionné des amendes, dommages, et intérêts et frais exorbitans, dont ils demandent la restitution.

Fixation pour l'avenir des amendes en cas de délit, attendu que celles prononcées jusqu'à présent à raison de vingt livres de France par chacune bête, sont excessives et ruineuses.

Confirmation du régrat établi à Liepvre, en cas que le commerce libre du sel n'auroit pas lieu.

Sainte-Croix

Pareil établissement d'un regrat sous la meme réserve.

Abolition du droit d'imal délivrable annuellement au curé, consistant en un boisseau de seigle par chaque laboureur, un demi-boisseau par demi-laboureur, et trois sols six deniers par manoeuvre, outre la dîme ordinaire.

Vizembach, La Croix-aux-Mines, Laveline, Verpelière, Quebrux et Bonnipaire

Confirmation de leurs anciens droits d'acensements sur les forêts royales.

La Croix-aux-Mines, Verpellière, Allegoutte, Laveline, Bonnipaire, Gainfosse, Raves, Remomeix et Ste. Marguerite

Modération sur les tailles de ces communautés ou toutes autres indemnités, a raison du dommage qu'elles souffrent dans leurs prairies, par la mauvaise qualité des eaux des mines de la Croix, qui servent seules à les arroser.

Laveline, Verpellière, Quebrux et la Croix-aux-Mines

Confirmation dans tous les droits à eux accordés par Lettres-patentes du Duc Leopold, du 13 juillet 1705.

Suppression de deux scieries, les bois étant à ménager, tant pour les usagers que pour les mines royales.

Quebrux, la Croix-aux-Mines et le Chipal.

Restitution de leurs bois communaux.

La Croix-aux-Mines

Demande d'être réintegrée dans la propriété de ses forêts, et que les religeux de l'abbayge de Moyenmoutier, possesseurs de métairies dans son finage, soient obligés de contribuer avec elle au paiement de la redevance, due à raison du droit de parcours dans les forêts dont les fermiers de ces religieux profitent comme elle.

Ste. Marguerite

Demande l'abornement de ses forêts, contre les communautés voisines.

Gemaingotte

Rétablissement intégrale de ses droits sur les forêts de son seigneur; il est bien juste, sans doute, qu'en acquittant la redevance, on jouisse pleinement de ce qui en fait l'objet.

Exécution d'une ordonnance, qui prescrit l'abornement du finage de cette communauté contre celle de Vizembach.

Lusse-Dolot, Bilistain, Lesseux, Changeur et Les Merlusses

Réintégration dans leurs anciens droits sur les forêts seigneuriales, révocation du partage qui en a été fait.

Réduction dans la délivrance des bois d'affouage aux Seigneurs, proportionnement à celles des habitants.

Exemption des corvées pour construction et réparation du moulin seigneurial.

Lusse-Dolot, Lusse-Bilistain et Lusse-Changeur

Construction d'un moulin, si la bannalité subsiste.

Bertrimoutier

Reconstruction d'un moulin à la charge du Chapitre de St. Diez, dans le cas que la bannalité ne seroit pas abolie, attendu que ce Chapitre oblige les habitants à aller moudre dans un village éloigné de leur demeure, où ils ne peuvent le plus souvent parvenir à cause des eaux.

Acensements dans les forêts royales, pour bois d'affouage, maronnage et autres, aux offres de payer le cens exigé des autres usagers.

Colroy et Lubine

Restitution de leurs forêts communales, dont Sa Majesté se trouve aujourd'hui en possession par le malheur des guerres, et en cas que ce retour ne pourroit s'effectuer, réduire les quarante sols de Lorraine de redevance à treize sols même cours, taux auquel elle se payoit il n'y a pas longtemps.

Abolition du droit de parcours, qui a lieu entre ces deux communautés et les voisines.

Lubine

Construction d'un moulin, en cas que la bannalité subsiste.

Provenchères et Frapelle

Demandent la suppression du droit de parcours.

Sur quoi protesté au contraire par les communautés voisines.

Frapelle

Rétablissement dans ses droits d'usage sur les forêts royales, sans redevances comme les autres communautés usagères et dans la même forêt.

Beulay

Réintegration de ses anciens droits sur les forêts seigneuriales et par lui prétendues communales.

Abornement de ses terreins communaux, contre les terres dépendantes du Château de Spitzemberg.

La Grande-Fosse et la Bonne-fontaine

Suppression du droît de menantie perçue par le Chapitre de St. Diez, à chaque mutation de Propriétairé, à peine de perte du fonds.

Rétablissement dans leurs biens communaux, fixation de la quotité du jour de terre, à deux cents cinquant toises comme anciennement et comme par tout ailleurs.

Réduction du cens à un gros par jour de terre comme autrefois, et delivrance du bois d'aissis dans les forêts seigneuriales, dont ces villages sont privés sans motifs.

La Petite-Fosse

Anéantissement du droit de parcours dans ses biens communaux, exercés par les habitants de la Grande-Fosse, à moins de réciprocité de la part de ces derniers.

Exécution de l'acensement de Fleurigoutte en tous ses points, à l'effet de quoi, délivrance au censitaire de tous les bois que son titre lui accorde dans les forêts qui y sont désignées.

Remomeix

Cession du droit d'affouage, marronage, et autres dans les forêts royales qui avoisinent cette communauté surchargeé de l'entretien de plusieurs ponts et manquant de forêts, aux offres de payer le même cens que les usagers actuels.

A laquelle demande il y a opposition de la part des communautés de Spitzemberg, des hautes et basses Fosses et du ban d'Anould, attendu que Remomeix a vendu les forêts, ce qui a été désavoué par ce dernier, qui assure n'en avoir jamais eu en sa possession et persiste à sa demande.

Mandray

Interdiction du droit de parcours sur son finage aux communautés voisines. Sur quoi il a été protesté au contraire par les bans de Fraize et d'Anould.

Rétablissement dans la propriété de quatre cents jours de terre situes à la basse de Bénifosse, et dans ses droits d'usage sur la forêt de la Behouille et celle du Frenat.

St. Leonard

Réintégration dans ses anciens droits sur les forêts de la Bourse, au chapitre de St. Diez, et pour la pêche dans la rivière de Meurthe.

Abornement de ses biens communaux, contre le ban de Saulcy, la Vard et le Chenois.

Vanemont

Restitution de dix-huit jours de terre, pour lesquels il paie redevance au Chapitre de St. Diez, malgré qu'il ne jouisse pas ce terrein.

Reconstruction de deux moulins par le même Chapitre, en cas que la bannalité ne seroit pas abolie.

Vain parcours dans les taillis de St. Léonard.

Ban de Taintrux

Rétablissement de tous ses droits sur les forêts, tant seigneuriales que communales, conformément à l'arrêt de la cour souveraine de Lorraine, du 5 aout 1734.

Ce voeu est d'autant plus important, que plusieurs maisons, qui tombent en ruine, ne peuvent être réparées à défaut de délivrance de bois, depuis huit ans, contrairement aux prescrits du même arrêt.

Augmentation d'un moulin, en cas que la bannalité ne seroit point abolie.

La Bourse

Rétablissement dans ses droits contre le Chapitre de St. Diez, pour affouage, maronnage et autres dans ses forêts seigneuriales, dont ce village est privé, quoiqu'il paie annuellement le cens pour en jouir; objet d'autant plus intéressant, que les maisons tombent aussi en ruine, et que déja il y en a de détruites.

Réintégration dans son droit de parcours dans les taillis de St. Léonard et autres.

Ban de Saulcy

Rétablissement dans ses anciens droits sur les forêts seigneuriales du ban de Taintrux, à raison desquels il paie une redevance, et cependant il en est frustré.

Protesté au contraire par le ban de Taintrux.

La Varde de Saulcy

Réintégration dans ses anciens droits de pêche dans la rivière de Meurthe, et d'usage dans les forêts royales, dites d'Ormont et d'Erigouttes.

Le Chenois de Saulcy

Même demande sur les forêts d'Ormont et d'Erigoutte.

Surquoi il a été protesté par les habitants de Spitzemberg, des hautes et basses Fosses et ban d'Anould, à l'égard de la forêt d'Ormont.

Indemnité à ces trois communautés, à raison de l'entretien de plusieurs ponts à leurs charges, sur différents bras de la rivière de Meurthe, qui leur enlève toute communication avec leurs voisins.

Défense au fermier de la Bergerie de conduire ses moutons dans les héritages des habitants.

Le Petit-Valtin

Réintégration dans ses anciens droits d'usage sur les forêts seigneuriales, et interdiction du droit de parcours aux communautés voisines, à moins qu'elles ne contribuent à la redevance et à charge de réciprocité. Sur quoi il a été protesté par ces dernières.

Fraize

Restitution des fonds délivrés par la paroisse de Fraize aux ci-devant Jesuites d'Epinal, pour les missions, et application de ces fonds aux Soeurs d'écoles de la même paroisse ou a toutes autres oeuvres pies.

Même voeu pour Plainfaing.

Opposition au partage des Forêts seigneuriales, sur la totalité desquelles ces deux communautés ont différents droits d'usage, tant pour affouage, que maronnage, et autres qui doivent être maintenus, puisqu'elles acquittent annuellement les redevances dues à cet égard, et qui sont considérables en exécution des arrêts de la cour de 1727 et 1765.

Indemnité à Fraize des frais de reconstruction de son église paroissiale incendiée en 1782, ce qui l'a constitué dans des dettes considérable encore subsistantes.

Même voeu pour Plainfaing, nouvelle paroisse.

Ban d'Anould et Ban-le Duc

Décharger les maires de ces communautés de l'obligation dans laquelle ils sont de garantir la totalité des cens et redevances dues au domaine de Sa Majesté par les habitants de ces bans, dont les possessions varient si souvent et depuis si longtemps, qu'il est impossible à ces officiers d'en connoitre les vrais détenteurs, ce qui leur cause une perte de trois à quatre cents livres par année et nécessitent un remembrement.

Décharger pareillement les maires de toutes les autres communautés domaniales, de faire et garantir la même collecte, sauf aux Etats-provinciaux à y pourvoir.

Ban d'Anould

Rétablissement de son droit de pêche dans tous les ruisseaux du ban, et de ses usages dans le bois communaux.

Même voeu que la paroisse de Fraize pour les missions.

Ban-le-Duc

Rétablir ce ban dans la possession de 18 jours de terre, autrefois labourable, qui ont été negligés par les malheurs des guerres et percrus actuellement en bois, pourquoi il en est privé, quoiqu'il paie annuellement le cens qui y est affecté.

Même demande pour la pêche dans le ruisseaux de Straiture, qui a été acensé à ce ban en 1614, et dont il est aussi frustré.

Confirmation de ses anciens droits d'usage dans les forêts du Roi, dont on prive ce ban d'année à autre par de menues ventes, que les officiers de maîtrise y font, sans arrêt du conseil et sans avoir préalablement consulté l'intérêt de ce ban, d'où résulte la dégradation entière de ces forêts et la privation du vain pâturage, si necessaire à cette contrée, qui ne se soutient que par son commerce de fromage et de bétail.

Nullité des ventes faites dans la même forme l'année dernière, de deux mille trois cents neuf arpents de bois, ce qui consommeroit la ruine des habitants, et les obligeroit à démigrer, si ces ventes pouvoient avoir lieu.

Réduction à deux francs barrois payables par habitant et à un franc pour les veuves, au lieu de 35 sols de Lorraine exigés depuis 1762 pour la redevance due au domaine par ce ban.

Clevecy

Confirmation de ses anciens droits d'usage dans les forêts du chapitre de St. Diez.

Partage du produit des fermes, construites dans ce siècle par ce Chapitre, au moyen des défrichements qu'il a fait dans ses forêts, et qu'il étend d'une année à l'autre, au prejudice du bien public et des usages acquis à cette communauté.

Ban d'Etival

Nullité du partage de ses forêts avec les Sieurs Abbé et religieux de l'Abbaye du même lieu, et confirmation des droits qui lui sont acquis par sa chartre confirmée par arrêt de la cour souveraine de Lorraine de 1709.

Restituition de la part avenante à ce ban dans le prix des ventes faites de toutes espèces de bois, des ladite année 1709 jusqu'à present; sur la représentation des procès-verbaux de vente et défense d'en faire d'autres à l'avenir, sans la participation des habitants.

Rétablissement de ses droits de parcours dans toutes les forêts du ban, et dans celles limitrophes et de la grasse pâture, en tout temps.

Sur quoi opposition, de la part des députés de la ville de St. Diez, pour ce qui concerne ses forêts qui sont contigues à celles de ce ban.

Liberté d'ouvrir des carrières dans toutes les forêts du ban, d'après une simple déclaration au greffe des lieux et sans frais.

Construction d'une scierie.

Interdiction du commerce personnel des bois au monastère.

Contribution aux frais de constructions et répartations du pont de la Fosse, de la part des religieux d'Etival et des habitants du ban de Moyenmoutier, qui profitent de ce pont.

415

Sur quoi il a été protesté au contraire par les députés de Moyenmoutier.

Suppression des corvées personnelles, très-multipliées et ruineuses par les frais des procès qu'elles entrainent.

Fixation de la grosse dîme au taux le plus bas de la province.

Continuation du droit de faire célébrer l'office paroissial dans l'église de ce monastère par les habitants du Vivier, et fourniture des cloches, sans rétribution.

Fondation et construction d'un hôpital, par les Sieurs Abbé et Religieux d'Etival, pour les pauvres du ban qui ne sont pas admis dans celui de St. Diez, parceque le ban n'a pas contribué à sa construction, au moyen de la promesse qui lui a été faite par ce monastère de lui en établir un; si mieux n'aiment fonder des places dans celui de St. Diez.

La Salle

Réduction à un franc barrois du cens convenu, et fixé à ce taux sur chaque jour de terre d'un canton dit à la roie Duhan, de la consistance d'environ 140 jours, suivant la transaction de 1713, perçu et élevé insensiblement, par l'effet de l'injustice la plus criante, jusqu'à trois livres ou trois quarterons d'avoine par chacun jour et par année.

St. Remy

Construction d'un moulin audit lieu par le seigneur, dans le cas que l'on n'obtiendroit pas l'abolition absolue de la bannalité.

Ban de Moyenmoutier

Réintégration dans tous ses anciens droits contre l'Abbaye de ce nom, et suppression de droit d'avoine, de regain, que chaque habitant paie annuellement à ce monastère, pour pouvoir faire du regain dans son propre héritage.

Abolition de toute corvée personnelle.

Restitution des biens communaux, que le Sieur Abbé a vendu et dont il a perçu le prix.

Ban d'Hurbache

Restitution d'environ 120 jours de terres communales, lieudit ès brulées, dont les habitants de la Voivre se sont emparés.

Surquoi, opposition de la part de ces derniers.

Rétablissement de leurs droits de pêche dans la rivière de Meurthe, et d'usage dans les bois seigneuriaux.

St. Jean d'Ormont

Même voeu que pour Hurbache.

Ban-de-Sapt

Construction d'un moulin, par son seigneur, dans la colline de Chata.

Le Paire de Grandrupt

Défense au habitants de Remomeix d'enlever des terres dans un continent de terre dit à la Rappe, sauf à eux à jouir du droit de parcours, qui leur a été acensé sur ce continent et sans plus, conjointement avec ceux dudit lieu du Paire de Grandrupt.

Proteste au contraire par les députes de Remomeix.

Enfin, pour terminer le cahier de ces doléances par une observation très-importante, pour un grand nombre de communautés, il conviendroit pourvoir en faveur des adjudicataires de l'entretien des routes, en 1787, des sous traitans et manoeuvres qui y ont travaillé, à la juste indemnité qui leur est due, et que la plupart n'ont pu obtenis jusqu'ici, malgré leurs démarches et sollicitations réitérées.

Les doléances particulières aux différentes communautés n'ont été insérées et jointes au present cahier, que d'après leurs voeux et pour leur donner une espèce de satisfaction, nonobstant toutes les remontrances de M. le Lieutenant-général à cet égard.

Lesquelles doléances, plaintes, remontrances et demandes ayant été lues en l'Assemblée générale des représentants du Tiers-état du bailliage royal de St. Diez, ont été approuvées et arrêtées, sauf à y ajouter dans la suite, s'il échet.

Fait en la Grand'salle de l'Auditoire du bailliage royal de St. Diez, cejourd'hui 22 mars 1789. Et signé par Nous Lieutenant-général, Président, tous les députés et notre greffier.

De Bazelaire de Colroy[69]
[One hundred and twelve signatures][70]

[69] This is the name of the lieutenant-general.

[70] Since the names were printed in the text, and there would be no errors of interpretation, the list is given in full. J. J. Marchal, fils, J. N. Boulanger, J. G. Màire, N. Ruyer, J. B. Bella, Petitmengin, Haxo, Mengin, Fachot, Gerard, J. D. Phulpin, Kest, M. Thirion, Rubin, Huin, Litaize, Jean Hyocom, J. B. Sertelet, N. J. Pierson, J. B. Clement, J. F. Picard, J. B. J. Droüel, N. Humbert, J. Michel, Joseph David, J. Fade, S. Georges, V. Baly, J. N. Urbain, N. Noël, Jacques Marchal, Benoît Cunin, J. B. Colin, J. Mainbourg, N. Mandray, J. B. Rovel, S. Toussaint, N. Villemin, J. D. Thiébaut, J. B. Mettemberg, A. Bolfe, N. Aubry, Jacques Anthoine, G. Pierre, J. B. Valdejo, J. Riette, J. G. Lemaire, N. Mettemberg, Laur. Benoit, J. Petitdidier, J. Germain, M. Blaise, François Noël, S. Jacquemin, J. S. Kemberg, N. Henry, N. Grandjean, Marc Lecomte, N. Chanal, J. N. St. Dizier, Q. Simon, J. F. Colin, J. Dargot, J. B. Fleurent, N. Georgeon, J. B. Duchamp, C. Colin, J. B. Flayeux, N. Ferry, N. Marchal, J. F. Vichard, J. B. Husson, C. Bernard, A. Léonard, J. N. Pierrat, N. Durand, Barthel, Vincent, J. Pechey, J. B. Houssemand, N. Jeandel, J. Michel, J. Thiriet, Léopold Ory, F. Mathis, J. B. Barbe, N. André, J. J. Divoux, J. B. Gerardin, Joseph Maugenre, N. Demenge, S. Vallance, N. Lamaze, J. P. Didier Michel, M. Cuny, N. Husson, C. Henneman, N. Jacquot, J. L. Jaunet, J. H. Didelot, J. B. Baderot, Hydulp, Jacquot, N. Parisot, F. Gerard, J. Ruyer, J. B. Colin, J. François, N. Colin, Laur. Ferry, J. Bodaine, J. Rataire, L. Claudel, J. Poirel, J. B. Bonnissant, F. Petit-Demenge, J. Houssemand, F. Houssemand, D. Flayeux. Simon, greffier.

UNEDITED TEXTS OF GENERAL CAHIERS

NO. 33. THE COLONY OF SAINT DOMINIGUE

Cf. supra, p. 27 on the convocation and elections of St. Dominigue. The committee in Paris did not make a cahier. This address for admission to the Estates-General in some measure takes the place of a cahier. The text is reprinted from the MS text, *Arch. Nat.* C 86/15.
Convocation: 7th type.

ADRESSE DES DEPUTÉS DE LA COLONIE DE
ST. DOMINIGUE PAR LAQUELLE ILS DEMANDENT D'ÊTRE ADMIS AUX
ETATS GÉNÉRAUX. 8 JUIN 1789

Au moment où, pour le bonheur de la France, le Sénat de la Nation vient enfin de se former, Une des plus grandes Provinces de l'Empire une des plus puissantes, la plus productive, sans doute, vient suspendre un instant les délibérations— importantes des Etats généraux, et fixer sur ses justes réprésentations les regards des Pères de la Patrie.

Ces augustes représentans de 24 millions d'hommes à peine revenus de l'étonnement que leur cause une réunion presque inespérée, l'ame ouverte à toutes les sensations délicieuses que la confraternité procure, n'ont pû sans doute au premier coup d'oeil, s'appercevoir que la famille entière n'étoit pas réunie, vérité dont ils vont convenir, lorsqu'ils observeront que leurs frères, les représentans des Colonies françaises ne Siègent point encore à leurs côtés.

De toutes les Isles, qui, depuis les derniers Etats, ont étendu sur les Mers, le Territoire français, la Corse seule a le bonheur, aujourd'hui d'être admise dans la Sanctuaire de la Patrie; la justice qu'on lui à rendue est un sur garant de celle qu'on ne sauroit refuser aux autres Isles ses soeurs.

C'est à l'ainée d'elles toutes, c'est a la plus étendüe, c'est à la plus considérable par sa population, son Commerce, son inflüence politique, à celle enfin qui, sans ostentation, peut s'appeler la Capitale de nos Colonies à se presenter la première au souverain Tribunal de l'Empire, pour y réclamer l'exercice honorable d'un droit—imprescriptible auquel est attaché l'honneur et la felicité de ses habitans.

Tel est, Messieurs, le rapport sous lequel Saint Dominique, jamais conquise, jamais acquise, Jadis indépendante, volontairement Française, apporte en ce jour, à la Nation, l'offrande de son respect, et vient lui payer le tribut si doux de ces mêmes sentimens dont elle offrit, il y a plus d'un siecle et demi, les prémices à Louis Le Grand. Ses députés, à qui les Mers, les Tempêtes, un Eloignement de 2.000 lieues, n'ont rendue que plus chère la mission flatteuse qui devoit les approcher de vous, en borneront les fonctions préliminaires, à obtenir de votre équité, un moment d'attention dont ils n'abuseront pas.

De ces places élevées où les suffrages de la Nation ont placé chacun de vous, daignez étendre vos regards au delà du Royaume; Franchissez l'océan,

Embrassez l'immense pays que nous représentons; dans un espace de 200 lieues de côtes couvertes des productions les plus riches, comptés Trois Capitales, soixante villes, ou Bourgs, Six mille habitations qui sont autant de Villages; voyez quarante mille Fêtes françaises qui font agir un million de bras africains; voyez le Commerce vivifié par nous, La Navigation encouragée par nous; vingt mille matelots employés par nous; voyez six cent millions chaque année, mis en circulation par nous; voyez tous les ans 500 vaisseaux français—chargés de nos denrées, voguer sur toutes les Mers et approvisionner les Marchés et de l'Europe, et de l'afrique et de L'asie; voyez en tems de guerre nos biens, nos personnes, les premieres victimes de l'Ennemi; voyez nous en cet instant les premiers défenseurs de l'Etat; voyez sur un sol destructeur nos jours s'écouler loin d'un Roy plein de bontés, sous l'empire immédiat de l'abus et du pouvoir arbitraire qu'il déteste et qui nous opprime; et frappés à la vérité de ce grand tableau, daignez sur la présentation et l'examen de nos pouvoirs, de nos Titres, de nos droits, nous assigner la place que votre justice—s'empressera d'accorder à St. Dominigue dans l'assemblée actuelle de la grande famille.

Voilà. Nosseigneurs, la demande noble et fraternelle qu'une immense Province a chargé ses députés de soumettre à l'assemblée respectable de la Nation. Ils attendent avec Empressement, tranquillité, confiance, l'issüe d'une démarche, dont le résultat va serrer à jamais les liens indissolubles qui, pour le bonheur de l'Empire, doivent unir, intimement les Colonies à la Métropole.

Nous sommes avec Respect
Nosseigneurs,

Vos freres, vos enfants

Les Députés de la Colonie de St. Dominigue
      Signé le Mis de Gouy d'arsy, Reynaud, De Villebranche, Perrigny, Douge, Peyrac, Cocherel, Rouvray Bodkin-fitzGerald, Magallon
Versailles le 8 Juin 1789.

NO. 34. THE THIRD ESTATE OF THE SÉNÉCHAUSSÉE OF TOULON

Cahier MS, *Arch. Nat.* Ba81 copy by registrar. The cahier given by the *Archives parlementaires,* Vol. V, p. 788 is the cahier of the town of Toulon under a false title.

P.V.—MS, *Arch. Nat.* B III 146, p. 148. There was a committee, but according to the p.v., the assembly itself did the major part of the composition (*cf.* Havard, *Histoire de la Révolution dans les états de guerre,* Vol. I., p. 26, for influences.) The cahier was voted April 4 by the assembly. Convocation: 2d type, reunion at Toulon.

Constitution

1.—La constitution du Royaume sera fixée avant toute autre proposition.

2.—Aucune loi ne pourra être executée si elle na été consenti ou demandée par les états généraux qui s'assembleront régulièrement tous les trois ans dans la ville et en la forme qui sera reglée sans qu'il soit besoin d'autre convocation ni qu'il puisse y être apporté aucun obstacle.

3.—Dans les états généraux il sera voté par tête et non par ordre.

4.—Nul impôt ou subside ne pourra être accordé par les états généraux qu'après la connoissance détaillée qu'ils prendront de la Situation des finances et des besoins de l'état rigoureusement demontrée et après les réductions dont la dépense sera susceptible.

5.—L'égalité de la répartition des impôts généralement quelconques mis et à mettre entre les Citoyens de tous les ordres sans distinctions réelles n'y personeles en acceptant comme contrat irréfragable la soummission de deux premiers ordres à toutes les charges et contributions royales et locales mises et à mettre par le Roy, la province, ou les communautés sans exception.

6.—Réclamer une représentation toujours mieux proportionnée aux droits de l'ordre national et jusques alors déclarer constitutionnelle son égalité aux deux premiers ordres réunis.

7.—Ne voter aucun impôt qu'autant qu'ils seront universel et proportionnels aux propriétés et faculté en conservant à notre province le droit constitutionnel d'abonnement et de répartition.

8. Les impôts ou Subsides ne pourront être accordées que jusque à la première assemblée des états généraux qui auront le droit d'hypotéquer aux créanciers de l'état, les impôts ainsy déterminé, et en cas de besoin qui pourroient survenir dans l'intervalle des états généraux, le roy fairoit une convocation extraordinaire pour y pourvoir.

9.—La propriété déclarée inviolable, et nul ne pourra en être privé qu'a la charge d'une entière indemnité ou de reprise de l'immeuble depuis au choix du propriétaire notamment en fait d'ouvrages publics chemin et embellissement des villes et demander une lois générale qui soulage les communautés et les propriétaires des injustices qu'ils éprouvent à cet égard.

10.—Liberté individuelle des citoyens destruction des prisons d'état; Suppression des lettres de cachet portant exil ou emprisonnement, révocation de celles à expédier, nul ordre pour s'assurer de la personne d'un citoyen, ne pourra etre expédiée que d'aprés un jugement domestique visé par le juge local que sera tenu de recevoir la justification du prévenu par la révocation du dit ordre apres son exécution.

11.—La Liberté legitime de la presse.

12.—Demander incessement l'assemblée des trois ordres de la province pour sa reconstitution légitime et vraiment représentative et y porter les chefs des doléances relatifs aux vices de notre administration.

13.—Nul changement dans les Taux et le titre des espéces ne pourra être fait par le gouvernement.

14.—Nouveau plan d'éducation plus à portée du peuple réformation des études dans les universités.

15.—Suppression des impositions sur les comestibles du piquet et de la double capitation notamment pour les personnes employées au service du Roy.

Legislation

1.—Les cours Supérieurs ni aucune autorité représentative de l'autorité souveraine, ne pourront modifier, interpréter, entendre ou resteindre la loi, ni moins encore en promulguer de 1er chef sous le titre d'arrêt, régle-mens, et autre disposition imperatives, toute loi derivant essentiellement de la nation et de son Chef.

2.—Réformation du code criminel et du code civil abbréviation et sim-plicité dans les formes, précision et clarté dans la rédaction adoucissement et proportion dans les peines, suppression de toutes distinction de peine entre les différens ordres de l'etat sans ménagement pour l'ordre plus étroite-ment soumis aux lois de l'honneur, et pour éviter que le supplice déshonnore plus que le crime.

3.—Les peines envers les contrebandiers seront adoucies, abrogation des lois fiscales qui mettent en compensation la fortune avec l'honneur et la liberté, consacrent l'impunité du comis assassin et donnent à ses procés verbaux une foy souvent dangereuse.

4.—La où les états généraux n'adopteroient point le jugement par pairs et la procédure par jurés qui est le voeu de plusieurs paroisses, les pro-cédures criminelles ne seront plus secrétes mais pour éviter le désordre et la confusion qui pourroient distraire le magistrat, le cabinet des instruc-tions ne sera ouvert qu'au seul deffenseur, et le juge sera spécialement chargé d'avertir les accusés, qu'ils ont le droit d'en choisir un et à def-faut tenu de lui en nommer un d'office.

5.—Renvoyer aux états généraux la question sur la Surséance des arrêts de mort et sur la nécessité de la confirmation du Souverain pour leur exécu-tion en faveur de laquelle quelques paroisses ont voté.

6.—Indemnité accordée à l'accusé reconnu innocent, selleté [sellette], question et serment de l'accusé abolit.

7.—Collection des ordonnances, réduction des lois, et traduction des lois romaines en langue françoise.

8.—Deux rapporteurs dans chaque affaire qui auront une égalle communication de Sacs.

9.—Tous jugemens en matière civile et criminelle seront motivés et il sera ajouté en queue des Sentences et des arrets, un verbal d'opinion dans lequel les juges qui auront été d'un avis contraire au jugement donneront les motifs particuliers de leurs opinions.

10.—Demander que les jurisdictions municipales qui seront substitués aux justices Seigneuriales puissent juger souverainement jusque à quinze livres et s'en rapporter à la sagesse des états généraux sur la mesure de souveraineté à accorder aux tribunaux inférieur qui pourroit être portée jusqu'a la somme de trois cents livres et nonobstant l'appel jusque à celle de mille livres.

11.—Une loy unique sur la pêche, et faveur à la pêche Nationale.

12.—Abolition de la vénalite des charges san lésion quelconque pour les titulaires.

13.—La vénalité étant supprimée les provinces rembourseront la finance des officiers Supérieurs, et les communautés, celle des judicatures locales.

14.—La justice comme dette royale sera rendue gratuitement et il sera substitué aux épices des gages mesurés sur la nature et le mérite des fonctions.

15.—A chaque mutation les états ou commissions intermédiaires pour les cours supérieurs et les villes et bourgs pour les juges locaux, présenteront trois sujets d'une capacité bien reconnue parmi lesquels le Souverain fera son choix après la justification de huit années de profession au barreau, pour les judicatures subalternes; et en outre de la dite profession de quatre années d'exercice dans un tribunal inférieur pour pouvoir être admis dans les cours souveraines.

16.—Les Tribunaux Supérieurs un partie de la Noblesse et du Tiers-Etat.

17.—Droit d'aubaine, attribution committimus, Tribunaux d'exception et huissiers priseurs abolis en remboursant qui de droit et sans lésion.

18.—Il doit être pourvu par les États généraux au moyen de juger et de punir tous les représentans du Souverain sans exception qui auront abusé de leur pouvoir et tous les juges Supérieurs et subalternes pour deni de justice acceptation de personnes, sollicitations accueillies et autres abus de ce genre.

19.—S'en rapporter au Roy et aux états généraux pour la suppression des justices Seigneuriales et leur retour dans la main du Roy, solliciter par le voeu général de toutes les paroisses et demander dans tous les cas l'exercice de la police et l'établissement des jurisdictions municipales telles que sa Majesté trouvera convenable pour le bien de l'état et l'avantage de ses Sujets.

20.—Le décret d'ajournement personnel n'enportera plus une interdiction de droit, mais après l'intérrogatoire de l'accusé le tribunal sur le vû des charges et la conclusion du ministère public pourra prononcer un décret d'interdiction provisoire pendant proies.

21.—Renouveller les loix contre les banqueroutes frauduleuses.

22.—Prescrire des formalités moins couteuses pour l'aliénation des bien des pupilles.

23.—Révocation de toutes les loix réglemens déliberation et décision qui excluent le tiers-état des places de magistrature et emplois militaires et civile avec faculté aux membres du Tiers-état d'être promu à toutes les places et dignités sans exception.

Clergé

1.—Augmentation de la portion congrue des curés et vicaires qui sont les ministres de la religion les plus laborieux abolition et du casuel forcé.

2.—Cannonicats, dignités des églises, métropoles et cathédrales données aux curés et vicaires pour leur servir de retraite après un exercise dont la durée sera déterminée par les états généraux; et en conséquence abolition de toutes résignation, permutations et collations de bénéfices en cours de Rome ou à la légation d'avignon et abrogation des Taxes relatives aux Dispenses apostoliques avec facultés aux ordinaires de les octroyer.

3.—Suppression des chapitres des églises collégiales et les prêtres qui les composent employés à la desserte des paroisses.

4.—Évêchés, abbayes et autres places éminentes du clergé accordée au mérite reconnu des écclésiastiques pris sans distinction de naissance et en y admettant surtout ceux des curés et vicaires qui se seroient distingués par leurs service et par leurs vertus.

5.—Incompabilité de plusieurs bénefices sur une même tête quand ils exéderont deux milles livres de revenus.

6.—Obligation des Évêques et grands bénéficiers de résider dans les lieux de leur bénéfices.

7.—Les cures et Succursales seront érigées par les Evêques en cours de visite pastorale et à defaut les frais des procédures des erections seront à leur charge.

8.—Les dimes étant une obligation volontaire demander leur suppression en se chargeant de pouvoir à l'entretien des ministres des autels.

9.—Suppression des abbayes inutiles réductions des revenus immenses des archevêques et évêques et leur application au soulagement de la nation.

10.—Renouvellement de la pragmatique sanction.

11.—Les ordres militaires devant servir l'état gratuitement sans réunir à leurs riçhes revenus des apointemens et dispensions dont ils doivent être privés par incompatibilité et qui grévent la caisse de l'état.

12.—Un employ plus utile des biens ecclésiastiques en cas de suppres-

423

sion sans que les Supérieurs en détournent la destination à d'autres usages qu'au soulagement des pauvres ou du second ordre.

Administration

1.—La dette de l'état declarée nationale et consolidée.

2.—La publicité par la voye de l'impression de l'état actuel des finances lorsqu'il aura été présenté aux prochains états généraux, visé et arrêté par eux.

3.—Le résilement actuel de tous les baux des biens domaniaux exposition aux enchéres judiciares adjudication pour le tems déterminé dans les états généraux.

4.—Rachat des domaines alienes et réunion des domaines concédés.

5.—L'incompatibilité de plusieurs places quelconques sur une même tête et réduction des apointemens immenses au moyen desquels un seul homme engloutit les contributions de plusieurs paroisses.

6.—Suppression des Intendans de province pouvoirs sur les Communautés transférés aux états provinciaux et par provision aux commissions intermédiaires.

7.—Suppression des receveurs généraux, les caisses provinciaux les devant verser directement dans le Trésor Royal.

8.—Suppression de la loterie Royale et Militaire.

9.—Les corporations ou assemblée de citoyens réunis par l'exercice des mêmes fonctions érigées en jurande avec attribution de la police intérieure, de leur corps, et pouvoir de diriger les réglemens nécéssaire à leurs organisation pour n'être néanmoins exécuter qu'après avoir reçu dans le lieu de leur établissement l'aprobation d'un conseil de tous les chefs de famille et l'autorisation gratuite du Souverain.

10.—Abrogation des priviléges dérogatoire aux droits de jurande et notamment de ceux des universités connue encore des priviléges exclusif en fait d'imprimerie pour proportionner le nombre des imprimeurs aux besoins des villes ou il y a évêché ou Sénéchaussée.

11.—Défense aux provinces, aux communes et à tous les corps en général d'emprunter sans pourvoir en même tems au remboursement dans un délay fixé par une imposition avec établissement d'une caisse d'amortissement dans chaque corps écclésiastique ou civil pour l'amortissement des emprunts faits jusqu'à ce jour.

12.—Sa Majesté suppliée de ne pas oublier sa promesse de supprimer l'impôt désastreux de la gabelle.

13.—Suppression des droits de contrôlle et centième denier en conservant la formalité, et la, où les droits seroient maintenus, en excepter les successions en ligne directe, et les legs d'usufruit entre conjoints, fixer un tarif modéré clair et uniforme et proscrire les abus des vérificateurs.

14.—La permission de stipuler les intérêts des sommes à jour.

15.—Les lettres confiées à la poste respectées dans toutes les occasions punition exemplaire contre ceux qui effeindront cette régle.

16.—Suppression du droit et faculté de rachat des droits féodaux et Seigneuriaux généralement quelconques notamment des bannalités.

17.—Défense aux Seigneurs de fiefs de céder à l'avenir leur droit de prélation ou de l'exercer pour autruy obligation lorsqu'ils voudront l'exercer par eux même de le faire dans un court délay fixé par les états généraux.

18.—Les Seigneurs particuliers soumis à la même loy que les Seigneurs possédents fiefs par rapport à leur directe faculté de rachat des directes particulieres en faveur des propriétaires qui y sont soumis que les reconnoissances féodales ne supplient plus au titre.

19.—Défense aux Seigneurs directe de mettre les immeubles retraits hors de leur main pendant un tems qui sera déterminé par les états généraux même règle pour les retrayans lignagers.

20.—Suppression ou modération du demy-lods à la main morte jusque au rachat de la directe.

21.—Un réglement contre la mendicité, une loy de secours pour les pauvres valides, une loy de soulagement pour les infirmes, chaque communauté obligée de nourrir ses pauvres, application du quart des revenus ecclésiastiques au soulagement des pauvres suivant le canon.

22.—Un réglement imprimé, public et affiché, pour fixer les honoraires des Notaires, greffiers, et autres ministres inférieurs de la justice et le renouvellement des réglemens pour veiller à la sûreté des dépôts et régitres public.

Comerce

1.—Qu'il soit établi une jurisdiction consulaire dans toutes les villes ou il y a bailliage Sénéchaussée ou présidial.

2.—Que l'arrêt du conseil du Trente Août 1784 concernant le comerce étranger dans les iles de l'Amérique soit révoqué.

3.—La suppression et révocation des priviléges de comerce exclusif accordée à diverses compagnies.

4.—Suppression des douanes intérieur et seulement des bureaux aux frontières.

5.—Examen du traité de comerce avec l'Angleterre renvoyé aux états Généraux.

6.—Que le tarif du droit des fermes soit uniforme, et qu'il soit imprimé et affiché annuellement après avoir été signé par le juge local.

7.—Un seul poids, une même mesure dans chaque province, et si la chose paroit practicable dans tout le royaume.

8.—Option à la ville de Marseille d'être étrangère, ou nationale et abolition du privilege qui la constitue l'une et l'autre.

9.—Suppression du droit de fret sur l'importation des grains et sur l'exportation des vins ainsi que des autres droits établi sur les grains.

425

10.—Suppression de droit de foraine sur les marchandises expédiées de provence pour les provinces des cinq grosses fermes par le détroit de Gibraltar.

11.—Que les foires franches accordées a la ville de Toulon pour services particuliers rendus à la nation soient rétablis dans leurs exemption primitives, et qu'a cet effet le reculement des barrières ne porte aucune atteinte aux franchises de ces foires dont un Terme sera fixé a lamy janvier et l'autre subsistera en novembre avec concession d'une pareille foire franche au bourg de la Seyne et autres de la côte telle que Bairdol et Saint Nazaire.

12.—Que les arrêts du conseil permettant le fabrication de draperies commune sur les dimensions arbitraires, soient révoquées à l'exception de celle de Colmar, et de la vallée de Barcelonnette, et que la place d'inspecteur des manufactures de provence payées par la province soit accordée à un ancien fabricant provençal.

13.—Liberté entière aux taneries, suppression de l'impôt excessif dont elle sont grévées, encouragement accordée aux fabriques nationales pour que nos cuirs puissent soutenir la concurrence des cuirs étrangers.

14.—Que l'exemption de tous droits sur les articles nécessaires à la construction équipement et approvisionnement des navires du comerce soit accordée à Toulon, et à tous les ports du ressort ainsi qu'en jouit dejà celui de la Ciotat.

15.—Que la perception des droits sur les amidons et poudres ne soit pas un obstacle à l'établissement des fabriques.

16.—Moderation des impôts sur les papiers et cartons.

17.—Remplacement de ces suppressions par des impositions sur des objets de luxe.

18.—Que defense soit faites à tous proprietaires ou conducteur de troupeaux d'employer du goudron à la marque distinctive de leurs troupeaux.

19.—Que les orfévres soient seuls autorises à vendre tous les objets d'or et d'argent ouvrés en france avec prohibition des ouvrages Étrangers.

20.—Les navires expédiés des ports de france forcés à leur retour des colonies et à leur attérage en france d'entrer dans les ports nationaux reputés étrangers seront autorisés à y verser les marchandises destinées à ces ports et à transporter dans ceux de leur départ primitif les denrées et marchandises coloniales qui y sont destinées sans qu'elles soient soumises à de plus forts droits que ceux dûs à leur importation directe.

21.—La suppression des péages établis sur les routes et rivières.

22.—Encouragement en faveur de l'agriculture et notamment par des exemptions accordées aux pères de famille à raison du nombre de leurs enfants, et par des récompenses en faveur des agriculteurs qui se distingueront.

Marine

1.—Conservation des bois par une nouvelle loy sur les défrichemens des lieux montagneux par la plus exacte observation des réglemens sur chêvres, et de l'ordonnance des eaux et forêts, et par un nouvel ordre dans les maitrises.

2.—Suppression des entreprises, et prix faits dans l'arsenal, exactitude dans les payemens, fixation d'un fonds déterminé et suffisant pour le salaire des ouvriers afin d'éviter à cette classe précieuse de sujets le danger de s'expatrier, et de porter leurs utiles services à la première puissance qui veuille leur donner du pain cette émigration devient chaque jour plus frappante, et les suites politiques plus à craindre.

3.—La ville de Toulon ne peut voir avec indifférence qu'un intéret moral dirigé du fisc s'oppose à l'entretien économique de la partie des forces de la marine royale déposés dans le port de cette ville, et jugeant cette représentation étroitement liée au bien général de la chose publique, elle expose aux états généraux la necessité pressante d'attirer dans la ville de Toulon, le plus grand nombre possible de fabriques de savon et de tannerie dont les lessives et les égouts préservent efficasement les vaisseaux et les bois autrefois si bien conserves, et aujourd'hui dévores des vers, par la diminution de ces fabriques, protégées à Marseille par des privilèges, et abandonnées à Toulon par la raison contraire.

4.—La santé publique exige que les préposés pour donner l'entrée aux navires qui arrivent sur nos cotes, ne soient qu'à la nomination et sous la dépendance des bureaux principaux de l'arrondissement avec déffense aux Seigneurs de s'immiscer dans cette partie.

5.—Que le bureau de la santé de la ville de Toulon soit établi hors des murs de la ville afin que toutes communication entre les bâtimens à rame qui viennent du lazareth, et ceux du pays soit plus séverement inspectée.

6.—Qu'il soit établi hors des murs de la ville un carenage pour les navires particuliers, afin d'écarter des accidents du feu les vaisseaux de la marine royale enfermés dans la darce [darse] du comerce.

7.—(Supprimé)

8.—Qu'il y ait une différence dans les capitaines du grand et petit cabotage quant aux examens.

Guerre

1.—L'abolition d'une discipline exotique et opposée au caractère de la nation françoise les coups de plat de sabre.

2.—Le rétablissement de l'ancienne institution militaire seule faite pour conserver à nos troupes les vertus guerrières qui les caractérisent toujours malgré les vices du régime actuel.

3.—Suppression du conseil de Guerre comme trop dispendieux ainsi que celui de la marine.

4.—Réduction du nombre des apointemens des officiers généraux Suppression des apointemens aux gouverneurs particuliers des forts et citadelles du royaume avec conservation du titre et démolition des places inutiles.

Articles communs à la Guerre et à la Marine

1.—Suppression des milices gardes côtes et Levées de matelots qui pezent uniquement sur le tiers-état, en les remplacant par tel moyen que les états généraux croiront devoir y substituer pour que le poids en soit également réparti sur les trois ordres.

2.—Même observation sur les exemptions des logemens et des gens de guerre.

3.—Que les fonds assignées aux deux départemens soyent annuellement détermines pour chaque objet particulier de dépenses et que les comptes en soient rendus dans la même forme.

4.—Qu'en tems de paix la poudre à canon ne soit plus déposée dans l'intérieur des villes.

5.—Amnistie générale en faveur des deserteurs soldats et matelots et délivrance de ceux détenu à la chaine ainsi que des contrebandiers.

6.—Recomandation aux députés du tiers état de soutenir la dignité de leur ordre et défense à eux de recevoir aucune grace du Gouvernement.

7.—Monument a ériger par la nation au Souverain, et témoignage de gratitude à son digne ministre.

Objets particuliers

Sa Majesté sera tres humblement suppliée en présence des états généraux, d'accorder une attention particulière à la demande qui lui sera faite incessement d'un nouveau réglement qui régle avec sagesse le destin de trente mille habitans gouvernés jusqu'ici par le régime vitieux [vicieux] et abusif de cette municipalité, à l'effet de quoi il sera convoqué une nouvelle assemblée du tiers état en la même forme que celle convoquée pour la députation.

Le résiliment du bail des casernes avec restitution des avances faites lors d'icelui.

Ollioules

Demandes de levées de l'interdit des Dames clairistes et ursulines.

Sollies

Demande à rentrer sous la puissance immédiate du roi, comte de provence, et que le fief, concédé par nos comtes soit réuni au Domaine du Roi; demande à laquelle toutes les communautés qui se trouvent dans un cas pareil ont adhére.

La Revest

Demande en cas de suppression de justice Seigneuriales à avoir ses causes portées directement au Lieutenant de Toulon, attendu sa proximité de la ditte ville.

Cogolin

Demande la suppression d'un degré de jurisdiction attendu qu'elle est sujette à quatre degrés, cogolin, grimaud, Toulon et Aix; et l'embarquement de ses denrées sur la plage la plus proche.

Réclame contre la route des gens de guerre contre la compascuité de la chartreuse de laverne et contre les prétentions de son Seigneur.

Pierrefeu

Demande l'évocation de ses proies avec son Seigneur, et l'établissement d'un notaire au dit lieu, ou il n'en existe aucun.

La Seyne

Réclame contre la construction de son port et implore le secours du Gouvernement.

La Vallette

Se réserve de retirer la directe et la bannalité des mains de son Seigneur, Ecclésiastique qui les a usurpées sans titre et demande un nouveau réglement municipal.

Bandol

Réclame contre les conditions onéreuses de l'acte d'habitation de mil sept cent quinze et contre les arrêts surpris au conseil par leur Seigneur.

Le Baussett

Demande l'incompatibilité des fonctions de notaire et de procureur. Les Doléances particulières des communautés ayant été en outre remises aux députés pour leur servir de plus amples instructions.

Paraphé ne varietur par nous, président du tiers état à Toulon, le 4 Avril 1789, Signés, Granet Lieutenant Général. . . .[71]

[Forty-five signatures.]

Collationné.

Guérin.[72]

No. 35. The Third Estate of the Bailliage D'Ustaritz

On the *procès-verbal* and cahier, *cf.* Brette, *op. cit.*, Vol. IV, pp. 385-86. The original was burned in a fire at the archives at Bayonne. The volume of the reprint, cited by Brette, is missing at the *Bibliothèque Nationale*. It therefore seemed useful to reprint a text which is so inaccessible. The only known public text is the reprinted text in the Municipal Archives at Bayonne.

[71] President of the assembly.
[72] Secretary of the assembly.

UNEDITED TEXTS OF GENERAL CAHIERS

The present text is copied from a rare example of the reprinted text acquired by the author, by the kind assistance of the archivist of Bayonne, M. Detchepare. The reprint was published by P. Cazals: printer, Bayonne, in 1874. It consists of 39 pages, in 8°, with cover. The French text of this cahier appears on the lefthand pages, and the Basque on the right. Only the French text will be given here.
Convocation: 1st type.

CAHIER DES VOEUX ET DES INSTRUCTIONS DES BASQUES-FRANÇOIS DU LABOURT, POUR LEURS DEPUTES AUX ETATS GENERAUX DE LA NATION

Pénétrés du plus profond respect et de la plus vive reconnoissance pour les grandes vues de justice et de bienfaisance qui ont déterminé leur Souverain à convoquer les Etats-généraux de son Royaume, les Basques-François du Labourt ses fidelles Sujets, les seconderont autant qu'il leur sera possible, par les voeux que leurs Députés seront chargés d'y faire entendre.

Un Roi qui aime plus la vertu que l'autorité, douze cens Représentans choisis dans une des Nations les plus éclairées de la terre, un Ministre qui n'a pour politique que les grandes vues du génie; voilà quels seront les grands coopérateurs de la régénération d'un vaste Empire; quels motifs d'espérer que nous allons laisser à nos descendans un sort plus heureux que celui que nous avons reçu de nos pères!

Les voeux des Basques-François s'arrêteront d'abord sur la Constitution nationale, sur les Finances du Royaume, et sur l'Administration de la justice.

Ce ne sera qu'après avoir présenté leurs idées sur les objets nationaux, qu'ils se permettront de faire entendre leurs réclamations particulières pour l'amélioration de leur province, qui, comme frontière du Royaume, mérite, à ce seul titre, de fixer tous les tems, les regards du gouvernement.

Constitution fixe à donner à la Nation

De quelque manière qu'on nomme son gouvernement, une Nation ne peut se dire libre, si elle ne fait elle-même ses loix; si la propriété et la sûreté personnelle de chacun de ses membres ne sont mises sous leur garde inviolable; si chaque citoyen n'y a la faculté de manifester toutes les pensées qu'il croira utiles au maintien et au perfectionnement de l'ordre public.

Il faut donc que les assemblées de la Nation se renouvellent; que leurs retours soient périodiquement fixés; et que l'on prenne des mesures certaines pour que leurs convocations, aux époques convenues, ne puissent jamais être empêchées.

Il faut que les loix destinées à régir la Nation avec un voeu de permanence, se délibèrent, soit sur les propositions de ses représentans, soit sur celles du Souverain dans ces assemblées de la Nation, et que celles qu'on y aura ainsi délibérées se publient et s'exécutent aussi-tôt.

Cependant, comme il pourra absolument arriver que, dans l'intervalle d'une assemblée de la Nation à une autre, des loix provisoires deviennent nécessaires, soit à tout le Royaume, soit à quelques-unes de ses provinces, ce sera au Souverain seul qu'il appartiendra, dans ces circonstances imprévues et urgentes de delibérer dans son Conseil de pareilles loix. Il les fera vérifier dans ses Cours de Parlement, qui sur les inconvénients qu'elles croiront y apercevoir, pourront lui présenter des premières et des secondes remontrances; mais qui, si le Souverain persiste, malgré cela, à vouloir les maintenir, et sur la simple manifestation de sa volonté à cet égard, par des lettres de jussion, seront tenues de les publier aussi-tôt, pour être exécutées provisoirement, jusqu'à la prochaine assemblée de la Nation; à moins que leurs inconvéniens ne se rendent trop sensibles dans l'exécution; auquel cas les Cours de Parlement pourront encore avoir recours, auprès du Souverain, à de nouvelles remontrances.

Il faut que chaque sujet du Roi n'ait rien à craindre, ni pour ses propriétées, ni pour sa liberté individuelle, tant que les loix et leurs Ministres se taisent à son égard; qu'il ne puisse dès-lors y être attaqué que dans les cas et les formes que traceront les loix du Royaume; qu'il ne soit plus fait aucun usage de lettres de cachet; que, hors des cas qui regarderont le service militaire, les Gouverneurs et les Commandans des provinces ne puissent plus, sous peine d'être poursuivis comme coupables du crime de lese-liberté civile, expédier des ordres arbitraires d'emprisonnement, ni les géoliers des prisons, ou les Commandans des châteaux, enfermer des citoyens arrêtés en vertu de tels ordres, sans être punis comme complices du même crime.

Il faut que chaque citoyen ait la liberté de répandre, par la voie de l'impression, toutes les idées qu'il peut croire utiles, ou à la chose publique, ou même aux loisirs et aux délassemens de sa Nation; qu'en conséquence les fonctions des censeurs soient supprimées, et que la presse reste libre avec cette précaution, qui paroit suffisante pour en détourner les abus, que l'Auteur et l'Imprimeur seront obligés de se nommer dans les ouvrages.

Il faut enfin que, hors le Souverain, il n'y ait aucun dépositaire de quelque portion de la puissance publique, qui ne soit desormais obligé de répondre ou devant les assemblées de la Nation, ou devant ses Tribunaux, des abus qu'il se sera permis d'en faire; et qu'a ces égards, le cours de la Justice ne puisse plus être interverti par des évocations et par des établissemens momentanés de Tribunaux de commission, qui ne peuvent servir le plus souvent qu'à sauver des coupables, ou à perdre des innocens.

Pour rendre ou pour donner à l'Etat cette constitution tutélaire des propriétés et des libertés de chacun des Sujets du Roi, et pour la lui assurer à jamais, il faut que les assemblées de la Nation soient invariablement soumises au principe du droit commun qui doit régir toutes les assemblées délibérantes; et que les opinions s'y prennent par tête et non par ordre.

La constitution nationale une fois établie sur ces maximes fondamentales des Gouvernemens légitimes, opérera d'elle-même dans les détails de l'administration, toutes les réformes qu'y solliciteront les droits imprescriptibles de la justice et de l'humanité, et l'intérêt général de la Nation.

Les habitans de nos Colonies seront admis à une représentation aux assemblées générales de leur Métropole.

L'esclavage des Nègres sera aboli dans nos Colonies.

Les loix, qui dans les armées de terre et de mer affectent exclusivement à la Noblesse les premières places, seront abrogées.

Les annates seront supprimées.

Les dispenses pour les mariages, les provisions pour les résignations en faveur et pour les autres titres de bénéfices, seront données par nos Evêques dans leurs diocèses respectifs, et notre argent n'achètera plus à Rome toutes ces choses qui doivent se donner.

Ces maximes fondamentales de la constitution de l'Etat, et ces réformes dans son administration, une fois consacrées par l'adhésion des Représentans de la Nation, et du Souverain, l'objet public dont s'occupera ensuite la Nation, sera sans doute celui des dépenses nécessaires à l'entretien de la force publique, qui doit maintenir l'ordre dans l'Etat, et faire respecter sa puissance au dehors.

L'Impôt

Le désordre des finances du Royaume est-il tel, que, pour préserver la Nation de l'opprobre d'une banqueroute, et pour subvenir aux dépenses nécessaires du Gouvernement, il faille, à la masse énorme des impôts déja établis, en ajouter d'autres?

Ne seroit-il pas possible d'atteindre ce double but en substituant aux impôts établis, d'autres subsides d'une perception plus facile et moins dispendieuse, en les répartissant également sur tous les Sujets du Roi indistinctement, en simplifiant leur régie, en modérant les bénéfices des principaux Agens du Fisc, en diminuant leur nombre et celui de tous leurs Agens en sous-ordre, en les supprimant même tous, en faisant subir aux dépenses de l'Etat, jusqu'ici estimées nécessaires, toutes les réductions qu'y exigeroient peut-être leur juste comptabilité avec l'honneur du trône, la puissance de l'Etat au-dedans et au dehors, et le bonheur du peuple, le premier voeu d'un Souverain chéri?

Sur tout cela, les Députés du Tiers-état du Labourt devront entendre les instructions que le Souverain fera donner à la Nation par son Ministre des finances.

Les vertus et les lumières connues de ce Ministre assurent d'avance le

Tiers-état du Labourt, que la Nation pourra livrer sa confiance à ces instructions; qu'elles lui présenteront un tableau fidelle de l'état de ses finances; qu'on ne lui demandera pas de nouveaux subsides, si l'Etat peut absolument s'en passer; que, si même on a pu trouver des moyens pour alléger le poids des impôts actuels, on tiendra à honneur et gloire de les indiquer et de les faire adopter à la Nation assemblée; mais si des états bien vérifiés y démontraient la nécessité d'établir de nouveaux impôts pour les engagemens de l'Etat et ses besoins indispensables, alors sans doute les Députés du Tiers-état de toutes les autres provinces du Royaume voteront pour y souscrire; l'on ne peut guère en douter d'après les sentiments patriotiques qu'elles ont déjà manifestés à cet égard; et alors le Tiers-état du Labourt auroit trop à souffrir de faire exprimer par ses Députés des voeux contraires dans l'assemblée de la Nation. Ils s'uniront donc dans ce cas au voeu général de la Nation: mais ils ne devront pas rougir de solliciter des ménagemens dans la répartition, en faveur de la pauvreté de leur Pays. Ils représenteront que le sol y est montueux, ingrat, stérile et long-tems rebelle aux efforts les plus opiniâtres et les plus dispendieux de la culture; qu'aussi beaucoup de terreins y restent en friche de tous les tems; que d'ailleurs la province, comme pays frontière, entretient un corps de milice permanent de mille hommes, dont son Bailli d'épée est le Colonel-né, et qui, dans les tems de guerre, est prêt à suppléer les garnisons militaires à Bayonne, et dans les autres postes du Pays où le Gouvernement peut le croire utile: que par toutes ces considerations, le contingent du Pays aux subsides de l'Etat étoit resté borné, jusques vers le milieu du dernier siècle, à un abonnement de 253 liv., appelé de subvention; que depuis, son abonnement a été porté, en y comprenant l'ancien, à plus de 60,000 liv; et qu'un accroissement de cet impôt, pour peu qu'il s'y rendit sensible, pourroit forcer ses habitans aux émigrations, et amener la ruine entière de cette contrée limitrophe de l'Espagne.

Vraisemblablement ce sera au moment où s'entamera cette deliberation sur les subsides de l'Etat, que les Représentans de la Nation réclameront le renouvellement et la confirmation de ce principe tutélaire de la propriété, auquel la justice souveraine du roi a elle-même rendu hommage dans ces derniers tems; qu'aucun impôt ne puisse désormais s'établir dans le Royaume, que de l'aveu de la Nation assemblée.

Ce sera aussi dans cette partie des délibérations de la Nation assemblée, que les Députés qui la représenteront demanderont que cette loi, si digne du trône, que s'est déjà imposée le Souverain, de faire vérifier chaque année les comptes de finances du Royaume, et de publier par la voie de l'impression, les résultats de ces vérifications; devienne encore, pour l'avenir, l'une des lois fondamentales de la constitution. Les Députés du Tiers-état du Labourt s'uniront à ces demandes si intéressantes des autres Représentans de la Nation.

Administration de la Justice

La position du Pays de Labourt ne permet guère peut-être à ses habitans de juger, si parmi les Parlemens du Royaume, autres que celui dont il dépend, il s'en trouve quelques-uns, dont les ressorts sont trop étendus, et exigeroient des demembremens, pour une expédition plus facile, plus active et moins dispendieuse des causes d'appel.

Cependant l'inconvénient de la distance où se trouvent les Cours souveraines d'appel de quelques-unes des contrées de leur ressort, ne peut-il pas être modéré par des moyens moins extraordinaires et moins dangereux que celui du démembrement de leurs territoires, qui tendroit à donner à leurs justiciables actuels de nouveaux Magistrats, en qui ils ne pourroient avoir la même confiance que dans les anciens, et qui, selon toutes les apparences, en pourroient la mériter de long-tems?

Que désormais tous les procès civils se portent en première instance devant les Bailliages et les Sénéchaussées, et que les appels de leurs jugemens, dans les causes reconnues assez importantes pour devoir en être susceptibles, se portent directement aux Cours du Parlement, d'où ils ressortissent.

Ce sera supprimer du même coup ces distinctions, déshonorantes peut-être pour la justice, que l'Edit de Crémieu avoit établies entre les causes civiles des Nobles et celles des autres Sujets du Roi.

Que sans faire changer de nom aux Bailliages et aux Sénéchaussées, les jugemens qu'ils rendront dans les contestations civiles purement pécuniaires, soient rendus souverains, toutes les fois que l'objet de la discussion n'excédera pas une certaine somme, et que dans chacun de ces Tribunaux la quotité de cette somme soit fixée eu égard aux ressources plus ou moins étendues du pays pour le numéraire.

On n'ose tracer le même plan pour les contestations civiles qui rouleroient sur des propriétés immobiliaires, parce qu'il faudroit en assujettir l'objet à des estimations préalables qui compliqueroient la procédure et que d'ailleurs ces sortes de choses ont un prix d'affection, qui peut s'accroître encore par le litige même, et qui échappe presque toujours aux estimations.

Que les Tribunaux même des Bailliages et des Sénéchaussées soient fermés à toutes les petites contestations pécuniaires qui n'excéderont pas une somme de 12 liv. ou même le double de cette somme; que ces modiques différends soient renvoyés aux Officiers-municipaux des lieux, et qu'ils soient autorisés à les juger définitivement, par manière de police, sans forme ni figure de procès.

Mais qu'on rende en même-tems aux Bailliages et Sénéchaussées les matières des eaux et forêts qu'on leur a enlevées, pour créer ces Tribunaux du même nom, dont l'inutilité et la surcharge pesent trop long-tems sur la Nation.

Qu'on leur rende encore les causes contentieuses des Communautés et des Paroisses, qui se portent devant les Intendans.

Que dans les matières criminelles même, les Bailliages et les Sénéchaussées soient chargés en première instance de leur jugement; et qu'après les premières informations faites, les Juges des lieux soient tenus de les leur envoyer avec les plaintes. Il y a trop long-tems qu'on reconnoit que l'innocence est trop exposée dans ces petites jurisdictions, à y laisser achever ces sortes de procédures, et que le crime y trouve trop de ressources pour l'impunité.

Que dans ces affaires du petit-criminel, qui naissent des injures, des rixes, les Bailliages et les Sénéchaussées puissent sans règlement à l'extraordinaire, prononcer des dommages et intérêts jusqu'à concurrence de 100 liv., et que leurs jugemens, lorsque la peine pécuniaire n'excédera pas cette somme, et qu'ils ne tendront d'ailleurs qu'à des réparations civiles, restent définitifs.

Par ces légers changemens de l'ordre de procéder en premiere instance, dans les matieres civiles et criminelles,[73] par ces médiocres accroissemens de la jurisdiction des Bailliages et des Sénéchaussées dans les affaires de l'un et l'autre genre, l'autorité publique prémunira l'homme autant que cela lui est permis peut-être, contre la triste manie du litige; la plupart des procès se termineront dans les Tribunaux des contrées où ils auront pris naissance; les Tribunaux souverains n'auront plus a juger des appels que pour des affaires d'une importance digne de cette réclamation extraordinaire; et leur distance de quelques-unes des contrées de leurs ressort deviendra encore, dans ces causes même, un frein utile contre la licence des appellations.

Les réformes que la Nation paroît desirer depuis long-tems dans la législation civile et criminelle, pourront sans doute, une fois effectuées, remplir encore mieux les voeux d'un Gouvernement bienfaisant pour l'administration de l'une et l'autre Justice.

Mais, pour achever ce grand ouvrage, ce ne sera pas trop vraisemblablement de l'intervalle qui séparera la prochaine Assemblée de la Nation de celle qui suivra; et en attendant, ne pourroit-on pas, dans les Etats-généraux qui vont se convoquer, faire subir à notre code criminel quelques réformes partielles, qui peut-être intéressent d'une maniere urgente l'innocence des accusés, victimes de l'erreur ou de la calomnie, et l'honneur de la Justice?

Ne pourroit-on pas faire disparoître des actes de l'instruction criminelle, cette clandestinité trop dangereuse qu'on y exige à l'égard des accusés, et qui ne s'observe qu'à l'égard des accusés pauvres?

Ne pourroit-on pas bannir de l'ordre judiciaire que l'on suit maintenant au criminel, cette distinction trop répugnante à la raison, entre les faits appelés *péremptoires*, et les faits justificatifs; les établir également proposables et susceptibles de preuve de la part des accusés en tout état de cause, et les affranchir encore d'une partie au moins des gênes auxquelles on assujettit les accusés pour la production des témoins par lesquels ils pourront les prouver?

---

[73] The accents were apparently omitted in the reprint of this line of the original text.

Ne pourroit-on pas faire cesser ce privilége étrange qui semble outrager la Justice en faveur des Prêtres et des Nobles, en leur attribüant la faculté arbitraire de faire juger leurs causes criminelles aux Parlements, par la Tournelle seulement, ou par la Tournelle et a la Grand-chambre réunies?

Ne pourroit-on pas supprimer les distinctions qu'amenent certains crimes, pour les peines publiques à décerner contre les Nobles ou contre les Roturiers qui s'en rendent coupables?

Enfin ne pourroit-on du pas titre des *Récusations,* commun aux procédures civiles et criminelles, supprimer certaines dispositions, qui, pour honorer excessivement la dignité du Magistrat, deviennent trop favorables à ses passions, comme homme?

Demands particulières du Tiers-état du Labourt

1. Par rapport à l'Administration de la Justice dans son Pays, le Tiers-état demandera qu'en même-tems qu'on maintienne sa contrée dans le ressort du Parlement de Bordeaux, ses causes d'appel y soient néanmoins expediées sans aucune acception de personnes, selon le rang de date où elles arriveront; et que pour assurer cet ordre de leur expédition, le Gouvernement veuille prendre des mesures rigoureuses, et s'il se peut, incorruptibles.

Qu'en matiere civile, les jugemens de son Bailliage, dans les contestations pécuniaires, dont l'objet principal n'excédera par la somme de 300 liv., restent définitifs, et que la voie de l'appel soit fermée contre ces jugements.

Que dans les affaires du petit-criminel, son Bailliage puisse sans règlement à l'extraordinaire, prononcer des dommages et intérêts jusqu'à concurrence de 100 liv., et que les Jugemens qui n'excéderont pas cette peine pécuniaire, et qui d'ailleurs n'ordonneront que des réparations civiles, restent également définitifs et non sujets à l'appel.

Que les appels des autres jugemens qui s'y rendront en matiere civile et criminelle, se portent directement au Parlement de Bordeaux; qu'en réintégrant son Bailliage dans l'intégrité de sa primitive jurisdiction, on lui rende la partie des cas royaux dont on l'a privé; et qu'on lui restitue les trois Paroisses de Bardos, de Guiche et d'Urt, démembrées autrefois de son territoire pour les unir à la Sénéchaussée ducale de Cames.

L'Assemblée-générale des Basques-François n'a pu céder, sur ce point, aux représentations contraires des Députés particuliers de ces trois Paroisses; parceque leur attachement pour la maison de Gramont a pu seul les leur suggérer, et que le Pays de Labourt, en partageant avec eux le même sentiment pour cette maison respectable, y trouve un motif de plus d'espérer que la justice toujours généreuse des Gramont appuyera elle-même, s'il le faut, cette demande si intéressante pour les Basques-François.

Que les procès en regle soient interdits dans le Pays pour des contestations purement pécuniaires qui n'excéderont pas la somme de 12 liv., et que ces modiques différends soient renvoyés aux Officiers-municipaux des lieux, pour les régler définitivement, par manière de police, sans forme ni figure de procès.

Que les lois contre le vagabondage soient renouvelées, confirmées et publiées, et qu'il soit enjoint au Tribunaux de tenir une main rigoureuse à leur exécution.

2. Par rapport à la manière de contribuer aux impôts, et de se régler entr'eux pour l'administration intérieure de leurs Communautés respectives, les habitans du Tiers-état du Labourt demanderont qu'on leur conserve la constitution particulière que leur assignent les arrêts du Conseil du 3 juin 1660, du 10 fevrier 1688, du 17 juillet 1769, et du 1 mai 1772. Ils se trouvent assez bien de ce régime; ils craindroient d'en changer.

Si les voeux qui se font entendre dans la Nation pour la suppression des Intendans étoient remplis, ce régime dans lequel les Basques du Tiers-état demandent à être maintenus, n'en deviendroit vraisemblablement que plus avantageux pour leur contrée. Mais si les Intendans conservés devoient continuer d'y avoir l'inspection qu'on leur a reconnue jusqu'à présent, les Basques du Tiers-état demanderoient que, dans ce cas, on leur donnât pour Subdélégué un Basque qui résidât dans le Labourt, qui entendit leur langue, et qui pût avoir pour leurs intérêts communs, ce zèle d'affection que n'affoiblissent point des intérêts personels opposés.

Après même ces réformes adoptées et sanctionnées par le Gouvernement, peut-être faudroit-il d'autres moyens encore pour encourager l'agriculture dans un pays où la sterilité des terres est telle qu'à peine elles rendent le tiers des grains nécessaires aux besoins du pays. Des loix récentes ont accordé en général aux defrichemens des terres incultes, des exemptions d'impôt et de dîme plus ou moins longues; il seroit de la justice et de l'intérêt du Gouvernement, que ces exemptions fussent prolongées pour le Pays Basques, et qu'à l'époque où elles cesseroient, les terres défrichées ne payassent la dîme qu'au 50me des fruits.

3. Par rapport à leur Coutume locale, en prévoyant que la réforme de quelques-unes de ses dispositions pourroit ranimer dans leur Pays l'activité de l'industrie, et favoriser les progrès de l'agriculture, les Basques-François pensent néanmoins que le plan de cette réforme doit être concerté avec beaucoup de réflexion; et tout ce qu'ils croient pouvoir, à cet égard, demander maintenant au Gouvernement, c'est qu'il leur soit permis de former dans le Pays un Comité d'hommes sages et instruits, pour travailler au plan de cette réforme, et lui obtenir la sanction du Gouvernment s'il est adopté par la majorité des Paroisses du Pays.

4. Les Députés des Basques-François dénonceront à la Nation Assemblée, les recherches vexatoires auxquelles se trouvent journellement exposés, de la part des Agens du Fisc, les habitans des Paroisses de leur Pays situés entre la Nive et l'Adour; ils seront chargés d'un memoire qui les détaillera et dont le tableau suffira pour intéresser la Nation et la Souverain à en arrêter le cours.

Ils dénonceront encore les concussions que les Agens du Fisc entreprennent d'exercer sur le Pays, en exigeant sur les cuirs et le fers ouvrés dans les manufactures des mêmes Paroisses, ainsi que les insinuations des donations entrevifs, des droits que la Province a déjà payés par son abonnement pour les impôts de tous genres.

Ils dénonceront l'atteinte que le Fisc a entrepris de porter dans ces derniers tems à l'allodialité de tous les tems reconnue de la Province.

5. Ils demanderont pour la partie maritime du Pays, et pour la Nation, intéressée à conserver ses meilleurs matelots, que pour l'encouragement de la pêche de la Morue, il soit fait des réglemens fixes, auxquels soient assujettis les armateurs et les matelots, relativement aux avances que les derniers reçoivent à leur départ.

Qu'il soit accordé des primes pour ces expéditions maritimes:

Que les Morues de la pêche circulent librement dans le Royaume, en exemption de tous droits, même des droits d'octroi des villes;

Qu'enfin l'entrée du Royaume soit fermée aux Morues de pêche étrangère.

6. Ils demanderont que le Gouvernement fasse reconstruire le pont de Saint Jean-de-Luz, qui menace une ruine prochaine; qu'il rembourse à la Paroisse de Cambo les frais d'un pont de pierre déjà commencé sur la partie de la Nive qui la traverse, et qu'en même-tems il fasse construire deux autres ponts de pierre, l'un sur la Nive encore à Itxassou, l'autre sur l'Adour, à prendre d'Urt vers le borde opposé.

On demande ces dépenses au Gouvernement, parcequ'elles ne seront pas considérables, et qu'elles sont nécessaires, non-seulement au commerce du Pays avec les Provinces voisines, mais encore à la Nation pour les passages des troupes.

7. La ville de St. Jean-de-Luz n'est défendu contre les ravages de la mer qui a déjà emporté plusieurs de ses maisons, que par une estacade en bois. La justice et l'humanité réclament du Gouvernement, qu'à cette barrière trop foible, il substitue un mur solide, qui puisse rassurer les habitans de Saint Jean-de-Luz contre les irruptions nocturnes de ce terrible élément.

8. La justice et l'humanité réclament encore du Gouvernement, que le port de Biarrits soit rétabli, et que les fanaux qui éclairoient autrefois, la nuit, les navigateurs dans ces côtes dangereuses, y soient replacés.

Un cordon d'Invalides établi depuis Itxassou jusqu'à la riviére de Bidassoa, pour empêcher la desertion, n'y peut remplir que foiblement cette destination; et cependant son entretien est très-onéreux au Pays.

Le Tiers-état demande qu'on le remplace par trois brigades de Maréchaussée, qui distribuées convenablement dans la contrée, rempliront bien mieux la même destination, et rendront encore au Pays d'autres services importans, comme ceux d'en imposer aux malfaiteurs, et de contenir les brigandages des Bohemes-vagabonds.

9. Un bureau établi sur le bord espagnol du Pas de Béhobie, perçoit des

droits sur tous les François qui viennent d'Espagne en France, et qui de la France passent en Espagne. La loi de la réciprocité ne voudroit-elle pas qu'on accordât aux Basques-François, sur qui pèse le plus cette fiscalité espagnole, un bureau sur le bord françois, où se perçussent les mêmes droits sur les Espagnols qui viendroient en France et qui retourneroient chez eux, et dont le produit fût réparti proportionnellement entre les Paroisses du Labourt, pour aider ce pauvre Pays à acquitter sa contribution aux subsides de l'Etat?

10. Tous les revenus presque du Chapitre de Bayonne se composent de dîmes qu'il tire du Pays de Labourt, ne seroit-il pas juste qu'un certain nombre des prébendes canoniales de ce Chapitre fût exclusivement affecté aux Prêtres Basques?

11. Enfin les habitans de Bonloc et Lahonce sont accablés sous d'énormes redevances seigneuriales. Ce sont les seules traces de féodalité oppressive qu'on remarque avec effroi dans le Pays de Labourt, de tous les tems noble, c'est-à-dire, libre et allodial. Leur origine peut paroître d'autant plus suspecte, que les habitans de la Province ont toujours été très-religieux, et que les Seigneurs qui les perçoivent sont des Ecclésiastiques. Ils gémissent eux-mêmes d'avoir à les recouvrer, et ils accepteroient avec reconnoissance l'union de quelque bénéfice à leur manse, qui remplaçant à-peu-près ces droits dans leur revenu, pût leur procurer la satisfaction d'en affranchir les habitans de ces Paroisses.

Tels sont les objets des réclamations générales et particulières que ses fidelles Sujets du Tiers-état du Labourt chargent leurs Députés de faire parvenir au Souverain, dans l'Assemblée de la Nation. En leur donnant la mission de les proposer dans cette Assemblée, ils les revêtent, conformément au voeu énoncé par Sa Majesté dans l'article 45 du règlement du 24 janvier, de tous les *pouvoirs généraux et suffisans pour proposer, aviser et consentir,* à tout ce qui s'y délibérera à la pluralité des voix, sur ces objets, ainsi que sur tous les autres qui s'y discuteront. Ce n'est pas qu'ils pensent, ni que leurs Députés, dès le choix qu'ils en auront fait, se transforment en Représentans de la Nation, ni que, comme leurs mandataires, leurs pouvoirs ne pussent être valablement limités; mais toute limitation de ce genre seroit essentiellement contraire à l'objet de leur mission. Ils sont envoyés à une Assemblée de la Nation, non pour y imposer des loix à ses autres Représentans, mais pour y délibérer avec eux les meilleures loix possibles, soit sur la constitution de l'Etat, soit sur toutes les parties de son administration. Il faut dès-lors s'abandonner à leur conscience et à leurs lumières, et que, sur les voeux et les réclamations même qu'ils sont chargés d'y présenter, comme sur tous les autres qui s'y proposeront, ils soient libres de se ranger du parti où une discussion calme et patriotique leur fera reconnoître la vérité, la justice et le bonheur général de la Nation.

Lu, revisé et approuvé en l'Assemblé générale du Tiers-état, tenue dans

439

l'auditoire du Bailliage du Labourt, avec autorisation aux Commissaires d'y apposer leurs signatures, pour garantir la fidélité de la transcription, le 23 avril, 1789.

Signés sur l'original,

Gorostarsou, Commissaire.

d'Aguerresar, Commissaire.

Dithurbide, Commissaire.

d'Hiriart, Commissaire.

Harriet.

Haranboure.

d'Elissalde, Commissaire.

Diesse, Commissaire.

BIBLIOGRAPHY

INTRODUCTION

The bibliography which follows aims to give essential information about original and reprinted texts of the general cahiers, a full list of all volumes or articles discussing critically those documents, and a selected list of the most helpful volumes for an understanding of the electoral period. An alphabetical list of books would be of little use. The titles have been classified into the following groups: I. Original sources; II. Reprinted texts of cahiers; III. Manuals and guides; IV. The early States-Generals; V. The convocation and elections of 1789, general volumes; VI. Analyses, criticisms, and summaries of the cahiers of 1789; VII. Essential volumes for an understanding of the general cahiers, listed by district; VIII. Sources for France in 1789.

Any study of the general cahiers should start with the little volume by Champion (see *supra*, p. *x*) and with the introduction and reprinted sources in Brette's four volumes (see *supra*, p. *x*). With these two authors, and the official inventory of texts (see *infra*, p. 449 under Hyslop), the present volume completes the necessary tools for a comprehension of the general cahiers. Each of these publications overlaps the others to a certain degree. The subject is so complex and the number of books dealing in any way with the cahiers is so large, that it would be impractical to repeat information that could be gained in any of the foregoing volumes. There has been no attempt, for example, to indicate all volumes which reprint a given cahier, as was done in the *Repertoire critique*. In the present volume, the best reprint has been indicated. Similarly, not all volumes dealing with the elections in a given area have been listed, but only those which are most helpful or reliable. Titles referring exclusively to preliminary cahiers have also been omitted. All essential material for an understanding of the general cahiers has been included, but this volume does not aim to be a complete bibliography of all books or articles dealing with *cahiers de doléances*.

ORIGINAL SOURCES[1]

Archives Nationales

Three large series of documents contain the royal regulations, correspondence, *procès-verbaux*, cahiers, and related source materials: Ba 1— Ba 90; C 14— C 34; B III 1—B III 174. Brette gave a helpful inventory of these series (*op. cit.*, Vol. I, pp. cxxix *et seq.*), but the Tuetey inventory (see *supra*, p. 449), is more detailed for series C. The *Repertoire critique* cites the existence of all *procès-verbaux* and cahiers in these collections, classified un-

---

[1] Although several libraries in the United States (e.g., Cornell University, Harvard University, etc.), have numerous examples of printed editions of cahiers, there are none that cannot be found in the French collections.

der each electoral district. The series AD I 9—AD I 11 contains printed editions of cahiers. A few other series contain isolated texts, which are cited in the table of sources, *supra,* pp. ooo *et seq.*

Bibliothèque Nationale

The Collection of printed texts of *procès-verbaux* and cahiers in series Le 23. and Le 24. overlaps with the texts at the *Archives Nationales,* but also contains some texts that the latter does not. An inventory of the texts is given in the official *Catalogue de l'histoire de la France,* Vol. VI, and Supplement, Vol. XIII. Citations to these texts are included in the *Repertoire critique.*

Departmental and Communal \Archives and Libraries

In 1789, one set of electoral documents was taken by the deputies to the States-General, and these papers are now found in the *Archives Nationales* described above. Another set of the documents was kept in the local registry, whose papers were eventually turned into the *Departmental Archives,* or, in the case of parish materials, into the *Communal Archives.* The *Repertoire critique* . . . illustrates the duplication of the chief electoral documents in the *Archives Nationales* and the various *Departmental Archives.* In the present study, research in the latter was undertaken to fill gaps in documents preserved at Paris. While preparing the *Repertoire critique,* the author had recourse to information supplied by the departmental archivists, but in addition, the following archives and libraries were visited:

Besançon	*Arch. Doubs, Bib. Mun.*
Bourg-en-Bresse	*Arch. Ain.*
Dijon	*Bib. Mun.* (The *Arch. Côte d'Or* were closed at the time, but information was obtained by correspondence).
Grenoble	*Arch. Isère, Bib. Mun.*
Laon	*Arch. Aisne.*
Lons-le-Saunier	*Arch. Jura,* Private Collection of M. Cernesson.
Nancy	*Arch. Meurthe-et-Moselle, Bib. Mun.*
Rouen	*Arch. Seine-Inférieure, Bib. Mun.*
Strasbourg	*Arch. Mun., Bib. Mun. et Universitaire de Strasbourg.*
Tours	*Arch. Indre-et-Loire, Bib. Mun.*

Correspondence and the loan of certain documents to be used at the *National Archives* made possible the discovery of, and utilization of numerous hitherto unedited documents.

British Museum

The Croker Collection on the French Revolution, series R and F.R., was consulted, but with one exception (C. Toulouse) no printed texts not already seen in French collections were discovered.

REPRINTED TEXTS OF CAHIERS DE DOLEANCES OF 1789

The titles of all books necessary for consultation of the full number of known general cahiers are given here. References to specific texts are given under each cahier in the composite table, pp. 116 *et seq.*

Archives parlementaires de 1787 à 1860, edited by J. Mavidal and E. Laurent, 1st series, 1787-1799 (Paris, 1867-75, 7 vols.).

This publication, which contains the majority of the general cahiers is very defective. A searching criticism of the method and results was made by Brette (*op. cit.,* Vol. I, pp. xci *et seq.*). With the help of page references to each cahier, given in the composite table, *infra,* pp. 116 *et seq.,* and the textual corrections for texts in the *Archives parlementaires, infra,* pp. 158 *et seq.,* these volumes may be used with accuracy.

The Official Series of Volumes: Documents inédits sur l'histoire économique de la Révolution française.

A commission, under the auspices of the French Ministry of National Education has undertaken the careful publication of source materials, chiefly of three types: *cahiers de doléances,* documents relating to feudal rights, and documents relating to the sale of national lands. A survey of the volumes which had appeared up to 1928 was given by H. E. Bourne, "The Economic History of the French Revolution as a Field of Study," in *American Historical Review,* January, 1928 (pp. 315 *et seq.*).

Editions of cahiers are based upon the *bailliage,* and not all of the volumes reprint the general cahiers. Nevertheless, it has seemed desirable to give the complete list of volumes that have appeared thus far, for each is authoritative, and the introductions should be studied for the descriptions of the elections in the particular district. Page references to texts of general cahiers are cited in the composite table of cahiers, *infra,* pp. 116 *et seq.*

Volumes are listed alphabetically by editors. Starred volumes(*) reprint the general cahiers. Attention has been called to any introductions which contain valuable contributions to the discussion of the value of *cahiers de doléances.* A dagger(†) has been placed after volumes that deal only with cahiers of secondary *bailliages.*

Balencie, G., Les Cahiers de doléances de la sénéchaussée de Bigorre. Dépt. des Hautes-Pyrénées. Tarbes, 1925.

Bligny-Bondurand, E., Cahiers de doléances de la sénéchaussée de Nîmes pour les Etats-Généraux de 1789. Dépt. du Gard. Nîmes, 1908-9, 2 vols.*

Bloch, Camille, Cahiers de doléances du bailliage d'Orléans pour les Etats Généraux de 1789. Dépt. du Loiret. Orléans, 1906-7, 2 vols.*

Boissonnade, Prosper, Cahiers de doléances de la sénéchaussée d'Angoulême et du siège royal de Cognac. Dépt. de la Charente. Paris, 1907.*

Boissonnade, Prosper, and L. Cathelineau, Cahiers de doléances de la

sénéchaussée de Civray pour les Etats-Généraux de 1789. Dépt. de
la Vienne. Niort, 1925.† Secondary to Poitiers.

Bondurand, E. Bligny—, see Bligny-Bondurand.

Bridrey, Emile, Cahiers de doléances du bailliage de Cotentin. Dépt. de
la Manche. Paris, 1907-12.*

Cathelineau, Léonce, Cahiers de doléances de la sénéchaussée de Niort et
des communautés et corporations de St. Maixent pour les Etats Généraux de 1789. Dépt. des Deux-Sèvres. Niort, 1912.† Secondary to
Poitiers.

Etienne, Charles, Cahiers de doléances des bailliages des généralités de
Metz et de Nancy. Dépt. de Meurthe-et-Moselle. Nancy, 1907-30. Vol.
I, Bailliage de Vic. Vol. II, Bailliage de Dieuze.* Vol. III, Bailliage de
Vézelise.*

Fourastie, Victor, Cahiers de doléances de la sénéchaussée de Cahors.
Dépt. du Lot. Cahors, 1908.

Fournier, Joseph, Cahiers de doléances de la sénéchaussée de Marseille pour
les Etats Généraux de 1789. Dépt. des Bouches-du-Rhône. Marseille,
1908.*

Gandilhon, Alfred, Cahiers de doléances du bailliage de Bourges et des
bailliages secondaires. . . Dépt. du Cher. Bourges, 1910.
  This volume does not give the general cahiers, but the author's comments on the text of the general cahier of the clergy are invaluable.

Godard, M., and Léon Abensour, Cahiers de doléances du bailliage d'Amont.
Dépt. de la Haute-Saône. Besançon, 1918-27, 2 vols.

Godfrin, Jean, Les Cahiers de doléances du bailliage de Nancy. Dépt. de
Meurthe-et-Moselle. Paris, 1933.*

Guillaume, Abbé, Récueil des réponses faites par les communautés de
l'élection de Gap. . . . Dépt. des Hautes-Alpes. Paris, 1908.† Section of
the Dauphiné.

Jouanne, René, Cahier de doléances des corps et corporations de la ville
d'Alençon pour les Etats Généraux de 1789. Dépt. de l'Orne. Alençon,
1929.†

Laurent, Gustave, Cahiers de doléances pour les Etats Généraux de 1789.
Dépt. de la Marne. Vol. I, Bailliage de Châlons-sur-Marne, Epernay,
1906.* Vols. II, III, Bailliages de Sézanne et Châtillonsur-Marne, Epernay, 1911.* Vol. IV, Bailliage de Reims, Reims, 1930.

Le Moy, A., Cahiers de doléances des corporations de la ville d'Angers et
des paroisses de la sénéchaussée particulière d'Angers pour les Etats
Généraux de 1789. Dépt. de Maine-et-Loire. Angers, 1915-16, 2 vols.

Le Parquier, E., Cahiers de doléances du bailliage d'Arques. Dépt. de la
Seine-Inférieure. Lille, 1922.† Secondary to Caudebec.

———— Cahiers de doléances du bailliage du Havre. Dépt. de la Seine-
Inférieure. Epinal, 1929.† Secondary to Caudebec.

Le Parquier, E., Cahiers de doléances du bailliage de Neufchâtel-en-Bray. Dépt. de la Seine-Inférieure. Rouen, 1908.† Secondary to Caudebec.

Lesueur, F., and A. Cauchie, Cahiers de doléances du bailliage de Blois et du bailliage secondaire de Romorantin. . . Dépt. de Loir-et-Cher. Blois, 1907-8, 2 vols.*

Martin, E., Cahiers de doléances du bailliage de Mirecourt. Dépt. des Vosges. Epinal, 1928.*

Maurel, Blanche, Cahiers de doléances de la colonie de Saint Domingue pour les Etats Généraux de 1789. Paris, 1933.*

Mourlot, Félix, Le Cahier d'observations et doléances du tiers-état de la ville de Caen en 1789, Dreux, 1912. The introduction to this volume is very useful.

Pasquier, F., and Fr. Galabert, Cahiers paroissiaux des sénéchaussées de Toulouse et de Comminges en 1789, Toulouse, 1925-28.

This volume was published under the supervision of the committee of Haute-Garonne, and not of the national committee. It is a less satisfactory publication than other volumes of the official series.

Porée, Charles, Cahiers de curés et des communautés ecclésiastiques du bailliage d'Auxerre. . . Dépt. de l'Yonne. Auxerre, 1927.

——— Cahiers de doléances du bailliage de Sens. Dépt. de l'Yonne. Auxerre, 1908.*

Savina, J., and D. Bernard, Cahiers de doléances des sénéchaussées de Quimper et de Concarneau. . . Dépt. du Finistère. Rennes, 1927.*

Sée, Henri, and André Lessort, Cahiers de doléances de la sénéchaussée de Rennes. Dépt. d'Ille-et-Vilaine.* Rennes, 1909-12, 4 vols.

The introduction to these volumes is invaluable for the study of the cahiers as sources, and also for remarks on the district of Rennes.

Vernier, J. J., Cahiers de doléances du bailliage de Troyes et du bailliage de Bar-sur-Seine. Dépt. de l'Aube. Troyes, 1909-11, 3 vols.*

Semi-official editions of cahiers

Chassin, Charles L., Les Elections et les cahiers de Paris, Paris, 1888-89, 4 vols.

This appears in the series called *Collection de documents rélatifs à l'histoire de Paris,* published under the auspices of the Municipal Council.

Dorvaux, N., and Abbé Lesprand, Cahiers des bailliages de Boulay et de Bouzonville, in the series *Documents sur l'histoire de Lorraine,* Metz, 1908, Vol. IX.

——— Cahiers de doléances des communautés de Metz, in the same series, Metz, 1918, Vol. X.

Lesprand, Abbé, in the *Annuaire de la Société d'histoire et d'archéologie lorraine,* Metz, Scriba. Vol. XV, 1903, "L'Election du député et cahier du tiers-état de la ville de Metz en 1789," pp. 158 et seq. Vol. XVI, 1904, "Cahiers lorrains de 1789," pp. 175, et seq. This gives some texts not reprinted elsewhere.

Unofficial publications of texts

Consult the list by *bailliage* for titles dealing with particular districts. The titles that follow are those which give texts for several districts.

Cauna, Armorial des Landes (Bordeaux, 1863-65, 2 vols.).

Duhamel, L., Documents rares ou inédits de l'histoire des Vosges (Paris, 1869, Vol. II).

Hippeau, C., Le Gouvernment de Normandie aux dix-septième et dix-huitième siècles (Caen, 1863-69, 9 vols.).

Jérome, L., Les Elections et les cahiers du clergé lorrain aux Etats Généraux de 1789, Paris, 1899.

Contains the texts of several cahiers of the clergy from districts in Lorraine which are not reprinted elsewhere, and whose texts have disappeared since the sale of the library of the Seminary of Nancy, where M. Jérome found the originals.

Proust, Antonin, Archives de l'Ouest, Série A, Paris, 1867-69, 5 vols.

Révolution française, revue d'histoire, moderne et contemporaine, La, Paris, from 1880 on.

Vol. XXXII (1897), Texts of the cahiers of N. Bar-le-duc and T. Verdun. This quarterly, started in 1880 and after 1887 published under the direction of A. Aulard, was continued by a society founded by him. The publication of the quarterly has now been taken over by the Centre d'études de la Révolution française, of the Université de Paris, under the title: *La Révolution française, revue d'histoire contemporaine.*

Vic, Dom Claude de, and Vaissete, J., Histoire de Languedoc, Toulouse, 1872-92, Vol. XIV.

MANUALS, GUIDES, INVENTORIES, DICTIONARIES, ATLASES AND SIMILAR MISCELLANEOUS LITERATURE

Annales historiques de la Révolution, Paris, 1908 on. Published six times a year by the Société des Etudes Robespierristes, founded by Albert Mathiez.

Boursin et Challamel, A., Dictionnaire de la Révolution française, Paris, 1893.

Brette, Armand, Recueil de documents rélatifs à la convocation des Etats Généraux de 1789, Paris, 1894-1915, 4 vols.

These four volumes are indispensable. They contain an inventory of documents, a reprint of the most important ones for the convocation of 1789, and an extensive introduction and scholarly footnotes. Volume

I deals with the convocation of the States-General. Volume II gives complete information upon the deputies to the States-General. Volumes III and IV give analyses of the elections by district, with critical information on the assemblies, officials, procedure, and texts, for sixteen generalities. Brette intended to continue the publication and to add volumes for the other seventeen generalities, but he died prematurely. The gaps have been partly filled by separate volumes in the official series of *Documents inédits . . .*, but much remains to be done.

Brette, Armand, Atlas des bailliages ou juridictions assimilées . . . , Paris, 1904. This is a separate folio volume to accompany the four volumes cited above.

———— Les Limites et les divisions territoriales de la France en 1789, Paris, 1907.

An indispensable description of the geographic and administrative character of France in 1789, with a few useful maps.

Caron, Pierre, Manuel pratique pour l'étude de la Révolution française, Paris, 1912.

Catalogue de l'histoire de France, Paris, 1855-. Vols. VI and XIII are especially useful.

Catalogue général des manuscrits des bibliothèques publiques de France, Paris, 1886-1911, 44 vols.

Garrett, Mitchell B., A Critical Bibliography of the Pamphlet Literature Published in France between July 3 and December 27, 1788, Birmingham, 1925.

Hyslop, Beatrice, *Documents inédits . . . ,* Repertoire critique des cahiers de doléances pour les Etats Généraux de 1789, Paris, 1933.

This inventory indicates all known manuscripts, printed and reprinted texts of all types of cahiers, preliminary and general. For corrections and subsequent discoveries, see historical reviews and regional publications.

Lasteyrie, P., et Vidier, A., Bibliographie des travaux historiques et archéologique, Paris. 1880-.

Marion, Marcel, Dictionnaire des institutions de la France au dix-septième et dix-huitième siècles, Paris, 1923.

Sanson, Victor, Repertoire bibliographique pour la période dite "révolutionnaire" (1789-1801) en Seine-Inférieure, Rouen, 1911-12, 3 vols.

La Révolution française, revue. . . . Cf. supra, p. 448.

Société de l'histoire de la Révolution française. *Les Manuscrits rélatifs à l'histoire de la Révolution et de l'Empire dans les bibliothèques publiques des départements,* Paris, 1913.

Tuetey, Alexandre, Les Papiers des Assemblées de la Révolution aux Archives Nationales, Paris, 1908.

Shepherd, William R., Historical Atlas, New York, 1929, 7th edition.

THE EARLY STATES-GENERALS

Sources

It would require extensive research to discover all existing texts of cahiers drawn up for the early States-Generals. The following are items that have come to the attention of the author, and which form a workable bibliography.

Archives Nationales: K 672: minutes of sessions; T. cahier (1614); T. Paris *intra-muros* (1588); T. Vendôme (1614); T. Paris *intra-muros* (1614); T. Rouen (1596).

Isolated examples of cahiers: Ba 49—T. Mâcon (1560, 1675, 1588); Ba 50—T. Marseille (p. v. 1576, 1588, 1614); Ba 1—T. Méry-sur-Seine (1576); B III 3—Amiens (papers).

Bibliothèque Nationale: Le 12.10—T. Troyes (1561); Le 17.10—University of Paris (1614). Other items at the *Bibliothèque* duplicate K 674 of the Archives. See the general catalogue of the history of France, Vol. VI, for items.

Reprinted sources

Lalourcé and Duval, Récueil des cahiers généraux des trois ordres aux Etats-Généraux, Paris, 1789, 4 vols.

Contains reprints of all the national cahiers of the States-Generals from 1560 to 1614.

——— Forme générale et particulière de la convocation et de la tenue des Assemblées nationales ou Etats-Généraux de France, Paris, 1789, 3 vols.

Reprint of documents on the convocation, accompanied by explanations. Reprint of several cahiers: T. Blaigny (1576), Vol. II, pp. 103 *et seq.*; T. Blois (1614), Vol. II, pp. 184 *et seq.*; T. Blois (1588), Vol. II, pp. 188 *et seq.*

Mayer, Charles J., Des Etats Généraux, et autres assemblées nationales, La Haye et Paris, 1788-89, 18 vols.

Contains text of the national cahier for 1484 not given by Lalourcé and Duval, *op. cit.*, as well as most of the subsequent national cahiers.

Descriptive works

Danjou, F., and Cimber, L., Archives curieuses de l'histoire de France (Louis XI—Louis XVIII), Paris, 1837, Vol. I, 2ᵉ série.

Picot, Georges, Histoire des Etats Généraux, Paris, 1888, 2nd edition; 5 vols.

This work was written to comply with the request of the commission for historical works for a study showing the demands of the French people for the States-Generals, and the effect of the States-Generals on French law and custom. It is a thorough and scholarly study. In view of this excellent work, it seems unnecessary to list other books on the early States-General, which are all fragmentary, biased, or inadequate.

THE CONVOCATION AND ELECTIONS OF 1789

General works

Delannoy, L., La Convocation des Etats-Généraux de 1789, Paris, 1904. Good summary. Emphasizes the haste in composition of cahiers, and denies that they are a good gauge of public opinion.

Desjardins, Gustave, Le Beauvoisis, le Valois . . . en 1789, Beauvais, 1869.

Duchâtellier, A., Histoire de la Révolution dans les départements de l'ancien Bretagne, Paris, 1836, 6 vols.

Garrett, Mitchell B., "The Call for Information concerning the States-General in 1788," in *The American Historical Review*, April, 1932, pp. 506 *et seq.*

Lesort, André, "La Commission de la convocation des Etats-Généraux," in *La Révolution française, revue*, 1930, Vol. LXXXIII, pp. 5 *et seq.*

By districts

The following books are supplementary to bibliography given by Brette. Special effort has been made to give necessary references for the convocation, elections, and cahiers of districts which Brette and official volumes of the *Documents inédits* . . . have not treated. Districts are listed alphabetically by *generalities*, and the order of the latter is the same as that recommended for reading the general cahiers (*cf. supra*, p. 92, and table in Appendix, p. 145). If a district is not listed, that signifies that no additions to the bibliography given by Brette (at the end of his treatment of each electoral district in volumes III and IV), or to the volume of the *Documents inédits* . . ., are necessary. Where a district has not been treated by either, and does not appear in the list, that signifies that no pertinent volumes were discovered. It is obviously not feasible to list all local histories. Local reviews and learned journals should always be consulted. Under each *generality* are given first, books that may deal with several bailliages, and then works dealing with specific districts preceded by the name of the *bailliage*.

Generality of Paris (Brette)

Beauvais: Desjardins, Gustave, Le Beauvoisis, le Valois, . . . en 1789, Beauvais, 1869.

Montfort-l'Amaury: "Cahiers de Montfort-Amaury" in *Mémoires de la société archéologique de Rambouillet;* 1902, Vols. XVI, XVII.

Sens: *D.I.*, see Bibliography under Porée.

Generality of Orléans (Brette)

Blois: *D.I.*, see Bibliography under Lesueur and Cauchie.

Orléans: *D.I.*, see Bibliography under Bloch.

Generality of Bourges (Brette, D.I.)

Generality of Moulins (Brette)

Generality of Lyon (Brette)

Generality of Riom (Brette)

Mège, Francisque, "Les Cahiers des bailliages et sénéchaussées d'Auvergne en 1789," in *Revue d'Auvergne*, 1903, Vol. XX.

Mège, Francisque, "La Dernière Année de la province d'Auvergne," in *Mémoires de l'Académie des sciences, belle-lettres et arts de Clermont Ferrand*, 1904.
Saint Flour: Serres, J. B., Histoire de la Révolution en Auvergne, Paris, 1895.

Generality of Montpellier
Mathieu, André, La Convocation des Etats-Généraux de 1789 en Languedoc, Montpellier, 1917.
Vic, Dom Claude de, and Vaissete, J., Histoire de Languedoc, Toulouse, 1872-92, Vol. XIV.
Mende: Burdin, Gustave, Documents historiques sur la province de Gévaudan, Toulouse, 1847, Vol. II.
Delon, J. B., Les Elections de 1789 en Gévaudan, Mende, 1922.
Montpellier: Aigrefeuille, Charles d', Histoire de la ville de Montpellier, Montpellier, 1837, 4 vols.
Nîmes: *D.I.*, *supra*, under Bligny-Bondurand.
Villeneuve-de-Berg: Vaschalde, Le Vivarais aux Etats-Généraux, Paris, 1889.

Generality of Toulouse
See *supra*, under "Montpellier," Vic, Dom Claude de, and Vaissete, J., *op. cit.*; Mathieu, *op. cit.*
Castres: La Jonquière, Les Cahiers de 1789 . . . de Castres, Paris, 1867.
Toulouse: *D.I.*, *supra*, under Pasquier and Galabert.

Generality of Perpignan (Roussillon)
Vidal, Pierre and Calmette, Joseph, Bibliographie roussillonnaise, Perpignan, 1906.

Generality of Auch (Brette)

Generality of Bordeaux (Brette)
Couture, L., "Les Trois Ordres aux assemblées électorales de Dax et de Tartas en 1789," in *Revue de Gascogne*, 1864.
Périgord: Ampoulange, Lucien, Le Clergé et la convocation aux Etats-Généraux de 1789 dans la sénéchaussée principale de Périgord, Montpellier, 1912.
Bussière, G., Etudes historiques sur la Révolution en Périgord, Bordeaux, 1885.

Generality of Montauban (Brette)
Cahors: *D.I.*, *supra*, under Fourastie.

Generality of Limoges (Brette)

Generality of La Rochelle (Brette)
St. Jean d'Angely: Mesnard, A., St. Jean d'Angely sous la Révolution, Paris, 1910.

Generality of Poitiers (Brette)
There are volumes of the *D.I.* dealing with secondary bailliages of Poitiers. *Cf. supra,* p. 446.

Generality of Tours (Brette)
Tours: Faye H., Le Cahier du clergé de Touraine pour les Etats-Généraux de 1789, Tours, 1899.
Massereau, T., *Documents d'Archives sur l'histoire économique de la Révolution française:* Cahiers de doléances de Tours et de Loches Orléans, 1915.
This volume did not have the approval of the central committee for the publication of the official series, and is inferior to other volumes. It does contain a useful analysis of the elections.

Generality of Caen
See *supra,* under Hippeau; Caen: *D.I.,* Mourlot; Coutances: *D.I.,* Bridrey

Generality of Alençon
See *supra,* under Hippeau
Alençon: see also *supra, D.I.,* under Jouanne
Courtilloles, E. F. L. de, Recueil de documents rélatifs à la tenue des Etats-Généraux du grand bailliage d'Alençon, Cherbourg, 1866.
Mourlot, Félix, Département de l'Orne, documents inédits . . . du district d'Alençon, 1788-an IV, 1907-10, 3 vols.

Generality of Rouen
See also *supra,* under Desjardins; under Hippeau.
Sanson, Victor, Repertoire bibliographique pour la période dite "révolutionnaire" (1789-1801) en Seine-Inférieure, Rouen, 1911-12, 3 vols.
Le Parquier, E., "Thouret et les cahiers du tiers-état normand en 1789," in *La Normandie,* 1905, août.
Le Parquier, E., Etudes sur la Normandie en 1789, Sotteville-lès-Rouen, 1906.
Caudebec-enCaux: *D.I.* of secondary bailliages, *supra,* p. 446.
Rouen: Hyslop, B., "Le Cahier de doléances du tiers-état du grand bailliage de Rouen en 1789," in *Révolution française,* January, 1932. This article should soon be superseded by a volume by M. Le Parquier. For secondary *bailliages,* see Hippeau, *op. cit., supra,* p. 448.

Generality of Amiens (Brette)
Sagnac, P., and St. Leger, Les Cahiers de la Flandre maritime en 1789, Bailleul, 1896, 3 vols.

Generality of Lille
See also *supra,* under "Amiens," Sagnac, and St. Leger.
Coussemaker, C. E. de, Les Elections aux Etats-Généraux en 1789 dans la Flandre maritime, Paris, 1864.

Lepreux, Georges, Nos Représentants pendant la Révolution, 1789-99, Lille, 1898.

Lefebvre, Georges, Les Paysans du Nord pendant la Révolution, Lille, 1924.

Loriquet, Henri, Cahiers de doléances de 1789 dans le département du Pas-de-Calais, Arras, 1891, 2 vols.

Lille: Belval, "Les Elections de Lille en 1789," in *Arch. hist. et litt. du Nord de la France*, 1829, 1st série.

Generality of Soissons (Brette)

See also *supra*, under "Paris," p. 451, and Desjardins, *op. cit.*

Soissons: Perrin (Périn), Cahiers du clergé et du tiers-état du bailliage de Soissons (Soissons, 1868). Especially valuable since original of cahier of third estate has been lost. Brette assigned this volume in the collection of the *Bibliothèque Nationale* an erroneous call number. Its correct number is 8° Le 24.230.

Generality of Châlons (Brette)

Poinsignon, Maurice, Histoire générale de la Champagne et de la Brie, Châlons-sur-Marne, 1885, 3 vols.

Châlons-sur-Marne: *D.I., supra*, under Laurent.

Troyes: *D.I., supra*, under Vernier.

Vitry-le-françois: Torcy, Charles de, Recherches sur la Champagne, Troyes, 1832.

Generality of Dijon

Cochin, Augustin, and Charpentier, Charles, La Campagne électorale de 1789 en Bourgogne, Paris, 1904.

Dubois, Eugène, Les Préliminaires de la Révolution dans l'Ain, Bourg, 1913.

Le Duc, Philibert, Curiositiés historiques de l'Ain, Bourg, 1877, 2 vols.

Lex, Léonce, Cahiers de doléances pour les Etats Généraux de 1789, Mâcon, 1910.

Autun: Charmasse, A. de, Cahiers des paroisses et communautés du bailliage d'Autun pour les Etats Généraux de 1789, Autun, 1895.

Auxerre: *D.L., supra*, under Porée.

Demay, Charles, Cahiers des paroisses du bailliage d'Auxerre, Auxerre, 1885.

Bar-sur-Seine: *D.I., supra*, under Vernier.

Belley: Recamier, E., Les Députés des communes du Bugey en 1789 et en 1876, Paris, 1876. Especially valuable since it reprints the only known text of the third estate.

Bourg-en-Bresse: Dubois, Eugène, article in *Soc. de l'émulation de l'Ain*, 1911.

Dijon: Guérin, A., article in *Bull. d'hist. du diocèse de Dijon*, Années 1886, 1887. Reprint of documents of clergy.

Gex: Baux, *Nobiliaire de l'Ain*, Vol. II.

Generality of Besançon
Maréchal, Philippe, La Révolution en Franche-Comté, Paris, 1903.
Amont: *D.I., supra,* under Godard and Abensour.
Besançon: Richlin, Révendications du bailliage de Besançon en 1789, Dijon, 1910.
Dôle: Fromond, Abbé, *Mémoires de la Soc. d'Emulation du Jura,* 1906, 7th série.

Generality of Grenoble
Champollion-Figéac, A., Chroniques dauphinoises, 1754-94, Vienne, 1884, 3 vols.
Chassin, C., article in *Le Progrès,* Dec. 9, 1862.

Generality of Aix
Viguier, Jules, La Convocation des Etats-Généraux en Provence, Paris, 1896.
Mireur, F., Procès-verbaux des élections des députés des sénéchaussées de Draguignan, Grasse, et Castellane, Draguignan, 1891.
Lauvergne, H., Histoire de la Révolution dans le Var, Toulon, 1839.
Marseille: *D.I., supra,* under Fournier.
Toulon: Harvard, Oscar, Histoire de la Révolution dans les ports de guerre, Paris, 1911-13, Vol. I.

Generality of Rennes
D.I., supra, under Sée and Lessort. This is an excellent study.
Duchâtellier, A., Histoire de la Révolution dans les départements de l'ancien Bretagne, Paris, 1836, 6 vols.
Pommeret, H., L'Esprit public dans le département des Côtes-du-Nord pendant la Révolution, St. Brieuc, 1921.
Quimper: *D.I., supra,* under Savina and Bernard.
Rennes: *D.I., supra,* under Sée and Lessort.

Generality of Valenciennes
Lepreux, see *supra,* under "Lille."

Generality of Nancy
Supra, Duhamel, p. 448; Lesprand; in *Annuaire* . . . p. 447, Jérome, p. 448.
Mathieu, F. D. (Cardinal) L'Ancien Régime dans la province de Lorraine et Barrois, Paris, 1907
Chevreux, Cahiers des doléances du tiers-état des villes et villages, Epinal, 1889-91.
Kastener, Jean, Les Cahiers de doléances des bailliages et des communautés ayant formé le département des Vosges, Epinal, 1931. This is an inventory of the cahiers that have been preserved.
Bar-le-duc: *Révolution française, revue,* 1897, Vol. XXXII.
Bruyères: Lemasson, Les Cahiers de doléances du bailliage de Bruyères in *La Révolution dans les Vosges,* Paris, 1910-11.

Dieuze: *D.I., supra,* under Etienne.

Lunéville: Baumont, H., Histoire de Lunéville (Lunéville, 1900).

Mirecourt: *D.I., supra,* under Martin.

Nancy: *D.I., supra* 446, under Godfrin.

Thiaucourt: in *Annales de l'Est,* 1904.

Vézelise: *D.I., supra, under Etienne.*

Generality of Metz

Supra, Dorvaux and Lesprand, Lesprand.

Metz, see *supra,* under Lesprand.

Verdun: *Révolution française, revue,* 1897, Vol. XXXII.

Vic: *D.I., supra,* under Etienne.

Generality of Strasbourg

Hermann, Auguste, Elsassische Monatschrift für Geschichte und Volkskunde 1912, Vol. III.

Krug-Basse, M. J., L'Alsace avant 1789, Paris, 1876.

Reuss, R., Alsace pendant la Révolution, Paris, 1880, 2 vols.

Strasbourg: Reuss, R., Histoire de Strasbourg, Paris, 1922.

    Seinguerlet, E., Strasbourg pendant la Révolution, Paris, 1881.

Corsica

Franceschini, E., and Franceschini, J., "Les Elections aux Etats-Généraux de 1789," in *Bull. de la Soc. des Sciences hist. et nat. de la Corse,* Année 1920.

Jollivet, Maurice, La Révolution française en Corse, Paris, 1892.

Letteron, Abbé, Osservazioni storiche sopra la Corsica dell' Abbate Ambrogio Rossi, in *Bull. de la Soc. des Sciences hist. et nat. de la Corse,* 1896, Vol. XIV.

Villat, Louis, La Corse de 1769 à 1789, Besançon, 1924-25, 2 vols.

The French Colonies

Deschamps, Léon, La Constituante et les colonies, Paris, 1898.

Gaffarel, Paul, La Politique coloniale en France de 1789 à 1830, Paris, 1908.

Pondichéry: Labernadie, Marguerite, La Révolution et les établissements français dans l'Inde, Paris, 1930.

St. Domingue: Boissonnade, Prosper M., St. Domingue à la veille de la Révolution, Paris, 1906.

D.I., Supra, p. 447 under Maurel.

SELECTED LIST OF ELECTORAL PAMPHLETS

Antraigues, Emanuel L. H. de L., Mémoire sur les Etats-Généraux, s.l. 1789, 8°, 279 pp.

————Second Mémoire sur les Etats-Généraux, s. l. 1789, 8°, 112 pp. This sometimes appears under the title, Mémoire sur la constitution des états de la province de Languedoc.

Barère de Vieuzac, Bertrand, L'Esprit des séances des Etats-Généraux, s. l. 1789, 8°.

Barnave, Antoine P. J. M., L'Esprit des édits enregistrés, Grenoble, 1788, 8°, 24 pp. Anon.

——Coup d'oeil sur la lettre de M. de Calonne (28 mars, 1789), 8°, 29 pp. Anon.

Bergasse, Nicolas, Considérations sur la liberté de commerce, La Haye, 1780; new edition, London, 1788, 8°, 78 pp.

——Discours sur l'humanité des juges dans l'administration de la justice criminelle . . ., Paris, 1788, 8°, 48 pp.

——Mémoire sur les Etats-Généraux, s. l. 1789, 8°, 47 pp. Anon.

Brissot de Warville, Jean P., Le Moniteur, see Condorcet.

——Plan de conduite pour les députés du peuple aux Etats-Généraux de 1789, s. l. 1789, 8°, 268 pp. and supplement. Anon.

——Précis addressé à l'assemblée générale des électeurs de Paris, s. l. n. d., 8°, 19 pp. Anon.

Carra, Jean L., Cahier de la déclaration des droits du peuple, et contrat de constitution de l'Etat, Paris, 1789, 8°, 18 pp. Anon.

——Considérations, recherches, et observations sur les Etats-Généraux, s. l. 1789, 8°, 91 pp. Anon.

——Projet de cahier pour le tiers-état de Paris, Paris, 1789, 8°, 20 pp. Anon.

Cérutti, Joseph A. J., Mémoire pour le peuple français, s. l. 1788, 8°, 66 pp. Anon.

——Vues générales sur la constitution française, Paris, 1789, 8°, 165 pp.

Condorcet, Marie J.A.N.C. de, Oeuvres (Paris, 1847): Déclaration des droits . . ., Vol. IX; Examen sur cette question: est-il utile de diviser une assemblée nationale en plusieurs chambres, Vol. IX; Idées sur le despotisme, Vol. IX; Lettre d'un gentilhomme à Messieurs du tiers-état, Vol. IX; Lettres d'un citoyen des Etats-Unis à un français, Vol. IX; Réflexions sur l'esclavage des nègres, Vol. VII; Réflexions sur les pouvoirs et instructions à donner par les provinces à leurs députés aux Etats-Généraux, Vol. IX; Sentiments d'un républicain sur les assemblées provinciales et les Etats-Généraux, Vol. IX.

——Le Moniteur, Londres, 1788, 8°, 50 pp. Attributed to Condorcet, Clavière, and Brissot.

Eprémesnil, J. J. D. de, Réflexions d'un magistrat sur la question du nombre et celle de l'opinion par order ou par tête, s. l. 1789, 7 pp.

Gohier, Louis J., Mémoire pour le tiers-état de Bretagne, s. l. 1789, 8°, 188 pp.

Gouy d'Arsy, Louis M., Au nom de la patrie, monsieur, daignez lire ceci, Paris, 1789, 8°, 16 pp. Anon.

Gouy d'Arsy, Louis M., Mémoire a,u roi, en faveur de la noblesse française, Paris, 1789, 8°, 34 pp.

Grégoire, Abbé, Lettre d'un curé à ses confrères députés aux Etats-Généraux, Paris, 1789, 8°, 40 pp. Anon.

——Essai sur la régéneration physique, morale et politique des juifs, Metz, 1789. Anon.

Guibert, Jacques Antoine de, (under "Abbé Raynal"), L'Abbé Raynal aux Etats-Généraux, Marseille, 1789, 8°, 64 pp. Anon.

Lanjuinais, Jean D., Oeuvres, Paris, 1832: Le Préservatif, Vol. I; Réflexions patriotiques sur l'arreté de quelques nobles de Bretagne, Vol. I.

Le Révellière-Lépeaux, Louis M. de, Doléances, voeux et pétitions pour les représentants des paroisses . . . aux assemblées de la nation pour les Etats-Généraux; Plaintes et désirs des communes tant de ville que de campagne. Anon. Reprints in Le Moy, D.I., Cahiers de doléances des corporations de la ville d'Angers et des paroisses de la sénéchaussée particulière d'Angers pour les Etats-Généraux de 1789, Introduction, in Vol. I.

Linguet, Simon, N. H., Seroit-il trop tard? Aux trois ordres, s. l. 1789, 43 pp. Anon.

Malouet, Pierre L., Avis à la noblesse, décembre, 1788 (in Dugour). Anon.

——Mémoire sur l'esclavage des nègres, Paris, 1788, 8°.

Mirabeau, Honoré G. R., Comte de, Oeuvres, Paris, 1834: A la nation provençale, Vol. I; Sur la liberté de la presse, Vol. III.

——Dénonciation de l'agiotage de Paris (s. l. 1787); Suite de la dénonciation . . . , s. l. 1788.

——Réponse aux alarmes des bons citoyens, s. l. n. d., 8°, 49 pp.

Mounier, Jean J., Considérations sur les gouvernments . . ., Versailles, 1789, 66 pp.

——Nouvelles considérations sur les Etats-Généraux de France, s. l. 1789, 8°, 282 pp.

Orléans, Duc d', Instructions envoyées par S.A.S. Mgr. le duc d'Orléans suivie de Délibérations à prendre . . . , s. l. 1789, 4th edition, 8°, 75 pp.

Pétion de Villeneuve, Jérome, Avis aux français sur le salut de la patrie, s. l. 1788, 254 pp. Anon.

Rabaut de St. Etienne, Jean Paul, Considérations très-importantes sur les intérêts du tiers-état . . .,s. l. 1788, 8°, 72 pp.

——Question de droit public: doit-on recueillir les voix dans les Etats-Généraux par ordres ou par têtes de déliberans? En Languedoc, 1789, 8°, 77 pp. Anon.

——Prenez-y-garde, ou Avis à toutes les assemblées d'élections, s. l. 1789, 8°. Anon.

Robespierre, Maximillian, M. I. de, A la nation artésienne sur la nécessité de réformer les états d'Artois, s. l. 1789, 8°, 83 pp. Anon.

————Au peuple de l'Artois, par un habitant de la province. (Ascribed to Robespierre, copy not found.)

Servan, Joseph M. A., Adresse à M.M. les curés, s. l. 1789, 8°, 30 pp. Anon.

————Avis au public, et principalement au tiers-états, Paris, [1788], 8°, 55 pp. Anon.

————Avis salutaire au tiers-état . . ., s. l. n. d., 8°, 52 pp. Anon.

————Idées sur le mandat des députés aux Etats-Généraux, s. l. 1789, 8°, 19 pp.

————Exhortation pressante aux trois ordres de la province de Languedoc, s. l. 1788, 8°, 44 pp. Anon

Siéyès, Abbé, Essai sur les privilèges, s. l. 1789, 8°, 54 pp. Anon.

————Qu'est-ce que le tiers-état? S. l. 1789, 8°, 130 pp. Anon.

See also Orléans, Duc d', second part of his Instructions, Délibérations à prendre . . .

Talleyrand-Périgord, Charles M.de, Adresse aux français par l'éveque d'Autun, s. l. 1789, 8°. This was written after the elections.

Target, Guy J. B., Les Etats-Généraux convoqués par Louis XVI, s. l. 1789.

————Suite de l'Ecrit, Les Etats-Généraux convoqués par Louis XVI.

————Ma pétition, ou Cahier du bailliage de 1788, s. l. 1788 in 8°.

Thouret, Jacques G., Avis des bons normands à leurs frères tous les français, Rouen, 1789, 8°, 55 pp. Anon.

————Suite de l'avis des bons normands . . ., Rouen, 1789 in 8°, 60 pp., followed by

————L'Essai d'un cahier de pouvoirs et instructions projeté pour une des assemblées de l'ordre du tiers-état. Anon. [See summary of latter in Lebegue, E., La vie et l'oeuvre d'un constituant, Thouret, Paris, 1910, p. 105.]

Miscellaneous anonymous pamphlets (unidentified)

Aux Français sur les instructions de M. le duc d'Orleans, s. l. n. d., 8°.

Instruction ou si l'on veut, Cahier de l'assemblée du bailliage de . . . 28 fév. 1789, s. l. n. d., 32 pp.

Projet de procès-verbaux d'élection de députés, et d'instructions et pouvoirs à donner aux dits députés . . ., Paris, 1789.

Réponse aux instructions envoyées par le duc d'Orléans . . ., s. l. 1789.

Revue des principaux écrits sur les Etats-Généraux, s. l. n. d., 63 pp.

This is a summary of the pamphlets which the author considers the most influential, and of a few that he wishes to call to the attention of the electorate.

Seconde suite de la revue des principaux écrits sur les Etats-Généraux, s. l. n. d., 70 pp.

ANALYSES, CRITICISMS, AND SUMMARIES

Collection of pamphlets

Dugour, A. J. (editor), Collection de pièces interessantes sur les grands évenements de l'histoire de France, 1789-91, Paris, 1801, 12 vols. Contains reprints of many pamphlets, etc.

ANALYSES, CRITICISMS, AND SUMMARIES OF THE CAHIERS

Practically every general volume dealing with the Revolution has more or less to say about the cahiers. The volumes listed here are those whose center of interest is the cahiers, or whose comments are of particular interest. None of the volumes, except my own, distinguish between general and preliminary cahiers in their general treatment.

Aubin, Raoul, L'Organisation judiciaire d'après les cahiers de 1789, Paris, 1928. A thesis, but contributes little original analysis.

Aulard, Auguste, "Quels sont les cahiers de 1789 qui nous manquent?" in *La Révolution française, revue,* 1895, Vol. XXIX, pp. 150 *et seq.*

Bloch, Camille, L'Assistance et l'état en France à la veille de la Révolution, Paris, 1908. Excellent analysis.

Bonnassiaux, P., Examen des cahiers de 1789 au point de vue commercial et industriel, Paris, 1884.

Bourrilly, L., Les Cahiers de l'instruction publique en 1789, Paris, 1901.

Brette, A. "La Population de la France en 1789," in *La Révolution française, revue,* 1904, Vol. XLVI, pp. 481 *et seq.*

"Les Cahiers de 1789 et les Archives parlementaires," *ibid.,* 1904-5, Vols. XLVII, XLVIII.

"Les Cahiers de 1789 considérés comme mandats impératifs," *ibid.,* 1896, Vol. XXXI, pp. 123 *et seq.*

"La Vérification des pouvoirs à l'Assemblée constituante," *ibid.,* 1893, 1894, Vols. XXV, XXVI.

Buirette, Denys- see Denys-Buirette.

Champion, Edme, Esprit de la Révolution française, Paris, 1887.

———"La Conversion de la noblesse en 1789," in *La Révolution française, revue,* 1895, Vol. XXVIII, pp. 5 *et seq.*

———La France d'après les cahiers de 1789, Paris, 1897. Excellent and indispensable analysis, though not exhaustive.

Chassin, Charles, Le Génie de la Révolution, Paris, 1864.

———Les Cahiers des curés en 1789, Paris, 1882.

Chérest, Aimé, La Chute de l'ancien régime, Paris, 1884-86, 3 vols. Although this is an early work, it contains much helpful information on the convocation, elections, and cahiers.

Clermont-Tonnerre, Comte Stanislas de, "Rapport du comité de constitution, contenant le résumé des cahiers rélatifs à cet objet," in *Procèsverbal de l'Assemblée nationale constituante, op. cit., infra,* p. 462; séance of July 27, 1789.

Denys-Buirette, A., Les Questions religieuses dans les cahiers de 1789, Paris, 1919.
    A most scholarly and useful study of the cahiers, with an excellent bibliography.
Desjardins, Albert, Les Cahiers et la législation criminelle, Paris, 1883.
Duméril, A., Des voeux des cahiers de 1789 rélatifs à l'instruction publique, Toulouse, 1880.
Dupont de Nemours, Tableau comparatif des demandes contenus dans les cahiers des trois ordres . . ., Paris, 1789.
Grille, François, J., Introduction aux mémoires sur la Révolution française ou Tableau comparatif des mandats et pouvoirs . . ., Paris, 1825, 2 vols.
Hyslop, Beatrice, French Nationalism in 1789 according to the General Cahiers, New York, 1934.
Lesprand, Abbé, "Quelques mots sur les cahiers de doléances des communes en 1789," in Annuaire de la Soc. d'hist. et d'arch. lorraine, 1906, Vol. XVIII, pp. 165-204.
Mornet, Daniel, Les Origines intellectuelles de la Révolution française, Paris, 1933.
    The final chapter contains a useful analysis of the cahiers on the subjects of education and intellectual development. There is also a handy bibliography of reprints of cahiers, arranged alphabetically by district.
Onou, A., "La Valeur des cahiers de 1789 au point de vue économique et social," in La Révolution française, revue, Vol. XLIX, 1905, pp. 385 et seq.
    "Les Elections de 1789 et les cahiers du tiers-état," ibid., Vols. LVI, LVII; 1909.
Picard, Roger, Les Cahiers de 1789 et les classes ouvrières, Paris, 1910.
    This volume also appears under the title, Les Cahiers de 1789 au point de vue industriel et commercial (same publisher and date of publication). This is a good analysis.
Poncins, Léon de, Les Cahiers de '89, Paris, 1866.
Principes de 1789 et la liberté de la presse, Les, Paris, 1867. Anon.
Prudhomme, L. M., and Mezières, Laurent de, Résumé général ou Extrait des cahiers des pouvoirs, instructions, demandes et doléances . . ., Paris, 1789, 3 vols.
Résumé des cahiers de doléances, pouvoirs et instructions des différents bailliages de la Lorraine, s. l. n. d., in 8°, 6 pp. Anon.
Sagnac, P., "De la méthode dans l'étude des institutions d'ancien régime," in Revue d'histoire moderne et contemporaine, Oct., 1904, Vol. VI, pp. 13 et seq.
    "Les Cahiers de 1789 et leur valeur," in Revue d'histoire moderne et contemporaine, 1907, Vol. VIII, pp. 329 et seq. Excellent.

Sée, Henri, "La Redaction et la valeur historique des cahiers de paroisse," in *Revue historique,* 1910, Jan.-Avril, pp. 292 *et seq.*

Souriau, M., "Etude litteraire sur les cahiers," in *Bull. de la Faculté des Lettres de Poitou,* 1891.

Tocqueville, Alexis de, The State of Society in France before the Revolution, London, 1888. Translation by H. Reeve. 3d edition. Special analysis of Cahiers in Appendix.

Vialay, Amedée, Les Cahiers de doléances du tiers-état aux Etats-Généraux de 1789, Paris, 1911.

Wahl, Adalbert, Studien zur Vorgeschichte der franzosischen Revolution, Tubingen, 1901.

FRANCE IN 1789
LAWS

Bulletin des lois, supplemented after the first publication by *Collection des lois depuis 1789 jusqu'au 22 prairial, an II, formant le commencement du Bulletin des Lois* (Paris, an XII-1906, 7 vols.).

Duvergier, J. B., Collection Duvergier, Paris, 1825-, 24 vols.

Isambert, F. A., Récueil général des anciennes lois françaises . . ., Paris, 1822, 29 vols.

Anderson, Frank Maloy, The Constitutions and other select Documents illustrative of the History of France (1789-1901), Minneapolis, 1908.

NEWSPAPERS

Le Moniteur universelle, May 5, 1789-Dec. 1789. The numbers prior to November 24, 1789 were reconstructed later by Thuau-Grandville.

Le Point du jour, June 19-Dec. 1789.

Journal des débats et décrets, Aug. 29-Dec. 1789.

Journal des Etats Généraux (appeared under different titles), April 27, 1789-Dec. 1789.

Mercure de France, nos. for 1788 and 1789.

Gazette de France, nos. for 1788 and 1789.

MINUTES OF THE STATES-GENERAL AND NATIONAL ASSEMBLY

Procès-verbal de l'Assemblée nationale constituante, imprimé par son ordre, Paris, s. d., 75 vols.

Aulard, F. A., Récit des séances des députés des communes de 5 mai à 12 juin, 1789, Paris, 1895.

Biron, Armand L., de G., Lettres sur les Etats-Généraux de 1789, Paris, 1865.

Crévecoeur, Robert de, Journal d'Adrien Duquesnoy, Paris, 1894, 2 vols.

Houtin, Albert, Les Séances des députés du clergé aux Etats-Généraux de 1789, Paris, 1916.

Reports in the newspapers cited above, and the collection of printed minutes, reports, etc.—*Bib. Nat.* Le 27.10, Le 27.11, etc.

MÉMOIRES, DIARIES, TRAVELS

Bailly, Jean Sylvain, Mémoires d'un témoin de la Révolution, Paris, An XII-1804, 3 vols.

Barère, de Vieuzac, Bertrand, Mémoires, Paris, 1842-44, 4 vols.

Browning, Oscar, Despatches from Paris, London, 1909-10, Vol. II.

Desmoulins, Camille, La France libre, s. l. 1789.

Grönvelt, H. F. Letters containing an Account of the late Revolution in France, London, 1792. These letters are attributed to Pierre E. L. Dumont, a friend of Mirabeau.

Jefferson, Thomas, Writings, New York, 1895, Vols. II, III.

La Révellière-Lépeaux, Louis Marie de, Mémoires, Paris, 1895, 3 vols.

Mallet du Pan, Jacques, Memoirs and correspondence . . ., London, 1852, 2 vols.

Malouet, Pierre L., Mémoires, Paris, 1874, 2 vols.

Mirabeau, Gabriel-Honoré de Riquetti, comte de, Lettres à ses commetants, Paris, 1791.

Morris, Gouverneur, Journal pendant les années 1789, 1790, 1791 et 1792. French translation by E. Pariset, Paris, 1901. English editions do not give the diary in consecutive form.

Mounier, Jan J., Exposé de la conduite de Mounier (1790); Recherches sur les causes qui ont empeché les français de devenir libres (1792): De l'Influence attribuée aux philosophes, aux francs-maçons (1801).

Rabaut St. Etienne, J. P., The History of the Revolution in France. Translation by James White, London, 1893, 2d edition.

Staël, Baroness de, Considerations on the Principal Events of the French Revolution, New York, 1818.

Young, Arthur, Voyages en France en 1787, 1788 et 1789, Paris, 1931, 3 vols.

This work is a part of the series of *Les Classiques de la Révolution française,* directed formerly by Albert Mathiez. The introduction and annotations by Henri Sée are invaluable.

CORRECTIONS AND ADDITIONS, 1967

It is well to repeat here that the corrections and additions are designed to bring up to date the statistics and information on general cahiers available since 1936, when this volume was first published. The author could have added to the bibliography on the cahiers, but this would have involved more revision than a new edition usually permits. The substance of the text remains valid, as it was in 1936.

The same abbreviations will be used as in the original publication. See p. xvi.

Map facing p. 46. It is not feasible to redraw this map. The hatching needs to be changed for the nine cases of cahiers that have been found. Since these nine were scattered and represented different classes, the general map would not be altered drastically. There would still be important gaps for Alsace, Lorraine, Brittany, Provence, and the Pyrenees region. With the discovery of the texts of N, Puy-en-Velay, C, Villefranche-en-Rouergue, and T, Hennebont, the districts numbered 36, 70, and 160 become white on the map. Tartas would remain white, since the cahier of the clergy had not been considered missing. With the finding of the cahiers of the third estate of Brignoles and Hyères in Provence, districts numbered 143 and 149 would still be indicated as missing the cahiers of the clergy and the nobility. Although the cahiers of the nobility of St. Dié, the joint cahier of the nobility and the third estate of Carignan, and the cahier of the third estate of Quesnoy were discovered, the cahiers of the clergy are still missing for the districts numbered 208, 215, and 178, respectively. See explanation of maps, p. 155.

47   Note 32. The statistics referred to for p. 150 will be corrected hereafter. There were nine cahiers of the colonies, six surviving.

Note 33. Four *Procès-verbaux* have been found: N, Bigorre, N, Clermont-en-Beauvoisis, N, Tartas, and C, Vannes. See corrections to table, pp. 120, 124, 140, and 141 respectively.

57   Note 51. See also by the author, *L'Apanage de Philippe Egalité, Duc d'Orléans, 1785-1791,* Paris: Société des Etudes robesierristes; 1965, pp. 248-52 and 252-58, additional references in index under "Elections."

88   See also corrections for U, Bassigny-Barrois, *infra,* p. 118.

91   Notes 192 and 193. See also corrections of statistics given for table, pp. 116, *et seq.*

97   Paragraph 1, Line 4. Correct to read 265.

Note 215. See corrections, pp. 128, 132, and additions to list on pp. 151-52. N, St. Dié and T, Hennebont must now be added, making the total number of general cahiers printed 265.

98   Note 220. Same addition as for note 215.

100   Note 246. Add: and col. 7 of table (with corrections), pp. 116-42 and pp. 471 *et seq.*

101-2   Note 246. Add to the list: N, Haguenau, Perpignan, Quesnoy, Rouen. Correct figure for nobles to 86 in text, next to last line.

107   Paragraph 3. Correct the numbers to 616 and 532, respectively.

Corrections and additions to
Comprehensive Table of General Cahiers, pp. 116-42.

117   N, Armagnac, col. 7: read I (for Imperative Mandate), not S. Since the nobles held a new assembly to grant wide powers, they must have considered the mandate imperative. See list of new assemblies, p. 102 and note 246.

T, Auray, col. 11: read VI, 112-16.

C, Autun, col. 6: add new powers; col. 7: omit G, read I.

N, Autun, col. 6: add new powers; col 7: read I.

118   N, Auxerre, col. 6: add new powers; col. 7: read I.

T, Auxerre, col. 7: read I, not S.

N, T, Aval: M. Cernesson is no longer living. The author believes that texts have been returned to the Arch. dép. Jura.

U, Bassigny-Barrois, col. 9: The cahier cited in cols. 9, 10, 11 is one drafted in May. A text drafted in April is copied in Arch. Nat. B III 22, pp. 484-92. This has not been counted as a cahier found, but rather that the May text is a supplement. The April text is not printed in the AP.

119   N, Besançon, col. 11: read VI, 515-19.

120   N, Bigorre, col. 5: omit Missing, read Arch. dép. Hautes-Pyrénées, C 265.

T, Boulay, col. 7: read I.

U, Bourg-en-Bresse, col. 11: read II, 453-64.

121   N, Bourges, col. 15: add Mandate, AP, II, 323.

T, Bourges, col. 7: read I, not S.

T, Brignoles, col. 9: omit Missing; col. 11: add *Bull. soc. études sci. et arch. du Var*, t.44, 1942-43, pp. 22-35.

122   NT, Carignan, col. 9: omit Missing; col. 11: add H. Rouy, *Souvenirs sedanais*, t.II, 1888, 4e. série, pp. 270-75 (under the name of Yvois-Carignan).

N, Castelmoron d'Albret (not Albert), col. 11: read 543-44.

N, Castelnaudary, col. 11: add 555-57 to pages for cahier.

N, Châlon-sur-Saône, col. 15: add AP, II, 605-6 (Mandate).

123   T, Château-Salins, col. 6: add p.v.; col. 7: add I.

N, Château-Thierry, col. 6: add AP, II, 667-68; col. 7, read S.

Col. 15. This mandate might be called imperative, but it had to do with the deputy not receiving favors from the court rather than adherance to articles of the cahier.

C, Chatellerault, col. 11: read 686-90.

124 C, Clermont-en-Beauvoisis, col. 7: omit G, add I.

N, Clermont-en-Beauvoisis, col. 5: omit Missing, add Arch. dép. Oise (extract).

T, Corsica, col. 11: read III, 41-46.

125 T, Dax, col. 15: The *Supplément* referred to in Brette appears to be the text reprinted in AP, III, 107-10.

T, Dijon, col. 11: read III, 130-40.

126 N, Dôle, col. 7: read I.

128 N, Haguenau, col. 6: add new powers; col. 7: add I.

T, Hennebont, col. 9: omit Missing; col. 10: Bib. Tribunal Pontivy; col. 11: add edition by Thomas Lacroix, in *Mém. soc. d'hist. et arch. de Bretagne*, t.XXV, 1955, pp. 75-104.

T, Hyères, col. 9: omit Missing; Col. 11: add *Bull. soc. études sci. et arch. du Var*, t.44, 1942-43, pp. 36-41.

129 N, Lille, col. 6: add p.v.; col. 7: add I.

N, Limoges, col. 7: omit G, add I.

Lixheim, see texts also in P. Lesprand and L. Bour, *Cahiers de doléances de Sarrebourg . . . et de Lixheim* (Annuaire de la société d'histoire et d'archéologie de la Lorraine, 1935, 1936, 1937), Metz, 1938.

Longuyon and Longwy. See also d'Arbois Jubainville, *Cahiers de doléances des bailliages de Longuyon, Longwy et de Villers-la-Montagne*, Nancy, 1952.

130 T, Lyon, col. 7: omit S, add I.

C, Meaux, col. 11: add see text, *Guide*, pp. 180-84.

131 T, Mende, col. 7: omit G, add S.

C, Mirecourt, col. 6: add p.v.; col. 7: add I.

C, Mont-de-Marsan, col. 7: omit S, add I.

132 T, Morlaix, col. 11: read IV, 72-75.

133 C, Nîmes, col. 6: add new powers; col. 7: omit G, add I.

N, Orléans, col. 6: add p.v.; col. 7: add I.

134 N, Péronne, col. 7: read S, not G.

135 T, Pont-à-Mousson, col. 15: add see Z. E. Harsany, *Cahiers de*

doléances du bailliage de Pont-à-Mousson (Cahiers de doléances des généralities de Metz et de Nancy, t.V), Paris, 1946.

N, Puy-en-Velay, col. 9: omit Missing; col. 11: add ms. Arch. dép. Haute-Loire, I B 1759.

N, Quesnoy, col. 7: omit S, add I.

T, Quesnoy, col. 9: omit Missing; col. 11: add *Bull. soc. études provinciales de Cambrai,* t.VIII, 1906, pp. 232-44.

T, Reims, col. 11: read V, 530-35.

136   U, Remirement, col. 6: add N, p.v.; col. 7: add I.

T, Rochefort, col. 11: read AP, III, 486-90.

T, Rouen, col. 15: see also Marc Bouloiseau, *Cahiers de doléances du Tiers Etat du bailliage de Rouen* (Rouen, 1960) t.II.

137   U, Rustaing, col. 4: read U, not T.

N, St. Dié, col. 9: omit Missing; col. 10: add text printed, Bib. mun. St. Dié, vol. 5543.

St. Domingue, Paris, col. 11: add Blanche Maurel, *Cahiers de doléances de la colonie de Saint-Domingue* (Commission de recherche et de publication des documents relatifs à la vie économique de la Révolution), Paris, 1933. Colony, see Maurel, *op. cit.* pp. 263-82. The information is for a cahier drafted by the North, but adhered to also by the West; therefore it may be called the general cahier of the Colony. West, col. 5: PR. Arch. Min. Col., F[3]193, pièce 13; col. 9. Arch. Min. Col., Bib. de Moreau St. Méry, t.XXIX; col. 11: Maurel, *op. cit.,* 299-302. South, col. 5: Papiers Gérard; col. 9: Missing, unofficial cahier, Bib. Nat. Le[24] 203, col. 15: Maurel has given p.v., pp. 246-50; col. 9: Missing.

Col. 15. A Plan, "Le Projet de formation des états coloniaux et provinciaux," given by Maurel, pp. 282-98, should be read as part of the general cahier adhered to by all sections.

N, St. Jean d'Angely, col. 6: add p.v.; col. 7: add I.

C, St. Mihiel: The cahier of the clergy has not been published.

138   Sarrebourg and Phalsbourg. P. Lesprand and L. Bour have published a complete edition: *Cahiers de doléances des prévotés bailliagères de Sarrebourg et Phalsbourg et du bailliage de Lixheim pour les Etats généraux de 1789* (Annuaire de la société d'histoire et d'archéologie de la Lorraine, 1935, 1936, 1937), Metz, 1938.

N, and T, Sarrebourg, col. 11: see Lesprand et Bour, *op. cit.*

139   N, Sedan, col. 6: p.v.; col. 7: G; col. 15: see H. Rouy, *Souvenirs sedanais*, t.II, 1888, 4e. série, for summaries of documents now lost. He gives the part of the p.v. that elected a committee of correspondence, pp. 239-40. See also Hubrecht, in *Nouvelle Revue de Champagne et de Brie*, t.XII, 1934, pp. 90-102, on the clergy. Col. 8: add N.

       N, Semur, col. 10: add Bib. Nat. (two editions).

140   C, Tartas, col. 9: omit Made no cahier; col. 11: add *Bull. soc. Borda*. t.V, 1881, p. 285. This text appears to be an authentic text. Since former information led to the conclusion that no cahier was made, this cahier was neither counted among the total made nor among those missing. It is now counted among the number made, raising the total to 616, but it does not decrease the number reported as missing.

       N, Tartas, col. 5: omit Missing, add Arch. comm., edition by Abbé Départ, *Bull. soc. Borda*, 1881, p. 289.

       T, Thionville, col. 11: read III, 776-80.

141   T, Valenciennes, col. 7: read I.

       C, Vannes, col. 5: omit Missing, add Arch. Nat. H 419, pièce 402.

       T, Vannes, col. 11: read VI, 107-112.

       C, Verdun, col. 11: read VI, 127-30.

142   C, Villefranche-en-Rouergue, col. 9: omit Missing; col. 11: add *Mém. soc. des lettres, sci., et arts de l'Aveyron*, t.XVII, 1906-11, pp. 253-81.

       U, Villers-la-Montagne. See edition of all documents by d'Arbois de Jubainville, *Cahiers de doléances des bailliages de Longuyon, Longwy et de Villers-la-Montagne*, Nancy, 1952.

143-44   List of General Cahiers. The cahiers that have been found should now be indicated in Roman type: T, Brignoles, NT, Carignan, T, Hennebont, T, Hyères, N, Puy-en-Velay, T, Quesnoy, N, St. Dié, C, Tartas, C, Villefranche-en-Rouergue. (T, Rouen had been found between the publication of *French Nationalism* in 1934 and the *Guide* in 1936.)

144   Correct the summary statistics to read:

       Made: 195 C, 182 N, 213 T, 18 U, 3 CN, 1 CT, 4 NT—616[1]
       Lost: 35 C,   26 N,   18 T,   4 U,   1 NT—84
       Extant: 160 C, 156 N, 195 T, 14 U, 3 CN, 1 CT, 3 NT—532[1]
       Recently found: 2 C, 2 N, 4 T, 1 NT—9

       Colonial Cahiers: Made 9, Lost 3, Extant 6.

[1] See footnote on p. 471.

Corrections to *List of General Cahiers by Generality,* pp. 145-50.

Add, and take out under missing.

145-46   *Generality* of Montpellier. Extant (20): add N, Puy-en-Velay; N7. Missing (1); N0.

146   *Generality* of Bordeaux. (36). Extant (34): add C, Tartas; C11. Missing (2); C1. Total: 36.

Generality of Montauban. Extant (9): add C, Villefranche-en-Rouergue; C3. Missing (none): omit entire line.

148-49   *Generality* of Aix. Extant (26): add T, Brignoles, T, Hyères; T10. Missing (13); T3.

149   *Generality* of Rennes. Extant (21): add T, Hennebont; T14. Missing (8); T5.

Generality of Valenciennes. Extant (8): add T, Quesnoy; T4. Missing (2); T0.

Generality of Nancy. Extant (65): add N, St. Dié; N19. Missing (28); N10.

Generality of Metz. Extant (27): add NT, Carignan; NT 1. Missing (6); NT0.

Colonies. (9). Extant (6): add St. Domingue, N, W. Missing (3). Add St. Domingue, S. Total: 9.

Correct the summary statistics to read:

Extant: 160 C, 156 N, 195 T, 14 U, 3 CN, 1 CT, 3 NT—532[1]
Missing: 35 C, 26 N, 18 T, 4 U,   1 NT—84
Made: 195 C, 182 N, 213 T, 18 U, 3 CN, 1 CT, 4 NT—616[1]
Colonial: Extant 6; Lost 3; Made 9.

Correction for *List of General Cahiers that were Printed, by Generality,* pp. 151-52.

152   *Generality* of Rennes: add T, Hennebont; 12 printed; 7 T.

Generality of Nancy: add N, St. Dié; 17 printed; 8 N.

Total: Printed: 265. 54 C, 106 N, 93 T, 8 U, 1 CN, 1 CT, 2 NT.

Alphabetical List of Imperative Mandates.

C, N, T, Agen; T, Aix; N, Alençon; N, Amiens; N, Amont; N, T, Angers; N, Angoulême; N, Annonay; NT, Arles(ville); N,

----

[1] The cahier of the city of Paris (V.) was counted as U, but erroneously counted with T, thereby reducing the U count in the statistics originally given in the *Guide,* and adding 1 to the T column. These figures have now been corrected for the line of cahiers made, at the same time that the figures for Extant and Made for the clergy have been increased by 1—C, Tartas.

Armagnac; N, Artois; N, T, Auch; T, Auray; C, N, Autun;
N, T, Auxerre; N, T, Aval; T, Avesnes; C, Bailleul; C, Bar-
celonnette; N, T, Bar-sur-Seine; C, N, T, Bazas; CN, T, Béarn;
N, Beauvais; N, T, Belfort; C, N, T, Bellême; N, T, Belley; C,
N, Besançon; C, Beziers; C, N, Bigorre; C, Blamont; N, Blois;
N, Bordeaux; T, Boulay; C, T, Boulogne; N, Bourg-en-Bresse;
N, T, Bourges; N, Bourmont; C, Bouzonville; N, T, Briey; T,
Brignoles; CT, Bruyères; N, T, Caen; C, N, Cahors; N, Calais;
C, N, Cambrèsis; N, Carcassonne; C, N, T, Castelmoron; N,
Castelnaudary; N, T, Castres; N, Caudebec; N, Châlon-sur-
Saône; N, Charmes; C, N, T, Charolles; C, N, T, Chartres; T,
Château-Salins; T, Château-Thierry; C, N, T, Châteauneuf-en-
Thimerais; N, T, Chatellerault; T, Châtel-sur-Moselle; N, T,
Châtillon-sur-Seine; N, T, Chaumont-en-Bassigny; N, Chau-
mont-en-Vexin; C, N, Clermont-en-Beauvaisis; C, N, T, Cler-
mont Ferrand; N, Colmar; N, Comminges; C, N, T, Condom;
N, Couserans; N, T, Coutances; N, Crépy; N, Darney; U,
Dauphiné; C, N, Dax; T, Dieuze; C, N, T, Digne; C, N, T,
Dijon, N, Dôle; N, Dorat; C, N, T, Douai; N, Dourdan; N,
Epinal; N, Etain; N, T, Etampes; C, N, T, Evreux; U, Fené-
trange; N, Foix; C, Forcalquier; N, T, Forez; T, Fougères;
C, N, T, Gex; N, T, Gien; N, T, Guéret; N, Haguenau; N,
La Marche; N, Langres; N, La Rochelle; N, T, Libourne; C, N,
Lille; N, T, Limoges; C, N, T, Limoux; CN, Lixheim; N,
Loudun; C, N, Lunéville; N, T, Lyon; N, T, Mâcon; N, Le
Mans; C, T, Marseille; N, Meaux; C, Melun; N, Mende; T, V,
Metz; C, N, T, Mirecourt; U, Mohon; C, N, T, Montargis;
C, N, Mont-de-Marsan; U, Montfort l'Amaury; N, Montpellier;
N, Montreuil; N, Moulins; Cl, T, Nantes;[1] C, N, T, Nemours;
C, N, Nérac; N, T, Neufchâteau; C, N, Niverais; C, N, Nîmes;
C, N, Orléans; N, Paris-hors-les-murs; N, Paris-intra-muros;
C, N, Périgord; T, Péronne; N, T, Perpignan; T, Ploërmel; N,
T, Poitiers; C, N, Pont-à-Mousson; N, T, Ponthieu; C, N, T,
Puy-en-Velay; N, T, Quesnoy; Cl, T, Quimper;[1] N, Reims; N,
Remiremont; Cl, Rennes;[1] T, Rhuys; C, N, Riom; N, T,
Rivière-Verdun; N, Rodez; N, Rouen; U, Rozières; U, Rus-
taing; T, St. Brieuc; N, T, St. Dié; N, St. Flour; N, T, St.
Jean d'Angely; N, Saintes; N, Sarrebourg; N, T, Sarreguemines;
T, Sarrelouis; T, Saumur; T, Sedan; N, T, Semur-en-Auxois;
N, T, Senlis; N, Sézannes; C, Sisteron; C, N, Soule; N, Toul;
N, Toulon; C, N, Toulouse; N, T, Trévoux; N, Troyes; N,
Tulle, C, Ustaritz; T, Valenciennes; T, Vannes; N, Vendôme;
N, Verdun, N, Villefranche-de-Beaujolais; N, Villefranche-en-

[1] Cl—lower clergy.

Rouergue; N, T, Villeneuve-de-Berg; C, N, Villers-Cotterêts; N, Vitry-le-françois.

Total: Correct to read 279 cahiers, 53 C, 135 N, 81 T, 6 U, 1 NT, 2 CN, 1 CT.

154-56 There is no change in this material for the reading of the maps. Note, however, correction that should be made for Map III, facing p. 46, *supra.*

448 Official volumes:

Marc Bouloiseau, *Cahiers de doléances du Tiers Etat du bailliage de Rouen,* Rouen, 1960, 2 vols.

Semi-official editions of cahiers. Add:

P. d'Arbois de Jubainville, *Cahiers de doléances des bailliages de J. Godfrin, Cahiers de doléances du bailliage de Nancy,* Paris, *Longuyon, Longwy, et de Villers-la-Montagne,* Nancy, 1952. 1934.

Z. E. Harsany, *Cahiers de doléances du bailliage de Pont-à-Mousson* (Cahiers de doléances des généralités de Metz et de Nancy, t.V), Paris, 1946.

P. Lesprand and L. Bour, *Cahiers de doléances des prévotés bailliagères de Sarrebourg et Phalsbourg et du bailliage de Lixheim pour les Etats généraux de 1789* (Annuaire de la société d'histoire et d'archéologie de la Lorraine, 1935, 1936, 1937), Metz, 1938.

INDEX

References to the districts (*bailliages, sénéchaussées, comtés*, etc.) that sent general cahiers to the States General and to cahiers from the districts follow references to the name of the district. If there are special references to a particular cahier of the district, the letter of the class (C, N, T, V) precedes the page reference. For example, see Agen.

INDEX

INDEX

Rousseau, 65, 75
Royal officers, 14, 34, 53-55, 86
Rozières, 17, 136, 144, 149, 152, 156, 157, 197
Rustaing, 23, 24, 73, 137, 144, 146, 156

St. Aubin-le-Cormier, 25 n. 93, 137, 144, 149, 156, 157
St. Brieuc, 25, 137, 144, 149, 152, 156, 157; C, 25 n. 89, 149; T, 197
St. Dié, 17, 137, 144, 149-50, 152, 156, 157; text of T cahier, 398-417
St. Domingue, 26, 27-28, 62, 137, 144, 150 and n. 4; petition to National Assembly, 418-19
Saintes, 138, 144, 147, 151, 156, 157; T, 198
St. Flour, 49, 137, 144, 145, 156, 157
St. Jean d'Angely, 137, 144, 147, 156, 157
St. Malo, 25 n. 89, 137, 144, 149, 152, 156, 157
St. Mihiel, 17, 137, 144, 149-50, 152, 156, 157; T, 197
St. Pierre-le-Moutier, 138, 144, 145, 151, 156
St. Pol-de-Léon, 25 n. 89, 138, 144, 149, 156, 157
St. Quentin, 138, 144, 147, 152, 156, 157; C, 197-98
Sarrebourg et Phalsbourg, 17, 73, 138, 144, 150, 156, 157
Sarreguemines, 17, 138, 144, 149, 156, 157; C, N, 198; text of T cahier, 38, 391-97
Sarrelouis, 17, 138, 144, 150, 156, 157; text of CN cahier, 397-98
Saumur, 138, 144, 147, 151, 156, 157; T, 198
Schlestadt, 23. See also Colmar
Scope of cahiers, 40, 45, 89. See also Length of cahiers
Seal on manuscript, 35, 37
Secondary bailliages, 15, 16, 17, 25, 42
Secretary of assemblies, 37, 55
Sedan, 17, 139, 144, 150, 152, 156, 157
Sée, M., 66
Semur-en-Auxois, 139, 144, 148, 152, 156, 157; C, N, 198
Sénéchaussée, see Bailliage
Senlis, 139, 144, 145, 151, 156
Sens, 139, 144, 145, 151, 156
Servan, vii, 67, 71, 73, 75
Sézanne, 139, 144, 148, 152, 156, 157
Siéyès, 58, 67, 102-3

Signatures of cahiers, 38, 159, 203
Similarity of cahiers, 91, 108
Sincerity of cahiers, 77-84
Sisteron, 17, 139, 144, 149, 156, 157
Société des Amis des Noirs, 62
Soissons, 73, 139, 144, 148, 156, 157; generality of, 148, 152
Soule, 139-40, 144, 146, 151, 156; C, 199
States-General: convocation of, see Convocation; of 1484, 4-5; of 1560, 5; of 1576, 5; of 1588, 5; of 1614, ix, 5-7, 30; of 1789, see Convocation, National Assembly
Strasbourg (town), 21, 22-23, 140, 144, 150, 152, 156, 157
Strasbourg (intendance), 46, 150, 152. See also Alsace
Subjective value, 44, 45, 105
Suffrage, 12, 13, 19, 21, 29-30
Summary of cahiers, 104-5, See also bibliography, 460-62

Table of cahiers, 113-42
Talleyrand, 102
Tartas, 140, 144, 146, 151, 156
Ten Imperial Cities, 21, 23 and n. 75, 126, 143, 150, 152, 155, 157; cahier, 266-83
Texts of cahiers, see Manuscripts, Printing of cahiers, Unedited texts
Thiaucourt, 17, 140, 144, 149, 156, 157
Thionville, 17, 140, 144, 150, 152, 156, 157
Third Estate, representation of, 9, 13, 14, 16, 19, 20, 21, 25, 30, 40, 49, 82
Thouret, 67, 70-71
Time element, 19-20, 24, 28, 29, 49-52, 86, 87, 95
Time influences on cahiers, see Time element
Title of cahier, 36
Toul, 17, 140, 144, 150, 152, 156, 157; C, T, 199
Toulon, 17, 140, 144, 149, 156, 157; text of T cahier, 419-29
Toulouse, 140, 144, 146, 151, 156; N, 199; T, 72, 199; generality of, 146, 151
Tours, 140, 144, 147, 151, 156, 157; N, 199; generality of, 147, 151
Towns, representation of, 14, 16, 21-23, 30. See also name of each town
Tradition, 3, 4, 6, 7, 10, 11, 29, 30, 39, 95, 96, 103
Tréguier, 25 n. 89, 141, 144, 148, 156, 157
Trévoux, 141, 144, 148, 152, 156, 157